FOOD

((‘‘FOOD’’))

A Dictionary of Literal and Nonliteral Terms

Robert A. Palmatier

GREENWOOD PRESS
Westport, Connecticut • London

Library of Congress Cataloging-in-Publication Data

Palmatier, Robert A. (Robert Allen)
    Food : a dictionary of literal and nonliteral terms / Robert A. Palmatier.
        p.   cm.
    Includes bibliographical references.
    ISBN 0–313–31436–5 (alk. paper)
    1. Food—Dictionaries.   I. Title.
  TX349.P353   2000
  641.3'003—dc21   99–088203

British Library Cataloguing in Publication Data is available.

Library of Congress Catalog Card Number: 99–088203
ISBN: 0–313–31436–5

First published in 2000

Greenwood Press, 88 Post Road West, Westport, CT 06881
An imprint of Greenwood Publishing Group, Inc.
www.greenwood.com

Printed in the United States of America

The paper used in this book complies with the
Permanent Paper Standard issued by the National
Information Standards Organization (Z39.48–1984).

10 9 8 7 6 5 4 3 2 1

Dedicated to:

My late mother,
Cecile Chase Palmatier,
born 1899, died 1997.

She learned to cook at a time when everything was made from scratch and was baked (or roasted) in, or boiled (or fried) on, a woodstove. On her family's Michigan farm she helped her aunt and mother do the canning, feed the threshers, bake bread and pies, and fix holiday dinners. Later, in the same farmhouse, she became widely known among archers, hunters, and conservationists for her own favorite dishes: chicken, biscuits, and gravy; pan-fried bass, blue gills, and perch; rabbit and squirrel stew; baked pheasant and goose; baked ham and turkey (with all the fixings); biscuits, muffins, and rolls; strawberry shortcake; apple, cherry, peach, and rhubarb pie; pineapple whip; homemade vanilla ice cream; iced tea and lemonade. And for snacks: fried cakes and molasses cookies.

I miss her, and I miss her cooking.

CONTENTS

PREFACE

Food: A Dictionary of Literal and Nonliteral Terms is based on a survey of thirty-three popular and scholarly books, most of them dictionaries, that identify, and in many cases discuss, the literal language of cooking and eating food. Only three of the books focus exclusively on the language of food, however; and only one of these, which is not a dictionary, deals extensively with the nonliteral language. These books are *The Dictionary of American Food and Drink*, *The Food Lover's Companion* (also a dictionary), and *The Philology of Taste: The Wayward Language of Food* (a book-length essay).

What is the difference between literal and nonliteral language? Literal language means what it says: A *roast* is a *roast*. Nonliteral language means something other than what it says: A nonliteral *roast* is a *toast* turned upside down—a friendly putdown of a famous person at a banquet in his/her honor. The guest of honor is *roasted* by his/her friends as if he/she were being turned on a spit over an open fire. The *roast* ends when the subject is *done to a turn*. ("Stick a fork in him and see if he's done.")

Nonliteral language includes both figurative and nonfigurative terms. All metaphors, such as *jellyfish*, are figurative, as are all similes, such as *like trying to nail jelly to a wall*, and all proverbs, such as *It must be jelly, 'cause jam don't shake like that*. Together, these terms are known as "metaphorical language." In contrast, idioms, clichés, and slang terms and expressions can be either figurative or nonfigurative. Together they are usually known as "idiomatic language."

What is the difference between metaphorical language and idiomatic language? For most scholars, metaphorical language is "analogical" language, based on the similarity between one thing and another, whereas idiomatic language is "unanalyzable" language, based on the impossibility of analyzing the meaning of the whole from adding up the sum of the meanings of its parts. For example, *yester-*

day, today, and tomorrow is an idiom (for "hash") but not a metaphor, whereas *a can of corn* is a metaphor, meaning "an easily catchable fly ball" (in baseball), but not an idiom.

Assistance in using the dictionary is provided by the Guide to Reading the Entries, which uses the metaphor *to lay an egg* as an illustration; and judging by the number of references works citing that phrase, it is one of the most popular terms in the dictionary. The references are represented in the entries by coded abbreviations (found in the Key to Works Cited), such as HND for *Have a Nice Day—No Problem!* The only works dealing specifically with metaphors are *Metaphorically Speaking* (MS), *Loose Cannons and Red Herrings: A Book of Lost Metaphors* (LCRH), and *Speaking of Animals: A Dictionary of Animal Metaphors* (SA).

The rationale for including both literal and nonliteral terms in the dictionary is that literal terms are the grist from which nonliteral terms are ground. The rationale for heading some of the entries with literal terms, even though the entries contain nonliteral terms within, is to emphasize the importance of the former in their transformation into the latter. When the nonliteral terms are especially numerous, however, they are often used as entry headings in their own right. In addition, some entries are headed by literal terms, even though they contain few or no nonliteral terms, because of either their broad nature (e.g., *cream soda*) or their unusual form (e.g., *snickerdoodles*).

The coverage of food terms and expressions in this dictionary is slightly broader than the actions of cooking and eating food. Included in the category of "cooking" are "gathering" (e.g., *cherry picker*), "preserving" (e.g., *home canning*), and "serving" (e.g., *full plate*); and included in the category of "eating" are "clearing the table" (e.g., *dessert*), "washing the dishes" (e.g., *pearl diver*), and "taking out the garbage" (e.g., *garbage in, garbage out*). The definition of "food" includes drink (e.g., water, milk, juice) but not alcoholic beverages, which deserve a book of their own.

Bon appétit!

ACKNOWLEDGMENTS

I wish to recognize the following persons for their generous support:

My brother, Malcolm, who supplied me with a "sorting board," mailed me lots of clippings from the *Los Angeles Times*, and generally kept me posted on the food scene on the West Coast.

My daughter, Denise, who shared with me the language of the kitchen that she picked up during five years as a cook in various restaurants. Also her daughter, Kelly, and Kelly's husband, Andrew.

My daughter-in-law, Linda, whose specialty is lasagna but who prepares delicious holiday dinners for the entire family, including her husband (my son), David, and their sons, Justin and Daniel.

My former colleagues in the Department of Foreign Languages and Literatures at Western Michigan University—especially Daniel Hendriksen, Peter Krawutschke, John Benson, and Jorge Febles.

Harry Randall, author of *The Philology of Taste*, who critiqued the manuscript and recommended several corrections and additions.

And, finally, the resourceful Reference Librarians and Children's Librarians at the Portage (Mich.) District Library and Western Michigan University's libraries, and the helpful clerks at the Portage branches of Barnes and Noble and the John Rollins Bookstore.

Thank you all.

ABBREVIATIONS AND SYMBOLS

GENERAL ABBREVIATIONS

A.	answer
adj.	adjective
adv.	adverb
Amer.	American
approx.	approximately
Brit.	British
ca.	around
cent.	century
dim.	diminutive
esp.	especially
equiv.	equivalent
fig.	figuratively
fr.	from
gen.	generally
immed.	immediately
lit.	literally
n	noun
N.D.	no date
neg.	negative
orig.	originally
past part.	past participle

pl.	plural
poss.	possibly
prep.	preposition
pres. part.	present participle
prob.	probably
Q.	question
q.v.	which see
sing.	singular
specif.	specifically
trad.	traditionally
U.S.	United States
usu.	usually
v	verb
vs	versus
WWI	World War One
WWII	World War Two
X.	first speaker
Y.	second speaker

Language Abbreviations

Amer. Eng.	American English
Ar.	Arabic
Braz. Port.	Brazilian Portuguese
Brit. Eng.	British English
Du.	Dutch
Eng.	English
Fr.	French
Frank.	Frankish
Ger.	German
Gk.	Greek
Gmc.	Germanic
Heb.	Hebrew
Hung.	Hungarian
I.E.	Indo-European
It.	Italian
Lat.	Latin
L.Lat.	Late Latin
M.E.	Middle English

M.Fr.	Middle French
M.H.G.	Middle High German
M.Lat.	Medieval Latin
Mod. Eng.	Modern English
Mod. Fr.	Modern French
O.E.	Old English
O.Fr.	Old French
O.H.G.	Old High German
O.It.	Old Italian
O.N.	Old Norse
O.N.Fr.	Old North French
O.Prov.	Old Provençal
Port.	Portuguese
Prov.	Provençal
Rus.	Russian
Skt.	Sanskrit
Sp.	Spanish
V.Lat.	Vulgar Latin
Yid.	Yiddish

Symbols

→	becomes
=	equals
(*)	not a food metaphor
+	plus
(?)	questionable source

KEY TO WORKS CITED

AID   Richard A. Spears. *NTC's American Idioms Dictionary*. Lincolnwood, Ill.: National Textbook Company, 1987.

ATWS   Darryl Lyman. *The Animal Things We Say*. Middle Village, N.Y.: Jonathan David Publishers, 1983.

BDPF   Ivor H. Evans, ed. *Brewer's Dictionary of Phrase and Fable*, rev. Centenary ed. New York: Harper & Row, 1981.

CE   Richard Lederer. *Crazy English*. New York: Pocket Books, 1989.

CI   E. M. Kirkpatrick and C. M. Schwarz, eds. *Chambers Idioms*. Edinburgh: W. & R. Chambers, 1982.

CODP   John Simpson and Jennifer Speake. *The Concise Oxford Dictionary of Proverbs*, 3d ed. Oxford: Oxford University Press, 1998.

DAFD   John F. Mariani. *The Dictionary of American Food and Drink*, rev. ed. New York: Hearst Books, 1994.

DAI   Adam Makkai, ed. *A Dictionary of American Idioms*, 2d ed. Hauppauge, N.Y.: Barron's Educational Series, 1987.

DAP   Wolfgang Mieder, Editor in Chief; Stewart A. Kingsbury and Kelsie B. Harder, eds. *A Dictionary of American Proverbs*. New York: Oxford University Press, 1992.

DAS   Richard A. Spears. *NTC's Dictionary of American Slang and Colloquial Expressions*, 2d ed. Lincolnwood, Ill.: National Textbook Company, 1995.

DC   James Rogers. *The Dictionary of Clichés*. New York: Facts on File, 1985.

DEI   Daphne M. Gulland and David G. Hinds-Howell. *The Penguin Dictionary of English Idioms*. London: Penguin Books, 1986.

DEOD   Hugh Rawson. *A Dictionary of Euphemisms and Other Doubletalk.*
                New York: Crown Publishers, 1981.

EWPO   Robert Hendriksen. *The Facts on File Encyclopedia of Word and
                Phrase Origins.* New York: Facts on File Publications, 1987.

FLC   Sharon Tyler Herbst. *Food Lover's Companion.* Hauppauge, N.Y.:
                Barron's Educational Series, 1990.

HB   Charles Earle Funk. *Heavens to Betsy and Other Curious Sayings.* New
                York: Harper & Row, 1955.

HDAS   Johnathan E. Lighter, Editor; J. Ball and J. O'Connor, asst. eds.
                Random House Historical Dictionary of American Slang, 2 vols. (Vol.
                I: A–G, Vol. II: H–O). New York: Random House, Vol. I: 1994,
                Vol. II: 1997.

HF   Charles Earle Funk. *Horsefeathers and Other Curious Words.* New
                York: Harper & Row, 1958.

HI   Charles Earle Funk. *A Hog on Ice and Other Curious Expressions.*
                New York: Harper & Row, 1948.

HND   Christine Ammer. *Have a Nice Day—No Problem!* New York:
                Penguin Books USA, 1993.

IHAT   Stuart Berg Flexner. *I Hear America Talking: An Illustrated History of
                American Words and Phrases.* New York: Simon and Schuster, 1976.

IRCD   Christine Ammer. *It's Raining Cats and Dogs . . . and Other Beastly
                Expressions.* New York: Dell Publishing, 1989.

LA   Stuart Berg Flexner. *Listening to America.* New York: Simon and
                Schuster, 1982.

LCRH   Robert Claiborne. *Loose Cannons and Red Herrings: A Book of Lost
                Metaphors.* New York: W. W. Norton, 1988.

MDWPO   William Morris and Mary Morris. *Morris Dictionary of Word and
                Phrase Origins*, 2d ed. New York: Harper & Row, 1988.

MS   N. E. Renton. *Metaphorically Speaking.* New York: Warner Books,
                1992.

MWCD   Frederick C. Mish, Editor in Chief. *Merriam-Webster's Collegiate
                Dictionary*, 10th ed. Springfield, Mass.: Merriam-Webster, 1994.

NSOED   Lesley Brown, Editor in Chief. *The New Shorter Oxford English
                Dictionary*, 2 vols. Oxford: Oxford University Press, 1993.

PT   Harry Randall; illustrations by Betty Beeby. *The Philology of Taste:
                The Wayward Language of Food.* Eastport, Mich.: Suwalsky
                Publishers, 1995.

SA   Robert A. Palmatier. *Speaking of Animals: A Dictionary of Animal
                Metaphors.* Westport, Conn.: Greenwood Press, 1995.

SHM   Teri Degler. *Straight from the Horse's Mouth . . . and Other Animal
                Expressions.* New York: Henry Holt, 1989.

THT   Charles Earle Funk. *Thereby Hangs a Tale: Stories of Curious Word Origins*. New York: Harper & Row, 1950.

WNWCD   Victoria Neufeldt, Editor in Chief; David B. Guralnik, Editor in Chief Emeritus. *Webster's New World College Dictionary*, 3d ed. New York: Macmillan, 1996.

NOTE: MWCD was used as the primary source for spellings, dates, etymologies, and meanings. WNWCD was used as the primary source for Americanisms and as the secondary source for spellings, etymologies, and meanings. Biblical quotations are from the King James (Authorized) version of the Bible (1611).

GUIDE TO READING THE ENTRIES

A typical entry in the dictionary has the following parts: an entry *heading*, consisting of the common form of the term or expression; an illustration of its *grammatical use*; a definition of its literal or nonliteral *meaning*; the *date* of its first recorded use in English (where possible); the name of the food (cooking, eating) *source* on which the term or expression is based; the *date* of the first recorded use of the name of the food source (where possible); an attempt to establish a *connection* between the literal meaning of the source and the nonliteral meaning of the metaphor, idiom, or proverb; coded *references* to the published works (*see* Key to Works Cited) that recognize the terms and expressions as nonliteral language; and informative and comparative *cross-references* to other entries in the dictionary. The entry for *lay an egg*, which is both an idiom and a metaphor, illustrates all of these elements:

LAY AN EGG   *to lay an egg.* To fail miserably. HDAS: 1861. Source: EGG. MWCD: 14th cent. This expression originated in England in the 1850s in reference to the failure of a cricket team to score any points in an inning: *to lay a duck's egg,* i.e., to deposit an egg-shaped "zero" on the scoreboard. American baseball adopted the expression in 1866, modifying it to *to lay a goose egg* (HDAS: 1866), i.e., to get a big fat "zero" for a scoreless inning. In the late-19th cent. the expression passed into the legitimate (and illegitimate) theater, where it signified either a bad performance by an actor (who was pelted with hen's eggs) or a total failure of the entire production. The expression was so far removed from sports by 1929 that the show business organ *Variety* could declare that Wall Street had *laid an egg,* i.e., had allowed the stock market to crash. In that same year, 1929, an imperative form of *lay an egg* developed: *Go lay an egg!* (HDAS: 1928)—"Get lost!" ATWS; AID;

DAI; DAS; DC; EWPO; HND; IRCD; LA; LCRH; MDWPO; PT; SA. *See also* Love. *Compare* Go Fry an Egg; Go Suck an Egg.

"LAY AN EGG" is the common form of the expression in America. "*To lay an egg*" illustrates that the expression is a verb phrase. "HDAS: 1861" indicates that the first recorded use of the metaphor or idiom in English was in 1861, according to *The Historical Dictionary of American Slang*. "Source: EGG" attributes the food source of the expression to the egg. "MWCD: 14th cent." indicates that the earliest recorded use of *egg* for a hen's production was in the 14th cent., according to *Merriam-Webster's Collegiate Dictionary*. The body of the entry presents a history of the development of the idiomatic and metaphorical use of the expression— first in baseball, then in the theater, and finally on Wall Street. The thirteen coded references at the end of the body of the entry indicate that *lay an egg* is a popular and familiar expression. (Codes used in the body of an entry are not repeated at the end of the entry.) "*See also* Love" is an invitation to the reader to turn to the entry *Love* for another use of the egg as metaphor and idiom. "*Compare* Go Fry an Egg; Go Suck an Egg" directs the reader to two other entries that have *egg* as a base.

A

ABOVE THE SALT   *See* Salt of the Earth.

ACADEMIA NUT   *See* Nut.

À CHACUN SON GOÛT   *See* Everyone to His Own Taste.

ACORN DOESN'T FALL FAR FROM THE TREE   *See* Acorn Squash.

ACORN SQUASH   *an acorn squash.* A squash that resembles an acorn. MWCD: 1937. Source: ACORN (MWCD: O.E.); SQUASH (MWCD: 1634). An acorn squash is a "winter" squash, one that ripens in the late fall and can "keep" for several months during the winter. An acorn also "ripens" in the fall; i.e., it changes color and falls to the ground, where small rodents "squirrel" it away to their nests for winter storage. However, the resemblance ends there: Acorns grow on trees (oak trees), whereas squash grow on vines (ground vines); acorns are small (about the size of a marble), whereas acorn squash can grow up to half a foot long and weigh up to two pounds; acorns are light brown and smooth, whereas acorn squash are dark green and ribbed; inside the acorn are tan nutmeats, whereas inside the squash is orange pulp; and, most importantly, some acorns are poisonous, whereas no acorn squash has ever been accused of being so. When the colonists arrived in America, they were already familiar with the acorn, but they were unfamiliar with the acorn squash (which they named with the Eng. word *acorn* and the final syllable of the Narraganset word *askutasquash* "squash"). The Native Americans ate both the squash and the acorns, whose poison they neutralized by cracking them open, grinding up the contents, rinsing them several times in flowing water, and boiling or roasting them. Acorns figure in such proverbs as *The acorn doesn't fall far from the tree* ("Like father, like son; like mother, like daughter") and *Mighty oaks from little acorns grow* ("There's hope for you yet"). CODP; DAFD; DAP; FLC; NSOED. *See also* Vine Apple. *Compare* Apple Doesn't Fall Far from the Tree.

ACQUIRE A TASTE FOR   *See* Acquired Taste.

ACQUIRED TASTE   *an acquired taste.* An appreciation for something that must be developed over time. MWCD: 1858. Source: TASTE (n). MWCD: 14th cent. Among foods, caviar is the dish most often cited as an *acquired taste*, prob. because, to the uninitiated, it looks "alien" and tastes salty. In Shakespeare's *Hamlet* (Act II, Scene 2), the Prince of Denmark refers to a play that "pleas'd not the million" as being *caviary to the general*, i.e., too sophisticated for the general public. Oysters are also cited in literature as an *acquired taste*: Johnathan Swift observed, "He was a bold man that *first ate an oyster*," implying that because the man found the bivalve "exotic," he had to screw up his courage before he could actually down one. To those for whom eels and squid are "foreign," these seafood are an *acquired taste*; but *acquired tastes* can be found right at home, inside the bodies of familiar farm animals: the brain, heart, kidneys, liver, tongue, tripe, etc.—known as *variety meats* (MWCD: ca. 1946) in the United States, and as *offal* in Great Britain. Metaphorically, anything that you were not brought up with is an *acquired taste*—e.g., ballet, baseball, hockey, and opera. If you get to like it, you will then have *acquired a taste for* it. AID; DEOD; FLC.

ADAM AND EVE ON A RAFT   *See* Coddle; Lunch-counter Jargon.

ADAM'S APPLE   *an Adam's apple.* A bony projection midway up the front of the neck. MWCD: ca. 1775. Source: APPLE. MWCD: O.E. Before the second half of the 18th cent., neither laypersons nor physicians had a name for the bony projection from the throat of both men and women. However, because the bulge, which is actually the anterior cartilage of the larynx, is much more prominent in men than in women, a name was given to it that recalls an event involving Adam in the Garden of Eden. In chapter three of Genesis, the serpent talked Eve into eating of the fruit of the tree of the knowledge of good and evil, even though God had told Adam that if they did so they would surely die. Eve did not die, and, in fact, she gave some of the fruit to Adam, who also ate, and who also did not die. A folk interpretation of this development held that a piece of the fruit that Adam ate stuck in his throat, and it remains there as a reminder to us of original sin. Different cultures have identified the fruit according to their different geographical orientations. To some it was an apple, to others an apricot, to others a pomegranate, and to still others a fig. Western physicians settled on the apple and gave the protuberance the name *pomum Adami*, Lat. for "Adam's apple." BDPF; CE; EWPO; HF.

AIR-SUCKER   *See* Sucker.

À LA CARTE   *See* Menu.

ALASKA STRAWBERRIES   *See* Strawberry Mark.

ALBANY BEEF   *See* Beefeater.

AL DENTE   *See* Spaghetti Squash.

ALIKE AS TWO PEAS IN A POD   *See* Like Two Peas in a Pod.

ALL HANDS AND THE COOK!   All able-bodied men are needed to respond
to an emergency! EWPO: early-19th cent. Source: COOK, n. MWCD: O.E. On a
New England whaling ship in the early 1800s, a cry of "All hands and the cook!"
meant "All hands on deck, including the cook!"; i.e., every man on the ship was
needed to help butcher the whale that had been harpooned and dragged on board.
Later, the same cry was uttered on cattle drives out West, when every cowhand,
even the cook, was needed to quell a stampede and herd the cattle back in the
proper direction. From these examples it can be concluded that both the cook in
a ship's galley and the cook in a Western chuckwagon were not sailors or cowboys
but were specialized members of the group whose job it was to feed the "hands."
Calling on the cook to wrangle a whale or a steer must have meant that the
situation was desperate indeed. BDPF; MDWPO.

ALLIGATOR PEAR   *an alligator pear*. An avocado. MWCD: 1763. Source:
PEAR. MWCD: O.E. The *alligator* in *alligator pear* is either (1) a mispronunciation
of *aguacate*, the Sp. name for the Mexican fruit, or (2) a metaphor based on the
similarity between the bumpy green skin of the alligator and that of the avocado.
The *pear* in *alligator pear* reflects the fact that the fruit is pear-shaped, although
Nahuatl *ahuacatl*, the source of Sp. *aguacate*, meant "testicle," not "pear." Thus,
the avocado is a fruit that has the skin of an alligator but the shape of a pear (or
a scrotum). (*Avocados* is also slang for a woman's breasts—HDAS: 1932.) The
nickname *alligator pear* developed in the 18th cent., when avocado trees were
first planted in Florida (the land of the alligators); but most Americans associate
the fruit with the state of California, which began marketing them widely in the
Northwest and Midwest after WWII. Now the avocado is popular throughout the
country in desserts, salads, and dips because of its buttery texture and nutty flavor.
The dip known as *guacamole* (MWCD: 1920, fr. Nahuatl *ahuacamōlli* "avocado
sauce") consists of mashed or pureed avocados seasoned with chili peppers.
ATWS; BDPF; DAFD; EWPO; FLC; IHAT; MDWPO; PT; SA.

ALL STEAMED UP   *See* Pressure Cooker.

ALL THAT MEAT AND NO POTATOES   *See* Meat-and-potatoes.

ALL THE TRIMMINGS   *See* Cape Cod Turkey.

ALPHABET SOUP   The initials and acronyms that are used as shorthand names for government organizations. MWCD: 1934. Source: SOUP. MWCD: 14th cent. Sometimes it seems that the initials, such as I.R.S., and acronyms, such as HUD, are the real names of these government agencies; and, in fact, the shorthand forms are the names most frequently used. A parlor game could prob. be developed to teach schoolchildren the real and unfamiliar names attached to such initials as CIA, DOD, FBI, INS, OMB, SSA, etc. Then, when they ate their *alphabet soup* (DAFD: ca. 1900), which contains pasta cutouts of the letters of the English alphabet, the children could practice up for the big game. (Advice: If the last three letters in your soupbowl spell FLY, call the waiter.) DAFD; DAS; DC.

AMBROSIA   A food that is fit for the gods. MWCD: 15th cent. Source: FOOD. In Greek (and Roman) mythology, ambrosia was both the food—the only food— and the fragrance—or perfume—of the gods (and goddesses). The literal meaning of *ambrosia* was "immortality" (fr. Gk. *ambrotos* "immortal," fr. *a-* "not" + *mbrotos* "mortal"); and not only was it eaten by the gods, but anyone who ate it *became* a god. Understandably, in Mod. Eng. the word has come to mean a food that is "fit for the gods" in respect to taste and aroma. One such dish bearing the name *ambrosia* is a 19th-cent. dessert consisting of chilled oranges (plus or minus bananas) mixed with grated coconut. The beverage of the gods, called nectar (NSOED: mid-16th cent.—fr. Gk. *nektar* "overcoming death"), was also believed to confer immortality on anyone who consumed it; and the word *nectar* has come to mean both (1) a drink that is "fit for the gods" and (2) the sweet liquid secreted by plants and collected by bees to become the basis for "nectar on earth" (i.e., honey). The name *nectarine* (MWCD: 1611) for a "smooth-skinned peach" seems to imply that if peaches didn't have all that fuzz, they would be "heavenly." DAFD; FLC; WNWCD.

AMERICAN AS APPLE PIE   *as American as apple pie*. As American as baseball and hot dogs. Source: APPLE PIE. IHAT: 1760s. Americans regard apple pie as a uniquely American product, a symbol of American values: honesty, simplicity, and wholesomeness. However, apple pies—and the apples themselves—were brought to America from England, where the same values were no doubt held. America *has* become the world's largest producer of apples, and it *has* invented baseball and hot dogs; but the apple pie is uniquely American only if it is accompanied by a top crust and either a large chunk of cheddar cheese or a large scoop of vanilla ice cream. (The English apple pie is actually a topless tart.) DAFD.

AMERICAN PLAN   *See* Meal.

AND ONE FOR GOOD MEASURE   *See* For Good Measure.

AND ONE FOR THE POT   *See* For Good Measure.

ANGEL CAKE   *See* Angel Food Cake.

ANGEL FOOD CAKE   A cake that even an angel couldn't resist. MWCD: 1920. Source: FOOD (MWCD: O.E.); CAKE (MWCD: 13th cent.). Angel food cake is so called because it resembles an angel in color (white) and texture (light as a feather). However, it is so light and airy that it is not very filling: One must eat half a cake in order to be satisfied. To solve this problem, bakers sometimes apply vanilla frosting or add strawberry coloring to the batter—and strawberry frosting to the finished product. The unadorned cake has been around since the 1880s, when it was made without a hole in the center and called an *angel cake*. DAFD; FLC; IHAT; NSOED; PT. *See also* Angel-hair Pasta; Angels on Horseback. *Compare* Devil's Food Cake.

ANGEL-HAIR PASTA   *See* Spaghetti Squash.

ANGELS ON HORSEBACK   Oysters wrapped in bacon strips, cooked, and served on toast points as hors d'oeuvres. EWPO: early-20th cent. Source: OYSTER. Although *angels on horseback* is prob. a translation of Fr. *anges à cheval*, there is no clue to the connection between angels/horses and oysters/bacon. (The name of the hot-sauce version, *devils on horseback*, doesn't help either, although it is reminiscent of the *angel food cake/devil's food cake* contrast.) A more familiar dish of this sort, at least in the Midwest, is *pigs in the blanket*, a home-cooked entrée consisting of wieners (the "pigs") wrapped in biscuit dough (the "blanket") and baked in the oven. This recipe has its variants, also called *pigs in the blanket*: (1) Vienna sausages wrapped in pie dough, baked, and served as appetizers, and (2) link sausages wrapped in thin pancakes and served as breakfast. FLC; SA.

ANIMAL CRACKERS   Small cookies in the shapes of circus and zoo animals. MWCD: 1898. Source: CRACKER. DAFD: 1739. Animal crackers are an American product, first produced in the home—by cutting somewhat larger animals out of rolled cookie dough—and later produced in the factory and marketed by the National Biscuit Company. (Note that the *crackers* produced by the *biscuit* company were really *cookies*.) The box in which these cookies were first sold was a marvel of design. On each side it had pictures of a railroad car, with the animals peering through the bars; and on the top was a shoestring to carry the animals with you wherever you went. *Animal crackers* is also a slang term for "crazy." (HDAS; 1992). SA.

ANOTHER KETTLE OF FISH   *See* Kettle of Fish.

ANOTHER TABLE WITH THE SAME SETTING   *See* Set the Table.

ANTIPASTO   Italian hors d'oeuvres. MWCD: 1590. Source: PASTA. MWCD: 1874. *Antipasto* is It. "before the pasta"—i.e., as a first course in a typical Italian meal, whose main course almost always features pasta, whether as a main dish or a side dish. The antipasto usu. consists of provolone cheese, prosciutto ham, pickled vegetables, black olives, olive oil, and slices of Italian bread. The pasta consists of some type of wheat-flour dough cut or squeezed into strings (spaghetti), cut and shaped into forms (macaroni), or cut into narrow or wide ribbons (noodles). The word *pasta* is related to several other words derived from L.Lat. *pasta* "dough or paste," one of which is the word *paste* (MWCD: 14th cent.), which first referred to the high-fat dough used to make pie crusts and sweet rolls and then to the foods themselves (now called *pastry*, MWCD: 1538). *Paste* also came to refer to the low-fat dough used to make spaghetti, macaroni, and noodles. The French inherited the Lat. word *pasta* as O.Fr. *paste* (borrowed into Eng. as *pasty* "meat pie turnover," MWCD: 13th cent.), which took two forms in Mod. Fr.: *pâte* "paste or dough" and *pâté* "pie or meat spread." English borrowed *pâté* as *patty* (MWCD: 1710) to designate a small round pie, a small flat piece of chopped meat (a *hamburger patty*—NSOED; early-20th cent.), or a small round piece of candy (a *peppermint patty*—NSOED; early-20th cent.). Both the French and the English use *pâté de foie gras* (MWCD: 1827) to refer to "goose liver paste." DAFD; FLC; PT.

APOSTLE SPOON   *See* Born with a Silver Spoon in Your Mouth.

APPETITE   *an appetite for culture, knowledge, work, etc.* An intense interest in or desire for culture, knowledge, work, etc. Source: APPETITE. MWCD: 14th cent. When you have an appetite for something, you just can't seem to get enough of it, or you can't enjoy it as many times as you would like. That is also the case with the original meaning of *appetite*: "to have a strong desire for food, or for certain foods" (fr. Lat. *appetitus* "an eager desire for," fr. *appetere*, "to strive after"). Food that satisfies your appetite is *appetizing* (MWCD: 1653), and the same adj. can be used to describe objects of your desire that are not food. People who have an abnormal craving for food (or pleasure) are said to have a *canine appetite* (MWCD: 1623), a *ravenous appetite* (MWCD: 15th cent.), or a *voracious appetite* (MWCD: 1635)—all based on the intensity with which a wolf devours its prey. (Watching such an act could also make you *lose your appetite*.) In contrast, something that causes you to increase your desire for food or other pleasure is said to *whet* (often pronounced "wet") *your appetite*. To *whet* a knife (MWCD: O.E.) is to sharpen its cutting edge by rubbing it on an abrasive stone—or rubbing the abrasive stone on the knife. The result of this operation is an implement with improved ability to perform its primary task: to cut. An appetite is like the dull edge of a knife: it can be "sharpened" by exposing it to samples of tempting food such as *appetizers* (q.v.). The appetite is then ready to do justice to the main course. (Sometimes just the sight, even in a photograph, or the smell of the entrée can have the same effect.) A *champagne appetite* is a taste for the life of luxury. Champagne, the sparkling wine from the Champagne region of France, is usu. regarded as the finest of wines, suitable to be served on the finest of occasions. However, French champagne is expensive in the United States, and it is beyond the means of someone who has not only a *champagne appetite* but a *beer-belly pocketbook*. Such a pocketbook is big enough to buy beer but not big enough to buy imported champagne. This is the plight of many former "royals" who have fallen on hard times but try to keep up the appearance of wealth. CE; CI; HDAS; MS; SA; WNWCD.

APPETIZER *an appetizer.* A tempting preliminary to an even more satisfying main event. Source: APPETIZER. MWCD: 1859. An edible appetizer is a *finger food* (q.v.) that is served before a meal in order to stimulate the appetite. The two main types of appetizers—*canapés* (fr. Fr. for "couch"), MWCD: 1890, and *hors d'oeuvres* (fr. Fr. for "apart from the main work"), MWCD: 1714—are strictly distinguished in Europe but are practically synonymous in the United States. What they have in common, on both continents, is that they are small, eaten with the fingers, served before the first course of a meal, and designed to *whet the appetite* (q.v.). The only obvious difference is that canapés always involve a bread (toasted or untoasted), cracker, or pastry base that is topped with a savory spread of cheese, a pâté of meat or fish, egg salad, smoked salmon, anchovies, caviar, sliced olives or pickles, or Vienna sausages wrapped in pastry (called *pigs in the blanket*, q.v.). The appetizers called *angels on horseback* (oysters wrapped in bacon) and *devils on horseback* (chicken livers wrapped in bacon) are wrapped, but not in pastry, and come closer to crossing the semantic field of *hors d'oeuvres*, which includes chicken livers and water chestnuts wrapped in bacon. *Hors d'oeuvres* are not served on bases: they are either eaten as is (e.g., olives or radishes) or on a toothpick (e.g., Vienna sausages or meat balls) or they are dipped into a salad dressing (e.g., celery or carrot sticks) or into a seafood sauce (e.g., shrimp or prawns). *Canapés* are usu. served on trays carried by waitpersons; *hors d'oeuvres* are usu. found on a buffet-type side table. DAFD; FLC; HF; MDWPO; SA.

APPETIZING *See* Appetite.

APPLE *an apple.* Any small, round, edible fruit. Source: APPLE. MWCD: O.E. Apples are not native to North America, but after the seeds that the Pilgrims brought with them in 1620 were planted and produced trees that produced fruit, the apple became the most popular fruit on the continent and remained so through the 20th cent. Apples have provided us with both food (fresh apples, dried apples, applesauce, apple butter, apple cobbler, apple pie, etc.) and drink (apple juice, sweet apple cider, hard apple cider, applejack, etc.). Because the apple is so familiar, it has become a symbol not only of fruit in general—as in *Adam's apple* (q.v.), the *apple of discord* (q.v.), and the *love apple* (i.e., a tomato)—

but of our favorite pastime, baseball, which is *as American as apple pie* (q.v.). In fact, a baseball was called an *apple* back in the 1920s, and the ballpark was called an *apple orchard*. (An *apple orchard* is now a "speed trap"—HDAS: 1970. In Europe, Wilhelm Tell shot an apple off his son's head, Isaac Newton based his law of gravitation on the fall of an apple ("Newton's Apple"), and the Beatles named their record company after the apple's core ("Apple Corps"); and in America the inventors of the personal computer named their company after the apple ("Apple Computer Inc"), the symbol of which is an apple with a "byte" taken out of it. Around the world, *apple* has become a name for things that are simply round, such as the *pomegranate* (Fr. for "seedy apple"), *pomme de terre* ("earth apple," Fr. for "potato"), *oak apple* (a gall on oak leaves), and *road apple* (horse manure). BDPF; DAFD; DAS; EWPO; IHAT; NSOED.

APPLE A DAY KEEPS THE DOCTOR AWAY   *an apple a day keeps the doctor away*. Apples are good for your health. DAP: ca. 1630. Source: APPLE. MWCD: O.E. This proverb exaggerates the value of the apple to your health, but not by much. Fresh, ripe, washed apples are a great source of fiber and, combined with other fruits, should make up approx. one-fifth of your daily diet. Another proverb warns against eating unripe apples: Q. "How sure are you?" A. *"As sure as God made little green apples"* (IHAT: 1909—i.e., absolutely sure). God's *little* green apples are "green" because they're not yet ripe. Children who eat them are certain to get a bad stomach ache. (*Big* green apples are simply apples that turn—or stay—green when they ripen.) Any doctor would be pleased to have a young patient, esp. a girl, whose cheeks were the color of red apples—i.e., one who was *apple-cheeked* (MWCD: 1864), a condition that was also highly regarded in Victorian times. CODP; DEI; EWPO; HND; IHAT.

APPLE BRANDY   *See* Applejack.

APPLE BROWN BETTY   *See* Brown Betty.

APPLE BUTTER   A spread consisting of apples cooked in cider, along with sugar and spices. MWCD: ca. 1774. Source: APPLE; BUTTER. MWCD: O.E. Apple butter is not *real* butter (processed from milk or cream), but it *spreads* like real butter; and though not yellow, it is yellowish brown (ranging to dark brown) in color. Apple butter is thought to have originated as a Pennsylvania Dutch dish (ca. 1765), somewhere between a puree and a preserve, and darker than it is now. The "apples" to be cooked were prob. the pulp left over from cider-making. DAFD; FLC. *Compare* Cocoa Butter; Crab Butter; Maple Butter; Peanut Butter.

APPLECART   *See* Upset the Applecart.

APPLE-CHEEKED   *See* Apple a Day Keeps the Doctor away.

APPLE CIDER   *See* Applejack.

APPLE DOESN'T FALL FAR FROM THE TREE   *See* How Do You Like Them Apples?

APPLE DUMPLING   *See* Dumpling.

APPLE FOR THE TEACHER   *See* Apple-polisher.

APPLEJACK   Apple brandy. MWCD: 1816. Source: APPLE. MWCD: O.E. *Apple juice* is the expressed, strained, and usu. pasteurized juice of apples. *Sweet apple cider* (MWCD: 13th cent.) is unstrained, sometimes unpasteurized, and sometimes carbonated apple juice. *Hard apple cider* (MWCD: 1789) is unstrained, unpasteurized, and fermented apple cider. *Applejack* is either hard cider that has been distilled into *apple brandy* (IHAT: 1780) or hard cider that has been frozen and the liquid siphoned off. The *jack* in *applejack* may derive from the 17th cent. term for corn liquor, *John Barleycorn* (MWCD: ca. 1620), or from the name of the type of apple first used to make the brandy, the "John apple." (An early name for *applejack* in New England was "apple-john.") *Cider vinegar* (MWCD: 1851) is apple brandy turned sour. In Colonial times, cider was also pressed from cherries, peaches, and pears. The word *cider* derives ultimately from Heb. *shēkhār*. BDPF; DAFD; EWPO; FLC; HF; NSOED; PT; WNWCD.

APPLE-KNOCKER   *an apple-knocker*. A rustic; a stupid person. MWCD: 1919. Source: APPLE. MWCD: O.E. There is no such thing as a literal apple-knocker, i.e., someone who harvests apples by knocking them off the tree with a stick. Such an act would be foolish because apples bruise easily, and unless you could catch them in your hands or a sack before they hit the ground, they would be ruined for eating (although they could still be used for making applesauce or cider). The pejorative term *apple-knocker* was invented by city people who wished to disparage country people. The joke is on them, however, because a machine that is based on the same principle is now used to shake the trunks of small fruit trees and catch the fruit in a net before it hits the ground. Nuts, of course, have been harvested for centuries by knocking them loose with a stick, although they are not damaged when they hit the ground. DAFD; EWPO; HDAS; IHAT.

APPLE OF DISCORD   *an apple of discord*. A cause of disagreement, dispute, rancor, or revenge. Source: APPLE. MWCD: O.E. In Greek mythology, the *apple of discord* was a golden apple that was thrown among three goddesses who were attending the wedding of the future parents of Achilles. The thrower was Eris, goddess of discord and strife, who was angry about not having been invited to the wedding. (She showed up anyway.) The wedding partners were Thetis, a sea-goddess, and Peleus, King of Phthia. The three goddesses were Hera, wife of Zeus;

Athena, goddess of wisdom and warfare; and Aphrodite, goddess of love and beauty. The golden apple was a cause of discord because on it was written "For the Fairest," and the question was, which of the three goddesses deserved the prize. One of the guests at the wedding, Paris, son of Priam (King of Troy), was chosen to judge the matter, and in spite of tempting promises of power and authority from Hera, and victory in battle from Athena, he chose Aphrodite as the fairest goddess of them all. Her promise was the hand of Helen, wife of Menelaus, who was the fairest *mortal* at the wedding, and the rest is history (or at least mythology). BDPF; CI; DC; EWPO; HI. *Compare* Bone of Contention.

APPLE OF LOVE   *See* Love Apple.

APPLE OF YOUR EYE   *the apple of your eye.* What you hold most dear. Source: APPLE. MWCD: O.E. In O.E., the word *æppel* meant both "apple" (or "fruit" generally) and "eyeball"; i.e., the eyeball was the "fruit" of your eye. Because the eye was indispensable for sight, the eyeball (and later, and more specifically, the pupil of the eye) was regarded as something both cherished and treasured. By the early Mod. Eng. period the expression *apple of your eye* had undergone a more abstract and figurative extension to "anything, or anyone, that is treasured and cherished," as in the King James version of the Bible (1611), Deuteronomy 32: 10, where Moses describes the Lord as having cherished Jacob (Israel) as the *apple of his eye*: "He found him in a desert land, and in the waste howling wilderness; he led him about, he instructed him, he kept him as the *apple of his eye*" [italics added]. Today, the expression is usu. used to refer to a person's child, esp. a man's daughter: "She is the *apple of her father's eye*" (i.e., he will do anything for her). BDPF; CE; CI; DAI; DAP; DC; EWPO; HI; HND; IHAT; LCRH; MDWPO; MS.

APPLE ORCHARD   *See* Apple.

APPLE-PIE BED   *an apple-pie bed.* A bed that has been "short-sheeted." Source: APPLE PIE. IHAT: 1760s. "Short-sheeted" is a WWII American GI term for what the British call an *apple-pie bed*: a bed whose top sheet, instead of extending all the way to the foot, is doubled back under the pillow by a prankish bunkmate. When the unfortunate serviceperson (camper, etc.) climbs into bed, his/her feet go only halfway down, causing him/her great puzzlement and consternation. Calling a short-sheeted bed an *apple-pie bed* reinforces the notion that *apple-pie*, in the expression *apple-pie order* (q.v.), may have derived from the Fr. term *nappe pliée* "a folded napkin or sheet," in the following steps: *a nappe pliée—an appe pliée—an apple-pie* (bed, order). BDPF; CI; MDWPO. *Compare* Humble Pie.

APPLE-PIE ORDER   *See* In Apple-pie Order.

APPLE-POLISH   *See* Apple-polisher.

APPLE-POLISHER   *an apple-polisher.* A sycophant. HDAS: 1927. Source: AP-PLE. MWCD: O.E. The original apple-polisher was a grade-school pupil who polished a red apple until it was bright and shiny, took it to his/her one- (or two-) room schoolhouse, and placed it on the desk of the teacher (usu. a schoolmarm), who was about to start the day's lessons. The motivation of the pupil to provide *an apple for the teacher* was to exchange a gift (the apple) for a favor (a better grade on the next report card). The metaphor *apple-polisher* "a bold flatterer" derives from the phrase *to polish the apple,* i.e., "to curry favor" (HDAS: 1901); and *to apple-polish* (MWCD: 1935) is a back-formation from *apple-polisher.* The term *an apple for the teacher* now means "a bribe," and *apple-polishing* (HI: mid-20th cent.) is now practiced more often in the business world than in the halls of ivy. BDPF; CE; DAI; DAS; EWPO; IHAT; PT; WNWCD.

APPLE-POLISHING   *See* Apple-polisher.

APPLES AND ORANGES   *See* Compare Apples and Oranges.

APPLESAUCE!   Nonsense! IHAT: 1910. Source: APPLE. MWCD: 14th cent. Literally, *applesauce* (MWCD: 1739) is a cooked puree of apples and sugar, with the texture ranging from smooth to chunky, and the taste from bland to sweet. Smooth, bland applesauce is one of the cheapest foods around, a fact that prob. led to the figurative meaning "nonsense." In its metaphorical history, *applesauce* has also meant "flattery," or insincere praise, a sense that may have developed in early-20th cent. boardinghouses, where the expression "They have great apple-sauce" meant that they served little of anything that was more substantial. DAFD; DAS; EWPO; FLC; HDAS; PT.

APRON   *See* Tied to Your Mother's Apron Strings.

APRON STRINGS   *See* Tied to Your Mother's Apron Strings.

ARMY MARCHES ON ITS STOMACH   *An army marches on its stomach.* Sol-diers can't fight unless they are fed. DAFD: late-18th cent. Source: STOMACH. MWCD: 14th cent. This maxim has been attributed to both Frederick the Great, King of Prussia (died 1786), and Napoleon Bonaparte, Emperor of France (died 1821). The leaders were prob. trying to convince their people that their dreams of victory could not come true unless they coughed up more taxes to finance another campaign. Actually, a modern army *does* "march on its stomach"—when soldiers are advancing, flat on their stomachs, under barbed wire, with machine gun bullets flying overhead. CODP; DAP. *See also* Way to a Man's Heart Is through His Stomach.

ARROWROOT   *See* Take the Starch out of.

AS SLOW—OR THICK—AS MOLASSES IN JANUARY   *See* Slow as Molasses in January.

ASS-OVER-TEAKETTLE IN LOVE   *See* Kettledrum.

AS SURE AS GOD MADE LITTLE GREEN APPLES   *See* Apple a Day Keeps the Doctor away.

ATHLETIC CUP   *See* Cup (n).

ATLANTIC CITY TAFFY   *See* Taffy.

AUTOMAT   *an Automat* (or *automat*). An automated restaurant. DAFD: 1902. Source: RESTAURANT. The automat had a short life. It was created in Philadelphia in 1902 as "Horn and Hardart's Automat," spread to New York City in 1912, reached its peak there in 1939, and disappeared from the scene in 1991. An automat is hard to classify. Some sources refer to it as a buffet, some as a cafeteria, and some as a giant *vending machine* (MWCD: ca. 1895). The last description is prob. the most accurate. As you entered the single large room and walked among the tables and chairs, you came to an entire wall covered, from waist-high to chest-high, with foot-square glass doors, next to which were coin slots, and behind which were enough types of food to make up a hearty meal. Peering through the particular door of your choice, you could see the actual item that you wanted to purchase—by putting the correct coin(s) in the slot, opening the door, and carrying the food to your table. You couldn't see them—except for a hand once in a while—but there were people behind the "wall" whose job it was to restock the bowls of soup and stew, the plates of meat and mashed potatoes, and the cups of coffee and hot chocolate. However, the "wall" didn't look so much like a giant vending machine as a series of large-doored mailboxes in the lobby of an apartment building, or the metal-doored safe-deposit boxes in the vault of a bank. Eating in an automat was a little like eating in a buffet or smorgasbord because you went to a particular "station," picked up the food yourself, and carried it back to the table. The process was also a little like that in a cafeteria, however, because you could move down the counter, from station to station, before returning to your table. But you'll never know, because the automat is gone forever. LA; WNWCD. *See also* Buffet; Cafeteria; Restaurant.

AVOCADO   *See* Alligator Pear.

B

BABE DU JOUR   *See* Menu.

BABYCAKES   *See* Cupcake.

BACK BACON   *See* Canadian Bacon.

BACK TO THE SALT MINES   *See* Old Salt.

BACON BAROMETER   *See* Pork.

BAD APPLE   *See* One Rotten Apple Spoils the Barrel.

BAD EGG   *a bad egg.* A dishonest, disreputable, no-good, rotten person (usu. male). HDAS: 1855. Source: EGG. MWCD: 14th cent. Nothing smells quite as bad as a rotten egg. However, an egg can be "bad" even if it doesn't smell, the weight seems normal, the shell isn't cracked, and the shell's color is normal. Egg farmers used to "candle" their eggs—hold them in front of a candle—to determine their "goodness." They now send them, en masse, on rollers over a bright light to reveal the same thing. Unfortunately, there is no "candling" process to determine the "goodness" of humans. *Bad eggs* are humans who look good on the outside but, on the inside, are *rotten to the core* (q.v.). BDPF; CI; DAP; DAS; DEI; EWPO; HI; HND; LA; MS; PT; SA. *See also* Rotten Egg. *Compare* Good Egg.

BAD TASTE IN   *See* Good Taste.

BAD TASTE IN YOUR MOUTH   *See* Leave a Bad Taste in Your Mouth.

BAGEL   *a bagel*. A "ring." Source: BAGEL. MWCD: 1932. A culinary bagel is a yeast bun, the size of a large doughnut with a hole in the center, that is eaten with the hands. However, that's where the similarities between the bagel and the doughnut end. The differences are numerous: A doughnut is a cake roll; a bagel is a bread roll. A doughnut is deep fried in oil; a bagel is boiled in water and then baked. A doughnut is soft; a bagel is chewy. A doughnut is an accompaniment to coffee; a bagel can be eaten alone or cut in two and made to serve as "sandwich bread." A favorite bagel "sandwich" is *lox and bagels*: Slit a bagel into two rings, spread cream cheese on the "cut" side of each ring, cover the cream cheese with thin slices of smoked salmon (i.e., *lox*), and eat. The noun *bagel* (fr. Yid. *beygl*) is a metaphor, deriving from the M.H.G. *bougel*, meaning "ring." The late-1900s verb *bagel* (to *bagel out*—HDAS: 1976) is also a metaphor, meaning to be "shut out" (i.e., score no points) in a tennis game. DAFD; EWPO; FLC; MDWPO; NSOED; PT. *Compare* Love.

BAGEL OUT   *See* Bagel.

BAKE (v)   *to bake in the sun; to bake something into the budget*. To bask in the sunshine; to include something in the budget. Source: BAKE (v). MWCD: O.E. *Baking in the sun* (NSOED: late-17th cent.) is something that sunbathers do. The sun's rays are not hot enough to bake bread, at least not without reflectors or magnifiers. Nevertheless, people can receive second-degree burns from too much exposure to a summer sun without sun screen or sun block. *Baking something into the budget* is based on the preparation of a food for baking, at which time all of the necessary ingredients must be included, as well as optional ones such as nuts and raisins. Too much baking in the kitchen can also be dangerous, leading to what is called *baker's knees*, or "knock-knees," which bakers are said to develop from kneading too much dough. FLC; MDWPO.

BAKED ALASKA   *a baked Alaska*. A baked sponge cake containing ice cream and meringue. DAFD: ca. 1905. Source: BAKE (v). MWCD: O.E. How does one bake ice cream? And why is the result called an Alaska? The answer to the first question is to bake the meringue-covered ice-cream cake in a very hot oven until the meringue begins to brown. The meringue protects the ice cream from the heat and keeps it from melting. The answer to the second question is that although the term first appeared in print about 1905, the dish itself goes back to the 1860s, when the United States purchased Alaska from Russia (1869). Presumably the dessert was created to commemorate that event. FLC.

BAKER'S DOZEN   *a baker's dozen*. Thirteen. MWCD: 1596. Source: BAKE (v). MWCD: O.E. *Baker's dozen* is a 16th cent. phenomenon. Fed up with bakers "shortweighting" the vendors who came to pick up their bread, the English Parliament passed a law regulating the wholesale weight of bread and imposing penalties for violating it. The bakers responded by adding a thirteenth loaf, called a *vantage loaf*, to each dozen supplied to the vendors, to ensure that no one was shortchanged. However, because thirteen was an unlucky number, the augmented dozen came to be called either a "Devil's dozen" or a *baker's dozen*. The latter term survived, and now the moderator of a meeting might look out at the small crowd and say, "Ah! We have a baker's dozen." BDPF; CI; DAI; DC; DEI; EWPO; HI; HND; LCRH; MDWPO; NSOED.

BAKER'S KNEES   *See* Bake (v.).

BALLPARK MUSTARD   *See* Mustard.

BALONEY!   Nonsense! Rubbish! HDAS: 1922. Source: BOLOGNA. MWCD: 1596. *Bologna* is the name of a sausage, *bologna sausage*, that originated in Bologna, Italy, and became known to the English-speaking world in the late-16th cent. Made of a mixture of precooked, seasoned, and smoked beef, veal, and pork, the sausage became popular in America in the 1870s, where its name was soon pronounced *baloney* (or *boloney*). The first metaphorical use of *baloney* was for an old bull or cow that wasn't good for much of anything but making sausage, and the second was for a worn-out, punch-drunk boxer, also known as a "palooka." Governor Al Smith of the State of New York contributed the metaphorical expressions *baloney dollar* (in reference to the devaluated dollar of 1934) and *No matter how you slice it, it's still baloney* (which may have been the model for Carl Sandburg's similar usage in *The People, Yes*, 1936). In 1943 Claire Booth Luce, a federal congressperson, created the term *globaloney* (from *global* + *baloney*) to refer to aid to certain foreign allies of the United States during WWII; and sometime after the 1950s a cute little boy sang a jingle on television for the first time that illustrated the contrast between the American pronunciation of the name of the sausage ("My buh-LOH-niy has a first name . . .") and the Italian spelling of the word (". . . with B-O-L-O-G-N-A"). Other metaphorical uses of *baloney* include "That's a *bunch of baloney*," "That's *no baloney*," "You're *full of baloney*," and "You're a *phoney baloney*." The literal definition of *bologna* has also been altered recently by the use of turkey meat as a substitute for, or additive to, beef and pork. The slang term for boneless turkey is *bleached boloney*. (HDAS: 1974). BDPF; CE; DAI; DAS; DEOD; EWPO; FLC; HND; MDWPO; NSOED; PT.

BALONEY DOLLAR   *See* Baloney!

BANANA   *See* Banana Boat; Twinkie Defense.

BANANA BOAT   *a banana boat*. A cargo ship used to transport bananas and emigrants from the Caribbean and Gulf countries to the United States. IHAT: 1916. Source: BANANA. MWCD: 1597. If you came to America on a banana boat, as General Colin Powell's father did (from Jamaica), you were prob. poor and determined because the ship was stereotypically dirty and decrepit. The countries from which the banana boats came were known as *banana republics* (MWCD: 1935), which were also sterotyped as economically poor, politically unstable, and financially dependent on a single crop (bananas) and a single currency (American). *Banana republic* has become the name of a chain of upscale clothing stores and has also become incorporated into the term *banana-republic politics*: volatile and despotic; and *Banana Boat* has become the trademark for both a tanning oil and a plastic dish in which banana sundaes are served. A *banana split* (MWCD: 1920) is a sundae consisting of a lengthwise-split banana covered with three scoops of ice cream and topped with fruits, nuts, syrups, whipped cream, and maraschino cherries. The lunch-counter jargon for a banana split in the 1920s was *houseboat*, which was based on the resemblance of the oblong glass bowl and its contents to a shallow-draft boat with a small "house" on top. If filled with pieces of fruit alone, minus the ice cream and toppings, the glass bowl was referred to in lunch counters as a *fruit boat* or *canoe*. DAFD; DAS; DEI; MS.

BANANA PEPPER   *See* Fruit with Appeal.

BANANA REPUBLIC   *See* Banana Boat.

BANANA-REPUBLIC POLITICS   *See* Banana Boat.

BANANA SEAT   *See* Fruit with Appeal.

BANANA SPLIT   *See* Banana Boat.

BAND SHELL   *See* Shell out.

BANQUET   *See* Feast.

BAR AND GRILL   *See* Grill a Suspect.

BARBECUE (v)   *to barbecue meat.* To roast or broil meat on a grate or spit over an open fire. NSOED: mid-17th cent. Source: BARBECUE (n). The verb *barbecue* (*barbeque* or *Bar-B-Q*) is derived from the noun *barbecue* (MWCD: 1709), in spite of the fact that the noun is first recorded several decades after the verb. The noun is derived from Sp. *barbacoa*, which is a rendering of the word used by 16th-cent. Haitian Indians for a wooden framework on which meat (orig. poultry or fish, later pork) was roasted over an open fire (perhaps in a pit). American colonists borrowed the word *barbacoa* from the Spanish, altering it to *barbecue* and allowing it to function also as a verb. As the practice of barbecuing spread throughout the colonies, the outdoor barbecue became a social gathering (LA: 1733); and as the practice moved westward, in the 19th cent., beef (often an entire steer) became the meat of choice at a *Western barbecue*. In the 20th cent., a sandwich containing barbecued beef or pork came to be called a *barbecue*, and the sauce that had been used all along to baste the meat came to be called *barbecue sauce* (DAFD: 1939). The outdoor barbecue of a whole hog is now usu. called a *pig roast*, and the outdoor barbecue of a whole steer is now often called an *ox roast*. BDPF; EWPO; FLC; IHAT; MDWPO; PT; THT.

BARBEQUE (n)   *See* Barbecue (v).

BAR-B-Q   *See* Barbecue (v).

BATTER CAKE   *See* Pancake (n).

BATTERY ACID   *See* Java.

BEAN   *to bean someone on the bean*. For a baseball pitcher to hit a batter on the head with a ball. HDAS; 1908. Source: BEAN (n). MWCD: O.E. In baseball, the *beanball* (MWCD: ca. 1905), if thrown intentionally, is an illegal pitch and can lead to a warning for both managers, esp. if it follows a home run by the preceding batter, or to a brouhaha, esp. if the hit batter walks out to the pitching mound, esp. with his bat in his hand, to "have a word with the pitcher." If a beanball is thrown unintentionally, i.e., as a brushback pitch, esp. if the preceding batter has just homered, and if the batter walks out to the mound, even without his bat, to visit the pitcher, the same results usu. follow. The verb *bean* can also be applied to the action of striking someone who is not a batter with something other than a baseball; e.g., a batter can *bean* a catcher by releasing one hand from the bat while swinging at a pitched ball, thereby lengthening his swing and catching the catcher on the head, shoulder, or mask. Outside of baseball, a customer at a bar can *bean* another customer with a beer bottle, a pedestrian can *bean* another pedestrian with an umbrella, etc. The noun *bean* has been a metaphor for "head" since the late-19th cent (LA: 1880s), as illustrated by the green skullcap, with or without horizontal propellar on top, that used to be required wearing by college freshmen from the beginning of the fall semester until homecoming (approx. two months): the *beanie* (HDAS: 1918). Sometimes the noun *bean* seems to apply more to the contents of the head, i.e., the brain, than to the container itself, as in the expression "That's *using the old bean*" or "Smart people *use their beans*." CE; DAS; MDWPO.

BEANBALL   *See* Bean.

BEAN COUNTER   *See* Bean Eater.

BEANEATER   *See* Bean Eater.

BEAN EATER   *a Bean Eater*. A resident of Boston, Mass. HDAS: 1867. Source: BEAN; EAT. MWCD: O.E. Residents of Boston (*Bean Town*) are called *Bean Eaters* because the city is famous for its *Boston baked beans* (DAFD: 1850s). The name became so popular with Bostonians that the 1891 Boston National League baseball team was called the *Beaneaters*, and the modern American League Boston Red Sox are sometimes referred to by broadcasters as the *Beaneaters*. Boston baked beans are made with pea beans (however, outside of New England, with navy beans) and salt pork or bacon, molasses, and brown sugar. According to Puritan custom, the beans are baked in a crock on Saturday, eaten for "supper" on Saturday night, and eaten as leftovers for "brunch" on Sunday—with Boston brown bread, of course. Outside of the home, beans are the specialty at cheap restaurants called *beaneries* (MWCD: 1887), and beans were once used to mark the squares at *Beano* ("bingo") *parlors* (MWCD: 1935). Boston not only has bean eaters but *bean counters* (MWCD: 1975): financial analysts and statisticians who are far removed from the man or woman on the street; business and financial managers who hate to spend money; and accountants and bookkeepers who simply "count the beans" (i.e., the figures) to make sure the books balance. *Counting beans* prob. derives from the centuries-old association of beans with coins, although the invitation to count the beans in a glass jar at the general store, and win a handsome prize, may have had some influence also. Beans are jocularly referred to as *the musical fruit*: The more you eat, the more you toot (HDAS: 1919). DAFD; DAS; FLC; LA; PT; WNWCD. *See also* Not Worth a Hill of Beans.

BEANERY   *See* Bean Eater.

BEANIE   *See* Bean.

BEANO   *See* Bean Eater.

BEAN POLE   *a bean pole*. A tall, thin person. LA: 1836. Source: BEAN. MWCD: O.E. Literally, a *bean pole* (MWCD: 1798) is a tall wooden pole, up to eight feet in height, that is set in the ground next to a climbing "pole bean" plant and up which the bean vine, heavy with pods, grows to reach the sunlight. (A growing corn stalk works just as well.) Metaphorically, a *bean pole* is a lanky or skinny person, male or female, whose height emphasizes his or her slenderness (and vice versa). Another name for a tall, thin person is *string bean*, an Americanism that was based on the name of a variety of bean, a *string bean* (MWCD: 1759), and was prob. coined before the end of the 19th cent., when a stringless variety of the bean was developed and the bean was given the name of other, existing beans—snap beans, green beans, wax beans, and even French beans—for euphemistic reasons. (Some people disliked the stringy bean pods so much that they shelled them and boiled the beans as if they were peas.) CE; DAFD; DAS; EWPO; FLC; HDAS; LA; PT.

BEAR FRUIT   *See* Be Fruitful and Multiply.

BEAR GREASE   *See* Grease.

BEAT THE STUFFING OUT OF   *See* Knock the Stuffing out of.

BECOME TOAST   *See* Toast (n).

BED AND BOARD   *See* Boardinghouse Reach.

BED AND BREAKFAST   *See* Boardinghouse Reach.

BEEF (n)   *a beef*. A complaint. HDAS: 1899. Source: BEEF (n). MWCD: 14th cent. To *have a beef* with or about someone or something is to have an argument, complaint, grudge, or protest with or about them. The metaphor prob. derives from the vocal "complaints" made either by cattle who have waited too long to be fed or let out of the barnyard or by cows who have waited too long to be milked or let back into the barn. Literally, *beef* is a modified form of Fr. *boeuf* "beef" (fr. Lat. *bou-* "head of cattle"). It contrasts with Eng. *cow* (Mid. Eng. *cou*) the way *pork* (fr. O.Fr. *porc* "pig") contrasts with Eng. *pig* (M.E. *pigge*) and *mutton* (fr. O.Fr. *moton* "ram") contrasts with Eng. *sheep* (M.E. *sheep*); i.e., the Fr. word denotes the edible meat from the animal, whereas the Eng. word denotes the live animal itself. Among domesticated mammals, *beef* is the meat of adult bovines— bulls, cows, and steers—whereas *veal* (MWCD: 14th cent.) is the meat of very young, specially fed calves. Beef is often called *red meat*, as opposed to chicken or turkey breast, which is called *white meat* (q.v.), and pork, which is referred to in advertisements as "The other white meat." A television commercial in 1984 asked its competitors, "Where's the beef?"—in regard to the alleged shrinking size of fast-food hamburgers back in the 1980s. *Beef* is normally associated with "substance," as with the adj. *beefy* (MWCD: 1743), which describes a large, heavy, powerful man—e.g., a *beefy bodyguard*. ATWS; BDPF; DAFD; DAS; FLC; LA; NSOED; PT; SA. *Compare* Beef (v).

BEEF (v)   *to beef* ("build") *something up* (MWCD: 1860); *to beef* ("complain") *about something* (LA: 1880). Source: BEEF (n). MWCD: 14th cent. Beef cattle, or steers, are *beefed up*, or fattened, before they are sent to the slaughter house, in order to increase their weight and their value on the market. From this practice has developed the metaphor *to beef up* something in order to increase its strength, size, or substance (HDAS: 1944). For example, a bodybuilder might *beef up* his/her muscles before a competition; a company might *beef up* its staff or workload in order to cope with a large order; a business might *beef up* its advertising campaign before introducing a new product; a campaign manager might *beef up* the number of his/her candidate's television appearances just before an election; and a corporation might *beef up* its offer to buy another corporation before someone else does. The contrasting phrase *to beef about something* derives from the behavior of cattle complaining loudly when they are hungry or haven't been milked on time. People *beef about* just about anything, to just about anybody, esp. when they know that their complaints are going to fall on deaf ears. AID; ATWS; CE; DAI; DAS; DEI; LCRH; SA.

BEEF ABOUT   *See* Beef (v).

BEEFALO   *See* Beefeater.

BEEF BACON   *See* Canadian Bacon.

BEEFCAKE   *See* Cheesecake.

BEEFEATER   *a Beefeater*. A Warden of the Tower of London. MWCD: 1671. Source: BEEF (MWCD: 14th cent.); EAT (MWCD: O.E.). The Wardens of the Tower of London are Yeomen Extraordinary of the Guard who were first assigned to the Tower during the reign of Edward VI (1547–1553) and still wear uniforms reminiscent of the Tudor court of Edward's father, King Henry VIII. The Beefeaters were so named because they were issued a daily ration of beef—not, as once supposed, because they served as *buffetiers*, i.e., "table waiters," in the Tower. In recent years the slang term *Beefeaters* has developed in America to include all Englishmen, who are targeted for their appetite for beef. In America, beef is what "real" men eat—*red meat* (q.v.), *meat and potatoes* (q.v.)—as opposed to *quiche* (q.v.), which "real" men don't eat. When a "real" man in America gets a black eye, he slaps a raw *beefsteak* (MWCD: 1710) on it; if he wants a change of pace, he can switch to *beefalo* (MWCD: 1973), the meat of a cross between an American buffalo (or "bison") and a cow; and if he runs out of beef, he can transfer the name to a substitute, as in *Albany beef* (HDAS: 1779), i.e., sturgeon from the Hudson River. BDPF; DEOD; EWPO; FLC; MDWPO; NSOED; SA. *Compare* Limey.

BEEF JERKY   *See* Chipped Beef.

BEEFSTEAK   *See* Beefeater.

BEEFSTEAK TOMATO   *See* Tomato.

BEEF TARTARE   *See* Steak Tartare.

BEEF UP   *See* Beef (v).

BEEFY   *See* Beef (v).

BEEN THROUGH THE MILL   *See* Through the Mill.

BEER-BELLY POCKETBOOK   *See* Appetite.

BEET RED   *See* Red as a Beet.

BEET SUGAR   *See* Red as a Beet; Sugar.

BE FRUITFUL, AND MULTIPLY   Be productive, and bring forth many progeny. Source: FRUIT. MWCD: O.E. In Genesis 1:27, God created man and woman (detailed later in 2:1 and 2:22), and in 1:28 "God said unto them, *Be fruitful, and multiply*, and replenish the earth" [italics added]. A plant that is *fruitful* bears much fruit, whether in the narrow definition of the word *fruit* (e.g., peaches, apples, berries, and melons) or in its broad definition (including nuts, beans, seeds, etc.). Animals and humans who are *fruitful* (MWCD: 14th cent.) are able not only to produce progeny but to build tangible things (such as domiciles) and to achieve intangible results (such as security). For humans, however, it is plans and schemes that are esp. *fruitful, bearing fruit* in the form of acquisitions and profits. When these plans and schemes do not *bear fruit*, i.e., do not reach *fruition* (MWCD: 15th cent.), then it is *fruitless* (MWCD: 14th cent.) to pursue them any further. NSOED.

BEGGING BOWL   *See* Panhandle (n).

BE IN HOT WATER   *See* Look like a Boiled Lobster.

BELGIAN WAFFLE   *See* Waffle (v).

BELLY BACON   *See* Canadian Bacon.

BELOW THE SALT   *See* Salt of the Earth.

BEND YOUR MIND INTO A PRETZEL   *See* Human Pretzel.

BERRIES   *the berries.* (*You're the berries!*) The greatest. EWPO: 1902. Source: BERRY. MWCD: O.E. In early-20th cent. American slang, *the berries* was a term of approval for both people and things: "He/she's *the berries*"; "This place is *the berries*"; "That band is *the berries*." Berries are a category of fruit, along with other categories, such as drupes (single-seeded fruits, such as peaches) and pomes (central-cored fruits, such as apples). Strictly speaking, berries are small, globular, soft, juicy, multiseeded fruits that usu. contain the word *berry* in their name. Most berries are edible, and quite a few berries—such as blackberries, raspberries, and strawberries—are regarded as the most delicious of fruits. However, the *berry* category has become a catchall for the leftovers in the fruit field, collecting not only tomatoes, which are multiseeded but are popularly grouped with the vegetables, and bananas, which seem to contain no seeds at all. Furthermore, the term *berry* is used for true vegetable products such as coffee beans, and for shellfish products such as lobster eggs. The expression *brown as a berry* (EWPO: 1386) derives from Chaucer's Prologue to the *Canterbury Tales*, which describes the Monk's horse as being *as broun as eny berye*. Since berries are seldom brown (unless they are starting to spoil), and since the brown coffee bean had not yet been introduced into England by 1386, Chaucer either was referring to brown cedar-tree berries or making a sarcastic remark about the monk's steed. CE; DAS; DEI; HDAS; HND; MDWPO; NSOED; PT; WNWCD.

BEST THING SINCE SLICED BREAD   *See* Greatest Thing since Sliced Bread.

BET DOLLARS TO DOUGHNUTS   *See* Doughnut.

BETTY   *See* Brown Betty.

BEYOND YOUR SALAD DAYS   *See* Salad Days.

BIG APPLE   *The Big Apple*. New York City. HDAS: 1946. Source: APPLE. MWCD: O.E. In jazz musicians' slang of the 1930s, there were *big apples* (i.e., "big cities") and *little apples* (i.e., "little cities") where jazz was popular. One of the *big apples* of the time was New Orleans, which went by that nickname until it was replaced by "The Crescent City" and, later, "The Big Easy." New York City, of course, was the biggest apple of them all, and the nickname *The Big Apple* caught on there sometime between the 1930s and the 1960s. A popular dance of the 1930s, not among jazz fans but among swing fans, was also called *The Big Apple*, although it is not certain how the two terms are related. It seems clear, however, that the name *The Big Apple* for New York City was not influenced by the Unisphere—a hollow, spherical, forty-foot-diameter, stainless steel framework with the continents of the Earth attached that was installed in Flushing Meadow(s), Queens, for the 1964 World's Fair and donated to the city by the U.S. Steel Corporation. For the average visitor to New York City, *The Big Apple* prob. connotes a city that is full of opportunity and ripe for the picking. CI; DAS; EWPO; IHAT; MDWPO; WNWCD.

BIG CHEESE   *See* Cheesehead.

BIG ENCHILADA   *See* Chili Today, Hot Tamale.

BIG FISH EAT LITTLE FISH   *See* Food Chain.

BIGGER THAN A BREADBOX   *See* Is It Bigger than a Breadbox?

BIG PRETZEL   *See* Human Pretzel.

BING CHERRY   *See* Cherry (adj).

BIRCH SYRUP   *See* Cough Syrup.

BIRDSEED   *See* Chicken Feed.

BISCOTTI   *See* Biscuit.

BISCUIT   *a biscuit*. A twice-baked bread or cake. Source: BISCUIT. MWCD: 14th cent. Before the 19th cent., biscuits were flat, hard, and dry, like Amer. cookies—or flat, crisp, and dry, like Amer. crackers. The modern Amer. biscuit, emanating primarily from the South, is high, soft, and moist, like bread. The word *biscuit* (fr. Fr. for "twice baked," fr. Lat. *bis-* "twice" + *coqtum* "cooked") is a misnomer for all of these products except crackers (in the Amer. sense) because cookies (in the Amer. sense), biscuits (in the Amer. sense), and breads are never baked twice. (Of course, already baked bread can be sliced and browned, but then it is usu. given a different name, such as Eng. *toast*, Du. *rusk*, or Ger. *Zwieback*—lit. "twice baked"). The It. word *biscotti* "cookie" also lit. means "twice baked," although biscotti really are baked twice. (They are popular in America for dunking in tea, coffee, hot chocolate, or wine.) In Britain, *biscuit* now refers to what in America would be called a cookie or a cracker—a sense that prob. derives fr. the much earlier *sea biscuits* (MWCD: ca. 1690), later known as *hardtack* (MWCD: 1836), which were unsalted, unleavened, unshortened breads that were baked (only once!), dried, and then stored on board ship for the crew to munch on during a long voyage. *Soft tack* (DAFD: 1833) referred to shortened bread. BDPF; DAS; EWPO; FLC; HDAS; IHAT; PT; WNWCD.

BISCUIT ROLLER   *See* Biscuit Shooter.

BISCUIT SHOOTER   *a biscuit shooter*. A waitress in a lunch counter (HDAS: 1893); a cook on a ranch (HDAS: 1912). Source: BISCUIT. MWCD: 14th cent. It is not clear why cooks and waitresses were once characterized as "shooters of biscuits." Perhaps the biscuits were so hard in those days that they could be thrown by the cook to the ranch hand—or by the waitress to the diner—without breaking apart. However, an earlier name for a biscuit shooter was *biscuit roller* (DAFD: 1870s), a name that suggests that the hard biscuits could be rolled to the cowboy or the customer. From the term *biscuit shooter* developed the word *shooter*—not for the cook or the waitress but for the biscuit itself. (Waitresses at lunch counters also asked for biscuits by the slang term *clinkers*.) All of these terms disappeared ca. 1925. IHAT; LA. *See also* Hardtack.

BITE (n)   *a bite*. A small amount of food. Source: BITE (n). MWCD: 15th cent. Literally, a bite is the act of biting off a piece of bread, meat, fruit, vegetable, etc., with the teeth. The bite produces an amount of food somewhere between a morsel and a mouthful. A bite can also be the amount of food taken into the mouth by the point of a knife or the tines of a fork, even though the teeth (and lips) are used only to strip the food from the utensil. Figuratively, a *bite* is the amount ("bite-size") of (semisolid) food that comes to reside in the mouth, regardless of how it gets there. For example, a diner who is "full"—or dislikes what he/she is eating—may tell the host or hostess that he/she *can't eat another bite*; or that same person may use the excuse that he/she *had a bite* before leaving home or *stopped for a bite* on the trip over.

BITE (v)   *to bite.* To go along with a joke or riddle. Source: BITE (v). MWCD: O.E. A fish *bites* when it claps its jaws onto either the bait alone (a."nibble") or the bait and the hook to which the bait is attached (a "true" *bite*). If the fish manages to evade the hook's barb, its reward is food (unless the bait is artificial); however, if the fish's mouth becomes impaled on the barbed hook, the fish becomes the loser, and the reward (also food) goes to the angler. The "straight man" (*sic*) on a comedy team is like the fish who gets caught on a hook: He never gets the reward (i.e., the laughs). For example, if Lou Costello had said to Bud Abbott (the straight man), "What did the pot say to the kettle?" Abbott might have said, "I'll *bite.* What *did* the pot say to the kettle?" ("Don't get all steamed up!"); or if Gracie Allen had said to George Burns (the straight man), "What has four wheels and flies?" Burns might have said, "I'll *bite.* What *does* have four wheels and flies?" ("An old-fashioned garbage truck.") The one who *bites* in a "knock knock" game is the one who says, "Who's there?" ATWS; CI; DAS; DEI; SA.

BITE OFF MORE THAN YOU CAN CHEW   *to bite off more than you can chew.* To attempt more than you can accomplish. Source: BITE; CHEW. MWCD: O.E. This metaphorical expression dates from either the late medieval period in England (alluding to food) or the late-19th cent. in America (alluding to tobacco). To bite off more *food* than you can chew is something that both animals and humans are prone to do, although animals are more likely to cough the food up, whereas humans are more likely to swallow it (sometimes with fatal results). Biting off more tobacco than you can chew is restricted to humans (esp. males), who tear off a "chaw" from the "cake" with their teeth and position it in one of their cheeks. (Swallowing a chaw of tobacco can also be fatal.) Humans who metaphorically *bite off more than they can chew* are too ambitious, greedy, overconfident, or reckless for their own good. AID; BDPF; CE; CI; DAI; DEI; HB; HND; NSOED. *Compare* Eyes Are Bigger than Your Stomach.

BITE SOMEONE'S HEAD OFF   *to bite someone's head off.* To respond angrily, curtly, or sharply to a simple question, answer, or request. Source BITE. MWCD: O.E. X: "Good morning!" Y: "What do you mean by that?" X: "You don't have to bite my head off!" One animal, an insect, actually *does* bite the head off another. During courtship, the female praying mantis sometimes bites off the head of the male, which then mounts her, copulates with her, and is eaten by her. Among humans, there once were performers who bit the heads off small animals. Such persons were called *geeks* (MWCD: 1914, fr. Du. *gek* "fool"). At carnivals and sideshows during the early part of the 20th cent., *geeks* were "freaks" whose specialty was biting off the head of a chicken or a snake. (This practice was revived by the rock star Ozzy Osbourne in the late-20th cent.) The word *geek*, however, has now come to mean an adolescent male who is so engrossed in computers, mathematics, or other sciences that he is regarded as "weird" or simply antisocial. BDPF; DAS; DEI; HND; MS. *Compare* Toadeater; Toady.

BITE THE HAND THAT FEEDS YOU   *to bite the hand that feeds you.* To turn on your benefactor. DC: 1711 (Joseph Addison's *The Spectator*). Source: BITE; FEED. MWCD: O.E. The dog may be "man's (*sic*) best friend," but that friendship can turn to enmity if the owner teases the dog mercilously, harasses it endlessly, abuses it physically, or even wakens it suddenly out of a sound sleep. As a result, in spite of the fact that the the human feeds and shelters the dog, the animal may turn on its owner and attack him/her viciously, *biting the hand that* (regularly) *feeds it.* People are sometimes tempted to do the same thing to their "superiors" who discriminate against them or abuse them verbally or physically. Those who advise against taking any action against the offenders warn the victim that if they *know which side their bread is buttered on* (q.v.), they will not *bite the hand that feeds them*; otherwise they might lose their jobs. (Those who *do* take action are regarded as heroes by all of the other victims.) AID; ATWS; BDPF; CI; DAP; DEI; HND; MDWPO; MS; SA. *Compare* Kill the Goose That Laid the Golden Eggs.

BITTER   Harsh; intense; severe. Source: BITTER. MWCD: O.D. *Bitter* is one of the four basic taste sensations, along with *salt, sour,* and *sweet* (all of which *see*). The harshness of the metaphors based on *bitter* is attributable to the fact that this sense of taste is variously described as "acrid, astringent, and sharp" and because the adj. *bitter* is prob. related to the verb *bite*. The Old Testament book of Proverbs (5:4) states of a "strange woman": "But her end [i.e., her death] is *bitter as wormwood*, sharp as a two-edged sword" [italics added]. This sharpness is evident in metaphorical phrases such as *bitter death* (with severe pain and suffering), *bitter enemies* (showing intense animosity), *bitter contempt* (featuring cynicism and rancor), *bitter cold* (helped by a raw and piercing wind), and *bitter tears* (from severe grief and loss). Generally speaking, a person who is bitter is angry and resentful over something that has occurred in the recent or distant past. CE; DEI; EWPO; HF; IRCD; SA; WNWCD.

BITTER COLD   *See* Bitter.

BITTER CONTEMPT   *See* Bitter.

BITTER DEATH   *See* Bitter.

BITTER END   *to the bitter end*. To the very end of a long and difficult struggle. MWCD: 1849. Source: BITTER (*). *Bitter end* is not a food metaphor. It derives from the sea. On old sailing ships, a *bitter* (HND: 1627) was a turn of an anchoring cable on a *bitt* (MWCD: 1593), the post on board the ship on which the cable was secured. If all that remained of the cable on the bitt was the *bitter end*, the cable had been fully deployed and the anchor was now "at the end of its rope." When people are "at the end of their rope," they have a choice of giving up or struggling *to the bitter end*, i.e., until defeat or death, regardless of how "bitter." AID; CI; EWPO; HB; LA; MDWPO.

BITTER ENEMIES   *See* Bitter.

BITTER FRUITS   *See* Fruits of Your Labors.

BITTER PILL TO SWALLOW   *a bitter pill to swallow*. A negative occurrence that is hard to accept. EWPO: 1779 (Horace Walpole). Source: BITTER; SWAL-LOW. MWCD: O.E. Bitter-tasting pills were once coated with honey in order to mask their bad taste; otherwise, they would have been too bitter to swallow. (Now they are *sugarcoated*, q.v.) Swallowing a pill is like receiving news. Swallowing a coated pill is like receiving good news: you're delighted and happy; but swallow-ing a *bitter pill* is like receiving bad news: you're disappointed and distressed. The disappointment occurs if you or someone close to you fails to reach a goal, but it turns to distress if someone close to you betrays your trust. Such behavior is *hard to swallow* (q.v.). CI; DEI; MS.

BITTERSWEET   *See* Take the Bitter with the Sweet.

BITTERSWEET CHOCOLATE   *See* Take the Bitter with the Sweet.

BITTERSWEET VICTORY   *See* Take the Bitter with the Sweet.

BITTER TEARS   *See* Bitter.

BLACK AND WHITE   *See* Black Cow.

BLACK-AND-WHITE   *See* Salt-and-Pepper; White Chocolate.

BLACKBERRIES ARE RED WHEN THEY'RE GREEN   Blackberries—and blueberries—are red-colored when they're immature. Source: BLACKBERRY. MWCD: O.E. The blackberry is a clustered-berry fruit: Each "berry" is really a cluster of tiny berries that contain the seeds. Blackberries are related to black (and red) raspberries but are much larger than raspberries; in fact, the blackberry is the largest of all wild berries. The *loganberry* (MWCD: 1893) is a cross between the blackberry and the red raspberry, and the *boysenberry* (MWCD: 1935) is a cross between the blackberry and the loganberry. All of these berries—the black-berries, raspberries, loganberries, boysenberries, and the related *dewberry* (MWCD: ca. 1578)—grow on trailing brambles and are closer in color to purple than to black. A *blackberry winter* (DAFD: ca. 1900) is a cool May when black-berries bloom, and a *blackberry summer* is a warm September when blackberries ripen. DAP; EWPO; FLC.

BLACKBERRY SUMMER   *See* Blackberries Are Red When They're Green.

BLACKBERRY WINTER   *See* Blackberries Are Red When They're Green.

BLACK-BOTTOM PIE   *See* Mud Pie.

BLACK-BOTTOM SUNDAE   *See* Sundae.

BLACK CHERRY   *See* Cherry (adj.).

BLACK COW   *a black cow.* (Lunch-counter jargon.) A chocolate soda or root beer float containing chocolate ice cream. Source: SODA. The *black cow* is also known as a "double chocolate soda," or a *mud fizz.* If vanilla ice cream is substi-tuted for chocolate, the soda is called a *black-and-white*, and the float is called a *brown cow* or a *Boston cooler. Black cow* was also a lunch-counter term for just plain root beer in the 1930s, and for chocolate milk ca. 1920. DAFD; HDAS; IHAT; SA.

BLACK-EYED PEA   *See* Pea Bean.

BLACK JELLY BEAN   *See* Jelly Bean.

BLACKSTRAP MOLASSES   *See* Slow as Molasses in January.

BLANCH (v)   *to blanch.* To turn pale. NSOED: mid-18th cent. Source: BLANCH. MWCD: 15th cent. When a person *blanches* from fear, he/she experi-ences loss of blood in the capillaries of the face. (The condition is the opposite of blushing, in which case the capillaries fill with blood and turn the face red or rosy.) The intransitive form of the verb *blanch* is derived from the transitive form, which once described the method of preventing celery, endive, and rhubarb from assuming their natural color. The vegetables were covered with earth or boards to prevent the development of chlorophyl and thereby enhance their appearance. Nowadays, to *blanch* food means to scald it briefly in order to firm up the flesh, loosen the skin, or set in the flavor in preparation for freezing. FLC; WNWCD.

BLOODCURDLING SCREAM   *See* Curdle Your Blood.

BLOOD PUDDING   *See* Pudding.

BLOOD SAUSAGE   *See* Pudding.

BLOODTHIRSTY   *See* Thirst (n).

BLOW THE LID OFF   *to blow the lid off something.* To expose something criminal or scandalous. Source: LID. MWCD: O.E. A *lid* (fr. O.E. *hlid*) is the removable cover of a pot. When the liquid in a full pot is brought to a hard boil, the pressure can build up and force the lid either to float off (if it is lightweight and not tightly fitted) or to blow off (if it is mediumweight and tightly fitted). The latter case is the basis for the expression *to blow the lid off something*, although in the metaphor the cause of the "blowing" seems to be an individual, such as an investigative reporter or whistle-blower, who has become aware of the impending danger and has chosen to *uncover* (MWCD: 14th cent.) it before it "blows" on its own. The objects of "lid blowing" are usu. the corrupt practices of politicians, the illegal operations of businesses, and the sexual behavior of celebrities. A similar metaphor, *to flip your lid* (HND: 1951), means "to become angry" (like the boiling liquid) and "lose control" (like the blowing lid). In contrast, *to put a lid on it* means to "shut your mouth" (an open "pot") by closing it with your lips and jaws (the "lids"); and *to keep the lid on* means "to keep quiet about something" or keep it under control. *Potlids* is a slang term for "cymbals," and *lid* alone is slang for both a "hat" and "an ounce of marijuana." CI; DAI; DAS; HDAS; MS; PT.

BLT   *See* Lunch-counter Jargon.

BLUEBERRY   *See* Blackberries Are Red when They're Green; Huckleberry.

BLUE CHEESE   Cheese that has been treated with mold. MWCD: 1925. Source: CHEESE. MWCD: O.E. Most people are repulsed by the sight of a piece of moldy cheese that has been left in the refrigerator too long. However, these are the same people who gladly eat cheese that is moldy on the *inside* and call it the "king of cheeses." Blue cheese is cheese that has been skewered several times to hasten the growth of *Penicillium roqueforti* deep within. After aging for three to six months, the cheese displays several bluish-green (or greenish-blue) veins that penetrate throughout. The most famous of the blue cheeses is the trademarked Roquefort, from Roquefort, France, which is also the only one made from sheep's milk. The others, all made from cow's milk, are Danablu (from Denmark), Gorgonzola (from Gorgonzola, Italy), Stilton (from Stilton, England), and, of course, the generic "blue cheeses" that Americans call "Roquefort" until they are informed by their server how much real Roquefort costs. FLC. *Compare* Moon Is Made of Green Cheese.

BLUE PLATE SPECIAL   *See* Full Plate; Lunch-counter Jargon.

BOARD (n)   *See* Boardinghouse Reach.

BOARD (v)   *See* Boardinghouse Reach.

BOARDER   *See* Boardinghouse Reach.

BOARDINGHOUSE   *See* Boardinghouse Reach.

BOARDINGHOUSE REACH   *a boardinghouse reach.* An ability to grasp objects
that are beyond most people's reach. DAFD: 19th cent. Source: BOARD (v).
MWCD: early-1500s. In the 16th cent., to *board someone* was to provide that
person with three square meals a day at your house—for a fee, of course. That
person, called a *boarder* (MWCD: 1530), was usu., but not always, also provided
with lodging, for a larger fee. In time, such a house came to be called a *boardinghouse* (MWCD: 1728), as opposed to what eventually came to be called a *rooming
house* (MWCD: 1893). In order to survive at a boardinghouse, the residents found
it necessary to perfect their *boardinghouse reach.* The secret was to be in your shirt
sleeves, with the sleeves rolled up, and to rise from your chair and lean forward—
or to the right or left—and grasp that last leg of chicken before anyone else had
a chance to grab it. Nowadays, a *boardinghouse reach* can be practiced in any
environment, just as long as there is competition to possess something almost
unreachable. One of the early terms for food and lodging was *bed and board*,
employing the noun *board*, which was the source of the verb *board.* This expression orig. referred to the rights of the lady of the house: a *bed* to sleep in and a
board (a "table") to eat on (HND: ca. 1400). Today, a *B & B* is a *bed and breakfast*
(MWCD: 1910), a large house or inn at which people who stay there receive a
free breakfast; and bed and board is now referred to as *room and board* (MWCD:
1955). HDAS; WNWCD.

BOIL DOWN TO   *for something to boil down to something else.* For something
complex to be reduced to something simple; for something long to be reduced
to something short. HND: late-19th cent. Source: BOIL (v). MWCD: 13th cent.
In cooking, liquid is sometimes heated to a temperature of 212° Fahrenheit, i.e.,
is boiled, to convert it into something more concentrated, as when maple sap is
reduced to maple syrup, or maple syrup is converted into maple sugar. *What it
all boils down to* is an expression used by a speaker to summarize the contents of
his/her speech, or by a commentator to capture the gist or essence of a series of
remarks by others. The expression is also used by editors to instruct writers to
"make a long story short." CE; CI; DAI; MS.

BOILING MAD   *See* Reach the Boiling Point.

BOILING (OVER) WITH ANGER   *See* Reach the Boiling Point.

BOILING (OVER) WITH RAGE   *See* Reach the Boiling Point.

BOILING POINT   *See* Reach the Boiling Point.

BOIL WATER WITHOUT BURNING IT   *See* Can't Even Boil Water.

BOLOGNA SAUSAGE   *See* Baloney!

BOLONEY   *See* Baloney!

BOLT DOWN   *See* Devour.

BOMBAY DUCK   *See* Mock Duck.

BOMBER   *See* Submarine Sandwich.

BONE OF CONTENTION   *See* Have a Bone to Pick with Someone.

BONE TO PICK   *See* Have a Bone to Pick with Someone.

BONFIRE   *a bonfire.* A large outdoor fire. MWCD: 15th cent. Source: BONE; FIRE. MWCD: O.E. The modern *bonfire* is usu. built in the Northern states in the fall to celebrate events related to nature or football. The natural event is the falling of leaves in October and November, which is celebrated with a leaf burning— where permitted by law—and the roasting of marshmallows and hot dogs. The football event is the annual homecoming game, which is preceded, on the night before, by a huge wood fire—where permitted by local law and school policy— and accompanied by singing, dancing, cheerleading, and the verbal roasting of the next day's opponents. These autumn activities are a far cry from the original *bonfire* (MWCD: O.E. *bān* "bone" + *fȳr* "fire"), which occurred in England every spring to celebrate the end of winter by burning the huge collection of animal bones that had accumulated over the past year. Originally a pagan festival, it was adopted by the Christian Church and henceforth held on June 24, St. John's Day. EWPO; NSOED; SA.

BORN WITH A SILVER SPOON IN YOUR MOUTH   *to be born with a silver spoon in your mouth.* To be born into a wealthy family. DAP: 1639. Source: SPOON. MWCD: 14th cent. The silver spoon that the baby of a wealthy family is born with is not actually in its mouth, but it soon will be. The spoon in question is a christening spoon, or *apostle spoon*, that is customarily given to the infant at its baptism by the godparents, as has been done in continental Europe since at least the early-17th cent., and in England and America since the early-18th cent. Godparents who could afford it in those days actually gave twelve spoons, each with a likeness of one of the apostles on its handle; those who were not quite so wealthy gave four spoons, each with a likeness of one of the four Gospel writers; and godparents who were not quite so well off gave only one spoon, which had no biblical figure on its handle but was still called an *apostle spoon*. The silver spoon became a symbol of a family's wealth, and of wealth in general; however, although the custom continues, esp. among Roman Catholic families, the spoon is no longer associated with the wealth of the baby's family or the godparents' family. *Born with a silver spoon in your mouth* has even taken on a negative connotation in recent years, implying that you acquired your money by inheritance rather than by hard work. AID; BDPF; CI; DAI; DC; DEI; EWPO; HND; MS; NSOED; WNWCD.

BORSCHT BELT   *the borscht belt* (or *borscht circuit*). The Jewish summer resorts in the Catskills. HDAS: 1936. Source: BORSCHT. MWCD: 1829. *Borscht* (Yid. *borsht*, fr. Rus. *borshch*) is the name of a beet-and-cabbage soup (orig. parsnips or turnips and cabbage), served hot or cold, with a dollop of sour cream on top. It is a traditional favorite of Russian and Polish Jews in New York City and was a traditional offering at the Jewish hotels in the Catskill Mountains of southeastern New York State that made up the *borscht belt*. Jewish entertainers from New York City and other parts of the country made the rounds of the nightclubs in these hotels, beginning in the 1930s, thus establishing a *borscht circuit* within the *borscht belt*. Another traditional Jewish dish is *chicken soup*, which has been dubbed *Jewish penicillin* (HDAS: 1968) because of its reputed healing powers over colds and the flu, although it may simply be that the heat and steam unclog the sinuses. DAFD; FLC; MDWPO; NSOED; PT.

BORSCHT CIRCUIT   *See* Borscht Belt.

BOSSY IN A BOWL   *See* In a Stew; Lunch-counter Jargon.

BOSTON COOLER   *See* Black Cow.

BOSTON CREAM PIE   A two-layer spongecake with a custard filling. DAFD: 1855. Source: CREAM; PIE. MWCD: 14th cent. Why this "cake" is now called a *pie* is a mystery. It was orig. called a "cream cake," but the name was changed to "pudding-cake pie," then to *Boston cream pie*, or, if iced with chocolate, to "Parker House chocolate pie," in honor of the hotel in Boston where it was created. At any rate, this "pie" consists of a bottom layer of half a round sponge cake (sliced horizontally), a filling of thick custard, and a top layer of the other half of the sponge cake (coated with powdered sugar or, optionally, with chocolate icing). FLC; IHAT; PT.

BOSTON STRAWBERRIES   *See* Strawberry Mark.

BOTTLE GOURD   *See* Gourd.

BOTTLENECK   *a bottleneck.* An impasse or obstruction; a constriction or congestion. MWCD: 1907. Source: BOTTLE. MWCD: 14th cent. The most distinctive feature of a bottle is that the neck is narrower than the body. (A bottle also has no handle and is designed for pouring from rather than drinking from.) When the contents of a bottle—orig. wine or oil—are poured out, they do not all rush out at once, as from a glass or jar, but are slowed by the restraining influence of the narrow neck. (Champagne shoots up toward the ceiling when the cork is popped because it is under great pressure, unlike nonsparkling wines.) The constrictive effect of the neck of the bottle has been applied, metaphorically, to the impedence of progress of anything that is intended to move forward at a steady rate, as on the line of a factory, which is completely held up if some of the equipment fails, or on a multilane highway, when an accident blocks one of the lanes. In the former case, the products begin to pile up behind the point of obstruction, and in the latter case the cars are forced to occupy one less lane than before. Result? Gridlock. Another "bottle" metaphor is *to bottle up* (HND: mid-19th cent.), i.e., hold in your feelings, as of anger or indignation, rather than let them out by expressing them (HND: mid-19th cent.). *Bottled up* is also used to describe congestion of cars on the highway, boats in a harbor, planes on a runway, and tanks on a battlefield. AID; BDPF; CE; CI; DAI; DEI; MS.

BOTTLE UP   *See* Bottleneck.

BOTTOM FEEDER   *a bottom feeder.* A human scavenger. Source: FEED (v). MWCD: O.E. Among fish, a bottom feeder, or "bottom fish" (MWCD: 1561), is a toothless "sucker" that feeds on the bottoms of lakes and oceans, vacuuming up the scraps left over by the predator fish. This underwater "garbage collector" has an unusual appearance—mouth on the bottom of its head, barbels in front of the mouth—and an unusual size, the white sturgeon measuring up to twelve feet and weighing up to more than 1,300 pounds. Human *bottom feeders* are not identified by their appearance or size but by the fact that they are small-time operators who clean up after the big-time operators, "feeding" on the crumbs that float down to them from the top. Scavengers on dry land, such as the hyena and the rat, and in the air, such as the buzzard and the crow, feed primarily on the corpses of animals that were the victims of predators, although human garbage is also popular. Human *scavengers* (MWCD: 1530) do not lit. feed on other humans, but they do feed on human garbage or salvage usable material from the dump that can be sold to buy food. SA. *Compare* Parasite.

BOTTOMS UP!   *See* Here's Mud in Your Eye!

BOTULISM   *See* Sausage Dog.

BOWL OF CHERRIES   *See* Life Is just a Bowl of Cherries.

BOWSER BAG   *See* Brown-bag Lunch.

BOX LUNCH   *See* Business Lunch.

BOYSENBERRY   *See* Blackberries Are Red When They're Green.

BRAIN FOOD   Fish. Source: FOOD. MWCD: O.E. The term *brain food* has been around since at least the Great Depression of the 1930s, when fish were among the cheaper and more accessible foods. As children began to weary of a monotonous diet of fish, fish, and fish, their parents came up with the idea of telling them that fish were *good for them*: "They're *brain food*." It had worked for carrots (to improve the eyesight) and spinach (to increase strength), so why not fish (to sharpen the mind)? It turns out that the parents were right. Some fish contain an amino acid that helps humans to manufacture more neurotransmitters, giving them greater mental abilities, stronger concentration, and a longer attention span. That discovery has been confirmed by the remarkable achievement in American schools of children from families that originated in the fish-and-rice cultures of the Asian Pacific Rim. A more abstract kind of *brain food* is *food for thought* (DC: 1825): "something to think about"; "something worth thinking about." In the mid-1990s the CBS-TV *Early Show* was advertised as providing *Breakfast for Your Head*," i.e., ideas to stimulate your thinking. Just as *soul food* (q.v.) is food for the soul, *brain food* is food for the brain. AID; BDPF; CE; DAI; HND; MS.

BRAIN IS FRIED   *See* Fried.

BRANCH   *See* Water, Water, Everywhere, but Not a Drop to Drink.

BRAN MUFFIN   *See* Graham Flour.

BRASSIERE CUPS   *See* Cup (n).

BRATWURST   *See* Sausage Dog.

BRAUNSCHWEIGER   *See* Chopped Liver.

BREAD   Money. EWPO: ca. 1935. Source: BREAD. MWCD: O.E. Bread has long been regarded as the *staff of life* (q.v.), a *staple* of the diet (q.v.), and what sustains us through the day: our *daily bread* (fr. the Lord's Prayer, Matthew 6:11). In the late-19th cent., *bread* also took on the meaning of "livelihood" (in an Arthur Conan Doyle Sherlock Holmes mystery); and in the early-20th cent. it acquired the meaning "money" (prob. originating among musicians). The latter sense was modified by two other terms meaning "a lot of money": *long bread* (poss. influenced by the Fr. *baguette*) and *heavy bread* (poss. influenced by unleavened bread).

"Could I borrow some bread?" is not as easy a question to answer as it once was. DAS; EWPO; FLC; MDWPO; NSOED; PT.

BREAD ALWAYS FALLS BUTTERSIDE DOWN   *See Bread Always/Never Lands Butterside Up.*

BREAD ALWAYS/NEVER LANDS BUTTERSIDE UP   *His/her bread always/never lands butterside up* Things always/never seem to turn out right for him/her. Source: BREAD; BUTTER. MWCD: O.E. If you drop your slice of buttered bread (or toast) while sitting at the table, it will prob. fall on your plate or the tablecloth. In either case, if the *bread always falls butterside down* (DAP: 1834), there will be a mess, and you can consider yourself very unlucky. If it *always falls butterside up*, you can consider yourself lucky indeed. However, if you drop your bread butterside down on the floor, or if you have *buttered your bread on both sides* (q.v.), you might just as well crawl under the table. You'll never be invited to eat there again. CODP.

BREAD AND BUTTER (1)   *Your bread and butter.* Your living or livelihood; the source of your income or sustenance. MWCD: 1732. Source: BREAD; BUTTER. MWCD: O.E. Bread and butter are foods found in the diets of most of the cultures of the world. Just as bread and butter are basic to one's diet, the tools of one's trade are basic to one's livelihood. A hammer and saw are the *bread and butter* of a carpenter, words and music are the *bread and butter* of a songwriter, and pots and pans are the *bread and butter* of a cook. More abstractly, building buildings is the carpenter's *bread and butter*, writing songs is the songwriter's *bread and butter*, and cooking food is the cook's *bread and butter*. AID; CI; DAI; DAS; DEI; MS; NSOED.

BREAD AND BUTTER (2)   *Bread and butter!* Good luck! Source: BREAD; BUTTER. MWCD: O.E. Bread and butter go together like love and marriage (or a horse and carriage): They are meant for each other. When two lovers (or siblings or close friends) encounter a vertical obstacle (such as a tree or a telephone pole) while walking hand in hand, each may release the other's hand and say, "*Bread and butter!*" thereby promising that the separation (by the obstruction) will be only temporary. It is a harmless superstition meant only to reaffirm the affection that the couple have for each other. DAI. *See* Bread and Butter (1).

BREAD-AND-BUTTER (1)   *bread-and-butter issues or activities.* Basic or fundamental issues or activities. MWCD: ca. 1837. Source: BREAD; BUTTER. MWCD: O.E. *Bread-and-butter* issues in many communities include jobs, safety, education, and transportation. *Bread-and-butter* activities in many communities include working, housekeeping, and raising children. In other words, they are the issues and activities that are the most important to one's livelihood. A more recent (1990s) use of the compound occurs in an expression such as *bread-and-butter science*, i.e., science made simple, science for laypersons. MS. *See also* Bread-and-butter (2).

BREAD-AND-BUTTER (2)   *a bread-and-butter product or skill.* Something that you can depend on for your livelihood. MWCD: ca. 1837. Source: BREAD; BUTTER. MWCD: O.E. In the case of a bakery that is famous for its cookies, its *bread-and-butter* item is cookies; and in the case of a boxer who relies on his/her jab, his *bread-and-butter* punch is his/her jab. The *bread-and-butter* programs on a television network might be its soap operas; the *bread-and-butter* scenes in movies might be those containing violence; and the *bread-and-butter* books on a publisher's list might be those dealing with true romance. *See also* Bread-and-butter (1).

BREAD-AND-BUTTER LETTER   *a bread-and-butter letter (or note).* A thank-you letter or note. IHAT: 1890s. Source: BREAD; BUTTER. MWCD: O.E. In the late-19th cent. it was expected that a departed houseguest would write a *bread-and-butter letter* to the hostess, thanking her for her hospitality—and, presumably, for her delicious food (including bread and butter). Such visits are less common these days, when the visit is more likely for a luncheon or reception. The *bread-and-butter letter* is still required, however, although it is now called a "thank-you note." DAI; DEI; IHAT. *See also* Bread-and-butter (1).

BREAD AND CIRCUSES   Free food and entertainment to pacify the masses. MWCD: 1914. Source: BREAD. MWCD: O.E. According to Juvenal's *Satires* (early-2nd cent. A.D.), "bread and circuses" (Lat. *panis et circenses*) were what the Roman people wanted the most; so the government fed them (with bread, cheese, and wine) and entertained them (with games and chariot races) in order to keep them happy and peaceful. Modern palliatives of this sort consist of *pork* (q.v.) and politics. BDPF; EWPO; HND; WNWCD.

BREAD AND WATER   The reputed diet of criminal and political prisoners throughout history; the "staff of life" (MWCD: 1638). Source: BREAD; WATER. MWCD: O.E. A diet consisting only of bread and water would sustain a prisoner for a little while, but not for very long. The lack of necessary proteins, vitamins, and minerals would eventually outweigh the benefits of water, which is the more vital of the two ingredients. In the Old Testament book of Isaiah (3:1), Isaiah describes bread and water as *the staff of life:* "For, behold, the Lord, the Lord of hosts, doth take away from Jerusalem and from Judah the stay and the *staff*, the whole stay of *bread*, and the whole stay of *water*" [italics added]. Parents sometimes threaten to put a child on a diet of bread and water for misbehaving, and young women (esp.) sometimes limit their diet, temporarily, to bread and water in order to lose weight. BDPF; DAP; DC; HND; NSOED.

BREADBASKET   *the breadbasket.* The abdomen (stomach, belly) of a human being (MWCD: 1753); the major grain-producing area of a nation. Source: BREAD. MWCD: O.E. Literally, a breadbasket is a wicker basket in which loaves of bread are carried home from the bakery or served to the family at dinnertime. The "abdomen" metaphor is based either on a person carrying a basket of bread in front of him/her, making the basket look like an extended abdomen, or on the fact that the stomach is where the bread, broadly meaning "food," goes when eaten. To *hit someone in the breadbasket* is to hit that person in the abdomen. The "grain" metaphor is based either on the central location of the basket of bread on the dinner table or on the comparison of a nation to a dinner table, with the major grain-producing area prominently located thereon. Kansas was once regarded as the *breadbasket of America.* BDPF; DAI; DAS; HDAS; IHAT; NSOED; PT.

BREADBASKET OF AMERICA   *See* Breadbasket.

BREADWINNER   *the breadwinner of the family.* The wage earner of the family, the one who provides its major financial support. Source: BREAD. MWCD: O.E. In this metaphor, *bread* stands for "food," and *winner* for "earner": the "earner of the food." If a man is the *breadwinner* of the family, and the man dies, then the man's wife becomes the *breadwinner* (and vice versa). *Breadwinner* orig. meant not the person who earned the bread but the tool or craft of that person (MWCD: 1818); e.g., it might be a saw or the craft of sawing: "My *breadwinner* is my saw," said the carpenter. CE; CI; DEI; EWPO; MS; NSOED. *See also* Bring Home the Bacon. *Compare* Lady; Lord.

BREAK BREAD   *to break bread with someone.* To dine with someone, not necessarily on bread. Source: BREAD. MWCD: O.E. This metaphor derives from three of the Gospels of the New Testament—Matthew, Mark, and Luke—the most frequently quoted of which is Luke (22:19). Jesus and his disciples were in the upper room of a house in Jerusalem, about to celebrate the Passover feast: "and he took *bread*, and gave thanks, and he *brake* it, and gave unto them, saying, This is my body which is given for you: this do in remembrance of me" [italics added]. The meal is now referred to as the Last Supper, or the Lord's Supper, and the breaking of bread is known as the Eucharist, or Holy Communion (which also involves the drinking of wine). In Mod. Eng. a person who keeps company with another person—or accompanies or serves that person—is known as that person's *companion* (MWCD: 13th cent.), lit. one who breaks *bread* (fr. Lat. *panis* "bread, food") *with* (fr. Lat. *com-* "with, together with") him or her. BDPF; NSOED.

BREAKFAST (n)   The first—and most important—meal of the day. MWCD: 15th cent. Source: FAST (n). MWCD: O.E. To eat *breakfast* is lit. to *break* the *fast* that occurred during your overnight sleep. Consequently, even for people who work nights, breakfast is the first meal taken during the daytime, and night workers often eat breakfast with the rest of their family. However, in recent years some short-order restaurants and diners have started to serve breakfast at any time of the day (or night), although this favor is not accorded to *brunch* (q.v.), *lunch* (q.v.), *dinner* (q.v.), or *supper* (q.v.). Therefore, the definition of *breakfast* seems to be shifting from the time of day at which the meal is taken to the type of food that is offered under that name. The English colonists' first breakfasts consisted of food introduced to them by the Native Americans: cornbread, cornmeal mush, and cornmeal porridge. In the 18th cent., breakfasts were light—toasted or untoasted bread, tea or coffee—but in the 19th cent. they became much heavier and more varied: oatmeal or porridge with milk; bacon, ham, or sausage with eggs; pancakes or waffles with maple syrup; grits or fried potatoes; biscuits, muffins, or rolls with butter; and coffee or tea. The modern breakfast in America is comparatively light—cereal with milk and fruit, toast with butter and jam or jelly, orange juice, and coffee—although many mothers feel that it is still *the most important meal of the day*. The argument may be that breakfast tends to "jumpstart" a sleepy body and provide it with enough nutrition to last it through the day, if necessary, or at least until the *brown-bag* (q.v.) lunch at school or work. In America, breakfast is sometimes combined with a business meeting, as in the *power breakfast* (DAFD: 1980), or with TV-watching, as of the CBS-TV *Early Show*, which was advertised in the 1994–1995 season as being *Breakfast for your head*—i.e., *food for thought* (q.v.). DAFD: LA; PT.

BREAKFAST BUFFET   *See* Meal.

BREAKFAST FOR YOUR HEAD   *See* Breakfast (n).

BREAKFAST NOOK   *See* Dine (v).

BREAST   *See* Drumstick; Tough Old Bird.

BREWER'S YEAST   *See* Yeasty.

BRIMFUL   *See* Filled to the Brim.

BRIM OVER   *See* Filled to the Brim.

BRINE   *See* Pickle (n).

BRING HOME THE BACON   *to bring home the bacon*. To win a prize; to support a family. HDAS: 1909. Source: BACON. MWCD: 14th cent. The origin of this metaphorical expression is obscure, and the date of its first appearance in print is surprising. The earliest suspected source is the case of a man winning a whole side of bacon as a prize and taking it home to his wife. The place was Dunmow (Essex), England, and the prize was called the Dunmow Flitch. The man knelt on the steps of the church and was able to swear that he had been happily married for the past year and a day. Between A.D. 1244 and 1772, only seven other men won the Flitch—an average of one winner every sixty-six years! The second suspected source is the appearance in a 1725 Eng. dictionary of thieves' cant of the word *bacon*, defined as "loot" from a robbery. It is possible, of course, considering that the Dunmow Flitch was still being offered in 1725, that the thieves stole the term from the Church, or that one of the happily married winners of the Flitch had turned into a happily married crook and took the expression with him to jail. The third suspected source is an American one, prob. originating in the 19th cent., which involved the (continuing) practice of turning children loose in a pen of one or more greased pigs at a country fair. The child who caught the pig was awarded it as a prize and allowed to take it home, where his/her parents could then have it butchered and turned into pork, ham, and bacon to feed their family. AID; BDPF; CE; CI; DAS; DC; DEI; EWPO; HI; HND; LCRH; MDWPO; MS; NSOED; PT; SA; SHM.

BROCCOLI   *See* Cauliflower Ear.

BROWN AS A BERRY   *See* Berries.

BROWN-BAG   *See* Brown-bag Lunch.

BROWN-BAGGER   *See* Brown-bag Lunch.

BROWN-BAGGING   *See* Brown-bag Lunch.

BROWN-BAG IT   *See* Brown-bag Lunch.

BROWN-BAG LUNCH   *a brown-bag lunch.* A lunch prepared at home, packed in a brown paper bag, carried to work, and eaten at a desk or in a lunchroom. Source: LUNCH. MWCD: 1812. Factory workers have their *dinner pails*, school-children have their *lunch boxes*, and office workers have their *brown bags*. The bag is not usu. carried in plain sight to the office—although there seems to be no stigma for doing so—but is packed in a briefcase, an attaché case, or a large purse. The paper bag is not waterproof, so the contents—perhaps a sandwich, some chips, an individually wrapped dessert, and some juice or soda pop—are wrapped in plastic wrap or aluminum foil if they are not already packaged. (The wrap or foil also comes in handy for disposing of the leftovers.) A person who carries a brown-bag lunch is a *brown-bagger* (HDAS: 1968), and the practice is known as *brown-bagging* (MWCD: 1959). If an office worker is asked by a fellow employee if he/she is going out to lunch at a nearby restaurant, he/she may reply, "No, I'm going to *brown-bag it*" (HDAS: 1987). Carrying consumables in a brown bag is thought to have derived from persons carrying a bottle of liquor in a brown bag *into* a restaurant that served no liquor. Diners may also carry food *out* of a restaurant after eating there: the leftover food that is packed in a bag (not usu. brown) by the waitperson. The package, which at fancy restaurants sometimes consists of aluminum foil shaped in the form of an animal, is called a *doggie bag* (MWCD: 1963) or a *bowser bag* (HDAS: 1965), as if there were a general agreement that everyone would pretend that you are taking the food home to your pet dog. BDPF; DAFD; DAS; SA.

BROWN BETTY   *a brown betty*. A baked pudding of spiced apples and buttered crumbs. MWCD: 1864. (Also called *apple brown betty* and *betty*.) Source: PUDDING. A *brown betty* is regarded as a pudding because it has no crust; if it did have a crust, it would prob. be classified as a deep-dish pie. The apples are sliced and placed in alternating layers with the buttered bread crumbs, brown sugar, and spices. The mixture becomes soft during baking, and it can be eaten with either a fork or a spoon. The origin of the name *brown betty* is uncertain, but the fact that it is sometimes spelled *brown Betty* suggests that the dessert may have been named after the female cook who first prepared it. DAFD; FLC; WNWCD.

BROWN BREAD   *See* Graham Flour.

BROWN COW   *See* Black Cow.

BROWNIE   *a brownie*. A flat square of thick, rich, heavy, moist, chocolate sheet cake. DAFD: 1897. Source: CAKE. In spite of the belief of some contemporary journalists that brownies are a product of the 20th cent., arising from a baker's inadvertent omission of one ingredient (baking powder) or the accidental addition of another (chocolate pudding), brownies prob. developed back in the 19th cent. as the result of a "fallen" or undercooked chocolate cake—and have been one of America's favorite desserts or snacks ever since. More recently, nuts have been added, and a butterscotch recipe has been developed. Bakeries sell brownies by the square (or rectangle) or as a sheet of "brownie cake" (for the customer to cut as desired). FLC; HDAS; MWCD; PT; WNWCD.

BROWSE (n)   *See* Browse (v).

BROWSE (v)   *to browse*. To casually, leisurely, or randomly examine, inspect, or sample an assortment of things. EWPO: 1823. Source: BROWSE (v). MWCD: 15th cent. Animals such as deer, elk, and moose "browse" when they nibble leaves, shoots, and twigs—i.e., *browse* (n)—from bushes, shrubs, and trees. Humans *browse* when they look over the contents of a department store, a bookstore, a library, or even an individual book, magazine, or newspaper. For them it is a kind of indoor windowshopping. Clerk: "May I help you?" Customer: "No, I'm just browsing." *Browsing through* a book (NSOED: late-19th cent.) is equivalent to "skimming" it: flipping the pages until you find something that catches your interest. It is not unusual for libraries and bookstores to welcome visitors with a sign saying, "Come in and *browse*." ATWS; MDWPO; SA. *Compare* Graze.

BROWSE THROUGH   *See* Browse (v).

BRUNCH   A late morning, noontime, or early afternoon meal, esp. on Sunday. MWCD: 1896. Source: BREAKFAST (MWCD: 15th cent.); LUNCH (MWCD: 1812). Brunch is a portmanteau word, a blend of the first two consonants of *breakfast* and all but the first consonant of *lunch*. The word developed after the name for the weekday noon meal changed from *dinner* to *lunch* and the "weight" of the meal changed from heavy to light. A light lunch was sufficient for a weekday (or Saturday) because it usu. followed a hearty breakfast; but it was redundant on a Sunday because it followed a hearty and also late breakfast. To the managers of hotels and restaurants, it made sense to combine breakfast and lunch into one meal, *Sunday brunch*, and either to serve only one other meal that day (a late *Sunday dinner*) or to serve no other meal at all. Brunch is now served between 11:00 A.M. and 2:00 or 3:00 P.M., and it is usu. served buffet style, with visits necessary to several different "stations" for egg dishes, pancakes or waffles, quiches, meats, potatoes, salads, desserts, etc. This menu fits neither a breakfast nor a lunch, but it does fit the two together: a *brunch*. A *champagne brunch* is a lavish Sunday brunch at which champagne is served. DAFD; EWPO; FLC; LA; MDWPO; PT.

BRUSSELS SPROUTS   *See* Cabbage.

BUCKWHEAT CAKE   *See* Pancake (n).

BUFFALO CHIP   *See* Cow Pie.

BUFFET   *See* Smorgasbord.

BUFFET SUPPER   *See* Supper.

BULIMIA   An eating disorder characterized by bingeing and purging. Source: HUNGER; OX. To have *bulimia* is lit. to have the appetite (Gk. *limos* "hunger") of an ox (Gk. *bous* "ox"). In the 14th cent., *bulimia* simply meant an abnormal hunger, but in recent times it has come to mean an abnormal craving for food followed by an abnormal fear of gaining weight. The result is a medical condition (bulimarexia) that involves bingeing on a large quantity of food (e.g., an entire cake or pie) and then purging it (by inducing vomiting) before it adds any nu-trition to the body. Another eating disorder, "anorexia nervosa," is almost the exact opposite of bulimia; i.e., it involves fear of gaining weight that is so extreme that the person (usu. a young woman) almost starves herself to death. NSOED; SA; WNWCD.

BULLY BEEF   *See* Corned Beef.

BUNCH OF BALONEY   *See* Baloney!

BUNCH OF GARBAGE   *See* Garbage.

BUNCH OF TRIPE   *See* Tripe.

BURGER   *See* Make Hamburger of.

BURNED TO A CRISP   *See* Slow Burn.

BURN ONE   *See* Slow Burn.

BURN THE TOAST   *See* Warm as Toast.

BURRITO   *See* Tortilla.

BUSHEL AND A PECK   *See* In a Peck of Trouble.

BUSHEL OF TROUBLE   *See* In a Peck of Trouble.

BUSHELS OF MONEY   *See* In a Peck of Trouble.

BUSINESS LUNCH   *a business lunch.* A midday meal at a restaurant during which business is conducted. DAFD: 1950s. Source: LUNCH. MWCD: 1812. The businesspersons at a working lunch of this sort prob. order the *businessman's* (sic) *lunch*, which is so called on the menu because it can be served and eaten within an hour. If the businesspersons are really high powered, the meal could be referred to as a *power lunch* (DAFD: 1979). In the past, all of these types of lunches have been accompanied by two or three drinks apiece and have been classified, informally, as a *two-martini lunch* or a *three-martini lunch* (DAFD: 1960s), with the martinis being written off as part of the business expense. (Those days are gone forever.) Before the small-businessperson leaves his/her shop to join the others, he/she hangs a sign in the window saying *Out to Lunch* (parodied in cartoons about NASA as "Out to Launch"), which has become a metaphorical expression for "not all there" or "out of touch with reality" (HDAS: 1955). To make the appointment to *lunch* (MWCD: 1823) with the others, the businessperson says, "*Let's do lunch*," and states a specific time and place. When, however, at the end of a meeting this expression is used by one person who is not well acquainted with—or impressed by—the other, in the form of "*Let's do lunch sometime*," it simply means "Goodbye." If the invitee takes umbrage at the insincerity and causes enough trouble, he/she might be told, "*You'll never eat lunch in this town again*" (the title of a 1991 book by Julia Phillips). On a business outing or excursion, the members of the party might be given *box lunches* (MWCD: 1950), each containing a sandwich or cold chicken, an apple or orange, a candy bar or dessert, plasticware and a napkin, and a small carton of milk or soda pop—all in a white box the size of a shoe box. AID; CE; DAS; LA; NSOED.

BUSINESSMAN'S LUNCH   *See* Business Lunch.

BUTCHER (n)   *a butcher.* An incompetent tradesperson, surgeon, writer, etc. HDAS: mid-19th cent. Source: BUTCHER. MWCD: 13th cent. The 13th cent. *butcher* (fr. O.Fr. *bouchier*, fr. *bouc* "he-goat") was a slaughterer of goats and a dresser of their carcasses. In modern times the butcher has given up slaughtering entirely and has broadened his/her attention to the carcasses of all kinds of animals—chopping, cutting, and sawing them up into meal-size or bite-size pieces. (The first line of Carl Sandburg's 1916 poem "Chicago" confirms this: "Hog Butcher of the World . . ."). Unlike surgery, butchering does not demand great precision, and for that reason an incompetent surgeon—i.e., one who *butchers* an operation—is sometimes called a *butcher.* The same principle applies to the incompetent bricklayer or carpenter who *butchers,* or "botches," the construction of a building—and to the incompetent writer who *butchers* the English language. Incompetent actors, dancers, and musicians—i.e., those who interpret the creative works of others—are also sometimes said to *butcher* the creation of the playwrights and composers. Finally, persons who murder other persons brutally or ruthlessly are said to be *butchers,* although it is usu. their mental competence that is called into question. DEI; EWPO; NSOED; SA; THT; WNWCD.

BUTCHER (v)   *See* Butcher (n).

BUTTER (n)   "Cow's cheese." Source: BUTTER. MWCD: O.E. Butter started out as "cow's cheese" (Gk. *boutyron,* fr. *bous* "cow" + *tyros* "cheese"); and, in a sense, butter and cheese have a lot in common: Butter and skim milk are the outcome of churning sweet cream; and cheese curds and whey are the outcome of pressing sour milk. At the same time, *butter* disassociated itself from *cheese,* just as it would disassociate itself much later from *margarine.* However, a number of other soft (or semisolid), yellow (or yellowish brown), spreads (or condiments) have developed that declare themselves to be a kind of "butter": *apple butter, cocoa butter, crab butter, maple butter,* and *peanut butter.* DAFD; FLC; LA; NSOED.

BUTTER-AND-EGG MAN   *a (big) butter-and-egg man.* A big spender, esp. one who is a member of the nouveau riche. HDAS: 1924. Source: BUTTER (MWCD: O.E.); EGG (MWCD: M.E.). "Butter-and-Egg Man" was the title of a play by

George S. Kaufman that was first produced on Broadway in 1925. In approx. that same year, during the height of Roaring Twenties prosperity, the title was applied also to rich out-of-towners who brought their newfound wealth to the Great White Way to lavish it on chorus girls and nightclub entertainers. The transfer of title was made either by New York columnists or by speakeasy owner Texas Guinan, who introduced one such big spender, a dairy farmer who had made a fortune from selling butter and eggs, as "my butter-and-egg man." EWPO; HB; LA; MDWPO; NSOED. *See also* Butter-and-egg Money.

BUTTER-AND-EGG MONEY   Pin money. LA: 1942. Source: BUTTER (MWCD: O.E.); EGG (MWCD: M.E.). In the first half of the 20th cent. many American farms were of the all-purpose variety, featuring both crops (grasses, grains, etc.) and animals (livestóck and dairy cows). The farmer was responsible for the major crops, whereas the farmer's wife was responsible for the garden crops. The farmer looked after the livestock and milked the cows, whereas the farmer's wife gathered the eggs and churned the butter. Money raised from the sale of the excess butter and eggs—and the excess garden produce—became the farmwife's only income: her *butter-and-egg money*. HB; LA.

BUTTERBALL   *a butterball*. A chubby child or young adult. HDAS: 1860. Source: BUTTER. MWCD: O.E. A chubby baby is often referred to as a "little *butterball*," and the appellation can stick through childhood, adolescence, and young adulthood. Oddly enough, a "ball" of butter is usu. quite small, about the size of a melon ball, and is fashioned by the chef from a "crock" of butter. Butter is sold in the market in one-pound boxes containing four quarter-pound "sticks," not in the form of "balls." WNWCD. *Compare* Buttercup.

BUTTERCUP   *a buttercup*. A yellow-flowered herb commonly found in pastures. MWCD: 1777. Source: BUTTER. MWCD: O.E. English dairy farmers named this herb a *buttercup* either because (1) they believed that the butterfat in their cows' milk became a deeper yellow after the cows had eaten the herb's flowers or (2) they noticed the obvious resemblance between the color of the flowers and the color of the butter. The word *cup* appears in this compound because the petals of each flower are arranged in a circle. Butter is sometimes served in little ceramic "cups" in fine restaurants—and in little plastic "tubs" at less expensive ones. BDPF; EWPO; LA; NSOED; WNWCD. *Compare* Butterball.

BUTTERFINGERED   *See* Butterfingers.

BUTTERFINGERS   (Pl. in form, sing. in usage.) *a butterfingers*. A person who cannot catch something thrown to him/her or to hold onto something already in his/her hands. HDAS: 1837. Source: BUTTER. MWCD: O.E. A *butterfingers* behaves as though his/her fingers were covered with, or made of, butter, the semi-solid butterfat of milk. A chronic *butterfingers* is sometimes addressed by this term—"Hey, *Butterfingers!*"—or, more politely, is said to be *butterfingered* (MWCD: 1615). The noun *butterfingers* prob. developed in the sport of cricket. The Butterfinger candy bar is a chocolate-coated "finger" of peanut butter candy. BDPF; CI; DAS; DEI; LA; MS; NSOED.

BUTTERFLY   *a butterfly.* A colorful flying insect of the order Lepidoptera. MWCD: O.E. Source: BUTTER. MWCD: O.E. The origin of the word *butterfly* is uncertain. The name may derive from the fact that many butterflies—such as the swallowtail, sulpher, and monarch—are partially or mostly yellow, the color of butter; and butterflies, unlike moths, are diurnal and must open their wings to the sun before flying, so they are easily seen by humans. However, many butterflies are *not* yellow, so the name has also been suggested to have come from (1) the color of the butterfly's excrement, (2) the belief that butterflies steal butter, or (3) a spoonerized form of the words *flutter by.* At any rate, the tiny butterfly has produced its share of secondary metaphors, such as "a social *butterfly,*" "the *butterfly* stroke," "a *butterfly* table," "a *butterfly* valve," "*butterflied* shrimp," and "to have *butterflies* in your stomach." ATWS; BDPF; FLC; HDAS; NSOED; SA.

BUTTERMILK   Cultured and fermented milk. Source: BUTTER; MILK. MWCD: O.E. Originally, *buttermilk* (MWCD: 15th cent.) was the milk left over after butter was churned from it—a little like the whey that is left over after cheese is pressed from it. Original buttermilk actually had pieces of butter floating about on it; however, since homogenization (ca. the 1930s), real buttermilk has disappeared from stores and menus, and in its place is a product called "buttermilk" but consisting of skim milk to which bacteria have been added to thicken it and give it a tangy flavor. A nice touch is that tiny pieces of real butter are sometimes added to make it seem authentic. DAFD; FLC; HDAS; IHAT; NSOED; WNWCD.

BUTTERNUT   *a butternut.* A nut of the butternut tree. IHAT: 1741. Source: BUTTER; NUT. MWCD: O.E. The butternut tree of eastern North America is a member of the walnut family and is also known as the "white walnut." The name *butternut* derives from the oiliness of the nutmeats and the yellowish brown color of the nut casings and the tree's bark. Dye from the tree's bark, also called *butternut,* has been used in the South since before the Civil War to color homespun fabric, and Confederate soldiers were nicknamed "Butternuts" because some of them wore uniforms made of such fabric. FLC; HDAS; NSOED.

BUTTERNUT SQUASH   *a butternut squash.* A variety of squash bearing some resemblance to a nut of the butternut tree. MWCD: 1945. Source: BUTTERNUT (MWCD: 1741); SQUASH (MWCD: 1634). The nut of the butternut tree is egg-shaped and yellowish brown (or "butternut") in color. The fruit of the butternut squash is pear-shaped and yellowish camel in color. Because the butternut tree grows only in the eastern United States, and most people have never seen a butternut, the analogy is prob. based on the color alone. The color "butternut" has been associated with the nut since 1810. FLC; IHAT; NSOED.

BUTTER UP   *See* Buttery (adj.).

BUTTER WOULDN'T MELT IN YOUR MOUTH   *to look as if butter wouldn't melt in your mouth.* To appear cool, calm, and collected despite your guilt—like the cat that ate the canary. DC: 1546. Source: BUTTER. MWCD: O.E. Butter melts easily in the mouth of a warmhearted person but apparently not in the mouth of a coldhearted one. Dishonest people who appear innocent, polite, and friendly are probably too good to be true. (What is needed is a scientific experiment to test the veracity of this claim: Place a pat of better under the tongue of a known innocent person, and another under the tongue of a known guilty one who professes innocence, and see which pat melts first.) Tender meat is also said to *melt in your mouth.* AID; BDPF; CI; DAI; DEI; EWPO; HND; LCRH; MDWPO; MS; NSOED; WNWCD.

BUTTERY (adj.)   *to be buttery.* To be like butter in color, consistency, or taste. MWCD: 14th cent. Source: BUTTER. MWCD: O.E. Nothing is more like butter than margarine, which is yellow, spreadable, and sweet. This was not always so: *Oleomargarine* (q.v.) was once white, stiff, and tasteless—at least until the little "color pellet" was broken and mixed in. Since the 14th cent. the adj. *buttery* has also taken on the meaning "flattery," although more in the sense of ingratiating than congratulating. *To butter someone up* (MWCD: 1819) is to praise someone excessively, or to flatter someone insincerely, in order to gain his/her favor. In this metaphor, the *buttering up* of a boss, for example, is compared to the buttering of a piece of bread or toast: the thicker the butter, the greater the effect. The metaphorical expression *to spread it on thick,* however, does not necessarily derive from buttering bread: It could just as well have come from bricklaying, painting, or plastering. AID; BDPF; CE; CI; DAS; DEI; DC; EWPO; LTA; NSOED; PT; WNWCD. *Compare* Polish the Apple.

BUTTERY (n)   *a buttery.* A pantry or larder. DAFD: 1654. Source: BUTTER (*). The noun *buttery* derives, not from the familiar word *butter,* but, indirectly, from the same source as the word *bottle*—i.e., fr. L.Lat. *bottis* "cask." A *bottle* is a "little cask" (fr. M.Fr. *bouteille*), and a M.E. *boterie* (fr. M.Fr. *boterie*) was a room where little casks were stored. By the middle of the 17th cent., in England, *boterie* had become *buttery,* and the room was now used for storing food—a kind of pantry. The *butteries* at some English colleges are still used to store wine and ale (as well as bread and butter) for sale to the students. NSOED; PT. *Compare* Larder.

BUTTER YOUR BREAD ON BOTH SIDES   *to butter your bread on both sides.* DAP: 1678. To engage in wasteful extravagance. Source: BREAD; BUTTER.

MWCD: O.E. Someone who lit. butters his/her bread on both sides is doing something unnecessary—buttering on only one side is sufficient—and prob. impossible. It's like trying to *eat your cake and have it too* (q.v.). However, someone who metaphorically *has his/her bread buttered on both sides* is enjoying the good life, perhaps made possible by "working both sides of the street"—another sense of the metaphor. To *want your bread buttered on both sides* is to desire this state of luxury. BDPF; CI; DEI; NSOED.

BUZZARD MEAT   *See* Meaty.

BY THEIR FRUITS YOU SHALL KNOW THEM   *See* Tree Is Known by Its Fruit.

C

CABBAGE   Money; folding money. HDAS: 1903. Source: CABBAGE. MWCD: 15th cent. Cabbage leaves range in color from green to white or red, and the green leaves range in shade from dark green to light or pale green. The latter shade just happens to match the color of American paper money, or "greenbacks," which, along with the long, thin, flat appearance of both the leaves and the bills has inspired the development of the metaphor *cabbage* for "folding money." *Cabbage* itself is the product of a reverse metaphor, based on the resemblance of a cabbage "head" (M.E. *caboche*) to a human head (Lat. *caput*), a similarity that was overlooked in the naming of the "head" of *lettuce* (q.v.). The association of *cabbage* with *head* can be found in such metaphorical expressions as the phrase *to come to a head* "to reach the peak of development" (EWPO: 16th cent.), the compound noun *cabbagehead* "a stupid person" (LA: 1682), and the proverb *Two heads are better than one* (HND: 1546), to which is sometimes added *even if one is a cabbage head*. Cabbage can be prepared hot, as cabbage soup or collard greens, or cold, as sauerkraut or cole slaw. *Sauerkraut* (Ger. for "sour cabbage") is shredded white cabbage fermented in a salt brine made of its own juice. It has been known in England since the early-17th cent. (MWCD: 1617) but in America only since the Revolution, although it has become a necessary condiment for hot dogs in many parts of the country since the turn of the 19th cent. During WWI, the term *liberty cabbage* was substituted for *sauerkraut* by Americans who reserved the word *Kraut* for Germans in general. *Cole slaw* (MWCD: 1794), an Amer. loan translation from Du. *koolsla* "cabbage salad," denotes chopped white cabbage with shredded carrots and mayonnaise (or vinegar). Some Americans erroneously refer to cole slaw as *cold slaw*, although it is sometimes served warm or hot. *Skunk cabbage* (MWCD: 1751) is not cabbage at all but a swamp plant with leaves that resemble those of the cabbage—and a smell that resembles that of a skunk. *Brussels sprouts* (MWCD:

1796)—also spelled *brussels sprouts*—are "little cabbages," growing on the surface of a stalk, whose leaves can also be eaten as mustard greens. DAFD; DAP; DAS; DEOD; EWPO; FLC; IHAT; IRCD; MDWPO; NSOED; PT; SA; THT.

CABBAGEHEAD   *See* Cabbage.

CABBAGE WITH A COLLEGE EDUCATION   *See* Cauliflower Ear.

CACTUS PEAR   *See* Pear-shaped.

CAESAR SALAD   *See* Salad Days.

CAFÉ   *See* Café Society.

CAFÉ SOCIETY   The wealthy patrons of expensive restaurants, cabarets, and nightclubs. MWCD: 1939. Source: CAFÉ. MWCD: 1802. *Café* is a borrowing from French, where it means both "small, informal restaurant" and "coffee." The earliest form of this eating and drinking establishment in England was the *coffee-house* (MWCD: 1612), which appeared only a few years after the introduction of coffee into England. The coffeehouse not only was a place of refreshment for ordinary citizens but became their meeting place for conversation and socializing. In France, the same sort of establishment was called a *café*, because it served coffee, and by the beginning of the 19th cent. this term began to compete with *coffeehouse* in both England and America. By the late-19th cent. (LA: 1893), *café* was applied to informal establishments that also served alcoholic beverages, such as bars and saloons; and in the early-20th cent. it took a giant leap to become the name for small but expensive restaurants, cabarets, and nightclubs, the wealthy patrons of which were referred to as *café society*—lit. "the coffee people," but fig. "the fashionable people." DAFD; FLC; NSOED.

CAFETERIA   *a cafeteria.* An assembly-line dining facility. MWCD: 1839. Source: COFFEE. *Cafeteria* is a Sp. Amer. word for coffeehouse, coffee shop, or coffee store. By the early-20th cent. the cafeteria had become not only a successful commercial operation but an integral part of many American institutions. In the schools, new buildings included a kitchen and a cafeteria, sometimes combined with an auditorium and called a *cafetorium* (MWCD: 1952). Colleges installed cafeterias in their dormitories, companies set them up for their employees, and hospitals established them for their visitors and staff. Though convenient, some of these institutional dining facilities acquired a bad reputation, earning names such as *ptomaine domain* and *ptomaine palace.* Yet the word *cafeteria* became so familiar that its suffix, *-teria*, was borrowed to form other institutional names, such as *drugeteria* (a drugstore) and *shaveteria* (a barber shop). The entire word has been adopted by higher education, where a *cafeteria-style curriculum* is one from which you can choose the courses you want; *cafeteria-style benefits* can be selected from a complete list of benefits; and choices can be made from the *cafeteria-style* options on an ATM machine or a television set. (This selection process is also called *menu-driven*, q.v.) In recent years, as the cafeteria has become more popular in colleges and universities, it has become less popular as a commercial restaurant, giving way to buffets and smorgasbords, which are self-serve restaurants, not cafeterias. But the wonderful thing about all these restaurants is that you can always go back for seconds. DAFD; DAP; DAS; LA.

CAFETERIA-STYLE   *See* Cafeteria.

CAFETORIUM   *See* Cafeteria.

CAJUN CUISINE   *See* Cuisine.

CAJUN POPCORN   *See* Popcorn Shrimp.

CAKE (n)   *a cake of ice, mud, etc.* A block or lump of something orig. soft that has become hard over time. Source: CAKE. MWCD: 13th cent. This hardening is based on the process that turns liquid cake batter into semisolid food. The word *cake* developed from O.N. *kaka* (!), which was borrowed in the 13th cent. to fill a void in the Eng. lexicon. The new word was first applied to Scottish pancakes, made of oatmeal; but in the 14th cent. it was also applied to English sweet cakes, made of wheat flour. The verb *to cake* came along in the 17th cent. (MWCD: 1607), meaning "to be encrusted with something" (e.g., being *caked* with dirt, mud, ice, or snow) or to be in the process of becoming so. DAFD; DAS; EWPO; FLC; NSOED; THT. *See also* Cupcake; Fish Cake; Pancake.

CAKE (v)   *See* Cake (n).

CAKES AND ALE   Fun; good times. MDWPO: 1602. Source: CAKE (n) (MWCD: 13th cent.); ALE (MWCD: O.E.). *Cakes and ale* first appeared in this metaphorical sense in Shakespeare's *Twelfth Night* (Act II, Scene 3), where Sir Toby Belch chastizes Malvolio for trying to break up a wild party at a friend's house: "Dost thou think, because thou art virtuous, there shall be *no more cakes and ale?*" [italics added]. The cakes referred to were not layer cakes, which hadn't been invented yet, but more likely individual rolls, such as scones, made of bread dough. At any rate, the *cakes and ale* represented a good time, and *no more cakes and ale* represented "gloom and doom." In more recent times, *Cakes and Ale* became the title of a book by W. Somerset Maugham (1930); and the proverb *Life is not all cakes and ale*, with which Malvolio should have countered Sir Toby, has developed to convey the meaning "There is more to life than fun and games." BDPF; DC; EWPO; NSOED; PT. *Compare* Beer and Skittles.

CAKEWALK   *a cakewalk*. An easy task. HDAS: 1897. Source: CAKE (n). MWCD: 13th cent. The *cakewalk* was orig. an African American promenade, or stepping contest, of the mid-19th cent. (EWPO: 1840s), in which participants displayed fancy steps in a circle around the prize—a cake. The winning couple would *take the cake* (q.v.). By the late-19th cent. (IHAT: 1890s), *cakewalk* had become the name for a strutting style of dance that was performed on stage but without the cake or the competition. By the turn of the 19th cent. *cakewalk* still referred to a type of dance but also developed the meaning "a cinch" or "a snap"— i.e., *a piece of cake* (MDWPO: 1936). The implication was that winning that mid-19th cent. contest was not so difficult after all; otherwise, it would have been *no piece of cake*. AID; BDPF; CE; CI; DAFD; DAI; DAS; DC; DEI; HND; MS; NSOED.

CALABASH   *See* Gourd.

CALF FRIES   *See* Lamb Fries.

CANADIAN BACON   Back bacon. MWCD: ca. 1934. Source: BACON. MWCD: 14th cent. *Canadian bacon* is an Amer. term for a product that is called *back bacon* in Canada. Back bacon is not the regular bacon that Americans have been familiar with throughout their history: a two-inch high slab of pork from the side of the pig that is equal parts lean and fat, with or without rind, and that is cured and smoked, cut into foot-long strips, and fried as an accompaniment to eggs, pancakes, waffles, etc., for breakfast. Back bacon, however, is cut from the center of the back of the pig (i.e., the loin); it has little or no fat (and no rind); it is also cured and smoked; it is sold as a "log" (rather than a slab); it can be cut into three-to-four-inch diameter "rounds"; and because it is precooked, it can be eaten "as is" in a sandwich or fried like regular bacon. Even within the United States, some people prefer "bacon" from a location other than the side, or from an animal other than a pig. For example, *belly bacon*—also called *white bacon*— is cut from the belly of the pig and is really just fat *salt pork* (MWCD: 1723). *Beef bacon* is cut from the belly of a beef, cured, and used like pork bacon; and *turkey bacon* consists of turkey meats that are cured, pressed, and made to look like the "real" thing. DAFD; FLC; PT.

CANAPÉ   *See* Appetizer; Whet Your Appetite.

CANDY   Illegal drugs. Source: CANDY. MWCD: 15th cent. Illegal drugs can be bought at a *candy store* or on the street, where they are sold by a *candy man* (HDAS: 1969). Purchases can include *nose candy* (powdered cocaine or heroin that can be inhaled), *needle candy* (liquid drugs, esp. heroin, that can be injected directly into a vein), and *rock candy* (crystallized cocaine—"crack"—or heroin that can be smoked in a pipe). All of these drug-related terms developed in the 20th cent., long after the confection called *candy* (orig. *sugar candy*) was created in the Middle East by boiling down sugar syrup to form crystals. The 14th cent.

product was called *qandi*, Ar. for "made from sugar," but the name was preceded by *sugar* when the term passed into O.It. (*zucchero candi*) and then M.Fr. (*sucre candi*). Today, candy is the most popular between-meal snack in most parts of the world, where a *candy store* is simply a place where you can buy "sweets," and where *ear candy* (HDAS: 1984) and *eye candy* are simply "sweet music" and "saccharine cinemas," respectively. A compulsive shopper is *like—or as happy as—a kid in a candy store*, and something that is too easy is *like—or as easy as—taking candy from a baby* (IHAT: 1930s). A *candy striper* (MWCD: 1963), i.e., a high school girl who volunteers for work at a hospital, is so called because her uniform was orig. a red-and-white-striped dress, like a candy cane. A *candy apple*, which can be purchased at any amusement park, carnival, circus, or country fair, is an apple (on a stick) that has been dipped in warm, red-colored sugar syrup that coats it like wax. *Candy-apple red* is the bright red color that every young man wanted for his hot rod back in the 1950s, and *candy-coated* (i.e., "sugar-coated") is what the television shows for young men and women seemed to be in the 1950s. *Cotton candy* (MWCD: 1926), i.e., spun sugar on a cardboard stick, has become a metaphor for anything that is attractive but lacks substance; and *cotton-candy clouds* are fluffy white cumulus clouds that remind us of the confection. Finally, a *candy-ass* (HDAS: 1966) is an *apple polisher* (q.v.), a coward, a new recruit in the army, or a man who orders a "woman's" drink at a bar. CE; DAFD; DAS; FLC; LA; NSOED; PT.

CANDY APPLE   *See* Candy.

CANDY-APPLE RED   *See Candy*.

CANDY-ASS   *See* Candy.

CANDY-COATED   *See Candy*.

CANDY MAN   *See* Candy.

CANDY STORE   *See* Candy.

CANDY STRIPER   *See* Candy.

CANE SYRUP   *See* Cough Syrup.

CANINE APPETITE   *See* Appetite.

CAN IT   *See* In the Can.

CANNED APPLAUSE   *See* In the Can.

CANNED LAUGHTER   *See* In the Can.

CANNED MUSIC   *See* In the Can.

CANNED SALES PITCH   *See* In the Can.

CANNED SPEECH   *See* In the Can.

CANNIBAL   *See* Cannibalize.

CANNIBALISM   *See* Cannibalize.

CANNIBALIZE   *to cannibalize something.* To take parts from one machine in order to give "life" to another of the same type. MWCD: 1943. Source: CANNI-BAL. MWCD: 1553. *Cannibalism* (MWCD: 1796) is lit. the eating of one human by another—or the eating of one animal by another of the same species. Human cannibalism has historically served either a ritualistic or a survivalistic purpose. In either case, the victim is already dead, and the survivor, although still alive, lacks the strength or nutrition that the body of the victim can provide. The word *cannibalism* can also be used to describe the taking of the words of one writer by another (i.e., plagiarism) and the competition between products of two divisions of the same company that results in the demise of the weaker product—and damage to the entire company. SA. *Compare* Eat Someone Alive.

CANNON FODDER   Infantry troops in a ground war. MWCD: ca. 1891. Source: FODDER. MWCD: O.E. *Fodder* is the coarse feed fed to farm animals, esp. cattle, sheep, and goats. It consists of ground-up cornstalks from the silo and dried hay from the barn loft. During a ground war, infantry troops become the corn and hay that the "cannons" (artillery) "mow down" in order to "feed" the cause. *Fodder* also feeds other causes; e.g., scandal is *fodder* for gossip columnists; corruption is *fodder* for political debates; and discoveries are *fodder* for scientists. A special kind of fodder is *farrago,* a mixture of cattle feed in ancient Rome but a "confused mixture of elements" in Mod. Eng. (MWCD: 1632): e.g., a *farrago* of doubts, fears, or nonsense. DEI; EWPO; MDWPO; SA; WNWCD.

CANOE   *See* Banana Boat.

CAN OF CORN   *See* In the Can.

CAN SHE MAKE A CHERRY PIE?   *Can she make—or bake—a cherry pie?* The acid test for a potential wife in the 18th or 19th cent. Source: CHERRY (MWCD: 14th cent.); PIE (MWCD: 14th cent.). This question is from an English ballad about a young man named Billy Boy. The questioner is Billy Boy's mother, and the subject is Billy Boy's girlfriend: "*Can she make a cherry pie, /* Billy Boy, Billy

Boy, / *Can she make a cherry pie*, / Charming Billy?" [italics added]. Billy Boy answers in the affirmative, but he confesses that she is unavailable: "*She can make a cherry pie* / Quick's a cat can wink its eye; / (But) she's a young thing / And cannot leave her mother" [italics added]. Being able to make a cherry pie—from "scratch," that is—is no longer a criterion for wifehood. If it were, far fewer women would be married. *See* also Way to a Man's Heart Is through His Stomach.

CANTALOUPE   *See* Slice of the Melon.

CAN'T BOIL WATER WITHOUT BURNING IT   *See* Can't Even Boil Water.

CAN'T CUT IT   *See* Cut the Mustard.

CAN'T CUT THE MUSTARD   *See* Cut the Mustard.

CAN'T EAT ANOTHER BITE   *See* Bite (n).

CAN'T EVEN BOIL WATER   *He/she can't even boil water*. He/she doesn't know the first thing about cooking. Source: BOIL (MWCD: 13th cent.); WATER (MWCD: O.E.). This expression is not as ridiculous as it sounds. A person from the mile-high city of Denver, Colorado, may assume that a quart of water always comes to a boil in a certain number of minutes, only to move to New Orleans, Louisiana, and discover that the same amount of water is not yet boiling at the same amount of time—because water boils at approx. 202° Fahrenheit in Denver but at approx. 212° in New Orleans. A related expression, "He/she *can't boil water without burning it*," is also not totally impossible, for the same reason. A person who moves from New Orleans to Denver and walks away from a quart of water boiling on the stove, assuming that the water will take a certain number of minutes to boil, may return to find the water gone and the bottom of the metal pot on fire.

CAN'T STOMACH SOMETHING   *See* Have No Stomach for.

CAPE COD TURKEY   Baked codfish. EWPO: mid-19th cent. Source: TURKEY. MWCD: 1555. At Thanksgiving time in the mid-1800s, families that barely made a living netting cod, and therefore could not afford to buy a turkey, substituted baked codfish for the holiday bird, calling it by the euphemism *Cape Cod turkey*. Over half a cent. later, during the Great Depression of the 1930s, poverty-stricken residents of Boston served corned beef and cabbage for Thanksgiving and called it *Irish turkey*; and, during the same period, hungry residents of Texas killed what had previously been a nuisance animal, the armadillo, and called it either *Texas turkey* or *Hoover hog* (after Herbert Hoover, president of the United States from 1929 to 1933, during the early years of the Great Depression). Presumably, these substitute "turkeys" were served with *all the trimmings* of a real turkey dinner:

mashed potatoes and gravy, sweet potatoes or yams, dressing, cranberry sauce, pumpkin pie, and bread or rolls. Supposedly, also, the senior member of the family was asked to *do the honors*, i.e., to carve the "turkey," although *do the honors* could also have been an invitation to say grace or make the first "toast." AID; DAI; DEOD; HDAS; LA; MDWPO; SA. *Compare* Albany Beef; Welsh Rabbit.

CARIBBEAN BUFFALO   *See* Mock Turtle Soup.

CARNIVAL   The period of partying and feasting before the Lenten period of penitence and fasting. MWCD: 1549. Source: FLESH. MWCD: O.E. The word *carnival* is derived fr. Lat. *carne* "flesh" + *levare* "to remove" by way of It. *carnevale* (orig. *carnelevare*). An alternative explanation, that *carnival* is derived fr. Lat. *carne* "flesh" + *vale* "farewell" ("Farewell, flesh!"), is prob. attributable to false etymology. *Carnival* (or *Carnaval*) is celebrated in certain predominantly Roman Catholic communities on the last day (Shrove Tuesday) before the first day of Lent (Ash Wednesday). The most prominent example in America is New Orleans, where the festival is called *Mardi Gras* (Fr. for "fat Tuesday") and the merrymaking goes on all day and night. The word *carnival* has continued to broaden its meaning to include other events that have little or nothing to do with religion or fasting. For example, a traveling amusement show, with games, rides, and sideshows, is also called a *carnival*, the operators are called *carnies*, and they sell cotton candy and elephant ears, just as they do on the "midway" of a circus or fair. Elementary schools sometimes hold their own *carnivals*—often inside, often moneyraisers, often at Halloween time—with each classroom offering a game or test of skill, and food such as popcorn balls and candy apples. Cities also get into the act, combining fun and games with special events such as a *water carnival* or a *winter carnival*. EWPO; MDWPO; WNWCD.

CARNY   *See* Carnival.

CARROT-AND-STICK APPROACH/POLICY   *See* Carrottop.

CARROTTOP   *a carrottop*; *Carrottop*. A redhead; a term of address for a redhead. HDAS: 1889. Source: CARROT. MWCD: 1533. *Carrottop* is a rather strange name for a redhead. A "carrot top" is the lacy *green*—not red—foliage that extends aboveground from the *orange*—not red—root. (There may be a French-Canadian influence here: In the 1970s a redheaded American baseball player, Rusty Staub, who was traded to the Montreal Expos, was immediately dubbed *Le Grand Orange*!) During the 1940s, many young American males began to feel like *carrottops* because they had read that carrots contained vitamin A (actually beta carotene, which converts to vitamin A in the liver), which was essential to good eyesight, which, in turn, was essential for getting into the U.S. Army Air Corps (rather than the infantry) or the U.S. Navy (rather than the Marines)—so they ate lots of raw carrots, every day, right up until the time they were drafted. Nevertheless, raw carrots—whole or cut into "sticks"—do make a delicious snack; boiled carrots—esp. with butter—do make a delicious side dish; and baked—or roasted—carrots do make a delicious accompaniment to a beef roast. (Some people also like carrot cake topped with cream cheese.) Animals, esp. equines, also like (raw) carrots—so much so that the carrot is often used to entice a horse, mule, or donkey to do something that it would not otherwise do: move forward. When combined with a stick used to paddle the animal, the result is a very effective *carrot-and-stick approach* that has become an international metaphor (MWCD: 1951). This approach, or policy, involves simultaneous or alternating reward (the carrot) and punishment (the stick). Such a reward is *like a carrot to a donkey* (the stubbornest of the three equines); and offering such a reward is *like holding out a carrot to a donkey*. CE; CI; DAFD; DAI; DAS; DEI; EWPO; FLC; MDWPO; MS; NSOED; PT; SA.

CARRYOUT   *See* Restaurant.

CASH COW   *See* Milk a Cash Cow.

CASTANETS   *See* Chestnuts.

CAST YOUR BREAD UPON THE WATERS   Don't be afraid to take a chance: You'll probably get your entire investment back—and more. Source: BREAD. MWCD: O.E. The model for this advice appears in the Old Testament book of Ecclesiastes (11:1): "*Cast thy bread upon the waters*: for thou shalt find it after many days" [italics added]. The preacher, Ecclesiastes, seems to be saying that if we give freely of our time, energy, and money now, without expectation of future reward, that reward will come. It is a call for charity. Casting bread upon the waters was also a mid-19th cent. means of locating drowned bodies. In Mark Twain's *Huckleberry Finn* (Chapter VIII), Huck, who is running away and is thought to have been murdered, hides out on an island in the Mississippi River watching loaves of bread, each stuffed with a vial of mercury, float by. The loaves were supposed to stop floating downriver when they reached the spot where a body had come to rest, but Huck snagged one, removed the mercury, remarked that it was "baker's bread," not "corn-pone," and ate it. Also, observers of the Jewish New Year cast bread upon the nearest water on Yom Kippur as a symbol of the cleansing of their sins. BDPF; DAP; DC; HND; MS; NSOED.

CATCH MORE FLIES WITH HONEY THAN WITH VINEGAR   *See* Honey.

CATCH OF THE DAY   *See* Menu.

CATER   *See* Restaurant.

CAT SOUP   *See* Catsup.

CAT'S PAW   *See* Pull Someone's Chestnuts out of the Fire.

CATSUP   Seasoned tomato sauce. EWPO: ca. 1730. Source: KETCHUP. MWCD: ca. 1690. *Catsup* is a variant spelling of *ketchup*, although the word has always been pronounced "ketchup"—except by children who call it *cat soup*— and no one knows how or why the alternative spelling developed. *Ketchup* is from the Chinese word *ke-tsiap* for the pickled fish sauce (or mushroom sauce) that was discovered in Malaysia (or Singapore) by Dutch (or English) sailors in the 17th cent. The Malay version of the word, *kechap*, was rendered as *ketjap* by the Dutch sailors who brought it back to Europe, but the English changed the spelling to *ketchup* (EWPO: ca. 1710). The Americans changed the basis of the sauce from brine to tomato and called it *tomato ketchup* (LA: 1831), a name that stuck until the end of the 19th cent., by which time it was simply assumed that ketchup was a tomato product. Now, ketchup competes with salsa as the most popular sauce in America, but at the ballpark it's mustard and ketchup that are called for by most hotdog lovers. DAS; FLC; HDAS; MDWPO; PT; SA; THT.

CAUGHT WITH YOUR HAND IN THE COOKIE JAR   *to be caught with your hand in the cookie jar.* To be caught stealing money from your employer. Source: COOKIE. MWCD: 1703. This metaphor is based on the childhood experience of being caught while reaching for a cookie in the cookie jar—where cookies were stored to keep them fresh—after being told, time and time again, that you were not supposed to snack between meals or after dinner. For adults, the cookie jar becomes the cash register, and the hand is reaching for cash that doesn't belong to you. You are "caught stealing forbidden fruit," "caught red-handed," "caught with a smoking gun." The assumption, which is prob. wrong, is that children who steal cookies will grow up to be adults who steal cash. *Compare* Cook the Books.

CAULIFLOWER EAR   *a cauliflower ear.* A human ear whose cartilage has been thickened and disfigured in the boxing or wrestling ring. HDAS: 1896. Source: CAULIFLOWER. MWCD: 1597. *Cauliflower ears* are uncommon these days among boxers because amateurs now wear headgear and both amateur and pro- fessional boxers wear heavily padded gloves. However, in the early-1900s, when boxers wore gloves that were no more than leather mittens, and in the 18th and 19th cents., when they wore no gloves at all, it was not uncommon for a boxer to develop cauliflower ears as a result not only of the blows but of the deliberate gouges applied during clinches. In wrestling, the cauliflower ear is uncommon among amateur wrestlers because like amateur boxers, they wear headgear; how- ever, it is quite common among "professional" wrestlers who have never worn headgear and who find the ear to be an inviting appendage to grab hold of, twist, and attempt to rip off. Cauliflower is the "elegant" member of the cabbage family because its "head" is not simply made up of tightly wrapped green leaves but of tightly packed white flowers, as reflected in its Lat. name: *caulis* "cabbage" + *fiore* "flower." In "Pudd'nhead Wilson's Calendar," from *Pudd'nhead Wilson*, Mark Twain observed that in spite of its elegance, "Cauliflower is nothing but cabbage with a college education." *Broccoli* (MWCD: 1699) is It. for "little cabbage sprouts"; however, the small, single-stemmed sprouts are flowers, not leaves, and therefore are usu. classified with the cauliflower by gardeners and green grocers. BDPF; CE; DAFD; DAP; DEI; EWPO; FLC.

CAVIAR TO THE GENERAL   Too sophisticated for the general public to appreciate. (Shakespeare's *Hamlet*, ca. 1602.) Source: CAVIAR. MWCD: ca. 1560. Caviar, the strained and salted eggs (or "roe") of sturgeon (and other large fish), is an expensive delicacy, not experienced by most people—and prob. not enjoyed by them even if they could afford it. In Shakespeare's *Hamlet* (Act II, Scene 2), Hamlet recalls to one of the visiting players at Elsinore Castle: "I heard thee speak me a speech once, but it was never acted; or if it was, not above once; for the play, I remember, pleas'd not the million, 'twas *caviary* (sic) *to the general*" (i.e., to the masses). Caviar was not always such an *acquired taste* (q.v.): In 19th cent. saloons in the Northeast it was a regular part of the *free lunch* (q.v.)—the saltiness causing a thirst for something to "wash it down with," just as the salted "beer nuts" in modern bars do. Children of affluent families who have been told that caviar is "fish eggs" have been known to use the term *fish eggs* (HDAS: 1921) for their *tapioca pudding*, which bears a strong resemblance to caviar. BDPF; DAFD; EWPO; FLC; HI; IHAT; MDWPO; NSOED; PT; SA.

CAYENNE PEPPER   *See* Pep (n).

CENTER CUT   *See* Cutting Edge.

CEREAL   Breakfast food. NSOED: late–19th cent. Source: CEREAL. DAFD: 1832. The word *cereal* derives from the name of the Roman goddess of agriculture, *Ceres*. It orig. referred to the edible seeds of grasses such as barley, oats, rye, and wheat but was later applied also to corn and rice. The first use of cereal grains as breakfast food in this country consisted of porridgelike hot dishes of cornmeal, oatmeal, and wheat germ—including *pabulum* (MWCD: 1733), a bland cereal for infants, and, based on the name of a much later commercial product, *Pablum* (MWCD: 1948), an adult word for "tasteless language": *pablum*. Two of the first packaged, ready-to-eat, dry cereals in America were Post's Grape-Nuts (DAFD: 1898) and Kellogg's Toasted Corn Flakes (DAFD: 1907)—both developed in Battle Creek, Mich., the "Cereal City." Many other commercial cereals followed, including Shredded Wheat (Nabisco), Wheaties (General Mills), and Wheat Chex (Ralston Purina). Following decades of targeting the children's market, several companies are now offering *granola* (MWCD: 1970)—a mixture of rolled oats, nuts, raisins, and brown sugar or honey—to a more mature level of customers. EWPO; FLC; LA.

CHACUN À SON GOÛT   *See* Everyone to His Own Taste.

CHACUN À SON GOÛT   *See* Everyone to His Own Taste.

CHAMPAGNE APPETITE   *See* Appetite.

CHAMPAGNE BRUNCH   *See* Brunch.

CHEESECAKE   Revealing photographs of attractive female models. EWPO: 1912. Source: CHEESE (MWCD: O.E.); CAKE (MWCD: 13th cent.). Literally, *cheesecake* (DAFD: 1440) is not a cake at all but a pie, consisting of smooth cream cheese in a graham-cracker-crumb shell. Cream cheese is the most luscious of all unripened cheeses, and it is the basis not only for cheesecake—and for the spread used for lox and bagels—but for the metaphorical expression *smooth as cream cheese*. *Cheesecake photographs* picture the most luscious female models showing off their legs and curves, which is about all that was allowed in 1912. The same effect was achieved in the drawn—not photographed—pinup posters of the 1930s and 1940s and can still be seen in calendar drawings hanging on the walls of auto repair shops. The masculine counterpart of the feminine *cheesecake* is *beefcake* (MWCD: 1949): "photographic displays of the physiques of muscular males—or the muscular males themselves." *Beef* alludes to the sleek, well-muscled bodies of prime steers; and *cake* refers to the delicious dessert. The muscular male torso can be viewed at gyms, beaches, and bodybuilding competitions. *Beefcake* photographs can be seen in bodybuilding magazines, adult magazines for women, and the high school lockers of ninety-seven-pound weaklings. CE; DAFD; DAI; DAS; EWPO; FLC; HDAS; HF; LA; MDWPO; NSOED; SA.

CHEESE-EATER   *See* Rat Trap Cheese.

CHEESEHEAD   a *Cheesehead*. A resident of Wisconsin. Source: CHEESE. MWCD: O.E. Residents of Wisconsin are called *Cheeseheads* because they reside in the Dairy State, and cheese is a major by-product of milk production. However, some Wisconsinites have taken the nickname lit. by wearing wedges of cheddar cheese (also called *Cheeseheads*) on their heads at Green Bay Packers football games and Milwaukee Brewers baseball games. These wedges, which are actually made of foam, are shaped like the tricorne hats worn by soldiers during the American and French Revolutions. The foam is orangeish yellow in color and has large holes on all surfaces. *Cheesehead* is not to be confused with *headcheese* (MWCD: 1841), a jellied pork (or veal) loaf that is harvested from the head of a pig (or calf), along with the feet, heart, and tongue. The pieces of meat are combined with gelatin, molded, and cooked. The resulting loaf, or sausage, can then be sliced for luncheon meat. Furthermore, *headcheese* should not be confused with *head cheese* (HDAS: 1913), an expression comparable to *big cheese* "big shot" (MWCD: 1920), which in turn is derived from Eng. *big* + Urdu *chiz* "important person." The appearance of another Eng. metaphor, *big wheel* (ca. 1942), suggests that the Urdu origin was either unknown or forgotten by most Americans, and another source—real, edible cheese, esp. a big wheel of it—replaced it. BDPF; CE; DAFD; DAI; DAS; DC; EWPO; FLC; HND. *Compare* Top Banana.

CHEESE IT!   *See* Say Cheese.

CHEESE SOUFFLÉ   *See* Flat as a Cheese Soufflé.

CHEESE STANDS ALONE   *The cheese stands alone.* You're the only one left. Source: CHEESE. MWCD: O.E. This is the last line of the children's song "The Farmer in the Dell," which accompanies the "round game" of the same name. Seven children form a circle around a single child in the center who has been chosen as the "Farmer." They hold hands and sing the first verse: "The farmer in the dell, / The farmer in the dell, / Hi, Ho, the derrio, / The farmer in the dell." Then they sing the second verse: "The farmer takes a wife, / The farmer takes a wife, / Hi, Ho, the derrio, / The farmer takes a wife." The "farmer" then selects a "wife" from among the circlers, and "she" joins "him" in the center. Then the wife takes a child, the child takes a nurse, the nurse takes a dog, the dog takes a cat, the cat takes a rat, and the rat takes the "cheese," which by then is the only child left standing (i.e., circling around the others). The last verse of the song is "*The cheese stands alone, / The cheese stands alone, / Hi, Ho, the derrio, / The cheese stands alone*" [italics added]. The *Dick Van Dyke Show* Christmas episode featured two different (adult) versions of this game, set to different words and music. The children's game of musical chairs works pretty much the same way, because when the music finally stops, one child is left standing alone.

CHEESY   Cheap, crummy, flimsy, shabby, or tacky. HDAS: 1863. Source: CHEESE. MWCD: O.E. In this metaphor, things of poor quality are compared to cheese, esp. cheese that is overripe (and smelly), extremely dry (and crumbly), or extremely old (and moldy). Things that can be described as *cheesy* are shabby clothes, flimsy buildings, crummy neighborhoods, tacky decor, and cheap tricks. Cheese was prob. chosen as the basis for all these unpleasantries because it comes in so many different forms. Limburger cheese has a bad odor; Parmesan cheese is dry and crumbly; and Roquefort cheese contains veins of blue-green mold. Nevertheless, there is nothing *cheesy* about the cheese industry, which supplies us with a food that is vital to many modern recipes, such as pizza. CE; DAS; FLC; MDWPO; NSOED.

CHEF DE CUISINE   *See* My Compliments to the Chef.

CHEF'S SALAD   *See* Salad.

CHERRIES JUBILEE   *See* Cherry (adj.).

CHERRY (adj.)   In mint condition. IHAT: 1930s. Source: CHERRY. MWCD: 14th cent. A used car has long been advertised as being *cherry*, i.e., undamaged, unmodified, untouched—the way it came off the assembly line. In addition, the noun *cherry* has been a slang term for "virginity" for about three centuries. (HDAS: 1700). In the 1930s the word *virgin* was lunch-counter jargon for a "cherry Coke"; and during the Persian Gulf War in early-1991, the term *desert cherry* (a probable pun on *dessert cherry*) was used to refer to a soldier who was experiencing desert warfare for the first time. *Cherry tart*, the name of a small cherry pie, esp. one without a top crust, is also a slang term for a "novice prostitute"; and a *cherry farm* is a minimum security correctional institution for first offenders. DAI; DAS; NSOED.

CHERRY (n)   *a cherry.* A single, small, round, reddish fruit of the cherry tree. Source: CHERRY. MWCD: 14th cent. The word *cherry* is interesting because it derives from a misinterpretation by English speakers of the O.N.Fr. word *cherise* (Mod. Fr. *cerise*) for "cherry." The English took that to be a plural, subtracted the *s*, and came up with M.E. *chery* (now Mod. Eng. *cherry*). The French inherited the word fr. Lat. *cerasus*, a borrowing fr. Gk. *kerasos*. Of the two types of modern cherries, the European variety was prob. what is now called the *sour cherry*, *tart cherry*, or *cooking cherry*—a small, round, red fruit with a soft flesh and a some-what sour taste that is used as a filling in pies, etc. The other modern cherry is the *sweet cherry*, *black cherry*, or *eating cherry*, a larger, heart-shaped, dark red fruit with a firm flesh and a sweet taste that is used to make *maraschino cherries* and for eating out of hand. The American sweet cherry prob. originated in Asia, since it was introduced to this country by a Chinese farmer named Bing, who harvested the first *Bing cherries* in Oregon in 1875. *Sweet cherries* are the variety used for making *cherries jubilee*, a dessert consisting of cherries, sugar, and brandy flambéed and poured over vanilla ice cream. DAFD; DAS; EWPO; FLC; PT; WNWCD.

CHERRY ANGIOMA   *See* Cherry Tomato.

CHERRY BOMB   *See* Cherry Tomato.

CHERRY FARM   *See* Cherry (adj.).

CHERRY LIPS   *See* Cherry Tomato.

CHERRY PICK   *See* Cherry Picker.

CHERRY PICKER   *a cherry picker.* A large plastic bucket hanging from the end of a telescoping crane. MWCD: ca. 1944. Source: CHERRY. MWCD: 14th cent. The original "cherry picker" was a worker who placed his/her short ladder into the branches of a cherry tree, climbed the ladder with an empty pail in his/her hand, picked cherries until the pail was full, descended the ladder, and emptied the pail into a nearby wagon. Cherry picking is still done that way, but the term *cherry picker* has been borrowed by another set of climbers—telephone company workers, electric company workers, cable company workers, and fire company workers—to describe a collapsible (or jackknifing) crane mounted on the back of a truck and having a large plastic bucket hanging from the end. No more climbing up a pole to get to the lines, or to rescue a person from a burning building or a cat from a tree, or to put the star on the top of the municipal Christmas tree. *Cherry picker* is also used to denote a person who transfers savings from a lower-interest account to a higher-interest account; and to *cherry-pick* witnesses for a trial is to pick only the safest ones, esp. if you represent the prosecution. HDAS; MDWPO; NSOED; WNWCD.

CHERRYSTONE CLAM   *See* Cherry Tomato.

CHERRY TART   *See* Cherry (adj.).

CHERRY TOMATO   *a cherry tomato.* A tomato, about the size of a sweet cherry, that is often used in salads. MWCD: 1847. Source: CHERRY (MWCD: 14th cent.); TOMATO (MWCD: 1604). This tiny tomato is named for the cherry because of its reddish color, its globular shape, and its small size (about one inch in diameter). The *cherrystone clam* (MWCD: 1880), a quahog clam of the East Coast, is also likened to the cherry because of its round shape and small size (approx. two and one-half inches in diameter). A *cherry bomb* (MWCD: 1953) is a powerful firecracker that is red, spherical, and small (about one inch in diameter). *Cherry angioma* is a condition associated with aging in which clusters of bright red spots appear on the surface of the skin of the upper body. *Cherry lips* are lips that are as red as a tart cherry, either by nature or because of the application of lipstick. CE; FLC; NSOED; WNWCD.

CHESHIRE CAT   *See* Grin like a Cheshire Cat.

CHESTNUT (n)   *See* Old Chestnut.

CHESTNUTS   Castanets. Source: CHESTNUT. MWCD: 14th cent. Castanets (MWCD: ca. 1647) are not really chestnuts, but they have been made from the wood of the chestnut tree since the 17th cent. The word *castanet* derives from Sp. *castañeta*, the dim. of Sp. *castaña* "chestnut." However, the percussion instruments known as *castanets* are certainly not "little chestnuts"; in fact, they are even larger than horse chestnuts, which were first discovered in the Americas. Nevertheless, castanets do look as though they were made from oversize halves of chestnuts, and they are often carved from chestnut wood (or other hard wood or ivory). Castanets are worn on the hands of Spanish dancers, who hang the two pieces of wood over one thumb, with the hollowed-out sides facing each other in the palm of the hand, and strike them with their fingers. Another *chestnut* that is not really a chestnut is the *water chestnut* (MWCD: 1854), the tuber of an Asian water plant that is sliced for oriental cooking and that is so called because the "nut" is white and crunchy and the "skin" is dark brown. EWPO; FLC; PT; WNWCD.

CHEW FACE   *See* Eat Nails.

CHEW ON   *See* Chew Your Cud.

CHEW OUT   *to chew someone out.* To reprimand someone severely. HDAS: 1937. Source: CHEW. MWCD: O.E. Predatory mammals, such as the grizzly bear, the mountain lion, and the wolf, feast on their prey as soon as they have downed it—i.e., while it is still alive. One of the prime areas of attack is the torso, which contains vital organs such as the heart, liver, kidneys, stomach, and intestines. Among humans, the U.S. Army or Marine drill sergeant most closely resembles the predator when he/she "dresses down" a recruit for violating even the most minor of rules. The recruit must feel like the prey whose insides are being eaten up while he/she is still alive. The metaphor originated in the military during WWII but has softened considerably since being adopted by the business world (where it now amounts to being "called on the carpet") and the family (where it is equivalent to being "bawled out"). Another kind of animated chewing is when an actor/actress *chews up the scenery* (HDAS: 1895), i.e., "overacts." AID; CE; DAI; DAS; DC; NSOED; SA; WNWCD.

CHEW OVER   *See* Chew Your Cud.

CHEW SOMEONE UP AND SPIT THEM OUT   *See* Eat Someone Alive.

CHEW THE FAT   *to chew the fat.* To chat with friends; to make small talk. HDAS: 1907. Source: CHEW (MWCD: O.E.); FAT (MWCD: 14th cent.). The origin of this expression may have been sailors who chewed salt pork (while working together aboard ship) and talked at the same time. It's quite a leap from the ship to the farmhouse, but that's where the expression became a metaphor— when women gossiped at length at a quilting bee, although no actual fat was being chewed. Nowadays, people *chew the fat* when they talk informally with their friends and relatives over coffee and doughnuts, talking about anything that comes to mind, from gossip to sports. The Brit. version of the metaphor, to *chew the rag* (same meaning), calls into question the nautical origin of the expression but adds nothing to determining its real origin. AID; CE; CI; DAI; DAS; EWPO; HB; HND; LA; MDWPO; MS; NSOED; PT.

CHEW THE RAG   *See* Chew the Fat.

CHEW UP THE SCENERY   *See* Chew out.

CHEW YOUR CUD   *to chew your cud.* To turn something over and over in your mind. DC: 1547. Source: CHEW; CUD. MWCD: O.E. This metaphor is based on the peculiar chewing activity of "ruminants," such as bison, deer, goats, sheep, and (esp.) cows. Ruminants have a series of stomachs for digesting their food, the first of which produces a *cud,* or portion of partially digested food, that can be brought back to the mouth and chewed again. When a cow is chewing its cud—moving its lower jaw sideways, with its "lips" closed—it appears to be preoccupied, concerned only with the matter at hand. People who *chew their cud* (or *ruminate*—MWCD: 1533) do not bring their food back from their stomach and turn it over and over in their mouth; instead, they bring back thoughts from their memory and turn them over and over in their head. While *ruminating,* people often assume a contemplative look, as if they are *chewing on something* or *chewing something over* in their mind (MWCD: 1939)—i.e., reflecting or meditating on it. ATWS; BDFF; CE; CI; DAS; DEI; HI; HND; IRCD; LA; MDWPO; MS; NSOED; SA.

CHICAGO SUNDAE   *See* Pineapple; Sundae.

CHICKEN-AND-EGG QUESTION   *See* Which Came First, the Chicken or the Egg?

CHICKEN COFFEE   *See* Coffee.

CHICKEN FEED   A paltry sum of money. MWCD: 1836 (Davy Crockett). Source: CHICKEN (MWCD: 14th cent.); FEED (MWCD: 1576). Barnyard chickens are usu. fed by throwing them kernels of corn and wheat that are too small or too old for human consumption. To Davy Crockett, this "throwaway food" was like the "small change" (or *birdseed*—MWCD: 1840) that gamblers tossed on the table for the "card sharps" to gobble up. Nowadays, a poor person who *works for chicken feed* works for practically nothing, an insignificant amount of money; and to someone who is rich enough to light his/her cigars with hundred-dollar bills, the C-notes are *chicken feed.* The expression "That's *(strictly) for the birds*" (DC: 1951—J. D. Salinger's *Catcher in the Rye*), meaning that something is insignificant or worthless, may derive from the grain (rye?) thrown to birds (prob. pigeons) in the park. AID; ATWS; BDPF; CI; DAI; DAS; DEI; EWPO; HDAS; IRCD; LA; MS; SA.

CHICKEN IN EVERY POT   *a chicken in every pot.* Prosperity for all. LA: 1928. Source: CHICKEN (MWCD: 14th cent.); POT (MWCD: O.E.). *A chicken in every pot* was a slogan of Herbert Hoover's (successful) presidential campaign in 1928. Hoover himself did not make this claim: It was conceived and publicized by his election committee, which was attempting to capitalize on the relatively prosperous past seven years of Republican administration. However, the phrase may have been used in Scotland as early as the mid-1800s, and the message may even have been expressed (in French) by Henry IV when he was crowned King of France in the late-1500s (DC: 1589). Nowadays, a promise of prosperity might specify "a chicken in every microwave" rather than *a chicken in every pot*. EWPO; FLC; IRCD; SA.

CHICKEN OF THE SEA   *See* Tastes Just like Chicken.

CHICKEN SALAD   *See* Salad.

CHICKEN SOUP   *See* Borscht Belt.

CHICK PEA   *See* Pea Bean.

CHIEF COOK AND BOTTLE WASHER   *the chief cook and bottle washer.* The only employee of a small business; a jack-of-all-trades at a large business. DAFD: 1840. Source: COOK (MWCD: O.E.); BOTTLE (MWCD: 14th cent.). In the kitchen of a large restaurant there are many cooks, one of whom is the chief cook, and many other employees, some of whom wash dishes. Chief cooks, who may qualify as chefs, do not wash dishes; and dishwashers, who have the lowest status in the kitchen, do not prepare meals. If one person actually did both jobs, it would mean that he/she was either the owner of the restaurant or the only employee in the kitchen. The kitchen then becomes a metaphor for the roles of people in the business world. Bosses are expected to be familiar with the entire operation and capable of stepping in at any level if needed. When the operation is tiny, the boss has no choice: He/she is also the receptionist, the telephone operator, the typist, the bookkeeper, the accountant, etc. DAS; HDAS.

CHILI   *See* Chili Today, Hot Tamale.

CHILI CON CARNE   *See* Chili Today, Hot Tamale.

CHILI-DIP   *See* Chili Today, Hot Tamale.

CHILI DOG   *See* Hot Dog.

CHILI PEPPER   *See* Pep (n).

CHILI POWDER   *See* Chili Today, Hot Tamale.

CHILI SAUCE   *See* Chili Today, Hot Tamale.

CHILI TODAY, HOT TAMALE   Chilly today, hot tomorrow. (A parody of a weather report from a Tex-Mex radio station.) Source: CHILI (MWCD: 1604); TAMALE (MWCD: 1854). *Chili* (fr. Nahuatl *chilli*) is the name of a hot pepper—

sometimes spelled *chile*—that is native to Mexico and Central and South America. The heat quotient of chilies ranges from mild (read "hot") to strong (read "hot hot"). Chilies can be eaten alone (fresh or roasted), dried and ground into a powder for use as a condiment (*chili powder*—MWCD: 1938), chopped up for use in a tomato-based sauce (*chili sauce*—MWCD: 1880), or combined with meat, beans (optional), and sauce to form a stew (*chili con carne*—MWCD: 1857). Served at room temperature, the chili sauce (or *salsa*—MWCD: ca. 1962) can be used as a dip for tortilla chips (or *nachos*—MWCD: 1969). The expression "to *chili dip* a golf shot" (an LPGA term) means to hit a short-iron shot "fat," i.e., taking too much turf, like a nacho scooping up too much salsa and causing it to drip back into the bowl. When meat, cheese, and other ingredients are rolled into a soft tortilla, covered with chili sauce, and baked, the result is an *enchilada* (MWCD: 1887), lit., "chilied." Metaphorically, a *big enchilada* (HDAS: 1973) is a big boss, esp. of the underworld, and *the whole enchilada* means "all of it, everything, the whole ball of wax, the whole Magilla, etc." In contrast, a *tamale* (fr. Nahuatl *tamalli*—MWCD: 1854) is more of a Mexican food than a Mexican-American food. It consists of chopped meat and vegetables in a cornmeal dough, wrapped in corn husks, steamed, and served only on special occasions. DAFD; DAS; FLC; IHAT; LA; PT; WNWCD.

CHIMICHANGA *See* Tortilla.

CHINESE GOOSEBERRY *See* Kiwifruit.

CHINESE GRITS *See* Grits.

CHIPPED BEEF Thin-sliced, salted, smoked, dried beef. MWCD: 1859. Source: BEEF. MWCD: 14th cent. Chipped beef has a strange appearance (it is red, like ham) and a strange name (which implies that the beef looks like potato chips). Nevertheless, it has been a popular *trail food* since the early-19th cent. because it is so well preserved; and it has been a popular dinner food—on toast, covered with a hot cream gravy—because it is so inexpensive. However, *creamed chipped beef on toast* was served so often in U.S. Army mess halls in WWII that it acquired the nickname *shit on a shingle* (abbreviated as *S.O.S.*), although it is still available as a frozen dinner. Another beef product with a strange name and appearance is *beef jerky* (NSOED: mid-19th cent.—*jerkin beef*), a trail food consisting of inch-wide, half-inch-high strips of beef dried in the sun. The name *jerky* is an Eng. pronunciation of Sp. *charqui*, which is a Sp. pronunciation of Quechuan (Peruvian Indian) *ch'arki* "dried meat." (The verb *jerk* "to prepare meat by cutting it into strips and drying it in the sun"—MWCD: 1707—is a back-formation from the noun *jerky*.) In the late-20th cent., *beef jerky* became popular again among hikers, climbers, canoeers, truckers, and just plain travelers, and a jerky made of dried turkey meat was introduced: *turkey jerky*. Another form of trail food is *pemmican* (MWCD: 1791), a Native American (Cree) mixture of dried meat, fat, and berries ground up and formed into small cakes that remain nutritious and unspoiled on long journeys. BDPF; DAFD; EWPO; FLC; LA; PT.

CHIVES   *See* Onionskin Paper.

CHOCOHOLIC   *a chocoholic.* A lover of chocolate. MWCD: 1968. Source: CHOCOLATE. MWCD: 1604. A *chocoholic* is not an alcoholic who is also addicted to chocolate but a chocolate lover who is as addicted to chocolate as an alcoholic is to alcohol. The history of chocolate contains about as many surprises as Forrest Gump's box of chocolate creams: "You never know what you're gonna get." For example, what we now call the *cocoa bean* (MWCD: 1855) was orig. called the *cacao bean* (MWCD: 1555). Sometime during the past three centuries, and for reasons unknown, the vowels of the word *cacao* switched places (*a* → *o, o* → *a*), producing modern *cocoa.* (*Cocoa butter*, as in "*cocoa butter* body lotion," developed after the vowel changes had taken place.) During WWII there were two quite different meanings for the familiar term *Hershey bar* in the U.S. Army. One was the hard, flat, milk chocolate candy, produced by M. S. Hershey, the inventor of the candy bar; and the other the small gold bar worn horizontally on the bottom of the left sleeve to signify six months of overseas service—not to be confused with the larger, diagonal "service stripes," nicknamed *hash marks*, worn higher up on the left sleeve, which signified three years of overall service each. The soldiers' *Hershey bar* (HDAS: 1945) was named for Gen. L. B. Hershey, the director of the Selective Service, but it is pretty obvious that the name of the service bar was modeled after the name of the familiar candy bar. BDPF; DAFD; DAS; FLC; IHAT; NSOED.

CHOCOLATE CREAM   *See* Cream Puff.

CHOP-CHOP   *See* Chop Suey.

CHOP HOUSE   *See* Chopping Block.

CHOPPED LIVER   *What am I, chopped liver?* What about me? Don't I deserve some credit (praise, recognition, respect)? HDAS: 1954. Source: LIVER. MWCD: O.E. *Chopped liver* is a descriptive term for *liverwurst* "liver sausage" (MWCD: 1869): chopped pork livers, pork meat, and other meats, finely ground, seasoned, cooked in loaves, and served in sandwiches or on canapés. If also smoked, liverwurst is also called *Braunschweiger*, after the orig. Ger. name *Braunschweiger Wurst* "Braunschweiger sausage." Because liverwurst is a common sausage, not a delicacy like *pâté de foie gras* (MWCD: 1827) "goose liver paste," it has become a metaphor for the person who "gets no respect" (like Rodney Dangerfield), such as a younger brother compared to an older brother, or a woman compared to a man. Comparing yourself to chopped liver, as opposed to *foie gras*, is like comparing yourself to beer as opposed to champagne. The expression prob. developed in America in the late-19th cent. among German immigrants. DSFD; FLC; IHAT.

CHOPPED STEAK   *See* Salisbury Steak.

CHOPPER   *See* Chopping Block.

CHOPPING BLOCK   *to have your head—or neck—on the chopping block.* To be about to be fired. Source: CHOP. MWCD: 14th cent. A *chopping block* (MWCD: 1703) is a large block of wood—hard or medium-hard, solid or laminated—on which a butcher cuts up a carcass into meal-size pieces—such as roasts, steaks, and chops. *Chop*, therefore, is not only the name of a blow from a meat cleaver to a carcass but the name of the resulting piece of meat and bone: a *lamb chop, pork chop*, or *veal chop*. Since the late-17th cent., *chop house* (MWCD: ca. 1690) has been a restaurant that specializes in steaks and chops. However, from the point of view of a barnyard fowl, such as a chicken, duck, or turkey, a *chopping block* is a stump on which the bird will eventually lose its head. For humans, a *chopping block* is the means by which an employee is separated from his/her job—reminiscent, no doubt, of the ax with which executioners once separated heads from bodies. Even within an inanimate corporation, the expression "to put something on the *chopping block*" means to separate it from the "corpus," i.e., the body of the organization. And the "chopper"? The *chopper* (HDAS: 1951) is the helicopter in which the enforcers fly away. BDPF; DAFD; FLC; WNWCD.

CHOPSTICK   *See* Chop Suey.

CHOP SUEY   A Chinese-American dish of chopped meat (usu. chicken or pork) and vegetables (of both Chinese and American extraction), stewed together and served over rice or noodles. MWCD: 1888. Source: CHOP. MWCD: 14th cent. The term *chop suey* appears to reflect the mixed origin of the dish: *chop*, English; *suey*, Chinese. However, the name is strictly Chinese (Cantonese *tsaâp sui* "miscellaneous bits") and the dish is strictly American: Even the people of China are not familiar with it. The most reasonable explanation for its conception in America is that Cantonese cooks working in the gold mining camps and among railroad-building crews chopped up leftover meat and vegetables and cooked the "odds and ends" in a fashion that both the Chinese workers and the American bosses could appreciate: a stew. After the Gold Rush was over and the Union Pacific Railroad was completed, many of the Cantonesee cooks started up restaurants in San Francisco and other large cities, advertising their presence with a large CHOP SUEY sign outside. Eventually this American dish became the basis for the popularity of Chinese food throughout the country, even in smaller towns. The *chop* in *chop suey* is not the same as the *chop* in *chopsticks* (MWCD: 1699). The latter *chop* is Pidgin Eng. for "quick" or "fast," as in *Chop-Chop!* (MWCD:

1834) "Quickly!" It is linked with *sticks* because the Asian utensils move so quickly in the hands of an expert, and the word *chopsticks* has also been applied to a simple piano piece because it is so fast and "choppy" (NSOED; late-19th cent.). BDPF; DAFD; EWPO; FLC; HF; PT; WNWCD.

CHOW   *See* Chow Hound.

CHOWCHOW   *See* Chow Hound.

CHOWDERHEAD   *a chowderhead.* A clumsy or stupid person: a "blockhead." MWCD: 1833. Source: CHOWDER (*). MWCD: 1751. Chowder is historically a thick, rich, creamy stew made with milk, potatoes (and other vegetables), salt pork, and (esp.) seafood, such as clams or fish. However, a "food fight" of sorts has developed between the defenders of the original *clam chowder*, called "New England clam chowder" (or "Cape Cod clam chowder"), as described above, and those of "New York clam chowder" (or "Manhattan clam chowder"), which is made with tomato sauce rather than milk and is consequently thinner and closer to a soup than a stew. The term *chowder* derives fr. Fr. *chaudière*, a kettle into which 17th cent. Breton fishermen threw scraps of fish and vegetables to make a soup or stew. Clams replaced fish as the favorite seafood in American chowder in the late-19th cent. (LA: 1880s), but the unfortunate people who lived in the Wild West never got a chance to experience either kind—and prob. had no idea what a chowder was. Lack of knowledge was also a problem with the word *chowderhead*: It has nothing whatsoever to do with *chowder* but is a false etymology based on an attempt to make sense of the 18th cent. word *cholterhead* "blockhead," which was in turn an attempt to make sense of a 17th cent. word *jolterhead* (same meaning). These Eng. dialectal words all sounded like *chowderhead*, which was rationalized to mean someone who had chowder in his/her head instead of brains. DAFD; DAS; EWPO; FLC; HDAS; HF; MDWPO; PT.

CHOW DOWN   *See* Chow Hound.

CHOW HOUND   *a chow hound.* The first one in the chow line. HDAS: 1917. Source: CHOW. MWCD: 1856. *Chow* is a borrowing from Mandarin Chinese *ch'ao* "to fry or cook"—compare Cantonese Chinese *chàau-mihn* (*chow mein*) "fried noodles"—presumably by way of Chinese Pidgin English *chowchow*, orig. "a Chinese fruit preserve or pickle relish" (MWCD: 1850). The shortened form, *chow*, was prob. picked up in America from Chinese laborers who were imported to build the western half of the transcontinental railroad. For both the bosses of the work crews and the Chinese workers themselves, *Chow!* came to mean "Food!" or "Come and get it!" By WWI, compound terms such as *chow time* "mealtime," *chow down* "eat heartily" (MWCD: 1917), and *chow line* "food line" (MWCD: 1919) had become standard fare for servicemen, and in 1917 the term *chow hound* was added to the list. Since WWII the word *chow* has continued in use, but it is slowly passing out of general usage, allowing even the earlier term *grub* (IHAT: 1807) to return. ATWS; DAFD; DAS; EWPO; FLC; HDAS; MDWPO; NSOED.

CHOW LINE   *See* Chow Hound.

CHOW MEIN   *See* Chow Hound.

CHOW TIME   *See* Chow Hound; First Come, First Served.

CHRONIC VEGETATIVE STATE   *See* Vegetable.

CHUCK WAGON   *a chuck wagon.* A Western food wagon. HDAS: 1887. Source: CHUCK. MWCD: 1723. *Chuck wagon* was the original "meals-on-wheels." The "wagon" was simply a farm wagon carrying a huge box filled with food, utensils, supplies, and firewood that was pulled by a team of horses or mules and driven by the cook ("Cookie") himself. The meals were for the cowhands who were either on a cattle drive or working so far away from the ranch house that it would have been impossible for them to ride back and forth just to eat. The cooking was done not in the wagon but over a fire built nearby, enabling the cowboys to have a hot meal of meat, vegetables, biscuits, and coffee three times a day. The word *chuck* is sometimes linked to the noun meaning "an inexpensive cut from the neck or shoulder of a steer," but it is also associated with the verb meaning "to pitch, throw, or toss something into or onto something else." This latter sense is conducive with the work that the cook had to do when the cowhands moved to another locations: toss everything back onto the wagon, put out the fire, hitch up the team, and drive away. *Chuck wagon* became a popular name for a roadside diner following WWII, and the name has recently been borrowed for a brand of dog food, although the wagon in those commercials is a covered wagon. DAFD; LA; NSOED; WNWCD.

CHURN (v)   *to churn.* To agitate; to be agitated. Source: CHURN (n). MWCD: O.E. The O.E. *churn* was a cylindrical wooden vessel into which whole milk or cream was poured and agitated until the fat solidified into butter. In the 15th cent., a verb developed from the noun to describe the process of making butter. By the turn of the 19th cent., home butter-making declined, and by WWII it was cheaper to buy butter than to make it at home. The butter churn, and the noun that identified it, both became obsolete; but the verb that described the obsolete process was reborn as a metaphor for various types of agitation: for a paddle-wheel boat to *churn up* the water and a law school to *churn out* lawyers; and for thoughts to be *churning in* your head and acids to be *churning in* your stomach. FLC; NSOED; WNWCD.

CHURN IN/OUT/UP   *See* Churn (v).

CIDER   *See* Applejack.

CIDER VINEGAR   *See* Applejack.

CITY CHICKEN   *See* Mock Chicken.

CLAMBAKE   *a clambake*. An outdoor social gathering, often for political purposes. HDAS: 1941. Source: CLAM (MWCD: ca. 1520); BAKE (MWCD: O.E.). The traditional *clambake* (MWCD: 1835) was a seaside outing (or picnic) at which clams and other seafood were baked (or steamed) on hot rocks covered with seaweed. The practice was strictly American, having been introduced to colonists in New England by the Native Americans. In the mid-20th cent., however, and on the Pacific Coast, the event became more of an annual party, accompanied by fun and games. The most famous example was prob. the former Bing Crosby Golf Tournament at Pebble Beach, Calif., which was always referred to by Crosby's close friends as a *clambake*. Nowadays, a clambake requires neither a seashore nor clams, and the guests of honor are neither colonists nor crooners, but politicians. ATWS; DAFD; NSOED; PT; SA.

CLAM CHOWDER   *See* Chowderhead.

CLAM COCKTAIL   *See* Shrimp Cocktail.

CLARIFY   *to clarify something*. To make something clear, understandable, and free of confusion. NSOED: late-M.E. Source: CLARIFY. MWCD: 14th cent. To *clarify* a statement derives from "clarifying" a liquid that contains sediment or other impurities. The liquid, such as beef or chicken stock, is usu. "clarified" by adding eggshells, heating briefly, and straining thoroughly. Fat can be "clarified" by adding water, boiling, and straining; and butter can be "clarified" by heating it and then separating the liquid on top from the milk solids on the bottom. Ideas can be *clarified* by reorganizing them, illustrating them, or restating them in a simpler way. FLC; WNWCD.

CLEAR THE TABLE   *See* Set the Table.

CLINGING VINE   *See* Wither on the Vine.

CLINGSTONE PEACH   *See* Peach.

CLINKERS   *See* Biscuit Shooter.

CLOVE   *See* Onionskin Paper.

COCKTAIL TABLE   *See* Coffee.

COCOA BUTTER   Yellow vegetable fat processed from cocoa beans. MWCD: ca. 1891. Source: COCOA (MWCD: 1788); BUTTER (MWCD: O.E.). Although cocoa butter is valuable for cooking because it has a low melting point, it also has become a popular addition to skin-care products such as suntan lotion and hand and body lotions. FLC; NSOED.

COCONUT CREAM   *See* Coconut Milk.

COCONUT MILK   The natural juice of a coconut; the liquid prepared by mixing shredded coconut with water. Source: COCONUT (MWCD: 1613); MILK (MWCD: O.E.). The natural juice of a coconut is obtained by puncturing two of the three "eyes" at the base of the coconut and draining it. The juice is sweet and milklike, but thin, like skim milk. The prepared liquid is made by cooking equal parts of water and shredded coconut until foamy, then straining and squeezing it. Both of these liquids can be called *coconut milk*, but purists insist that only the prepared liquid deserves the name. Everyone agrees that *coconut cream* is a stronger form of the prepared liquid. FLC.

CODDLE   *to coddle someone*. To pamper someone. Source: EGG. *Coddling* people is a derivative of coddling (or "poaching") eggs. Eggs are coddled (or "poached") when they are cooked in hot water just below the boiling point. Because the water is not boiling—and the eggs are usu. in individual containers, not even touching the water—the eggs are cooked slowly and gently. Coddled eggs were once recommended for babies and invalids because they are soft and easy to chew and digest. The association with tenderness led to the use of *coddle* to refer to "babying" an older child or young adult—treating them as if they were helpless, like a baby or an invalid. The *poaching* of eggs may be derived from the poaching of game. Just as the egg is placed in a container to cook, the game is put into a bag or pouch (Fr. *poche*) to become part of an illegal meal. Furthermore, the *poacher* of game (MWCD: 1614) predates the *poacher* of eggs (MWCD: 1861) by almost two and one-half centuries, so the *poaching* of wild animals is prob. not a food metaphor. In lunch-counter jargon, a breakfast of poached—or "coddled"—eggs on toast was called *Adam and Eve on a raft* (HDAS: 1909). The book of Genesis doesn't record any trip on a raft by Adam and Eve; but if they did take such a trip, and it was before they ate of the fruit of the tree of the knowledge of good and evil, they would have been naked, like two eggs out of the shell. In this breakfast dish, two eggs are cracked open, poached, and turned out onto a large piece of toast. The eggs are Adam and Eve, and the toast is their "raft." DAFD; FLC; IHAT; MDWPO; NSOED; WNWCD.

COFFEE   *a coffee*. A social gathering; a reception for a celebrity or dignitary; a promotion for a social or political cause. Source: COFFEE. MWCD: 1598. Coffee was more available than tea following the Boston Tea Party of 1773 and the subsequent Revolution and cessation of trade with England. The Eng. *coffeehouse*

(MWCD: 1612) and *coffee room* (MWCD: 1712) were replaced in America by the *coffee shop* (MWCD: 1836), a small restaurant that sold coffee and light refreshments and served as a meeting place for people of the neighborhood. The coffee that was drunk there was prob. much stronger than that served in today's coffee shops and restaurants. During the Civil War, when coffee was scarce, dried, ground, roasted roots of the chicory herb were used to make *chicory coffee* (DAFD: early-1860s), or *chicken coffee*, which was both strong and bitter. Other "mock coffees" have been made from dried peas, bread crumbs, and cereals (e.g., Postum). Iced coffee was created in Philadelphia in the 1870s (DAFD: 1876) and became popular throughout the country until about WWII, after which it yielded to iced tea and is no longer on the menu of most restaurants. American servicepersons brought back a taste for *espresso* (MWCD: 1945) from Italy after WWII, and this hot drink of "pressed-out" coffee—called "cappuccino" (MWCD: 1948) if topped with foamy hot milk or cream—has taken the country by storm. The *coffee table* (MWCD: 1877) was named almost seventy years before the *cocktail table* (MWCD: 1946), but the *coffee-table book* (MWCD: 1962)—a large, heavy, expensive book meant for "show" rather than for reading—is fairly recent. (So far, there has been no coffee-table book about coffee tables.) EWPO; FLC; LA; NSOED; WNWCD. *Compare* Tea.

COFFEE BREAK   *a coffee break.* A short, spontaneous recess for taking refreshments and visiting the bathroom. MWCD; 1951. Source: COFFEE. MWCD: 1598. The *coffee break* was orig. a midmorning or midafternoon cessation of work in order to consume coffee and doughnuts (or rolls). The term prob. derives from Ger. *Kaffeeklatsch* (MWCD: 1888), lit., "coffee gossip," which denoted a more structured gathering of neighborhood housewives socializing over coffee. The Ger. term has been Americanized as *coffee klatch* (MWCD: 1895) and updated as *coffee hour* (MWCD: 1952), a usu. scheduled period, following a meeting, for relaxation, conversation, and refreshments. The drinking of coffee is no longer required on any of these occasions, despite their names; however, coffee is always available (regular or decaf), as well as tea (hot or cold) and sometimes soft drinks. The *coffee break* for American factory workers is more like a "pop break." DAFD; EWPO; LA; NSOED; PT; WNWCD.

COFFEE GRINDER   *See* Java.

COFFEE HOUR   *See* Coffee Break.

COFFEEHOUSE   *See* Café; Coffee.

COFFEE KLATCH   *See* Coffee Break.

COFFEE MILL   *See* Through the Mill.

COFFEE ROOM   *See* Coffee.

COFFEE TABLE   *See* Coffee.

COFFEE-TABLE BOOK   *See* Coffee.

COFFEE, TEA, OR ME?   *See* Wake up and Smell the Coffee.

COLANDER   *See* Leak like a Sieve.

COLD AS A CUCUMBER   *See* Cool as a Cucumber.

COLD DUCK   Pink sparkling wine. MWCD: 1969. Source: DUCK. MWCD: O.E. *Cold duck* is "sparkling" because it is a mixture of two sparkling wines: sparkling burgundy and champagne; and it is pink because it is a mixture of a red wine (the burgundy) and a white wine (the champagne). *Cold duck* refers to a drink instead of a fowl because it is a mispronunciation (and misspelling) of Ger. *kalte Ende* "cold end" as *kalte Ente* "cold duck," prob. in the early part of the 20th cent. in Germany, before the mixture was introduced into America. It seems that German waiters used to pour the various wines left over at banquets into single bottles, and the leftovers (or *Ende*) of sparkling red burgundy and champagne were found to have produced a wine of attractive taste (sweet) and appearance (pink). The mixture was first sold in America under the Eng. name *cold duck* in the 1960s, it became very popular in the 1970s, and it practically disappeared in the 1980s. DAFD; FLC; MDWPO; SA.

COLD SHOULDER   *a cold shoulder*. A cool reception; a snub. MWCD: 1816. Source: MUTTON. According to Sir Walter Scott, the *cold shoulder* that was given as a sign of unfriendliness in the early-19th cent. was an actual cold shoulder of mutton. If a hostess, who was accustomed to serving hot food to her welcome guests, encountered one who was unwelcome, she would serve that person a cold shoulder of mutton. It was unlikely that such a guest would not take the hint or get the message. Out of this practice developed the expression *to give someone the cold shoulder*, which is usu. applied nowadays to a woman attempting to discourage the advances of an amorous man, although both women and men can *give the cold shoulder* to people with whom they do not wish to become friendly. Some people would call it a "brush-off" or a "put-down." AID; CI; DAI; DAS; EWPO; HND; MS; SA.

COLD SLAW   *See* Cabbage.

COLD TURKEY   *See* Quit Cold Turkey.

COLE SLAW   *See* Cabbage.

COME AND GET IT!   *See* Chow Hound; First Come, First Served.

COME TO A HEAD   *See* Cabbage.

COME UP CHERRIES   *See* Life Is Just a Bowl of Cherries.

COME UP FOR A CUP OF COFFEE   *See* Wake up and Smell the Coffee.

COMFORT FOOD   Food that reminds you of your childhood. Source: FOOD. MWCD: O.E. Food (including drink) is one of the three basic *creature comforts* (MWCD: 1659) that are enjoyed by both animals and humans, the others being shelter and warmth. The food that brings back the most pleasant memories to most adult humans is what they ate as a child—both at the table and as snacks. The homecooked meals were hot and heaping, and there was little worry about salt, sugar, fat, or cholesterol content. (The good old days!) Even if the child refused to eat his/her vegetables, he/she could make up the calories by snacking (or *piecing*) between meals, usu. on cookies and fried cakes, or later on pretzels and chips. *Comfort food* is often *forbidden fruit* (q.v.) these days—the food that you wish you could eat but know that you shouldn't. It's prob. what you would order for your final meal if you were a prisoner on death row. DAFD; SA; WNWCD.

COMING UP   *See* Maître d'Hôtel.

COMPANION   *See* Break Bread.

COMPARE APPLES AND ORANGES   *to compare apples and oranges*. To compare unlike, and therefore incompatible, entities. Source: APPLE (MWCD: O.E.); ORANGE (MWCD: 14th cent.). It is hard to imagine why these two fruits were selected to illustrate a contrast of features. Apples and oranges are both fruits, they are both rather round, they are about the same size, they both have seeds, they are both edible, and the flesh of both is sweet and juicy. It seems more logical to contrast apples (round) and pears (bell-shaped), or oranges (sweet) and lemons (sour); but metaphors are not based on logic. Apples and oranges *do* have some differences, of course: Apples are not really spherical; some oranges are much larger than apples; the skin of apples is thin, whereas the rind of oranges is sometimes quite thick; and the flesh of apples is firm, whereas the flesh of oranges is soft. The two fruits are sometimes used to characterize a contradiction ("That's *apples and oranges*" = Brit. "chalk and cheese") or an odd couple ("They're *like apples and oranges*"). MS.

CONCOCT   *See* Cook the Books.

CONEY ISLAND   *See* Hot Dog.

CONSERVE   *See* Preserve.

CONTINENTAL BREAKFAST   *See* Meal.

COOKBOOK   *a cookbook.* A set of detailed instructions. HDAS: 1965. Source: COOKBOOK. MWCD: 1809. The metaphorical cookbook is the set of instructions that you receive with a toy or appliance for which "some assembly [is] required." You are expected to follow the instructions, without questioning their rationale, in order to put together the desired product—with fewer than two screws left over. This application of step-by-step procedures is known as the *cookbook approach* (MWCD: 1944). The literal *cookbook* (fr. Ger. *Kochbuch* or Du. *kookboek*) was first published in America in 1809. It was a collection of recipes for preparing foods according to a set of instructions that incorporated the ingredients. (In 1896 the instructions and the ingredients were listed separately, with the ingredients appearing first.) Before 1809, cookbooks were called *recipe books* (or *receipt books*) and were simply collections of handwritten instructions for preparing a family's favorite foods, handed down from mother to daughter. Modern cookbooks also give information about calories and cholesterol, weights and measures, times and temperatures, and advice on meals and menus. DAFD; IHAT. *See also* Recipe.

COOKBOOK APPROACH   *See* Cookbook.

COOK FROM SCRATCH   *See* Make from Scratch.

COOKIE   *a cookie.* A "little cake." MWCD: 1703. Source: CAKE. The Eng. word *cookie* derives from the Du. word *koekje*, the dim. form of *koek* "cake." The word appears to be an Americanism, presumably borrowed from Dutch settlers in old New Amsterdam, because the word *cookie* is not in popular use in England. (There, cookies are variously called either *cakes* or *biscuits*.) The defining feature of the American cookie is that it is capable of being picked up by, held in, and eaten from the hand. Cakes are softer, moister, and messier. Crackers are brittler, drier, and messier. Nevertheless, the term *cookie* has a very broad range, including hand-held snacks that can be either large or small, hard or soft, filled or unfilled, frosted or unfrosted, single or double (the *sandwich cookie*, q.v.), flat or ball-shaped, edged or cut from a loaf (the "bar cookie"), etc. In contrast, what are really cookies sometimes go by other names, such as the *Moon Pie* (q.v.), the *Oreo* "Sandwich" (q.v., orig. "Biscuit"), the tea cake, and the fig newton. An example of *cookie* as a metaphor is the term *death cookie* "a frozen lump of snow on a ski run." DAFD; FLC; IHAT; MDWPO. *See also* Smart Cookie; That's the Way the Cookie Crumbles.

COOKIE-CUTTER (adj.)   *Cookie-cutter houses* (etc.). Houses (etc.) that all look alike. MWCD: 1963. Source: COOKIE (MWCD: 1703); CUT (MWCD: 13th cent.). The metal or plastic device known as a *cookie cutter* (MWCD: 1903) was designed to cut out pieces of rolled dough in the exact same shape and size and in as large a quantity as desired. (A rolling-pin cookie cutter can do the same job in a fraction of the time.) The result is a number of rabbits, stars, turkeys, trees, etc., that are identical at this stage of production and will show originality only when frosting and colored sugar are added. The adj. *cookie-cutter* has been applied to such look-alike architectural projects as shopping malls and hotels, and to such nondistinctive entertainment projects as TV sitcoms and talk shows. FLC.

COOKIE-CUTTER HOUSES   *See* Cookie-cutter (adj.).

COOKIE PUSHER   *a cookie pusher.* A waitress. HDAS: 1936. Source: COOKIE. MWCD: 1703. Why would cookies need pushing? Literally, on the production line of a cookie factory, workers with gloves on *do* push (or pull) deformed cookies off the belt coming out of the oven. But the workers are not called "cookie pushers." BDPF defines the term as a junior diplomat who functions as a roving waiter at an official reception, presumably "pushing" appetizers on people who don't really want them. That comes close to *cookie pusher* as a slang term of the mid-20th cent. for a waitress in a restaurant who both lit. and fig. "pushes" cookies (and other desserts) on a cart from the kitchen to the table. (Waitresses have also been called *biscuit rollers* and *biscuit shooters*, both of which *see*.) The late-20th cent. definition of a *cookie pusher* as a "cog in a wheel, an interchangeable part, a robot," comes from the assembly line of a factory but is directed at the management in the offices. It is practically synonymous with *bean counter* (q.v.). BDPF; DAFD; DAS; PT.

COOKING BANANAS   *See* Fruit with Appeal.

COOKING CHERRY   *See* Cherry (n).

COOKING WITH GAS   *See* What's Cooking?

COOK SOMEONE'S GOOSE   *to cook someone's goose.* To spoil someone's plans. DC: 1851. Source: COOK (v) (MWCD: 14th cent.); GOOSE (MWCD: O.E.). The simplest—and most likely—source of this metaphor is the stealing of someone's Christmas goose and cooking it as your own. Not only have you lit. "cooked that person's goose," you have also spoiled that person's Christmas. That is prob. what the supporters of the Church of England had in mind in 1851 when they opposed the Pope's appointment of a new cardinal in England by singing: "If they come here, we'll *cook their goose/*The Pope and Cardinal Wiseman." However, the metaphor may also have been influenced by the Aesop fable of the *goose that laid the golden eggs*. The farmer who owned the goose grew so impatient to "get rich quick" that he killed the goose, hoping to find a cache of unlaid eggs inside. There were none, and the most he could salvage from this unfortunate experience was the goose itself, which he gave to his wife to cook. When the bird was done, the farmer's wife may have said to him, "*Your goose is cooked!*"—meaning something like "You really blew it this time!" AID; ATWS; BDPF; CI; DAI; DEI; EWPO; HDAS; HI; HND; IRCD; LCRH; MDWPO; MS; SA; SHM. *See also* Goose Hangs High.

COOK SOMETHING UP   *See* Cook the Books.

COOK THE BOOKS   *to cook the books*. To falsify the accounts. HDAS: 1848. Source: COOK (v). MWCD: 14th cent. *Cooking the books* is what dishonest book-keepers do to make financial accounts appear to balance when they really don't. Such crooked accountants are able to "doctor" the records so skillfully that no one—they hope—will notice the difference. Skillful cooks do the same thing, albeit legally, when they substitute a cheaper ingredient for a more expensive one or create a dish that is so well disguised that no one can identify it. Butchers and restaurateurs are also prone to label foods in a way that makes them appear to be one thing when they are really another; e.g., *city chicken* and *pigs in the blanket* (both of which *see*). A metaphor that is similar to *cook the books* is *to cook something up*—i.e., to concoct a scheme or plot to get yourself into money or power and out of poverty or trouble (NSOED: early-17th cent.). Even schoolchildren have been known to *cook up* an excuse when they are unable to come up with an assignment on time. ("The printer ate it.") The verb *concoct* (fr. Lat. *concoctus*, past part. of *concoquere* "to cook together") is also a metaphor when it is used to mean "to devise a scheme or fabricate an excuse" (NSOED: late-18th cent.). AID; BDPF; CE; DAI; DAS; DEI; LCRH; MS.

COOK UP   *See* Cook the Books.

COOL AS A CUCUMBER   *to be as cool as a cucumber*. For someone in a situation of confusion, danger, or fear to be calm, collected, and composed; undisturbed, unemotional, and unruffled; neither anxious, nervous, nor upset. DC: 1838. Source: CUCUMBER. MWCD: 14th cent. This simile is derived from an earlier one, *to be as cold as a cucumber* (DC: 1615), which meant "to be uncompassionate, unsociable, and unsympathetic." What does a *cucumber*, or "cuke" (HDAS: 1903), have to do with being *cool* (or *cold*)? Mostly the initial letter *c*, which makes for a nice alliteration, reinforced by the following rounded back vowel *u*. In addition, the cucumber—the only totally edible member of the gourd family (flesh, rind, seeds, and all)—has long been associated, as have its cousins, the melons, with summer picnics alongside the cool waters of a lake or stream. The picnic might also include another food associated with cool water—the pickle, which is a cucumber that is picked at a young age and immersed in cold salt or vinegar brine for many days. The smaller pickles are called *gherkins* (MWCD: 1661), a poor rendition of Du. *gurken* "cucumber pickle." The term *cucumber pickle* is almost a redundancy because when people think of pickles, they automatically think of cucumbers; furthermore, other pickled foods are usu. called "pickled _____," as in *pickled herring* and *pickled pig's feet*. (*Watermelon pickles* is an exception.) Unfortunately, when people think of cucumbers—those foot-long, two-inch-diameter "gourds"—they seldom think of pickles: Q. "Do you like cucumbers?" A. "Not really." Q. "Do you like pickles?" A. "Oh yes, I love pickles." *Cucumber eyes* is not exactly a metaphor, but it is food-related. It's what a young man makes when he's bothering a young woman who is cutting cucumber slices for a salad. The young man puts a cucumber slice on each eye and walks around the kitchen like a zombie. Imitation "cucumber slices" are now being manufactured by Pond's for applying to the eyes to reduce puffiness. BDPF; CE; CI; DAFD; DAI; DEI; EWPO; FLC; HF; NSOED.

CORDON BLEU   *See* My Compliments to the Chef.

CORKSCREW   *See* Pop Your Cork.

CORN   *a corn; corn.* A granule; a grain. NSOED: O.E. Source: CORN. MWCD: O.E. *Corn* meaning "granule" survives in very few terms in Eng., three of which are *peppercorn* (MWCD: O.E.), a dried berry of the pepper plant; *corned beef* (DAFD: 18th cent.), beef that has been preserved either by rubbing *with grains* ("corns") of salt or storing in salt brine; and *corn snow* (MWCD: 1935), snow that is so characterized by skiers because it has become granular as a result of thawing and freezing. *Corn* "grain" (i.e., having hard, granular "seeds") means different things to different people. Before the English colonists came to America, *corn* denoted only the wheat of England and the oats of Scotland and Ireland; but when the colonists encountered Native American grain, they extended the meaning of the word *corn* to include the local variety by referring to it first as *corn* (IHAT: 1608) and later as *Indian corn* (IHAT: 1617). However, Indian corn was so different from wheat and oats that eventually the British (and most other Europeans) adopted the word *maize* (fr. Taino *mahiz* by way of Sp. *maíz*). Nowadays, *Indian corn* is an Amer. term referring to dried ears of corn with multicolored kernels, whereas *maize* is now a golden yellow color used in the expression "maize and blue." Two modern metaphors employing the word *corn* are *rough as a (corn) cob*, which is based on the use of dried corncobs as "toilet paper" in the 19th and early-20th cents., and *cornrow* (MWCD: 1946), which refers to a hairstyle in which the hair is tightly braided in rows that resemble a cornfield as seen from above. (The "corn" on your toe is derived fr. Lat. *cornu* "horn," not fr. Eng. *corn* "grain.") BDPF; EWPO; FLC; HDAS; PT.

CORNBALL (adj.)   Countrified, old-fashioned, unsophisticated; banal, hackneyed, trite. MWCD: 1951. Source: CORNBALL (n). MWCD: 1949. The adj. *cornball* was orig. applied to a countrified, old-fashioned, or unsophisticated person—someone who lacked urbanity, modernity, and style. Soon after its origin, however, the semantic field of the adj. was broadened to include the lack of these qualities in persons who were engaged in the performing arts (dance, film, music, theater) and eventually to the productions of both the performing arts (ballet, movies, concerts, plays) and the fine arts (scores, scripts, canvases, sculptures). An artistic performance or production was regarded by critics as *cornball* if it lacked originality, freshness, and novelty or was superficially or trivially senti- mental. In the rural areas—esp. of the South and Midwest, where corn was one of the big-three cash crops: corn, cotton, and tobacco—corn was associated with hogs, which brought a higher price if they were cornfed. *Cornfed humor* came to be regarded as corn-country humor—broad, lacking in subtlety, but always wholesome—the sort of humor that was appreciated by *cornfed* audiences or was "fed to them" by visiting humorists. The adj. *cornfed* is thought to have been the source of the more popular term *corny* (HDAS: 1932), which applies not only to humor—a *corny* joke—but to any performance or production that is clichéd, hackneyed, simpleminded, or tiresome. A final *corn*-based adj., *cornpone*, also describes corn-country humor but has not been used widely or generally. CE; DAS; DEI; EWPO; IHAT; MDWPO; NSOED; WNWCD.

CORNBALL (n)   *a cornball*. A countrified, old-fashioned, or unsophisticated person. MWCD: ca. 1949. Source: CORN. IHAT: 1608. *Cornball* is another name for a hayseed, hick, or hillbilly of the sort that used to populate the *Beverly Hillbillies* TV show. The word prob. derives from a blend of *corn* "maize" and (screw) *ball* "an eccentric person," i.e., a kook from the corn country. However, there really is such a thing as an edible cornball—or corn "cake"—made of the same ingredients (cornmeal, water, salt) as Northern *corn bread* (MWCD: 1750) and Southern *corn pone* (MWCD: 1859). In fact, there have been several "corn- balls" since the early-19th cent.: the *corn dodger* (MWCD: 1834), the *corn fritter* (IHAT: 1862), and the *hush puppy* (MWCD: ca. 1918)—all of which are pan-fried or deep-fried chunks of cornmeal dough. The *corn dodger* gets so hard that you'd better "dodge" it if somebody throws one at you in a food fight. The *corn fritter* is more of a sweet cake than a ball, but it is deep-fried in the same way as a breakfast-roll fritter. The *hush puppy*, like the other two "cornballs," is a Southern delicacy. It was created following the Civil War—but named much later—when possum hunters kept the meat for themselves but threw *corn dodgers* to their hungry dogs, saying, "Hush, puppy!" In the second half of the 20th cent., *hush puppies* migrated north to become a standard accompaniment to America's answer to Britain's "fish and chips" (fried white fish and french fries). Also in the North, when wheat or potato flour is substituted for cornmeal and the resulting dough balls are deep-fried, the product is called a *doughnut hole* (q.v.). ATWS; DAFD; DAI; EWPO; FLC; HDAS; HF; MDWPO; NSOED; PT; SA.

CORN BREAD   *See* Cornball (n).

CORN DODGER   *See* Cornball (n).

CORN DOG   *See* Hot Dog.

CORNED BEEF   Beef cured in salt brine. DAFD: 18th cent. Source: BEEF. MWCD: 14th cent. *Corned beef* is so called because orig. the beef was cured by rubbing it with grains (or "corns") of salt; now it is usu. preserved by curing it in a seasoned salt brine. The beef that is so treated is usu. the *brisket* (MWCD: 14th cent.—fr. M.E. *brusket*), the meat from the breast. This meat is best known for its role in *corned beef hash* and *corned beef and cabbage*. A similar beef product is *pastrami* (MWCD: 1936—fr. Yid. *pastrame*, fr. Romanian *pastrama*), which is also salt-cured or brine-cured and can come from the brisket (or plate or round). However, after curing, pastrami is then smoked and cooked, giving it a darker reddish color than corned beef, and it is more highly seasoned. Pastrami sandwiches on rye are extremely popular on the East Coast (esp. in New York City delicatessens), and pastrami sandwiches on a French roll, dipped in beef gravy, are extremely popular on the West Coast. Another product similar to pastrami is *bully beef* (MWCD: 1753), which is so called because it is simply corned beef that is boiled (Fr. *bouilli* → Eng. *bully*) and then canned. (The term *bully beef* is not often used in America.) BDPF; DAFD; EWPO; FLC; MDWPO; NSOED; PT; SA; WNWCD.

CORNFED   *See* Cornball (adj.).

CORN FRITTER   *See* Cornball (n).

CORNISH PASTY   *See* Pasty.

CORNMEAL MUSH   *See* Grits; Johnnycake.

CORN MILK   *See* Milk (n).

CORNPONE (adj.)   *See* Cornball (adj.).

CORN PONE (n)   *See* Grits; Johnnycake.

CORNROW   *See* Corn.

CORN SNOW   *See* Corn.

CORN STARCH   *See* Take the Starch Out of.

CORN SYRUP   *See* Cough Syrup.

CORNY   *See* Cornball (adj.).

CORRODE   *See* Eat away at.

COTTAGE CHEESE   *See* Cottage-cheese Thighs.

COTTAGE-CHEESE THIGHS   Lumpy, bumpy, fatty thighs. Source: COT-
TAGE CHEESE. MWCD: 1848. *Cottage-cheese thighs* are the bane of overweight
persons (esp. women) whose upper legs and buttocks develop lumps and bumps
on the back and sides that resemble the semisolid curds that rise to the top of
the whey during the process of producing cheese from soured skim milk. This
product, when skimmed off and washed, is called *cottage cheese* because such
cheese was orig. made at home, i.e., in the "cottage." Other names for cottage
cheese are *Dutch cheese* (MWCD: 1829) and *smearcase* (MWCD: 1829). Further
draining of the moist cottage cheese produces a semifirm *pot cheese* (MWCD:
1812); and even further draining and pressing produce *farmer cheese* (MWCD:
1949). *Ricotta* (MWCD: 1877) is the Italian version of cottage cheese, but
smoother and made from the whey of an entirely different cheese, i.e., in a second
processing. (*Ricotta* lit. means "recooked.") Some people believe that "whey
cheeses" are not really cheeses at all, but don't tell that to the lovers of lasagna
and cheesecake, a primary ingredient of which is ricotta. DAFD; FLC; HF;
NSOED. *Compare* Biscotti; Biscuit.

COTTAGE PIE   *See* Porkpie Hat.

COTTON CANDY   *See* Candy.

COTTON-CANDY CLOUDS   *See* Candy.

COUCH POTATO   *a couch potato.* A TV junkie. MWCD: 1982. Source: PO-
TATO. MWCD: 1565. A *couch potato* is a person who spends most of his/her time
glued to the TV set regardless of whether anything is worth watching and obliv-
ious to anyone else in the house except when he/she runs out of snacks. Then
the call goes out for more sacks of potato chips, popcorn, and pretzels and more
bottles or beer or pop. Besides being lazy, *couch potatoes* tend to be slovenly and
grossly overweight, prob. because of their inactivity and consumption of a huge
number of calories. The selection of a potato to represent this TV zombie is
understandable: Potatoes are round and fat, they are sedentary, they have "eyes,"
and they can easily "go to seed." An alternative name for the *couch potato* is *sofa
spud*, based on the nickname for the potato, *spud* (LA: 1870s), which is the name
of the spade that has, since the 17th cent. (MWCD: 1667), been used to dig
potatoes out of the ground. The figurative *spud* was first applied by the English
to the Irish who wielded it (LA: 1870s), and later to the potato itself. With the
advent of the computer "mouse" in the 1980s, the term *mouse potato*, patterned
after *couch potato*, has been coined to describe a computer junkie: someone who

is hopelessly hooked on computers—another sedentary, single-focus occupation. CE; DAFD; DAS; EWPO; HDAS; MDWPO; THT.

COUGH SYRUP   A medicated liquid for relieving coughing. MWCD: 1877. Source: SYRUP. MWCD: 14th cent. Cough syrup is swallowed, but it is not a food; it is ingested not for the purpose of supplying sugars and calories to the body but specifically to treat a sore or congested throat. The original *syrup* (fr. Ar. *sharāb* "a drink," by way of M.Lat. *sirupus* and M.Fr. *sirop*) was a sweet, thick liquid, consisting of boiled, flavored sugar water that was taken as a drink, not as a medicine. Since the 14th cent. many other syrups have been created—not for drinking, but for use in cooking or as toppings. (Sweet, thick syrup has become so popular that the metaphor *syrupy*—NSOED: early-18 cent.—has developed to refer to music, literature, and rhetoric that are excessively sweet or sentimental.) The simplest of the syrups are *sugar syrup*, which is the foundation for many candies; *cane syrup*, from sugar cane, which is used in Creole cooking; and *corn syrup* (MWCD: 1903), from cornstarch, which is used in candy, frosting, and jellies and as a *pancake syrup*. The best-known syrup in America is prob. *maple syrup* (MWCD: 1849), the boiled-down sap of the sugar-maple tree, because it is used not only as a flavoring in many foods but as a do-it-yourself topping for such breakfast items as pancakes, French toast, and waffles and such desserts as ice cream, sherbets, and *sorbets* (a related word). The mid-19th cent. date for *maple syrup* seems extremely late, considering that (1) there are plenty of hard ("sugar") maple trees in Mother England that could have been "tapped" (although there may not have been enough freezing nights in late winter), (2) the sap of birch trees has been boiled down to *birch syrup* in northern Europe for hundreds of years (although the birch fructose is less sweet than the maple fructose), (3) the Native Americans of the North East had manufactured both *maple syrup* and *maple sugar* for hundreds of years before the colonists arrived (and taught the colonists how to do it), and (4) the date for *maple sugar* (MWCD: 1720) is almost 130 years earlier than that for *maple syrup*. *Maple sugar* is made by boiling down maple syrup until it crystallizes. Between maple syrup and maple sugar in the boiling-down process are *maple honey* (a thick liquid) and *maple butter* (a thick spread). All this work is done in the *sugar shack*, which is located among the *sugar maples* (MWCD: 1731) in the *sugar bush* (MWCD: 1823). CE; DAFD; EWPO; FLC; IHAT; PT; WNWCD.

COUNT THE SILVERWARE!   *See* Silverware.

COUNT YOUR CHICKENS BEFORE THEY HATCH   *See* Don't Count Your Chickens before They Hatch.

COVERED-DISH SUPPER   *See* Take Potluck.

COW CHIP   *See* Muffin.

COW PAT   *See* Cow Pie.

COW PATTY   *See* Cow Pie.

COWPEA   *See* Pea Bean.

COW PIE   *a cow pie*. A single, fresh deposit of cow manure. HDAS: 1977. Source: PIE. MWCD: 14th cent. This inedible "pie" is so called because it is round and flat and steamy, just like a pie from the oven. The cow pie was orig. called a *cow patty* or *cow pat* (MWCD: 1937), and when dried, it may even have been called a "cow chip," in line with the *buffalo chip*, which is a single dried deposit of buffalo manure. Buffalo chips were once used as firewood by Native Americans and European pioneers on the Western plains, where trees were few and far between. Currently, there is also a candy bar called a Cow Pie: a large, flat "turtle" consisting of chocolate-coated caramel and pecans.

CRABBURGER   *See* Fish Cake.

CRAB BUTTER   The yellowish fat under the back shell of a crab. Source: CRAB; BUTTER. MWCD: O.E. *Crab butter* is not a spread, like *lobster butter* and other pseudo butters, but an addition to other foods, such as sauces and salad dressings. This delicacy is called a "butter" because it is soft and yellow. It is similar in appearance to *calipee*, a yellowish fat found inside the lower shell of a green sea turtle and used in making green turtle soup. DAFD; WNWCD. *Compare* Apple Butter; Cocoa Butter; Maple Butter; Peanut Butter.

CRACKER-BARREL PHILOSOPHER   *a cracker-barrel philosopher*. A small-town expounder of truth and wisdom. MWCD: 1916. Source: CRACKER (DAFD: 1739); BARREL (MWCD: 14th cent.). Cracker-barrel philosophers are professors without degrees, politicians without offices, and (usu.) retired farmers without jobs. They once gathered around the pot-bellied stove in the general store, sitting on cracker barrels, and talked about the problems of the day and how to solve them. The cracker barrels really did hold crackers, in bulk, for sale by the pound. Those were the days before paper boxes, when the choice of container was a cloth sack, a wooden box, or a wooden barrel. Crackers were sold in large barrels, as were apples, pickles, and beer. BDPF; EWPO; LA.

CRACKERJACK (adj.)   *a crackerjack shot (etc.)*. An excellent shot. Source: CRACKERJACK (n). MWCD: 1895. A *crackerjack shot* is a *crackerjack* (HDAS: 1895) at shooting, and the adj. usage prob. derived from that of the noun. The noun *crackerjack* prob. derived from the name of the candied peanuts-and-popcorn confection that was first sold at the Columbian Exposition in Chicago in 1893: *Cracker Jack*. Until Cracker Jack arrived—with a prize in every box!— "Peanuts! Popcorn!" was the cry of vendors hawking snacks at the old ballpark.

Cracker Jack combined these two foods with molasses (now caramel), and the new cry became "Peanuts! Popcorn! Cracker Jack!" Cracker Jack also made it into the most popular baseball song of all time: "Take Me out to the Ball Game." CE; DAS; LA; NSOED.

CRACKERJACK (n)   *See* Crackerjack (adj.).

CRACKERJACK   *See* Crackerjack (adj.).

CRACKERJACK SHOT   *See* Crackerjack (adj.).

CRACKERS   *See* Drive Someone Crackers.

CRACKLINGS   *See* Tub of Lard.

CRACKPOT   *See* Crock.

CRAYFISH   *See* Little Shrimp.

CREAM (n)   Something having the color, consistency, or quality of real cream. Source: CREAM. MWCD: 14th cent. Cream is the high-butterfat part of milk. It is pale yellow in color and relatively thick in consistency. In spite of its thickness, it is lighter than skim milk, and in pre-WWII glass milk bottles it was the part of the product that occupied the top one-quarter of the bottle. Cream is highly valued for its ability to thicken sauces, dilute coffee, form the basis for ice cream, and be whipped into a topping. An example of *cream* as a color metaphor is *creamware* (MWCD: 1780): earthenware with a glaze that is the color—yellow, pale yellow, yellowish white—of cream. It is surprising that cream is still used as a basis for describing the color of familiar objects (*cream-colored*) because children in America have not seen the contrast between milk and cream in the same bottle since before WWII. *Cream rinse* (late-20th cent.) is an example of the use of *cream* as a "consistency" metaphor for a hair-care product that is *creamy* (NSOED: early-17th cent.), i.e., is soft, smooth, and thick like cream, as opposed to milk. Paint, which is *creamy* in texture, can also be mixed in a *creamy* color, i.e., one that has a hint of yellow in it. Among skin-care products, a *cream* is a soft, white, light, fluffy mixture that is not pourable (like a lotion), not sticky (like a paste), and not oily (like an ointment). An example of a "quality" metaphor based on *cream* is *cream of the crop* (q.v.). DAFD; FLC; NSOED; WNWCD.

CREAM (v)   *See* Cream Puff.

CREAM ALWAYS RISES TO THE TOP   *See* Cream of the Crop.

CREAM CHEESE   *See* Cheesecake.

CREAM-COLORED   *See* Cream (n).

CREAMED   *See* Cream Puff.

CREAMED CHIPPED BEEF ON TOAST   *See* Chipped Beef.

CREAMER   *See* Cream in My Coffee.

CREAM IN MY COFFEE   *You're the cream in my coffee.* You make my life worth living. (From the 1928 Broadway musical *Hold Everything*.) Source: CREAM (MWCD: 14th cent.); COFFEE (MWCD: 1598). "You're the cream in my coffee" is the first line of the refrain sung by a young man and a young woman in love. (The second line declares, "You're the salt in my stew.") At the end of the refrain, they proclaim that they would be lost without each other. Nowadays, the "cream" in your coffee might be a *nondairy creamer* (NSOED: late-20th cent.), which sounds like an oxymoron: If it's a *creamer*, how can it not be a dairy product? The answer is that this cream substitute does to coffee almost exactly what dairy cream does: sweeten it, weaken it, cool it, and lighten it. Such a product is important to persons who are allergic to milk products or to those whose dietary laws forbid combining meat and milk (or cream) at the same meal. (The label *pareve* signals that the creamer is kosher.) When your host(ess) pours cream (or "cream") in your coffee (or tea), he/she may utter the words "*Say 'When'* " meaning "Tell me when I've added enough." (The presumption is that the host(ess) is not familiar enough with you to know exactly how much cream you prefer.) You are then expected to say the word *When!* when the mixture reaches the proper color or level. (You may substitute "That's fine," "That's good," or "That's enough" for the word *When!*) FLC. *Compare* Say Cheese!

CREAM OF SOCIETY   *See* Cream of the Crop.

CREAM OF TARTAR   *See* Cream Soda.

CREAM OF THE CROP   *the cream of the crop.* The "pick of the litter"; the "top of the line." HND: 17th cent. Source: CREAM. MWCD: M.E. The *cream of the crop* is the "best of the bunch": the most outstanding student in a graduating class, the most beautiful woman in a beauty contest, the most muscular man in a bodybuilding competition, etc. The "crop" can also consist of animals (the best of breed in a cat or dog show), plants (the best flowers at a garden show), and even inanimate objects (the best automobile at a car show). The French expression for "the cream of the crop" is *la crème de la crème* (MWCD: 1848), lit., "the cream of the cream," and, fig., "the best of the best." Among wines, champagne is the *crème de la crème*; among cheeses, Roquefort is the *crème de la crème*; and among caviars, beluga is the *crème de la crème*. Both the English and the French expressions are used to describe the kind of people who are invited to attend galas, receptions, openings, etc. (the *cream of society*), and the kind of athletes invited to participate in the Olympics (the *cream of athletes*). The reason for the choice of *cream* for these metaphors is that in the days before homogenization (ca. the 1930s), the glass bottle of milk that the milkman (*sic*) delivered in the morning looked as if it contained two different liquids: a thick yellow liquid at the top and a thin white liquid at the bottom. The yellow liquid was *cream* (the butterfat of milk), and the white liquid was "skimmed milk" (the nearly fat-free portion of milk). Even if you shook the bottle (producing "buttermilk"), the two layers would eventually separate, and the cream would rise to the top again. From this phenomenon developed the proverb *The cream always rises to the top*, meaning that "the best man/woman always wins"—i.e., always comes out on top. The saying is used in connection with all kinds of struggles, but it is esp. popular in sports, where it is usu. predicted that a perennial winner will finish first regardless of the competition because *The cream always rises to the top*. AID; BDPF; CE; DAI; DC; HND; MS.

CREAM PUFF   *a cream puff.* A wimp (HDAS: ca. 1914); a used car in great condition (HDAS: 1949). Source: CREAM (MWCD: 14th cent.); PUFF PASTRY (MWCD: 1611). Literally, a cream puff is a puff pastry shell filled with whipped cream, Bavarian cream, or custard. Figuratively, a *cream puff* is (1) a person who is lacking in backbone or is soft in the center, like a *chocolate cream* (candy); (2) an issue that is lacking in importance; or (3) a used car that lacks the usual bumps, bruises, and other signs of age. A person who is a *cream puff* is not likely to *cream* someone else (i.e., soundly defeat an opponent) or to *cream* a car (i.e., to totally wreck it). To *cream* a bowlful of ingredients in the kitchen is to beat them until the mixture is *creamy* (q.v.), i.e., is soft and smooth and the individual ingredients are unrecognizable. To *cream* an opponent is to "beat him/her to a pulp." To *cream* a car is to turn it into an unrecognizable pile of junk. (NSOED: early-20th cent.) Not only can opponents and cars be *creamed*, but you yourself can become *creamed* (i.e., intoxicated) if you drink too much alcohol. CE; DAS; FLC; PT. *See also* Cream (n).

CREAM RINSE   *See* Cream-colored.

CREAM SODA   *a cream soda.* A vanilla-flavored soft drink. MWCD: 1854. Source: CREAM (MWCD: 14th cent.); SODA (MWCD: 1558). A cream soda contains soda water and vanilla flavoring, but it usu. lacks coloring and never contains any real cream. Coincidentally, the sweet liqueurs *crème de cacao* and *crème de menthe* also contain no cream, they can both be colorless, and the former is flavored with vanilla. All of these beverages are prob. called *creams* because they are sweeter than average, like sweet cream. *Cream of tartar* (MWCD: 1662) is not a drink but an additive that makes candy and frosting *creamier*. It is derived from salt crystals that are deposited on the inside of wine barrels by the juice of grapes. (The crystals are similar in color—reddish brown—and consistency—

crusty—to the tartar deposited on teeth by food and drink.) When the crystals are purified and pulverized, they form a *baking powder*—with the addition of yeast—that is essential to the *creaminess* of candies and frostings and the volume and stiffness of egg whites. FLC; NSOED; WNWCD.

CREAMWARE   *See* Cream-colored.

CREAMY   *See* Cream (n).

CREATIVE JUICES   *See* Juice.

CREATURE COMFORTS   *See* Comfort Food.

CREDENZA   *See* First Come, First Served.

CRÈME DE CACAO   *See* Cream Soda.

CRÈME DE LA CRÈME   *See* Cream of the Crop.

CRÈME DE MENTHE   *See* Cream Soda.

CREOLE CUISINE   *See* Cuisine.

CROCK   *a crock.* A lie. Source: CROCK. MWCD: O.E. A *crock* is a thick-walled earthenware pot that is used either for cooking foods (a *crock pot*) or for holding liquids or dry foods (a "jar"). The journey from *crock*, meaning "cooking pot," to *crock*, meaning "lie," is a tricky one, but it may have occurred something like this: Someone who was unhappy with the food that had been cooked in a *crock* referred to the vessel and its contents as a *crock of shit* (HDAS: 1945—later shortened to a *crock*), meaning that it was disgusting and worthless, and that calling it "food" was an outright lie. (There may also have been some influence from the porcelain "chamber pot.") At any rate, *crock pot* has become a trademark, *Crock-Pot* (DAFD: 1971), for a lidded electric crockery cooker that cooks moist foods slowly, for several hours, without any attention required. Various metaphors, beside *crock*, have developed from these terms. *Crockery* (HDAS: 1910) can refer to one's teeth, whether they remain in the mouth or come out at night, like the stars. *Crocked* (HDAS: 1917) means "falling-down drunk," and *half-crocked* means "stumbling drunk"—both presumably as a result of drinking all or part of a crock of moonshine. The juice in the crock pot after cooking greens and pork is called *pot liquor* (MWCD: 1744) or *potlikker*, which is a staple of soul-food cooking. A *crackpot* (MWCD: 1883) is an eccentric person whose *crackpot* (HDAS: 1934) ideas are about as good as a cracked pot: Neither one holds water. DAI; DAS; FLC; MDWPO; WNWCD.

CROCKED   *See* Crock.

CROCKERY   *See* Crock.

CROCK OF SHIT   *See* Crock.

CROCK POT   *See* Crock.

CROWN OF OLIVES   *See* Hold out an Olive Branch.

CRUMB   *a crumb.* A despicable, disgusting, filthy, lousy, mean, miserable, re-
pellent, or worthless person. HDAS: 1919. Source: CRUMB. MWCD: O.E. A
crumb (fr. O.E. *cruma*) is a tiny bit of bread that falls to the table (or the floor)
when the bread is cut, and also when it is toasted. Unfortunately, there is more
than one crumb, sometimes up to one hundred or more, and cleaning up these
useless, insignificant little particles is an unpleasant task. The metaphor is based
on both the uselessness of the crumb and the unpleasantness of the cleanup. A
person who is a *crumb bum* (HDAS: 1934) or a person, place, task, or action that
is as disgusting as a pile of crumbs is referred to as being *crummy* (or *crumby*).
Something that falls into small pieces, like breadcrumbs, is said to *crumble*
(MWCD: 1570); and if it is likely to do so, like friable soil, it is said to be *crumbly*
(MWCD: 1523). When someone *throws you a few crumbs*, you are the recipient
of a symbolic, rather than a substantial, gift. BDPF; CE; DAS; HF; MS; NSOED;
WNWCD.

CRUMB BUM   *See* Crumb.

CRUMB CRUST   *See* Graham Flour.

CRUMBLE   *See* Crumb.

CRUMBLY   *See* Crumb.

CRUMBY   *See* Crumb.

CRUMMY   *See* Crumb.

CRUMPET   *See* English Muffin.

CRUST   *a crust.* A hard surface. NSOED: late-M.E. Source: CRUST. MWCD:
14th cent. In the 14th cent., a crust was the hard surface of a loaf of bread or a
top-crusted pie. Since that time, *crust* has spawned a number of metaphors outside
the field of food. For example, deep snow on which rain has fallen and frozen is
said to have a *crust*; the outer layer of our planet is called the earth's *crust*; and a

deposit of organic salts on the inner surface of an old bottle of wine is known as a *crust*. A person who is hard on other people, showing no respect for their feelings or opinions, is said to have *some crust*; and an elderly person, esp. a man, who is grumpy, gruff, and ill-tempered is sometimes described as being *crusty*, as in Shakespeare's *Troilus and Cressida* (ca. 1603), (Act V, Scene 1), where Achilles uses the word to address Thersites: "How now, thou core of envy? Thou *crusty* batch of nature, what's the news?" [italics added]. BDPF; CE; DAS; FLC; MDWPO. *See also* Upper Crust.

CRUSTY   *See* Crust.

CRY OVER SPILLED MILK   *to cry over spilled (or spilt) milk.* To get upset over something that you caused but can't correct. DC: 1659. Source: MILK. MWCD: O.E. Spilling the milk from a glass at the table, or a pail in the barn, is neither a serious offense (there's a lot more where that came from) nor a correctable one (the milk can't be collected and returned to the container). It's best to adopt the philosophy "What's done is done and cannot be undone" or follow the wisdom of "You can't unring a bell." The expression is often used as a neg. imperative: *Don't cry over spilled (or spilt) milk.* Another metaphor, *to spill the milk* "to mess up," is quite different from *to cry over spilled (or spilt) milk.* In the former, there is no regret over the action, which was most likely not an accident; and the spiller has no desire to make amends for it. In the latter, the spiller shows remorse over the action, which was most certainly an accident; and he/she would like to make amends for it if that were possible. AID; BDPF; CE; CI; CODP; DAI; DAP; DEI; EWPO; HB; HND; MS; NSOED; SA. *Compare* Spill the Beans.

CRY OVER THE SPILT MILK   *See* Cry over Spilled Milk.

CRYSTAL   *See* Glass Is Half Empty.

CRY WITH A LOAF OF BREAD UNDER YOUR ARM   *to cry with a loaf of bread under your arm.* To feel sorry for yourself when you really have a lot to be thankful for. Source: LOAF; BREAD. MWCD: O.E. This early-19th cent. expression is similar to the story of the man who complained that he had no shoes until he met a man who had no feet. The picture of a person with a long loaf of bread under one arm is typical of a scene in France of someone carrying a baguette home from the boulangerie. *Compare* Half a Loaf Is Better than None.

CUBAN SANDWICH   *See* Submarine Sandwich.

CUCUMBER EYES   *See* Cool as a Cucumber.

CUCUMBER PICKLE   *See* Pickle (n).

CUCUMBER SLICES   *See* Cool as a Cucumber.

CUISINE   A manner of cooking or preparing food; the food so cooked or prepared. MWCD: 1786. Source: COOK; KITCHEN. *Cuisine* is a figure of speech because it derives from the Fr. word for "kitchen," *la cuisine*, which, in turn, is derived from Lat. *coquere* "to cook." The most common meaning of *cuisine* in English is the way food is cooked or prepared in a particular place—e.g., *French cuisine*—or by a particular ethnic group—e.g., *Creole* or *Cajun cuisine*. The traditional form of French cooking is known as *haute cuisine* (MWCD: 1928), the style that once spared no time, ingenuity, resourcefulness, expense, or calories to set the most elegant table. In response to these excesses, a group of young French chefs developed, in the 1960s and 1970s, a new style of cooking called *nouvelle cuisine*, which featured fewer, lighter, simpler, fresher, healthier dishes. In the 1980s *nouvelle cuisine* was exported to California, where it was sometimes called *new American cuisine* because it emphasized the use of American ingredients and techniques. *Creole* and *Cajun cuisine* were developed in Louisiana in the 18th cent. by immigrants from other parts of the Americas: speakers of French Creole from Haiti (the "Creoles") and speakers of Canadian French from Nova Scotia (the "Acadians"). The two cuisines are somewhat similar, although Creole is said to be more "sophisticated" (and to use more butter and tomatoes) and Cajun is said to be more "country style" (and to use more fat and spices). Both cuisines use plenty of green peppers, onions, celery, and filé powder. A favorite Creole dish is *shrimp Creole*; a favorite Cajun dish is *jambalaya*. DAFD; FLC; WNWCD.

CULINARY ARTS   The art(s) of cooking. Source: KITCHEN. The culinary arts are those that are practiced in the *kitchen* (fr. L.Lat. *culina* "kitchen," fr. Lat. *coquere* "to cook"). The recognition of cooking as an art is prob. attributable to the French, who have supplied many of the terms, most of the chefs (and sous chefs), and two of the most influential styles of cooking: *haute cuisine* and *nouvelle cuisine*. The *art* of cooking contrasts with the *science* of cooking—the basis for what is found in most cookbooks, which prescribe a list of ingredients, a set of steps to be followed, and the exact measurements to be used. Master cooks fly pretty much by the seat of their pants, imposing their own personalities on the preparation of their dishes. MWCD; WNWCD.

CUP   *a cup*. A golf hole; an athletic protector; a breast supporter; a cooking measure. Source: CUP. MWCD: O.E. When a golf ball rolls into the hole, it actually rolls into a metal or plastic "cup" that has been "planted" there. Unlike the drinking cup, however, it lacks a handle, is quite large, and has holes in the bottom to permit drainage in case of heavy rain. In other words, the golf cup is much more like the Lat. *cupa* "tub," which is the ancestor of Eng. *cup*, than the modern drinking cup, considering its size, round bottom (with one or more holes), and lack of a handle. The handles on cups were prob. borrowed from the 15th cent. pewter tankard, which was a large, single-handled vessel with a hinged lid, used for drinking beer or ale. Besides being made of clay, as in primitive times, cups have been molded from silver, glass, tin, paper, thin plastic (no handles), and Styrofoam (no handles). The *loving cup* (MWCD: 1812), which was once passed around for ceremonial drinking, had four handles; but now, when it is given away as a prize, it usu. has only two. The *cupboard* (MWCD: 1530) was so called because it consisted of shelves ("boards") with hooks underneath from which cups were hung, indicating that they had handles by that time. In modern times we have seen the invention of the *athletic cup*, to support and protect the genitals of male athletics, and *brassiere cups*, to support and protect the breasts of females. An unfortunate expression, *Her cups runneth over*, based on the line in Psalm 23:5 "My cup runneth over" (with joy), is sometimes used to describe a full-breasted woman, with a low-cut top, who is wearing "C" cups when she should be wearing "Ds." The use of the cup as a "measure" is also found in cooking, where a *cup* (or *cupful*) amounts to half a pint (eight fluid ounces, or sixteen tablespoons). The proverb *There's many a slip twixt the cup and the lip* (HI: 1539) means that nothing is certain, success is not guaranteed, secrets can be revealed. Things have gone very wrong if you are *in your cups*—i.e., drunk—prob. from collapsing forward into your beer. The verb *to cup* (MWCD: 14th cent.), which is derived from the noun, means not only for a doctor to *cup a patient* but for people to *cup their hands* (NSOED: mid-19th cent.)—as under a pump, to get a drink of water; behind their ears, to hear better; or over their mouth, to stifle a scream. BDPF; CI; DAFD; DAP; DC; DEI; EWPO; MS; PT; WNWCD.

CUPBOARD   *See* Cup (n).

CUPCAKE   *a cupcake; Cupcake.* An attractive young woman; a term of address or endearment for a wife or daughter. Source: CUP (MWCD: O.E.); CAKE (MWCD: 13th cent.). Literally, a *cupcake* (MWCD: 1828) is one of the small cakes baked in a pan that has an even number of approx. two-inch depressions into which the batter is poured. Metaphorically, when used as a common noun, *Cupcake* is equiv. to "chick" or "babe"; but when used as a term of address or endearment, *Cupcake* is equiv. to "Honey" or "Sweetheart." In this latter use, *Cupcake* is always singular; but three other cake "noms d'amour"—*Babycakes* (HDAS: 1967), *Honeycakes*, and *Sweetcakes*—are always used in the plural, suggesting a reference to a soft part of the anatomy: breasts or buttocks, for example. In the world of business, politics, and sports, a *cupcake*, or "softy," is an easy-to-defeat opponent: a "pushover." DAS; PT. *Compare* Honey Bun; Sweetie Pie.

CUP OF COFFEE   *See* Wake up and Smell the Coffee.

CUP OF JAVA   *See* Java.

CUP OF JOE   *See* Java.

CUP OF TEA   *See* Not for All the Tea in China.

CUPPA JOE   *See* Lunch-counter Jargon.

CUPS RUNNETH OVER   *See* Cup (n).

CUP YOUR HANDS   *See* Cup (n).

CURATE'S EGG   *the curate's egg.* A mixed blessing. MWCD: 1905. Source: EGG. MWCD: 14th cent. The term *curate's egg* derives from a story about a British "curate" (a clergyman) who was served a stale egg by his host (either the bishop or a parishoner). When asked how he liked his egg, the curate, not wanting to offend his host, replied that "parts of it" were "excellent." (EWPO reports that the story appeared in *Punch* in 1895, ten years before the term was admitted into the dictionary.) Today, something that is *like the curate's egg* has both good and bad features. NSOED; PT.

CURDLE YOUR BLOOD   *for something to curdle your blood.* For something to frighten or terrify you. Source: CURDLE. MWCD: 1590. In this metaphor, human blood is compared to cow's milk, which *curdles*—i.e., "separates" into *curds and whey* (q.v.)—when it turns sour. Human blood does not actually *curdle* when things "turn sour," but it must seem that way to the victim. A *bloodcurdling scream* (MWCD: 1904) is either what a terrified person utters or a scream from someone else that causes you to do likewise. WNWCD.

CURDS AND WHEY   Coagulated milk. Source: CURD (MWCD: 15th cent.); WHEY (MWCD: O.E.). Curds and whey were what Little Miss Muffet was "eating" while seated on a "tuffet" (a stool) in the nursery rhyme of the same name: "Along came a spider/ And sat down beside her/ And frightened Miss Muffet away." Note that Miss Muffet was more frightened of the spider than she was of the "bonny-clabber" that she was eating, prob. with a little sugar sprinkled on it. She could have been *drinking* the clabbered milk instead, if it was in the first stages of coagulation. That was the more popular way of ingesting it in the 17th cent., so the nursery rhyme was prob. written in the 18th or 19th cent. *Curds* are the coagulants, and *whey* is the liquid, in the process of turning milk (or buttermilk) into cheeses of various sorts. The metaphor *whey-face* (MWCD: 1605) describes a person with a face the color (grayish white) of whey, either by nature or as a result of fear or illness. However, because cheeses such as *cottage cheese* (q.v.) are no longer made at home (in the "cottage"), few people are aware of the meaning of *whey*, and the word *whey-face* is becoming obsolete. FLC; NSOED. *Compare* Pizza-faced.

CURE (v)   *to cure meat.* To prevent meat from spoiling by using physical or chemical means. Source: CURE. NSOED: early-17th cent. *Cure*, in curing meat, derives from the same source as *cure* "to save souls" and *cure* "to save patients"; however, in this reverse metaphor, *cure* "to cure meat" is an attempt to *prevent* abnormalities, not to correct them. The preservation of meat by *curing* it takes several different forms, depending somewhat on the type of meat being treated. The oldest method of curing meat is to cut it into thin slices, hang it out of the reach of animals, and let it dry (or *air dry*) in the sun and wind. The trouble with this method, which is used esp. with red meat and fish, is that it is slow and hazardous: birds fly down, and squirrels (etc.) climb up. Another early method of food preservation by curing it is *salting* it (MWCD: O.E.), which involves rubbing the meat with salt, possibly combined with drying it in a protected place—a method that is used esp. with fish (*salted fish*). A third method of preservation by curing is to salt meat and then soak it in *brine* (MWCD: O.E.), as is done with *corned beef* (q.v.) and *salt pork* (q.v.). If soaked in brine without first being salted, the meat is said to be *pickled* (q.v.), as with *pickled herring* (q.v.). The last form of preservation by curing is *smoking* the meat, esp. pork and fish, in a smokehouse for several days, over a low, hardwood fire, as with bacon and ham. More modern methods of preserving meat, such as canning it and freezing it, are not regarded as "curing" it. FLC.

CUSTARD APPLE   *See* Papaya.

CUSTARD PUDDING   *See* Pudding.

CUT ABOVE THE REST   *See* Cutting Edge.

CUTIE PIE   *See* Sweetie Pie.

CUT IT CLOSE   *See* Cut to the Bone.

CUT NO ICE   *See* Put on Ice.

CUT OUT THE FAT   *See* Fat (n).

CUT THE FEED   *to cut the feed.* To cut off the electronic transmission of a radio or television signal to a particular audience. Source: CUT (MWCD: 13th cent.); FEED (n) (MWCD: 1576). In Colonial times, the phrase *to cut the feed* prob. meant "to cut off the food given to the livestock." The noun *feed* is derived from the verb *feed* (fr. O.E. *fēdon*), and both words are related to the noun *food* (fr. O.E. *fōda*). The noun *food* has developed as a more general term than the noun *feed*, covering not only human nourishment but nourishment of flowers ("plant food") and pets ("cat and dog food"). The noun *feed* has developed as a more specific term, covering nourishment for all farm animals ("cattle feed," "chicken feed") except pets. *Feed* has also come to be associated with mechanics and electronics: A person who has had his/her television signal "cut" has *lost his/her feed*.

CUT THE MUSTARD   *to cut the mustard*. To perform satisfactorily; to live up to expectations. HDAS; 1902. Source: CUT (v); MUSTARD. MWCD: 13th cent. Mustard in the jar—used as a dressing for hamburgers and hot dogs—is a soft, yellow condiment that does not need to be "cut": It can easily be applied with a butter knife or squeezed from a plastic bottle. Therefore, the association of *mustard* with *cut* has always been a mystery. In order to solve this mystery, scholars have investigated several leads: (1) The verb *cut* can also mean "to adulterate," as in to *cut a drink* with water in order to weaken it. The only reason to adulterate mustard would be to reduce the "bite," but anybody could do that. (2) The word *mustard* is sometimes confused with the word *muster*, as in "to pass muster," i.e., to meet the required standards. This lead sounds promising, except that *cut* is used with *muster* only in the sense of "to skip the examination." (3) Since WWI, the negative form of this expression, *can't cut the mustard* or *can't cut it*, has meant an inability to perform successfully. The implication is that such an inept individual can't *even* cut the mustard, i.e., can't even perform the simplest task. (4) A variant of the preceding expression, *too old to cut the mustard*, refers to sexual impotence. Perhaps the original metaphor, *to cut the mustard*, was a euphemism for successful sexual performance all along. CE; DAI; DAS; DC; EWPO; HB; HND; LA; LCRH; WNWCD; PT.

CUTTING EDGE   *the cutting edge*. The avant-garde of art, design, style, etc. MWCD: 1951. Source: CUT (v). MWCD: 13th cent. A literal *cutting edge* is the sharp edge of a single-bladed knife, designed for dressing wild game, butchering it, and cutting it up at the table. (The double-bladed dagger is used for dispatching people.) The *cutting edge*—as opposed to the blunt edge—is where the action is, and every artist and artisan, as well as researcher and developer, wants to be working *on the cutting edge*. A butcher who is cutting up an animal carcass is careful not to waste any meat and therefore cuts as close to the bone as possible. A budget director who *cuts costs*—expenses, allowances, allotments, etc.—*to the bone* lowers the amounts to the bare minimum, eliminating everything that is not essential. The architect or contractor who *cuts it close* allows barely enough time or space for the building to be built. The butcher is also aware that the higher up on the animal, the better the quality of the meat (e.g., *sirloin* "upper loin"); and a person who is "first class" is said to be *a cut above the rest*. Within a chunk of meat, such as a tenderloin, the tenderest portion is in the center; and the term *center cut* has been borrowed by sportscasters to describe everything from a baseball that is thrown precisely over the middle of the plate to a golf ball that is putted into the very center of the cup. Finally, all of us play butchers when we say that the atmosphere—meteorological or psychological—is *so thick that you could cut it with a knife*. AID; CI; DAI; DEI; MS; WNWCD.

CUT TO THE BONE   *See* Cutting Edge.

D

D'   *See* Maître d'Hôtel.

DACHSHUND SAUSAGE   *See* Hot Dog.

DAGWOOD   *See* Dagwood Sandwich.

DAGWOOD SANDWICH   *a Dagwood sandwich.* A foot-high, multilayered sandwich of various meats, cheeses, vegetables, and condiments—all between two slices of bread. DAFD: 1936. Source: SANDWICH. MWCD: 1762. The *Dagwood sandwich* is named for Dagwood Bumstead, the husband of Blondie in the comic strip of the same name. Dagwood's two excesses are eating and sleeping, and he sometimes wakes up hungry at night, goes down to the kitchen, and makes himself a *dagwood*. Another sandwich with a popular name is the *Denver sandwich* (MWCD: 1950)—also called a *Western sandwich*—which is actually a small omelette (containing chopped ham, green peppers, and onions) between two slices of bread. The *Monte Cristo* sandwich (presumably named after the Count of) is composed of sliced ham, chicken, and Swiss cheese between thick slices of bread. The sandwich is either dipped into beaten eggs and pan-fried in butter or dipped into beer batter and deep-fried in oil. Another eponym is the *Reuben sandwich*, or *Reuben*, which is named after either a New York City restaurateur with the last name of *Reuben* (DAFD: 1914) or an Omaha grocer with the first name of *Reuben* (WNWCD: 1930). Whatever the origin, the Reuben sandwich always consists of corned beef, Swiss cheese, sauerkraut, and dressing between slices of rye bread, and it is pan-fried in butter like a grilled cheese sandwich. DAS; FLC; HDAS; MDWPO; NSOED.

DAILY BREAD   *See* Bread.

DAILY GRIND   *See* Through the Mill.

DANISH   *See* Pastry.

DARK MEAT   *See* Drumstick.

DARK MOLASSES   *See* Slow as Molasses in January.

DARNING EGG   *See* Nest Egg.

DASH OF HUMOR   *See* For Good Measure.

DEAD MEAT   *See* Meaty.

DEADPAN   *See* Pan out.

DEATH COOKIE   *See* Cookie.

DEEP-FRY   *See* Fried.

DELAYED FEEDBACK   *See* Feedback.

DENTAL PLATE   *See* Full Plate.

DENVER SANDWICH   *See* Dagwood Sandwich.

DESERT CHERRY   *See* Cherry (adj.).

DESKTOP DINING   *See* Dine (v).

DESSERT CHERRY   *See* Cherry (adj.).

DEVILED EGGS   Hard-boiled eggs that have been halved (lengthwise) and the yolks removed, mixed with a spicy seasoning (such as mustard), and returned to the centers of the upturned halves. MWCD: 1800. Source: EGG. MWCD: 14th cent. Deviled eggs are so called because they taste as hot as the Devil's hell. Other foods that have been spiced in this fashion are oysters (*devils on horseback*) and ham (*deviled ham*). *Devil's food cake* (MWCD: 1905) is not "hot," but its dark color and rich flavor make it so tempting that it might as well have been made by the Devil. ("The Devil made me eat it.") Also bearing the name *Devil's food* are chocolate cookies and brownies. DAFD; FLC; IHAT. *Compare* Angel Food Cake; Angels on Horseback.

DEVILED HAM   *See* Deviled Eggs.

DEVIL'S FOOD CAKE *See* Deviled Eggs.

DEVILS ON HORSEBACK *See* Angels on Horseback; Deviled Eggs.

DEVOUR *to devour something.* To eat something greedily or ravenously. MWCD: 14th cent. Source: EAT. Literally, to *devour* something is to "swallow it whole" (fr. Lat. *vorare*), as a wild animal might. However, the Eng. uses of the verb are all figurative, involving a lesser (as above) or greater degree of abstraction. For example, natural resources, such as land and water, can be *devoured* by cities and highways; books and music can be *devoured* by the eyes and ears of readers and listeners; and people themselves can be *devoured* by grief and guilt. Of course, people can still *devour* an entire cake or a whole chicken by *gobbling it up* (MWCD: 1601) or *bolting, scarfing* (MWCD: ca. 1960), or *wolfing* (MWCD: 1862) it down (or even *inhaling* it). BDPF; DAS; DEI; MDWPO; NSOED; SA; WNWCD.

DEWBERRY *See* Blackberries Are Red When They're Green.

DIE ON THE VINE *See* Wither on the Vine.

DIFFERENT KETTLE OF FISH *See* Kettle of Fish.

DIGEST (n) *See* Digest (v).

DIGEST (v) *to digest spoken or written material.* To assimilate spoken or written material mentally; to condense spoken or written material verbally. Source: DIGEST (v) (*). MWCD: 14th cent. The verb *digest* orig. meant to condense portions of written material and then classify and arrange them systematically. The modern use of the word focuses on the condensation aspect of the earlier definition but also recognizes the assistance that systematization can provide to the mind and memory. For example, in order to *digest* (absorb, assimilate, comprehend, internalize, understand) a large body of work, it is very useful to have the contents logically arranged for you. The noun *digest* (MWCD: 14th cent.), meaning "an abstract, condensation, summary, or synopsis," has developed from the verb *digest*. Abstracts of scholarly papers and books, and condensations of popular articles and books, as in the *Reader's Digest*, have proved very useful and profitable. The meaning "to assimilate and condense food" is derived from these literary senses, rather than vice versa. That is, *digest* is not a food metaphor, as one might suspect. BDPF; WNWCD.

DIG YOUR GRAVE WITH A KNIFE AND A FORK *See* Fork in the Road.

DILL PICKLES AND ICE CREAM *See* Pickle (n).

DIN DIN *See* Dinner.

DINE (v)   *to dine.* To eat dinner; to provide dinner for others. Source: DINE (v). 13th cent. The Eng. verb *dine* is derived fr. the Fr. verb *dîner* "to dine," which is also the basis for the Fr. noun *le dîner* "dinner" and the Eng. noun *dinner* (q.v.). The surprise here is that the Fr. words derive fr. Lat. *disjejunare* "to break one's fast" (i.e., "to eat breakfast"), which is also the basis for the Fr. noun *le déjeuner* "lunch" and the Fr. noun phrase *le petit déjeuner* "breakfast." When an American family eats dinner, they usu. have it in the *dining room* (MWCD: 1601); however, when they eat lunch or a late supper, they usu. have it at the kitchen table or in a *dinette* (MWCD: 1925); and when they eat breakfast or brunch, they usu. have it at the kitchen table or in a *breakfast nook*. When the family *dines out* (MWCD: 1816), they eat their meal, usu. dinner, at a restaurant or at the home of a friend. When they *wine and dine* someone else, they entertain their guests at an elaborate dinner at home or at an expensive restaurant, where wine may or may not be served. If the *breadwinner* (q.v.) of the family eats his/her lunch out of a *brown bag* in the office, that is called *desktop dining.* EWPO.

DINE OUT   *See* Dine (v).

DINER   *a diner.* A roadside restaurant resembling a railroad dining car. LA: 1930s. Source: DINE (v). MWCD: 13th cent. Literally, a *diner* is one who dines—i.e., one who *eats*, esp. dinner. Metaphorically, the word *diner* was applied in the early-20th cent. to the *dining car* (MWCD: 1838) of a train; and when the design of the railroad dining car was copied for a roadside restaurant in the 1930s, the name was borrowed also. The diner resembled the dining car from the outside only: long and narrow; clad in aluminum; bright and shiny. On the inside, the diner resembled a *lunch counter* (q.v.) (MWCD: 1869), with padded stools, napkin holders, and sugar shakers. The patrons faced a wall, separating the dining area from the kitchen, which had a wide window cut into it for the waitresses (*sic*) to shout their orders to the cook, and the cook to set out the plates of food. Behind the seats at the counter were booths along the windowed front of the diner; and between the booths and the counter there were sometimes tables and chairs. With the birth of drive-ins and fast-food restaurants after WWII, the diner just about disappeared from the scene, but now it is coming back and gaining in popularity. DAFD; NSOED.

DINETTE   *See* Dine (v).

DINING CAR   *See* Diner.

DINING ROOM   *See* Dine (v).

DINING SALON   *See* Restaurant.

DINNER (1)   The main meal of the day. Source: DINNER. MWCD: 13th cent. The Eng. word *dinner* comes fr. Fr. *dîner*, which is fr. O.Fr. *disner*, which is fr.

the same Lat. source as Fr. *déjeuner: dis-* "away" + *jejenus* "fast," i.e., "breakfast."
To complicate the picture, in America *dinner* used to be the noon meal; now it is
the early evening meal. The serving of the most substantial meal of the day at
noontime (12:00 to 2:00 P.M.) was attributable solely to the demands of life on a
diversified farm in the 18th, 19th, and early-20th cents. A diversified farm had
not only crops and livestock but also cows to milk: twice a day, at approx. daybreak and sunset. Therefore, the milkers ate either before or after milking, or
both; and the noon meal was the only one at which they could be predicted to
show up on time. (Threshers also ate at noon.) However, even from the beginning
there were some members of the family who did not have a main meal of the day
at all: (1) the women who prepared and served the food and cleaned up after the
diners, and (2) the children who carried their noon meal to school in a *dinner
pail* (LA: 1856). The practice of serving the main meal of the day in the evening,
and still calling it *dinner*, came about as a result of the Industrial Revolution,
which attracted many men, most of them former farmers, to the factories, which
were located in the cities. At first these men, like the schoolchildren from the
farms, carried their noon meal to work in a *dinner pail*, whose name reflected the
fact that (1) the meal was intended to be the largest one of the day and (2) it was
packed hot. By the end of the 19th cent., most families of factory workers had
given up packing hot, heavy noon meals and had moved the main meal of the
day, still called *dinner*, to the early evening. Only farmers, esp. dairy farmers, and
those who were raised on a diversified farm, still use the word *dinner* for the noon
meal, even if it is a light meal, now called *lunch* (q.v.) by most other people. The
Sunday meal, served in the afternoon, is still called *dinner* by almost everyone, as
is *Thanksgiving dinner*. Young children sometimes refer to dinner as *din din*, and
they ask if they can have *din din* in their *jammies* ("pajamas"). DAFD; NSOED.
Compare Supper.

DINNER (2)   The evening meal. Source: DINNER. MWCD: 13th cent. When
a spouse comes home from a long, hard day at work, one of the first questions
he/she asks is, "*What's for dinner?*" The time at which dinner is served has been
early evening (6:00 to 8:00 P.M.) for most urban American families since the
second half of the 19th cent. Exceptions to this *dinnertime* (MWCD: 14th cent.)
are usu. indicated by qualifiers such as *early* and *late*. An *early dinner* is a full
meal taken at 6:00 o'clock or so in order to make it on time to the theater or to
a reception or party. A *late dinner* is a full meal taken at 8:00 o'clock or later
following a reception or party—or a play presented in the same restaurant: a
dinner theater (MWCD: 1960). Formal evening wear for men is called a *dinner
jacket* (MWCD: 1891), and *dinnerware* (MWCD: 1895) includes the numerous
plates of all sizes necessary for a formal dinner. The packaged *TV dinner* (MWCD:
1954—orig. a trademark of the Swanson Company) was designed to allow people
to watch television in the evening without spending a lot of time in the kitchen
or going out to a restaurant. This *frozen dinner* contained meat and potatoes—all
located in an appropriate section of an aluminum tray that could be heated in the
oven. A popular method of dining in the 1950s was the *progressive dinner*, by

which the families in a neighborhood—or the members of a club or other group—shared the production of an evening meal by assigning one course to each of half a dozen different families or members. First all of the families would go to House A for soup, then to House B for fish, etc., until they reached House F for dessert. Although breakfast is hailed by nutritionists as *the most important meal of the day* (q.v.), dinner is prob. the most popular one: Q. "What should I call you?" A. "Call me whatever you like, but *don't forget to call me for dinner.*" DAFD; LA; NSOED. *Compare* Late Supper; What's Cookin'?

DINNER JACKET   *See* Dinner (2).

DINNER PAIL   *See* Dinner (1); Lunch (n).

DINNER THEATER   *See* Dinner (2).

DINNERTIME   *See* Dinner (2).

DINNERWARE   *See* Dinner (2).

DIP INTO   *to dip into a book; to dip into your savings.* To sample—or "skim"—a book; to remove a portion of your savings. Source: DIP (v). MWCD: O.E. The verb *dip* orig. meant to immerse something briefly in water (or another liquid); e.g., to dip your big toe into the water to determine its temperature, or to dip a red-hot piece of iron into water to cool and harden it. However, the meaning was soon extended to dipping a ladle into hot soup to test its taste, and to dipping a *dipper* (MWCD: 1611) into cold water in order to drink it. Dipping into a book is like dipping a ladle into hot soup: You're just sampling it. Dipping into your savings is like dipping a dipper into cold water: You're transferring it. CI. *See also* Double-dipper.

DIPLOMA MILL   *See* Grist for the Mill.

DISH (n)   *(a) dish.* A pretty woman (HDAS: 1606); a favorite activity; a satellite or microwave antenna (NSOED: mid-20th cent.); dirt or gossip (HDAS: 1676). Source: DISH (n). MWCD: O.E. Eng. *dish* is derived fr. Lat. *discus* "dish," which is fr. Gk. *diskos* "discus." The ancient Greeks threw the discus at the Olympic Games, but the ancient Romans modified the discus into serving and eating dishes (and other tableware). Unlike the Greek discus, which was slightly convex on both sides, the Roman plate was noticeably concave on one side, the better to hold semisolid foods. In Eng., *dish* gradually acquired a number of figurative meanings, such as (1) the "contents" of the dish rather than the dish alone ("We have a new *dish* on the menu"), (2) a particular type of food ("My favorite *dish* is potatoes au gratin") and (3) an entire course of the evening meal ("the main *dish*"). Somehow the noun *dish* came to mean "whore" in Elizabethan times, although it has since acquired the much softer meaning of "pretty woman": "She's *some dish.*"

In the 1970s the word *dish* was first applied to a satellite or microwave antenna, which resembled the dish in shape; and in the 1970s *dish* also acquired the meaning of "dirt" or "gossip": "What's the *dish* on the new boss?" (The *dish* on the tableware is that the dish ran away with the spoon, but they later broke up because of irreconcilable differences.) DAS; DEI; EWPO; PT; WNWCD.

DISH (v)   *See* Dish It out.

DISH DIRT   *See* Dish It out.

DISH IT OUT   *to dish it out.* To dispense something freely, plentifully, or forcefully. MWCD: 1641. Source: DISH (v). MWCD: 14th cent. Literally, what was "dished out (or up)" before the mid-17th cent. was food, which was ladled out of a kettle into a dish. In the early-20th cent. the phrase *dish out* became a metaphorical expression for handing out such things as advice, criticism, gifts, gossip, lies, money, punches, and punishment (HDAS: 1926). Sometime during this period it was noticed that some people could *dish it out, but they couldn't take it* and, conversely, some could *take it, but they couldn't dish it out*. The alternative form, *to dish up*, is used more narrowly, and positively, in the sense of "to come through," "to bring to fruition." Another variant, *to dish off* (HDAS: 1980), means to pass off the basketball to a teammate, esp. if the teammate makes the basket and you are therefore credited with an assist. *To dish dirt about someone* is to spread gossip or rumors about a person, whether or not they are false or without foundation. *To dish someone* (HDAS: 1941), i.e., "to criticize or spread rumors about a person," may be the source of the slang verb *to dis* (HDAS: 1992), which has the same meaning. DAI; DAP; DAS; DEI; NSOED.

DISH OFF   *See* Dish It out.

DISHPAN HANDS   *See* Taste like Dishwater.

DISH RAN AWAY WITH THE SPOON   *See* Dish (n).

DISH SOMEONE   *See* Dish It out.

DISH UP   *See* Dish It out.

DISHWATER   *See* Java.

DISHWATER BLOND   *See* Taste like Dishwater.

DISTASTEFUL   *See* In Good Taste.

DOG-EAT-DOG   *It's dog-eat-dog out there; It's a dog-eat-dog world.* It's every person for him/herself in the highly competitive world of business. MWCD: 1834.

Source: EAT. MWCD: O.E. Dogs do not ordinarily eat other dogs, but someone observing a dogfight might think that that was exactly what they were trying to do: kill the other dog and then eat it. People do not ordinarily eat each other either, but when they fight for a sale item at a store, a bid on the stock market, or an interview with a celebrity, they appear to be as ruthless as the dogs. For both dogs and people, "It's a jungle out there," where individuals will do just about anything to get what they want, and where "only the fittest survive." ATWS; BDPF; CI; DAI; DAP; DAS; DC; HND; SA; SHM.

DOGGIE BAG   *See* Brown-bag Lunch.

DOG MEAT   *See* Variety Meats.

DO GOOBERS EAT GOPHERS, OR DO GOPHERS EAT GOOBERS?   *See* Peanut.

DOLLOP OF SATIRE   *See* For Good Measure.

DO LUNCH   *See* Business Lunch.

DONE TO A TURN   *See* Spit.

DONE UP BROWN   *See* Do up Brown.

DON'T COUNT YOUR CHICKENS BEFORE THEY HATCH   Don't count on something happening until it happens. MDWPO: ca. 1578. Source: CHICKEN. MWCD: 14th cent. This warning is usu. attributed to an Aesop fable about a farmmaid who, while carrying eggs to market, daydreams about how she will use the eggs to trade up and become rich—until she suddenly trips, falls, and drops all the eggs, thus ending all of her dreams. A simpler explanation would be that a farmmaid collected ten eggs and immed. bought a new basket on credit, promising ten chickens in payment. But only five eggs hatched, so the farmmaid had "hanged herself upon the expectation of plenty." ATWS; CODP; DAI; DC; EWPO; HND; IRCD; MS; SA. *Compare* Don't Put All Your Eggs in One Basket.

DON'T CRY OVER SPILLED MILK   *See* Cry over Spilled Milk.

DON'T EAT YELLOW SNOW   *See* Eat Nails.

DON'T EAT YOUR HEART OUT   *See* Eat Your Heart out.

DON'T FORGET TO CALL ME FOR DINNER   *See* Dinner (2).

DON'T FRET ABOUT IT   *See* Fret (v).

DON'T MAKE/TAKE TWO BITES OF THE CHERRY   *See* Two Bites of the Cherry.

DON'T PUT ALL YOUR EGGS IN ONE BASKET   *See* Put All Your Eggs in One Basket.

DON'T UPSET THE APPLECART   *See* Upset the Applecart.

DONUT   *a donut.* A doughnut. Source: DOUGHNUT. MWCD: ca. 1809. *Donut* is a variant spelling of *doughnut* (q.v.), prob. originating in the post-WWII period as a shortened (or "phonetic") form for advertising purposes. Nevertheless, *donut* has taken on a life of its own, bearing most of the weight for metaphorical uses. For example: (1) the inflatable, ring-shaped "pillow" used as a seat by persons suffering from a sore bottom is sometimes referred to as a *donut*; (2) the round iron weight that is slipped onto a baseball bat and used by a batter in the on-deck circle for warming up is usu. called a *donut*; and (3) the small, emergency tire, on a regular-size wheel, that is stored in the trunk of your car is almost always identified as a *donut* (NSOED: early-20th cent). A major influence on the spelling of real *doughnuts* as *donuts* has been the Dunkin' Donuts chain of coffee shops, found throughout the United States. *Compare* Bagel.

DO THE HONORS   *See* Cape Cod Turkey.

DOUBLE-DECKER   *See* Sandwich (n).

DOUBLE-DIPPER   *a double-dipper.* A person who receives a government salary while at the same time receiving a government pension (MWCD: ca. 1974); a person who dips a morsel of food (e.g., a cracker or a shrimp) into the communal dip, takes a bite of it, then dips the remainder of the same morsel into the dip again. Source: ICE CREAM. Both of these *double-dippers* are looked at unfavorably—the government one because the person is being paid twice by the same organization, and the party one because returning food from the mouth to the bowl of dip is unsanitary . The basis for the metaphor is the number of scoops (two) of ice cream on an ice-cream cone, resulting from a *double dip* into the ice-cream tub. In baseball, a *double-dipper* (or *double dip*) is a doubleheader: two games played on the same day against the same team. DAS; FLC; WNWCD.

DOUGH   Money. NSOED: mid-19th cent. Source: DOUGH. MWCD: O.E. In baking, dough is a mixture of flour (or meal) and water (or milk) that is too stiff to pour (like *batter*) but pliable enough to knead. The connection between dough and money is not readily apparent, but it may be that *dough* is *kneaded*, and *money* is also *needed*. (Bakers' rally: "What do we knead?" "Dough!" "When do we knead it?" "Now!") Another possibility is suggested by the phrase "to be *rolling in dough*," i.e., to have more money than you need. It is also possible that bakers, who bake a lot of bread, must *make a lot of dough*, i.e., make a lot of money, in the process. CE; DAP; FLC; PT. *Compare* Bread; Cabbage; Lettuce.

DOUGHBOY   *a doughboy*. A foot soldier in the U.S. Army before WWII. MWCD: 1865. Source: DOUGH. MWCD: O.E. A *doughboy* was orig. a cornmeal dumpling (DAFD: 1753), then a ball of fried dough (BDPF: early-19th cent.), then a name for one of the round brass buttons on an infantryman's uniform (BDPF: late-1840s), then a nickname for the infantryman himself (late in the American Civil War). The moniker stuck with the American footsoldier through the Spanish-American War and WWI but was replaced by "G.I." in WWII. In the late-20th cent. "doughboy" became a pejorative term of address for a pudgy young man, perhaps influenced by the pudginess of the Pillsbury Doughboy in television commercials. In contrast, the term *doughface* (MWCD: 1830) designated a Northerner who was sympathetic to slavery before the Civil War, or to the South during that war. Now it simply signifies a person who is *dough-faced*, or has a pale, perhaps even unhealthy complexion; i.e., his/her face is the color of dough. HDAS; IHAT; MDWPO; NSOED; WNWCD. *Compare* Half-baked.

DOUGHFACE   *See* Doughboy.

DOUGH-FACED   *See* Doughboy.

DOUGHNUT   *a doughnut*. A ring-shaped cake fried in deep fat. NSOED: late-18th cent. Source: DOUGH; NUT. MWCD: O.E. One would expect a ring of dough to be called a "doughring" rather than a *doughnut*. The reason for the latter name is that the original doughnuts were actually "nuts" of "dough," or what are now called *doughnut holes* (q.v.). These deep-fried "dough balls" were brought to America by the Pilgrims, who learned how to make them in Holland before setting out for Plymouth in 1620. The "nut" shape of the doughnut was reinforced in America by the Dutch in New Amsterdam (1625–1664), but it was abandoned in the early-19th cent. because of influence from the "Dutch" (actually Germans) of eastern Pennsylvania. The "Pennsylvania Dutch" observed the custom of serving *fastnachts* on the night (*nacht*) before the Lenten fast (*fast*) began. Fastnachts had a hole in the middle to allow the hot fat to properly cook the center of the doughnut as well as the perimeter. (Another, less credible, story is that the ring-shaped doughnut was invented by a New England sea captain who redesigned the ball as a ring so that it would fit over the spoke of a helmsman's wheel.) Because of some confusion arising from the fact that *doughnut* could now refer to either a ball or a ring, the term *fried cake* (MWCD: 1839) appeared, and is still in use, to refer to the doughnut with a hole. In lunch counters of the 1920s, "ring" doughnuts were called *sinkers* (IHAT: ca. 1925), perhaps because they were so heavy—or because they were so stale that they had to be immersed in coffee to soften them up. The expression *to bet dollars to doughnuts* (i.e., *my* dollars to *your* doughnuts—HDAS: 1893) illustrates how low on the food chain the dough-

nut has sunk. A single doughnut is one of the cheapest snacks you can buy.
DAFD; DAS; EWPO; FLC; MDWPO.

DOUGHNUT HOLE   *a doughnut hole.* A ball of dough deep-fried in fat or oil.
DAFD: 1960s. Source: DOUGHNUT. MWCD: ca. 1809. *Doughnut holes* were the
original *doughnuts* (q.v.). They were not the dough from the center of a small,
ring-shaped cake but "nuts" of dough, formed by hand, deep-fried, and enjoyed
in the 17th cent. by the English in the Plymouth Colony and the Dutch in New
Amsterdam. When the word *doughnut* first appeared (ca. 1809), it referred to
these balls of dough, not to rings of dough. When ring-shaped doughnuts were
developed in the early-19th cent., they were called *fastnachts* (q.v.) or *fried cakes*
(q.v.) to contrast them with the traditional cake balls; however, the name *doughnut*
stuck for both the balls and the rings. With the invention of the cookie cutter in
the early-20th cent. (MWCD: 1903), both a ring and a hole could be cut out at
the same time, with the same instrument; and the dough in the hole could be
deep-fried, along with the ring, and legitimately be referred to as a *doughnut hole.*
A similar deep-fried ball of dough, but made from cornmeal rather than wheat
flour, is a *hush puppy* (MWCD: ca. 1918), which was once fed to dogs to keep
them quiet but is now sold to people to accompany their fish. The expression
Watch the doughnut, not the hole, meaning to think positively rather than negatively,
refers to the actual ring of dough and the actual hole in the center of it, not to
the metaphorical *doughnut hole.* CE, DAFD; EWPO; IHAT; MS.

DOUGHY   *See* Doughboy.

DO UP BROWN   *to do something up brown.* To do something carefully and
completely. Source: BAKE. The metaphor is based on the baking of food in the
oven, where it usu. turns brown on the outside. In fact, the appearance of a brown
color on the exposed part of a loaf of bread or a batch of rolls or biscuits is a
pretty good—but not infallible—sign that they are "done." The same is true of
meats (such as roasts), vegetables (such as squash), and casseroles. Something
that is properly baked or properly executed is said to be *done up brown*—not to
be confused with the Brit. expression "to be *done brown,*" i.e., to be taken in or
deceived. BDPF; DC; MDWPO; MWCD; PT.

DOWN THE HATCH!   *See* Here's Mud in Your Eye.

DO YOU EAT WITH THAT MOUTH?   *See* Garbage in, Garbage out.

DO YOU KNOW HOW SAUSAGE IS MADE?   *See* Sausage Dog.

DRAG A RED HERRING ACROSS SOMEONE'S PATH   *See* Red Herring.

DRESSER   *See* First Come, First Served.

DRESSING   *See* Knock the Stuffing out of.

DRINKING GLASS   *See* Glass Is Half Empty.

DRINK OF WATER   *See* Long Drink of Water.

DRIVE-IN   *See* Fast Food.

DRIVE SOMEONE BANANAS   *See* Go Bananas.

DRIVE SOMEONE CRACKERS   *to drive someone crackers.* To drive someone crazy. MWCD: 1928. Source: CRACKER. DAFD: 1739. A person who is "driven crackers" falls apart like a handful of soda crackers being crumbled into a bowl of tomato soup. Before the word *cracker* denoted a small, thin, flat wafer, it meant, in order, (1) a braggart (MWCD: 15th cent.), (2) a safecracker, (3) a firecracker, (4) a nutcracker, and (5) a party favor. What all of these senses had in common was the loud sound involved, starting with the braggart, who wanted everyone to hear how good he/she was. A third of the way into the 18th cent. *cracker* came to mean an unleavened, unsweetened, wheat-flour wafer that made a cracking sound when broken. A century later, when crackers began to be leavened with bicarbonate of soda, they came to be called *soda crackers* (MWCD: 1830); and when they were also sprinkled with salt, they were called *saltines* (MWCD: 1907). To complete the derivational circle, *crackers* now not only means "crazy" but, as a proper noun, *Cracker*, can refer, pejoratively, to a poor white male in the Deep South, esp. in Georgia and Florida (NSOED: mid-18th cent.). BDPF; CE; HDAS; LA; WNWCD.

DRIVE SOMEONE NUTS   *See* Nuts about.

DROP LIKE A HOT POTATO   *See* Hot Potato.

DRUGETERIA   *See* Cafeteria.

DRUMSTICK   *a drumstick.* The portion of a fowl's leg between the "knee" and the "thigh." PT: 1763. Source: FOWL (*). *Drumstick* is neither a food metaphor nor an animal metaphor: It is a musical-instrument metaphor. The original drumstick was simply a wooden stick used to beat on the animal-hide head of a drum (MWCD: 1589). However, the resemblance between a chicken (or turkey) leg and a drumstick is so slight that one must wonder whether the analogy was not to the meatless bone itself, which might have been used by children in the 18th cent. to beat on toy drums. In the 19th cent., the Victorians used *drumstick* as a euphemism for the taboo word *leg*—animals and humans having been declared to have *limbs*—and the phrase *dark meat* (for the meat of the drumstick) was used as a contrast to *white meat* (PT: 1752), which had already replaced another taboo word, *breast.* BDPF; DEOD; EWPO; NSOED.

DUCK'S EGG   *See* Lay an Egg.

DUCK SOUP   *See* Easy as Duck Soup.

DULL AS DISHWATER   *See* Taste like Dishwater.

DUMB WAITER   *See* Maître d'Hôtel.

DUMPLING   *a little dumpling.* A pudgy little girl or young woman. Source: DUMPLING. MWCD: ca. 1600. *Dumpling* is a term of endearment or address that is often used by a doting father to a chubby—or not so chubby—young—or not so young—daughter: "Hi, Dumpling! How's my little dumpling?" The term is meant to be flattering, in spite of the fact that in cooking, a dumpling is a small (note the *-ling*) "lump" (the probable source of *dump-*) of soft dough that is dropped into boiling soup (in which case it is usu. stuffed with meat or cheese) or stew and allowed to expand there. (Dessert dumplings, such as *apple dumplings*, which consist of pastry dough stuffed with fruit, are baked.) Pennsylvania "Dutch" and other German immigrants to the Midwest are said to have turned the area into a *dumpling culture.* Other cultures have provided America with the *matzo ball* (MWCD: 1952—a Jewish dumpling), the *pierogi* (a Polish dumpling), and the *wonton* (a Chinese dumpling). CE; DAFD; FLC.

DUMPLING CULTURE   *See* Dumpling.

DUNK (n)   *See* Dunk a Basketball.

DUNK (v)   *See* Dunk a Basketball.

DUNK A BASKETBALL   *to dunk a basketball.* To force a basketball into the basket with one hand. NSOED: mid-20th cent. Source: DUNK (v). MWCD: 1919. This metaphor is based on the act of dipping (i.e., "dunking") a doughnut into a cup of coffee with one hand. The purpose is to soften a stale doughnut or to warm a cold one. (Doing this cools the coffee, however, and leaves a deposit of crumbs in it.) The process of dunking was prob. invented by the Pennsylvania "Dutch," who also invented the ring-shaped doughnut. (That doughnut was easier to dunk than the original ball-shaped variety.) The verb *dunk* is from Pennsylvania Ger. *dunke*, which had approx. the same meaning. The noun *dunk* (MWCD: ca. 1944), which derives from the basketball sense of the verb, refers to the act of *dunking* a basketball with one hand. A *slam dunk* (MWCD: 1972) is a one-handed dunk while on the run; a *monster slam* is a one-handed dunk that follows a huge leap, straight at the basket, with great "hang time"; and a *stuff* is a two-handed dunk. A football player who scores a touchdown sometimes attempts to "dunk" the ball over the crossbar of the goal posts, in imitation of the basketball dunk. DAFD; IHAT.

DUTCH CHEESE   *See* Cottage-cheese Thighs.

DUTCH OVEN   *a Dutch oven.* A nontraditional oven. MWCD: 1769. Source: OVEN. MWCD: O.E. The original Dutch oven was a three-sided metal box that was placed on the hearth of a fireplace, with the oven side facing the fire, and used for roasting meat. A later version of the Dutch oven was a compartment built into the brick wall of a large fireplace, which heated up enough to bake bread or cook foods. A still later version of the Dutch oven, the one that may have given it its name, was a large, heavy, cast-iron pot or kettle, with a high, tight-fitting, domed lid, that was hung from an iron bar, swung into the fireplace above the coals, and used to slow-cook pot roasts and stew. The final version of the Dutch oven was a high, thin, metal dome, with a handle on top, that was placed over a thick, round wire grid, which, in turn, was placed on an opening in a cookstove or a burner on a gas stove for the purpose of toasting bread or making toasted sandwiches. These older ovens have been replaced by modern ovens such as the convection oven, the wall oven, the electric crock pot, and the toaster oven, respectively. The fact that Dutch ovens are not "real" ovens suggests that the word *Dutch* may have been applied in the same sense as in *Dutch treat* (q.v.), i.e., no treat at all. A *microwave* is also a nontraditional oven, so if you can't find a Dutch oven, just *Nuke it!* DAFD; FLC; WNWCD.

DUTCH TREAT   Each person pays for his/her own meal. MWCD: 1887. Source: RESTAURANT. *Dutch treat,* which originated in English as a not-so-gentle gibe at the Dutch people—as with *Dutch courage* ("false courage," induced by alcohol) and *Dutch oven* (a "false oven," utilizing the fireplace)—is now so commonly used that *Dutch* is often spelled *dutch.* What is false about Dutch treat is that it seems to be no treat at all: You still have to pay for your own meal—plus tax and tip. However, by agreeing, ahead of time, to *go Dutch treat* (or *go to Dutch*—NDAS: 1978), you have saved yourself the burden of paying the cost of both meals put together—plus tax and tip. (Although the expression began as an arrangement for the paying of a meal bill, it is often used, even by children, for the payment of tickets to a movie—and then, once inside, for the purchase of popcorn and soda pop.) Waitpersons dislike *Dutch-treaters* because they either have to make out separate checks for them or wait around while one of the guests figures out what everyone ate and collects the exact amount—plus tax and tip— from each individual. They much prefer that one of the diners *pick up the tab,* i.e., pay the entire bill without deliberation—and leave a healthy tip. A *tip* (MWCD: 1755) is a gratuity equal to a certain percentage of the total bill (including tax), the exact amount depending on the times, the status of the restaurant, the quality of the food and service, the cleanliness of the table and tableware, etc. Before credit cards, diners did not have to reveal the amount of their tip to the waitperson, but now there is no way to avoid it except to pay the tip in cash. Cash tips are picked up by the *busboy* (MWCD: 1913) or *busgirl*, a "waiter's helper" who *buses* (i.e., "clears") the table after a meal, cleans it, and resets it with dishware, silverware, and glasses. The busperson is interested in the size of the tip because he/she receives a share of it, along with the waitperson and sometimes the cook. DAFD; DAI; DEOD; EWPO; NSOED.

E

EAR CANDY   *See* Candy.

EARLY-BIRD SPECIAL   *See* Menu.

EARLY DINNER   *See* Dinner (2).

EARN YOUR SALT   *See* Old Salt.

EARTH NUT   *See* Peanut.

EASTER EGG   *an Easter egg.* A hard-boiled, decorated hen's egg. MWCD: 1804. Source: EGG. MWCD: 14th cent. Decorating hard-boiled eggs on the evening before Easter Day—by dipping them in various colors of vegetable dye (which shows up better on white eggs than on brown ones)—is almost as much fun for children as the *Easter-egg hunt* (on Easter Day) and the *Easter-egg roll* (on the day after). The Easter-egg hunt is a game in which the parents of a family, or the teachers of a Sunday school, hide Easter eggs throughout the house or school, or throughout the yard and grounds, for the children to collect in "Easter baskets." An *Easter-egg roll* (or *egg rolling*) is an event in which the children are present when the Easter eggs are rolled down the slope of a well-manicured lawn (as at the White House) and are then expected to retrieve them, also in Easter baskets. However, the name *Easter egg* also applies to chocolate and candy "eggs" that are sold at Eastertime and are advertised as being laid by the "Easter Bunny," not the traditional hen. BDPF; NSOED.

EASTER-EGG HUNT   *See* Easter Egg.

EASTER-EGG ROLL *See* Easter Egg.

EASY AS DUCK SOUP *as easy as duck soup.* Child's play: a "cinch." HDAS: 1902. Source: DUCK (MWCD: O.E.); SOUP (MWCD: 14th cent.). Recipe for duck soup: "First catch your duck!" That's the difficult part. Turning the duck into soup is relatively easy because duck contains more fat than chicken, and the fat and juices combine quickly to form a hearty broth. However, the metaphor may be based on another metaphor, "sitting duck," i.e., an animal or human that is an easy target—as easy to shoot as a duck sitting on the ground or water. The sitting duck becomes a "dead duck," which soon becomes *duck soup.* AID; ATWS; CE; DAI; DC; HB; HND; IRCD; LA; NSOED; PT; SA. *Compare* Can of Corn; Easy as Pie; Piece of Cake.

EASY AS PIE *as easy as pie.* A cinch. IHAT: 1920. Source: PIE. MWCD: 14th cent. There is nothing easy about making a pie, although some pies are easier to make than others, and the job has become less demanding over the years. Therefore, the simile prob. refers to the *eating* of a piece of pie, which is about as easy as eating a *piece of cake* (q.v.), esp. if you hold the food in your hand, as children do, rather than eating it from a plate. AID; CE; DC; HND; MDWPO. *Compare* Can of Corn; Easy as Duck Soup.

EASY AS TAKING CANDY FROM A BABY *See* Candy.

EAT A BULLET *See* Eat Nails.

EAT A HORSE *See* Eat like a Horse.

EAT A SOUR GRAPE *See* Sour Grapes.

EAT AWAY AT *to eat away at something.* For wind or water (liquid or frozen) to destroy earth or stone; for chemicals to deface or destroy metal; for disease to destroy flesh and bone. NSOED: M.E. Source: EAT. MWCD: O.E. *To eat away at* is a translation of the verb *erode* (MWCD: 1612), fr. Lat. *erodere* (fr. *e-* "away" + *rodere* "to gnaw like a rodent"). A rodent is a gnawer, and although some of that gnawing is for the purpose of securing food, most of it is for digging holes and felling trees. Natural erosion is caused by wind shaping the dunes and shores, running water carving valleys and canyons, and glaciers creating hills and lakes. Just as wind and water *erode,* or *eat away at,* earth and stone, chemicals *corrode* (MWCD: 14th cent.), or *eat away at,* metals, causing rust on iron and steel, pitting on aluminum, tarnish on silver, and a patina on copper and bronze. Diseases such as cancer and gangrene *eat away at* tissues of the body, and, more abstractly, anxiety and worry *eat away at* both your body and your mind. AID; DAI; SA; WNWCD.

EAT CROW *to eat crow.* To admit your error; to accept defeat. DC: ca. 1870. Source: EAT; CROW. MWCD: O.E. *To eat crow* is comparable to the metaphors *to eat humble pie* (q.v.), in the sense of voluntarily doing something that is distasteful, and *to eat your hat* (q.v.), in the sense of voluntarily doing something that is ridiculous. The origin of *to eat crow* is uncertain, but there are three possibilities: (1) The crow is a scavenger, and there is no telling where it has been and what has passed through its gullet. (Eating crow meat would be a disgusting punishment.) (2) Crow meat tastes so bad that it was once used as initiation food for young men trying to make it on the frontier. (Eating crow meat proved that you could "take it.") (3) In the War of 1812 an American soldier crossed the Niagara River to the British side and shot a crow. A British soldier saw the shooting and approached the American soldier, asking if he could examine the gun that had made such a wonderful shot. The American soldier complied, and the British soldier pointed the gun at him and forced him to eat some of the crow. When the British soldier returned the gun, the American soldier then pointed the gun at *him*, making him eat the rest of the crow. This anecdotal account is prob. apocryphal, developing orally during the decades following the war and serving as propaganda for the superiority of America over Britain. AID; ATWS; BDPF; CE; DAI; DAS; EWPO; HI; HND; IRCD; LCRH; MS; SA; SHM.

EAT DIRT *to eat dirt.* To put up with insults and other verbal abuse; to humiliate yourself as punishment for making an error. HND: 1859. Source: EAT. MWCD: O.E. *To eat dirt* is comparable to *to eat humble pie* (q.v.), which once involved eating a real pie, and *to eat crow* (q.v.), which could really happen in a period of near starvation; and it is similar to *to eat your hat* (q.v.), which is impossible unless it is really a gingerbread hat, and *to eat your words* (q.v.), which is also impossible unless the words are written down or recorded. Actually, it *is* possible to *eat dirt* (HDAS: 1933), as when a husband is made to grovel (i.e., lie with his face in the dirt) as a result of having cheated on his wife ("She *made him eat dirt*") or when a resident of the American South maintains an African tradition by eating dirt for its mineral content (HDAS: 1840). *To eat someone's dirt*, in contrast, is to trail a horse, human, automobile, or motorcycle in a race on a dirt track, thereby "eating" the dirt that is kicked up by the feet or wheels. BDPF; DAFD; DAI.

EAT, DRINK, AND BE MERRY *See* Let Us Eat, Drink, and Be Merry, for Tomorrow We Die.

EAT FACE *See* Eat Nails.

EAT HIGH ON/OFF THE HOG *to eat high on—or off—the hog.* To live well and prosperously. HND: 19th cent. Source: EAT; HOG. MWCD: O.E. In the American South of the mid-1800s, the food animal of choice was the hog—not the sheep or goat, and not the steer. The most expensive meat on a hog—the bacon, hams, and loins—is found on the sides, upper legs, and shoulders. The lower and less expensive portions are the feet (the knuckles and hocks), the belly ("sow belly"), and the jowls. If you ate *high on—or off—the hog* in the 1850s, you were thought to be *living high on/off the hog* as well. A century and a half later, bacon and hams, at least, were more moderately priced; pig's feet were regarded as delicacies, and beef was competing with pork for "meat of choice." AID; ATWS; BDPF; DAI; EWPO; IRCD; LCRH; MDWPO; SA.

EAT HUMBLE PIE   *to eat humble pie.* To humble yourself; to apologize under pressure. MWCD: 1830. Source: EAT (MWCD: O.E.); PIE (MWCD: 14th cent.). Before this phrase became a metaphor, it simply meant to eat a meat pie containing the innards of a deer. This *humble* fare (MWCD: 13th cent.) was served to the huntsman and servants of the manor, whereas the lords and ladies ate the venison. However, *humble* had a dual meaning, referring both to the humility associated with eating deer's innards and to the innards themselves. In the 15th cent. the viscera of deer were called *umbles* (pl.), an alteration of earlier *nombles* (pl.). The journey from *nombles* to *humble* may have gone something like this: (1) The initial n- of the noun was absorbed by the possessive article: *min nombles → min ombles* ("my humbles"); (2) the initial vowel of the noun was raised: *min ombles → min umbles*; (3) the final -s of the noun was dropped in combination with *pie*: *umbles pie → umble pie*; and (4) an initial h- was added to *umble*, at least in the spelling: *umble pie → humble pie.* Nowadays, *eating humble pie* is more offensive to the pride than to the palate. AID; ATWS; BDPF; CE; CI; DAFD; DAI; DC; DEI; EWPO; FLC; HI; HND; MDWPO; MS; PT; SA. *Compare* Eat Crow; Eat Your Hat; Eat Your Words.

EATING CHERRY (v)   *See* Cherry (n).

EAT IT UP   *to eat something up.* To enjoy or appreciate something immensely. Source: EAT. MWCD: O.E. To eat up your food is to chew it and swallow it. However, the act of ingesting can be trasferred, metaphorically, to cars (eating up gas), expenses (eating up profits), printers (eating up homework), small talk (eating up lunch hours), etc. People are also known to *eat up* things other than food, such as sales pitches and tall tales, flattery and praise, and genuinely enjoyable activities and performances. If the audience really likes the performance, they may be said to *eat it up with a spoon.* Without *up*, the expression has an unpleasant connotation: "The financial loss was our fault, so we had to *eat it*," i.e., absorb it, bear the expense of it. AID; DAI; DAS.

EAT IT UP WITH A SPOON   *See* Eat It Up.

EAT LIKE A BIRD   *to eat like a bird.* To eat very little; to "pick" at your food. HND: 1930. Source: EAT; BIRD. MWCD: O.E. Small birds who feed at the bird-feeder in your backyard seem to eat very little, and that is prob. where the simile originated. The birds spend most of the daylight hours pecking at seeds, dropping them, looking around to see if anyone noticed, picking them up again in their beaks, swallowing them, looking around again, etc.—and this is also how some young children and distracted teenagers address their food. Nevertheless, a bird can easily eat 100 percent of its bodyweight every day, whereas a human eats only a tiny fraction of his/her bodyweight (approx. two percent) each day. Therefore, a person who *eats like a bird* eats about the same amount as a bird but not the same percentage of his/her weight. A person with the eating disorder *anorexia nervosa* (an abnormal fear of gaining weight) *eats like a bird* almost to the point of starvation, whereas one with the eating disorder *bulimia* (q.v.) (an abnormal craving for food) *eats like an ox*, then counters the "binging" with "purging" as a result of the same abnormal fear of gaining weight that an anorexic has. AID; DAI; SA; WNWCD. *Compare* Eat like a Horse; EAT like a Pig.

EAT LIKE A HORSE   *to eat like a horse.* To eat a lot; to eat heartily. HND: 18th cent. Source: EAT; HORSE. MWCD: O.E. Horses are large animals with large appetites. They are also herbivorous, and their diet consists mostly of grasses and grains. In the course of one day, a 1,500-pound horse may eat two percent of its bodyweight, i.e., approx. thirty pounds of hay and oats. If a 150-pound human ate two percent of his/her weight per day, he/she would consume approx. three pounds of food—a reasonable amount that would be equivalent to *eating like a horse*. Yet if you are *so hungry that you could eat a horse*, you might mean that you could either consume 1,500 pounds at one sitting or that you would be willing to eat meat that was sold during the 1930s and 1940s in America but is no longer considered appetizing. AID; ATWS; DAI; DEI; MS; SA. *Compare* Eat like a Bird; Eat like an Ox; Eat like a Pig.

EAT LIKE AN OX   *See* Eat like a Bird.

EAT LIKE A PIG   *to eat like a pig.* To eat rapidly, greedily, noisily, and indiscriminately. Source: EAT (MWCD: O.E.); PIG (MWCD: 13th cent.). Pigs are messy eaters—from the time they are piglets, fighting for the last available teat, until they are shoats, fighting for the last place at the feeding trough. They don't care how much food they spill or how much noise they make, just as long as the food keeps coming. They have absolutely no manners whatsoever. Teenagers are somtimes like this. Their parents warn them not to *make pigs of themselves*, but they seldom pay attention. In contrast, *to pig out* (MWCD: 1978), or *to pork out*, is to eat a lot of your favorite food, though not necessarily noisily or messily. *Pigging out* often follows fasting or dieting; and for bulimics, such a "binge" is usu. followed by a "purge." CI; DAS; DAFD; DEI; IRCD; SA. *See also* Eat like a Bird; Eat like a Horse; Eat like an Ox.

EAT NAILS   *to be mad enough to eat—or chew—nails.* To clench your teeth so hard that you feel as though you could chew on nails. HDAS (fingernails): 1976.

Source: EAT. MWCD: O.E. People eat the strangest things. For example, if some-one *looks good enough to eat*, you might get in the back seat with that person to *eat face* (HDAS: 1968) or *chew face* (HDAS: 1980), i.e., to "neck." And they eat it in the strangest places. For example, when a guest remarks that the host's *floor looks clean enough to eat off of*, the host must wonder what goes on back at the guest's own home. *It must have been something I ate* is a convenient explanation for a hangover, and *Don't eat yellow snow* is good advice for discriminating eaters. *To eat punches* is what a boxer does when he/she absorbs the numerous blows of his/her opponent; *to eat a bullet* is for someone to be shot by a pistol or rifle; and *to eat your gun* is for a police officer to commit suicide by sticking the barrel of his/her gun in his/her mouth and pulling the trigger.

EAT OUT OF YOUR HAND(S)   *See* Have Someone Eating out of Your Hand(s).

EAT PUNCHES   *See* Eat Nails.

EAT, SLEEP, AND DRINK   *See* Let Us Eat, Drink, and Be Merry, for Tomorrow We Die.

EAT SOMEONE ALIVE   *to eat someone alive.* To completely dominate or defeat someone. HDAS: 1960. Source: EAT. MWCD: O.E. Metaphorically, *to eat someone alive* is to treat the person as if he/she were the mouse in a cat-and-mouse game: completely in your control. However, the expression takes various forms, from *eating (or chewing) someone up and spitting them out* (HDAS: 1940) to *eating (or having) someone for breakfast (or lunch)*. In sports, *Their running back is eating our defense alive*; in theater, *Broadway will eat you up and spit you out*; in the armed services, *Admirals eat ensigns for breakfast*; and in business, *The businessman ate his competitor for lunch (or ate his competitor's lunch—HDAS: 1959)*. EWPO; MS; PT. *Compare* Cannibalize; You Are What Your Eat.

EAT SOMEONE FOR BREAKFAST   *See* Eat Someone Alive.

EAT SOMEONE FOR LUNCH   *See* Eat Someone Alive.

EAT SOMEONE OUT OF HOUSE AND HOME   *to eat someone out of house and home*. To bankrupt someone by eating everything he/she has in stock and store. DC: ca. 1598 (Shakespeare's *Henry IV, Part II*, Act II, Scene 1). Source: EAT. MWCD: O.E. This expression is used when one spouse complains that the other spouse's live-in relative is consuming more than his/her share of food; but it is used humorously when a proud mother and father boast to a friend that their child (esp. a son) is *eating like a horse* (q.v.) and growing like a weed. Shakespeare had the former, near-literal, meaning in mind when he had the hostess of the Boar's Head tavern, Mistress Quickly, explain to the Lord Chief Justice why she had Sir John Falstaff arrested: "He hath *eaten me out of house and home*; he hath put all my substance into that fat belly of his" [italics added]. AID; BDPF; HND; MS; NSOED.

EAT SOMEONE'S DIRT   *See* Eat Dirt.

EAT SOMEONE'S LUNCH   *See* Eat Someone Alive.

EAT SOMEONE'S SALT   *See* Salt of the Earth.

EAT SOMEONE UP AND SPIT THEM OUT   *See* Eat Someone Alive.

EAT TENDERLOIN   *See* Tenderloin.

EAT WITH RELISH   *See* Relish (n).

EAT YOUR CAKE AND HAVE IT TOO   *See* You Can't Eat Your Cake and Have It Too.

EAT YOUR FIRST PEACH   *to eat your first peach.* To take your first risk. SA: 1915 (T. S. Eliot's "The Love Song of J. Alfred Prufrock"). Source: EAT (MWCD: O.E.); PEACH (MWCD: 14th cent.). Prufrock asked himself, "Do I dare to eat a peach?" But he didn't need to answer the question because he never dared to try anything new. A peach is about the tamest fruit that Eliot could have picked because it is sweet (but not too sweet), tender (but not too tender), and fuzzy (but not too fuzzy). If Prufrock couldn't get up enough nerve to eat a peach, it's pretty obvious what he would have done with an oyster. Jonathan Swift observed, in the early-1700s, "He was a bold man that first ate an oyster." That act of courage was rewarded not only with a satisfied palate but with a recharged libido, according to those who believe that the oyster is the ultimate aphrodisiac. FLC.

EAT YOUR GUN   *See* Eat Nails.

EAT YOUR HAT   (Usu. first person sing.) *I'll eat my hat if I'm wrong.* I'll humble myself in some appropriate way if my prediction doesn't come true. HB: 1837 (Dickens' *Pickwick Papers*). Source: EAT. MWCD: O.E. *To eat your hat* is comparable to *to eat humble pie* (q.v.) or *to eat crow* (q.v.), both of which describe an act of contrition following a major faux pas. However, humble pie and crow are at least potential food—albeit distasteful—whereas hats are made of inedible cloth, leather, plastic, or straw. Some persons who have been forced to make good on their pledge to *eat their hat* have substituted a hat made of cookie or cracker dough, but the promise is usu. not taken seriously, and no punishment is usu.

required. Dickens used the phrase in the conditional form rather the indicative: "If I knew as little of life as that, I'd *eat my hat*" [italics added]; and the phrase can also be used in the conditional to indicate indignation at the thought of doing something repugnant: "I'd eat my hat before I'd run for office." AID; BDPF; DAS; DC; EWPO; HND; MS. *Compare* Eat Your Words.

EAT YOUR HEART OUT   *to eat your heart out.* To suffer excessive worry or grief (DC: 1535); to be consumed by envy or jealousy. Source: EAT. MWCD: O.E. It is not possible, of course, to lit. *eat your heart out*; but it is possible to metaphorically consume yourself with sorrow or remorse to such an extent that you eventually waste away. (That may be the source of the metaphor *What's eating you?*—HDAS: 1892.) That is what the 6th cent. Greek philosopher and mathematician Pythagoras warned against in the negative form of the metaphor: *Don't eat your heart out.* Today, that advice would be given after a less serious loss of face or love and would mean something like "No big deal." Nowadays, the positive form of the metaphor is used to produce an effect of envy or jealousy in someone close to you who won't take offense, as when you send a postcard from Hawaii, with a picture of a tropical beach, to a friend or relative back in the frozen Midwest, saying, "*Eat your heart out!*" AID; BDPF; CE; CI; DAI; DAS; DEI; HND; MS; NSOED.

EAT YOUR WORDS   *to eat your words.* To be forced to take back what you have said. EWPO: 1571. Source: EAT. MWCD: O.E. *To eat your words* is comparable to *to eat crow* (q.v.), *to eat humble pie* (q.v.), and *to eat your hat* (q.v.), although these other metaphors are based on concrete object (*crow, pie, hat*), whereas *words* are abstract and formless. The only way you could lit. "eat" your words would be to eat the paper on which they are printed or the tape on which they are recorded; and that is exactly what some victims do, albeit in fun, in order to achieve the proper humiliation. "*I'll make you eat your words*" is a typical threat against someone who has made a false accusation against the threatener. What is demanded is a withdrawal, or retraction, of the statement, specif. a negation of the words that were orig. uttered. AID; BDPF; CE; DAI; DEI; HND; MS; NSOED.

EGGBEATER   *an eggbeater.* A helicopter. HDAS: 1945. Source: EGG. MWCD: 14th cent. The kitchen utensil called an *eggbeater* (MWCD: 1828) is a hand-held appliance consisting of two interlocking sets of curved blades, each on a metal post connected to a set of gears turned by a knob attached to a vertical plate. The function of the eggbeater is to beat eggs, but the appliance is also used for mixing ingredients and whipping cream and potatoes. In the 20th cent. the eggbeater has pretty much been replaced by the electric mixer and the food processor, but it is still useful when those appliances are busy or the electricity goes off. The helicopter is prob. nicknamed an *eggbeater* because it looks a little bit like the utensil turned upside down. However, the blades are straight, and the metal post connects to a set of gears turned by the engine of the aircraft. Military and industrial freight helicopters look the most like an eggbeater because they have two sets of blades extending outward. DAS; FLC.

EGG CREAM   *an egg cream.* A soda fountain drink consisting of milk, chocolate syrup, and soda water. MWCD: 1954. Source: EGG; CREAM. MWCD: 14th cent. *Egg cream* is falsely named: It contains neither eggs nor cream. However, when soda water is shot into the chocolate-flavored milk, the result is a topping of frothy, *egg-white* foam. The date of first appearance in print, 1954, is surprising: Egg cream has been popular in New York City since the 1930s, and the drink is thought to have been invented ca. 1890. Another egg-drink term is *eggnog* (MWCD: ca. 1775), which orig. denoted a Christmastime drink consisting of eggs, milk, sugar, nutmeg, and strong Norfolk, England, ale. Today, most eggnog sold in the United States is alcohol free, and it can be drunk "as is" by children and teetotalers; and those adults who prefer may add whiskey, brandy, or wine—but never beer or ale. Because commercial eggnog contains milk, it must be pasteurized; and because it contains raw eggs, it must be refrigerated. DAFD; EWPO; FLC; HF; NSOED.

EGGHEAD   *an egghead.* A bald man (HDAS: 1907); a male intellectual (LA: 1918). Source: EGG. MWCD: 14th cent. This metaphor developed in two stages. First, a man with little or no hair was said to have a head shaped like an egg (roundish and smooth): an *egghead*. Second, because intellectuals often had little or no hair, they were also called *eggheads*. In the presidential campaign of 1952, Adlai Stevenson, a Democrat who was both bald and intellectual, was called an *egghead* by his Republican opponent, who regarded him as "brittle on the outside and soft on the inside," like an egg. ATWS; BDPF; CE; DAS; DEI; MDWPO; SA.

EGG IN YOUR BEER   *See* What Do You Want, Egg in Your Beer?

EGGNOG   *See* Egg Cream.

EGG ON   *to egg someone on.* To urge someone to do something that he/she will prob. regret. MWCD: 13th cent. Source: EGG (*). *Egg on* is not a food metaphor. The verb *egg* is a borrowing into English from O.N. *eggja* "to edge." (The noun *egg*, also from O.N., was not borrowed until the following century.) Literally, *to egg someone on* is to drive them closer to the "edge." The confusion between the verb and the noun prob. leads people to believe that the person being driven is being pelted with eggs. Metaphorically, *to egg someone on* has come to imply that the person being *egged on* is not a criminal being punished but an innocent victim being manipulated. Children often engage in this kind of behavior, daring—or double daring—a younger child to do something foolish or unwise. AID; BDPF; CE; CI; DAI; DEI; EWPO; LA; SA.

EGG ON YOUR FACE   *to have egg on your face*. To be embarassed, humiliated, or chagrined as a result of your own foolish actions. HDAS: ca. 1952. Source: EGG. MWCD: 14th cent. There are three possible sources for this metaphor: (1) a diner eating eggs so sloppily that portions of them remain on his/her face; (2) an entertainer performing so poorly that he/she is pelted on the body and face with raw eggs; (3) a weasel crawling out of a henhouse with egg on its muzzle after spending the night eating and sucking eggs. All three qualify because they exhibit the consequences of unacceptable behavior. *Hen fruit* (HDAS: 1854) is a slang term for egg. AID; ATWS; CI; DAS; DC; DEI; HND; MS; NSOED; SA.

EGGPLANT   *an eggplant*. A large berry of the nightshade family, related to the potato (usu. regarded as a vegetable) and the tomato (variously regarded as a vegetable, a fruit, or a berry). MWCD: 1767. Source: EGG. MWCD: 14th cent. The eggplant is so called because the white variety of the plant is egg-shaped. The deep purple variety, which is more common in America, is pear-shaped, but the "egg" analogy has stuck. The eggplant has provided America with the name of a color (*eggplant*: deep, dark, blackish purple) and the main ingredient for a native "Italian" dish (*eggplant parmigiana*: breaded, sautéed, and baked). Although not shaped like a chicken (or turkey) egg, the eggplant is smooth and shiny and somewhat resembles a dinosaur egg. DAFD; EWPO; FLC; SA.

EGG ROLLING   *See* Easter Egg.

EGG SALAD   *See* Salad.

EGG-SHAPED   *See* Love.

EGGSHELL   *See* Walk on Eggs.

EGG-SUCKER   *See* Teach Your Grandmother to Suck Eggs.

EGG-WHITE   *See* Egg Cream.

ELBOW GREASE   *See* Grease.

ELEPHANT EAR   *an elephant ear*. A large, thin, honeyglazed cookie. Source: COOKIE. Elephant ears are perennial favorites at carnivals and fairs, where they are made and sold by professionals at food wagons. (Do not try to make them at home!) They are called *elephant ears* because they are approx. the same shape and size as the ears of a baby elephant. At one foot in diameter and approx. three-eights of an inch in thickness, an *elephant ear* is almost an entire meal in itself. *Compare* Mule Ear.

ENGLISH MUFFIN   *an English muffin.* A flat, round, yeast-raised bread roll. MWCD: 1902. Source: MUFFIN. MWCD: 1703. The name of this "bread" implies that it is a British product that has been imported into the United States. The truth is that there has never been such a "muffin" in Great Britain, either in fact or in name: *English muffin* is an Americanism. These breakfast (or brunch) bread rolls are sold "whole" but are fork-split into two halves before toasting. If prepared in a toaster oven, they can be buttered on the "rough" side before toasting; if prepared in a pop-up toaster, they must be buttered after toasting. The buttered "muffins" are then topped with jelly or jam. The closest thing the British have to the English muffin is the *crumpet* (MWCD: 1769), which is sometimes also split, toasted, and "jammed," though not necessarily so—and certainly not for breakfast. BDPF; DAFD; FLC; NSOED; PT.

ENTRÉE   *See* Pièce de Résistance.

ERODE   *See* Eat away at.

ESPRESSO   *See* Coffee.

EUROPEAN PLAN   *See* Meal.

EVERYONE TO HIS OWN TASTE   Everyone is entitled to his/her own likes and dislikes; to each his own. MDWPO: mid-1500s. Source: TASTE (n). MWCD: 14th cent. *Everyone to his own taste* is prob. either a literal translation of the Fr. phrase *chacun à son goût* or a mistranslation of one or another of these other Fr. phrases: (1) *chacun à son goût* ("everyone has his own taste") or (2) *à chacun son goût* ("to each his own taste"). To complicate the history, there is another expression involving taste, *There's no accounting for taste*, which dates back to ca. 1600 and prob. derives from Lat. *De gustibus non est disputandum* (same meaning); and there is a similar expression, without *taste*, that first appeared in late-16th cent.: *One man's meat is another man's poison*—sometimes jokingly rendered as *One man's meat is another man's poisson* (*poisson* being Fr. for "fish"). Modern versions of any or all of these proverbs are "Different strokes for different folks," "One man's trash is another man's treasure," and "There are horses for courses." AID; BDPF; CI; CODP; DAP; HND; MDWPO; MS; PT.

EVERYTHING BUT THE KITCHEN SINK   Almost everything you own; almost everything you can think of. HDAS: ca. 1944. Source: KITCHEN. MWCD: O.E. *Everything but the kitchen sink* is used in such expressions as "We own everything but the kitchen sink" (renters); "We take everything but the kitchen sink" (movers); "We steal everything but the kitchen sink" (burglars); and "We sell everything but the kitchen sink" (retailers). The reason that the kitchen sink is the one thing not owned, moved, burgled, or sold is that it is attached to the house by water pipes, a fact not true of ranges, refrigerators, and washing machines in the early-20th cent. In the 19th cent., even the kitchen sink was not necessarily piped to the wall. In farm houses it often stood next to an indoor hand pump, although the used water did flow out of a drain to the cistern. As an adj., *kitchen-sink* (MWCD: 1941) can be used to describe anything that is made up of a hodgepodge of elements: e.g., a *kitchen-sink* approach to interior decorating. HND; MS.

EVERYTHING BUT THE OINK   Every part of the pig except the squeal. Source: PIG. The pig has been the domesticated animal of choice for settlers in North America since the 16th cent., and it remains the favorite source of meat and meat products in the American South. At one time or another almost every part of the pig has been put to good use as food for humans: the belly, the feet, the hams, the hocks, the intestines, the jowls, the knuckles, the loins, the shoulders, and the sides. Sometimes an entire pig (minus the head, feet, tail, and internal organs) is roasted on a spit in a large gas-fired barbecue oven; and in Hawai'i, on special occasions, an entire pig (including the head, feet, and tail but excluding the internal organs) is barbecued over coals in a pit dug in the ground. In the 1990s a company named Oink-Oink, Inc., was founded in Detroit, Mich., to produce treats for dogs from the various parts of pigs, such as the heart, hooves, liver, and snout, as well as the original product: roasted pig ears. The company's slogan is "Everything But The Oink." DAFD; DAS; FLC.

EVERYTHING ELSE IS GRAVY   *See* Ride the Gravy Train.

EVERYTHING FROM SOUP TO NUTS   Everything that you could possibly imagine. LA: late-1920s. Source: SOUP (MWCD: 14th cent.); NUT (MWCD: O.E.). The early-20th cent. all-purpose department store carried everything you could possibly want, from corsets to cars, and from hardware to houses; i.e., they stocked and sold *everything from soup to nuts*. However, this metaphorical expression derives not from retail stores but from the multicourse dinners of the 18th and 19th cents., at which wealthy families dined on everything from soup (the first course) to nuts (the last course), with up to forty or more courses in between. A 20th cent. version of the multicourse meal—i.e., the six-course meal—has produced another metaphor, *soup and fish*, which refers, lit. to the first two courses of such a dinner and applies, fig., to the formal attire worn by men on such an occasion: white tie (cream soup) and tails (boiled fish). The modern formal dinner usu. begins with appetizers, which have spawned another metaphorical expression, *for starters*, referring, lit., to the antipastos, canapés, and hors d'oeuvres served at the beginning of the meal ("*For starters*, we'll have rumaki") and, figuratively, to whatever comes first in a private argument or an informal report ("*For starters*, let's take a look at our expenditures"). AID; CI; DAS; EWPO; HND; NSOED; PT; SA.

EXTRA VIRGIN   The finest grade of olive oil. Source: OLIVE. MWCD: 13th cent. Extra virgin olive oil is obtained from the first, light, cold pressing of tree-ripened olives. It is the "champagne" of olive oils: the lightest, fruitiest, least acid, and most expensive. Other grades, in ascending order of acidity, are *superfine* and *fine*. An additional grade, *pure* (or *virgin*) applies to oils that are chemically ex-tracted, lighter colored, and less flavorful. The importance of olive oil to humanity is reflected in the fact that the Eng. word *oil* derives not from animal fat or petroleum but from olives (M.E. *oile*, fr. O.Fr., fr. Lat. *oleum* "olive oil"); and the word *oleaginous* "oily" derives fr. Lat. *oleagineus* "of an olive tree" (fr. Lat. *olea* "olive tree"). It is not known how Popeye's girlfriend *Olive Oyl* got her name. DAFD; FLC.

EYE CANDY   *See* Candy.

EYES ARE BIGGER THAN YOUR STOMACH   *Your eyes are bigger than your stomach.* Your wishes are bigger than your wallet. DAP: 1580. Source: STOMACH. MWCD: 14th cent. Anatomically, the human stomach is much bigger than the two eyes put together, but the basis for the expression is that you sometimes take more food than you can eat, esp. at a family-style or buffet-style restaurant, where everything looks so good that you forget that your stomach has a limited capacity for a single meal. Beyond the restaurant, the expression has the more general implication that you are too ambitious, too greedy, or too unrealistic: You con-stantly *bite off more than you can chew* (q.v.). AID; DAI; MS.

EYES AS BIG AS SAUCERS   *See* Flying Saucer.

F

FABERGÉ EGG   *See* Walk on Eggs.

FALL FLAT AS A CHEESE SOUFFLÉ   *See* Flat as a Cheese Soufflé.

FALL FLAT AS A PANCAKE   *See* Flat as a Pancake.

FALL OFF THE CABBAGE TRUCK   *See* You Can't Get Blood from a Turnip.

FALL OFF THE TURNIP TRUCK   *See* You Can't Get Blood from a Turnip.

FARMER CHEESE   *See* Cottage-cheese Thighs.

FARRAGO   *See* Cannon Fodder.

FAST FOOD   Food prepared, packaged, and delivered in short order. MWCD: 1951. Source: FOOD. MWCD: O.E. The *fast-food restaurant* (MWCD: 1951) is the post-WWII answer to the post-WWI *short-order restaurant* (MWCD: 1920). The difference between the two types of restaurants is that (1) the customer sat on a stool at a *lunch counter* (MWCD: 1869) in the short-order restaurant and was served by a waitress standing between the counter and the window to the kitchen, whereas the customer at a fast-food restaurant is served either while standing at a counter inside the restaurant, while pulling his/her car up to a *drive-in* (MWCD: 1937) window of the restaurant, or while sitting in his/her car at a designated spot outside the restaurant; and (2) the food that was served in short-order res- taurants was traditional homestyle fare (e.g., meat loaf, mashed potatoes, and coffee), served on/in hard plates and cups that you left behind, whereas the food served at fast-food restaurants (e.g., burgers, fries, and pop) is what is pejoratively called *junk food* (MWCD: 1971), i.e., food high in calories but low in nutrition, served on/in disposable plates and cups. However, the term *junk food* is also used for such universal snacks as candy, ice cream, popcorn, potato chips, and pretzels, whereas some fast-food restaurants sell such standard fare as pancakes, sausages, and scrambled eggs. Pizza is referred to negatively as both *fast food* and *junk food*. DAFD; DAI; DAS; LA; WNWCD.

FAST-FOOD RESTAURANT   *See* Fast Food.

FASTNACHT   *See* Doughnut.

FAT (adj.)   Plump, obese; big, thick; large, substantial; full, rich; affluent, wealthy; lucrative, profitable; fertile, productive; foolish, stupid. Source: FAT. MWCD: O.E. *Fat*, meaning "having a large amount of fatty tissue," is derived fr. O.E. *fætt* "fattened," the past part. of the O.E. verb *fætan* "to fatten." The adj. *fat* may have produced more metaphors and metaphorical expressions than any other word connected with food. The minimal amount of figurative use of *fat* is found in the application of the word to overweight humans, as in the simile *as fat as a pig* "grossly overweight," or to a human who has received a *fat lip* (HDAS: 1944) "a swollen lip" as the result of a fight; but the amount is greater in reference to a person who has *grown fat* (i.e., "rich") on the production of war matériel, or has fat in his/her head instead of brains: a *fathead* (MWCD: 1842). Expressions such as a *fat book* (a thick and heavy one), a *fat pitch* (right over the middle of the plate), and the *fat part of the bat* (the big end) are figurative but still transparent; expressions such as a *fat wallet* (plenty of cash) and a *fat contract* (plenty of salary) are also figurative but are less transparent: the actual wallet and contract may not be "thick and heavy" at all. A *fat profit* is a big one; a *fat role* in a play (NSOED: early-19th cent.), or part in a movie, is a substantial one; and a *fat tone* is a deep, rich, and full one from a human voice or a musical instrument. A *fat year* on the farm is a bounteous and productive one in regard to crops and livestock. WNWCD. *See also* Fat Cat; Fat Chance; Fat Lot of.

FAT (n)   Abundance or plenty; wealth or luxury; excess or superfluity. NSOED: late-M.E. Source: FAT (n). MWCD: 14th cent. The noun *fat* derives fr. the adj. *fat* (q.v.). In the 14th cent., *fat* referred only to animal fat, such as suet, lard, and butter. However, it eventually came to be recognized that both animal fat and plant fat (as from seeds) are made up of the same glycerides of fatty acids—and that solid fat (i.e., saturated fats, mostly from animals) should be distinguished from liquid fat, or oil (i.e., unsaturated fats, mainly from plants). One of the earliest references to *fat* as a metaphor appears in Genesis 45:18, where the Egyptian Pharoah instructs Joseph to tell his brothers to go home to get their father and bring him back to Egypt: "and I will give you the good of the land of Egypt, and Ye shall *eat the fat of the land*" [italics added]. This expression has since been altered, in popular usage, to *to live off the fat of the land*—i.e., to live in abundance and luxury, with not only the best food but also the best clothing and shelter. Nevertheless, there can be too much of a good thing, and sometimes it is necessary to *trim—or cut out—the fat*, i.e., to reduce or eliminate unnecessary spending from a current or projected budget. In this case, *fat* is regarded as something that is unnecessary and even undesirable. Excess fat on humans is sometimes also regarded as undesirable, and people who can afford the expense go to a *fat farm* (MWCD: 1969) to *trim the fat* through diet and exercise. AID; CI; DAI; DEI; FLC; HDAS; MS; WNWCD. *Compare* Eat High on/off the Hog.

FAT AS A PIG   *See* Fat (adj.).

FAT BOOK   *See* Fat (adj.).

FAT CAT   A *fat cat*. A wealthy contributor, esp. to political campaigns. MWCD: 1928. Source: FAT. MWCD: O.E. A *fat cat* is so called because he/she is like a housecat that is too old and fat to catch mice but still remembers the thrill of the chase and wishes it could get back in action again. That is exactly what the human *fat cat* can afford to do, albeit vicariously, as a result of his/her financial support— not only of politics but of the arts, culture, the environment, etc. And what does the *fat cat* get out of spending all this money? The satisfaction of having made a difference—and the undying gratitude of the recipients of the money. Most of us have little chance of being benefactors; i.e., if someone asked us if we thought we would ever be *fat cats*, our reply would prob. be, "*Fat chance*" (HDAS: 1905), i.e., no chance at all. A similar term is *fat lot of* (HDAS: 1892), meaning "none at all," as in *a fat lot of good that'll do you* or *a fat lot of use that's going to be*. CI; DAI; DEI; HND; IRCD; MS; SA.

FAT CHANCE   *See* Fat Cat.

FAT CONTRACT   *See* Fat (adj.).

FAT FARM   *See* Fat (n).

FATHEAD   *See* Fat (adj.).

FAT IS IN THE FIRE   *The fat is in the fire.* The initial damage has been done, and serious consequences will follow. DC: 1562. Source: FAT (n). MWCD: 14th cent. In the 16th cent., meat was roasted on a spit over a low fire in a large fireplace. When the drippings from the fat of the roast fell into the fire, as was inevitable, the fire would snap and crackle, and the flames would rise up to the roast itself, charring it and possibly ruining the dinner. (The solution to the problem was simple: Raise the roast or lower the fire.) The fat in the fire was metaphorized as a sign of something much more serious to follow, like throwing the first stone, inciting a riot, or planting the seeds of insurrection. A much different interpretation has been suggested for this metaphor—that it derives not fr. M.E. *fat* "not lean" but fr. M.E. *fat* "vat." In that case, the proverb could refer to an entire vat of fat having fallen into the fire (which would certainly burn the entire building down) or, more seriously, to a vat of gunpowder (which would certainly blow the entire building up). It is true that a number of basic Eng. words beginning with *f-* changed to initial *v-* under Norman French influence in the early M.E. period, esp. in southern England (compare *fixen* → *vixen*), but this alternative suggestion is reminiscent of the mispronounced password in the movie *Under the Rainbow*: "The pearl is in the *river*" (for "The pearl is in the *liver*"). AID; BDPF; CI; DC; DEI; HB; HI; HND; LCRH; MS; NSOED; PT; WNWCD.

FAT LIP   *See* Fat (adj.).

FAT LOT OF   *See* Fat Cat.

FAT OF THE LAND   *See* Fat (n).

FAT PART OF THE BAT   *See* Fat (adj.).

FAT PITCH   *See* Fat (adj.).

FAT PROFIT   *See* Fat (adj.).

FAT ROLE   *See* Fat (adj.).

FATTED CALF   *See* Kill the Fatted Calf.

FATTEN (UP)   *See* Kill the Fatted Calf.

FAT TONE   *See* Fat (adj.).

FAT WALLET   *See* Fat (adj.).

FAT YEAR   *See* Fat (adj.).

FAUX APPLE PIE   *See* Mock Apple Pie.

FEAST   *a feast.* A periodic religious celebration; a special honorary dinner. Source: FEAST (n). MWCD: 13th cent. It is difficult to say whether the first *feast* was secular or sacred, or whether it featured feasting or fasting, because in Ancient Rome, where Lat. *festum* first appeared, the religious and popular worlds were totally entwined. Today, the Christian churches observe what are called, in Roman Catholic terms, "movable" and "immovable" feasts. A *movable feast*, such as Easter, which occurs anywhere from late March to late April, does not fall on the same date every year; whereas an *immovable feast*, such as Christmas, which always occurs on December 25, is one that does. The other *feast*, the eating kind, hearkens to the Roman feast in a wealthy person's villa, where the guests lay on benches and reached for viands on serving tables—or to an English feast at the court of Henry VIIIth, where noblemen sat on benches and reached for whole hams on the table in front of them. A *banquet* (MWCD: 15th cent.) of this latter sort is derived fr. O.It. *banchetto*, the dim. of *banca* "bench." Today, a *banquet* is a sumptuous *feast*, with lots of food, eaten by lots of people in semiformal attire, who are gathered to celebrate an occasion or to honor a person. The modern *feast* can also be something other than food that provides pleasure or delight. Bond (James Bond) said to Moneypenny, "You're a *feast for my eyes*." The same sentiment can be expressed by the verb *feast*, which developed from the noun *feast*: "*Feast your eyes on* that!" The abundance of food at a feast is contrasted with the scarcity of food during a drought in the phrase *feast or famine* (a modification of the earlier *feast or fast*—DC: 1732), which has become a metaphor for an alternation of successes and failures over a period of time: "It's been *feast or famine* for the team this year." Derived from the same source as *feast* are *festival* (MWCD: 1589) "an extended celebration of cultural events"; *festive* (MWCD: 1651) "suitably joyful for a feast"; and *-fest* (LA: 1856), a combining form for identifying various types of joyful gatherings: e.g., a *gabfest* (MWCD: 1897), a *songfest* (MWCD: 1912), and a *slugfest* (MWCD: 1916). BDPF; CE; DAI; DAP; DAS; DC; EWPO; HDAS; HI; HND; MS; NSOED; WNWCD.

FEAST FOR THE EYES   *See* Feast.

FEAST OR FAMINE   *See* Feast.

FEAST OR FAST   *See* Feast.

FEAST YOUR EYES ON   *See* Feast.

FED UP   *to be fed up.* To have had all you can take of someone or something. MWCD: 1900. Source: FEED (v). MWCD: O.E. To be *fed* (without *up*) is to be provided with enough food to amount to one meal, whether you eat it or not. To be *fed up* is strictly a metaphor. Instead of food, you are "fed" a steady "diet" of annoying, boring, disgusting, exasperating, or tiring data until you reach the point where you are *fed up to here* (patting the bottom of your chin with the back of your hand) with worthless information. "*Here*" is the place where the gills would be if people were fish, and Americans also say, "I'm *fed up to the gills* (with someone or something)." (The British say, "I'm *fed up to the back teeth*.") AID; CE; CI; DAI; DEI; HND; MS.

FED UP TO HERE   *See* Fed up.

FED UP TO THE BACK TEETH   *See* Fed up.

FED UP TO THE GILLS   *See* Fed up.

FEED (n)   *See* Cut the Feed.

FEED A COLD, STARVE A FEVER   *See* Starve (v).

FEEDBACK   Intentional or unintentional return of part of the output of an electronic system as part of the input. MWCD: 1920. Source: FEED (v). MWCD: O.E. Intentional feedback is (1) an automatic, self-correcting feature built into electronic systems to improve the quality of their output, or (2) an invited response by an audience to a speaker or writer. Unintentional feedback is either (1) the volume overload of a public address system, as when you speak into the microphone and the result is a loud humming sound, or (2) the *delayed feedback* in a large outdoor stadium when the amplified sound echoes off the stadium walls and returns to your ears while you are uttering the next sentence. (Singers of the National Anthem at baseball parks sometimes find it impossible to remember the words under such conditions.) Delayed-feedback machines are used in speech pathology laboratories to show students what it's like to stutter. NSOED; WNWCD.

FEEDING FRENZY   *a feeding frenzy.* A frantic scramble toward an attractive object or goal. MWCD: 1973. Source: FEED (v). MWCD: O.E. The feeding habits of certain predatory fishes, such as barracudas, piranhas, and sharks, feature mass attacks on live prey, such as other fish and even humans. If a large chunk of raw meat is thrown into the water, the fish not only attack it at once but attack each other in the process. The scene is not unlike that of a pack of wolves—or a flock of vultures—converging on a fresh carcass. Unfortunately, the scene is also like that of a crowd of adults fighting for a bargain at a blue-light special or a crowd of adolescents fighting for a spot in front of the stage at a rock concert. SA.

FEED SOMEONE A LINE   *See* Feed Your Face.

FEED THE BALL   *See* Feed Your Face.

FEED THE BULLDOG   *See* Feed Your Face.

FEED THE FIRE   *See* Feed Your Face.

FEED THE FISH(ES)   *to feed the fish (or fishes).* To drown at sea; to become *fish food.* Source: FEED (v); FISH. MWCD: O.E. Literally, to feed the fish(es) is simply to feed the tropical fish in a tank at home or go to the local lake or stream and toss in pieces of bread for the fish to eat. At sea, however, and in some of the large rivers of the world, carnivorous fish such as sharks, barracuda, and piranha prefer more substantial food, such as a human body. Metaphorically, a person who is now *feeding the fishes* either fell in the treacherous waters accidentally or was pushed in, murdered and thrown in, or fitted with concrete shoes and dumped in. Considering that *feed the fishes* is prob. a gangster term, the last three explanations are the most likely. Outside of the criminal world, the term also has the meaning "to throw up, or relieve yourself, over the side of a boat or ship" (HDAS: 1870). BDPF; DEI; NSOED; SA.

FEED THE IMAGINATION   *See* Feed Your Face.

FEED THE KITTY   *See* Feed Your Face; Sweeten the Kitty.

FEED YOUR FACE   *to feed your face.* To eat. Source: FEED (v). MWCD: O.E. Alliteration prob. had a lot to do with the development of this idiom; otherwise, it might have turned out as "feed your mouth" or "feed your stomach." Actually, it's the entire body that is fed, not a particular part of it. Other metaphors that employ the verb *feed* are (1) *to feed the fire* (of dissent, revolt, unrest, etc.) "to strengthen the efforts of an unpopular cause"; (2) *to feed the imagination* "to stimulate the imagination and help it to grow"; (3) *to feed the kitty* "to ante money into the pot before the next hand (of poker)"; (4) *to feed the bulldog* (usu. neg.: *That doesn't feed the bulldog*) "to solve—or not solve—the problem"; (5) *to feed someone a line* "to fill someone full of lies"; and (6) *to feed the ball* (to a teammate) "to pass off the basketball to a teammate instead of shooting it yourself." AID; CE; DAS; MS; NSOED; SA. *See also* Feed the Fish(es); Sweeten the Kitty.

FEEL LIKE A PIECE OF MEAT   *See* Meat.

FEEL LIKE A WET DISHRAG   *See* Taste like Dishwater.

FEEL LIKE DEATH WARMED OVER   *See* Look like Death Warmed over.

FEEL YOUR OATS   *to feel your oats.* For an animal or a human to feel eager, energetic, excited, exuberant, feisty, frisky, lively, peppy, playful, or spirited. Animal (HDAS: 1831); human (HDAS: 1908). Source: OATS. MWCD: O.E. The animal that lit. "feels its oats" is the horse, whose main diet is alfalfa or clover hay but whose special diet is high-energy oats, the kind of feed that is placed in its feed box or feed bag. After a meal of oats, a horse is likely to become friskier than usual and to behave more like a colt or filly than a gelding or mare. Oats are so closely associated with the horse—the only domesticated animal that prefers them—that the horse is sometimes referred to as the *oat-eater* (or *oat-burner*—HDAS: 1916), and a Western novel or film is sometimes called an *oater* (MWCD: 1946), a term that has never quite replaced *horse opera* (MWCD: 1927). *To know your oats* is for a person to be a good judge of talent, based on the reputation that an old cowboy has of being a good judge of horseflesh. *To sow your wild oats* (HI: mid-16th cent.) is for a young man to get his youthful urges out of his system so that they will not interfere with his life as an adult. *Wild oats* (MWCD: 15th cent.) are not oats at all but offensive weeds. AID; BDPF; CE; CI; DAFD; DAI; DAP; DC; DEI; EWPO; FLC; LCRH; MDWPO; MS; NSOED; SA. *Compare* Know Your Onions.

FEST   *See* Feast.

FESTIVAL   *See* Feast.

FESTIVE   *See* Feast.

FIG   *See* Not Worth a Fig.

FIG LEAF   *a fig leaf.* A camouflage, concealment, or cover-up of improper or illegal activities or materials. Source: FIG. MWCD: 14th cent. The large, triangular leaves of the fig tree were first used to "conceal" in the Garden of Eden, when Adam and Eve, who had just eaten the *forbidden fruit* (q.v.) of the tree of the knowledge of good and evil, realized that they were naked and sewed fig leaves together to hide their nakedness (Genesis 3:7). The practice was revived in the 19th cent. by painters and sculptors who covered the genitals of the figures of humans in their works of art with a single fig leaf each—in order to comply with the conservative morals of their Victorian patrons. Nowadays, *fig leaves* are feeble attempts by corrupt politicians and crooked entrepreneurs to cover up their illegal activities, although the public can see right through them. BDPF; EWPO; WNWCD.

FILLED TO THE BRIM   *to be filled to the brim.* To be chock-full of food and drink; to be showered with good fortune; to be overcome with emotion. HND: early-17th cent. Source: BRIM. MWCD: 13th cent. Refusing another helping of food or refill of drink, a guest might say to the host or hostess, "I'm *filled to the brim,*" an expression that is based on the condition of a cup or glass that is filled with liquid up to the very top. Like the vessel, the guest's alimentary canal is filled from the bottom of the stomach to the top of the esophagus. The earliest metaphorical use of this expression occurs in Shakespeare's *Antony and Cleopatra* (ca. 1607), Act III, Scene 13, lines 17–19, when Euphronius says to Antony: "To the boy Caesar send this grizzled head, / And he will *fill thy wishes to the brim* / With principalities" [italics added]. In this passage, Antony's wishes are likened to cups, which can be filled full with spoils. By the 19th cent., the metaphor had become associated with emotions, such as happiness and delight, pride and satisfaction. In Gilbert and Sullivan's *Mikado* (1885), the three little maids describe themselves as being "filled to the brim with girlish glee," and 20th cent. parents were often

pictured tearing up with pride and satisfaction at the high school or college grad-
uation of their "little maids." In this latter case, the emotion that *filled* the parents
to the brim has overflowed, resulting in falling tears. The adj. *brimful*, in the sense
of being *filled to the brim*, dates to the early-16th cent. (MWCD: 1530), and the
noun derived from it appears in a passage from Shakespeare's *Henry V* (Act I,
Scene 2, lines 146–150), in which King Henry says: "[M]y great-grandfather /
Never went with his forces into France / But that the Scot on his unfurnish'd
kingdom / Came pouring like the tide into a breach, / With ample and *brimfulness*
of his force" [italics added]. From the noun *brim* developed a verb *brim* (MWCD:
1611) that is now usu. used with *over*, as in *to be brimming over* (with enthusiasm,
passion, etc.). DC; NSOED.

FILL THE POT   *See* Go to Pot.

FILL UP ON SWEETS   *See* Sweets to the Sweet.

FIND SOMETHING HARD TO SWALLOW   *See* Hard to Swallow.

FINE KETTLE OF FISH   *See* Kettle of Fish.

FINE MESS   *a fine mess.* (An oxymoron.) A nice predicament. Source: MESS.
MWCD: 14th cent. Oliver Hardy (the tall, fat one in the Laurel and Hardy films
of the 1920s), used to say to Stan Laurel (the short, skinny one), "Now isn't this
a *fine mess* you've gotten us into!" The viewers were prob. not aware that *mess*,
meaning "trouble" or "difficulty," is derived, ultimately, from *mess* that once meant
"food," specifically that portion of food that was brought to the table at a single
time (i.e., a *course*) or the items of food of the same sort that made up a single
dish (e.g., a *mess of peas* or a *mess of fish*). Eventually, *mess* came to mean (1) a
mixture of things served and eaten together at a meal, (2) the mixed group of
people who partake of that meal (the *messmates*—MWCD: 1746), (3) the place
where such a meal is regularly served (a *mess hall*—MWCD: 1862), and finally,
(4) the condition that resembles an eating place after the meal is over: *a mell of a
hess* ("a hell of a mess"). Metaphorically, a dog can now *make a mess* on the rug,
a child can *make a mess* in the bathroom, and an adult can *make a mess* of his/her
life. In the book of Genesis (25:33), Esau, the older (by minutes) son of Isaac and
Rebekah, sold his birthright to his twin brother, Jacob, for *a mess of pottage*, i.e.,
a bowl of red soup. In the U.S. Army, a mess hall in the field is called a *mess tent*,
to which the soldiers are summoned by a *mess call*; in the U.S. Navy, the *officers'
mess* is both the place on the ship where the officers eat and the meal that they
eat there. Shortly after the noun *mess* was borrowed from M.Fr. *mes*, a verb *mess*
developed with the basic meaning of "to interfere with or bother." This verb
combined with different adverbs to form several idioms: to *mess (around) with*
(someone's car, someone's daughter), to *mess up* (your hair, your career), and to
mess in (someone else's affairs). *Mess up* can also be used without a complement

to mean "do something wrong," and *messed up* can mean both "confused" and "intoxicated." AID; BDPF; CI; DAFD; DAI; DAS; DEI; MDWPO; MS; NSOED; PT. *Compare* Kettle of Fish.

FINGER BOWL   *See* Finger Food.

FINGER FOOD   Food that is eaten while being held in the fingers. MWCD: 1928. Source: FOOD. MWCD: O.E. *Fingers were made before forks* (CODP: 1738), and before 1620, the year in which the table fork was introduced into England, all solid food was *finger food*. Before that time, breads and meats were either speared with a knife or reached for with the fingers. After that date, solid foods were divided into those that could be eaten from the fingers, such as chicken legs, and those that had to be cut up and raised to the mouth with a fork, such as a chicken breast. In modern times the number of *finger foods* has increased dramatically, primarily as a result of the invention of the *sandwich* (q.v.), the discovery of the *barbecue* (q.v.), and the advent of the *fast-food restaurant* (q.v.). Today, *finger sandwiches* (q.v.) are even eaten at formal teas, where *finger bowls* (MWCD: ca. 1860) are provided; *hors d'oeuvres* (q.v.) are picked up with the fingers at cocktail parties; corn on the cob is held with both hands at *picnics* (q.v.); and *pizzas* (q.v.) are eaten from the fingers at school cafeterias. However, some Americans still eat a sandwich or a slice of pizza by cutting it up with a knife and raising it to the mouth with a fork, in the Continental European style; and some teenagers regard just about any food, even cake and pie, as *finger food*, at least while their parents aren't watching. BDPF; DAFD; DAP; EWPO; WNWCD.

FINGER IN EVERY PIE   *See* Have a Finger in Every Pie.

FINGER IN THE PIE   *See* Have a Finger in Every Pie.

FINGER SANDWICH   *a finger sandwich.* A small, crustless sandwich served as an appetizer. LA: 1870s. Source: SANDWICH. MWCD: 1762. The *finger sandwich*, a type of *finger food* (q.v.), was orig. called a "reception sandwich" or "tea sandwich" in Britain. In America, the finger sandwich consists of either (1) a single piece of bread with the crust removed, cut in a geometric shape, and topped with *sandwich spread* (a mixture such as ham salad, egg salad, or tuna salad) or (2) a miniature sandwich of two pieces of crustless bread, untoasted, *sandwiched* around a spread, cream cheese, or watercress. The bread that is used for making finger sandwiches is called *sandwich bread* (DAFD: ca. 1930s): pre-cut, thin-sliced, white bread, which, under its original name, *sandwich loaf*, was synonymous with "sliced bread" in the 1930s. Nowadays, the term *sandwich bread* can also refer to a "square" (in cross-section) loaf of sliced white or wheat bread that is perfectly designed for holding square luncheon meat.

FINGERS WERE MADE BEFORE FORKS   *See* Finger Food.

FIRE-EATER   *a fire-eater.* A performer at a circus or carnival who sticks the burning end of a baton into his/her mouth with no apparent ill effect. MWCD: 1672. Source: EAT. MWCD: O.E. The *fire-eater* does not really *eat* fire, but it does disappear into his/her mouth and is gone when the baton is withdrawn. From this act has grown the application of the term *fire-eater* to a hot-tempered, pugnacious, violent, or militant person who always seems eager to start a quarrel or pick a fight—and the adj. *fire-eating* (MWCD: 1819) to describe such a person: a "*fire-eating* radical." (If the individual is an orator, the adj. *fire-breathing* is often used.) A *fire-eater* is not to be confused with a *smoke eater*: a fire-fighter who lives on a steady diet of smoke during the course of his/her career. DAS; DEI; WNWCD.

FIRE-EATING   *See* Fire-eater.

FIRST CATCH YOUR HARE   *See* Recipe.

FIRST COME, FIRST SERVED   The early bird gets the worm. DAP: 1545 Source: SERVE. MWCD: 13th cent. When *Come and get it!* is shouted out to campers and cowboys, it is equivalent to *Chow time!* for soldiers and U.S. Marines—and to "The buffet is now open" for ladies and gentlemen. In all cases, the first one in line is the first to be served—or to serve him/herself to—the food. Without the call, the saying is also true of children at a school cafeteria, adults in an industrial cafeteria, customers at a drive-through restaurant, and guests at a sit-down restaurant. In the last-mentioned case, the diners are seated by a host or hostess and then greeted by a *server*, formerly known as a waiter or waitress, who announces, "My name is Dan/Dawn, and I'll be your server this evening." If you are in an upscale restaurant, your server will bring your dishes in stages, such as soup or salad, meat and potatoes, and coffee and dessert. However, if you are in a family-style restaurant, your server will bring many—or most—of the dishes at once: large platters from which you will serve yourself as they are passed around—or rotated on a *lazy Susan* (MWCD: 1917)—just as at home or in a boarding house. Whatever the case, your service will not be like that in the 15th and 16th cents., when roasted meat was "dressed" on a kitchen sideboard called a *dresser* (now serving as a "chest of drawers"), then carried to a sideboard in the dining room called a *credenza*, where it was placed on a tray called a *salver* and taste-tested to make sure ("have credence") that it was not poisoned but was safe to eat. Nowadays, playwrights can also *serve up* a lot of laughs in a Broadway show, and pitchers can *serve up* a lot of fast balls at the old ball game. BDPF; CODP; DAI; DEI; EWPO; MDWPO; NSOED; PT.

FIRST FRUITS   *See* Fruits of Your Labors.

FIRST WATER   *See* Long Drink of Water.

FISH BOIL   *See* Kettle of Fish.

FISH EGGS   *See* Caviar.

FISH FOOD   *See* Feed the Fish(es).

FISHY   *to seem fishy.* To appear to be doubtful, dubious, questionable, or suspicious. DC: 1844. Source: FISH. MWCD: O.E. Food *tastes fishy* if it has been fried in an unwashed pan in which fish was previously fried, and a room *smells fishy* if fish is being fried there or has recently been fried there (MWCD: 15th cent.). (The room smells even "fishier" if the fish is spoiled to start with.) On a higher metaphorical level, a deal *sounds fishy* if it seems too good to be true, and a "like-new" car *looks fishy* if its fenders have been hammered out and its windshield is cracked. Either of these conditions might cause you to be suspicious of the quality of the offer being made or the merchandise being peddled. HND; IRCD; MS; SA.

FLANNEL CAKE   *See* Pancake (n).

FLAPJACK   *See* Pancake (n).

FLASH IN THE PAN   *a flash in the pan.* A person or thing that starts out with great success but ends up with disappointing failure a short time later. MWCD: 1901. Source: PAN. MWCD: O.E. A flash in a cooking pan is what occurs when hot grease reaches its ignition point and bursts into flames. However, in this idiom the *pan* is the depression below the hammer of a muzzle-loading flintlock musket that holds a small amount of gunpowder, and the *flash* is the flare-up of the powder in this pan when the trigger is pulled and the hammer causes a flint to strike a spark. When the primary powder ignites but is insufficient to travel through the small hole leading to the barrel, where the main charge is located, or when the main charge itself is damp or otherwise ineffective, the "flash in the pan" is the only explosion that occurs. That is, the process starts out well but ends in failure. When a hot new prospect explodes on the scene, everyone is excited to see how he/she will turn out; if he/she soon fizzles, then he/she is a *flash in the pan.* The same is true of a new business product that turns out to be only an overnight sensation. AID; CI; DAI; DC; DEI; EWPO; HI; HND; LCRH; MDWPO; MS; NSOED; SA.

FLAT AS A CHEESE SOUFFLÉ   *to be—or fall—as flat as a cheese soufflé.* To be as flat as a pancake; to fall from grace into disgrace. Source: SOUFFLÉ. MWCD: 1813. The *soufflé* (fr. Fr. *souffler* "to blow or puff up") is the king of high-rise baking, and the *cheese soufflé* is the highest riser of all. The lightness of the soufflé is caused by the large proportion of egg whites in the batter, which also includes an egg-yolk sauce, along with the milk-rich cheese. When baked, the dish begins to puff up, rising above the bowl like a huge popover. But the diners never see that because the minute the dish is taken from the oven, the top deflates, leaving what looks like the plastic over a swimming pool in wintertime. FLC.

FLAT AS A PANCAKE   *as flat as a pancake.* Extremely flat or thin. HND: 1542. Source: PANCAKE. MWCD: 14th cent. American pancakes are round and flat and vary in thickness from approx. one-quarter to approx. one-half inch. (Other "pancakes," such as blintzes, crepes, and tortillas, are much thinner.) Things that can be described as being *as flat as a pancake* include flat tires, women's chests, and Wile E. Coyote (after falling off a cliff or being run over by a steamroller in a Roadrunner cartoon). To knock someone *(as) flat as a pancake* (or *flatter than a pancake*) is to knock that person flat on his/her back. In the fall of 1996, a *pancake award* in college football was given to an offensive lineman who knocked his opponent *as flat as a pancake* with a *pancake block. To fall flat as a pancake* is what a joke does when nobody laughs at it. *Pancake ice* is small floes of ice in freshwater lakes in early or late winter. AID; BDPF; CE; DAI; DC; DEI; NSOED. *See also* Pancake (v).

FLATTER THAN A PANCAKE   *See* Flat as a Pancake.

FLATWARE   *See* Full Plate; Silverware.

FLAVOR   *See* Flavor of the Month.

FLAVOR OF THE MONTH   *the flavor of the month.* The person or thing that is recognized as being the most popular during the past month or judged to be the most promising during the coming month. Source: FLAVOR. MWCD: 14th cent. *Flavor* started out as a bad odor or smell but soon developed into a pleasant fragrance or aroma; then it became a combination of the smell and taste of food. The "flavor of the month" was orig. a variety of ice cream that was featured by a popular ice-cream parlor shortly after WWII. More recently, the phrase has been used fig. to describe (1) a celebrity who is judged to be the favorite personality of the month (or a companion with whom the celebrity has chosen to share his/her limelight for the coming month) or (2) a product that either achieves popularity for a brief period or is selected by the retailer to be featured in advertising for a short time. At any rate, the person or product enjoys only fleeting fame or fortune. MS. *Compare* Catch of the Day; Soup du Jour.

FLETCHERISM   *See* Fletcherize.

FLETCHERIZE   *to fletcherize your food.* To chew each bite of food thirty-two times (once for each tooth) before swallowing it. Source: CHEW. MWCD: O.E. *Fletcherism* (HI: 1903) was a program of nutrition promoted by American Horace Fletcher in his book *The ABC of Nutrition*, which was extremely popular throughout the country in the first two decades of the 20th cent. Of Fletcher's three main rules—(1) eat when hungry, (2) eat small amounts, (3) chew thirty-two times—the last one received the most attention and bore his name (although it really belonged to Brit. Prime Minister William Gladstone, who had advocated it in the preceding century). People took fletcherizing quite seriously; but besides the supposed nutritional benefits, it severely limited the amount of talk at the dinner table and considerably lengthened the amount of time it took to finish the meal. Fletcherism had some strong and influential supporters until the 1930s, when it rapidly faded away. Today, only persons born in the early-20th cent. remember the program—and still practice it! DAFD; EWPO.

FLIP YOUR LID   *See* Blow the Lid off.

FLOOR LOOKS CLEAN ENOUGH TO EAT OFF/ON   *See* Eat Nails.

FLOUR   The flower of meal. Source: FLOUR. MWCD: 13th cent. In early-M.E., *flour* and *flower* were both spelled *flour* (fr. O.Fr. *fleur* "flower") because the one destined to acquire the meaning "finely ground grain" was derived from the one that already had the meaning "blossom"—and was developing a figurative meaning "the finest." Specifically, M.E. *flour* developed fr. the O.Fr. phrase *fleur de farine* "the flower of meal," i.e., "the finest meal that could poss. be ground." As the two M.E. *flours* developed, it was the one meaning "blossom" that changed its spelling, to *flower*, not the one with the figurative meaning, which remained *flour*. At any rate, it was the grinding of grain beyond the stage of *meal* (MWCD: O.E.), which is coarse, and eliminating the unwanted matter, by sifting, that earned the new product the title of "the flower of meal": soft, silky, powdered grain, or *flour*. Modern wheat flour has been further refined by bleaching and eliminating the bran, although in the 1970 there began a movement to restore the original appearance and content of bread and rolls by discontinuing the bleaching and the elimination of bran. DAFD; FLC; MDWPO; NSOED; WNWCD. *See also* Grist for the Mill.

FLOWER   *See* Flour.

FLYING SAUCER   *a flying saucer*. A UFO. MWCD: 1947. Source: SAUCER. MWCD: 1607. Ever since the first unidentified flying object, or UFO, was reportedly sighted in 1947, this alien spacecraft has been described as looking like an inverted saucer, i.e., round, flat, and slightly domed on top. (It also reportedly has lights on the rim and can revolve, hover, and dart off at great speed.) The saucer that the UFO resembles is the normal accompaniment to a cup, as of coffee or tea, at upscale restaurants. There is a slight indentation on the inside of the saucer into which the matching cup fits precisely, ruling out the possibility of using an unmatched cup and saucer. Interestingly enough, the saucer was orig. designed not to hold a cup but to hold *sauce* (MWCD: 14th cent.), which is what it held in the late Middle Ages. Before that time, cups sat directly on the table, as they do today in many homes and family restaurants. It is also interesting to note that cups acquired handles at about the same time that they acquired saucers, although that may have been only a coincidence. In modern times, the term *saucer* has been applied not only to the UFO but to the satellite or microwave (TV) antenna, competing with the name of another piece of china: the *dish*. In the expression "The child's *eyes were as big as saucers*," the comparison is prob. to a demitasse (or "half-cup") saucer, which is still pretty big but is indicative of the child's amazement and delight at seeing, for example, a UFO. BDPF; DEI; WNWCD.

FLY IN MY SOUP   *See* Soup.

FODDER   *See* Cannon Fodder.

FOIE GRAS   *See* Chopped Liver.

FOOD CHAIN   *the food chain.* The hierarchy of predation. MWCD: 1926. Source: FOOD. MWCD: O.E. The *food chain* is characterized by the expression *Big fish eat little fish* (DAP: ca. 1200), with *fish* standing for animals in general (e.g., cats eat mice) and humans in particular (e.g., big companies eat little companies). An animal or human that is *low on the food chain* is known as a *bottom feeder* (q.v.), i.e., one who "preys" on nothing except garbage but is the "prey" of every other animal in the neighborhood. Animals or humans in the middle of the food chain are predators of those below and prey of those above; people in this category are called "middle management." At the top of the chain among animals are those that have no predators except humans, and for whom all other animals are prey; this would include the lion in Africa and the tiger in South Asia. Humans are at the top of the chain (or "ladder") on all continents, partly because of their wits, but mostly because of their weapons. CODP; NSOED; SA; WNWCD. *Compare* Food Pyramid.

FOOD FOR THOUGHT   *See* Brain Food.

FOOD FOR WORMS   *to be food for worms.* To be dead and buried—or dead and not buried. Source: FOOD. MWCD: O.E. In Shakespeare's *Henry IV, Part I* (ca. 1598), Act V, Scene 4, Henry (or Harry), the Prince of Wales, has mortally wounded Henry Percy (also known as Hotspur), who addresses himself in his final words: *Hotspur:* "No, Percy, thou art dust, and *food for*—" *Prince:* "*For worms,* brave Percy. Fare thee well, great heart!" [italics added]. The sentiment is expressed again a few years later in Shakespeare's *Hamlet* (ca. 1601), Act IV, Scene 3. A seemingly mad Hamlet is asked by his uncle, the new King of Denmark, the whereabouts of Polonius, whom Hamlet has just stabbed to death: *Hamlet:* "At supper." *King:* "At supper? Where?" *Hamlet:* "Not where he eats, but where he is eaten." (Hamlet then gives a description of a "cyclic," rather than a "ladder," food chain.) *Hamlet*: "A man may fish with the worm that hath eat of a king, and eat of the fish that hath fed of that worm." In spite of the allusion to fishing, the "worm" that feeds on dead bodies is not an angleworm but a maggot, the larva of a common housefly. An even earlier version of the metaphor, *wurmes fode* ("worm food," i.e., a dead body), can be found in the *Ancren Riwle* (ca. 1220). BDPF; DAS; HND; IRCD; NSOED; SA.

FOOD GUIDE   *See* Food Pyramid.

FOOD GUIDE PYRAMID   *See* Food Pyramid.

FOOD OF LOVE   *the food of love*. Music. (Shakespeare's *Twelfth Night*, ca. 1602). Source: FOOD. MWCD: O.E. This metaphor occurs in the very first line of the play as Orsino, Duke of Illyria, reclining in his palace and listening to music, speaks to his musicians: "If music be the *food of love*, play on, / Give me excess of it, that, surfeiting, / The appetite may sicken, and so die. / That strain again!" [italics added]. Orsino's appetite is for the Countess Olivia, whom he loves so much that it hurts. Just as an appetite for food can be satisfied by eating, perhaps his appetite for love can be satisfied by overdosing on what fuels it: music. It doesn't work. A few lines later, he countermands his order: "Enough, no more! / 'Tis not so sweet now as it was before. / O spirit of love, how quick and fresh art thou!"

FOOD PYRAMID   *the food (guide) pyramid*. The federal government's "guide to daily food choices." Source: FOOD. MWCD: O.E. The *food guide pyramid*, often referred to as the *food guide* or the *food pyramid*, and sometimes confused with the *food chain* (q.v.), is a "recommendation of daily allowances" for each of three, four, five, or six "food groups," depending on how you count them. When the *food guide* was introduced by the USDA in 1996, it was displayed in the form of a "pyramid" (actually, a triangle), divided into four horizontal "slabs," the middle two of which are divided into two approx. equal parts. The food group with the highest recommended daily allowance, "bread/cereal/rice/pasta," is at the bottom. On the second level from the bottom are "vegetables" and "fruits," with the former slightly exceeding the latter. On the next higher level are "dairy products" and "meat/eggs/beans/nuts," equally divided. At the top, in the smallest part of the pyramid, are "fats/oils/sweets," which may be eaten "sparingly" but are not really recommended at all. The *food guide pyramid* is sometimes printed on paper place mats in restaurants and can also be found on the side of a box of Ritz Crackers. DAFD.

FOR ALL THE TEA IN CHINA   *See* Not for All the Tea in China.

FORBIDDEN FRUIT   Illicit pleasure. DAP: ca. 1386. Source: FRUIT. MWCD: O.E. The term *forbidden fruit* was not used in the Bible, and its first appearance in the mid-17th cent. was as a metaphor; however, it is acknowledged that the metaphor was based on the story of Adam and Eve, the Garden of Eden, original sin, and the fall from grace. In Genesis 2:16–17, God informed Adam that he could eat the fruit of every tree in the Garden except that of the tree of the knowledge of good and evil, the penalty for which would be death. (Presumably Adam informed Eve, whose creation is described in 2:21–22.) In Genesis 3:1–5 the serpent convinced Eve that God had lied to Adam, and that instead of dying, she (and Adam) would become like gods, knowing good from evil. In Genesis 3: 6–7, Eve ate the fruit, Adam followed suit, they realized that they were naked, and they sewed fig leaves together for clothes. In Genesis 3:22–23, God banished Adam (and Eve) from Eden for fear that he would eat also of the tree of life and live forever. In modern times, *forbidden fruit* has become anything that is at the same time both (1) attractive, desirable, or tempting and (2) illegal, immoral, or sinful. For example, alcohol is attractive to a recovering addict, double chocolate cake is tempting to a dieter, and you may find your neighbor's spouse unbearably attractive; but these things are *forbidden fruit*. Incidentally, the type of tree that produced the biblical fruit has been thought to be an apple, an apricot, a pomegranate, or a fig. BDPF; DAS; DC; DEI; HND. *Compare* Adam's Apple.

FORCE MEAT   *See* Knock the Stuffing out of.

FOR GOOD MEASURE   *just for good measure.* Just to make sure that the minimum requirement has been met. Source: MEASURE. MWCD: 13th cent. In cooking, an extra amount is added to the ingredients by cooks just in case they have lost count of the number specified by the recipe: one, two, three, four, *and one for good measure.* The ingredient added is usu. a flavoring or seasoning, and the amount added is usu. what constitutes one shake from a bottle or jar (a *dash*), one heaping spoonful of a creamy substance (a *dollop*), or as much of a ground substance as can be held between the thumb and forefinger (a *pinch*). When the *good measure* is added to food cooking on the stove, it is sometimes expressed as *and one for the pot*; and when the bonus consists of an extra spank added to the posterior of a child at a birthday party, it is expressed as "and one to grow on." The measures themselves have become metaphors, as in *a dash of humor, a dollop of satire*, and *a pinch of jealousy* in a film, novel, or play. DAI, FLC; HND; NSOED.

FORKBALL   *See* Fork in the Road.

FORK IN THE ROAD   *a fork in the road.* The division of a road (or river) into two branches. IHAT: 1645. Source: FORK. MWCD: O.E. *Fork in the road* is a metaphor based on the resemblance between what happens to the road (or river, as in "South Fork") and what appears on the business end of a cooking utensil, such as a barbecue fork. The original *fork* was a primitive pitchfork, consisting of a sturdy stick from the end of which two smaller sticks branched off at a slight angle, forming a "V" (or a "Y," if the handle is counted). Most modern metaphors involving *fork* are of this sort, with two tines, or "prongs," in a "V" shape: (1) *to* *speak with forked tongue* (like the reptile's) is to deceive or mislead (MWCD: 1836); (2) *to fork over your money* (HDAS: 1839) with the fingers, or "forks" (HDAS: 1812), is to hand over money to a mugger or creditor; and (3) to throw a *forkball* (or "splitter") is to throw a baseball with the index and middle finger split apart. Even the humorous suggestion to *stick a fork in him and see if he's done* (i.e., has gotten enough sun) is based on the two-tined, medium-length fork for testing and turning the turkey at Thanksgiving, although the two tines are separated and form a "U" rather than a "V." (A *forklift*, MWCD: 1944, a machine for moving frozen turkeys around in a warehouse, also has two "tines" at the front in a "U" shape.) If the turkey is *fork-tender* (MWCD: 1973), it is *so tender you could cut it with a fork*; and if you eat too much turkey and fixings, you may be warned that you are *digging your grave with a knife and a fork* (EWPO: late-19th cent.), i.e., overeating to the point of gluttony. The multitined metal fork was the last of the three eating utensils—knives, forks, and spoons—to make it to the table in England, appearing as late as the 17th cent. (BDPF: ca. 1620), although it had prob. been used on the Continent as early as the 14th or 15th cent. AID; CI; DAI; DAS; DEI; MS.

FORKLIFT   *See* Fork in the Road.

FORK OVER THE MONEY   *See* Fork in the Road.

FORK-TENDER   *See* Fork in the Road.

FOR STARTERS   *See* Everything from Soup to Nuts.

FOR THE BIRDS   *See* Chicken Feed.

FRAGRANT MEAT   *See* Variety Meats.

FRANKFURTER   *See* Weenie.

FRANKLIN STOVE   *See* Slave over a Hot Stove All Day.

FRAPPÉ   *See* Milk Shake.

FREELOAD   *See* Parasite.

FREELOADER   *See* Parasite.

FREE LUNCH   *See* There's No Such Thing as a Free Lunch.

FREESTONE PEACH   *See* Peach.

FREEZER BURN   Discoloration of frozen food (esp. meat) as a result of improper wrapping. MWCD: 1926. Source: FREEZER. MWCD: 1847. *Freezer burn*
is an oxymoron, or "contradiction in terms": How can something be both cold
(i.e., freezing) and hot (i.e., burning up) at the same time? The answer is that
freezer burn is also a metaphor, meaning that the "burn" (or white spot) on a piece
of frozen meat looks very much like the burn (or white spot) on a person's flesh.
Freezer burns are caused when the material in which the meat is wrapped (paper,
foil, plastic) has allowed moisture to escape and caused the surface of the meat
to dry out. The original "freezer," an ice-cream freezer, was developed in the
1840s. It required ice for cooling and muscle for cranking. The modern version
still uses ice but offers an option of having an electric motor turn the beater. The
modern freezer, which freezes food solid rather than just chilling it, developed
after and from the first electric *refrigerator* (LA: 1916), part of which was eventually devoted to a freezer compartment. Following WWII, the freezer became a
separate home appliance, either as a "chest" or as an "upright" model. The material
in which the food (esp. meat) was wrapped was orig. waxed paper inside butcher's
paper or *tin foil* (MWCD: 15th cent.). Alternative materials now are plastic wrap
(inside butcher's paper) and *aluminum foil*. A sure way for a person to reveal
his/her age is to refer to a refrigerator/freezer as an *icebox* or to aluminum foil as
tin foil. CE; FLC; NSOED. *See also* Put on Ice.

FRENCH CUISINE   *See* Cuisine.

FRENCH-CUT   *See* French Fries.

FRENCH-FRIED ONION RINGS   *See* French Fries.

FRENCH-FRIED POTATOES   *See* French Fries.

FRENCH FRIES   *french fries* (or *French fries*). Deep-fried strips of potato.
MWCD: 1918. Source: FRY (v). MWCD: 13th cent. The *french* in *french fries* refers
not to the country (France) of their origin but to the method of cutting them into
narrow strips, also employed with *french-cut* green beans. The method was observed by Thomas Jefferson, ambassador to France, in 1785, who enjoyed the
deep-fried potato strips so much that he brought them back to America and called
them *French-fried potatoes*. The name was shortened to *French fries* during WWI
and was further reduced to *fries* (at least colloquially) in the late 1960s, at about
the same time that the capital *F* in *French* was reduced to lower case. In 1930,
the word *French fry* meant not only a "fried potato strip" but the process of frying
food in deep fat; and by 1945, battered and deep-fried circles of onion were called
French-fried onion rings. In Europe, what Americans call *french fries* are called
pommes frites ("fried potatoes") in France and *chips* (as in "fish and chips") in
England. DAFD; DAI; FLC; LA; MDWPO.

FRET (v)   *to fret.* To consume yourself with worry or anxiety. Source: FRET. MWCD: 12th cent. Humans consume themselves with worry or anxiety the way wild animals devour their prey: "voraciously," the original meaning of the word. On its journey from describing the eating habits of animals to the angst of humans, the verb *fret* also added the meanings "corrode, erode, fray, rub, chafe, grate, and gen. wear away." Eventually it developed the meaning "to cause someone to experience emotional strain" and "to become worried or anxious." In the early-20th cent., it was not unusual to hear someone say *Don't fret about it!* or *What are you fretting about?* This latter question has gen. been replaced today by *What's eating you?* which calls up an image of wolves or vultures feasting on your innards, but simply means "What's bothering you?" AID; BDPF; CE; CI; DAS; EWPO; SA. *Compare* Eat Your Heart out.

FRIDGE   *See* Icebox Cookies.

FRIED   *to be fried.* To be burned by the sun (NSOED: late-M.E.); to be executed in the electric chair (HDAS: 1928); to be high on drugs or alcohol (HDAS: 1923). Source: FRY (v). MWCD: 13th cent. Fried food is food that has been cooked in a large amount of fat (as in *deep-frying*) or a small amount of fat (as in *pan-frying*). The fat is absorbed into the surface of the food, and the heat of the fat changes the character of the food, shrinking it slightly and changing its color. A light-skinned person who has been severely burned by the sun not only has bright red skin but may even be suffering the disorienting effects of sunstroke. A person who is executed in the electric chair is subjected to a current that passes through the body and causes smoke to rise from the head. ("You're gonna fry for that" means that you're going to die for that, though not necessarily in the "chair.") A person who is high on drugs is sometimes out of his/her mind, talking and behaving wildly and uncharacteristically; i.e., his/her *brain is fried.* (A television commercial of the 1990s, warning against the use of drugs, displayed two eggs, representing the two hemispheres of the brain, and then showed the eggs snapping and crackling in a *frying pan*, representing the brain on drugs.) A person who is intoxicated is physically and mentally impaired by the overconsumption of alcohol. This last example may be the oldest of the four just given. DAI; DAS; FLC; IHAT.

FRIED CAKE   *See* Doughnut.

FRIED EGG   *a fried egg.* A "buried" lie (of a golf ball) in a sand trap, with only the top of the ball showing. HDAS: 1960. Source: FRY (v) (MWCD: O.E.); EGG (MWCD: 14th cent.). The partially buried golf ball looks very much like a fried egg, esp. one fried *sunny-side up* (MWCD: ca. 1901). The top of the ball (albeit white) represents the unbroken (yellow) yolk, and the clearly marked depression represents the (white) albumen. (*Sunny-side up* is itself a metaphor, comparing the yolk to the sun.) Telling someone to *go fry an egg* (HDAS: 1926) is not asking the person to hit a ball into a sand trap, but to "Beat it!" or "Get lost!" Similar imperatives involving *egg* are *Go lay an egg!* and *Go suck an egg!* (both of which *see*). When a pavement is *so hot you could fry an egg on it*, it is prob. at least 150°, which is so hot that you could also fry your bare feet on it. A *hobo egg* (DAFD: 1980) is an egg fried in a hole cut in the center of a piece of bread, a favorite dish for a camping trip. DAI; DAS; DC; IHAT.

FRIED GREEN TOMATO   *See* Tomato.

FRIES   *See* French Fries.

FROM SOUP TO NUTS   *See* Everything from Soup to Nuts.

FROM THE FRYING PAN TO THE FIRE   *See* Out of the Frying Pan into the Fire.

FROSTING   *See* Icing on the Cake.

FROSTING ON THE CAKE   *See* Icing on the Cake.

FROZEN DINNER   *See* Dinner (2).

FRUIT   *a fruit*. A male homosexual. HDAS: 1900. Source: FRUIT. MWCD: O.E. Horticulturally speaking, a fruit is the edible product of the flowering part of a plant. As a term for a human being, *fruit* was first applied to an adult male who was "gullible" (HDAS: 1894), and later to a homosexual or gay man. It is unclear why the word *fruit* was linked with homosexuals, although it may have had something to do with the association of the natural fruit with the flowering part of the plant and the negative stereotype of the homosexual male as an effeminate person. The adj. *fruity* orig. alluded only to the taste or aroma of ripe fruit (MWCD: 1657) but now can also describe anything that is excessively sweet or sentimental, such as a film, novel, or song. DAS; PT.

FRUIT BOAT   *See* Banana Boat.

FRUITCAKE   *a fruitcake*. A "nut"; a fool. MWCD: 1848. Source: FRUIT (MWCD: 12th cent.); CAKE (MWCD: 13th. cent.). A literal fruitcake is a winter holiday cake, in the shape of a small loaf of bread, that is noted for its weight, calories, and longevity. It contains a small amount of cake batter, mixed with fruit and nuts, and it can be made in a light (corn syrup, golden raisins, almonds, etc.) or dark (molasses, black raisins, walnuts, etc.) form. It is as heavy as a brick, loaded with calories, and able to survive in the back of the refrigerator for years (esp. if soaked in brandy or liquor and wrapped in aluminum foil). A person who is *as nutty as a fruitcake* (DC: 1935), or *nuttier than a fruitcake* (HND: ca. 1920), is either crazy or stupid, because nothing has as many nuts as, or more nuts than, a fruitcake. *Fruitcake* is also a derogatory term for a homosexual person. AID; CE; DAI; DAS; DC; FLC; HDAS; NSOED.

FRUIT COCKTAIL   *See* Shrimp Cocktail.

FRUITFUL   *See* Be Fruitful, and Multiply.

FRUITION   *See* Be Fruitful, and Multiply.

FRUITLESS   *See* Be Fruitful, and Multiply.

FRUIT OF THE LOOM   *See* Fruits of Your Labors.

FRUIT OF THE WOMB   *See* Fruits of Your Labors.

FRUIT SALAD   *See* Salad.

FRUITS OF YOUR LABORS   *the fruits of your labors.* The results of your hard work. Source: FRUIT. MWCD: O.E. The results of hard work can, like the fruits of trees (etc.), be either bitter or sweet. The *bitter fruits* result from either serious mistakes or evil intentions. For example, an incompetent architect can cause mass destruction as the result of the faulty design of a bridge or building, and a wicked dictator can cause the extinction of an entire minority of his/her subjects. The fruits are sweet when the labors are perfect and are based on good intentions. The *fruit of the loom* is a woven product resulting from long hours of hard work and tender care; and the *fruit of the womb* (as in the Roman Catholic "Hail Mary": "Blessed art thou among women, and blessed is *the fruit of thy womb*, Jesus" [italics added] fr. Luke 1:42) is the child born after labor. The *first fruits* (MWCD: 14th cent.) were orig. the first crops harvested, which were offered to the Lord, and are now, metaphorically, the first signs of success in a business or other endeavor. BDPF; DEI; EWPO.

FRUIT WITH APPEAL   *the fruit with appeal* ("a peel"). The banana. Source: BANANA. MWCD: 1597. The banana is an elongated tropical fruit with a soft, white, pulpy flesh and a soft yellow—when ripe—skin. It is usu. eaten by peeling the skin back a little ways and eating the flesh as if it were a Popsicle. When the banana is entirely consumed, the peel is carefully discarded because it is very slippery and can cause accidents such as those shown in cartoons or old movies, in which someone *slips on a banana peel* and falls over backwards. (Banana peels are so slippery that they have actually been used to launch large boats, such as tugboats.) The banana has a curved shape that resembles the profile of a sway-backed horse. The *banana pepper* is so named not only because it is soft and yellow but because it is long and curved; and the *banana seat* (MWCD: 1965) on a child's bicycle is an elongated seat with a pronounced curve from front to back. The *banana* (fr. Wolof *banāna*) was discovered in western Africa in 1482 by Portuguese explorers, who shared the discovery with the Spanish. Spanish explorers in the New World planted the first banana trees on the island of Hispaniola in 1516, where they competed with the native *plantain* trees, which produced what are now called *cooking bananas*. (The *pawpaw*, or *custard apple*, of North America is known as the *Indian banana*.) In Arabic, the *banana* is known as a "finger," and a bunch (or cluster) of bananas is known as a "hand." These terms have been borrowed by banana workers in the tropics of the Western Hemisphere, and the term *lady's fingers* has been coined to describe bananas that are about half the size of the regular, or "dessert," bananas. Another fruit, the *date* (MWCD: 14th cent.), is also named for a digit—Lat. *dactylus* "finger"—because of its size and shape. DAFD; EWPO; FLC; IHAT; NSOED; PT. *See also* Finger Food. *Compare* Ladyfingers.

FRUITY   *See* Fruit.

FRY (n)   *See* Small Fry.

FRYING PAN   *See* Fried.

FRY IN YOUR OWN GREASE   *See* Stew in Your Own Juice.

FUDGE (v)   *See* Fudge!

FUDGE!   *Oh, fudge!* Nonsense! (MWCD: 1766); Damn it! (HDAS: 1924). Source: FUDGE (v) (?). NSOED: early-17th cent. In this interjection, *fudge* appears to be a euphemism for some sort of expletive, but in the mid-18th cent. it simply meant "disbelief" or "disappointment." The noun *fudge* may have derived from the verb *to fudge*, meaning "to cheat or falsify," as in the expressions *to fudge the figures, to fudge the issue*, and *to fudge the rules*. However, it is quite a leap from cheating or falsifying to "nonsense," or, esp., to the soft chocolate candy made for the first time in the late-19th cent. (LA: 1890s). The story goes that *fudge* first acquired the meaning "hoax" in the early-19th cent. (LA: 1833), and this sense was applied to what the first fudgemakers did sixty years later. The "hoaxers" were students at various women's colleges in New England who used as their excuse for staying up late the fact that they were "making fudge" in their rooms. To make the hoax work, they actually did make what we now call *fudge* (DAFD: 1896)—the simplest possible combination of milk, sugar, butter, and chocolate flavoring (walnuts optional). In fact, a competition developed among the colleges regarding who could make the best fudge, which led to the creation of maple fudge, butterscotch fudge, and vanilla fudge. Eventually, the recipe was applied to *fudge frosting* (DAFD: 1898), *fudge brownies*, and *hot fudge sundaes* (DAFD: early-1900s), and no one cared any longer about the origin of the word or the "hoax" that the students were perpetrating. Today, the *fudge factor* (MWCD: 1962) shows up even in sophisticated mathematical calculations as a built-in "margin of error," lending justification to the notion of fudging. BDPF; CE; DAS; DEOD; EWPO; FLC; IHAT.

FUDGE BROWNIES   *See* Fudge!

FUDGE FACTOR   *See* Fudge!

FUDGE FROSTING   *See* Fudge!

FUDGE THE FIGURES   *See* Fudge!

FUDGE THE ISSUE   *See* Fudge!

FUDGE THE RULES   *See* Fudge!

FULL OF BALONEY   *See* Baloney!

FULL OF BEANS   *See* Not Worth a Hill of Beans.

FULL OF PISS AND VINEGAR   *See* Vinegar.

FULL OF PRUNES   *to be full of prunes*. To be full of hot air; to be talking nonsense. EWPO: ca. 1940. Source: PRUNE. MWCD: 14th cent. The expression *full of prunes* may have something to do with the fact that prunes are a natural laxative, and one of the consequences of laxative-taking is "natural" gas. Prunes are simply dried plums—plums that have been pitted and either allowed to dry in the sun or been forced to dry in a commercial dryer. The trick is to keep the plum/prune moist without spoiling or fermenting. The result is a small, chewy, bluish-black snack that stores well and tastes sweet—like raisins, which have the same relationship to grapes. However, whereas *plum* has a positive connotation ("My new car is a plum"), *prune* has a negative one. One of Dick Tracy's antagonists was the wrinkled Prune Face; oldsters with wrinkled skin are sometimes described as being *as wrinkled as a prune*; and an unpleasant adult of any age is sometimes referred to by children as an *old prune*. AID; CE; DAFD; DAI; DAP; FLC; NSOED; WNWCD.

FULL OF VINEGAR   *See* Vinegar.

FULL PLATE   *to have a full plate*. To have a busy schedule, a full agenda. Source: PLATE. WMCD: 14th cent. This metaphor is based on the dinner plate, which, when full of food, cannot hold any more. ("I won't offer you any more chicken because I can see that you have a full plate.") The predicament can also be expressed in such variations as "My *plate is full*"; "My *plate is a little full*"; "My *plate is too full* for me to take on any more responsibilities"; "I *have enough on my plate already*"; "My *plate is overflowing*"; and, the weakest of all, "I *have a lot on my plate at the moment.*" In most of these cases, the individual who is being offered more work is not necessarily being mean or indifferent and may really be sorry that he/she cannot accept the offer. The word *plate* (fr. O.Fr. *plate* "flat") is a cognate of Eng. *flat*, the base of the word *flatware* (MWCD: 1851), which refers not only to plates and platters but to knives, forks, and spoons in Amer. Eng. The reason for the grouping together of these serving and eating utensils is that the latter (the "silverware") were covered with silver *plate*, whereas the former (the "china") were simply flat. Modern examples of the metal plate are the ones that some people have in their heads (thin, but not flat), the "partial" *dental plate* (metal and plastic), the *printing plate* (for making real and counterfeit paper money), and the *license plate* (metal and flat). Nonmetal "plates" include *plate glass* (thick and flat), the *home plate* in baseball (thick, flat, hard rubber), the *blue plate special* (at an inexpensive restaurant or diner), and, of course, the *platter* (a vinyl record). *Platter* (MWCD: 13th cent.) lit. means "large plate," and platters come in both china and metal. Perhaps the most famous silver platter in history (actually a "charger") was the one that Herod's niece demanded that John the Baptist's head be brought to her on, as a reward for her "excellent" dancing. (And so it was.) A modern modification of that expression is the threat "I'll have your head on a (silver) platter (with an apple in your mouth)." In contrast, *to hand something to someone on a silver platter* is to give them a reward that was not earned, as Herod's niece's prob. wasn't. DAI; DEI; MS; NSOED; PT; WNWCD.

G

GABFEST *See* Feast.

GARBAGE *See* Garbage in, Garbage out.

GARBAGE IN, GARBAGE OUT Your output is only as good as your input. CODP: 1964. Source: GARBAGE. MWCD: 15th cent. If you feed *garbage* (inaccurate data) into your computer, it will spew *garbage* (useless information) out. The original meaning of *garbage* was "offal, refuse, or food waste," but the Eng. word prob. derives fr. It. *garbuglio* "confusion," which fits right in with the computer problem. In common language, *garbage* has come to mean "nonsense or gibberish," as in *to talk garbage* ("That's a *bunch of garbage*"); and a *garbage mouth* is someone who talks dirty or uses filthy language (*"Do you eat with that mouth?"*). A *garbologist* (EWPO: 1970s), in contrast, is an investigator who sorts through the garbage cans of celebrities to uncover their secrets ("You're *treating me like garbage*"). CE; DAP; DAS; NSOED; PT.

GARBAGE MOUTH *See* Garbage in, Garbage out.

GARBANZO BEAN *See* Pea Bean.

GARBOLOGIST *See* Garbage in, Garbage out.

GARDEN STATE *See* Truck Garden.

GARDEN-VARIETY *See* Truck Garden.

GARIBALDI   *See* Submarine Sandwich.

GARLIC   *See* Onionskin Paper.

GARLIC BREATH   *See* Onionskin Paper.

GARLIC EATER   *See* Onionskin Paper.

GARNET   *See* Pomegranate.

GARNISH (n)   *See* Garnish (v).

GARNISH (v)   *to garnish someone's wages.* For an employer to withhold, by order of the court, a certain amount of money from an employee's wages in order to repay a creditor. Source: GARNISH (v). MWCD: 14th cent. The original meaning of the verb *garnish* was "to decorate or embellish" (MWCD: 14th cent.), as in to add attractive and tasty touches to a plate of food before serving it. By the 16th cent. these edible adornments came to be known as either *garnishment* (MWCD: 1550) or simply *garnish (n)* (MWCD: 1596). (Today, popular garnishments are sprigs of parsley, wedges of lemon, cherry tomatoes, carved carrots, leaves of chocolate, etc.) By the 17th cent. the verb *garnish* had taken on the additional meaning of "to add an attachment to the wages of an employee, specifying that a portion of them be diverted to a creditor." The person whose wages were "attached" came to be known as the *garnishee* (n) (MWCD: 1627); and by the 19th cent. the act of attaching a person's wages could be expressed by the denominal verb *garnishee* (MWCD: 1876). FLC; NSOED, WNWCD.

GARNISHEE (n)   *See* Garnish (v).

GARNISHEE (v)   *See* Garnish (v).

GARNISHMENT   *See* Garnish (v).

GAS HOG   *See* Hog.

GEEK   *See* Bite Someone's Head off.

GEL (n)   *See* Gelatin.

GEL (v)   *See* Jell (v).

GELATIN   An animal-based "jelly." MWCD: 1800. Source: GELATIN. From the 14th cent. through the 18th cent., all foods that we now describe as "gelatins" and "jellies" were called *jellies*. After the word *gelatin* was borrowed from French in 1800, most animal-based "jellies" came to be called *gelatins*, and the word *jelly* was reserved for fruit-based "jellies." *Gelatin* now refers not only to the food produced by boiling down animal bones, hooves, horns, and skin but also to (1) the colloidal material resulting from the same process and used to thicken soups, puddings, ice cream, etc.; (2) a translucent sheet placed in front of a stop light; (3) a coating for photographic film (also called a *gel*); and (4) a soluble coating for pills and capsules. In recent years the short form, *gel* (NSOED: mid-20th cent.), has been applied to a shaving cream, a hairstyling mousse, and an antiperspirant ointment. DAFD; FLC; WNWCD.

GEORGIA ICE CREAM   *See* Grits.

GET ALL STEAMED UP   *See* Pressure Cooker.

GET BLOOD FROM A TURNIP   *See* You Can't Get Blood from a Turnip.

GET CANNED   *See* In the Can.

GET CAUGHT WITH YOUR HAND IN THE COOKIE JAR   *See* Caught with Your Hand in the Cookie Jar.

GET ON THE GRAVY TRAIN   *See* Ride the Gravy Train.

GET OUT OF MY KITCHEN   *See* Too Many Cooks Spoil the Broth.

GET THE CREATIVE JUICES FLOWING   *See* Juice.

GET YOUR FINGERS BURNED   *See* Slow Burn.

GET YOUR JUST DESSERTS   *to get—or receive—your just desserts.* To get what you deserve. Source: DESSERT (*). MWCD: 1600. Confusion surrounds this phrase. When it was first recorded (EWPO: before-1599), it was spelled *deserts*, as in the word from which it was derived (Fr. *deservir* "to deserve"), and it meant only punishment. However, because the word had always been pronounced like *desserts*, it came to be spelled that way by some writers, and it also broadened its meaning to include reward as well as punishment. Now, both spellings and meanings can be found. *Dessert* as a food is so called because it is the last course of a meal to be "served" (fr. Fr. *servir*) before the "table is cleared" (fr. Fr. *desservir*). That is, it follows the main course and precedes the clearing away of dishes from the table. Dessert usu. consists of a sweet dish such as cake, pie, or ice cream. AID; HND; IHAT; MDWPO.

GET YOUR TEETH INTO   *See* Sink Your Teeth into.

GINGER   Pep; spirit; vigor. HDAS: 1843. Source: GINGER. MWCD: O.E. The association of "pep" with *ginger* comes from the use of the ginger root, dried and powdered, as a seasoning, perfume, and medicine. As a seasoning, it is described as being pungent, aromatic, and spicy. The spiciness may have led to the use of the word *ginger* as a nickname for a girl or woman with bright red hair, although a case can also be made for a dropping of the first syllable of Virginia. At any rate, a light, reddish brown color now goes by the name *ginger*. It seems surprising that the adv. *gingerly* "carefully, cautiously" (MWCD: 1594) has such a contrasting meaning—until we learn that it is from an entirely different source: O.Fr. *genzor* "more delicate" + Eng.-*ly*. The spice *ginger* is, however, the basis for the words *ginger ale* "a sweetened, carbonated, ginger-flavored, nonalcoholic soft drink" (MWCD: 1886) and *ginger beer* (MWCD: 1809), which has the same ingredients as ginger ale except that the ginger extract is fermented. (Ginger beer is also a main ingredient, along with vodka, in the cocktail called a "Moscow mule.") BDPF; CE; DAFD; FLC; WNWCD. *See also* Gingerbread.

GINGER ALE   *See* Ginger.

GINGER BEER   *See* Ginger.

GINGERBREAD   Lavish, ornate, and superfluous ornaments, carvings, and other decorations on houses and furniture. NSOED: early-17th cent. Source: GIN-GERBREAD. MWCD: 15th cent. In baking, gingerbread is simply bread that is flavored with ginger and textured with molasses. However, the same dough that is used for the bread can be used to make *gingerbread cookies*, and these cookies are the basis for the application of the word to gaudy architecture. It seems that the favorite cookie in the 17th cent. was a *gingerbread man*: a spread-eagled man decorated with icing or cinnamon candies for the eyes, nose, mouth, buttons, belt, etc. Gingerbread figures were popular at Christmastime, and the most popular of all was the *gingerbread house*, made of hard, rectangular cookies "glued" together with icing and covered lavishly with both edible and inedible decorations. The association between the architecture of the Victorian-style house and the gingerbread house was first noticed in America in the 19th cent., and in the middle of the 20th cent. *gingerbread* had spread to jazz music to describe piano flourishes that were not art but simply decorations: fluff, filler. BDPF; IHAT; FLC; HDAS.

GINGERBREAD COOKIE   *See* Gingerbread.

GINGERBREAD HOUSE   *See* Gingerbread.

GINGERBREAD MAN   *See* Gingerbread.

GIRDLE CAKE   *See* Hot off the Griddle.

GIVE SOMEONE THE COLD SHOULDER   *See* Cold Shoulder.

GLASS IS HALF EMPTY   *The glass is half empty; the glass is half full.* We're in trouble; we're in good shape. Source: GLASS. MWCD: O.E. These two conflicting views of the same thing are characteristic of the positions of pessimists (*half empty*) and optimists (*half full*). Presumably they are both looking, from the side, at a transparent drinking glass in which the liquid contents are at the halfway mark. The pessimist worries that half of the liquid is already gone, assuming that the glass was once full in the first place; the optimist rejoices that half of the liquid is present, making no assumption about how it got there. The two would prob. argue the same way if they were looking at an *hourglass* (Time is running out; time is almost standing still) or through the *crystal* of a wristwatch (It's thirty minutes to eleven already; It's only half past ten). Although there is no correct answer to this conundrum, the evidence does seem to support the pessimist, because he/she is more aware of movement, whereas the optimist is more aware of status. Neither one of them noticed that the *glass* they were looking at was actually made of rigid plastic—and would be called a *cup* if it were opaque or flexible—or that the *eyeglasses* they were both looking through actually had plastic lenses. The *drinking glass* is named for the material—melted and cooled silicates, i.e., *glass*—that it is made from, but the actual date of the molding of the first drinking glass is unknown. Several other cooking, serving, and eating utensils have since been fashioned from glass, such as bowls, pans, pitchers, cups, saucers, plates, and even salad forks and spoons. When such glass is of a very high quality, it is referred to as *crystal* (NSOED: mid-17th cent.). CI; DAP; DEI; HND.

GLASS IS HALF FULL   *See* Glass Is Half Empty.

GLOBALONEY   *See* Baloney!

GLUTTON   *See* Glutton for Punishment.

GLUTTON FOR PUNISHMENT   *a glutton for punishment.* One who finds pleasure in service to others. Source: GLUTTONY. MWCD: 13th cent. The biblical *glutton* was someone who was obsessed with food and drink, and *gluttony* was one of the seven deadly sins. In modern times the word *gluttony* continues to refer to excessive eating and drinking but has added the meaning of excessive hunger for just about anything. A *glutton for punishment*, for example, likes hard, dirty work and is the first to volunteer for the job that nobody else wants. He/she is not exactly a masochist, who enjoys pain, or a martyr, who looks forward to death. When someone says, "I'm *no glutton for punishment*, but . . . ," it is usu. both a prelude to an acceptance of a difficult job and a disclaimer of any obsession with pain or death. CE; CI; MS; NSOED.

GLUTTONY   *See* Glutton for Punishment.

GO BANANAS   *to go bananas*. To go wild or crazy. MWCD: 1968. Source: BANANA. MWCD: 1597. Monkeys in the zoo go wild when they see the keeper approaching with a large bunch of bananas—the favorite tropical fruit of these tropical primates; and they go crazy if their keeper delays in handing out the bananas or if he/she teases them before giving up the goodies. The monkeys' emotions range from pleasure—in the realization that food is on the way—to frustration—over the fact that it is taking so long to get there. Children *go bananas* over the thought of going to the fast-food restaurant or the movies, and their parents *go bananas* if their team is winning the Super Bowl or the World Series. These are the pleasurable reactions. Children also *go bananas* when they have to clean their room or mow the lawn as a precondition to having fun, and their parents *go bananas* trying to enforce the conditions. These are the frustrating reactions. The situation becomes serious when the children actually start to behave like animals and the parents complain that they are *driving them bananas* (MWCD: 1968). Adults also can be *driven bananas* by loud music, loud parties, and loud cars. AID; CE; CI; DAI; DAS; DC; DEI; SA.

GOBBLE UP   *See* Devour.

GO DUTCH   *See* Dutch Treat.

GO FROM THE FRYING PAN TO THE FIRE   *See* Out of the Frying Pan into the Fire.

GO FRY AN EGG   *See* Fried Egg.

GO LAY AN EGG   *See* Lay an Egg.

GO NUTS   *See* Nuts about.

GOOBER   *See* Peanut.

GOOBER PEA   *See* Peanut.

GOOD EGG   *a good egg*. An agreeable, considerate, friendly, good-natured, kind, trustworthy, and wholesome person (usu. male). HDAS: 1871. Source: EGG. MWCD: 14th cent. A good chicken's egg is one that is not cracked, does not smell, and when held in front of a candle or other bright light reveals no evidence of a broken yolk, blood clots, or a tiny baby chick. A person who is a *good egg* is also observed to be without flaws in his/her behavior when viewed in the bright light of day. *Good egg* is often uttered reluctantly, however, as if such "nice guys" were regarded as being too good to be true. CE; DAI; HI; HND; LA; PT; SA. *Compare* Bad Egg; Rotten Egg.

GOOD FOR YOU   *See* Brain Food.

GOOD TASTE   *to have good taste.* To have excellent judgment of beauty and quality in the arts and entertainment, home decorating and furnishing, automobiles and clothing, food and drink, and male and female companions. Source: TASTE (n). MWCD: 14th cent. A good judge of beauty and quality, as evidenced by one's preferences and purchases, is known as a *person of good taste*. A person who has *bad taste* is one who attends all the wrong functions; buys all the wrong furniture, cars, and clothes; orders all the wrong food and drink; and hangs out with all the wrong people, i.e., "All his/her taste is in his/her mouth." Such a person is said to have *bad taste in* these areas, and the expression *There's no accounting for taste* (q.v.) applies to such people. AID; DEI; PT; WNWCD. *See also* In Good Taste; Leave a Bad Taste in Your Mouth.

GOOD TASTE IN   *See* Good Taste.

GOOSE EGG   *See* Lay an Egg.

GOOSE HANGS HIGH   *The goose hangs high.* All is well, and the future looks bright. LA: 1866. Source: GOOSE. MWCD: O.E. A hanging goose is a dead goose; and if the bird is hanging outside an inn, it may be a sign that either *goose* is on the menu that particular day or that the food in the inn is as good as that goose would taste if it *were* on the menu. Another explanation for the linking of *goose* and *goodness* is the possibility that the original expression was "The goose *honks* high," referring to the fact that migrating geese fly higher in good weather—and consequently *honk* higher. (They fly much lower and sound much louder in foggy or rainy weather.) The tradition of serving goose for Christmas dinner is long-standing in England but has never really caught on in America. ATWS; DAP; HI; MDWPO; PT; SA. *See also* Cook Someone's Goose.

GOOSE IS COOKED   *See* Cook Someone's Goose.

GO OUT OF THE FRYING PAN INTO THE FIRE   *See* Out of the Frying Pan into the Fire.

GORGE YOURSELF   *See* Make Your Gorge Rise.

GO SOUR (ON)   *See* Hit a Sour Note.

GO SUCK A LEMON   *See* If Life Hands You a Lemon, Make Lemonade.

GO SUCK AN EGG   *See* Teach Your Grandmother to Suck Eggs.

GO TOGETHER LIKE PEACHES AND CREAM   *See* Peach.

GO TO POT   *to go to pot.* To be ruined. EWPO: 16th cent. Source: POT. MWCD: O.E. During the Elizabethan era, game that was killed was divided between the lords and ladies, who got the finer cuts, and the servants and farmhands, who got the poorer ones. The latter pieces of meat were then thrown into a perpetually boiling pot to join the leftovers from the lords' and ladies' meal of the previous evening. As the pot boiled, the meat disintegrated, falling apart and losing its identity as a particular cut, so that the eaters of this stew could no longer tell a finer cut from a poorer one. This disintegration of the finer cuts of meat has become a metaphor for the process by which marriages fall apart, businesses collapse, and the lives and health of individuals are ruined, i.e., *go to pot.* The killing of the game that went to pot inspired another *pot* idiom, *potshot* (NSOED: mid-19th cent.): a shot taken at random at animals of the wrong age or sex, or birds resting on land or water, simply to *fill the pot*. Such unsportsmanlike conduct led to the modern metaphor *to take a potshot* at someone (MWCD: 1858), i.e., to ambush someone with a stinging and uncalled-for remark for which there may be no penalty, although there is also no excuse. AID; ATWS; BDPF; CI; DAI; DAS; DC; DEI; EWPO; HI; MDWPO; MS; SA.

GO TO SEED   *to go to seed.* To become decayed or decrepit, deteriorated or disreputable, shabby or squalid, uncared for or useless, weak or worn out. HND: at least-1740. Source: SEED. MWCD: O.E. People and their possessions *go to seed* (Brit.: "run to seed") in much the same way that a plant does. First, the plant produces flowers and "fruits"; then, unless the "fruits" are picked or harvested, they, in turn, produce seeds that, in their turn, can sprout, rendering the "fruit"— such as onions or potatoes—useless. In other words, neglect by the gardener has allowed the "fruits" to remain on the plant far beyond their prime, resulting in loss or reduction in value of the crop. When people allow themselves, their families, and their possessions to *go to seed*, they are putting themselves in danger of losing their friends, their reputations, and even their jobs. Things that have *gone to seed* are described as being *seedy* (NSOED: early-18th cent.): e.g., *seedy* ("shabby") clothes, a *seedy* ("squalid") neighborhood, and *seedy* ("lewd") entertainment. The sprouting of seeds is sometimes transferred to the *sprouting* of children, who are called *sprouts*, or *young sprouts*; when they grow up, the boys will *sprout antlers* (i.e., become sexually excited), and the girls will *sprout wings* (i.e., become little angels). Some of them may wind up in a tennis tournament in which the top players are *seeded* (NSOED: early-20th cent.), i.e., scattered, like seeds, in the two major brackets so that players next to each other in rank (such as the first-seeded and second-seeded players) do not meet each other before the finals. The *top-seeded* player is the *number one seed*. AID; ATWS; BDPF; CE; CI; DAI; DC; DEI; FLC; LCRH; MDWPO; MS; SA.

GO TO THE DOGS   *to go to the dogs.* For real estate to become run down or dilapidated; for people to become physically or morally disreputable. IRCD: 1619. Source: GARBAGE. On a farm, when food is left over from a meal, or the preparation of a meal, or when it has begun to spoil on the shelf or in the refrigerator, it is fed to the hogs or the dogs—the only two farm animals that will eat just about anything. The food that *goes to the dogs* has become a metaphor for (1) property that has become neglected to the point that it is rendered worthless and (2) people who have neglected themselves for so long that they are regarded as expendable. One particular favorite of the dog is a beef bone, from the soup or roast, which is thrown on the ground rather than placed in a bowl. The bone is nutritious, having a certain amount of meat left on the outside and containing marrow on the inside. The bone itself provides calcium and is beneficial for cleaning and strengthening the dog's teeth. The act of throwing a dog a bone has become a metaphor for human "altruism" to other humans: To *throw someone a bone* is for a boss to give his/her employees a minimum amount of encouragement or enticement, just enough to keep them happy, as if they were dogs. The expression is also used by persons who are in need of information that the provider has, e.g., by reporters to a "reliable source": "Throw us a bone!"—i.e., give us a hint or a clue. AID; ATWS; CI; DAI; DC; EWPO; HND; LCRH; MS; SA. *See also* Have a Bone to Pick with Someone.

GO TO THE WELL ONCE TOO OFTEN   *See* You Can Lead a Horse to Water, but You Can't Make It Drink.

GOURD   *your gourd.* Your head. HDAS: 1829. Source: GOURD. MWCD: 14th cent. *Gourd* is both the name of a family of vines—including the melon, pumpkin, and squash—and a member of that family that produces inedible "fruit" with an extremely hard shell, which, when dried, can be used as a utensil or container. Gourds come in various shapes, one of which is globular—hence the metaphor. To be *out of your gourd* (NSOED: mid-19th cent.) is to be crazy, empty-headed, or *out to lunch* (q.v.). To be *stoned out of your gourd* is to be either drunk or high on marijuana or some other drug. A bottle-shaped gourd is called a *bottle gourd* (MWCD: ca. 1828) because it resembles a short, fat, chianti bottle without the straw covering. An example of a bottle gourd is the *calabash* (MWCD: 1596—fr. Sp. *calabaza* "gourd"), which can, like Eng. *gourd*, also mean "empty-headed." The shell of the calabash can be used either as a bottle or, when cut in half, as a dipper. At the end of each of his TV shows, Jimmy Durante used to close with "Good night, Mrs. Calabash, wherever you are." No one besides Durante ever knew who or where Mrs. Calabash was. DAFD; DAS; EWPO; FLC.

GRAHAM BREAD   *See* Graham Flour.

GRAHAM CRACKER   *See* Graham Flour.

GRAHAM FLOUR   Coarse-ground, unrefined, unsifted, whole-wheat flour. MWCD: 1834. Source: FLOUR. MWCD: 13th cent. The *graham* in *graham flour* stands for the Reverend Sylvester Graham, of Boston, Mass., a self-taught nutritionist who joined the Temperance movement ca. 1830, maintaining that a diet of foods made from the entire kernel of wheat—bran and all, ground coarsely rather than fine—not only would improve a person's health but would lower that person's desire for alcohol (and other sinful pleasures). *Graham bread* (sometimes called *brown bread*) appeared on the tables of several boardinghouses that Graham had established in some of the larger Eastern cities in 1834, followed by *graham muffins* (now called *bran muffins*) and "graham wafers" (called *graham crackers* since 1882). *Graham crackers* are currently one of the basic ingredients of *s'mores* (q.v.), for which two of the crackers are sandwiched around a thin piece of flat chocolate with a roasted marshmallow sitting on it; and crumbled graham crackers are currently used to make *crumb crust*, an unbaked bottom crust with which custard pies and cheesecakes are made. The boardinghouses are long gone, but most nutritionists agree that eating food made of unrefined, unsifted, coarse-ground, whole-kernel wheat flour—i.e., *graham flour*—is a good idea. DAFD; EWPO; FLC; HF; LA.

GRAHAM MUFFIN   *See* Graham Flour.

GRAIN OF SALT   *See* Take with a Grain of Salt.

GRANOLA   *See* Cereal.

GRAPE BALLS OF FIRE   *See* Grapeshot.

GRAPE CAESAR'S GHOST   *See* Grapeshot.

GRAPEFRUIT   *a grapefruit*. A citrus fruit that grows in clusters, like grapes. MWCD: 1814. Source: GRAPE (MWCD: 14th cent.); FRUIT (MWCD: 12th cent.). In spite of the clustering, the often yellowish skin, the globular shape, and the fact that they are both berries, the grapefruit and the grape are unrelated. Aside from the other citrus fruits, such as the orange, lemon, and lime, the closest relative to the grapefruit is the *pomelo* (MWCD: 1858), or *shaddock* (MWCD: 1696). The English dates for these three fruits are misleading, however, because the one with the latest date, the *pomelo*, is the ancestor of the *shaddock*, which is merely a pomelo that was renamed for the Englishman Captain Shaddock, who brought the fruit from the East Indies to the West Indies in the late-17th cent.; and the shaddock is the ancestor of the grapefruit, which developed differently in the Caribbean and was further differentiated in Florida. The pomelo is much larger than the grapefruit (up to watermelon size), it is shaped like a pear, and it has a loose rind. The grapefruit, in contrast, is softball-size, is shaped like an orange, and has a hard-to-peel rind. The modern grapefruit comes seeded or seedless, and yellow or pink (and even red, in Texas). Note that American expressions relating to the pomelo, shaddock, or grapefruit use the term *grapefruit* rather than the other two: e.g., the *Grapefruit League* (HDAS: 1949—Major League

Baseball teams taking spring training in Florida) and *grapefruit-size hail* (q.v.) (hail the size of grapefruit). The "Pomelo league" and "shaddock-size hail" would be understood by very few Americans. DAFD; EWPO; FLC; MDWPO; NSOED; PT.

GRAPEFRUIT LEAGUE   *See* Grapefruit.

GRAPEFRUIT-SIZE HAIL   Hail the size of grapefruit. Source: GRAPEFRUIT. MWCD: 1814. *Grapefruit-size(d) hail* is the largest measure of hail—approx. four inches in diameter—used by American radio and television meteorologists along the Gulf and Pacific coasts where grapefruit are grown (esp. in Florida, Texas, and California). In the rest of the United States, the weather persons are divided between *grapefruit-size hail* and the more precise "softball-size hail" (named for the three and three-quarter inch missile used in the ball game by that name). The term *walnut-size hail* is used by meteorologists on the East and West Coasts for "medium-size hail," but they have different walnuts in mind. The *English walnut* (an Americanism) that is grown on the West Coast is approx. one and one-half inches in diameter—about the size of the golf ball for which such hail is named in the rest of the country: "golf-ball size hail." The American ("black") walnut that grows in the Eastern United States comes in two different sizes, depending on its stage of development. The stage at which the thick green husk has not yet been shucked is used as the name for "baseball-size hail" (two and three-quarter inch diameter hail), and the stage at which the green or brown husk has been removed is used as the name for "golf-ball size hail." There are no geographical parameters for the naming of small hail (one-half inch to one inch in diameter): It is called either *pea-size hail* (q.v.) (after the garden legume) or "marble-size hail" (after the regular-size marbles, not the "shooters").

GRAPE-NUTS   *See* Grapeshot.

GRAPESHOT   Small iron balls fired in a cluster from a cannon. MWCD: 1747. Source: GRAPE. MWCD: 14th cent. *Grapeshot* is named for the grape because each shot is approx. the size of a grape, and the shots are loaded into the barrel of the cannon in a grapelike cluster. When the cannon is fired, the individual "grapes" spread out in a wide pattern, killing or maiming the enemy forces. *Grapeshot* contrasts with *mustard-seed shot* (q.v.) in that the latter missiles are so small that they can be fired from a shotgun. Grape seeds are also small, much smaller than the individual *Grape-Nuts* that have been a popular Post breakfast cereal since 1898. Those "nuts" are actually little clusters of wheat and barley, which were orig. thought to produce *grape sugar* (MWCD: 1831), or dextrose, when baked. In the 1960s a fad swept the United States that involved substituting *grape* for *great* in such exclamations as *Grape Caesar's ghost!* and *Grape balls of fire!* BDPF; DAS; LA; NSOED.

GRAPES OF WRATH   *the grapes of wrath.* The seeds—or fruits—of discord and disaster. DC: 1910. Source: GRAPE. MWCD: 14th cent. The phrase *the grapes* *of wrath* is not from the Bible but from Julia Ward Howe's anthem, "The Battle Hymn of the Republic," which contains the line "He [the Lord] is trampling out the vintage where the *grapes of wrath are stored*" [italics added]. The sense is that the harvest contains seeds of dissension—to Christian ideals—that must be stomped out. (Recently the song, which is sung to the tune of "John Brown's Body," has been regarded as so militant that some Protestant congregations no longer sing it.) The phrase also appears in the title of John Steinbeck's novel *The Grapes of Wrath* (1939), in which the combination of drought and depression drives poverty-stricken Oklahoma farm families west to California. Their plight is the "fruit" of "seeds" that were planted ages ago by some evil force, not by these proud, godfearing folk themselves. (As late as the mid-1950s this novel was banned by certain school systems because of the scene at the end of the book in which a young mother lit. nurses a man to keep him alive.)

GRAPE SUGAR   *See* Grapeshot.

GRAPEVINE   *See* Hear It through the Grapevine.

GRAPEVINE TELEGRAPH   *See* Hear It through the Grapevine.

GRATE ON YOUR NERVES   *for something to grate on your nerves.* For a sound to irritate you to the point of illness. Source: GRATE (v). MWCD: 14th cent. In cooking, to "grate" a food is to rub it against a "grater," a metal utensil with a flat surface dotted with sharp-edged holes that convert the surface of the food into small particles: e.g., grated cheese and grated orange, lemon, or lime rinds. Grating food does not cause an irritating sound, so it is the damage to the surface of the food that has been transferred to the human reaction to certain other painful experiences. For example, the sound of fingernails raking down a blackboard can *grate on the nerves* of those who hear it—and chalk that is pushed rather than pulled on the same surface can cause the same displeasure. An experience that is less acute but longer lasting is to *have your nerves grated* by a person with a high-pitched or raspy voice, or by a group of people talking about a subject in which you have absolutely no interest. FLC; WNWCD.

GRAVEYARD STEW   *See* In a Stew.

GRAVY BOAT   *See* Ride the Gravy Train.

GRAVY TRAIN   *See* Ride the Gravy Train.

GRAZE (v)   *to graze.* To eat small portions of various foods at various times throughout the day. DAFD: early-1980s. Source: GRAZE (v). MWCD: O.E. Animals such as cattle, horses, sheep, and goats "graze" when they nibble *grass* (the basis of the word *graze*), weeds, and flowers that grow on the ground. The activity is random and unstructured, amounting to going where the ground cover is at whatever time of day the animals are hungry. Humans *graze* when they either snack, impulsively, on *junk food* at home or go to a *grazing restaurant* where there is a buffet stocked with a wide assortment of salads, meats, vegetables, fruits, breads, desserts, and beverages. Best of all, such restaurants are open all day long, with different buffets for breakfast, lunch, and dinner. Another verb *graze*, meaning "to touch in passing" (as in "The bullet merely grazed his scalp"), may have derived from the verb *graze* meaning "to nibble at grass." DAFD; NSOED; SA. *Compare* Browse.

GRAZING RESTAURANT   *See* Graze (v).

GREASE (n)   A viscous lubricant. Source: GREASE (n). MWCD: 13th cent. The thick lubricant called *grease*, used to lubricate (or *grease*) machinery such as automobiles, has a petroleum base and is not edible. The original *grease*, used for cooking, was derived from baking, broiling, frying, or roasting meat. That is, *grease* was a by-product of heating meat to the point where the fat "melted" and turned into a liquid. Before the 14th cent., no distinction was made between such incidental collections of melted animal fat (i.e., *grease*) and the deliberate conversion of animal fat (specif. pork fat) into what was later to be called *lard*. Before the development of petroleum lubricants (late-19th cent.), *bear grease* was used to lubricate the axles of the covered wagons, *ham fat* (q.v.) was employed as a base for the *greasepaint* used by performers in minstrel shows, and *elbow grease* (DAP: 1672) simply meant "hard work." In the 19th cent., *greaser* was a pejorative term for a Latin American immigrant, esp. one from Mexico; but following WWII the term *greaser* was applied to American-born men who wore their hair long and heavily greased and pretended to be tough and "cool." The adj. *greasy* (MWCD: 1514) no longer applies only to food that contains an excessive amount of grease from animal fat but also to (1) *greasy clothes* that are covered with petroleum-based lubricants and (2) *greasy smiles* that are a little too "oily" to be trusted. DAFD; DAI; DAS; HDAS; WNWCD. *See also* Greasy Spoon.

GREASEPAINT   *See* Grease (n).

GREASER   *See* Grease (n).

GREASY   *See* Grease (n); Greasy Spoon.

GREASY CLOTHES   *See* Grease (n).

GREASY-GREAZY LINE   *See* Grits.

GREASY SMILE   *See* Grease (n).

GREASY SPOON   *a greasy spoon*. A small, dingy diner that offers cheap, run-of-the-mill food to blue-collar workers at reasonable prices. HDAS: 1918. Source:

GREASE (n) (MWCD: 13th cent.); SPOON (MWCD: 14th cent.). The interesting thing about a *greasy spoon* is that the management is not ashamed to have it referred to as such (and sometimes even adopts the name for the establishment), and the customers are not at all ashamed to say that they patronize it (perhaps because it reminds them so much of home). At any rate, although the spoon that dishes out the chili and hash is greasy, *greasy spoons* are famous for their friendly atmosphere, the proximity of the cooks to the customers, their home cooking, their large portions, and the speed with which they deliver them. (The workers have only a half hour for lunch—one of only two meals, including breakfast, that are served there each workday.) Truckers know where the best highway diners are located; factory workers know where the best city diners are located. There's nothing like watching a grizzled old cook whip up bacon, eggs, and hashbrowns right in front of your eyes, albeit with a greasy spatula. DAFD; DAI; DAS.

GREATEST THING SINCE SLICED BREAD   *the greatest thing since sliced bread.* The best thing to come along in a lifetime. HDAS: 1966. Source: BREAD. MWCD: O.E. This expression is often used sarcastically of someone who thinks that he/she is superior to any other person, or that his/her ideas are superior to those of anyone else. The commercial bread-slicer was invented in 1928, and sliced bread was first sold in grocery stores in 1930. Presliced bread is certainly a time-saver, but it is not essential to human existence. People still buy unsliced bread at a bakery and slice it at home as needed. (The Brit. form of the expression is *the best thing since sliced bread.*) CE: DAFD; HND; MS; NSOED; PT.

GREEN CHEESE   *See* Moon Is Made of Green Cheese.

GREENHOUSE   *See* Truck Garden.

GREENHOUSE EFFECT   *See* Truck Garden.

GREEN ONION   *See* Onionskin Paper.

GREEN PEPPER STEAK   *See* Pepper (n).

GREEN THUMB   *See* Truck Garden.

GRENADE   *a grenade.* A handheld explosive. MWCD: 1591. Source: POME-GRANATE. MWCD: 14th cent. Pomegranate lovers may not be proud of the fact that the most famous spin-off from that fruit's name is *grenade*. A grenade, or *hand grenade*, is an antipersonnel weapon, like the rifle or bayonet, that is carried by a soldier into battle. To deploy the weapon, the soldier grasps the grenade and its lever in one hand, pulls the pin with the other hand (or his/her teeth), and throws the grenade toward the enemy. The grenade explodes according to a timed fuse, activated by the lever, and sends pieces of iron shrapnel, from the scored body of the grenade, flying out to maim or kill. (Some modern grenades produce only smoke or gas, or simply explode without producing shrapnel.) The *grenade* is named for the *pomegranate* because they are both spherical, both about the same size, both about the same weight, both filled with "seeds" (which, in the case of the hand grenade, are grains of gunpowder), and both expected to explode into a bloody mess when thrown. A 17th cent. British soldier was called a *grenadier* (MWCD: 1676), and the *Grenadiers* now make up a special regiment in the British army. EWPO; IHAT; LCRH; PT; THT. *See also* Pomegranate. *Compare* Pineapple.

GRENADIER   *See* Grenade.

GRENADINE   *See* Pomegranate.

GRIDDLE CAKE   *See* Hot off the Griddle.

GRILL (n)   *See* Grill a Suspect.

GRILL (v)   *See* Grill a Suspect.

GRILL A SUSPECT   *to grill a suspect.* For police to interrogate a suspected criminal intensely and at length in order to obtain a confession. HDAS: 1894. Source: GRILL (v). MWCD: 1668. To grill food—particularly meat—is to place it on a metal grate directly over hot coals, a gas flame, or electric coils and broil it there until it is done. Suspected criminals are not subjected to that kind of heat (although in old movies they were exposed to a hot lamp for many hours): They just *feel* as if they are being broiled on a hot grill. The verb *grill* is derived from the noun *grill* (MWCD: 1685), which orig. referred to the cross-barred grate—or *gridiron* (NSOED: M.E.)—on which meat was broiled, but now can also denote a hot flat metal surface that is found in the kitchen of most restaurants. The noun *grill* can also denote the food cooked (*hot off the grill*) on either surface (e.g., a *mixed grill*), and it can also refer to the restaurant in which it is located (e.g., a *bar and grill*). DEI; FLC.

GRINDER   *See* Submarine Sandwich.

GRIND IT OUT   *See* Through the Mill.

GRIN LIKE A CHESHIRE CAT   *to grin like a cheshire cat.* To grin inscrutably. (Lewis Carroll's *Alice's Adventures in Wonderland*, 1865.) Source: CHEESE. In *Alice*, the Cheshire Cat sat grinning on the limb of a tree until it gradually faded away, the grin being the last part of it to disappear. The cat and its grin are believed to derive from Cheshire County, England, home of the famous Cheshire cheese, where a cheese was once molded in the round face of a grinning cat. When the cheese was eaten, from outside in, the grin was the last part to disappear. There are various other theories, however, one of which is that the mold actually bore the coat of arms of a Cheshire nobleman that contained the figure of a regal lion that was mistaken for a grinning cat. IRCD; NSOED; SA; SHM.

GRIST FOR THE MILL   Raw material for the manufacturers; fuel for the fires; data for the scholars. Source: GRIST; MILL. MWCD: O.E. Literally, *grist* is the dried grain that is brought to the *mill* for grinding. The mill was orig. a stone that was rolled—by human power or animal power—over another stone, with the grain between them. Eventually, the power was supplied by flowing water (a *water mill*) or blowing wind (a *windmill*). All sorts of grain could be ground in this fashion, and it could be ground into either a coarse meal—e.g., oatmeal or corn-meal—or a fine flour—e.g., wheat flour or rye flour. Steel rollers have almost totally replaced stone rollers, and today *stone-ground flour* (MWCD: 1905) is so unusual that the feature is highlighted on the package and prob. adds a few cents to the price. Metaphorically, (1) wrecked cars are now *grist* for the recycling *mill*, where they are reduced to a fraction of their original size; (2) freshmen who enroll in unaccredited colleges are *grist* for the *diploma mill* (MWCD: 1914), which turns them out in record time; (3) any hint of scandal is *grist* for the *rumor mill*, which converts it into tabloid "news"; and more positively, (4) any unusual event or discovery is *grist* for the *mill* of the scholar, who analyzes and interprets it for the benefit of future generations. BDPF; CI; CODP; DC; DEI; HND; MS; NSOED.

GRITS   Ground, hulled kernels of corn. MWCD: 1579. Source: GRITS. MWCD: O.E. Just as birds must consume *grit*, i.e., sand or gravel, every day in order to digest their food, the people of the southern United States must consume *grits* every day in order to satisfy their craving for corn. This appetite was created for the early colonists by the Native Americans, who introduced them to the process of soaking kernels of corn in a mixture of water and ashes (to remove the hulls) and then drying the corn mixture and grinding it to produce what they called *homen* and the settlers called *hominy* (MWCD: 1629). *Hominy grits* (MWCD: 1879) are made by reconstituting hominy that is ground somewhere between "coarse," as for *cornmeal mush* (MWCD: 1671), and "fine," as for *corn pone* (MWCD: 1859). For example, for breakfast a Southerner might enjoy his/her hominy in the form of *grits* (hominy boiled in milk or water), *mush* (fried slices of chilled hominy), or *corn pone* (corn bread). From these terms come such metaphors as *Chinese grits* "rice," *mushy* "sentimental or romantic" (HDAS: 1839), and *cornpone* "down-home or rustic" (q.v.). Grits—sometimes called *Georgia ice cream*—are strictly a South-ern—and Southwestern—delicacy, not recognized or appearing on menus north of the *greasy/greazy line* that separates the Northern dialect from the North-Midland dialect. CE; DAFD; DAS; FLC; IHAT; LCRH; NSOED; SA; WNWCD.

GROUNDNUT   *See* Peanut.

GROUND PEA   *See* Peanut.

GROVES OF ACADEME   *See* Hold out an Olive Branch.

GROW FAT   *See* Fat (adj.).

GRUB (n)   Food. HDAS: 1659. Source: GRUB (v). MWCD: 14th cent. The verb *to grub* orig. meant to clear a field of roots and stumps so that it could be planted in food (for people) and feed (for animals). One of the implements used in this process was a "grub hoe," which was later used to dig up another kind of root— beets, carrots, and turnips—for human consumption. *To grub for food* has come to mean "to search about for something to eat," like the homemaker who answers the question "What's for dinner?" with the answer "I'll *see what I can dig up*." The noun *grub* developed in England in the mid-17th cent. (NSOED) as a slang term for "food" and surfaced in the American West in the early-19th cent. (IHAT: 1807) as a common term among cowboys, miners, and loggers. Among miners, the word *grubstake* developed to mean not only food but also the supplies necessary to conduct a search for gold (HDAS: 1863). For a merchant to *grubstake* (or "bank-roll") a prospector was for him to *stake* him to *grub*, on the condition that the merchant would receive a share of the value of the gold found (HDAS: 1879). Nowadays, *grub* competes with *chow* (q.v.) as a slang term for "food" in the armed services, and *grubstake* is used for investing in the future of starving artists (etc.). BDPF; DAFD; MDWPO; SA.

GRUB FOR FOOD   *See* Grub (n).

GRUBSTAKE   *See* Grub (n).

GRUEL   *See* Grueling.

GRUELING   Exhausting; punishing. MWCD: 1852. Source: GRUEL (?). MWCD: 14th cent. A *grueling* experience is one that is both taxing and tiring, like serving a sentence in jail or prison at hard labor. The word *grueling* is presumed to be the pres. part. of an obsolete verb *to gruel* "to suffer," which, if it really did exist, was in no way related to the noun *gruel* "thin oatmeal soup." The only connection between the noun and the participle is the fact that *gruel* was once a typical food for prisoners because it required so few ingredients (oatmeal and water) and so little preparation (boil and stir); i.e., it was cheap. Therefore, if you can convince yourself that pres. parts. can be derived from nouns, rather than obsolete verbs, then you are on your way to characterizing prison as a *gruel-ing* experience and employing *grueling* as a metaphor for anything that even comes close to being that bad: e.g., entertaining your in-laws for an entire weekend. The noun *gruel* is also associated with insubstantiality, as of ideas, prob. because of the thinness of oatmeal *porridge* (MWCD: ca. 1643) that it represents. Porridge is usu. more substantial, as with pease porridge (i.e., a "pea porridge") in the nursery rhyme. DAFD; EWPO; FLC; LCRH; PT. *See also* Like Two Peas in a Pod.

GUN SHELL   *See* Shell out.

GUSTO   Enjoyment; enthusiasm. NSOED: early-17th cent. Source: TASTE. Latin *gustus* "taste" is the source of It. *gusto* "taste," which has been much borrowed by other European languages, including English. At first, Eng. *gusto* (MWCD: 1620) was used as the object of the verb *have*: to *have gusto*, meaning to have a special or distinctive taste, applying principally to food. Later, the phrase was applied also to alcoholic beverages, particularly beer and ale, and the meaning of *gusto* broadened to include the senses of "vigor" and "vitality." Eventually, *gusto* came to be used as the object of the prep. *with*, as to eat or drink something *with gusto* (NSOED: early-17th cent.), i.e., "with relish." (Joke: "He ate his hot dog with gusto; she ate hers with relish.") Now the word *gusto* refers to the manner in which the food or drink is consumed rather than to the character of the consumables themselves. It can also apply to the enthusiasm with which someone engages in any other enjoyable activity: "They approached the job of cleaning out the garage *with gusto*." DAS; WNWCD.

GYRO   *See* Submarine Sandwich.

H

HAD IT UP TO HERE   *See* Have a Bellyful.

HALF A LOAF IS BETTER THAN NONE   Something is better than nothing. BDPF: 1546. Source: LOAF. MWCD: O.E. The *loaf* is a loaf of bread, and the advice is that if you foolishly give half of it away, or half of it accidentally breaks off and falls to the ground, you shouldn't feel too bad: You still have the other half. No doubt this is little consolation to a child who has suffered such a loss, esp. if he/she suffers the same loss of the remaining half. (Is half of a half loaf also better than none?) AID; BDPF; CI; CODP; DAI; DAP; DC; HND. *Compare* Cry with a Loaf of Bread under Your Arm.

HALF-BAKED   *a half-baked scheme, plan, or idea.* A poorly thought-out scheme, plan, or idea. MWCD: 1621. Source: BAKE (v). MWCD: O.E. Baked goods that are half-baked may be attractive on the outside but are not completely cooked on the inside. The conventional oven causes trapped gases to expand from the outside in, and partial baking may leave raw dough in the center. Ironically, the term was applied, as a metaphor, to dumb ideas and stupid people before it was applied, lit., to underdone baked goods. Nowadays, a *half-baked* person may not only be stupid but drunk. BDPF; CE; DAI; DAP; DAS; DEI; EWPO; MS; PT.

HALF-CROCKED   *See* Crock.

HALF-PINT   *a half-pint.* A small, short, or insignificant person. HDAS: 1926. Source: PINT. MWCD: 14th cent. In liquid measure, a *pint* is half a quart; so a *half-pint* (MWCD: 1611) is one-quarter of a quart. A human *half-pint* is *pint-sized* (MWCD: 1936), or small; so a *pint-sized* cop is shorter than average for a police officer. The expression *Mind your p's and q's!* "Be on your best behavior!" is thought by some to have once meant "Pay attention to your pints and quarts!" when spoken by a tavern owner to the bartender; however, most lexicographers believe that it was used by schoolmarms to remind their (dyslexic?) pupils to distinguish between a printed *p*, facing right, and a printed *q*, facing left. CE; WNWCD.

HALF-STEWED   *See* Stew in Your Own Juice.

HAM (1)   *A ham; a ham actor.* An overactor HDAS: 1881. Source: HAM. MWCD: M.E. *Ham* is a shortened form of *hamfatter* (HB: ca. 1875), a minstrel-show performer in the 19th cent. *Hamfatters*, whose name comes from the title of the song "The Ham-Fat Man," were so called because they were so poorly paid that they had to remove their lampblack with ham fat (i.e., *lard*, q.v.) rather than the more expensive cold cream. In the late-19th cent., the term *ham actor—ham* or *hambone* (HDAS: 1893)—came to be applied to any actor who did what the minstrel-show actors did: make faces, play to the audience, try to hog the *limelight* (q.v.), exaggerate movements, upstage other actors, speak in a very loud voice, etc.—the very things that Hamlet told his players he abhorred (*Hamlet*, Act III, Scene 2). Later in the 20th cent. (HDAS: 1950), *ham* acquired the additional, nontheatrical senses of "cutup," "show-off," and "clown" (as in "circus clown"). The theatrical senses survive in the verb phrase *to ham it up* "to overplay a part" (MWCD. 1933) and in the noun phrase *imported ham* "a Brit. actor performing in America." AID; BDPF; CE; DAI; DAS; EWPO; HB; HF; LCRH; MDWPO; NSOED; SA; WNWCD.

HAM (2)   A licensed amateur radio station operator. HDAS: 1922. Source: HAM (?). MWCD: M.E. The *ham* in *ham radio, ham radio station*, and *ham radio operator* may have derived from the first syllable of the word *amateur*, although the addition of an initial *h-* has not been satisfactorily explained. A better explanation may be the similarity between amateur radio operators, from the 20th cent. on, and professional telegraph operators, from the mid-19th cent. on. Both operators were required to learn International Morse Code; however, the professionals, including those at railroad stations and on ocean liners, used it all day long, became very proficient, and developed a fine touch at the key, whereas the amateurs were much slower and wielded a heavy hand. Professional telegraph operators of the early-20th cent. described their own trainees as being *ham-handed*, i.e., "clumsy" (MWCD: 1918), and the term was soon applied to amateur radio operators who tried to send and receive International Morse Code. *Ham-handed—* and its twin, *ham-fisted* (MWCD: 1928)—are based on the similarity between a very large human hand and the large upper hind leg of a hog. Besides referring to a lack of dexterity, both terms have also come to mean "heavy-handed," i.e., "inconsiderate, thoughtless, tactless, undiplomatic, lacking in restraint, unnecessarily tough, harsh, or cruel." CE; CI; DAI; DAP; DAS; DEI; MDWPO; MS; NSOED; PT; SA; WNWCD.

HAM ACTOR   *See* Ham (1).

HAM-AND-EGG   *See* Ham and Egg It.

HAM AND EGG IT   *to ham and egg it*. To plug away at it; to "nickel and dime" it. Source: HAM (MWCD: O.E.); EGG (MWCD: 14th cent.). Ham and eggs are the staples of both a traditional English breakfast and an old-fashioned American breakfast. Such breakfasts are hearty but not necessarily healthy, esp. if consumed every day of the week. An American breakfast of this sort is now more common among working-class people, who eat lunch out of a box or miss it altogether. The metaphor is based on the fact that a breakfast of ham and eggs is ordinary and routine. A *ham-and-egg* boxer is a "club" fighter with a minimum of talent. HDAS: 1916.

HAMBURGER   *See* Make Hamburger of.

HAMBURGER BUN   *See* Make Hamburger of.

HAMBURGER SANDWICH   *See* Sandwich (n).

HAMBURGER STEAK   *See* Make Hamburger of.

HAMFATTER   *See* Ham (1).

HAM-FISTED   *See* Ham (2).

HAM-HANDED   *See* Ham (2).

HAM IT UP   *See* Ham (1).

HAM LOAF   *See* Meat Loaf.

HAM RADIO   *See* Ham (2).

HAM RADIO OPERATOR   *See* Ham (2).

HAM RADIO STATION   *See* Ham (2).

HAM SALAD   *See* Salad.

HAND GRENADE   *See* Grenade.

HAND IT OVER ON A SILVER PLATTER   *See* Full Plate.

HAND-TO-MOUTH   *See* Live from Hand to Mouth.

HAPPY AS A KID IN A CANDY STORE   *See* Candy.

HARD-BOILED   Strict, tough, demanding, rigid, hardheaded; unfeeling, un-emotional, unsentimental, hard-hearted, heartless. MWCD: 1886. Source: BOIL (MWCD: 13th cent.); EGG. No one is as *hard-boiled* as a U.S. Army or Marine drill sergeant, but a *hard-boiled* cop and a *hard-boiled* detective come close. (*Hard-boiled* detectives were called *tough eggs* in 1930s novels and movies.) A person of this personality is also referred to as a *hard-boiled egg* (HDAS: 1899). Strangely enough, the verb *hard-boil* (MWCD: 1895), with the literal meaning "to boil an egg in the shell until its contents are solid," is derived, by back-formation, from the metaphorical expression *hard-boiled* (MWCD: 1886). This sort of delayed appearance may be attributable to the fact that the culinary term for solidified eggs is, and apparently always has been, *hard-cooked*. American dictionaries do not even recognize the term *hard-cooked*, but most American cookbooks prefer it to the exclusion of *hard-boiled*. BDPF; CE; CI; DAP; DAS; EWPO; LA; MS; PT; SA.

HARD-BOILED EGG   *See* Hard-boiled.

HARD CIDER   *See* Applejack.

HARD-COOKED   *See* Hard-boiled.

HARD NUT TO CRACK   *See* In a Nutshell.

HARDPAN   *See* Pan out.

HARDTACK   *See* Biscuit.

HARD TO SWALLOW   *to find something hard to swallow*. To find something difficult to believe or accept. Source: SWALLOW (v). MWCD: O.E. In this meta-phor, words or deeds are treated as if they were food—food too large or distasteful to ingest. The analogy is to an animal such as a bird, fish, or snake that attempts to swallow its prey whole, only to discover that its alimentary canal is too small to handle such a large meal. When a person asks, "Do you expect me to *swallow* that?" he/she is expressing doubt as to his/her ability to stretch his/her belief or imagination in order to accept a story that defies reason or logic. If that person is gullible enough to believe the story, however, he/she may *swallow it hook, line, and sinker*, i.e., totally, like a fish swallowing not only a baited hook but the leader line and lead sinker as well. ATWS; CE; DAS; DEI; HI; MS; SA.

HARVARD BEETS   *See* Red as a Beet.

HASH (n)   *a hash*. A hodgepodge or jumble; a mess or muddle. NSOED: mid-18th cent. Source: HASH (n). MWCD: ca. 1663. To *make a hash of something* is to bungle it or botch it up. The various senses of *hash* derive from the earliest recorded use of the word in *Pepys' Diary*, in the mid-17th cent. The reference there was to a "hash of rabbits," which presumably referred to a dish of chopped rabbit meat, potatoes, and other vegetables heated in a pot: a *shepherd's pie* (q.v.). In America, suppertime hash was likewise a mixture of ingredients, but they were almost always leftovers from the noontime dinner, and the meat was usu. roast beef or corned beef. The cold beef was chopped up into small pieces, and the cold boiled potatoes were diced with the sharp top of an opened tin can. The ingredients were then fried in a skillet with some butter or grease until brown, and were sometimes served with jelly on the side and a raw egg on top. (New England *red flannel hash* is made with beets, rather than beef, which contribute a reddish color that resembles the pinkness of corned beef.) Because hash was a mélange, because it consisted of leftovers, and because it was never served at dinner, it came to be regarded as a second-class dish. This reputation moved beyond the households to the eating establishments, where (1) *hash house* (HDAS: 1868) became a slang term for a cheap restaurant (implying that fancy restaurants would never serve hash), (2) *hash slinger* (LA: ca. 1868) became the name for an employee of such an eatery, and (3) *hashhouse Greek* (LA: 1930s) developed as a nickname for the *lunch-counter jargon* (q.v.) that was shouted to the cook by the waitresses (*sic*). (The jargon for "hash" was *yesterday, today, and tomorrow*—i.e., "prepared *yesterday*, served *today*, and prob. on the menu for *tomorrow*.") Hash has produced a number of other metaphorical expressions: *To settle someone's hash* (HDAS: 1803) is to punish someone for the mess he/she has made or to get even with someone for the problems he/she has created. *Hash marks* (MWCD: 1907) started out as the short stripes on a military person's lower left sleeve, denoting the number of years of service, but they have also become the short parallel lines on the football field, signaling where the officials should "spot" the ball before every "down." *Hash browns* (MWCD: 1951) resemble hash only in the sense that they consist of potatoes that have been cut (as cubes or strings) for deep- or pan-frying; they contain no meat but may be mixed with onions and peppers. BDPF; DAFD; DAI; DAS; DC; EWPO; FLC; HND; IHAT; WNWCD. *See also* Hash (v).

HASH (v)   *to hash something up, over, or out.* To make a mess of things; to talk things over; to work out a solution to a problem. HDAS: 1930. Source: HASH (v). MWCD: 1590. The verb *hash* is a borrowing fr. Fr. *hacher* "to chop or mince," which is derived fr. Fr. *hache* "battle-ax." *To hash something up* is, therefore, to demolish something, such as a perfectly good yard or a perfectly good project. When you're done, it looks like the chopped meat and potatoes of a beef or corned beef hash. *To hash something over* is not at all destructive: It simply means "to talk about something in some detail"—either to review something that recently took place or to speculate on something that could occur in the future. *To hash something out* (LA: 1931) is to try to put the pieces back together again, to come to an agreement or understanding. Once matters have been *hashed up, over, or out*, they can be *rehashed* (MWCD: ca. 1822), i.e., discussed and analyzed all over again.

A *rehash* (MWCD: 1849) of something is a repeat of it with a little change in form but very little change in substance: "That's just a *rehash* of the bill that I proposed two years ago!" CE; DAI; EWPO; LA; NSOED; WNWCD.

HASH BROWNS   *See* Hash (n).

HASH HOUSE   *See* Hash (n).

HASHHOUSE GREEK   *See* Hash (n).

HASH MARKS   *See* Hash (n).

HASH OUT   *See* Hash (v).

HASH OVER   *See* Hash (v).

HASH SLINGER   *See* Hash (n).

HASH UP   *See* Hash (v).

HASTY PUDDING   Cornmeal mush. IHAT: 1691. Source: PUDDING. MWCD: 13th cent. *Hasty pudding* is so called because it is a *pudding* (a soft boiled food) that can be made in great *haste* (fifteen or twenty minutes). Cornmeal is mixed with either water or milk; the mixture is sweetened with molasses, honey, or maple syrup; and the whole is boiled until the stirring spoon can stand alone. Hasty pudding was a favorite Colonial American breakfast (with the mush sliced, fried, and covered with syrup) or dessert (served hot, in a bowl, with milk and sweet sauce). Harvard University's famed literary society, the Hasty Pudding Club, was named for this dessert in 1795. (The club now awards a golden pudding pot to a male and female celebrity guest each year.) When cornmeal is mixed with water and baked instead of boiled, it is called *Indian pudding* (IHAT: 1722). In Britain, where *hasty pudding* first got its name (MWCD: 1599), it is made with boiled oatmeal, rather than cornmeal. DAFD; FLC.

HAUTE CUISINE   *See* Cuisine.

HAVE A BEEF WITH   *See* Beef (n).

HAVE A BELLYFUL   *to have a bellyful of something.* To have all you can take of something. MWCD: 1535. Source: STOMACH. The *belly* (fr. M.E. *belly* "bellows") is the abdomen, in which the stomach is located. As the stomach fills with food, the belly swells like a balloon, until the diner feels that he/she is "about to burst." To have a metaphorical *bellyful* is to have absorbed (i.e., "eaten") all of the offensive behavior (i.e., "junk") that you can hold (in your "stomach") from someone. A similar expression is *to have had it up to here*, accompanied by a hand held horizontally under the chin. The meaning is the same as *have a bellyful*, but the reference is to another metaphor, "to be *stuffed to the gills*"; i.e., not only is your stomach full, but also your esophagus and throat—all the way up to what would be your gills, if you were a fish. ATWS; BDPF; DC; DEI; MS; SA.

HAVE A BITE   *See* Bite (n).

HAVE A BONE TO PICK   *to have a bone to pick with someone.* To have an argument to settle with someone. HB: mid-19th cent. Source: BONE. MWCD: O.E. As long as a single dog has a single bone to pick on, there is no problem. The dog takes its time, removes every scrap of meat (usu. beef), and then starts to gnaw on the bone itself. In the early-16th cent., this peaceful activity of the dog became a metaphor for a philosopher mulling over an idea or a preacher delivering a sermon. However, when a second dog was added to the picture, the bone became a prize to be contested, leading to a violent dog fight. Later in the 16th cent., the object that the dogs were fighting over became a metaphor, *a bone of contention*, for the subject of a human quarrel. For example, two neighbors might quarrel over a barking dog or an overhanging tree, neither of which is life-threatening. In the mid-19th cent, the senses of *bone of contention* and *bone to pick* were combined into the expression *to have a bone* (of contention) *to pick with someone.* AID; ATWS; BDPF; CI; DAI; DEI; DC; EWPO; HI; HND; LCRH; MDWPO; MS; NSOED; SA. *See also* Go to the Dogs.

HAVE A BUN IN THE OVEN   *to have a bun—or a cookie—in the oven.* HDAS: 1960s. To be pregnant. Source: BUN (MWCD: 14th cent.); OVEN (MWCD: O.E.). *To have a bun in the oven* is one of the most descriptive euphemisms for pregnancy. The *bun* is the undeveloped dough (or "fetus") in the warm and nurturing *oven* (or "womb"). When the baking (or "gestating") process is complete, the dough will emerge (be "born") as a recognizable member of the bread (or "human") family. The expression is from the 20th cent., prob. post-WWII, and was preceded by the related expression *to put a bun in the oven*, i.e., "to make a woman pregnant." BDPF; CI.

HAVE A FINGER IN EVERY PIE   *See* Have a Finger in the Pie.

HAVE A FINGER IN MANY (DIFFERENT) PIES   *See* Have a Finger in the Pie.

HAVE A FINGER IN THE PIE   *to have a finger in the pie.* To be interested or involved in a project or activity. HND: 16th cent. Source: PIE. MWCD: 14th cent. This metaphor derives from the practice of sticking a finger in a pie that the cook of the house has just baked in order to discover what kind of pie it is and to determine whether it is up to the usual standards. (Sometimes that requires more than one taste!) *To have a finger in every pie* is, lit., to test every pie on the shelf in this way—or, as a metaphor, to be interested or involved in several different projects or activities at the same time. Shakespeare used this broader expression, adding a hint of meddling, in *Henry VIII* (1613), Act I, Scene 1, when the Duke of Buckingham says of Cardinal Wolsey: "The devil speed him! No man's *pie* is freed/ From his ambitious *finger*" [italics added]. Modern "renaissance" men and women *have a finger in many (different) pies*, some of them social, some commercial, and some political. AID; BDPF; CI; DAI; DC; DEI; EWPO; MS.

HAVE A FULL PLATE   *See* Full Plate.

HAVE A GREEN THUMB   *See* Truck Garden.

HAVE A LOT OF HUNGRY MOUTHS TO FEED   *to have a lot of hungry mouths to feed.* To have a large family that includes a lot of young children. Source: HUNGER; MOUTH; FEED (v). MWCD: O.E. This metaphor is based on the plight of many species of birds, whose large clutch of spring eggs all hatch at about the same time. For the following several weeks, until the offspring are ready to "fly the coop," the parents must feed each baby individually, and almost continuously during the daytime, by flying off and bringing back food, tearing it into pieces, and placing a single piece into each baby bird's mouth with their beak. (Some birds, such as pigeons, first swallow the pieces of food, partially digest them, and regurgitate them into the babies' mouths.) Human parents don't have things quite this bad, although breast or bottle feeding can go on both day and night for over a year, and parents often have to work at other jobs at the same time. The expression is usu. employed as an argument for getting a raise at one of those jobs. SA.

HAVE A LOT OF MOXIE   *See* Moxie.

HAVE A LOT ON YOUR PLATE   *See* Full Plate.

HAVE A LOW BOILING POINT   *See* Reach the Boiling Point.

HAVE A MEMORY LIKE A SIEVE   *See* Leak like a Sieve.

HAVE A SECOND BITE OF THE APPLE   *See* Two Bites of the Cherry.

HAVE A SECOND BITE OF THE CHERRY   *See* Two Bites of the Cherry.

HAVE A SLICE OF THE PIE   *See* Pie Chart.

HAVE A STRONG STOMACH   *See* Have No Stomach for.

HAVE A SWEET TOOTH   *See* Sweet Tooth.

HAVE BIGGER FISH TO FRY   *See* Have Other Fish to Fry.

HAVE EGG ON YOUR FACE   *See* Egg on Your Face.

HAVE ENOUGH/TOO MUCH ON YOUR PLATE   *See* Full Plate.

HAVE GUSTO   *See* Gusto.

HAVE ICE WATER IN YOUR VEINS   *See* Put on Ice.

HAVE LITTLE RELISH FOR   *See* Relish (n).

HAVE MORE IMPORTANT FISH TO FRY   *See* Have Other Fish to Fry.

HAVE NO STOMACH FOR   *to have no stomach for something.* To have no appetite or tolerance for something. Source: STOMACH. MWCD: 14th cent. A person who *has no stomach for* boxing—i.e., *can't stomach it*—can't tolerate it because it features too much violence. A person who *has no stomach for* opera *can't stomach it* because it is sung in a foreign language. The sight of blood *turns some people's stomachs*—i.e., makes them physically ill; but a doctor or nurse in an operating room must *have a strong stomach* to put up with all of the unpleasant sights, sounds, and smells. The stomach has been a symbol of various things since ancient times: strength, courage, fortitude—as witnessed by the modern expression "No guts, no glory." AID; CI; DAI; DAS; DEI; MS.

HAVE OTHER FISH TO FRY   *to have other fish to fry.* To have other matters to attend to. HND: 1552. (From an Eng. translation of Rabelais' *Pantagruel*.) Source: FISH (MWCD: O.E.); FRY (v) (MWCD: 13th cent.). Frying flour-coated fish in a pan of oil requires close attention because *pan fish* (MWCD: 1805) are small, cook quickly, must be turned at least once, and become tough if overcooked. If interrupted in this process, the cook might very well treat the interrupter as if he/she were a "fish" wishing to be "fried" (i.e., paid attention to) but then reject that wish in favor of dealing with the more important matter of frying the fish already in the pan. In fact, one variation of the metaphor is *to have more important fish to fry.* AID; ATWS; BDPF; CI; DAI; DEI; HB; IRCD; MS; SA.

HAVE POTATOES GROWING IN—OR BEHIND—YOUR EARS   *See* Slice of the Melon.

HAVE SAND IN YOUR CRAW   *See* Stick in Your Craw.

HAVE SAND IN YOUR GIZZARD   *See* Stick in Your Craw.

HAVE SCRAMBLED EGGS FOR BRAINS   *See* Scrambled Eggs.

HAVE SOMEONE EATING OUT OF THE PALM OF YOUR HAND   *See* Have Someone Eating out of Your Hand(s).

HAVE SOMEONE EATING OUT OF YOUR HAND(S)   *to have someone eating out of (the palm of) your hand(s)*. To have domination or control over someone. DC: 1921. Source: EAT. MWCD: O.E. According to Genesis 1:28, Adam was given dominion over the fish of the sea, the fowl of the air, and the four-legged creatures of the land. Adam's "dominion" at that time may have meant that all of the animals were tame, that they would lit. *eat out of his hands*. However, nowadays only domesticated animals and unthreatened—or starving—wild animals will do this; all of the rest would just as soon eat your hands, along with the food in them. Therefore, to have another human being *eating out of your hands*, or being completely submissive to you, is quite an accomplishment, giving you a real sense of power, esp. if that person is someone in possession of power him/herself. AID; BDPF; CE; DAI; DEI; HND; MS; NSOED; SA. *See also* Bite the Hand That Feeds You.

HAVE SOMETHING UNDER YOUR BELT   *to have something under your belt*. To have accomplished something that you never have to accomplish again. HND: before-1954. Source: STOMACH. The basis for this metaphor is the process of eating—i.e., of filling up your stomach, which is located under your belt. Once you have eaten breakfast, for example, that meal is now "under your belt" and need not be consumed again that day. Metaphorically, a goal that has been achieved is like food that has been chewed, swallowed, and digested: It is now part of your permanent record. The expression is used of artists (to have two plays *under your belt*), coaches (to have two wins *under your belt*), businesspersons (to have two major deals *under your belt*), etc. If you have *nothing* under your belt, i.e., are short on food because of a shortage of money, then the thing to do is to *tighten your belt*—or, if this has gone on for some time, to *tighten your belt another notch*. DAI; DEI; MS.

HAVE THE HUNGRIES   *See* Snack Bar.

HAVE THE MUNCHIES   *See* Snack Bar.

HAVE TWO BITES OF THE CHERRY   *See* Two Bites of the Cherry.

HAVE YOUR BREAD BUTTERED ON BOTH SIDES   *See* Butter Your Bread on Both Sides.

HAVE YOUR CAKE AND EAT IT TOO   *See* You Can't Eat Your Cake and Have It too.

HAVE YOUR HEAD ON THE CHOPPING BLOCK   *See* Chopping Block.

HAVE YOUR NERVES GRATED   *See* Grate on Your Nerves.

HEADCHEESE   *See* Cheesehead.

HEAD CHEESE   *See* Cheesehead.

HEAD LETTUCE   *See* Lettuce.

HEAR IT THROUGH THE GRAPEVINE   *to hear (or learn) it through (on, or by) the grapevine.* To receive unsubstantiated information, such as rumor or gossip, by word of mouth. HDAS: 1862. Source: GRAPE; VINE. MWCD: 14th cent. The grape is a berry that grows in clusters on a vine—a *grapevine* (MWCD: ca. 1736). During the American Civil War, soldiers distinguished between official information that came to them by the telegraph line (which was first employed in California in 1859) and unofficial information that reached them by the *grapevine telegraph* (HDAS: 1862), which was person-to-person communication. (Some sources believe that the *grapevine* was selected for the metaphor because a telegraph line sags, between poles, like a grapevine; others believe that the telegraph was selected because communication over the grapevine was just as fast as that over the wires.) *Grapevine telegraph* has since been shortened to *grapevine*, and the metaphor is still current, appearing in a 1990s commercial jingle for California raisins, which danced and sang to the music of "I Heard It through the Grapevine." BDPF; CE; CI; DAS; DC; DEI; LA; LCRH; MDWPO; MS; NSOED.

HEAVY BREAD   *See* Bread.

HEDGE APPLE   *See* Osage Orange.

HEINZ 57 VARIETIES   *See* Pickle (n).

HEN FRUIT   *See* Egg on Your Face.

HERB OF GRACE   *the herb of grace.* Rue. Source: HERB. MWCD: 14th cent. An *herb* (fr. Lat. *herba*) is a seed-producing (and sometimes flower-producing) plant or shrub whose fresh or dried leaves are used for medicinal and culinary purposes. *Rue* (MWCD: 13th cent.) is a strong-scented, yellow-flowered shrub with bittertasting leaves. It has been called the *herb of grace* since Shakespeare's time because the word *rue* coincides with another, similarly spelled Eng. word that functions either as a noun meaning "regret or sorrow" or as a verb meaning "to feel regret or sorrow," and the church is the place where such repentance takes place. Shakespeare illustrates this overlap in *Hamlet* (ca. 1602), Act IV, Scene 5, 175–185, where a delirious Ophelia mourns the death of her father, Polonius, by handing out symbolic herbs and flowers to members of the Danish court: *rosemary* (an herb symbolizing "remembrance") and pansies to her brother, Laertes; *fennel* (an herb symbolizing "deceit") and columbine to the King; and *rue* to the Queen and herself. Regarding *rue*, Ophelia says, "We may call it *herb of grace* o' Sundays" [italics added]—i.e., the symbol of God's forgiveness. Then she adds, "O, you [the Queen] must wear your *rue* with a difference" [italics added], meaning that the Queen should feel guilt (i.e., *rue*) about the circumstances of her husband's death and her hasty remarriage, whereas Ophelia should feel sorrow, but not guilt, over the death of her father. BDPF; EWPO; FLC; NSOED; WNWCD.

HERE'S MUD IN YOUR EYE!   *Here's to you!* (A drinking toast.) HDAS: 1927. Source: TOAST. It is not clear what *mud* and *eye* have to do with a good luck wish, but they may derive from the rare cup of lukewarm coffee (called *mud* in lunch-counter jargon) with which soldiers toasted each other in the trenches of WWI. Under such trying conditions, the "mud" from the canteen cup might spill over and hit the soldier in the eye on the way down. *Down the hatch!* (HND: 1933), in contrast, is a toast that clearly derives from sailors rather than soldiers. The sailor's mouth is equated with the "hatch," or the opening on the main deck of a ship that leads to the holds below. The toast *Bottoms up!* is neutral in respect to armed services: It simply wishes the drinker good luck in emptying the bottle, so that its bottom is pointed up in the air during the drinking of the last drop. An early Fr. toast was *Lampons!* "Let us drink!" which came into Eng. as *lampoon*, meaning "a personal satire" (MWCD: 1645). In modern times the word appears in the title of the *Harvard Lampoon*, a magazine devoted to satirical writing, and the *National Lampoon* films, which deal with stereotyped, rather than personal, satire. To *lampoon* someone (MWCD: ca. 1657) is to subject that person to ridicule. BDPF; DAFD; DC; EWPO; IHAT; WNWCD.

HERO   *See* Submarine Sandwich.

HERSHEY BAR   *See* Chocoholic.

HIDEBOUND   *to be hidebound.* To be narrow-minded, inflexible, or ultraconservative. Source: STARVE (v). Cattle that are hidebound have been starved to the point that their hide lit. "sticks to their ribs"; i.e., the flesh that ordinarily separates the skin from the bones has almost disappeared, and the ribs are visible enough to count. Hidebound skin is useless because it is inflexible and inelastic and practically bonded to the bone. People who are *hidebound* have minds that are as inflexible and inelastic as the hide, causing a kind of mental starvation that deprives them of fresh and diverse ideas. In contrast, food that *sticks to your ribs* (DC: 1670) is a *good* thing. It means that the food is filling enough to satisfy your hunger for several hours to come. AID; ATWS; DAI; EWPO; HF; HND; LCRH; SA.

HIDE THE PEA   *See* Like Two Peas in a Pod.

HIDE THE SILVERWARE!   *See* Silverware.

HIGH TEA   *See* Tea.

HILL OF BEANS   *See* Not Worth a Hill of Beans.

HIT A SOUR NOTE   *to hit—or strike—a sour note.* To change, for the worse, the entire complexion of an event or relationship. Source: SOUR (adj.). MWCD: O.E. In music, a *sour note* is either a "wrong" note or one that is sharp, flat, or otherwise mangled. In this sense, a "correct" note is like sweet milk, and a "sour" note is like milk turned sour. Outside of music, a *sour note* is something that is said or done that causes an abrupt—and negative—change in the mood of an audience or the relationship between two people or groups. At that point the mood or relationship is said to *turn—or go—sour* (or simply to *sour*), i.e., to become unpleasant and unpromising. People can also *go sour on* something that used to be one of their favorite pastimes (such as rollerblading after a painful spill); patients in the emergency room can *go—or turn—sour* if their condition begins to deteriorate rapidly; and a project or deal *gone sour* is one that once held great promise but now is about to be abandoned. AID; DAS; MS.

HIT SOMEONE IN THE BREADBASKET   *See* Breadbasket.

HIT THE CEILING   *See* Pressure Cooker.

HIT THE SAUCE   *See* Sauce.

HIT THE SPOT   *to hit the spot.* To be exactly what your mouth, throat, or stomach wants or needs. HND: mid-19th cent. Source: APPETITE. No one knows where the mysterious "spot" is that so quickly and completely satisfies hunger or thirst. In fact, there may be more than one "spot," depending on what kind of satisfaction is required. The stomach is the easiest to please because all it wants is hot and hearty food. The throat likes food that is soft and smooth, and liquid that is either hot or cold, not lukewarm. The mouth is the most difficult to please because that is where the taste buds are located, and the sense of smell is somewhat involved. Taste, smell, and the feel of tiny bubbles are what made Pepsi-Cola *Hit the Spot* in the 1930s and 1940s, according to the radio jingle. DAI; DC; WNWCD.

HOAGIE   *See* Submarine Sandwich.

HOBO EGG   *See* Fried Egg.

HODGEPODGE   *a hodgepodge*. A mixture, mess, or jumble. HF: 17th cent. Source: POT. MWCD: O.E. *Hodgepodge* is an Amer. corruption of Eng. *hotchpotch* (MWCD: 1583) "a stew of meat, potatoes, and vegetables"; and *hotchpotch* is a corruption of earlier Eng. *hotchpotch* (MWCD: 1552), which is closer to the original Fr. *hochepot* "shaking pot." A pot of stew would be much too heavy for a cook to shake, so O.Fr. *hochier* must have referred to the chunks of meat and vegetables shaking in the hot water and juices. On the basis of the variety of foods that were combined to create a stew, the judicial system in England applied the name *hotchpot* to the combining of properties of an estate into a single "pot" before distributing the resulting "stew" equally among the heirs. In America, a *hotchpotch* (or *hot pot*—MWCD: 1851) is a stew, whereas a *hodgepodge* is a mixture. (The metaphor of America as a "melting pot" has pretty much given way to America as a "stew.") On the European continent, the stew is still called *hochepot* in France and Belgium, where pigs' feet and ears are sometimes added, and it is called *hutspot* in the Netherlands, where the vegetables are usu. mashed. BDPF; FLC; PT. *See also* Stew.

HOECAKE   *See* Pancake (n).

HOG (n)   *a hog*. A greedy glutton. Source: HOG. MWCD: 14th cent. From the time that hogs are born, they seem to have insatiable appetites and little concern for their fellow beings. They fight with each other for the last vacant teat when they are piglets, they crowd each other at the feeding trough when they are pigs, and they bully each other over the choicest clover (or truffles) when they are fully grown hogs. Human *hogs* are people who either monopolize the available resources, use more than their fair share of them, or waste whatever portions they take. On a higher metaphorical level, people *hog* not only the food and drink but also the attention, the conversation, the *limelight* (q.v.), the publicity, and the road. A *road hog* (MWCD: 1891) has no intention of sharing the road with anyone, and it is more than likely that he/she is driving a car that "drinks gas as if it were water": a *gas hog*. DEI; SA.

HOG THE LIMELIGHT   *See* Hog (n).

HOGWASH   *See* Taste like Dishwater.

HOLD OUT AN OLIVE BRANCH   *to hold out an—or the—olive branch*. To make an offer of peace. Source: OLIVE. MWCD: 13th cent. The olive tree, along with its branches and fruit, was held in great esteem by the ancient civilizations in the eastern end of the Mediterranean. The first mention of the olive was in Egyptian records from the 17th cent. B.C. In Greek mythology, Athena was said to have planted the first olive tree, in the city that was to become her namesake, Athens. In time, a *crown of olives* (or olive branches) became the highest honor that could be bestowed on a citizen, and it was also the highest prize that was awarded in the Olympic Games. (Plato engaged his students under some olive trees near Athens: the *groves of academe*.) In Genesis 8:11, when the dove returned to Noah's ark for the second time, with an olive leaf in its mouth, Noah was delighted because he "knew that the waters [of the flood] were abated from off the earth" and that his people were again at peace with God. (The third time, the dove did not return at all.) Today, a peace offering is called an *olive branch* (MWCD: 14th cent.), and *to hold out an/the olive branch* is to extend an offer of peace. AID; ATWS; BDPF; CI; DC; DEI; LCRH; MS; NSOED; SA.

HOLD THE MAYO!   Don't add mayonnaise to my sandwich. HDAS: ca. 1910. Source: MAYONNAISE. MWCD: 1841. *Mayo* (MWCD: ca. 1960) is the clipped form of *mayonnaise*, which is a salad dressing containing egg yolks, vegetable oil, lemon juice or vinegar, and seasonings. Mayonnaise is the base for *tartar sauce* (q.v.) and for other dressings such as blue cheese, creamy French, Green Goddess, Ranch, Russian, and Thousand Island. *Mayo* got its name from waitresses (*sic*) in lunch counters shouting out *Hold the mayo!* when customers didn't want dressing on their meat or cheese sandwich. (The scene is reminiscent of Jack Nicholson's character in the film *Five East Pieces* who solved the problem of a waitress in a diner refusing to bring him toast—because it was "not on the menu"—by ordering a toasted chicken sandwich—which *was* on the menu—and telling her to "Hold the chicken!") The origin of the name *mayonnaise* is another story. Most sources agree that the word is the fem. form of a Fr. adj. derived from the Sp. name for the capital of Minorca: *Mahón*. Some of these sources cite, as evidence, the existence of an intermediate form, *Mahonnaise*, with capital *M* and an *h*, that appeared in use in Parisian restaurants in the mid-18th cent. What is the connection between a salad dressing with egg yolks and the capital of Minorca? American sources are less certain about that, but Brit. sources believe that the dressing was concocted by the Duc de Richelieu, a French officer who, in 1756, captured the Spanish port of Mahón, raided a kitchen there, mixed up everything he could get his hands on, and created mayonnaise. (Why it took eighty-five years for the dressing to get to England is anybody's guess.) BDPF; DAFD; DAS; EWPO; FLC; IHAT; LA; NSOED; PT; WNWCD. *See also* Salad; Salad Days.

HOLEY AS SWISS CHEESE   *as holey as Swiss cheese*. Full of holes. Source: CHEESE. MWCD: O.E. The *Swiss cheeses* (MWCD: 1822) that are referred to here are Emmentaler and Gruyère, which develop numerous large holes during the ripening process. The metaphor is used to describe something that has been partially eaten by worms (such as a woolen sweater attacked by moth larvae) or something that has been pierced by projectiles (such as a human body that has been shot through many times with bullets). A *Swiss-cheese infield* in baseball is a "leaky" one—one that is "full of holes." It is a collection of infielders who are unable to catch, stop, or make a play on any kind of ball hit their way. Such an error-prone infield has both literal "holes" (where the ball always seems to find its way) and figurative "holes" (where the ball always seems to pass directly through a player's glove). FLC.

HOME CANNING   *See* In the Can.

HOME PLATE   *See* Full Plate.

HOMINEY GRITS   *See* Grits.

HONEY   Sweetheart. NSOED: late-M.E. Source: HONEY. MWCD: O.E. *Honey* is a term of address and endearment for one's spouse or child, or someone else's child (esp. a girl). The association of honey with sweetness is a very old one, considering that honey was the principal sweetener in the world before the cultivation of sugar cane and sugar beets and the invention of artificial sweeteners. Based on the belief that a sweet taste is "good," but bitter, salty, and sour tastes are "bad," *honey* has appeared in several terms of endearment and address: *Honeybun, Honeybunch* (LA: 1904), *Honeycakes*, and *Honey Child. Honey* can also function as a superlative example of a human being ("Her grandchild is a *honey*") or of a thing ("That's a *honey* of a shot"—LA: 1888). The *honeysuckle* plant, which has flowers full of nectar ("honey"), attracts insects by the hundreds, proving that *You can catch more flies with honey than with vinegar* (HND: early-18th cent.). Honey is produced from the nectar of flowers by honey bees, which store the sticky sweet liquid in the hexagonal cells of the wax honeycomb in which they themselves were once incubated. Jonathan Swift, in his Preface to *The battle of the books* (1697), symbolized honey and wax as "sweetness" and "light," respectively. In the early- to mid-20th cent., the sweetest treat that any child could receive was a chunk of *honeycomb* (NSOED: O.E.) filled with liquid honey. The comb was chewed until all of the honey had been swallowed; then the wax was set aside for chewing on another day. Nowadays, all that people know about the word *honeycomb* is that it describes a strong, lightweight structural material that contains hundreds of air cells and keeps soda pop cold until you are ready to drink it. ATWS; BDPF; CE; CODP; DAFD; DAP; DAS; DC; DEI; EWPO; FLC; HDAS; HND; PT; SA.

HONEYBUN   *See* Honey.

HONEYBUNCH   *See* Honey.

HONEYCAKES   *See* Cupcake; Honey.

HONEY CHILD   *See* Honey.

HONEYCOMB   *See* Honey.

HONEYDEW MELON   *See* Slice of the Melon.

HONEYMOON   *a honeymoon*. A harmonious vacation for a newly married couple. MWCD: 1546. Source: HONEY. MWCD: O.E. The *honeymoon* for newlyweds is so called because it is *as sweet as honey* and lasts up to an entire month (a "moon"). When the "sweet month" is over, the couple return to the real world and discover that two people cannot live as cheaply, or as peacefully, as one; i.e., *The honeymoon is over*. The *honeymoon* metaphor has been extended in modern times to the relationship between a newly elected official, such as the president of the United States, and the loyal opposition with whom he/she must deal. It has become a custom to give the president a "break" from opposition during his/her first few months in office—i.e., a *honeymoon*. However, when the period of peace and harmony comes to an end, it is announced that *The honeymoon is over*, and the president is now fair game for whatever criticism he/she deserves. ATWS; DAI; DAP; DAS; DEI; HF; LCRH; MDWPO; MS; NSOED; SA.

HONEYMOON IS OVER   *See* Honeymoon.

HONEYSUCKLE   *See* Honey.

HOOVER HOG   *See* Cape Cod Turkey.

HORS D'OEUVRES   *See* Appetizer; Whet Your Appetite.

HORSE RADDISH   A large, white, pungent root of the mustard family. MWCD: 1597. (*Horseradish* is also used as an interjection meaning "Nonsense!"—HDAS: 1924.) Source: RADISH. MWCD: 15th cent. Horseradish is seldom seen by consumers in its raw form, which is impressive: up to a foot and a half in length. It is more often found on the table, as part of a pungent sauce, or as a condiment for meats, such as prime rib. The *horseradish* is so called because of its size—the horse being one of the largest of domestic animals—and its identification with the more familiar "common" radish. Many people believe that the horseradish is so called because its flavor and aroma are "as strong as a horse"; but the presence of *horse* in *horsechestnut*, which has neither flavor nor aroma, pretty much rules that out. *Horseradish* is therefore not a food metaphor but an animal metaphor. The common *radish* (fr. Lat. *radix* "root") is smaller (usu. one to two inches in length), more rounded, less pungent, and red. As a root, the radish is related to the beet, carrot, parsnip, and turnip. DAFD; DAS; EWPO; FLC; NSOED; SA.

HOTBED OF ACTIVITY   *See* Garden.

HOTCAKE   *See* Hot off the Griddle; Sell like Hotcakes.

HOTCHPOT   *See* Hodgepodge.

HOTCHPOTCH   *See* Hodgepodge.

HOT DIGGITY DOG   *See* Hot Dog (n).

HOTDOG (v)   *See* Hot Dog (n).

HOT DOG (n)   *a hot dog.* A show-off or exhibitionist. HDAS: 1897. Source: HOT DOG. HDAS: 1895. It is a long way from *hot dog*, meaning a "hot sausage in a bun," to *hot dog* meaning "a show-off or exhibitionist." One of the first applications of the word *hot dog* to a "hot sausage in a bun" was in the early 1900s, when the New York sports cartoonist T. A. Dorgan ("TAD") drew a cartoon of a dachshund lying in a bun and called it a *hot dog.* (The sausage in a bun had formerly been called a *red hot.*) This was no surprise to the vendors or fans at the home of the New York Giants baseball team, the Polo Grounds, where hot sausages in a bun had affectionately been called *dachshund sausages* for several years. To them, the cartoon was simply amusing. However, to the dispensers of hot frankfurters in a bun (called "Coney Islands") at the Coney Island Amusement Park, the cartoon suggested that their sausages were made of dog meat, and they retaliated by getting the Chamber of Commerce to ban the term *hot dog* from all billboards and signs on the boardwalk. Today, both *hot dog*, the generic term, and *Coney Island*, the term of the opposition, are familiar throughout the country. Other terms for "hot dog" are *chili dog* "a hot dog topped with chili meat" (MWCD: 1969); *corn dog* "a wiener dipped in cornmeal batter, deep-fried, and served on a stick" (MWCD: 1967); and *tube steak*, a slang term for a hot dog in New York City. *Hot dog* prob. acquired the sense of "show-off" or "exhibitionist" from the baseball players who liked to draw attention to themselves by performing fancy stunts for the benefit of the "hot dog eaters"—the fans. In addition, the fans got a certain thrill from hearing the vendors of the hot sausages shouting "Hot dogs! Get your hot dogs!" and from their own shouting of "Hot dog!" to get the vendor's attention. *Hot dog!* became a general exclamation of delight or approval (NSOED: late-19th cent.) and spawned the even more enthusiastic *Hot diggity dog!* (HDAS: 1923). When the term *hot dog* reached the West Coast, it developed into a verb associated with the sport of surfing—to *hotdog* "to perform unnecessarily dangerous maneuvers on a surfboard" (MWCD: 1962), and now a *hotdogger* (HDAS: 1961) is one who shows off on either water or snow. ATWS; CE; DAFD; DAI; DAS; EWPO; FLC; HB; IHAT; IRCD; MDWPO; NSOED; SA.

HOT DOG!   *See* Hot Dog (n).

HOTDOGGER   *See* Hot Dog (n).

HOT FUDGE SUNDAE   *See* Sundae.

HOT OFF THE GRIDDLE   Produced only minutes ago, with no delay in delivery: "Hot off the press!" Source: GRIDDLE. MWCD: 14th cent. One of the alternative names for *pancake* is *griddle cake* (MWCD: 1783). Griddle cakes are intended to be served hot—hence another alternative name: *hotcake*. A griddle cake that is *hot off the griddle* has developed from batter poured onto a hot iron plate (orig. circular, hence the alternative term *girdle cake*). The batter forms a round "cake" that is allowed to cook until brown on the bottom. Then it is flipped, allowed to cook on the other side, and immediately served to the mouth-watering diners. BDPF; FLC; PT.

HOT OFF THE GRILL   *See* Grill a Suspect.

HOT PEPPER   *See* Pep (n).

HOT POT   *See* Hodgepodge.

HOT POTATO   *a hot potato*. A controversial or embarrassing subject; a difficult or dangerous problem; a disagreeable or unpleasant person. HND: 1930. Source: POTATO. MWCD: 1565. A literal "hot potato" is a white potato that is baked in its skin until the flesh becomes soft and flaky. The reason why the potato was selected for this metaphor is that this tuber contains a large amount of water, which is held inside by the tough skin. If you were to hold a freshly baked potato in your hand, you would instinctively drop it at once; and if you tossed it to someone else, he/she would do the same thing. This reflex is the basis for the metaphor *hot potato* and also for the metaphorical expression *to drop something— or someone—like a hot potato*. A metaphorical *hot potato* is something that is dropped into your lap (or hands) that you don't want to touch for fear of getting burned. Social *hot potatoes* are usu. subjects that involve gender, politics, race, religion, or sex. Personal *hot potatoes* are people who are *too hot to handle*—either because they embarrass you, abuse you, harass you, lie to you ("Why didn't you tell me you were married?"), or simply no longer please or satisfy you. In "ball" sports, such as baseball, basketball, and football, in which a player is expected to be able to catch a ball, a *hot potato* is a ball that is batted, thrown, or kicked so hard that the receiving player can't handle it. In baseball, if a catcher tags a runner out at home plate—when there are other runners on base—and then tosses the ball to the umpire, thinking that there are three outs, the umpire will try *not* to catch the toss—i.e., will *drop it like a hot potato* because the ball is still in play. BDPF; CE; CI; DAI; DAS; DEI; MS; NSOED; PT.

HOT SANDWICH   *See* Sandwich (n).

HOT SAUCE   *See* Sauce.

HOT STUFF   *See* Java.

HOUSEBOAT   *See* Banana Boat; Lunch-counter Jargon.

HOW DO YOU LIKE THEM APPLES?   What do you think about *that*? HDAS: 1926. Source: APPLE. MWCD: O.E. The word *them* gives this question away as a colloquialism or slang expression. The *apples* in question were orig. real apples in a market, but now they are metaphors for anything large, outstanding, or unusually prominent, such as women's breasts ("She's got *some apples*!") or men's or women's talents ("He is *some apples*!"). A person who is esp. intelligent has been known as a *smart apple* (or *one smart apple*) since the early-1920s, but today the phrase can also mean "a smart alec or wise guy." If the smart alec's father was also like that, then the observation might be made that *the apple doesn't fall far from the tree* (CODP: 1839), i.e., "like father, like son." DAP; DAS; DC; DEOD; EWPO; IHAT.

HOW SWEET IT IS!   *See* Sweet Tooth.

HUCKLEBERRY   *a huckleberry*. A person of "little consequence" (e.g., Huckleberry Finn). HDAS: 1889. Source: HUCKLEBERRY. MWCD: 1670. The huckleberry is often confused with the *blueberry* (MWCD: 1709) because both are blue in color, grow on shrubs, are found in the wild, have many seeds, are eaten out of hand or with milk and sugar, and are used in baked goods such as muffins and pies. However, the blueberry is also cultivated, it is larger than the huckleberry, it has more seeds (and they are scattered throughout the berry rather than grouped together in the center, as with the huckleberry), it has a sweeter taste, and it sometimes grows on longer, higher shrubs. The word *huckleberry* prob. derives from the word *hurtleberry*, which is the source of Brit. Eng. *whortleberry* (MWCD: 1578), a name for the blueberry in England. DAFD; EWPO; HF; FLC.

HUMAN PRETZEL   *a human pretzel*. A contortionist. Source: PRETZEL. MWCD: ca. 1838. A contortionist is able to twist his/her supple body into a multitude of shapes, one of which is the *pretzel bow* (or *knot*), the most popular shape for a pretzel. The baker makes a pretzel bow by holding one end of a "rope" of pretzel dough in each hand, bringing his/her hands close together, letting the rounded loop fall on the board, crossing his/her hands (and optionally crossing them again), and placing the ends of the "rope" on the loop. The result looks somewhat like a person crossing his/her arms or sitting in the lotus position. The Eng. word *pretzel* derives fr. Lat. *brachiatus* "having branchlike arms," by way of Ger. *Brezel* "pretzel." The Romans may have invented the pretzel, but in modern times it has been associated with Rhineland Germany, whence it was prob. brought to America by the Pennsylvania "Dutch." This was the traditional large, soft, chewy, yeast pretzel, the kind that is sold from vendors' carts in New York City and is eaten with mustard in Philadelphia (the *Big Pretzel*). In the rest of the country the soft pretzel is catching on (esp. in the ring shape of a bagel), but the small, brittle, crisp, or hard pretzel is preferred, the pretzel stick is popular, and the surface of any pretzel is expected to be sprinkled with coarse salt. To *band someone's mind into a pretzel* is to twist it out of shape. DAFD; EWPO; FLC.

HUNGRIES   *See* Snack Bar.

HUNGRY AS A BEAR   *to be as hungry as a bear.* To be so hungry that you could eat just about anything, including garbage. Source: HUNGER. MWCD: O.E. American bears come in three varieties: black bears (mostly in the East), brown bears (mostly in the West and Northwest), and white bears (in the far North). Black bears are pretty much herbivorous, brown bears (such as the grizzly and Kodiak) are omnivorous, and white bears (i.e., polar bears) are carnivorous. American humans come in the same three varieties, but most of them are like the grizzly, which eats vegetables (esp. fruit and berries), fish (esp. salmon), fowl, and red meat. During periods of great hunger, as in the early winter (before hibernation), and the late winter (after hibernation), the grizzly may raid institutional garbage cans and even the city dump. People who are *as hungry as a bear* are desperate, and not discriminating. AID; SA.

HUNGRY FOR AFFECTION   *to be hungry for affection.* For a child to be starving for love. Source: HUNGER. MWCD: O.E. A child who is *hungry—or starved— for affection* needs to be *loved* as much as he/she needs to be *fed.* The same is true for a child who is *hungry for attention,* although this latter condition is not regarded as being as urgent as the former one. An older child may become *hungry for praise*—from parents, teachers, and coaches. An adult may become *hungry for money* (NSOED: M.E.), i.e., *money-hungry;* and an athlete, or team of athletes, may become just plain *hungry* (HDAS: 1962), i.e., craving a win in the worst way. BDPF; DAS; WNWCD. *Compare* Thirsty for Knowledge.

HUNGRY FOR ATTENTION   *See* Hungry for Affection.

HUNGRY FOR MONEY   *See* Hungry for Affection.

HUNGRY FOR PRAISE   *See* Hungry for Affection.

HUNK DU JOUR   *See* Menu.

HUSH PUPPY   *See* Cornball (n); Doughnut Hole.

I

ICE   *See* Put on Ice.

ICEBOX   *See* Icebox Cookies; Put on Ice.

ICEBOX COOKIES   Cookies made from dough that has been formed and chilled in the "icebox." LA: 1929. Source: ICEBOX (MWCD: 1846); COOKIE (MWCD: 1703). The dough for making icebox cookies is formed into a "log," wrapped in waxed paper, chilled in the "icebox," sliced into "rounds," and baked in the oven. Nowadays, logs of firm cookie dough, ready to slice and bake, can be found in the "cooler" section of the supermarket, where they are more likely to be called *refrigerator cookies*. The word *refrigerator* (MWCD: 1803), for an ice chest, preceded the word *icebox* by over forty years; but the term *icebox cookies* preceded *refrigerator cookies* by two decades. The *refrigerator* in *refrigerator cookies* refers to the electric refrigerator, which was invented in 1916. Generations who were born after WWII usu. call the food cooler a *refrigerator* and the cookies *refrigerator cookies*; those born earlier often use the terms *icebox* and *icebox cookies*. *Icebox pie* (DAFD: 1920s) consists of a bottom crust filled with a creamy mixture that is chilled until firm in the old-fashioned *icebox* or the modern *refrigerator*— also called a *fridge* (MWCD: 1926). People have wondered, ever since a light was first installed in the refrigerator, if the light went out when the door was closed, i.e., when no one was there to see it; however, in spite of considerable research, investigators are still in the dark about this matter. *Refrigerator art*—i.e., (1) kids' drawings attached to the door of the family refrigerator with magnets, (2) any kind of list, message, or reminder so attached, or (3) family photographs—has been around ever since refrigerators got metal doors, but the term dates from ca. the 1980s. DAFD; DAP; FLC; HDAS; LA; NSOED. *See also* Put on Ice.

ICEBOX PIE   *See* Icebox Cookies.

ICE CREAM   *See* Ice-cream Social.

ICE-CREAM CHAIR   *See* Ice-cream Pants.

ICE-CREAM CONE   *an ice-cream cone.* An edible holder, not necessarily cone-shaped, for—or containing—one or more scoops of ice cream. MWCD: 1909. Source: ICE CREAM. MWCD: 1744. The ice-cream cone was invented for the St. Louis World's Fair in 1904—but named five years later. The original "wafer cone" was created by rolling a large cookie wafer into a cone shape, and the "wafer" characteristics still show in today's cones. The *waffle cone* has the lightness and airiness of a wafer, and even some of its superficial "wafer" marks; but unlike the protocone, it is mass-produced in the form of a torch or cup. The *sugar cone* is more recent than the waffle cone, but it is more primitive in form: Not only are the "wafer" marks there, but the cone is actually made of a rolled-up wafer—darker, crispier, and sweeter than the waffle cone. Given a choice, a child will prob. pick a sugar cone. The ice-cream *scoop* may or may not have been the model for the "news" *scoop*, a hot story published or broadcast before a competitor has a chance to do so, or the fashionable *scoop neck*, a low, rounded neckline of a woman's dress, blouse, or sweater. DAFD; WNWCD.

ICE-CREAM PANTS   White flannel trousers. MDWPO: 1908. Source: ICE CREAM. MWCD: 1744. *Ice-cream pants* were de rigueur summer dress-up wear for adult men and young men in the 1920s and 1930s. They were so called because the wool flannel material of which they were made was the color of vanilla ice cream. (They became cream-colored, like French vanilla ice cream, after a few years.) They were also heavy and hot. They absorbed a lot of moisture in warm weather, but they could not be washed, and dry cleaning was very expensive. In the winter, they had to be stored in mothballs, and the smell of camphor lingered throughout the spring. Boys hated them; men tolerated them; and women loved them. When a young man took his date to the ice-cream parlor, wearing his ice-cream pants, he and his date would sit on *ice-cream chairs* (MWCD: 1949), which were standard furniture in such establishments in the 1930s and 1940s. The armless chairs had a round seat, and the back and legs were made of heavy wire. Four of them were set around a matching round table, at which the customers ate their sundaes and splits and drank their malts and shakes. The problem was that the floor of these parlors was usu. either hardwood or tile, and the wire legs of the chairs would spread-eagle under a heavy weight. They were not the sort of chairs—or tables—on which you could do a little dance. HDAS.

ICE-CREAM SANDWICH   *See* Oreo.

ICE-CREAM SOCIABLE   *See* Ice-cream Social.

ICE-CREAM SOCIAL   *an ice-cream social.* A social gathering at which home-made ice cream is the featured refreshment. Source: ICE CREAM. MWCD: 1774. A gathering of this sort was called a *sociable* in the early-19th cent. (NSOED), and in some parts of the country it still is. In the late-19th cent. the noun *social* began to replace the noun *sociable* for such gatherings (MWCD: 1870), and the compound *ice-cream* was added later. An *ice-cream social* (or *sociable*) was an excuse for rural families to relax, let their hair down, party, play games, socialize, and eat a lot of ice cream. It was usu. held at a church, a school, or the town hall—outside, weather permitting. In more recent times the ice-cream social has taken on a more serious purpose, serving as an occasion for churches, schools, and politicians to raise money for their various causes. Kids love ice cream, and the post-WWI jingle "I scream, you scream, we all scream for ice cream" was a play on the words *ice* and *cream*, which sound a lot like what children utter ("Ice scream!") at an ice-cream social (or ice-cream parlor, etc.). It is prob. not a coincidence that the original name of the Eskimo Pie (DAFD: 1921), an ice-cream bar covered with chocolate, was the "I-Scream Bar" (DAFD: 1920). DAFD; NSOED; WNWCD.

ICE-CREAM SODA   *See* Soda.

ICEHOUSE   *See* Put on Ice.

ICEMAN   *See* Put on Ice.

ICE WAGON   *See* Put on Ice.

ICE WATER IN YOUR VEINS   *See* Put on Ice.

ICING ON THE CAKE   *the icing on the cake.* (Also *the frosting on the cake.*) An unexpected bonus. NSOED: early-18th cent. Source: ICING (MWCD: 1769); CAKE (MWCD: 13th cent.). *Icing on the cake* is an unstrived-for goal, one that is almost as welcome as a strived-for goal. For example, if a baseball player is a member of the team that wins the World Series, and he is also named the MVP ("most valuable player"), then the MVP award is the *icing* (or *frosting*) on the *cake* (the championship). Of the two versions of the metaphor, *icing on the cake* is more appropriate because *icing* orig. meant the sugar-and-egg mixture (now called *royal icing*) that is used to decorate a cake (with flowers and writing) that is already coated with *frosting* (DAFD: ca. 1610). Since the mid-19th cent. (MWCD: 1858), at least in America, *icing* has become practically synonymous with *frosting* and has replaced it in the idiolects of many individuals. CE; DAS; DEI; FLC; HDAS; IHAT; MS.

IDIOT SANDWICH   *See* Jam Sandwich.

IF LIFE HANDS YOU A LEMON, MAKE LEMONADE   If you're faced with a stroke of bad luck, turn it into a stroke of good fortune. Source: LEMON. MWCD: 15th cent. In the movie *My Blue Heaven*, Steve Martin and his former mobster companions, now in the witness protection program, commandeer a truckload of empty plastic water-cooler bottles. Martin's buddies regard the haul as a worthless pile of junk, but he sees it as "potential"—by placing the jugs upright in local stores to collect money, ostensibly for a baseball park for the kids. (As it turns out, that's exactly how the money was used.) This upbeat sentiment appears in several different forms involving the lemon: "When you're dealt a lemon, make lemonade"; "Give him/her a lemon, and he/she'll make lemonade." It also applies to eggs: *If you break an egg, make an omelette*. In other words, be resourceful; make the most of the situation. *Lemonade* (MWCD: 1604), a mixture of lemon juice, sugar, and water, was the first of the citrus-juice drinks to become popular; it was followed by *orangeade* (MWCD: 1706) and *limeade* (MWCD: 1892). Of course, if you're in a hurry, you can cut the top off a lemon (the part with the bulge) and squeeze juice directly into your mouth. From this practice came the expressions *Go suck a lemon* (since you're so sour all the time) and *Suck the lemon dry* (i.e., get the most out of an unfavorable break for someone else). MS; NSOED; PT.

IF YOU BREAK AN EGG, MAKE AN OMELETTE   *See* If Life Hands You a Lemon, Make Lemonade.

IF YOU CAN'T STAND THE HEAT, GET OUT OF THE KITCHEN   If you can't put up with the pressures, get out of the business. (Attributed to President Harry S. Truman, 1945–1953.) Source: KITCHEN. MWCD: O.E. President Truman had plenty of pressures during his (almost) eight years in office, considering that he had to take over, during WWII, after the death of the longest-serving president in U.S. history (President Franklin D. Roosevelt, 1933–1945) and almost immediately was faced with the decision on whether to use the atomic bomb. His "kitchen" was the oval office, and his "heat" was the political pressures. President Truman also assumed more blame than most presidents, according to the motto that sat on his desk: "The buck stops here." CODP; DAS; DEI; MS. *See also* Pressure Cooker.

IF YOU SWALLOW WATERMELON SEEDS, THEY'LL GROW IN YOUR STOMACH   *See* Slice of the Melon.

I'M A LITTLE TEAPOT   *See* Tempest in a Teapot.

IMMOVABLE FEAST   *See* Feast.

IMPORTED HAM   *See* Ham (1).

IN A JAM   *to be in a jam.* To be in a bind, a fix, a tight spot; to be "between a rock and a hard place." HDAS: 1894. Source: JAM (*). MWCD: 1706. The phrase *in a jam* is not a food metaphor; i.e., it is derived not from the noun *jam* "a food" (MWCD: ca. 1736) but from the verb *jam* "to crowd," from which the noun *jam* "a crush" (MWCD: 1805) is also derived. The deverbal noun *jam* "a food" prob. gets its name from the act of crowding small whole fruit, such as cherries and strawberries, or pieces of large fruit, such as apples and pears, into a pot with sugar and pectin for boiling down. The resulting condiment is even more crowded because much of the fruit has turned to a puree by that time. Also eliminated from food-metaphor status because of the disparate *jams* are the compound nouns *ice jam, log jam, paper jam*, and *jam session* and the verb phrases *jam up the works, jam on the brakes, jam a batter*, and *jam a basketball*. Even *jampacked*, as in "The jar was *jampacked* with fruit," derives from the packing, not from the fruit. AID; BDPF; CE; DAS; DEI; FLC; HND; MS; NSOED. *See also* Jam Sandwich.

IN A NUTSHELL   Briefly; in summary; in a few words. HND: mid-19th cent. Source: NUTSHELL. MWCD: 13th cent. The words *in a nutshell* are usu. welcome ones to an audience that has sat through a long speech but now realizes that the end of it is finally near. The words are not welcome, however, if a person has been called into the boss's office, lectured, and then told, "*In a nutshell*, you're fired!" The nut whose shell is being referred to here is prob. an English walnut, because DC reports that ca. 1590 an Englishman produced a Bible that could fit into one. Most nuts have shells, but some of them are easier to crack open than others (coconuts prob. being the most difficult). The metaphor *a tough nut to crack* "a difficult problem to solve, a difficult person to deal with" (HND: early-18th cent.) is prob. based on the American ("black") walnut, which is so hard that it must be cracked on an anvil with a heavy hammer. Originally, the metaphor competed with *a hard nut to crack*, which was the form used by Benjamin Franklin and is still more common in Britain. AID; BDPF; CE; CI; DAI; DAS; DEI; HDAS; MS; NSOED.

IN A PECK OF TROUBLE   *to be in a peck of trouble.* To be in a predicament from which you may not be able to escape. Source: PECK. MWCD: 13th cent. In dry measure, a *peck* is an amount equivalent to two liquid gallons. Metaphorically, *a peck of trouble* is a lot of trouble, exceeded only by *a bushel of trouble*—fr. *bushel* (MWCD: 14th cent.), an amount equivalent to eight liquid gallons, or four pecks. Someone who has *bushels of money* has too much to count, esp. if it is in the form of coins. When one person loves another *a bushel and a peck*, that person loves the other more than a lot—actually, forty quarts' worth.

IN A PICKLE   *to be in a pickle.* To be in a difficult or troubling situation. MDWPO: late-15th cent. Source: PICKLE (n). MWCD: 15th cent. *To be in a pickle* is a loan translation of the Du. expression *in de pekel zitten* "to sit in the pickle," i.e., to sit in cold salt brine (the *pekel*). It was already a metaphor before it was borrowed into English. Shakespeare used the phrase in *The Tempest* (ca. 1611), Act I, Scene 1, when Alonzo, King of Naples, asks Trinculo, the jester, "How cam'st thou *in this pickle?*" and Trinculo replies, "I have been *in such a pickle . . . since I last saw you . . .*" [italics added]. The expanded metaphor *to be in a pretty pickle*, which adds sarcasm or irony to the situation (there is nothing pretty about brine), developed in England shortly after the original borrowing. *Pickle* as the name for a cucumber preserved in brine developed sometime after the metaphor, perhaps in America. AID; BDPF; CE; DC; DEI; EWPO; HB; HND; MS; PT.

IN APPLE-PIE ORDER   In perfect order. MWCD: 1780. Source: APPLE PIE. IHAT: 1760s. This phrase is used to describe the condition of a physical setting— such as a property, a building, or a room—or a social setting—such as a convention, a meeting, or a date. The connection between *apple pie* and orderliness has not been established to everyone's satisfaction. Some lexicographers have suggested a corruption of one or the other of two Fr. phrases, *cap-a-pie* "head to toe" and *nappes pliées* "folded linen," and the existence of the Brit. term *apple-pie bed* (q.v.) lends credence to the latter. However, the simplest explanation, at least for the popularity of the term in America, may be that the expression arises from the meticulous care that homemakers exert to arrange the apple slices "just so" on the bottom crust—and to the orderly appearance of the pie just before the top crust is added. AID; BDPF; DAI; DC; DEI; EWPO; HI; HND; MDWPO; MS; NSOED; PT. *See also* American as Apple Pie.

IN A PRESSURE COOKER   *See* Pressure Cooker.

IN A PRETTY PICKLE   *See* In a Pickle.

IN A STEW   *to be in a stew.* To be in a state of heated anger, high anxiety, deep confusion, serious difficulty, profound worry, etc. LA: 1806. Source: STEW. MWCD: 14th cent. Today, *to be in a stew* is to be under some kind of mental stress, but in the 13th cent. it would have meant to be in a cooking pot. In the 14th cent. the word *stew* went in two quite different directions: (1) it meant (a) a dish of cooked meat and vegetables and (b) a mixture of various and sundry things; and (2) it came to mean (a) a steam bath or public bathhouse and (b) a whorehouse or bordello. The senses in (1) were prob. influenced by the verb *stew*, which had developed in the 14th cent. for cooking food in a covered pot, over a low fire, for a long time—i.e., *stewing* it. Modern stew is something like a soup, but thicker, and the chunks of meat and vegetables are larger and more numerous. It is also somewhat like (1) chowder, but without the milk; (2) ragout, but thinner and not used as a sauce; and (3) chili or goulash, but with more liquid. In *lunch-counter jargon* (q.v.), the term for beef stew was *bossy in a bowl*. Other foods that have employed the word *stew* are *graveyard stew* (DAFD: 1911), lunch-counter jargon for *milk toast* (q.v.); *Mulligan stew* (MWCD: 1904), hobo slang for catch-

as-catch-can Irish stew; and *son-of-a-bitch stew* (DAFD: 19th cent.), an unidentifiable stew named after the cook—also called *son-of-a-gun stew*. The association
of the sense of "mixture" with *stew* can be seen in the borrowings *goulash* (MWCD:
1866—fr. Hung. *gulyás* "herdsman's meat") and *jambalaya* (MWCD: 1872—fr.
Fr. *jambon* "ham"). AID; BDPF; CI; DAP; DAS; DEOD; EWPO; FLC; IHAT; MS;
PT. *See also* Hodgepodge.

IN BAD/POOR TASTE   *See* In Good Taste.

IN COLD STORAGE   *See* Put on Ice.

INDIANA BANANA   *See* Papaya.

INDIAN BANANA   *See* Fruit with Appeal.

INDIAN CAKE   *See* Pancake (n).

INDIAN CORN   *See* Corn.

INDIAN PUDDING   *See* Hasty Pudding.

INDIAN RICE   *See* Rice Paper.

INDIAN SUGAR   *See* Sugar.

INDIAN TURNIP   *See* You Can't Get Blood from a Turnip.

IN GOOD TASTE   *to be in good taste*. To be fitting and proper. Source: TASTE
(n). MWCD: 14th cent. Something that is *in good taste* is respectful of public
standards and morals: e.g., a proper memorial service for someone who has died
or a fitting tribute for someone who has survived. Such an event is acceptable,
agreeable, considerate, pleasing, polite, and not in need of any alteration or cen-
sorship by the court of public opinion. In other words, it is *tasteful* (MWCD:
1611). In contrast, something that is *in bad—or poor—taste* is disrespectful of
public standards and morals; it is rude or crude, vulgar or obscene, like the off-
color jokes, dirty stories, and lewd behavior at the old burlesque and vaudeville
shows. In other words, it is *distasteful* (MWCD: 1607) or *tasteless* (MWCD: 1603).
AID; CE; DEI; NSOED; WNWCD. *Compare* Good Taste.

INHALE   *See* Devour.

IN HOT WATER   *See* Look like a Boiled Lobster.

IN SHORT ORDER   *See* Maître d'Hôtel.

INTERLARD   *See* Tub of Lard.

IN THE ALLEY   *See* Menu.

IN THE CAN   In the golf cup or hole; in the bathroom or washroom; in the basketball basket or hoop; in jail or prison. Source: CAN. MWCD: O.E. Before the tin can was invented in the late-18th cent. (MWCD: 1770)—and the sealed tin can in the early-19th cent. (LA: 1812)—a *can* was simply a cylindrical vessel for holding liquids: e.g., a milk can or a garbage can. The first *tin cans* (or *tins*), which were less than half the size of a milk can or a garbage can but were also made of metal and had tightly sealing covers, were designed to keep biscuits and crackers crisp and dry during long trips or voyages. The introduction of the sealed—and, later, hermetically sealed—tin can revolutionized food preservation, allowing everything from soup to fish—and everything else, from meat and milk to fruit and vegetables—to be stored for months and even years. Not a lot has changed in the function and appearance of the *tin can* since the Civil War, except that it is now made of tin-plated steel, aluminum, or rigid plastic and has become the nickname for a naval vessel of the destroyer class. True *canning* of food has always been a commercial operation, but when in the second half of the 19th cent. Mason and Ball invented their glass jars with removable lids, making home "canning" possible, the word *canning* was borrowed for that operation also. The noun *can* has also been metaphorized in several other ways besides *in the can*. For example, the baseball expression *a can of corn* (HDAS: 1937)—meaning "a pop fly that is easy to catch"—derives from the placement of canned goods in old-fashioned grocery stores: on the top shelf, where they could be tipped forward with a hooked pole and caught—by hand or in an apron—as they fell. *In the can* not only means "behind bars" but refers to an actual can: a flat, round tin can in which film or videotape is placed once a "shoot" is completed. Other media metaphors are based on the verb *can* (MWCD: 1861), which is derived from the noun *can*. *Canned applause, canned laughter*, and *canned music* (HDAS: 1903) are recordings, made in advance, that are played back during a TV show to enhance the excitement. A *canned speech* is a prepared speech that lacks originality, and a *canned sales pitch* is one that has been given, verbatim, many times before. To *get canned* is to be fired, and to *can it* is to sit down and shut up. AID; DAFD; EWPO; FLC; NSOED. *Compare* In the Cup.

IN THE CUP   *See* Cup (n).

IN THE SOUP   *See* Soup.

IN YOUR CUPS   *See* Cup (n).

IRISH POTATO   *See* Potato.

IRISH TURKEY   *See* Cape Cod Turkey.

IS IT BIGGER THAN A BREADBOX?   Are its dimensions greater than approx. one foot high, one foot deep, and one and one-half feet wide? Source: BREAD. MWCD: O.E. This question was a favorite of members of the panel of *What's My Line?*, a popular television quiz show in the 1960s. The question was asked by a panelist of a guest on the show who was involved with some kind of product. The idea was to narrow the identity of that product and, consequently, that person's occupation. A breadbox is a wooden, metal, or plastic box that has a door that can be lifted when depositing or returning bread or rolls. Its purpose is to help keep the bread fresh, but we all know that that is impossible to do in hot, humid weather. WNWCD. *See also* Breadbasket.

ITALIAN BEEF SANDWICH   *See* Submarine Sandwich.

ITALIAN PERFUME   *See* Onionskin Paper.

ITALIAN SANDWICH   *See* Submarine Sandwich.

IT MUST BE JELLY ('CAUSE JAM DON'T SHAKE LIKE THAT)   It must be fat because muscle isn't that soft. Source: JELLY (MWCD: 14th cent.); JAM (MWCD: ca. 1736). This observation is the title—and first two lines—of a blues-song parody from ca. 1940. The punch line of the parody identifies the "shaker" as a woman who is "so big and fat." (Note also the title of the Broadway musical *Jelly's Last Jam*, i.e., Jelly Roll Morton's last "gig.") Comparing jelly to fat, and jam to muscle, is a good way of contrasting these two fruit-based condiments. They are made in much the same way, by boiling fruit products with sugar and pectin; but the fruit product in jelly is fruit juice, whereas the fruit product in jam is real fruit—either small, whole fruit, such as cherries or strawberries, or pieces of larger fruit, such as apples and pears. The fruit boils down to a thick puree by the end of the process; otherwise it would be called a *preserve* (q.v.).

IT MUST BE THE WATER   *See* Long Drink of Water.

IT MUST HAVE BEEN SOMETHING I ATE   *See* Eat Nails.

IT'S A DOG-EAT-DOG WORLD   *See* Dog-eat-dog.

IT'S DOG-EAT-DOG OUT THERE   *See* Dog-eat-dog.

IT'S THE BERRIES   *See* Berries.

IT'S THE PITS   *See* Pits.

J

JAM (v)   *See* In a Jam.

JAMBALAYA   *See* Cuisine.

JAMPACKED   *See* In a Jam.

JAM SANDWICH   *a jam sandwich.* A bruise resulting from an accident in a baseball game. Source: JAM (n) (MWCD: ca. 1706); SANDWICH (MWCD: 1702). *Jam sandwich* is a baseball term for a reddening of the skin of a player who is involved in a "collision" with a ball, a bat, a bag or plate, a wall, or another player. *Sandwich* apparently relates to the player's bones as the lower "slice of bread," and the player's flesh and skin as the "filling" in between. The fact that the filling is meat and not jam, however, suggests that the word *jam* relates not to fruit but to the force of the blow that occurred to the player's body: He/she was *jammed.* A *knuckle sandwich* (HDAS: 1960) is a blow to the mouth, by which the attacker's knuckles find themselves *sandwiched* (q.v.) between the fist and the face. A *leather sandwich* is a stiff blow to the body in which the leather of the boxing glove is *sandwiched* between the fist of the opponent and the flesh of the victim. An *idiot sandwich* is created when a perfectly sane person is unfortunate enough to be seated between two "kooks" at a sporting event. DAS; NSOED. *See also* Sandwich.

JAVA   *a cup of java (or a java).* A cup of coffee. MWCD: 1850. Source: COFFEE. *A cup of Java*, or *a cup of Joe*, is lunch-counter jargon for a cup of the hot beverage that is brewed from the ground, roasted beans ("berries, seeds") of the coffee plant ("shrub, tree"). Coffee was introduced into England in the late-16th cent., approx. sixty years before the introduction of tea. Tea has competed successfully with coffee in England ever since, but it yielded ground to coffee in America following the Boston Tea Party and the subsequent Revolution. In spite of their similarity— both brewed from the product of a plant—the two beverages originated in widely separated locales: coffee in Ethiopia, and tea in China. Just as tea cultivation was introduced to other Asian countries by European explorers, the cultivation of coffee was introduced to Java, Indonesia, by the Dutch, and to Brazil by the Portuguese. It is a mystery why Americans would select *java* as a slang term for "coffee," rather than, say, *brazil*, because some of the other nicknames are quite sensible: *mud* (HDAS: 1875), because that's what it looks like when brewed strong; *dishwater*, because that's what it looks like when brewed weak; *hot stuff* (CB radio slang), because that's how coffee should be served; and *battery acid*, because that's what U.S. Army coffee tasted like in WWII. (A WWII U.S. Army portable emergency radio was called a *coffee grinder* because it had to be cranked like a coffee mill.) DAFD; DAI; DAS; EWPO; IHAT; NSOED.

JELL (v) *to jell.* For things to come together as expected, hoped, or planned. EWPO: 1949. Source: JELLY. MWCD: 14th cent. The verb *jell* is an Americanism, having first appeared in Louisa May Alcott's *Little Women* (1869), with the literal sense of "congeal." As the spelling suggests, it is a back-formation from *jelly* (MWCD: 14th cent.) "congealed fruit juice." Jelly is made by boiling fruit juice with sugar and pectin (a thickener) and then allowing the liquid to "set" (or congeal) in a container. If the right amount of ingredients has been used, and the fruit juice contains sufficient pectin of its own, the hot liquid will cool into a clear, translucent jelly. A companion term to *jell* (v) is *gel* (v) (MWCD: 1917), from *gelatin* (MWCD: 1800), which has the same literal meaning as *jell* (v) but whose metaphorical meaning is "to make sense" or "to be compatible," which applies more to ideas and personalities than to actions and events. FLC; MS; NSOED; PT.

JELLIED GASOLINE *See* Jelly.

JELLIES *See* Jelly Bean.

JELL-O *See* Nervous Pudding.

JELLY A gelatinous substance. Source: JELLY. MWCD: 14th cent. *Jelly*, orig. only a fruit-based food, and *gelatin*, orig. only an animal-based food, are both derived from the same Lat. verb, *gelare* "to freeze." The assumption is that the juice of boiled fruit (i.e., *jelly*) and boiled animal bones (i.e., *gelatin*) had to be frozen in ancient times in order to cause them to congeal. That is unlikely, how- ever, because bones contain enough colloid to cause the liquid to congeal on its own, when cooled, and fruit contains enough pectin to cause the juice to congeal if you boil it down before cooling. At any rate, anything that is like a jelly—i.e., is soft, clear, spreadable, and sticky—can also be called a *jelly*. One example is *petroleum jelly* (MWCD: 1897), a petroleum-based ointment that is soft, clear, spreadable, and sticky and is used for medical purposes; another is *jellied gasoline* (MWCD: 1944), or "napalm," which has the same properties but was used in Vietnam as an incendiary bomb. DAFD; EWPO; FLC; WNWCD. *See also* Aspic; Legs Turn to Jelly.

JELLY BEAN   *a jelly bean.* A small, egg-shaped candy with a hard sugar coating and a soft, sugary interior. DAFD: 1905. Source: JELLY (MWCD: 14th cent.); BEAN. (MWCD: O.E.). The *jelly bean*, which first went on the market in 1905, is not always bean-shaped, and it does not contain jelly. Nevertheless, everyone knows what jelly beans are, and everyone who can tolerate a high level of sugar enjoys eating them–from proletariats to presidents (e.g., President Ronald Reagan, who always kept a jar of gourmet jelly beans on his desk in the oval office). They come in many different flavors and colors (from white to black). The expression *black jelly bean* surfaced in 1996 as a pejorative term for an African American middle-management employee of a corporation. The jelly bean has inspired the development of *jelly bellies* (formerly a brand name), which are half-size miniatures in exotic colors and flavors, and *jellies*, which are plastic shoes and sandals that come in a variety of bright colors. DAFD; DAS; FLC; WNWCD.

JELLY BELLIES   *See* Jelly Bean.

JELLYFISH   *a (spineless) jellyfish.* A weak-willed person who lacks the courage of his/her convictions and can't make or maintain strong decisions. NSOED: early-19th cent. Source: JELLY (MWCD: 14th cent.); FISH (MWCD: O.E.). The human *jellyfish* is like the marine jellyfish—and they are both like *jelly*—because they both lack backbone (the jellyfish is an invertebrate), they are both wishy-washy (the jellyfish bounces up and down with the current), and neither one stands out in the crowd (the jellyfish is naturally transparent in the water). The marine jellyfish, however, can defend itself with its poisonous stingers, whereas the human *jellyfish* is practically powerless. (When attacked, his/her *legs turn to jelly*.) ATWS; CE; HDAS; LA; SA; WNWCD. *Compare* Waffle (v).

JELLY ROLL   Sex; the female genitalia. HDAS: 1914. Source: JELLY (MWCD: 14th cent.); ROLL (N.D.). The culinary *jelly roll* (MWCD: 1895) is a thin sheet of sponge cake spread with jam or jelly and rolled up. Jelly rolls make excellent snacks because they are not only delicious but clean: The cake is on the outside, and the jelly is on the inside. Before jelly rolls got their name, they were called *jelly cakes* (DAFD: 1860s), and in England they are called *Swiss rolls*. Jelly Roll Morton may have gotten his nickname from playing the piano in bordellos, where *jelly roll* was slang for sex or the female sex organs. FLC.

JELLY'S LAST JAM   *See* It Must Be Jelly.

JERK   *See* Chipped Beef.

JERKIN BEEF   *See* Chipped Beef.

JERKY (n)   *See* Chipped Beef.

JEWISH PENICILLIN   *See* Borscht Belt.

JIGGLY DESSERT   *See* Nervous Pudding.

JOE   *See* Java.

JOHN BARLEYCORN   *See* Applejack.

JOHNNYCAKE   Corn bread. MWCD: 1739. Source: CAKE. MWCD: 13th cent. *Johnnycake* is now the New England equivalent of Southern *corn pone* (MWCD: 1859). Originally, however, *johnnycake* was more like a Mexican tortilla: thin, flat, and round. This breakfast "pancake," dating from the late-1600s, may have been named for a similar food prepared by Native Americans in the Northeast (called *jonikin cake*) or in the Tennessee Valley (called *Shawnee cake*). It is unlikely that another name, *journey cake*, was the basis for the word *johnnycake*, for two reasons: (1) cornbread of any kind would be the worst possible food to carry on a journey because it crumbles instantly into hundreds of tiny pieces; and (2) *johnnycake* was more likely the basis for *journey cake*: To a speaker of an *r*-ful dialect, the *r*-less New England *johnnycake* could easily be misinterpreted as *journey cake*. DAFD; EWPO; FLC; HF; IHAT; MDWPO; NSOED.

JOURNEY CAKE   *See* Johnnycake.

JUICE (n)   The essence of something. Source: JUICE (n). MWCD: 14th cent. The Lat. noun *jus* "broth" remained unchanged in spelling and meaning as it passed through O.Fr. to early-M.E.; but in late-M.E. it acquired its modern spelling, *juice*, and in Mod. Eng. it has acquired numerous metaphorical senses, most of them based on the essential juices of animals, rather than those of plants. *Juice* has become a metaphor for strength (athletes *turn up the juice* at the Olympics), power (car racers *step on the juice* for greater speed), and influence (artists *get the creative juices flowing* when they're inspired). Electrical current is referred to as *juice*, and so is exorbitant interest charged on a loan. Something that is "succulent" is said to be *juicy* (MWCD: 15th cent.), and that adj. also carries the metaphorical senses of "interesting" (*juicy gossip*), "colorful" (*juicy details*), "racy" (*juicy passages*), "substantial" (a *juicy role*), and "rewarding" (a *juicy contract*). *To juice something up* (MWCD: 1955) is to make it more effective (e.g., *to juice up the engine*) or more interesting (e.g., *to juice up the plot*). CE; DAS; NSOED; WNWCD.

JUICE UP   *See* Juice (n).

JUICE UP THE ENGINE   *See* Juice (n).

JUICE UP THE PLOT   *See* Juice (n).

JUICY CONTRACT   *See* Juice (n).

JUICY DETAILS   *See* Juice (n).

JUICY GOSSIP   *See* Juice (n).

JUICY PASSAGES   *See* Juice (n).

JUICY ROLE   *See* Juice (n).

JUMBO SHRIMP   *See* Little Shrimp.

JUNKET   *a junket*. A vacation trip taken by a public official and financed either by the taxpayers or an interested corporation. Source: JUNKET. MWCD: 15th cent. The word *junket* orig. referred to a puddinglike dessert—consisting of co-agulated milk, sugar, and flavorings—that was served in a rush basket (Fr. *jon-quette*). Junket became a popular dessert, and feasts and banquets at which it was served came to be called *junkets*. On one such occasion, a *picnic* (q.v.), a basket of goodies was carried outside, where diners relaxed and had fun. The modern *junket* is prob. derived from this last sense, with the addition of financial support from lobbyists and ordinary citizens, although *curds and whey* (q.v.) are no longer on the menu. FLC; LCRH; PT; THT.

JUNK FOOD   *See* Fast Food.

JUST DESSERTS   *See* Get Your Just Desserts.

JUST FOR GOOD MEASURE   *See* For Good Measure.

JUST PEACHY   *See* Peach.

K

KAFFEEKLATSCH   See Coffee Break.

KEEP THE LID ON   *See* Blow the Lid off.

KEEP THE POT BOILING   *to keep the pot boiling*. (1) To put food on the table, make a living, or maintain a certain standard of living (DC: 1657); (2) to keep the ball rolling, sustain an activity, or maintain a momentum (DC: 1825). Source: POT (MWCD: O.E.); BOIL (v) (MWCD: 13th cent.). *Pot* is a metaphor for "livelihood" in sense (1) and for "activity" in sense (2). Providing a livelihood for your family is done either by operating a self-sufficient farm or working for someone else in order to make enough money to purchase the necessities of life. Sustaining an activity is achieved by working hard, focusing your attention, and maintaining the interest of others. The *pot* in question is the metal container in which food is boiled in liquid—over an open wood fire in the 17th cent. but on a wood- or coal-burning stove in the 19th cent. As long as the pot was boiling, the food was safe to eat, and the family could be kept alive. Two other metaphors that are derived from *keep the pot boiling* are *go to pot* (q.v.) and *potboiler* (MWCD: 1864) "an inferior piece of writing that is done chiefly for profit." *Potboilers* are usu. written by well-known authors, often under noms de plume, who use their reputations to get the works published. The *potboiler* does not gain the writer any more fame, but it does *put food on the table* (q.v.) and *keep the wolf from the door* (q.v.). BDPF; CE; CI; DAS; DEI; EWPO; HB; HI; LCRH; MS; NSOED; WNWCD.

KEEP THE WOLF FROM THE DOOR   *to keep the wolf from the door*. To barely ward off poverty or starvation. DAP: ca. 1470. Source: STARVE. In 15th-cent. England it was the wolf that was starving, not the people. Hungry wolves roamed the streets, seeking out, by smell, the houses where food was being prepared. The occupants may have thought that they themselves were the object of the wolves' search, leading to the birth of this metaphorical expression. Today, the "wolf" is poverty, followed by starvation. The safeguard against being devoured by ravenous "wolves" is not a door but a job: "It's not much of a job, but it *keeps the wolf from the door*"; i.e., it wards off the bill collectors, repo persons, and utility disconnectors and *puts food on the table*. ATWS; HI; LCRH; SA.

KEEP YOUR EYES PEELED   *See* Peel off.

KEEP YOUR EYES SKINNED   *See* Peel off.

KETCHUP   *See* Catsup.

KETTLEDRUM   *a kettledrum*. A musical percussion instrument. NSOED: mid-16th cent. Source: KETTLE (MWCD: 13th cent). The kettledrum in a symphony orchestra is a concave copper or brass hemisphere, the opening in which is covered with "parchment" (sheepskin or goatskin) that can be stretched to vary the pitch. The drum is so called because the hemisphere resembles the large, round-bottomed, metal vessel that has been used to heat water and cook food over an open fire for centuries. (The round bottom, which is a distinctive feature of the kettle, is not mentioned in most dictionary definitions.) The word *kettle* survives in only a few other words and contexts, such as *teakettle* (q.v.), which refers to an inverted kettle with a metal "bottom" that can rest easily on a flat surface; a geological *kettle* (or *pan*), which is a large, round-bottomed hole in the ground that is the remnant of a glacial iceball; the Salvation Army round-bottomed *kettle* (with little "feet") that is hung by a chain from a tripod and is used to collect donations at Christmas time; and a *kettle of fish* (q.v.). Considering that *kettle* is derived fr. Lat. *catillus*, meaning "little bowl," it is surprising that other round-bottomed kitchen vessels, such as the large (for bread dough) and small (for cake and cookie dough) mixing bowls, are not called *kettles*, although perhaps it is because no heat is applied to them. It is refreshing to note, though, that the colloquial expressions *to knock someone ass over teakettle* and *to be ass-over-teakettle in love* with someone recognize the upsidedownness of the teakettle. BDPF; DEOD; WNWCD.

KETTLE OF FISH   *a kettle of fish*. A sorry state of affairs: a "mess." LCRH: early-18th cent. Source: KETTLE (MWCD: 13th cent.); FISH (MWCD: O.E.). *A kettle of fish* was orig. the term for an outdoor picnic along the banks of a river or stream in northern England or southern Scotland, where the salmon swim upstream in the fall to spawn. The salmon were caught, cleaned, cut up into chunks, boiled over an open fire in a cast iron kettle of salted water, and eaten with the fingers. (It is comparable to the *fish boil* conducted in northern Michigan in the summer or fall, using coho salmon, whitefish, or lake trout, boiled in water spiked with beer, wine, or soda pop, and accompanied by white potatoes.) Eating the salmon apparently led to both a literal and figurative "mess," resulting in the association of *kettle of fish* with "a sticky situation." This meaning is also expressed in the phrases *a fine kettle of fish* and *a pretty kettle of fish* (DC: 1742—Henry Fielding's *Joseph Andrews*). Another expression, *a different kettle of fish*—or *another kettle of fish*—has quite a different meaning: "another matter entirely," i.e., *a whole nother kettle of fish*. AID; ATWS; BDPF; CE; CI; DAFD; DAI; DEI; HDAS; HI; HND; IRCD; MDWPO; MS; NSOED; PT; SA; SHM.

KEY LIME   *See* Limey.

KEY LIME PIE   *See* Limey.

KIELBASA   *See* Sausage Dog.

KILL THE FATTED CALF   *to kill the fatted—or fattened—calf*. To prepare an elaborate celebration for an honored guest. Source: FAT (v). MWCD: O.E. *Fatted* is an early-17th cent. form of the past part. *fætt*, of O.E. *fætan* "to fatten." The expression *to kill the fatted calf* is from the parable of the Prodigal Son (Luke 15: 23–24), in which the younger of two sons asked his father for his inheritance, received it, journeyed into a "far country," spent all of his money on "riotous living," went hungry, worked as a "swine feeder," repented, returned home, and was greeted with open arms by his father, who clothed him and ordered the servants to "bring hither the *fatted calf, and kill it*; and let us eat and be merry. For this my son was dead, and is alive again; he was lost, and is found" [italics added]. (This was a momentous occasion; anything less would have called for the slaughtering of a sheep or goat.) In modern times, *to kill the fatted calf* means to "go all out" to honor someone, whether a relative or a friend, whether after a long or short absence, and whether with an *ox roast* or a *fish boil*. We still *fatten up* livestock before selling or slaughtering them (MWCD: 1552), and a parent might even speak of *fattening up* a rather skinny child. AID; BDPF; CI; DC; DEI; EWPO; HB; HND; IRCD; LCRH; MS; NSOED; SA.

KILL THE GOOSE THAT LAID THE GOLDEN EGGS   *to kill the goose that laid—or lays—the goldern eggs*. To destroy a source of future revenue out of impatience for immediate wealth. HND: 15th cent. Source: GOOSE (MWCD: O.E.); EGG (MWCD: 14th cent.). This proverb derives from an Aesop fable about a farmer who raised a goose that laid a single egg of gold every day. Impatient to speed up the process, the farmer killed the goose, expecting to find a cache of golden eggs inside. Instead, he found nothing. Moral: If good fortune strikes, just remember: "Greed killed the goose that laid the golden eggs." AID; ATWS; BDPF; DAI; DAP; DC; LA; LCRH; MDWPO; MS; SA.

KIPPER   *See* Red Herring.

KIPPERED HERRING   *See* Red Herring.

KITCHEN CABINET   *a kitchen cabinet.* A group of friends whom a head of state relies on for advice more than he/she does the officially appointed secretaries or ministers. MWCD: 1832. Source: KITCHEN. MWCD: O.E. President Andrew Jackson (1829–1833) was the first American president to rely on a *kitchen cabinet,* which presumably met with him informally in the kitchen of the White House. All presidents since Jackson have relied on trusted but unofficial advisers, though not necessarily meeting with them in the kitchen; and the term *kitchen cabinet* has also come to apply to a group of advisers to the prime minister of England in the 20th cent. Surprisingly enough, the political meaning of *kitchen cabinet* preceded that of the architectural meaning: "cabinets in the kitchen." BDPF; DEI; WNWCD.

KITCHEN POLICE   U.S. Army mess hall duty. MWCD: ca. 1917. Source: KITCHEN. MWCD: O.E. *Kitchen Police,* or *KP* (MWCD: 1918), is not a detail of military police (or MPs) sent to the mess hall to inspect the food, but an assignment of enlisted men and women to the kitchen, where they peel potatoes, wash pots and pans, mop floors, etc. Soldiers "pull" KP either on a regular basis—about once a month—or when they have committed a misdemeanor that requires a mild form of punishment. The *police* in *Kitchen Police* is from the verbal form of the word, meaning "to clean up an area or put it in order." WNWCD.

KITCHEN-SINK   *See* Everything but the Kitchen Sink.

KITCHEN SPANISH   "Pidgin" Spanish used by an English-speaking householder to communicate with his/her predominantly Sp.-speaking kitchen staff. Source: KITCHEN. MWCD: O.E. Sometimes the only Spanish learned by a householder in a Sp.-speaking country—or in a part of the United States where Sp.-speakers are the only help available—is that which is necessary to communicate with the staff. The "pidgin" consists mostly of Sp. vocabulary that is forced to follow the rules of Eng. grammar and pronunciation, and the source becomes painfully evident when the householder uses it with a Sp.-speaking guest. Spanish is not the only language to be "pidginized" in this way; there is also Kitchen Chinese, Kitchen Japanese, Kitchen Italian, Kitchen French, etc.

KIWIFRUIT   The Chinese gooseberry. MWCD: 1966. Source: FRUIT. MWCD: O.E. The *Chinese gooseberry* is a large, brown, egg-shaped, downy-haired fruit with sweet-tart green flesh and edible black seeds. It may or may not have originated in China, but at least the fruit was imported into both the United States and New Zealand in the early-20th cent. and the vines were cultivated in both countries from approx. 1960. In spite of the usefulness of the fruit in salads and desserts, the association of the word *Chinese* with communism and the Korean War limited its popularity in the United States; so the New Zealand producers changed the name to *kiwifruit,* after the Australian nickname, *Kiwi,* for New Zealanders. The name was apt because the kiwi bird, which is a flightless resident of New Zealand, lays large eggs that hatch into downy brown chicks about the size of a kiwifruit. The strategy worked, and now the American growers of the fruit have changed the name also, producing Chinese gooseberries, renamed after New Zealanders, in California. DAFD; EWPO; FLC; NSOED; PT; SA.

KNOCK FLAT AS A PANCAKE   *See* Flat as a Pancake.

KNOCK SOMEONE ASS OVER TEAKETTLE   *See* Kettledrum.

KNOCK THE STUFFING OUT OF   *to knock—or beat—the stuffing out of some-one.* To trounce someone decisively. Source: STUFFING (?). MWCD: 15th cent. *Stuffing* is the seasoned mixture of bread, eggs, vegetables, etc., that is inserted into the cavities of meat, fish, and (esp.) fowl either before or after baking or roasting. It is so called because the mixture is lit. *stuffed,* or *forced,* by hand, into the abdomen or chest cavity of the animal, a procedure that led to the appearance of the word *forcemeat* (MWCD: ca. 1688), esp. in Britain, as a synonym for *stuffing.* The "revolting" nature of these terms led, in "Victorian" America, to the development of a third term, *dressing* (LA: 1880s), as an acceptable euphemism. *Dressing* had previously denoted a seasoned sauce for vegetables—e.g., *salad dressing* (MWCD: ca. 1839)—but it has now competed successfully with *stuffing* for over a century. The expression *to knock—or beat—the stuffing out of someone* prob. derives not from a stuffed turkey but from a stuffed toy, such as a teddy bear, although both *stuffings* have the same origin. CE; CI; DAFD; FLC; MS; NSOED.

KNOCKWURST   *See* Sausage Dog.

KNOW BEANS (ABOUT)   *See* Not Worth a Hill of Beans.

KNOW HOW MANY BEANS MAKE FIVE   *See* Not Worth a Hill of Beans.

KNOW WHERE YOUR NEXT MEAL IS COMING FROM   *See* Live from Hand to Mouth.

KNOW WHICH SIDE YOUR BREAD IS BUTTERED ON   *to know which side your bread is buttered on.* To know what's good for you; to know what's to your physical, social, or economic advantage. DC: 1546. Source: BREAD; BUTTER. MWCD: O.E. To know what is to your advantage is to know how to act—or not act—in an advantageous way toward others. If you "know what's good for you," you won't argue with your boss, cheat on your spouse, or wake up a sleeping dog. That would be self-defeating behavior. Bread is buttered on only one side, not two. You can't have it both ways. BDPF; CE; DAI; DEI; HND; MS; NSOED. *Compare* Butter Your Bread on Both Sides.

KNOW YOUR OATS   *See* Feel Your Oats.

KNOW YOUR ONIONS   *See* Onionskin Paper.

KNUCKLE SANDWICH   *See* Jam Sandwich.

KOSHER   *See* Not Kosher.

KOSHER FOOD   *See* Not Kosher.

KOSHER KITCHEN   *See* Not Kosher.

KOSHER LAWS   *See* Not Kosher.

KOSHER MEAT   *See* Not Kosher.

KOSHER PICKLES   *See* Not Kosher.

KOSHER RESTAURANT   *See* Not Kosher.

KP   *See* Kitchen Police.

L

LACTO-OVO-VEGETARIAN   *See* Vegetarian.

LACTO-VEGETARIAN   *See* Vegetarian.

LADY   *a lady*. A "kneader of loaves." MWCD: O.E. Source: LOAF. The O.E. noun *hlæfdīge* "lady" was a compound of the words *hlāf* "loaf" and *dīge* "kneader": "the kneader of the loaves." (O.E. *hlæfdīge* → *læfdīge* → *lavedi* → *lady*.) The "kneader of the loaves," or the lady, was the wife of the "keeper of the loaves," or the lord. In modern times, the word *ladies* competes with the word *women* for the titles of certain organizations. *Ladies* seems to be more popular with golfers (Ladies Professional Golf Association) and *women* with basketball players (Women's Professional Basketball Association). In politics, it seems to be a toss-up: the League of Women Voters, but the "First Lady." WNWCD. *Compare* Lord.

LADYFINGER   *a ladyfinger*. A small, light, finger-shaped pastry. MWCD: 1820. Source: CAKE. The ladyfinger was orig. called a *lady's finger* (pl.: *ladies' fingers*) or a *finger biscuit*. The implication is that these sponge-cake "fingers" were once much narrower than they are today. Today's ladyfingers look more like half-size hot dog buns than the delicate digits of 19th cent. dowagers. Ladyfingers are popular accompaniments to certain desserts, such as ice cream, and necessary ingredients in certain other desserts, such as charlottes. The shape and size of the ladyfinger have caused the name to be borrowed as a slang term for two unrelated items: a marijuana cigarette and a medium-sized firecracker—both of which are slim and approx. three inches long. DAFD; DAS; FLC; HF.

LADY'S FINGER BANANAS   *See* Fruit with Appeal.

LAMB CHOP   *See* Chopping Block.

LAMB FRIES   Fried lamb's testicles. DEOD: 1886. Source: LAMB (MWCD: O.E.); FRY (MWCD: 13th cent.). The term *lamb fries* first appeared in England (as *lamb's fries*) but was followed shortly in America by *calf fries* ("fried calf testicles"), both of which sometimes appear simply as *fries* on Western menus. ("Oh, and I'd like an order of *fries* with that chocolate shake!") The testicles are harvested from these animals at Western ranches during the annual spring castration, which is necessary to bulk the animals up and decrease their libido. American ingenuity has created another euphemism for animal testicles—*oysters*, appearing in such phrases as *prairie oysters, mountain oysters* (HDAS: 1890) and *Rocky Mountain oysters*, in spite of the fact that the mountains and prairies of the West are far from the oceans where real oysters are taken. (The name was chosen because of the resemblance between raw oysters and raw testicles.) Unfortunately, the term *prairie oyster* (IHAT: 1905) can also refer to a drink, orig. called a "prairie cocktail" (IHAT: 1905), that is used to relieve the symptoms of a hangover: a raw egg (the "oyster") dropped into tomato or fruit juice along with some Worcestershire sauce and a little beer or whiskey. (If a real oyster is used, the drink is called an *oyster shooter*.) DAFD; EWPO; FLC; NSOED; PT; SA.

LAMB'S FRIES   *See* Lamb Fries.

LAMPOON   *See* Here's Mud in Your Eye.

LAND FLOWING WITH MILK AND HONEY   *See* Land of Milk and Honey.

LAND OF MILK AND HONEY   *a land of milk and honey.* Paradise; heaven on earth. Source: MILK; HONEY. MWCD: O.E. This phrase appears in the Old Testament (Exodus 3:8) as *a land flowing with milk and honey*: "And I [God, speaking to Moses from a burning bush] am come down to deliver them [His people, the Israelites] out of the hands of the Egyptians, and to bring them . . . unto *a land flowing with milk and honey* [i.e., Israel: the Promised Land]" [italics added]. The Israelites must have pictured the Promised Land as a second Eden, a heaven on earth, with an abundance of everything, symbolized by the most basic food, *milk*, and the most basic sweetener, *honey*. The modern metaphor eliminates mention of the liquidity of the resources and carries with it a kind of callous familiarity with crooked real estate agents offering deals on swampland and desert. BDPF; CI; DC; DEI; HND; MDWPO; MS; NSOED.

LARD (n)   *See* Tub of Lard.

LARD (v)   *See* Tub of Lard.

LARD ASS   *See* Tub of Lard.

LARDER   *See* Tub of Lard.

LARDHEAD   *See* Tub of Lard.

LAST ONE IN IS A ROTTEN EGG   *See* Rotten Egg.

LATE DINNER   *See* Dinner (2).

LAY A DUCK'S EGG   *See* Lay an Egg.

LAY A GOOSE EGG   *See* Lay an Egg.

LAY AN EGG   *to lay an egg.* To fail miserably. HDAS: 1861. Source: EGG. MWCD: 14th cent. This expression originated in England in the 1850s in reference to the failure of a cricket team to score any points in an inning: *to lay a duck's egg,* i.e., to deposit an egg-shaped "zero" on the scoreboard. American baseball adopted the expression in 1866, modifying it to *to lay a goose egg* (HDAS: 1866), i.e., to get a big fat "zero" for a scoreless inning. In the late-19th cent. the expression passed into the legitimate (and illegitimate) theater, where it signified either a bad performance by an actor (who was pelted with hen's eggs) or a total failure of the entire production. The expression was so far removed from sports by 1929 that the show business organ *Variety* could declare that Wall Street had *laid an egg,* i.e., allowed the stock market to crash. In that same year, 1929, an imperative form of *lay an egg* developed: *Go lay an egg!* (HDAS: 1928) "Get lost!" AID; ATWS; DAI; DAS; DC; EWPO; HND; IRCD; LA; LCRH; MDWPO; PT; SA. *See also* Love. *Compare* Go Fry an Egg; Go Suck an Egg.

LAYER-CAKE EFFECT   *a layer-cake effect.* The resemblance of a building or a hierarchy to a layer cake. Source: CAKE. MWCD: 13th cent. A layer cake—as opposed to a pancake, a sheet cake, or a loaf cake—is one that consists of alternating layers of cake and frosting (or filling, such as jam or preserves), often of contrasting colors. A building that has a *layer-cake effect* is one that features alternating horizontal stripes of brick, stone, or metal of contrasting colors or textures. An organizational hierarchy resembling a layer cake is one that has many different levels of authority, from top to bottom. WNWCD. *See also* Pancake (v).

LAZY SUSAN   *See* First Come, First Served.

LEAD A HAND-TO-MOUTH EXISTENCE   *See* Live from Hand to Mouth.

LEAD A HORSE TO WATER   *See* You Can Lead a Horse to Water, but You Can't Make It Drink.

LEAF LETTUCE   *See* Lettuce.

LEAK LIKE A SIEVE   *to leak like a sieve.* To hold water (etc.) as well as a sieve does. Source: SIEVE. MWCD: O.E. A kitchen sieve is not designed to hold water but to allow water to pass through, as when draining water from a handful of washed berries. A metal pail, in contrast, is designed to hold water; but if its bottom is full of holes, it may do what a sieve is expected to do: leak water. A person who *has a memory like a sieve* is very forgetful—i.e., is unable to retain data, such as names, dates, appointments times, etc. The difference between a sieve and a *strainer* (MWCD: 14th cent.) is that the former is always made of fine-meshed screen, whereas the latter is sometimes made of perforated sheet metal, as is the case with the strainer in the kitchen sink. The difference between a sieve and a *colander* (MWCD: 14th cent.) is that the former always has one handle, whereas the latter always has two, is always perforated, and is larger than the sieve. A difference in use between a sieve and both a strainer and a colander is that the former is also used to *sift* (MWCD: O.E.) dry ingredients, such as flour and sugar, whereas the latter two are used only to drain liquids. The expression *to sift through the evidence* means to sort through notes, letters, reports, transcripts, etc., for information useful in a court case. CI; DEI; FLC; NSOED.

LEATHER SANDWICH   *See* Jam Sandwich.

LEAVE A BAD TASTE IN YOUR MOUTH   *for something to leave a bad taste in your mouth.* For the memory of something unpleasant to linger with you for a long time afterwards. Source: TASTE (n) (MWCD: 14th cent.); MOUTH (MWCD: O.E.). Experiencing something traumatic is like biting into an apple and finding *half* a worm in it: It will be quite a while before you get up the nerve to eat an apple again. The same reaction can take place when you drink a glass of milk, only to find that it is sour: You spit out the milk and approach your next glass with great caution. An appalling occurrence of bad manners or *bad taste* (q.v.), whether in speech or in action, can have the same effect, causing you to avoid or distrust the perpetrator in the future. It would be interesting to know whether dreadful experiences, other than with food or drink, actually do produce a *bad taste in your mouth* that is stored in the brain for your protection. AID; DEI; MS.

LEAVEN (v)   *to leaven something.* To alleviate, modify, temper, or lighten the tone of something. NSOED: mid-16th cent. Source: LEAVEN (v). MWCD: 15th cent. To leaven a bread or cake is to cause it to "rise," with the aid of a *leaven* (n) (MWCD: 14th cent.) or *leavener*, such as yeast, baking powder, or baking soda. When the leavener mixes with the water or milk in the dough or batter, it causes carbon dioxide bubbles to form, increasing the volume and consequently lightening the texture. In the theater, comedy is often used to *leaven*, or lighten the tone of, a serious play, as is the case with many of Shakespeare's plays. FLC.

LEAVE YOU TO STEW IN YOUR OWN JUICE   *See* Stew in Your Own Juice.

LEFTOVERS   *See* Look like Death Warmed over.

LEGS TURN TO JELLY   *See* Jellyfish.

LEMON   *a lemon*. A new car that turns out to be a dud. HDAS: 1924. Source: LEMON. MWCD: 15th cent. The word *lemon* began to be applied to a newly purchased new car that wouldn't run right—or at all—in the 1920s. The owner would take the car back to the dealer for repairs, under the warranty, and then the same—or a different—problem would appear within a few days. After going through this procedure several times, the owner would ask for a replacement or his/her money back. If the dealer refused, as was too often the case, the owner sometimes resorted to attaching a picture of a yellow lemon, or a sign reading *This car is a lemon*, to the back of the vehicle. Things got so bad that some states passed a *lemon law* (MWCD: 1982) forcing dealers to "repair, replace, or refund" unless defects were corrected within a certain period of time. These laws provided buyers with some relief until it was discovered, in the early 1990s, that some unscrupulous dealers were engaging in *lemon-laundering*: the resale of those same unrepairable *lemons* to other unsuspecting buyers—as "new" cars. The poor fruit known as a "lemon" has taken a bad rap here simply because it is "sour," and the buyers were getting a *sour deal*. Actually, of course, the *lemon* (fr. Ar., via Lat. and Fr.) is an important member of the citrus family, known for its vitamin C content; and its contribution to eating (lemon cake, lemon meringue pie, etc.) and drinking (a twist of lemon, lemonade, etc.) is large. CE; CI; DAFD; FLC; MS; NSOED; PT.

LEMONADE   *See* If Life Hands You a Lemon, Make Lemonade.

LEMON-LAUNDERING   *See* Lemon.

LEMON LAW   *See* Lemon.

LET OFF STEAM   *See* Pressure Cooker.

LET'S DO LUNCH   *See* Business Lunch.

LET THEM EAT CAKE!   That's *their* problem! EWPO: 1770. Source: CAKE. MWCD: 13th cent. Marie Antoinette may have said something like this about the poor people of Paris who were complaining to her husband, King Louis XVI, that they had no bread. "Then *let them eat cake!*" the Queen is alleged to have said [italics added]. However, the French version of the order translates as "Then let them eat *buns!*" (i.e., *brioches*), not "cake" (i.e., *gateau*). Considering the fact that the English and the French were not the best of friends during this period, the mistranslation of the Queen's words may have been deliberate in an effort by the

English to discredit her. At any rate, *Let them eat cake!* has established itself in English as a sarcastic response to an excessive demand.

LETTUCE   Money; folding money. HDAS: 1903. Source: LETTUCE. MWCD: 14th cent. Lettuce bears little resemblance to metal money, although coins do have "heads," like head lettuce; however, it has a lot in common with paper money, which is long, thin, flat, and green, like the leaves of both head lettuce and romaine. *Head lettuce* is so called because the leaves "ball up" to form a tight "head"—large, in the case of crisphead (or iceberg) lettuce, smaller in the case of butterhead (or Bibb) lettuce. *Romaine lettuce*, famous for its use in Caesar salad, forms a long "head" rather than a round one; and *leaf lettuce*, also popular in salads, forms no head at all. Almost all lettuces are green, but of different shades: Bibb lettuce and Romaine are dark green, iceberg is a lighter green, and leaf lettuce is either green or red. The word *lettuce* has a baffling etymology: It derives, by way of French, fr. Lat. *lac* "milk," supposedly because of its "milky juice"; however, the Romans must have been thinking of *romaine* (or "Roman") lettuce because head lettuce and leaf lettuce have no juice at all, milky or otherwise. The identity in pronunciation of *lettuce* and *Let us* has led to a few naughty puns, written on the walls above the urinals in men's rooms: *Lettuce spray!* (from the minister's "Let us pray!") and *Lettuce, turnip, and pea!* (a play on boys' "Let us turn up and pee!"). DAFD; DAS; EWPO; FLC; NSOED; PT; WNWCD. *Compare* Bread; Cabbage; Dough.

LETTUCE SPRAY!   *See* Lettuce.

LETTUCE, TURNIP, AND PEA!   *See* Lettuce.

LET US EAT, DRINK, AND BE MERRY, FOR TOMORROW WE DIE   Let's enjoy ourselves while we still have the chance. Source: EAT; DRINK. MWCD: O.E. This invitation sounds biblical, and it is. The first half of the quotation comes from *Ecclesiates* (8:15): "[A] man hath no better thing under the sun, than *to eat, and to drink, and to be merry*: for that shall abide with him of his labour the days of his life" [italics added]. And the second half is from Isaiah (22:13): "And behold joy and gladness, slaying oxen, and killing sheep, eating flesh, and drinking wine: *let us eat and drink; for tomorrow* (sic) *we shall die*" [italics added]. The sentiment may have been inspired by the ancient Egyptians, who "invited" a human skeleton to their banquets to remind the guests of their mortality; and it no doubt influenced German university students of the Middle Ages who sang, *Gaudeamus igitur, juvenes dum sumus* ("Let us be merry while we are young"). Another tripartite expression containing *eat* and *drink* is *to eat, sleep, and drink something*: i.e., to become totally absorbed in something, such as work, sports, or politics. BDPF; DAP; EWPO.

LIAISON   (a) *liaison*. An interrelationship; an illicit affair; military communication; pronunciation of.a normally silent final consonant. Source: COOK (v).

The word *liaison* is a borrowing from French, where it developed numerous extended meanings before it was taken into English. In cooking, a *liaison* (MWCD: 1759) is a binding agent—such as egg yolk, flour, or cornstarch—that is used to thicken soups, sauces, and gravies. The binding property has become a metaphor for various connections and relationships, illicit or otherwise, between people, military units, and words. *Liaison* in Fr. words refers to the pronunciation of the spelled but normally silent consonant of a word when the next word begins with a vowel: e.g., [*mo(n)* + *ami*] → [*monami*]. FLC; WNWCD.

LIBERTY CABBAGE   *See* Cabbage.

LIBERTY SANDWICH   *See* Make Hamburger of.

LICENSE PLATE   *See* Full Plate.

LICK YOUR CHOPS   *See* Make Your Mouth Water.

LICORICE STICK   *a licorice stick*. A clarinet. HDAS: 1935. Source: LICORICE. MWCD: 13th cent. A clarinet was called a *licorice stick* by jazz musicians in the 1920s and 1930s because it resembled the twisted "sticks" of this black, chewy candy sold in drug stores, grocery stores, and candy stores. The color of the candy derives from the black color of the extract made from the root of the licorice plant, which is also used to flavor liquors, medicines, and other confections. Licorice sticks now also come in the color red, which solves the problem of schoolchildren returning from recess with their teeth all black from chewing on "likwish." The sweet licorice flavor is found also in the seeds of the anise plant ("aniseeds"), which can be used as a substitute for licorice. DAS; FLC; PT.

LIFE IS JUST A BOWL OF CHERRIES   Life is good, great, wonderful! DC: 1931. (The title of a song from the musical *Scandals*.) Source: BOWL (MWCD: O.E.); CHERRY (MWCD: 14th cent.). A bowlful of cherries is attractive because of the color of the fruit ("cherry red"), the size of the fruit ("bite size"), the accessibility of the fruit (yours for the taking), the easy disposability of the fruit (just a stem and a pit), and the general knowledge that cherries are soft, juicy, and (sometimes) sweet. When life is like that, it's a bed of roses, like living on easy street, like *coming up cherries* on the slot machine (three cherries in a row: a "winner"!). When life is not like that, it's no bed of roses, i.e., *no bowl of cherries*. CE; DAI; DAP; DC; EWPO; HND.

LIFE IS NOT ALL CAKES AND ALE   *See* Cakes and Ale.

LIFE SUCKS   *See* Suck (v).

LIGHT MOLASSES   *See* Slow as Molasses in January.

LIKE A CARROT TO A DONKEY   *See* Carrottop.

LIKE A HOT KNIFE THROUGH BUTTER   Easily; without difficulty or impediment. Source: KNIFE; BUTTER. MWCD: O.E. The knife in this simile is prob. a butter knife—a short, dull, wide-bladed knife with a short handle that is used to transfer a chunk of butter from a communal butter dish to an individual butter dish—although it could just as well be a regular table knife. Neither of such knives is ordinarily heated for this purpose, although that would help if the butter were quite cold and hard. It is difficult to say whether the knife or the spoon was the first eating instrument to reach the table (the fork reached it fairly recently); however, the knife is definitely the older food-preparation instrument of the two. The knife was orig. an implement for "dressing" game animals—and cutting up the meat into suitable pieces for preservation or immediate cooking and eating—even before it was regarded as a weapon for killing the animals in the first place. Early knives were made of stone, bone, shell, or wood before the Bronze Age, after which they were fashioned from bronze, brass, iron, and steel. Spoons were orig. made of wood (or gourd or shell)—and they still are—and used for stirring the contents of a pot or kettle, although they are now also made of stainless, chromed, or plated steel. At the table, the knife orig. served the purpose of both knife and fork; i.e., it not only cut a piece of meat from a roast but transferred the piece to the plate, cut it up further, and transferred the smaller pieces to the eater's mouth. The spoon's role at the table was at first to transfer liquid and soft food from the serving bowls to the individual plate, after which it was either drunk (e.g., soup) or picked up and transferred to the mouth with the aid of a piece of bread. Today, there are table knives for almost every purpose—and table spoons (not *tablespoons*) for even more purposes. FLC; WNWCD.

LIKE A HOT POTATO   *See* Hot Potato.

LIKE A KID IN A CANDY STORE   *See* Candy.

LIKE APPLES AND ORANGES   *See* Compare Apples and Oranges.

LIKE HOLDING OUT A CARROT TO A DONKEY   *See* Carrottop.

LIKE TAKING CANDY FROM A BABY   *See* Candy.

LIKE THE CURATE'S EGG   *See* Curate's Egg.

LIKE THE POT CALLING THE KETTLE BLACK   Like a hypocrite. DC: 1699. Source: POT (MWCD: O.E.); KETTLE (MWCD: 13th cent.). A hypocrite (fr. Gk. for "actor") is a person who purports to be holier or more virtuous than another person, although the exact opposite is true. Both pots and kettles were blackened with smoke and soot in the days of "hearth" cooking—and, later, cooking on wood-fired stoves—and if we can suspend our disbelief that they could talk, neither would seem to be justified in calling the other black. However, there may be some extenuating circumstances here: (1) neither the pot nor the kettle can see itself or realize the condition of its own surface; and (2) the pot is prob. made of cast iron, which is black to start with, whereas the kettle is prob. made of copper or brass, which can be restored to a reflective shine. If the tables were turned, and a shiny kettle called the pot black, that would not be hypocritical—provided that the kettle knew it had been polished—because that would be true. However, if a dirty pot, seeing its own reflection in the shiny kettle, called the kettle black, that *would* be hypocritical because it would not be true. In modern times, such name-calling usu. takes place in political debates and courts of law, where it is difficult to tell the difference between a dirty pot and a shiny kettle. AID; BDPF; CE; CI; DAI; DAP; DC; DEI; EWPO; HND; LCRH; MDWPO; MS.

LIKE TRYING TO NAIL JELL-O TO A TREE   *See* Nervous Pudding.

LIKE TRYING TO NAIL JELLY TO A WALL   *See* Nervous Pudding.

LIKE TWO PEAS IN A POD   *to be like—or as alike as—two peas in a pod.* To be virtually indistinguishable. HND: 16th cent. Source: PEA (MWCD: 1611); POD (MWCD: 1688). This simile is usu. applied to human twins, who, like the peas, have identical sets of genes; however, it could as easily be applied to two kittens in a litter or two goobers in a shell. (The number of peas in a pod usu. ranges from four to eight.) The noun *pea* has such a late date of first appearance (17th cent.) because in M.E. the singular of the word was *pease*, as in the nursery rhyme: "*Pease porridge* [i.e., pea porridge] hot, / *Pease porridge* cold, / *Pease porridge* in the pot, / Nine days old" [italics added]. In early Mod. Eng., it was erroneously believed that because the pronounced word ended in a sibilant, it must be a plural; so a new singular, *pea*, was created by back-formation, to which a regular plural was added: *peas*. An early favorite of Americans was the *sugar pea* (MWCD: 1707), now usu. called the *snow pea* (MWCD: 1949), which can be eaten, pod and all, like the unopened string bean, which is known in French as *mange-tout* "eat it all." Peas are grown in "patches" in the South, and *to tear up the pea patch* means "to go on a rampage," at least according to the Georgia Peach, Red Barber, who broadcast Brooklyn Dodgers baseball games on the radio in the post-WWII years. The country singer Tennessee Ernie Ford used to refer to his fans as *pea pickers*, and the shell games that were played on the streets of large cities were called *Hide the Pea*. BDPF; CI; DAFD; DEI; EWPO; FLC; MDWPO; NSOED; PT.

LIME   *See* Limey.

LIMEADE   *See* If Life Hands You a Lemon, Make Lemonade.

LIME-JUICER   *See* Limey.

LIMELIGHT   *See* Limey.

LIMEY   *a Limey*. An Englishman. HDAS: 1917. Source: LIME. MWCD: 1638.
Limey is short for *lime-juicer* (HDAS: 1856), a pejorative term applied in the mid-
19th cent. by Americans and Australians to British sailors who had for the past
half century been issued lime juice as a preventive of scurvy. By the early-20th
cent. the term had been shortened to *Limey*, and by the end of WWI the shortened
form was being applied, without prejudice, to all Englishmen (*sic*), whether sailor
or not. (Nevertheless, the general nickname must have been about as easy to take,
for the average Englishman, as "Yank" was for the average Southern American.)
The lime juice did its job because limes, like all citrus fruits, are a good source
of vitamin C. A lime is smaller than a lemon (and, of course, green rather than
yellow), but both fruits have the same oval shape, with a bulge at the stem end
and a bump at the blossom end. The lime is an Asian fruit that was first encountered by Arabic traders, who called it *lim* and introduced it to Spanish traders,
who called it *lima* and brought it to the Caribbean in the 15th cent. The famous
Key limes (MWCD: 1929), the basis for the even more famous *Key lime pie*
(MWCD: 1954), were grown in the Florida Keys from the early-19th cent. (DAFD:
1835), but now they compete with the larger, seedless Persian variety in Northern
markets. The *lime* fruit is not the basis for the word *limelight* (MWCD: 1826),
which denotes a bright white light—caused by directing a flame at a cylinder of
quicklime in front of a mirror—that was used as a spotlight in theaters before the
invention of the light bulb. BDPF; EWPO; FLC; IHAT; NSOED; PT.

LIMP AS A DISHRAG   *See* Taste like Dishwater.

LION'S SHARE   *the lion's share*. The biggest part. MWCD: 1790. Source:
FOOD. In the Aesop fable that was the basis for this term, the *lion's share* meant
"all" of something, not just the "biggest part." The lion invited three other animals
to go on a hunt with him, and they were fortunate enough to kill a stag. The lion
then divided up the carcass into four piles, all of which he claimed for himself
by virtue of his being the bravest, the smartest, the strongest, and the most royal
(i.e., the king) of beasts. No one challenged his claims. During the ensuing mil-
lennia, the *lion's share* has come to mean the "*largest* part" of something *favorable*
(e.g., of awards, credits, presents, etc.), but more recently it has also come to
mean the largest portion of something *unfavorable* (e.g., the *lion's share* of the
work, the dishes, the cleaning, etc.). ATWS; CI; DAS; DEI; HI; LCRH; MS; SA;
WNWCD.

LITTLE APPLES   *See* Big Apple.

LITTLE PITCHERS HAVE BIG EARS   *See* Tempest in a Teapot.

LITTLE SHRIMP   *a little shrimp*. A small or puny person; a small or unimportant enterprise. NSOED: late-M.E. Source: SHRIMP. MWCD: 14th cent. *Little shrimp* is a redundancy: All shrimp are relatively small compared to their cousins, the lobsters. Both shrimp and lobsters are decapod crustaceans, but lobsters have claws, whereas shrimp have none. Both shrimp and lobsters are also saltwater crustaceans, but there are large freshwater shrimp, called *prawns*, and small freshwater lobsters, called *crayfish*. (Scampi and langostinos are really saltwater prawns, whereas rock lobsters and spiny lobsters are really saltwater crayfish!) Lobsters are identified with the New England coast, whereas shrimp and crayfish are identified with the Gulf Coast (the former with Creole cooking and the latter with Cajun cooking). At the opposite end of the spectrum from *little shrimp* is *jumbo shrimp* (MWCD: 1883), an oxymoron: How can something be mammoth, like Jumbo the Elephant, and minuscule, like a shrimp, at the same time? CE; DAFD; EWPO; FLC; LA; MDWPO; PT; SA. *See also* Shrimp Cocktail.

LIVE FROM HAND TO MOUTH   *to live from hand to mouth*. To have only enough food or money for the present. DC: 1509. Source: MOUTH. A person who *lives from hand to mouth* either (1) has no steady income, savings, or material wealth (and must therefore use whatever money he/she can earn for the next meal) or (2) has material wealth and a steady income but chooses to spend his/her money as fast as it comes in (rather than saving some of it for the future). Either type of person is said to *lead a hand-to-mouth existence* (MWCD: 1748), although this expression is more often used for the person in the first situation, i.e., the one who must put whatever food comes into his/her hand into his/her mouth immediately in order to survive. People in this condition are living from meal to meal by necessity, not by choice, and they *don't know where their next meal is coming from*. BDPF; CI; DAI; DEI; EWPO; HND; MS.

LIVE HIGH ON/OFF THE HOG   *See* Eat High on the Hog.

LIVE OFF THE FAT OF THE LAND   *See* Fat (n).

LIVERWURST   *See* Chopped Liver.

LOAF   *See* Meat Loaf.

LOBSTER BUTTER   *See* Crab Butter.

LOBSTER POT   *See* Potbelly.

LOGANBERRY   *See* Blackberries Are Red when They're Green.

LOLLIPOP   *a lollipop*. A Brit. crossing guard's sign; a pitcher's high toss to a base or the plate; a predictable encore selection at a concert. Source: LOLLIPOP.

MWCD: 1784. The candy called a *lollipop* (or *lollypop*) is a Brit. invention consisting of a small disc of hard candy (orig. pink and white), formed at the end of a stick, and named for the tongue (Brit. Eng. *lolly*) that licks it and the sound ("pop") that the candy makes when it is pulled from the mouth. The name was first expanded in England to include the round red-and-white sign on a long pole that traffic wardens (or *lollipop men*) carry to stop cars so that schoolchildren can cross the street. In America, crossing guards carry an octagonal sign with the word *STOP* in white letters on a red background, mounted on a short handle, that looks even more like a lollipop, although it is not called such here. When the lollipop was introduced into America in the early-20th cent., it was immediately nicknamed a *sucker*, and both names have persisted in this country. In baseball, it is only the top half of the lollipop that has become a metaphor—for the rainbow curve that a pitcher's lob to the catcher or the first baseman makes. The "predictable-encore" metaphor is based on the sweetness of the candy in the lollipop rather than its shape. A *lollipop dress*, a full-skirted party dress worn by young women in the 1950s, was so called because the colors of its material and matching heels were pink and white. The only improvements in the candy lollipop have been (1) to replace the wooden stick with a stiff, rolled, paper "rope" and (2) to bend the rope so that both ends are inside the disc. (Advice: *Never wave to a lollipop man*/"crossing guard" as you drive by!) BDPF; DAFD; DEI; EWPO; HDAS; HF; PT.

LOLLIPOP DRESS   *See* Lollipop.

LOLLIPOP MAN   *See* Lollipop.

LOLLYPOP   *See* Lollipop.

LONG BREAD   *See* Bread.

LONG DRINK OF WATER   *a long drink of water*. A person who is both tall and slim. HDAS: 1936. Source: DRINK; WATER. MWCD: O.E. A person who is extremely tall, like a seven-foot basketball player, no doubt drinks more water, i.e., a taller glass of it, than someone a foot shorter. If you should see two or more such persons from the same part of the country, you might conclude that *It must be the water*, i.e., that their height is attributable not to family genes but to environmental conditions. Water, of course, is the most basic of all ingredients for the survival of both animals and plants. (Humans can survive much longer without food than without water.) Water is so precious that the word has become a metaphor for the clarity of precious stones (e.g., a diamond of the *first water*) and for the excellence of human beings (e.g., a candidate of the *first water*). CS; DAFD.

LOOK AS IF BUTTER WOULDN'T MELT IN YOUR MOUTH   *See* Butter Wouldn't Melt in Your Mouth.

LOOK FISHY   *See* Fishy.

LOOK GOOD ENOUGH TO EAT   *See* Eat Nails.

LOOK LIKE A BOILED LOBSTER   *to look like a boiled lobster.* To have a severe case of sunburn. Source: BOIL (v) (MWCD: 13th cent.); LOBSTER (MWCD: O.E.). When the Maine lobster is in its natural habitat, the Atlantic Ocean, its shell is greenish brown; but when it is placed, live, in a pot of boiling water, its shell changes to a pinkish red. (The same is true of all lobsterlike shellfish, such as crayfish and langostinos, shrimp and prawns, and Alaskan crabs, although these other creatures are not boiled alive.) Persons who *look like a boiled lobster*, or are *as red as a boiled lobster*, have prob. been broiling in the hot sun, although the same effect can be produced by a hot winter sun reflecting off the cold ice or snow. The expression *to be in hot water* (DC: 1765), i.e., to be in big trouble, may also derive from the fate of the lobster, although boiling missionaries in hot water could have been the source. AID; DAI; DEI; HB; HDAS; HI; MS; SA. *Compare* Red as a Lobster.

LOOK LIKE DEATH WARMED OVER   *to look—or feel—like death warmed over.* To look—or feel—like a zombie. HDAS: 1939. Source: WARM (v). MWCD: O.E. A zombie is a member of the "walking dead," a person who has died and been brought back to a trancelike state like that of a robot or sleepwalker. The reanimation of the body is likened to the warming over of *leftovers* (MWCD: 1891) from a previous meal. Down on the farm, in the 1930s, *supper* (the evening meal) always consisted of food left over from *dinner* (the noon meal). Boiled potatoes were chopped up with the open end of a tin can, pieces of meat and some lard were added, and the whole was fried as a *hash*, sometimes with a soft-fried egg on top. (Breakfast on Sunday consisted of leftovers from Saturday night's leftovers.) The reheating—i.e., the *rewarming, warming over*, or *warming up*—of previously prepared food is still common today (e.g., reheating pizza, subs, and the leftovers that you brought home in the *doggie bag*), along with the rebaking or recooking of food before it is served for the first time. Examples of the latter are Eng./Fr. *biscuits*, It. *biscotti*, and Ger. *Zwieback*—all of which lit. mean "twice baked"—and Mexican Sp. *frijoles refritos*, or *refried beans*, which are beans that have been cooked, mashed, and then fried. Outside of cooking, the noun *warm-up* (MWCD: 1915) is used in both meteorology ("an increase in temperature") and baseball ("practice pitches before facing a batter"). *Leftovers* also have a life outside of cooking, as in the *leftovers* of a hurricane or tornado or the *leftovers* from a garage sale or a bazaar. FLC; NSOED; WNWCD.

LOOK LIKE THE CAT THAT ATE THE CANARY   *to look like the cat that ate—or swallowed—the canary.* To look smug or self-satisfied; to look sheepish or guilty. IRCD: 1871. Source: EAT. MWCD: O.E. A missing canary and a feline with a Cheshire-cat grin on its face add up to bird-slaughter. The assumption is that the cat somehow opened the door of the birdcage, caught the bird, killed it, and ate it. The cat looks smug and self-satisfied because it has successfully done what cats are supposed to do—eat mice, chipmunks, goldfish, and canaries. However, if the cat has been punished in the past for harassing the bird, then it will more likely look sheepish or guilty. People behave in the same way, grinning from ear to ear if they have been successful at permitted things, but looking away or at the floor if they have done something wrong. AID; ATWS; DAI; HND; SA.

LOOK LIKE THE CAT THAT SWALLOWED THE CANARY   *See* Look like the Cat That Ate the Canary.

LORD   *a lord.* A "keeper of the loaves." MWCD: O.E. Source: LOAF. O.E. *hlāford* "lord" was a compound of the words *hlāf* "loaf" and *weard* "keeper": "the keeper of the loaves." (O.E. *hlāford* → *lavord* → M.E. *loverd* → Mod. Eng. *lord*.) Even in O.E., *hlāf* meant not only "loaf" but "bread" and "food." The "keeper of the loaves" gradually evolved into the keeper of the place where those loaves were made and, eventually, to the keeper of the people who ate them. By the time of the publication of the King James version of the Bible (1611), the word *Lord* was used to refer to both God the Father and Christ the Son. NSOED; WNWCD. *Compare* Lady.

LOSE YOUR APPETITE   *See* Appetite.

LOSE YOUR FEED   *See* Cut the Feed.

LOSE YOUR LUNCH   *See* Lunch (n); Toss Your Cookies.

LOST IN THE SAUCE   *See* Sauce.

LOTUS-EATER   *a lotus-eater.* An indolent, self-indulgent person. Source: LOTUS (MWCD: ca. 1541); EAT (MWCD: O.E.). The term *lotus-eater* (MWCD: 1832) comes from Homer's *Odyssey* (Book IX), in which Odysseus and his men are attempting to sail home to Greece from Troy but are blown instead onto the northeast coast of Africa, the land of the lotus-eaters. The people there spend their days in total contentment, doing nothing but eating the sweet fruit (or berry) of the lotus tree (or bush) and living in the dreamy indolence that it produces. Given some of the fruit by the lotus-eaters, the sailors lose all desire to return home but want only to live out their lives there. Odysseus and the rest of the crew manage to take the affected crewmen back to the ship by force, lock them up, and sail away with them to their next adventure. The modern *lotus-eater* is at best a daydreamer, and at worst a drug addict, but the description matches very well with the flower children and hippies of the late-1960s and early-1970s. The home of the modern *lotus-eaters* is *Lotusland* (HDAS: 1980), a place that is as far from reality as possible: dreamland, La-La Land (HDAS: 1984), tinseltown, Hollywood. BDPF; EWPO; WNWCD. *Compare* Couch Potato.

LOTUSLAND   *See* Lotus-eater.

LOVE   Nothing; zero. NSOED: mid-18th cent. Source: EGG. *Love* is an Eng. mispronunciation of Fr. *l'oeuf* "the egg," which was once used by the French, in the game of tennis, to signify "no score" or "zero." The reason for the association of egg with zero was apparently the oval shape of both objects. The original Fr. word for "no score" was *zero*, and *l'oeuf* was a Fr. slang term for the same thing. When the English borrowed (court) tennis in the 1700s, they referred to "no score" by the slang term *love* rather than by the technical term *zero*. The English— and other Eng.-speaking people—still use *love* in tennis, but the French—and other Fr.-speaking people—have reverted to the more formal *zero*. The use of *egg* for "zero" has also occurred in cricket (a *duck's egg*) and in baseball (a *goose egg*, q.v.). The adj. *oval* (MWCD: 1577—fr. Lat. *ovum* "egg") is used to describe something that is *egg-shaped*, i.e., has the shape of an elongated spheroid, with one end wider than the other. (The larger end is positioned upward when storing in the refrigerator, whereas the smaller end is positioned upward in an egg cup.) In spite of the fact that the outline of an egg is not symmetrical, the noun *oval* (MWCD: 1570) has been applied to objects that *are*: e.g., a racetrack for horses or cars, which is really a rectangle with rounded corners. EWPO; MDWPO; SA.

LOVE APPLE   *a love apple*. A tomato. MWCD: 1578. Source: APPLE. MWCD: O.E. The tomato came to be identified with love, and with another fruit, the apple, because of a mistake in translation. When the tomato was first brought to Spain from Central America in the early-16th cent., it was called a *tomate* (fr. Nahuatl *tomatl*); but when the tomato reached Italy, it was given the nickname *pomo dei Moro* "Moorish apple" because the Italians had imported it from Spanish Morocco. When the French imported the tomato from Italy, they mistranslated *pomo dei Moro* as *pomme d'amour* "apple of love," and *love apple* became its popular name in England and America in the 17th cent. For several centuries people were afraid to eat the tomato because as a "love apple," it was thought to be a powerful aphrodisiac, and as a member of the nightshade family, it was feared to be poisonous. Now it is known that the tomato is neither an aphrodisiac nor a poison-bearer, and the "love" names have pretty much faded away. It is a *tomate* in France and Spain, and a *pomodoro* "golden apple" in Italy. BDPF; DAFD; EWPO; FLC; HF; MDWPO; PT.

LOVING CUP   *See* Cup.

LOW BOILING POINT   *See* Reach the Boiling Point.

LOW ON THE FOOD CHAIN   *See* Food Chain.

LOX AND BAGEL   *See* Bagel.

LUCK OF THE POT   *See* Take Potluck.

LUMBERJACK PIE   *See* Porkpie Hat.

LUNCH (n)   The midday meal; a light meal eaten at work or school. Source: LUNCH (n). MWCD: 1812. When *dinner* (q.v.) began to replace *supper* (q.v.) in the 19th cent., a new term was needed for the midday meal. Dinner at noon had been a substantial meal—the heaviest one of the day—but as more people moved from the farms to the cities and took jobs in the factories, it was no longer possible for the entire family to eat their main meal together at noon. As a result, the heavy meal of the day was moved to the early evening, when both the workers and the schoolchildren could attend; but it was now called *dinner*. (*Supper* was bumped up to an even later hour or became a special meal at a church or school; but it still remained light.) Workers still carried their noon meal—orig. packed hot, or intended to be heated up at work—in a *dinner pail* (DAFD: 1856). Schoolchildren, however, carried their cold noontime meal to school in a *lunch box* (DAFD: 1850) and ate it in a *lunchroom*. (Cafeterias were eventually established at many factories and schools to provide a hot lunch for everyone.) The word *lunch* has a disputed origin: It is either a shortening of the word *luncheon* (NSOED: late-16th cent.), which itself is of uncertain origin (it may be an alteration of dialectal *nuncheon* "a light snack"); or it is an Eng. pronunciation of Sp. *lonja* "a slice of ham" (leading to the early definition of *lunch* as "a thick piece of food"). At any rate, *lunch* is the word that caught on early in the 19th cent. and gradually filled the void left by the promotion of *dinner*. The replacement was complete for lifetime city dwellers by the early-20th cent. (DAFD: 1920s). *Lunch* now differs from *luncheon* in that the former is more casual and likely to be eaten alone, whereas the latter is more formal and likely to be eaten with friends. *Lunch*, however, is the word that is used in most of the metaphorical expressions, such as *to steal someone's lunch* or *to take someone to lunch* (HDAS: 1987) "to trounce someone in a game" or *to lose your lunch* "to throw up." NSOED. *Compare* Eat Someone's Lunch; Feed the Fishes; Toss Your Cookies.

LUNCH BOX   *See* Lunch (n).

LUNCH COUNTER   *See* Fast Food; Lunch-counter Jargon.

LUNCH-COUNTER JARGON   (Also *lunch-counter slang*.) The secret code in which customers' orders are shouted by the waitress (*sic*) to the cook at a lunch-counter restaurant. DAFD: 1852. Source: LUNCH. MWCD: 1812. A lunch-counter restaurant is a small, informal, inexpensive, short-order restaurant—also politely called a *luncheonette* (MWCD: 1924) or a *snack bar* (MWCD: 1930) and impolitely called a *hash house* (MWCD: 1869) or a *greasy spoon* (q.v.)—that has a *lunch counter* (MWCD: 1869). A lunch counter is a long, low bar—like a barroom bar or a soda fountain bar, but lower—at which customers sit on bar stools, sometimes with backs, facing the counter and the kitchen, which is usu. separated from the lunch counter by a wall with a wide-open window. It is through this window that the waitress shouts the order, in jargon, while she also deposits a written order in plain English. It is obvious to everyone that the oral order is redundant to the written one, and that the jargon is just part of the fun of eating at a lunch counter. No one would want to discourage the practice, because some of the orders are surprisingly creative and imaginative, like rock lyrics printed as poetry. Not only that, but customers start to use the jargon themselves, and it begins to pass into general usage. Examples are a *cuppa joe* (or *java* or *mud*) "a cup of coffee"; a *blue plate special* "the specially priced feature of the day"; a *BLT* "a bacon, lettuce, and tomato (toasted) sandwich"; a *houseboat* "a banana split"; and *Adam and Eve on a raft* "two poached eggs on a piece of toast" (HDAS: 1909). Other examples of lunch-counter jargon are (1) less familiar (e.g., *sinkers and suds* "doughnuts and coffee"), (2) more mysterious (e.g., *bossy in a bowl* "beef stew"), or (3) even a little naughty (e.g., *maiden's delight* "cherries"). DAFD and IHAT have extensive lists of such terms.

LUNCHEON   *See* Lunch (n).

LUNCHEONETTE   *See* Lunch-counter Jargon.

M

MACARONI *a Macaroni.* A "fop"; a "dandy." BDPF: ca. 1760. Source: MAC-ARONI. MWCD: 1599. The "foppish" young "dandies" of the mid-18th cent. Macaroni Club in London were named for the club itself, which was named after a food that represented one of the club's Continental interests: Italy, along with its macaroni, wine, women, and song. The upper-crust young Macaronis were not well respected in England; consequently, when the word appeared in the song "Yankee Doodle Dandy" during the American Revolution, it was difficult to tell whether the sarcasm was directed at a foppish young British soldier or a dandy young American one. (However, one American regiment was called the "Macaronies" because of their natty uniforms.) At any rate, the song, whether of British or American origin, is now associated with American soldiers during the Revolutionary War, and the word *Yankee* has progressively meant a New Englander, a Northeasterner, an American, and a member of the New York City American League baseball team: the Yankees. The song goes as follows: "Yankee Doodle went to town / Riding on a pony; / He stuck a feather in his cap / And called it *macaroni*" [italics added]. As a food, macaroni covers a broad category of pastas that are tube-shaped (such as the elbow macaroni that is used for macaroni and cheese), shell-shaped, twisted, and shaped in many other forms. Macaroni salad is a cold dish combining shaped macaroni with various vegetables and seasonings. The *macaroni penguin* (NSOED: mid-19th cent.) is so called because it has stringy yellow feathers hanging from its head. DAFD; EWPO; FLC; HDAS; LCRH.

MACARONIC VERSE Verse containing a mixture of words from two languages. MWCD: 1638. Source: MACARONI. MWCD: 1599. *Macaronic verse* is so called because it resembles a dish of macaroni mixed with vegetables, meats, sauces, and condiments. This type of verse was named, as one might expect, by an Italian poet who invented it in the early-16th cent. The verse is often comic, ludicrous, and nonsensical, but it has a sophistication that macaroni lacks: You have to be biliterate in order to enjoy it. The second language used, as opposed to the poet's own language, is usu. Latin, and the mixture sometimes involves using Lat. endings on native words (called "dog Latin"). Evidence that *macaroni* (fr. It. *maccherone*) was once the common word for all pastas lies in the comparison of the dates for the four major pasta terms—*macaroni* (MWCD: 1599), *noodle* (MWCD: 1779); *pasta* (MWCD: 1874), and *spaghetti* (MWCD: 1888)—and is reinforced by the fact that the Ger. word for *macaronic verse* is Nudelvers. BDPF; EWPO; MDWPO; NSOED.

MACARONI SALAD   *See* Salad.

MAD ENOUGH TO EAT NAILS   *See* Eat Nails.

MAGIC MUSHROOMS   *See* Spring up like Mushrooms.

MAIDEN'S DELIGHT   *See* Lunch-counter Jargon.

MAIN COURSE   *See* Pièce de Résistance.

MAÎTRE D'   *See* Maître d'Hôtel.

MAÎTRE D'HÔTEL   *a maître d'hôtel.* A headwaiter at an upscale restaurant. Source: RESTAURANT. *Maître d' hôtel* is French for "master of the house," equivalent to a head steward or head butler at a great house or palace (MWCD: 1538). In modern times, the *maître d'hôtel* has become the headwriter at a French restaurant—usu. referred to as the *maître* by the guests and simply the *d'* by the staff—or the headwaiter at a formal American restaurant. The *maître d*'s job is to accept reservations, by phone or in person; to assign the times and places of seating; and to seat the guests when their name is called. He—almost always *he*— is the gatekeeper for the restaurant, turning away riffraff, bumping regular guests when celebrities appear, making sure the celebs get the choice tables, enforcing the dress code, placating impatient guests, and arbitrating arguments over poor service or bad food. The *maître d'* at a less formal American restaurant is simply called a *host* or *hostess*, and his/her job is much easier—no dress code, everybody welcome, no preference given, etc. There is still the matter of poor service, but the problem of bad food usu. belongs to the "waitstaff," or *waitpersons* (MWCD: 1976), i.e., the *waiters* (MWCD: 15th cent.) and *waitresses* (MWCD: 1834), whose job it is to take the orders, serve the food, refill the water glasses and coffee cups, and deliver the bill. In a short-order restaurant, such as a diner, the expression *Coming up!* "Right away!" may have derived from a short-order cook's promise to have the waitress's order in the window toute suite, i.e., *in short order;* or it may have originated in the palace, with the pleasurable announcement that the *dumb* *waiter* (MWCD: 1749), loaded with food, was on its way up the service elevator from the kitchen. CI; DAFD; DAI; FLC; LA; WNWCD.

MAIZE   *See* Corn.

MAKE A HASH OF   *See* Hash (n).

MAKE A LOT OF DOUGH   *See* Dough.

MAKE A MESS   *See* Fine Mess.

MAKE A PIG OF YOURSELF   *See* Eat like a Pig.

MAKE A WISH   *See* Wishbone.

MAKE FROM SCRATCH   *to make something from scratch.* To make something—such as a cake or a birdhouse—from the basic ingredients. Source: SCRATCH. NSOED: late-16th cent. It is surprising that no one has marketed a prepared mix called "Scratch" so that a homemaker could legitimately claim that he/she had made their bread or cake "from Scratch." In the absence of such a product, a home cook must sift the flour, add the milk or water, and knead the dough (for bread), or sift the flour, break the eggs, add the milk, and beat the batter (for cake) all by him/herself—just to claim that the finished product is a *scratch bread* or a *scratch cake*—i.e., is *cooked from scratch.* The same homemaker, or his/her spouse, may use the same phrase to express pride over the birdhouse or doghouse that he/she made from lumber that had to be sawed, hammered, painted, shingled, etc.: "I *made it from scratch*!" The metaphorical *scratch*, however, derives from neither cooking nor carpentry but from sports, where "starting from scratch" orig. meant either starting a foot race from a line scratched in the dirt or starting—or resuming—a boxing match from a similar "scratch line." AID; DAI; MDWPO; MS; WNWCD.

MAKE HAMBURGER OF   *to make hamburger of someone or something.* To beat someone to a pulp; to defeat an opponent soundly. Source: HAMBURGER. MWCD: 1884. To "make hamburger of something" is what the early-19th cent. residents of Hamburg, Germany, lit. did to beefsteak, pounding it until it was tender, seasoning it, and then cooking it. German immigrants from Hamburg brought the recipe for Hamburger Hackfleisch ("minced meat of Hamburg") with them when they came to America in the mid-19th cent. In this country, the beef so prepared came to be called *hamburger* (short for the Ger. term) or *hamburg steak* (DAFD: 1884, if pounded; DAFD: 1902, if ground). The name *hamburger steak* appeared at the St. Louis Exposition of 1904, where a patty of cooked ground beef was served between two slices of bread. The *hamburger bun*, a split, round yeast roll, was invented in 1912, and by 1916 *hamburger* could refer to either the ground beef, the patty of uncooked or cooked ground beef, or the sandwich of cooked ground beef. During WWI, hamburger steak was sometimes advertised as a *Salisbury steak*, and the hamburger sandwich as a *Liberty sandwich*, in order to avoid the use of the name of an enemy city. Since WWI, the hamburger has become the most popular fast food in America, and the name *hamburger* has been redivided—not as *hamburg* + *er* but as *ham* + *burger*, as if the patty were made of ham. Other new combinations with *burger* (NSOED: mid-20th cent.) have resulted in such names as beefburger, buffalo burger, chicken burger, clam burger, crab burger, fish burger, lamb burger, soy burger, steerburger, turkey burger, veggie burger, and Wimpy burger—the last-mentioned from 1919. A variation on the beef hamburger is the *sloppy joe* (MWCD: 1961), which has the same ground beef and the same bun but instead of forming the beef into a patty and broiling, frying, or grilling it, the beef is fried loose in a skillet, combined with a tomato-based vegetable sauce, and spooned onto the bun—from which it soon spills onto the chest of the eater, the reason for "sloppy" in the name. AID; CE; DAS; DEOD; EWPO; FLC; IHAT; MDWPO; PT. *See also* Steak Tartare. *Compare* Make Mincemeat of.

MAKE IT HOT FOR   *See* Slave over a Hot Stove All Day.

MAKE MINCEMEAT OF   *to make mincemeat of someone or something*. HDAS: 1708. To defeat, demolish, destroy, or devastate someone or something. Source: MINCEMEAT. MWCD: 1663. Originally, *mincemeat* was meat (usu. beef) that had been *minced* (MWCD: 14th cent.), i.e., chopped up into very small pieces, somewhat like today's hamburger. However, by the 1800s, *mincemeat*—or *mince* (MWCD: ca. 1850)—had come to mean a filling for a pie (a *mincemeat pie*) that consisted of chopped fruit, nuts, and suet, but no meat at all. The metaphor *to make mincemeat of* is derived from the original sense of the word, in which a piece of beef is destroyed by a knife or cleaver. A person who vows to make *mincemeat*— or *hamburger*—of another person or persons doesn't really intend to cut them up into little pieces but simply to render them as ineffective as if they had been. A person who vows to *make mincemeat* of a company or organization doesn't necessarily intend to tear down its buildings, but to put it out of business. AID; BDPF; CE; CI; DAFD; DAS; DEI; FLC; MS; PT. *Compare* Make Hamburger of.

MAKE MUD PIES   *See* Mud Pie.

MAKE NO BONES ABOUT IT   *to make no bones about something*. To have no hesitation or doubt about doing or saying something; to speak frankly or bluntly about something. HB: 1548. Source: BONE. MWCD: O.E. The source of this metaphorical expression is unclear. It may refer to "meat" bones that are used to flavor soup and stew in the pot but sometimes wind up in individual bowls. That would be a mistake that the chief cook would take pains to correct, although he/she would prob. not tell his/her assistants to *make no bones about it*. However, the notion of "mistake" is interesting, because an alternative form of the expression is to *make no mistake about it*. Another possible source of the metaphor is games of chance, such as craps, that involve dice, which were orig. made of bone. Because the dice, or "bones," are not under the control of the shooter, he/she sometimes talks to them before shooting, urging them to "turn up" in his/her favor. There is no evidence, however, that someone who does *not* talk to the dice has been said to *make no bones about them*. It is also interesting to note that doubt or uncertainty is another of the possible meanings of *bones* in the metaphor. The jury is still out on this one. AID; BDPF; CI; DAI; DC; DEI; EWPO; HND; MDWPO; MS; NSOED. *See also* Bone of Contention.

MAKE SOMEONE EAT CROW   *See* Eat Crow.

MAKE SOMEONE EAT DIRT   *See* Eat Dirt.

MAKE SOMEONE EAT THEIR WORDS   *See* Eat Your Words.

MAKE SOMEONE'S BLOOD BOIL   *to make someone's blood boil*. To make someone very angry. LA: 1675. Source: BOIL (v). MWCD: 13th cent. The temperature of human blood is the same as that of the rest of the body: approx. 98.6° Fahrenheit. Raising it to 212° Fahrenheit, the temperature at which liquids boil at sea level, would destroy the blood, and the body as well. Nevertheless, this exaggerated metaphor catches the essence of anger: The blood pressure rises, the face becomes flushed, the sound level increases, and the subject becomes agitated—just like boiling water. AID; DAI; DC; DEI; MS.

MAKE YOUR GORGE RISE   *to make your gorge rise*. To make you angry, disgusted, or nervous. Source: GORGE. MWCD: 14th cent. The *gorge* is the pouch (or "crop") in a falcon's throat (or "gullet") in which food is stored for later digestion. If the falcon should eat too much, i.e., has *gorged itself* with meat, the food in the gorge might be regurgitated—angering, disgusting, and perhaps nauseating the handler. People have neither anatomical nor alimentary *gorges*, but some do become (1) sick at the sight of blood, (2) offended at the sight of pornography, or (3) revolted at a miscarriage of justice. In the first case, swallowed food may indeed be regurgitated (from the stomach, not the gorge), but in the second and third cases the reaction is more like covering your eyes (2) or shouting an obscenity (3). EWPO; NSOED; SA.

MAKE YOUR MOUTH WATER   *to make your mouth water*. For something to be so attractive that you want to have it—now. HND: 1663. Source: APPETITE. The appearance or aroma of freshly cooked or baked food can be so tantalizing that it lit. "makes your mouth water," i.e., excites your salivary glands and causes you to drool. Figuratively, and stereotypically, children's *mouths water* when they hear the calliope music of an ice-cream truck; men's *mouths water* at the newest line of tools; women's *mouths water* when they smell the latest perfumes; and everyone has a *mouth-watering experience* (MWCD: 1900) when they see a film of Hawai'i while they're freezing back home. Both humans and dogs *lick their chops* (i.e., "lips") in anticipation of undergoing the kind of experience that *makes their mouths water*. After enjoying the experience, humans—but not dogs—*smack their lips* (MWCD: 1557) as a sign of pleasure and satisfaction. Jazz musicians who warm up before a jam session are also said to be *licking their chops* (HND: 1930). AID; BDPF; DAI; DC; DEI; EWPO; HI; MDWPO; MS; SA.

MALT   *See* Malted Milk.

MALTED   *See* Malted Milk.

MALTED MILK   *a malted milk (or malted, or malt)*. A soda fountain drink made of malt powder, milk, ice cream, and flavored syrup—shaken, not stirred, and served in a tall, molded glass. LA: early-1900s. Source: MALT; MILK. MWCD: O.E. *Malted milk* was orig. not a soda fountain drink but a powder created by the Horlick Brothers in 1887 from wheat, malted barley, and milk and intended as a digestive aid for infants and the infirm. However, the combination of malted milk powder and fresh milk was too delicious to resist, and the powder was eventually added to the already existent *milk shake* (q.v.) and called a *malted milk shake*. The new beverage, called either a *malted* or a *malt* by 1910, competed with the milk shake in popularity; and by the 1930s a soda fountain not located in a pharmacy was called a *malt shop*. Since WWII the malt has lost ground to the shake, and persons now ordering a "malt" might be asked if they mean a "shake." Malts and shakes do not really taste that much alike, malts having a much stronger taste than shakes. DAFD; EWPO; FLC.

MALTED MILK SHAKE   *See* Malted Milk.

MALT SHOP   *See* Malted Milk.

MAN CANNOT LIVE BY BREAD ALONE   There is more to life than food. Source: BREAD. MWCD: O.E. This proverb is based on a passage from the book of Deuteronomy (8:3): "[A]nd he [the Lord] humbled thee [Israel] and suffered thee to hunger, and fed thee with manna . . . that he might make thee know that *man doth not live by bread only*, but by every word that proceedeth out of the mouth of the Lord doth man live" [italics added]. The message of this passage is that not only must a person's body be fed, but his/her spirit must be nourished as well. It is the *type* of nourishment of the spirit that has changed since the proverb first appeared in the King James Bible in 1611. CODP; DAP; EWPO. *See also* Manna from Heaven.

MANDARIN ORANGE   *a mandarin orange.* A small, loose-skinned orange with a deep reddish-yellow color. MWCD: 1771. Source: ORANGE. MWCD: 14th cent. The mandarin orange is so called because it is believed to have originated in China, and its skin and pulp have the color of the robes of a *mandarin*, an official of a former Chinese empire. The mandarin orange is the only member, along with its hybrids, of one of the three major categories of oranges: "loose-skinned." (The other categories are "sweet" and "bitter.") A loose-skinned orange is not only easy to peel but easy to "segment," i.e., to separate the dozen or so sections of the flesh from each other. Less than a century after the first mandarin oranges reached England from France, another mandarin orange, called a *tangerine* (MWCD: 1842), named for the city of Tangier(s), Morocco, entered by the same route. They are essentially the same fruit, but the name *mandarin* predominates in Europe and the name *tangerine* in America. The *tangerine* has been involved in the development of many hybrids of citrus fruits: (1) the *tangelo* (MWCD: 1904), a cross between a "*tangerine*" and a "pom*elo*" (or grapefruit); (2) the *temple orange*, believed to be a cross between a tangerine and an orange; and (3) the *Ugli fruit* (NSOED: mid-20th cent.)—Ugli being a trademark for an ugly but delicious hybrid of the tangerine, the grapefruit, and the orange. DAFD; EWPO; FLC; MDWPO; WNWCD.

MANGE-TOUT   *See* Like Two Peas in a Pod.

MANNA   *See* Manna from Heaven.

MANNA FROM HEAVEN   Unexpected help from a benevolent source. Source: MANNA. MWCD: O.E. For the Israelites who journeyed through the wilderness from Egypt to the Promised Land, the food that sustained them for forty years was *manna*. Moses called it "the bread which the Lord hath given you to eat" (Exodus 16:15); and later in the same chapter (16:31), *manna* is described as looking like "coriander seed," white, and tasty, like "wafers made with honey." This description seems to fit what the Egyptians called *mennu*, the sap of the tamarisk tree, because "when the sun waxed hot, it melted" (Exodus 16:21). In modern times, the closest thing to *manna from heaven* is a literal "windfall," i.e., a wind so strong that it blows the fruit or nuts right off the trees, eliminating your need to pick them. A figurative *windfall*—or *manna from heaven*—is a stroke of good luck or good fortune, something that you did not expect, a "reward" for something that you do not recall doing, a welcome "gift" from out of nowhere. BDPF; CI; DEI; HI; HND; LA; MS; NSOED.

MAN WHO FIRST ATE AN OYSTER   *See* Eat Your First Peach.

MAPLE BUTTER   A spread consisting of maple syrup boiled until almost all of the liquid has evaporated. Source: MAPLE (MWCD: 14th cent.); BUTTER (MWCD: O.E.). Maple butter is not *real* butter (processed from milk or cream), but it *spreads* like real butter; and though not yellow, it is yellowish tan in color (ranging to dark brown). Maple butter is the last stage that maple syrup goes through before it becomes maple sugar. The preceding stages are *maple honey* (barely runs) and *maple cream* (still spreadable). FLC. *Compare* Apple Butter; Cocoa Butter; Crab Butter; Peanut Butter.

MAPLE CREAM   *See* Maple Butter.

MAPLE HONEY   *See* Cough Syrup.

MAPLE SUGAR   *See* Cough Syrup.

MAPLE SYRUP   *See* Cough Syrup.

MARGARINE   *See* Oleomargarine.

MARSHMALLOW   *See* S'mores.

MASHED   *See* Mash Your Thumb.

MASHED POTATO   *the mashed potato.* A variation of the dance called the "Twist." Source: MASH (v) (MWCD: 13th cent.); POTATO (MWCD: 1565). The *mashed potato* originated in America in the early-1960s as a more subdued version of the contemporaneous Twist. In both dances the partners are separated, and their lower bodies—the feet, legs, and hips—do pretty much the same thing, i.e., "twist." The upper bodies are relatively inactive in both dances, although the arms are continuously pumped in the twist, whereas they are extended horizontally to the front or side for the mashed potato, with the hands facing palm down and moving up and down to imitate the action of a potato masher mashing boiled potatoes in a pot. Another musical use of the word *potato* was in the George and Ira Gershwin song "Let's Call the Whole Thing Off," from the 1937 film *Shall We Dance*, starring Fred Astaire and Ginger Rogers. The two stars sang their observations of the trivial differences in pronunciation between them, such as *eether/eyether, neether/neyether* and *potaytoes/potahtoes, tomaytoes/tomahtoes*. The "eether/eyether" and "neether/neyether" contrasts are as real today as they were in 1937, although they are certainly not serious enough to prevent marriage. The *potaytoes/potahtoes* and *tomaytoes/tomahtoes* contrasts can now be heard only in Boston, and their existence in Hollywood in the late-1930s was prob. due simply to an attempt at affectation, in the case of *potahtoes* and *tomahtoes*. (*Potaytoes* and *tomaytoes* have been the standard pronunciation since the 1880s.) Finally, a ritual use of the word *potato* occurs in the chant "One potato, two potato, three potato, four; five potato, six potato, seven potato, more." (The count can continue, and *banana* can be substituted for *potato*.) This rhyme is used in such children's activities as choosing sides (the chooser counting with closed fists) but can also be used in counting up to fifty (as in a game of hide and seek), counting the seconds (instead of saying "one thousand one," etc.), and perhaps skipping rope. LA; WNWCD.

MASHER   *See* Mash Your Thumb.

MASH YOUR THUMB   *to mash your thumb.* To hit the nail of your thumb—instead of the nail in the board—with the head of a hammer. Source: MASH (v). MWCD: 13th cent. The verb *mash* "to beat something to a pulp" is derived from the noun *mash* "ground up feed for livestock" (MWCD: O.E.). The noun was later applied to crushed malt, heated and stirred in water to produce a fermented liquid for the production of whiskey and beer; and the verb was used to describe someone who had become *mashed,* or intoxicated, by the same beverages. The utensil used to reduce boiled potatoes to a pulp is called a "masher" (MWCD: ca. 1500), but the human *masher,* who preys on unsuspecting women (MWCD: 1875), is from a different—and unknown—source. People from the Midland moonshine country like to surprise their Northern neighbors by asking, while on an elevator in the North, if the "locals" would *mash three* ("push the button for the third floor"), in which case the thumb becomes the *masher* rather than the mashee. The *mash* in the movie and TV show *M*A*S*H* is not related to any of the above uses but is an acronym for "Mobile Army Surgical Hospital." DAS; FLC; HDAS; NSOED; WNWCD. *See also* Mashed Potato.

MATSO BALL   *See* Dumpling.

MAYO   *See* Hold the Mayo!

MAYONNAISE   *See* Hold the Mayo!

MEADOW MUFFIN   *See* Muffin.

MEAL   *a meal.* One of the regular daily eating times. Source: MEAL. MWCD: O.E. *Meal* (fr. O.E. *mæl* "a set time") orig. referred only to the customary time at which a food was served during the day (e.g., *breakfasttime, dinnertime,* and *suppertime*) and only later came to refer also to the food that was eaten at those times ("Eat your *breakfast, dinner, supper!*"). In America, between the early-to-mid-19th cent. and the early-to-mid-20th cent., the regular meals changed to *breakfast* (q.v.), *lunch* (q.v.), and *dinner* (q.v.), with the morning meal becoming lighter, the noontime meal becoming much lighter, and the evening meal becoming much heavier. *Brunch* (q.v.) is a more recent development, and *supper* (q.v.) survives only as a late, light meal. In the 19th cent., men expected *three square meals* (or *three squares*) a day—a *square meal* (LA: 1836) being a complete, hot, hearty, nourishing meal that would *stick to your ribs,* metaphorically speaking. That expectation gradually changed in the early-20th cent. with the introduction of cold cereals for breakfast and cold sandwiches for lunch. Today, dinner is the only meal at which the *breadwinner* (q.v.) of the family can expect a *square meal*, and a hot one at that. Under the old *American Plan* (MWCD: 1856), the daily rate for a hotel room in America also covered the cost of three (square?) meals, but most American hotels now follow the (even older) *European Plan* (MWCD: 1834), by which the cost of a room includes no meals at all. However, many hotels today offer a free *continental breakfast* (MWCD: 1911), consisting of a pastry and coffee, and some even provide a free or reasonably priced *breakfast buffet*, esp. on weekends. The *meal ticket* (MWCD: ca. 1899) that was once a professional baseball player's only guarantee of one hot (i.e., cooked) meal a day survives only in college residence halls and collegiate dictionaries, where it is defined as one's "ultimate source of financial support." After college and career, you can retire and call *meals-on-wheels* (MWCD: 1961) to deliver your daily hot meal directly to your doorstep (provided that you are unable to go out and get it yourself). CE; CI; DAP; DAS; DC; DEI; HDAS; HND; MDWPO; NSOED; PT.

MEALS-ON-WHEELS   *See* Meal.

MEAL TICKET   *See* Meal.

MEALYMOUTHED   Devious; deceitful; dishonest. MWCD: ca. 1572. Source: HONEY. *Mealymouthed* is an adj. based on the Gk. noun *melimuthos*, lit. "honey" (*meli*) + "mouth" (*muthos*), which was orig. used to characterize someone with a voice *as sweet as honey*. In English, the word shifted in meaning from a "velvet-tongued orator" to "a soft-spoken person," one who, out of fear of giving offense, avoided being critical or direct. Later, the *mealymouthed* speaker developed into what we now call a *sweet talker* (MWCD: ca. 1928): "an insincere flatterer who can talk his/her way into or out of anything." Ironically, another borrowing based on the word *honey*, *mellifluous* (MWCD: 15th cent.—fr. Lat. *melli* "honey" + *flous* "flow"), has retained its favorable connotation and is now used in the phrase *a mellifluous voice* "a voice that flows like honey from the speaker's mouth." BDPF; CE; CI; DAI; DAP; DEI; EWPO; LCRH; MS; NSOED; SA.

MEAT   Food (as opposed to drink); kernel (as opposed to covering); animal flesh (as opposed to human flesh); flesh of mammals or fowl (as opposed to flesh of fish); flesh of mammals (as opposed to the flesh of fish or fowl). Source: MEAT. MWCD: O.E. In O.E. and M.E., the word *mete* simply meant "food" or "sustenance," as preserved in the early Mod. Eng. phrase *meat and drink*, as spoken by Touchstone in Act I, Scene 1, of Shakespeare's *As You Like It* (ca. 1599): "It is *meat and drink* to me to see a clown" [italics added]. In the 14th cent., *meat* was applied also to the edible part of a nut (a *nutmeat*) and the sweet part of a confection (a *sweetmeat*). The modern expression *to put some meat on your bones* "to put on some weight" reflects the status of *meat* in the early Mod. Eng. period, when the word was synonymous with *flesh*. In the 17th cent., *meat* narrowed its meaning to "the flesh of animals," as reflected in the modern term *meat market* "a shop where the flesh of mammals, fish, and fowl is sold." *Meat market* is also a modern metaphor for an environment in which people are treated as commodities rather than individual human beings (MWCD: 1896); and women, in particular, *feel like a piece of meat* when they find themselves in a relationship in which their lover *treats them like a piece of meat*, i.e., regards them as a sex object rather than a human being. In the 20th cent. the term *meat* narrowed further to "the flesh of mammals and fowl" (as in "white meat" and "dark meat") and also broadened again to "the flesh of mammals, fish, and fowl" (for people who are *fed up*, q.v., with such fine distinctions). To the latter group, people who won't eat "meat" are *vegetarians* (q.v.). BDPF; DAFD; DC; EWPO; FLC; HND; LA; MS; NSOED.

MEAT AND DRINK   *See* Meat.

MEAT AND POTATOES   *See* Meat-and-potatoes.

MEAT-AND-POTATOES   *a meat-and-potatoes* city; a *meat-and-potatoes* issue. MWCD: 1949. Source: MEAT (MWCD: O.E.); POTATO (MWCD: 1565). In the mid-20th cent., meat and potatoes were essential for any substantial meal—esp. if *meat* was interpreted to mean either "red meat" or poultry, and *potatoes* either sweet or white tubers. These basics then became a metaphor for (1) men who were "regular guys" (simple, uncomplicated, not demanding or expecting anything fancy); (2) cities that were known for their smokestack industries, blue-collar workers, and rough weather; and (3) issues or propositions that were fundamental and related to everyday life, such as housing and feeding. To solve these problems, the city would need to get down to *meat and potatoes* (MWCD: 1951), i.e., the nitty-gritty, the heart of the matter. Meat is no good without potatoes (and vice versa), as the expression *all that meat and no potatoes* suggests. (Unfortunately, this description usu. refers to a very fat woman as observed by a very fat man.) CE; DAS; HND; MDWPO.

MEAT-AX APPROACH   *See* Meaty.

MEAT BY-PRODUCTS   *See* Variety Meats.

MEAT HAND   *See* Meaty.

MEATHEAD   *See* Meaty.

MEATHEADED   *See* Meaty.

MEAT HOOKS   *See* Meaty.

MEAT LOAF   *a meat loaf.* Ground meat baked in the shape of a loaf of bread. MWCD: 1899. Source: MEAT; LOAF. MWCD: O.E. The conventional shapes of a loaf of bread are oblong and round, and these are the usual shapes of loaves of meat as well. The standard meat loaf is made of ground beef and pork; but *ham loaf* is made of ground ham, and *salmon loaf* is made of ground salmon. Another dish called a *loaf*, although it is neither shaped like a loaf of bread nor baked, is the *sugarloaf* (MWCD: 15th cent.). This mass of sugar, molded in the form of a cone, has given its name to Sugar Loaf Mountain in the harbor of Rio de Janeiro, Brazil. FLC; NSOED; WNWCD.

MEAT MARKET   *See* Meat.

MEAT PIE   *See* Porkpie Hot.

MEAT WAGON   *See* Meaty.

MEATY   *meaty hands; a meaty role; a meaty topic.* Large, heavy hands; a substantial role in a play; a profound topic. NSOED: late-19th cent. Source: MEAT. MWCD: O.E. The literal meaning of *meaty* is "full of meat" (MWCD: ca. 1787), which becomes metaphorical when applied to things that resemble meat in size, value, and weight. Two other meat metaphors have been used to describe hands: (1) a *meat hand* (HDAS: 1911) is the baseball player's hand on which he/she does not wear a glove; and (2) *meat hooks* "fingers" are so called because one's fingers resemble the hooks ("tenterhooks") on which meat is hung in a slaughterhouse. *Meathead* (HDAS: 1928) is a metaphor for a person who is stupid or dense, as Archie Bunker took his son-in-law, whom he called "Meathead," to be in the TV show *All in the Family*; and a *meatheaded* idea is one that is as simpleminded as the person who brought it up. *Dead meat* (HDAS: 1865)—or *buzzard meat*—is what you're going to be if you don't play along with the mob, who use a *meat-ax approach* to solving problems; and in that case you'll be hauled away in a *meat wagon* (HDAS: 1925) "a coroner's van." CE; DAS; EWPO; MDWPO; NSOED; PT.

MELBA SAUCE   *See* Melba Toast.

MELBA TOAST   Small, thin, crisp pieces of almost-burned toast. MWCD: 1925. Source: TOAST. MWCD: 15th cent. *Melba toast* is so called because it was named after Dame Nellie Melba, an opera singer from Australia who was inadvertently served such fare at London's Savoy Hotel. Surprisingly, she loved it, and it was added to the menu. The soprano also gave her name to a dessert called *peach Melba* (DAFD: 1906), which was prepared in her honor by the same French chef, Escoffier. The dish consists of two peach halves poached in vanilla syrup and served upside down on a large scoop of vanilla ice cream topped with a raspberry sauce called *Melba sauce*, also named for the singer. In contrast to low-calorie Melba toast, peach Melba is full of calories. BDPF; DAFD; EWPO; FLC; MDWPO.

MELLIFLUOUS   *See* Mealymouthed.

MELL OF A HESS   *See* Fine Mess.

MELONS   *See* Slice of the Melon.

MELTING POT   *See* Potbelly.

MELT IN YOUR MOUTH   *See* Butter Wouldn't Melt in Your Mouth.

MEMORY LIKE A SIEVE   *See* Leak like a Sieve.

MENU   *a menu.* A list of options displayed visually on a computer screen or spoken orally over a Touch-Tone telephone. NSOED: mid-20th cent. Source: MENU. MWCD: 1837. A computer program that allows the user to interact with it is *menu-driven* (MWCD: 1977); i.e., it offers a set of broad options, from which the user must pick one, then a set of narrower options, etc., until the desired goal is reached. (The ATM machine also has a menu-driven program of this sort, as do some television sets.) The telephone conversation between a caller and a set of recorded options occurs audially rather than visually, but it works pretty much the same way. (Banks, power companies, and mail-order houses also use such menu-driven programs on the telephone.) The original *menu* was a large card, posted in the front window of a restaurant, advertising the food that would be available for ordering on that particular day. In the 17th or 18th cents., that would have referred only to a complete meal, served *table d'hôte* (MWCD: 1617—lit. "host's table") to all diners, at a fixed time and price (*prix fixe*—MWCD: 1883). In the early-19th cent., however, restaurants began to allow diners to order *à la carte* (MWCD: 1826), i.e., from a menu that listed, and priced, dishes separately, so that the guests could pick and choose—often choosing items that added up to more than the "host's" dinner. The late-19th cent. saw a modification in the *table d'hôte* dinner that kept the complete meal and fixed price but dropped the single time and uniform offerings. By the 20th cent., diners could order as much or as little as they wanted, whenever they wanted, including during the "happy hour" (from 4:00 to 6:00 P.M.), when *early-bird specials* were offered at reduced prices to those who chose to eat. Some restaurant terms still stump diners. Diner: "What kind of soup is *soup du jour?*" (MWCD: 1969). Waiter: "That's 'soup of the day.' " Diner: "That sounds good. I'll have that." However, *du jour* has caught on outside of the food business, and we now have such expressions as *babe du jour* and *hunk du jour,* each of which sounds like "fish du jour," i.e., *catch of the day.* Meals ordered *à la carte* by lunch-counter diners in the 1920s and 1930s were identified by the term *in the alley* in lunch-counter jargon. DAFD; EWPO; FLC; HF; IHAT; LA; MDWPO; PT.

MENU-DRIVEN   *See* Menu.

MESS (AROUND) WITH   *See* Fine Mess.

MESS CALL   *See* Fine Mess.

MESSED UP   *See* Fine Mess.

MESS HALL   *See* Fine Mess.

MESS IN   *See* Fine Mess.

MESSMATE   *See* Fine Mess.

MESS OF FISH   *See* Fine Mess.

MESS OF PEAS   *See* Fine Mess.

MESS OF POTTAGE   *See* Fine Mess.

MESS TENT   *See* Fine Mess.

MESS UP   *See* Fine Mess.

MEXICAN GREEN TOMATO   *See* Tomato.

MEXICAN RAREBIT   *See* Welsh Rabbit.

MEXICAN WEDDING CAKE   *a Mexican wedding cake.* A ball-shaped butter cookie, containing finely chopped nuts, that is rolled in powdered sugar immediately after baking. Source: CAKE. MWCD: 13th cent. The *Mexican wedding cake* is not a cake, but it is certainly rich enough to be served at a wedding. Two other "cakes" that are made according to the same recipe, but are intended for serving at a "tea," are *Russian tea cakes* and *Swedish tea cakes*. The Ger. *Pfeffernüsse* (lit. "peppernuts"), which is also ball-shaped but contains no nuts (other than the ground peppercorns), is intended for serving at Christmastime. FLC.

MICHIGAN BANANA   *See* Papaya.

MIDNIGHT SNACK   *See* Snack Bar.

MIGHTY OAKS FROM LITTLE ACORNS GROW   *See* Acorn Squash.

MIKE AND IKE   *See* Salt-and-pepper.

MILK (n)   Any thin, white fluid that resembles cow's milk. NSOED: late-M.E. Source: MILK. MWCD: O.E. A lot of liquids resemble cow's milk, e.g., goat milk, sheep milk, buffalo milk, etc.; but the major metaphorical "milks" are *co-*

conut milk (q.v.), which is either the natural juice or the manufactured "milk" of a coconut; *corn milk*, the white liquid that hits you in the eye when you "pop" a kernel of unripe corn; *milk of magnesia* (MWCD: 1880), milky white magnesium hydroxide suspended in water and used as a laxative or antacid; *milkweed milk*, the white latex produced by milkweed plants and invaluable during WWII; *pigeon milk* (q.v.), the milky substance regurgitated into the mouths of baby pigeons by their parents; and *soy milk*, the artificial milk produced by combining ground soy beans with water. Soy milk is almost identical to cow's milk: milky white, rich in iron, high in protein. It can be used for cooking, creaming coffee, drinking, and making a cheese called *tofu*. Soy milk is also valuable for use by persons who are allergic to cow's milk, are opposed to the consumption of animal by-products, or require a strict kosher diet. BDPF; DAFD; FLC; WNWCD.

MILK (v)   *to milk something*. To drain the resources of something. Source: MILK. MWCD: O.E. *Milking* something can be as physical as *milking a snake* (NSOED: mid-18th cent.), i.e., extracting most of the venom from a poisonous snake by holding its fangs over the edge of a glass, or as fanciful as *milking a cash cow* (q.v.). Basketball players *milk the clock* (i.e., use up as much of the time remaining in a game as possible while they are in possession of the ball), and mine owners *milk a mine* (i.e., nearly exhaust its supply of ore) before selling it. Local merchants sometimes *milk* tourists (i.e., overcharge them for cheap souvenirs), and employees can *milk* a business (i.e., embezzle money or steal equipment from it). Houdini is said to have *milked* a stunt for all it was worth, and authors have been accused of *milking* metaphors for even less. BDPF; DAP; DAS; DEI; NSOED; SA *See also* Milk Dry.

MILK A CASH COW   *to milk a cash cow*. To use profits from a dependable source of revenue to finance less profitable investments in other parts of the organization. Source: MILK (v); COW. MWCD: O.E. A *cash cow* (HDAS: 1974) and a dairy cow are alike in the sense that they both turn out useful products (money, milk) on a regular basis with little coaxing and minimum upkeep. In business, a popular old product that just goes on and on can help a company diversify in other areas. In higher education, a consistently successful football program can help a college or university support teams in other (low-revenue or nonrevenue) sports. The danger of *milking a cash cow* is *milking it dry*, i.e., completely exhausting its supply of benefits. The same danger applies to basketball or football players *milking the clock dry*, to unscrupulous merchants *milking tourists dry*, and to unscrupulous companies *milking their employees dry*. BDPF; CE; DAS; DEI; IRCD; NSOED; SA. *See also* Milk (v).

MILK A MINE   *See* Milk (v).

MILK A SNAKE   *See* Milk (v).

MILK DRY   *See* Milk a Cash Cow.

MILK GLASS   *See* Milky.

MILK OF HUMAN KINDNESS   *the milk of human kindness.* Compassion; mercy. (Shakespeare's *Macbeth*, ca. 1606.) Source: MILK (n). MWCD: O.E. The phrase is from a soliloquy by Lady Macbeth, uttered after she reads a letter from her husband, a general in the army of Duncan, King of Scotland, announcing the King's visit to Macbeth's castle that evening. Lady Macbeth is very ambitious to have her husband replace Duncan as King, but she doubts that he has the nerve to make it happen (Act I, Scene 5): "Yet I do fear thy nature. / It is too full o' th' *milk of human kindness*/To catch the nearest way" [italics added]. The "nearest way," in Lady Macbeth's opinion, would be to assassinate Duncan that night in his sleep. That's exactly what happened, and Macbeth is the one who did it. BDPF; CI; DC; DEI; HND; MDWPO; NSOED.

MILK OF MAGNESIA   *See* Milk (n).

MILK RUN   *a milk run.* A routine flight of a military or commercial airplane. MWCD: 1925. Source: MILK (n). MWCD: O.E. The metaphor is based on the early morning delivery of milk in the 1920s, involving frequent stops at the homes of regular customers. This routine was first associated with airplane flights to deliver bombs or mail (HDAS: 1944) but was later extended to (1) commercial passenger flights that seem to stop at every airport, (2) passenger trains that seem to stop at every station, (3) buses that seem to stop at every corner, and (4) elevators that seem to stop at every floor. Thus, the meaning of the metaphor has changed gradually from "routine" to "annoyingly slow." BDPF; NSOED; WNWCD.

MILK SHAKE   *a milk shake.* A cold drink made of milk, ice cream, and flavored syrup, blended together. MWCD: 1889. Source: MILK (n). MWCD: O.E. The milk shake was already in existence when Horlick's Malted Milk was added to it ca. 1900 to form the *malted milk shake* (q.v.). Since then, the original *milk shake* (no malt) and the *malted milk shake* have competed for popularity, with the "malt" winning out during the first half of the 20th cent. and the "shake" returning strong in the second half. Malts were pretty much limited to two flavors, chocolate and vanilla; shakes also come in those two flavors (called a *mud shake* and a *white cow*, respectively) but now feature many more (e.g., strawberry and maple). A milk shake is also known as a *frappé* (or "frapp"), fr. Fr. *frapper* "to chill." DAFD; DAS; FLC; IHAT; PT.

MILK SNAKE   *a milk snake.* A common, harmless, multicolored snake of the Northeastern United States. MWCD: 1800. Source: MILK (n). MWCD: O.E. The milk snake is so called because it was once thought to frequent milkhouses in order to drink the cows' milk that was stored there. However, the snake was really there because that was where it could find its true supply of food: rodents, which actually *do* like to drink milk. The harmless milk snake is related to the "king snake," which is a six-foot-long constrictor. NSOED; WNWCD.

MILKSOP   *a milksop.* A sissy. MWCD: 14th cent. Source: MILK; SOP. MWCD: O.E. In the 14th cent., *milksop* (or "pap") was lit. "bread soaked in milk," an easily digestible dish fed to infants and invalids. Figuratively, it referred to a man or boy who behaved like a child sopping up milk with bread—i.e., one who lacked manliness and backbone: a "mollycoddle." The noun *sop*, alone, orig. referred to a piece of bread dipped into any tasty liquid, such as gravy or pan drippings. In the *Aeneid*, it was reported that cakes soaked in honey were placed in the hands of the dearly departed as a *a sop to Cerberus* (HB: 1513), i.e., a bribe to the three-headed dog that guarded the gates of Hades. In modern times, *a sop to Cerberus* is a bribe of any kind, a peace offering, or a gesture of friendship. A *sop* is now simply a drunk. BDPF; CE; DAFD; DAS; HF; MDWPO; NSOED; PT; WNWCD. *Compare* Milquetoast.

MILK THE CLOCK   *See* Milk (v).

MILK TOAST   *See* Milquetoast.

MILK TOOTH   *a milk tooth.* One of the twenty-four "baby teeth" of a human child. MWCD: ca. 1752. Source: MILK (n). MWCD: O.E. Baby teeth are presumably called *milk teeth* because they appear during the time when a baby is, or could be, nursing. Such teeth are sometimes called "deciduous" because they drop out, like leaves, while the child is in primary school, and are replaced by new, permanent teeth. A full set of *milk teeth* numbers twenty-four, rather than the adult's thirty-two, because children lack bicuspids and wisdom teeth. The term *milk teeth* has also been applied to the deciduous teeth of other young mammals. BDPF; NSOED; WNWCD.

MILKWEED MILK   *See* Milk (n).

MILKY   Resembling milk in color or consistency. MWCD: 14th cent. Source: MILK. MWCD: O.E. Things that are described as being *milky* are not milk but resemble milk in color (white) and transparency (opaque). An example of this resemblance is *milk glass* (MWCD: 1874), a type of glass that is as white as milk and only slightly more opaque. During the height of its popularity, from approx. 1875 to 1925, milk glass was used for "occasional" plates and bowls, such as candy dishes. The *Milky Way* is so called because it surrounds our galaxy with a white band of a myriad of opaque but twinkling stars. NSOED; WNWCD.

MILKY WAY   *See* Milky.

MILL   *See* Grist for the Mill.

MILL ABOUT   *See* Through the Mill.

MILLS OF THE GODS GRIND SLOWLY   *The mills of the gods grind slowly, but they grind exceeding fine.* Sooner or later you will be punished for your sins. Source: MILL; GRIND. MWCD: O.E. This modern proverb is a modification of a line from Henry Wadsworth Longfellow's translation (CODP: 1870) of a 17th cent. Ger. poem, "Retribution." The original Eng. version was "Though the mills of *God* grind slowly,/ Yet they grind exceeding *small*" [italics added]. *Retribution* is being interpreted here in its modern sense of "punishment" rather than in its early modern sense of "reward or punishment." The notion of God as a miller, grinding our lives on a millstone in order to examine every single transgression, is very Romantic. Today's youth might express the proverb as "You can run, but you can't hide." BDPF; DAP; DC; HND; MDWPO; MS.

MILQUETOAST   *a milquetoast.* A timid man. MWCD: 1935. Source: MILK (n) (MWCD: O.E.); TOAST (MWCD: 15th cent.). *Milquetoast* was the unusual spelling of the last name of a timid character, Caspar Milquetoast, in a comic strip of the 1920s: "The Timid Soul" (HDAS: 1924). Uncapitalized, it is now a metaphor for a man who has been described as apologetic, effeminate, mealymouthed, meek, shrinking, shy, and unassertive. The name derives from an American dish called *milk toast* (LA: 1857), consisting of toasted bread and warm milk. *Milk toast* differs from *milksop* (q.v.) in that the former consists of hot milk poured over toast in a bowl, whereas the latter consists of hot milk poured over untoasted bread on a plate. During the Depression of the 1930s, hot water was poured over toast on a plate, and the nameless dish was eaten for breakfast by everyone who couldn't afford ham and eggs. CE; DAS; FLC; IHAT; NSOED; PT; WNWCD.

MINCE (n)   *See* Make Mincemeat of.

MINCE (v)   *See* Mince Words.

MINCEMEAT   *See* Make Mincemeat of.

MINCEMEAT PIE   *See* Make Mincemeat of.

MINCE WORDS   *to mince words.* To use evasive language. Source: MINCE (v). MWCD: 14th cent. The verb *mince* orig. meant to chop up meat into small pieces in order to make it easier to chew, swallow, and digest. By the early-16th cent., *mince* had become a metaphor for *walking* with an affectation: taking short, dainty, delicate, or *mincing steps* (MWCD: 1530). By the early-17th cent., *mince* had become a metaphor for *talking* with an affectation, esp. when censuring someone: i.e., using equivocation, extenuation, and euphemism in order to soften the blow. In *Antony and Cleopatra*, Shakespeare used the metaphor in the neg. for the first time, *to not mince words*, i.e., to speak bluntly, plainly, and frankly; and that is the primary form in which it is used today: "I won't mince words: You're fired!" AID; BDPF; CE; CI; DC; HND; LCRH; MS. *See also* Make Mincemeat of.

MINCING STEPS   *See* Mince Words.

MIND YOUR P's AND Q's   *See* Half-pint.

MINED SALT   *See* Old Salt.

MISSISSIPPI MUD CAKE   *See* Mud Pie.

MISSISSIPPI MUD PIE   *See* Mud Pie.

MIXED GRILL   *See* Grill a Suspect.

MOCK APPLE PIE   *a mock apple pie*. (Also called a *faux apple pie*.) An "apple" pie made of Ritz Crackers rather than apple slices. DAFD: 1930s. Source: APPLE (MWCD: O.E.); PIE (MWCD: 14th cent.). This "false" apple pie was introduced during the Great Depression, when apples were scarce and Ritz Crackers had only recently appeared (DAFD: 1933). When broken into quarters, the well-browned crackers looked like cinnamon-coated apple slices; but it was the *taste* of the crackers, when coated with a hot syrup of water, sugar, cream of tartar, lemon juice, margarine, and cinnamon, that made the "mock" pie not only an acceptable substitute but a delicious dessert. As recently as 1996, the pie was mentioned on the *Murphy Brown* TV show (called *faux apple pie*), and the recipe was printed on the back of the Ritz Crackers box (called *"mock" apple pie*).

MOCK CHICKEN   Imitation chicken legs. Source: CHICKEN. MWCD: 14th cent. A request for *mock chicken* at a butcher's counter can result in (1) a blank stare; (2) an order of five-inch wooden sticks covered with a mixture of ground pork and veal, shaped in the form of the drumstick of a chicken, and coated with breadcrumbs (usu. called *mock chicken*); or (3) an order of five-inch pointed sticks on which are skewered, in shish-kebab fashion, alternating chunks of veal and pork (usu. called *city chicken*, but no chicken, and no drumsticks). Presumably, the last-mentioned term contains the word *city* to emphasize that it is not barnyard fowl that you're getting but a glamorous substitute for the real thing. Unlike *Cape Cod turkey* (q.v.) and *Texas turkey* (q.v.), however, the imitation is more expensive than the original. BDPF; SA.

MOCK COFFEE   *See* Coffee.

MOCK DUCK   An imitation duck roll. Source: DUCK. MWCD: O.E. *Mock duck* is one more example of the products of hard times. The dish contains no duck but is fashioned out of cube steak stuffed with cheese, breadcrumbs, and garnishes and cooked in tomato sauce. It can be used to replace duck or chicken in entrées or be served in place of meatballs with spaghetti. Another imposter is *Bombay duck*, which is not a duck at all but a dried fish. Bummalo fish, from India, is salted, dried, heated to a crisp, crumbled, and served on curry dishes. The word *Bombay* may refer to the city in India or it may simply be a mispronunciation of *bummalo*. MDWPO; PT; SA. *Compare* Mock Chicken; Mock Turtle Soup.

MOCK TURTLE SOUP   Imitation green turtle soup. MWCD: 1783. Source: TURTLE (MWCD: 1657); SOUP (MWCD: 14th cent.). In Lewis Carroll's *Alice in Wonderland* (1871), Part One: "Alice's Adventures in Wonderland" (1865), Chapter IX: "The Mock Turtle's Story," the Queen of Hearts explains to Alice what a Mock Turtle is: "It's the thing *Mock Turtle Soup* is made from" [italics added]. When Alice meets the Mock Turtle, she understands why he is so named: He has the body, shell, and front flippers of a sea turtle, but the head, tail, and hind feet of a calf. "Once I was a real turtle," says the Mock Turtle; and that is the case with green turtle soup. Once it was made of the flesh of the green sea turtle, which, along with some wine and spices, was cooked until it formed a thick, creamy, tasty soup—or, as the Mock Turtle sings in Chapter X, "Beautiful Soup, so rich and green, / Waiting in a hot tureen! / Who for such dainties would not stoop? / Soup of the evening, beautiful soup!" However, for various reasons, such as the low availability and high cost of green turtles, an imitation soup was created in the late-18th cent. that substituted—you guessed it!—a calf's head for the turtle meat, at least during the cooking. The head was then removed, the meat was cut off and returned to the broth, and the brains were used as a garnish. (For the squeamish, veal was substituted for the calf's head!) Despite the green turtle's current appearance on the endangered species list, it was once so plentiful that it was called the *Caribbean buffalo*. DAFD; FLC; PT; SA.

MOLASSES COOKIE   *See* Slow as Molasses in January.

MONEY-HUNGRY   *See* Hungry for Affection.

MONKEY NUTS   *See* Work for Peanuts.

MONTE CRISTO   *See* Dagwood Sandwich.

MOON IS MADE OF GREEN CHEESE   *The moon is made of green cheese.* ("You just won the lottery!" "Sure, and *the moon is made of green cheese*." That is, only a fool would believe that.) MDWPO: early-16th cent. Source: CHEESE. MWCD: O.E. It wasn't until 1969 that the Apollo astronauts Neil Armstrong and Buzz Aldrin walked on the moon, proving once and for all that the moon is not made of green cheese. Actually, no one had ever really believed that it was. What they believed, back in the early-16th cent., was that the moon was made of unripened or unaged cheese—"green" only in the sense of "immature." The reason for their belief was that a "wheel" of cheese looks very much like a full moon— perfectly round, and off-white in color. As you eat the wheel, it begins to look like a three-quarter moon, then a half moon, then a quarter moon, etc. BDPF; EWPO. *Compare* Blue Cheese; Grin like a Cheshire Cat; Pie in the Sky.

MOON PIE   *a Moon Pie.* A popular snack in the shape of a full moon. DAFD: 1919. Source: PIE. MWCD: 14th cent. Calling this snack a "pie" may be stretching it a bit. The confection consists of a marshmallow filling *sandwiched* (q.v) between two large, soft cookies. It originated in Chattanooga, Tenn., where customers regarded it as enough to serve as a complete lunch—until the manufacturer came out with a double-decker in 1969: another layer of marshmallow and another cookie on top! The snack may have been called a *Moon Pie* because it is as big as that heavenly body—a literal *pie in the sky* (q.v.). (It also "wanes" as you eat it.) DAFD.

MOST IMPORTANT MEAL OF THE DAY   *See* Breakfast (n).

MOTH-EATEN   *to be moth-eaten.* To be dilapidated, decayed, or decrepit; to be antiquated, out-of-date, or outmoded. NSOED: mid-16th cent. Source: EAT. MWCD: O.E. The moth that is responsible for all of these adjectives is the clothes moth, which flies into storage closets and lays eggs that turn into larvae, which hole up in animal by-products such as wool and fur. Undamaged clothes that have developed holes by other means, such as washing, wearing, and puncturing, are called *moth-eaten* because they look as though they have been attacked by moths or, more accurately, their larvae. In contrast, clothing that is in perfect physical condition can be called *moth-eaten* if it is out of style or fashion, i.e., if it looks as if it has been hanging in the closet for a number of years; and ideas that are out-of-date or old-fashioned can be called *moth-eaten* even if they are abstract, i.e., sheltering neither moths nor their larvae. The term *worm-eaten* has a similar history: The "worms" are really beetle larvae, not "true" worms; they eat wooden floors, furniture, and woodwork. Furniture that is old but not actually attacked by beetle larvae can also be called *worm-eaten*. ATWS; DEI; EWPO; MS; SA.

MOTHER OF VINEGAR   *See* Vinegar.

MOTHER'S MILK   The fundamental food. Source: MILK. MWCD: O.E. For many human babies, "formula" in a bottle has replaced mother's milk, but for animal babies it is still the only source of sustenance for the first several weeks of life. Metaphorically, *mother's milk* is something Americans cannot do without, such as television and fast food. In Britain, however, *mother's milk* has been a slang expression for "gin" since the early-1800s. DEI; NSOED.

MOUNTAIN OYSTERS   *See* Lamb Fries.

MOUSE POTATO   *See* Couch Potato.

MOUSSE   A foam used for styling hair: "styling mousse." Source: MOUSSE. MWCD: 1892. *Mousse* is derived fr. the Fr. word meaning "froth" or "foam," which in turn is derived fr. a Lat. word for "mead" or a Ger. word for "moss." Regardless of its exact origin, *mousse* was first applied in Eng. to a food that was based on cream or gelatin and was light and spongy. From that beginning has evolved the modern dessert, which is based on gelatin and either whipped cream or egg whites. The mixture is then sweetened, flavored, molded, chilled, and served in a fruit cup. Chocolate mousse is the most popular variety, but regardless of the flavor, the dessert is so light that it is tempting to order more—and more. *Styling mousse* is named for the dessert because it is also light and foamy when it comes out of the aerosol can. FLC; WNWCD.

MOUTHFUL   *See* You Said a Mouthful.

MOUTH-WATERING   *See* Make Your Mouth Water.

MOUTH WATERS   *See* Make Your Mouth Water.

MOVABLE FEAST   *See* Feast.

MOXIE   Nerve, courage; gall, guts; spunk, spirit; energy, pep; expertise, shrewdness. MWCD: 1930. Source: SODA. The metaphorical *moxie* is named for the beverage *Moxie* (MDWPO: 1884), which was one of the earliest of the current soft drinks to appear in the United States. Like the others, such as Hires Root Beer (MWCD: 1843) and Coca-Cola (IHAT: 1893), it started out as a medicinal drink. Moxie Nerve Tonic was a carbonated, bitter-flavored cola that was first produced in Lowell, Mass., but quickly became popular throughout New England. Its name ("nerve tonic") may have contributed to the belief that Moxie gave the drinker greater "nerve" (or courage), and the bitter taste may have contributed to the belief that you had to have a lot of nerve (or "guts") just to drink it. (The caffeine prob. also had something to do with it.) At any rate, *to have a lot of moxie* (EWPO: 1939) became a popular expression at the ball park, where Moxie was a best seller, and on the sports page. Not only has Moxie remained a popular soft drink, but the original name has branded anyone who asks, "Would you like a *tonic*?" as a current or former resident of eastern New England, esp. the Boston area. Of the two other century-old soft drinks, root beer, true to its name, was orig. flavored with roots and bark, whereas Coca-Cola, also true to its name, was orig. flavored with coca leaves and cola nuts. DAFD; DAS; FLC; HDAS; LCRH; MDWPO; NSOED.

MR. POTATO HEAD   *See* Potatohead.

MUD   *See* Java.

MUD FIZZ   *See* Black Cow.

MUD PIE   *a mud pie.* A handful of mud shaped like a small pie. Source: PIE. MWCD: 14th cent. *"Making mud pies"* is what children answer when a parent asks them what they're doing playing in the mud. It is also what bakers do when they pour dark chocolate custard or gelatin into a pie shell. The *Mississippi mud pie* (DAFD: 1980s) is as thick and dense as mud from the banks of that river, although it is sometimes referred to as a *Mississippi mud cake.* Add a layer of rum custard to the mud pie, and top it with whipped cream and chocolate parings, and you have a *black bottom pie* (DAFD: 1951). FLC. *Compare* Black-bottom Sundae.

MUD SHAKE   *See* Milk Shake.

MUFFIN   A term of endearment and address for a girl or young woman: "Hi, Muffin!" Source: MUFFIN. MWCD: 1703. The culinary muffin—or *popover* (MWCD: 1876)—is a "quick bread" that is baked in a "cupped" pan, like a cup-cake. *Muffin* derives fr. Low Ger. *muffen* "cakes," and it was once referred to in England as a *tea cake.* Plain muffins differ from *English muffins* (MWCD: 1902, an American invention) by being leavened with baking powder or baking soda rather than yeast. Unlike both English muffins and tea cakes, muffins can be served at any meal of the day. As is the case with other sweet pastries, such as *babycakes* (q.v.) and *sweetcakes* (q.v.), *muffin* is a term not only of endearment but of en-dowment: *Muffins* is slang for women's breasts; and a good-looking, sexually active man is sometimes referred to by the slang term *studmuffin.* A dropping of cow dung is called a *meadow muffin,* when fresh, or a *cow chip,* when dry. DAFD; DAS; FLC; HDAS; NSOED. *Compare* Dumpling; Sweetie Pie.

MUFFINS   *See* Muffin.

MULE EAR   *See* Pasty.

MULLIGAN STEW   *See* In a Stew.

MUNCHIES   *See* Snack Bar.

MUSHROOM (v)   *See* Spring up like Mushrooms.

MUSHROOM CLOUD   *See* Spring up like Mushrooms.

MUSHY   *See* Grits.

MUSICAL FRUIT   *See* Bean-eater.

MUST   *See* Mustard.

MUSTARD   "Heat." Source: MUSTARD. MWCD: 13th cent. The word *mustard* derives fr. O.Fr. *mostarde*, fr. Lat. *mustum* "must" + *ardens* "fiery." In other words, mustard is named, not for the powdered seeds of the mustard plant that are its basis, but for the unfermented grape juice, or *must* (MWCD: O.E.), that is used to convert the powder into a paste. Mustard also contains sugar, vinegar, and turmeric (to give it a yellowish color). Commercial mustard comes in several varieties, from the pungent, dark yellow Dijon mustard of France to the mild, light yellow American *ballpark mustard*—so called because of its use at baseball parks across the land: "That hot dog/pitch really had some *mustard* on it" (HDAS: 1971). Powdered mustard seed has also found uses in medicine, as a diuretic, emetic, and stimulant. The *mustard gas* (MWCD: 1917) that was used against the Allies in WWI was not made from mustard seeds, and it was an atomized liquid, not a gas. It was so called because it smelled like ground mustard seeds and left a mustard-colored residue on the skin. *Mustard-seed shot* (LA: 1812) is the name of an extremely small-gauge shot—smaller in diameter than *grapeshot* (MWCD: 1747)—that orig. was fired from cannons but later from shotguns. BDPF; DAFD; EWPO; FLC; NSOED; WNWCD.

MUSTARD GAS   *See* Mustard.

MUSTARD-SEED SHOT   *See* Mustard.

MUTT   *See* Muttonheaded.

MUTTON CHOPS   *See* Muttonheaded.

MUTTONHEAD   *See* Muttonheaded.

MUTTONHEADED   *to be muttonheaded*. To be dim-, dull-, or slow-witted. LA: 1768. Source: MUTTON (fr. Fr. *mouton* "sheep"). MWCD: 13th cent. A person who is *muttonheaded*—i.e., is a *muttonhead* (HDAS: 1803)—has the brains of a sheep. Sheep are not known for their intelligence: They fall down and can't get up; they bunch together so tightly they can smother each other; they follow the bellwether anywhere he goes; and they don't know enough to come in out of the rain. *Mutton* entered English during the occupation of England by the Fr.-speaking Normans, who brought about a change in the meaning of the word—from "sheep" to "meat of a sheep"—among the English people, who already had a word for "sheep": *scēap*. The same thing happened with *pork* (fr. Fr. *porc*) vs. Eng. *pig* (or *hog*), *beef* (fr. Fr. *boeuf*) vs. Eng. *steer* (or *ox*), and *veal* (fr. Fr. *veau*) vs. Eng. *calf*. In the early-20th cent. the word *muttonhead* was shortened to *mutt* "a stupid person" (LA: 1901), and soon afterwards *mutt* was applied also to "a mongrel dog" (LAS: 1904). A man doesn't have to be *muttonheaded*—or a *mutt*—to wear *mutton chops* (MWCD: 1865): "full side-whiskers or sideburns that extend from the temple almost to the chin." They are so called because they resemble (1) actual mutton chops placed bone-up on either side of the head (with the chin and upper lip clean shaven), and (2) the head of a full-grown sheep, on which the wool grows on the sides but not on the face or chin. BDPF; DAFD; DEOD; LA; MDWPO; PT; SA; WNWCD.

MY COMPLIMENTS TO THE CHEF   That was a delicious meal! Source: CHEF. MWCD: 1826. It is doubtful that such compliments are ever passed along to the chefs who create such delicious meals. In fact, the expression is often used at catered affairs, where nobody knows who the chef is, and at dinner parties, where the preparer of the meal may be the lady or gentleman of the house, who is sitting at the table along with the guests. The original *chef* was the head of the kitchen (*chef de cuisine*) at a large restaurant—the man (*sic*) in charge of the *cooks* who prepared the meals under his supervision. Today, a *chef* is a man or woman who is either in charge of the entire kitchen or in charge of one part of the meal— e.g., a grill chef, a pastry chef, a salad chef, a sauté chef, etc. (A *sous-chef*, or "under" chef, is the chief assistant to a chef.) In a small restaurant, the head cook is sometimes called a *chef*, and at a very small restaurant the *only* cook is sometimes addressed by that title. All "true" chefs are entitled to wear a *toque*, or *toque blanche*, a tall, white, brimless hat; but only the finest French chefs are awarded the *cordon bleu*, or "blue ribbon." (For most Americans, a "blue ribbon" is a first-place award at a country fair, and a *cordon bleu* is a baked chicken breast stuffed with ham and cheese.) EWPO; MDWPO.

MYSTERY MEAT   *See* Variety Meats.

N

NACHOS   *See* Tortilla.

NAPOLEON   *See* Pastry.

NECTAR   *See* Ambrosia.

NECTARINE   *See* Ambrosia.

NEEDLE CANDY   *See* Candy.

NEITHER FISH NOR FOWL   *to be neither fish nor fowl.* To be neither one thing nor another: "unclassifiable." HND: 1546. Source: FISH; FOWL. MWCD: O.E. The original phrase was *neither fish nor fowl nor good red herring,* and it had to do with the classification of 16th cent. European society according to the diet of its church members. The clergy, for example, ate fresh fish, the lay people ate fowl, and the paupers ate smoked herring. The phrase was later shortened to eliminate *red herring* but was extended in meaning to include anything, concrete or abstract, that could not be pigeonholed. The situation is one in which zoologists find themselves when they come across a new species: "Let's see. It's not a fish. It's not a fowl. It's . . ." AID; ATWS; BDPF; CI; DEI; HI; MDWPO; MS; NSOED; SA. *See also* Red Herring.

NEITHER FISH NOR FOWL NOR GOOD RED HERRING   *See* Neither Fish nor Fowl.

NERVOUS PUDDING   *Jell-O (or JELL-O).* HDAS: 1936. Source: PUDDING. MWCD: 13th cent. *Jell-O* (DAFD: 1897) is not a pudding, which has a base of flour or other meal, and it certainly doesn't have nerves. Instead, it is a gelatin, with fruit flavoring and coloring, that bears a strong resemblance to *jelly* (MWCD: 14th cent.), after which it was prob. named. However, jelly is sweeter, less firm, contains no pieces of fruit, and is used primarily as a spread or filling, whereas Jell-O is less sweet, more firm, elastic (the ads say that it "wiggles and wobbles," and it is sometimes referred to as the *jiggly dessert*), may contain pieces of fruit, and is prepared primarily as a dessert or salad, often in a mold. The confusion of the words *jelly* and *Jell-O* can be seen in the evolution of an analogy attributed to President Theodore Roosevelt regarding negotiations for the Panama Canal: *like trying to nail jelly to a wall*. The simile is now usu. expressed as *like trying to nail Jell-O to a tree*. EWPO; WNWCD.

NEST EGG   *a nest egg*. Money saved for retirement or "a rainy day." EWPO: 17th cent. Source: EGG. MWCD: 14th cent. A literal "nest egg" (MWCD: 14th cent.) is a real or artificial egg that's placed in a hen's nest to encourage it to lay more eggs in that same nest. A metaphorical *nest egg* is "seed" money set aside to encourage the saver to deposit more money there in the future. Artificial nest eggs, made of glass or porcelain, have two other uses: (1) they have become valuable collectors' items, and (2) they are also used as "darning eggs." A *darning egg* is a hard, egg-shaped object that is placed in a sock or stocking to facilitate darning. Darning eggs come in two forms: those *without* a handle and those *with* a handle. The ones *without* a handle were orig. glass or porcelain *nest eggs* or were modeled on the nest egg. The ones *with* a handle were orig. small, dried gourds but are now made of plastic and have a straight, rather than curved, handle. The handle is useful for holding the "egg" in place while darning. ATWS; DAS; MS; SA.

NEVER WAVE TO A LOLLIPOP MAN   *See* Lollipop.

NEW AMERICAN CUISINE   *See* Cuisine.

NEWS SCOOP   *See* Ice-cream Cone.

NO BOWL OF CHERRIES   *See* Life Is Just a Bowl of Cherries.

NO GLUTTON FOR PUNISHMENT   *See* Glutton for Punishment.

NO MATTER HOW YOU SLICE IT, IT'S STILL BALONEY   *See* Baloney!

NO MORE CAKES AND ALE   *See* Cakes and Ale.

NONDAIRY CREAMER   *See* Cream in My Coffee.

NOODLE (n)   *See* Wet Noodle.

NOODLE (v)   *See* Wet Noodle.

NO PICNIC   Difficult; unpleasant. HND: 1888. Source: PICNIC. MWCD: 1748. A picnic is ordinarily an enjoyable experience. It is held out of doors (in a neighbor's backyard or at a park or picnic grounds), it is informal (casual clothes, fun and games), and it features shared foods (barbecue, corn on the cob, watermelon, etc.). Consequently, something that is *no picnic*—or, worse yet, *no picnic in the park*—is not very easy at all ("Raising twins is *no picnic*") or no fun at all ("War is *no picnic*"). Picnicking has been around since ancient times, but the noun *picnic* (fr. Fr. *pique-nique*) didn't appear in Eng. until the mid-18th cent., and the verb *picnic* didn't arrive until the mid-19th cent. (MWCD: 1842). Since then the enjoyment of a picnic has been increased by the invention of the picnic table, the gas barbecue, the ice chest, and the thermos bottle. A picnic at which the food is served from the tailgate of a pickup truck or station wagon is called a *tailgate picnic* (MWCD: 1965). It usu. occurs in a parking lot before the start of a football game, and it may feature sandwiches made from a *picnic ham* (DAFD: ca. 1910), the smoked front boneless shoulder of a hog that looks very much like a "real" ham (from the back leg) but is less expensive and is perfect for a picnic. DAS; DEI; EWPO; FLC; MDWPO; MS.

NO PICNIC IN THE PARK   *See* No Picnic.

NO PIECE OF CAKE   *See* Cakewalk.

NOSE CANDY   *See* Candy.

NOSH (n)   *See* Snack Bar.

NOSH (v)   *See* Snack Bar.

NOSHER   *See* Snack Bar.

NO SUCH THING AS A FREE LUNCH   *See* There's no such Thing as a Free Lunch.

NOT AMOUNT TO A HILL OF BEANS   *See* Not Worth a Hill of Beans.

NOT CARE A FIG   *See* Not Worth a Fig.

NOT FOR ALL THE TEA IN CHINA   Not for any amount of money. HND: 1890s. Source: TEA. MWCD: ca. 1655. Tea is associated with China because that's where it was first discovered by European explorers—on the southeast coast, across from Taiwan. The Dutch explorers called it *te*, after the name in one Chinese dialect, and the Portuguese explorers called it *cha*, after the name in another.

Today *cha* is grown throughout coastal Asia: East Asia, Southeast Asia, and South
Asia (India, where it was introduced by the British); but it is called *tea* (*té, thé*)
throughout Europe, where it is not grown at all. Tea is associated with money
(*What does that have to do with the price of tea in China?* "What does that have to
do with anything?") because it is prob. the oldest beverage in constant use in the
world for the past four thousand years—although it has competed with coffee
since at least the 16th cent. When tea arrived in England in the mid-17th cent.,
it was called—and spelled—*tay*, after the Continental forms; but it was given its
present spelling by the end of that century. The English had to have their tea, at
any cost; but the American colonists protested the heavy tax on tea at the Boston
Tea Party in 1773 and were forced to switch to coffee—temporarily, at least. If
you wouldn't do something *for all the tea in China*, that means that that thing is
not your cup of tea (HND: 1920s), i.e., is not something you enjoy or are accomplished at: "Ice skating is *not my cup of tea*." In its positive form ("That's my *cup
of tea*"), the expression has been in use in Britain since the late 19th cent. AID;
BDPF; CE; CI; DAFD; DAI; DAS; DC; DEI; EWPO; FLC; MDWPO; MS; THT.

NOT GIVE A FIG   *See* Not Worth a Fig.

NOT HAVE A BEAN   *See* Not Worth a Hill of Beans.

NOT KNOW BEANS (ABOUT)   *See* Not Worth a Hill of Beans.

NOT KNOW WHERE YOUR NEXT MEAL IS COMING FROM   *See* Live
from Hand to Mouth.

NOT KOSHER   Not acceptable. Source: KOSHER. MWCD: 1851. *Kosher* is a
Yid. word derived fr. Heb. *kāshēr* "fit and proper," i.e., according to Jewish dietary
laws as specified in Leviticus 11 and Deuteronomy 14 and later interpretation.
These laws apply not only to which animals may or may not be eaten but to how
these permitted animals must be slaughtered, which foods may or may not be
eaten with other foods, etc. Food that is *kosher* is referred to as *kosher food* (e.g.,
kosher pickles, kosher meat, etc.), and a restaurant that adheres to *kosher laws* has
a *kosher kitchen* and is called a *kosher restaurant*. The term *not kosher* lit. refers to
food, meals, kitchens, or restaurants that are not permitted by Jewish dietary laws;
but fig. it is an American equivalent to the Brit. *not cricket*: i.e., not fitting or
proper according to certain secular "laws," written or unwritten. BDPF; DAFD;
FLC; HDAS; MDWPO; MS; WNWCD.

NOT MINCE WORDS   *See* Mince Words.

NOT MY CUP OF TEA   *See* Not for All the Tea in China.

NOT WORTH A BEAN   *See* Not Worth a Hill of Beans.

NOT WORTH A FIG   Worth nothing at all. Source: FIG. MWCD: 13th cent. A fig is the fruit of the fig tree, which originated in the Middle East but had spread throughout the Mediterranean area by the classical period, when figs were so plentiful that a single fig was worth practically nothing. English reflects the worthlessness of the fig in expressions such as *to not give a fig*, where the fig is the medium of exchange rather than the object for sale, and *to not care a fig*, where the fig is the degree of importance of something rather than its monetary value. The fig has also been a symbol of contempt, as expressed in the 16th cent. *Spanish fig* (or *sign of the fig*), a thrust of the thumb between the forefinger and the second finger—an obscene sexual gesture that has been replaced in northern Europe and America by "the finger" alone. The *Spanish fig* is so long forgotten by immigrants to America that such parents now play a game with their children in which the parent reaches out to the child with an outstretched hand, palm down, places the forefinger and second finger around the child's nose, withdraws the hand while sticking the thumb between the two fingers, and says to the child, "I've got your nose!" BDPF; CE; CI; DEI; EWPO; HI; MDWPO; MS; NSOED. *See also* Sycophant. *Compare* Sign of the Fig.

NOT WORTH A HILL OF BEANS   *not worth—or not amount to—a hill of beans*. Practically worthless. HDAS: 1863. Source: BEAN. MWCD: O.E. A hill of beans isn't worth very much, esp. if the beans have just been planted—in small mounds containing half a dozen beans each—and have not yet grown into plants and produced beans of their own. This is an Americanism, contrasting with the Brit. expression *not worth a row of beans*, both of which are expansions of the earlier *not worth beans* and *not worth a bean* (HB: 1297). The small value of the bean is reflected in the fact that *bean* is also a metaphor for a small amount of money, such as a small coin, as seen in the statement "He *didn't have a bean* when she married him." Metaphorical *beans* are not only worthless but can be trivial and unimportant as well, as in the observation that someone's advice, creation, decision, opinion, or proposal is *not worth beans*. This same person can be said to be *full of beans*, i.e., "full of nonsense" (LA: 1910), just as horses can be said to be *full of beans* "full of spirit" (HDAS: 1854) when too many leguminous plants have found their way into their hay; and children can be said to be *full of beans* when they simply act foolish and silly (HDAS: 1942). A person who *doesn't know beans* (LA: 1830s) knows practically nothing, and one who *doesn't know beans about* a subject knows practically nothing about it. Why the connection between beans and ignorance? The answer may be that British children were once taught to count by using beans. When they could count up to five, they were said to *know how many beans make five*; i.e., they had progressed from ignorance to intelligence. AID; BDPF; CE; CI; DAI; DAS; DC; DEI; EWPO; HI; HND; LA; LCRH; MS; PT.

NOT WORTH BEANS   *See* Not Worth a Hill of Beans.

NOT WORTH YOUR SALT   *See* Salt of the Earth.

NOUVELLE CUISINE   *See* Cuisine.

NOW YOU'RE (REALLY) COOKING   *See* What's Cooking?

NUKE IT!   *See* Dutch Oven.

NUMBER-ONE SEED   *See* Go to Seed.

NUT   *a nut.* A difficult problem (NSOED: mid-16th cent.); the heart of a matter; the partner to a bolt (NSOED: early-17th cent.); the top ridge of a violin (NSOED: early-17th cent.); an insane person (HDAS: 1908); a devotee or aficionado (HDAS: 1915); a person's head (HDAS: 1841); a male's testicle (NSOED: early-20th cent.); the capital invested in a Broadway show (HDAS: 1909). Source: NUT. MWCD: O.E. The nut that has spawned this myriad of metaphors is the hard-shelled fruit (such as a hickory nut) or seed (such as a Brazil nut) of a tree (such as a palm) or bush (such as a chestnut), which is sometimes contained in a soft outer rind (such as the black walnut) and always contains an edible kernel (though some, such as the cashew, must be roasted first). The "difficult problem" is a *tough nut to crack* (q.v.); the "heart of a matter," or *nut of a matter*, is the *kernel* inside the shell inside the rind; the "partner to a bolt" is the smaller of the two objects; the "top ridge of a violin" is the one at the head of the fingerboard; an "insane person" is one who is crazy in the head; a "devotee or aficionado" is one who is *nuts about something* (q.v.); a "person's head" is like a coconut; a "male's testicles" are like walnuts; and "the capital invested in a Broadway show is the "seed money" that will potentially grow and produce a profit for the backers if the show is successful. The *show* is said to be *on the nut* (HDAS: 1909) until it reaches the break-even point (*off the nut*—HDAS: 1939), but a *person* is said to be *off their nut* (HDAS: ca. 1889) if he/she is demented or insane. An insane person, i.e., one who is *nutty*, is sometimes called a *nutcase* (MWCD: 1959), i.e., one who belongs in a *nuthouse* (MWCD: 1900), a *nut factory*, or a *nut farm* (HDAS: 1940). An *academia nut*—rhymes with *macadamia nut*—is a perennial student or an absentminded professor. AID; BDPF; DAS; DEI; DEOD; FLC; LCRH; MDWPO. *See also* Nutty as a Fruitcake.

NUTCASE   *See* Nut.

NUT FACTORY   *See* Nut.

NUTHOUSE   *See* Nut.

NUTMEAT   *See* Meat.

NUT OF THE MATTER   *See* Nut.

NUTS (adj.)   *See* Nuts about.

NUTS (n)   *See* Nuts about.

NUTS!   *See* Nuts about.

NUTS ABOUT   *to be nuts about something or someone*. To be delighted, elated, or excited about something; to be crazy, mad, or wild about someone. MWCD: 1785. Source: NUT. MWCD: O.E. The adj. *nuts* developed its various metaphorical senses before the noun *nut*, from which it is derived, developed a single one. In fact, *nuts about* appeared even before the single adj. *nuts* (HDAS: 1846), meaning "crazy, insane, or mad." The association of *nuts* with insanity prob. grew out of an unrecorded resemblance between the head and a *nut* (q.v.), from which the notion of "crazy in the head" developed. *To go nuts* means "to go crazy," and to *drive someone nuts* is to "drive someone crazy." *Nuts to you!* (HDAS: 1928) means either "No!" or "You're crazy!" *Nuts!* is reported to have been the reply of an American general in the Battle of the Bulge (WWII) who, although his division was surrounded by German soldiers, refused to surrender the city of Bastogne. (His response to the enemy may have been something a little bit saltier.) AID; BDPF; CE; DAI; DAS; DEI; DEOD; EWPO; IHAT; MDWPO; MS.

NUTS TO YOU!   *See* Nuts about.

NUTTIER THAN A FRUITCAKE   *See* Fruitcake.

NUTTY   *See* Nut.

NUTTY AS A FRUITCAKE   *See* Fruitcake.

O

OAK APPLE   *See* Apple.

OAT-EATER   *See* Feel Your Oats.

OATER   *See* Feel Your Oats.

OCARINA   *See* Sweet Potato.

OD GRAVY   *See* Olive Drab.

ODs   *See* Olive Drab.

OFFICER'S MESS   *See* Fine Mess.

OFF YOUR FEED   *See* Put on the Feed Bag.

OFF YOUR NUT   *See* Nut.

OH, FUDGE!   *See* Fudge!

OIL   *See* Extra Virgin.

O.J.   Orange juice. HDAS: 1942. Source: ORANGE; JUICE. MWCD: 14th cent. *O.J.* (or *OJ*) as an abbreviation for "orange juice" goes back to lunch-counter jargon of the 1930s, when waitresses behind the lunch counter shouted out orders to the cook in the kitchen. Another example of lunch-counter jargon for "orange juice" was *Squeeze one!*—meaning to squeeze one glass of juice (not squeeze one orange). This latter order was ambiguous, however, because during the summer it could just as well apply to lemonade; therefore, *O.J.* was the call that survived. *O.J.* is also the nickname for O. J. (Orenthal James) Simpson; and the recognition of the similarity to *O.J.* (for "orange juice") can be seen in Simpson's other nickname, *Juice*. IHAT; WNWCD.

OLD CHESTNUT   *an old chestnut*. A hackneyed, overused, stale, or wornout adage, anecdote, joke, or story. LCRH: ca. 1875. Source: CHESTNUT. MWCD: 14th cent. *Old chestnut* is a redundancy—all metaphorical *chestnuts* are old—and the origin of *chestnut* as a "stale joke" is a mystery. The closest that anyone has come to solving the mystery is to suggest that the expression was taken from an obscure English play called *The Broken Sword* (BDPF: 1916), in which a long-winded character named Captain Xavier spins a familiar yarn that happens to involve a "cork" tree. His companion, a character named Pablo, corrects the captain, insisting that it is a "chestnut" and adding that he ought to know because he has heard the captain tell the story twenty-seven times. Nevertheless, in spite of the fact that the play was later produced in Boston, the evidence does not outweigh the fact that the term was regarded as a "recent" example of "American" slang in 1875, more than sixty years later. The origin is still uncertain, but the metaphor was extended to pieces of music in the 20th cent. CE; CI; DEI; EWPO; HF; HND; MDWPO; NSOED; WNWCD.

OLD PRUNE   *See* Full of Prunes.

OLD SALT   *an old salt*. An old sailor. Source: SALT. MWCD: O.E. The exact age of *old salt* is not known, but the term goes back to the days of sailing ships, when much of a sailor's life was spent on the open decks, exposed to the weather and the salt spray. After a time, the sun and the salt turned the sailor's skin red, rough, and wrinkled, identifying him as an *old salt* and leading to the development of several metaphorical meanings for the adj. *salty* (NSOED: mid-19th cent.) that were associated with old *salts*: crude, dirty, earthy language. The term *old salt* is not, but could have been, used to describe both types of consumable salt in use today: salt from the *sea*, like the sailor's; and salt from the earth, which is very *old*. *Sea Salt* results from the labor-intensive job of evaporating salt from sea water. *Mined salt* is extracted from veins of salt in the earth that were deposited there eons ago by drying seas. The current phrase *back to the salt mines* "back to work" (HND: 1890s) is a reminder of the familiarity that we once had with this latter type of salt extraction; and it is also an appropriate metaphor because "work" is where you *earn your salt*, i.e., your *salary* (q.v.), or "salt money." A *salt* mine is one thing, but a *salted* mine is something else: It is a worn-out precious gem or precious metal mine that has been "salted" (NSOED: mid-19th cent.), or deliberately sprinkled, with a few rich samples in order to increase the value of the mine for sale. *Rock salt* (MWCD: 1707) is mined salt that is crushed into small pieces much larger than grains, is not refined, and is not eaten, although it connects with food because it is used to harden the cream in ice cream and serves as a bed for the oyster shells in the serving of "oysters Rockefeller." BDPF; CE; DAI; DAP; DAS; DEI; FLC; PT.

OLEAGINOUS   *See* Extra Virgin.

OLEO   *See* Oleomargarine.

OLEOMARGARINE   "Pearl oil": a substitute for butter. Source: OLEOMARGARINE. MWCD: 1854. When margarine was invented in France in the mid-19th cent., it was called *oleomargarine* (fr. Lat. *oleum* "oil" + Gk. *margaron* "pearl") because it was made from oil extracted from the pearl-like lard of pork fat. When the product was introduced into the United States in the 1870s, the word *oleomargarine* was shortened, by some, to *margarine* (MWCD: 1873); then it was also shortened, by others, to *oleo* (MWCD: 1884), and the two short forms coexisted until after WWII. Sometime during this period the recipe was changed from oils extracted from animal fat to oils extracted from vegetables; and during the Great Depression of the 1930s, when butter was at a premium, a capsule of yellow dye was included with the *oleo/margarine* for kneading it into a brick that looked very much like butter. (That didn't make the dairy farmers very happy.) Nowadays, *margarine* (no longer called *oleo*) and butter are almost interchangeable, and some margarines even contain a little cream just to improve the flavor. FLC; LA; MDWPO; NSOED; PT.

OLIVE (adj.)   *See* Olive Drab.

OLIVE BRANCH   *See* Hold out an Olive Branch.

OLIVE COMPLEXION   *See* Olive Drab.

OLIVE DRAB   The color of U.S. Army nondress uniforms during WWII. Source: OLIVE. MWCD: 13th cent. WWII U.S. Army nondress uniforms consisted of shirts, pants, jackets, and caps of a medium-brown color that were issued in wool for the winter and in cotton for the summer. They were called *olive drabs* or *ODs*, even though the only olives that are medium brown are beyond the stages of unripe (green) and ripe (black). It is possible that there may have been some confusion with U.S. Army "fatigues," the all-season cotton uniforms that were worn in combat and on work duty and were of a medium-green color, because the dictionary definitions of *olive drab* run from "greenish brown" to "grayish olive." The clincher may be in the name that is given to brown gravy in some parts of the rural South: *olive drab gravy*, or *OD gravy*. *Olive drab* as a color has been around since the late-19th cent. (MWCD: 1897), and *olive green* since the mid-18th cent. (MWCD: 1757), but *olive*, as in *olive complexion*, has not been dated. It denotes the normal color of the skin of a Caucasian person from the Mediterranean basin, the Middle East, the Caribbean, or the South Pacific Islands. That color is usu. described as "dark," but it certainly is not "greenish" or "grayish," although it could prob. be labeled "yellowish brown." DAFD; FLC; NSOED; WNWCD.

OLIVE DRAB GRAVY   *See* Olive Drab.

OLIVE DRABS   *See* Olive Drab.

OLIVE GREEN   *See* Olive Drab.

ONE BANANA   *See* Mashed Potato.

ONE FOR GOOD MEASURE   *See* For Good Measure.

ONE FOR THE POT   *See* For Good Measure.

ONE MAN'S MEAT IS ANOTHER MAN'S POISON   *See* Everyone to His Own Taste.

ONE MAN'S MEAT IS ANOTHER MAN'S POISSON   *See* Everyone to His Own Taste.

ONE POTATO   *See* Mashed Potato.

ONE ROTTEN APPLE SPOILS THE BARREL   One corrupt person in a group tends to corrupt the other persons in the group. HND: at least 1736. Source: APPLE. MWCD: O.E. In the early-18th cent., barrels were used to ship and store just about everything, from molasses to rum, and from apples to crackers. Barrels were more maneuverable than boxes (they could be rolled rather than carried), and they could be sealed tighter than boxes. However, apples store longest and best in a cool, dark place, such as a fruit cellar, where they are separated from one another on a shelf and exposed to the air. When they are cooped up in a barrel, exposed to a variety of temperatures, touching each other, without any circulation of air, sooner or later bacteria are bound to grow, affecting one apple first and then spreading to another, until all of the apples in the barrel are rotten. In the case of people, the process is the result not of an act of nature but of the evil influence of one *bad apple* over the formerly upstanding members of the group. A crooked cop is sometimes referred to as a *rotten apple* among the fraternity of police officers, rendering them all tainted by association with him or her. A politician who is *rotten to the core* (DC: at least 1718) is like an apple that is diseased not only on the surface but all the way to the center. Cynics believe that *there is always one rotten apple in the barrel*, and parents often accuse their children of being *spoiled rotten* (q.v.). CE; CODP; DAP; DAS; DEI; FLC; HDAS; MS; NSOED; PT.

ONE SMART APPLE   *See* How Do You Like Them Apples?

ONE SMART COOKIE   *See* Smart Cookie.

ONIONSKIN   *See* Onionskin Paper.

ONIONSKIN PAPER   Strong, thin, light, glossy, translucent paper. MWCD; 1879. Source: ONION. MWCD: 14th cent. Onionskin paper (or *onionskin*), which was once used for carbon copies, has pretty much gone the way of the manual typewriter—i.e., into obsolescence. It was once highly valued because it was so thin that you could make several carbon copies, all of which, however, contained evidence of the many errors that had been corrected. Onionskin paper got its name because it resembled the thin, light outer skin of a dry onion, such as a Bermuda onion or Spanish onion, although that skin is not strong and is usu. of a golden color. The onion itself was named by the Romans (Lat. *unio*) for the remarkable uniting of its hundreds of leaves into a single ball, a growth process found also in the pearl, whose "leaves" are layers of mother-of-pearl, and which was also called *unio*. The term *pearl onion* (MWCD: ca. 1890) for a tiny, mild onion that is usu. creamed as a side dish or pickled for use in a Gibson cocktail is therefore a modern redundancy. The expression *to know your onions* "to be a specialist in a particular subject" (as C.T. Onions, Editor of the first *Shorter Oxford English Dictionary*, was in lexicography) is apt because there are many varieties of onions besides the globular "white" onion. For example, *green onions* (MWCD: 1847), like white onions, have a white flesh—the word *green* meaning that they are picked young, or immature, before they have a chance to "bulb," and are therefore cylindrical: a "stalk" only. Green onions are also known as "spring onions" or *scallions* (MWCD: 14th cent.). The ultimate cylindrical "onion" is the *leek* (MWCD: O.E.), or *Welsh onion* (the national symbol of Wales), which has a large, thick, stout, white stalk. (Onions are white because they are actually tightly packed "leaves" that grow underground.) In between the large cylindrical leek and the large globular onion is the *garlic* (MWCD: O.E. *garleac*, lit. "spear leek," after the shape of the leaves), which has a "bulb," but one that is divided into eight to twelve sections, or *cloves*. The cloves are so pungent that they were once banned from sailing ships because it was believed that they could demagnetize the compass; and even today some people, esp. in the Mediterranean area, wear garlic cloves around their neck to ward off germs (and vampires). Italians were once tagged with the pejorative term *garlic eaters* (HDAS: 1865), and in *lunch-counter jargon* (q.v.) garlic was known as *Italian perfume* (DAFD: ca. 1930). *Spanish garlic* was once a nickname for the *shallot* (MWCD: 1664), a "green" onion that produces multiple small cloves. *Chives* (MWCD: 14th cent.) are the green ("exposed") leaves of onion plants, cut up and used as seasonings. BDPF; CE; DAFD;

DAI; DEI; EWPO; FLC; MDWPO; MS; NSOED; PT; SA; WNWCD. *Compare* Rice Paper.

ON THE CUTTING EDGE   *See* Cutting Edge.

ON THE HALF SHELL   Open-faced. Source: OYSTER. An oyster is a "bivalve," meaning that it has two hinged valves, or "shells," that open and close so that the body of the oyster can feed on the passing nutrients in the water. Oysters are usu. served *on the half shell* (MWCD: 1860), i.e., on the interior side of the bottom valve—either raw (served on crushed ice) or cooked (served on rock salt, as with Oysters Rockefeller). From this practice comes the slang expression *on the half shell* for *open-faced sandwiches*, i.e., "sandwiches" consisting of the filling on a single slice of bread—like *chipped beef* (q.v.) or *Welsh rabbit* (q.v.) on a single piece of toast. The expression is sometimes also used for appetizers on a single cracker rather than in a "cracker sandwich." FLC; SA.

ON THE NUT   *See* Nut.

ON THE ROCKS   *See* Put on Ice.

ON THE SAUCE   *See* Sauce.

OPEN-FACED SANDWICH   *See* On the Half Shell; Sandwich (n).

ORANGE   *an orange.* The reddish yellow fruit of the orange tree. Source: ORANGE. MWCD: 14th cent. The color *orange* is named for the fruit, rather than vice versa. The orange is native to southern India, where Tamil *naru* "fragrant" became the basis for a Skt. word, *naranga*, meaning "orange tree." The word (and the fruit) passed through Persian (*narang*), Ar. (*naranj*), Prov. (*auranja*), and Fr. (*orange*) before it entered English. (Note that the initial *n-* was lost between Arabic and Provençal, prob. because it was absorbed into the final *-n* of the article, as in Mod. Fr. *une orange* "an orange.") The original form of the word is best preserved in Sp. *naranja*, poss. because the fruit was brought there by the Moors in the 8th cent. Also, the greatest cultivation of the fruit began in Spain, resulting in the *Seville orange*, a bitter, seedy orange used for sauces, relishes, marmalades, and flavorings, and the *Valencia orange* (MWCD: 1858), a sweet orange, with few seeds, that is used for eating and juicing. A third category of oranges, besides bitter and sweet, is "loose-skinned," which consists pretty much of the *mandarin orange* (q.v.), or *tangerine* (q.v.). Columbus brought the first orange seeds to America on his second trip, and the cultivation spread from the Caribbean Islands to Florida, which now shares production records with California. DAFD; EWPO; FLC; NSOED; PT.

ORANGEADE   *See* If Life Hands You a Lemon, Make Lemonade.

ORANGE PEEL   *See* Peel off.

OREO   *an Oreo.* An African American who adopts the culture, lifestyle, and values of middle-class White America: an "Uncle Tom." (Black slang.) MWCD: 1969. Source: COOKIE. *Oreo* is the name of a Nabisco "sandwich" consisting of a white cream filling sandwiched between two small, round, black cookies: "black on the outside, white on the inside." The *Oreo* "cookie" was first marketed in 1912 as a *biscuit* (in the Brit. sense of "cracker"), but the name was changed to *sandwich* in 1921. (It has never been marketed as a *cookie*.) A similar product, Hydrox, appeared even earlier (1910) but has not been used in a similar metaphor. A larger example of the black-white contrast is the *ice-cream sandwich* (DAFD: late-1890s): a rectangular slab of vanilla ice cream between two soft chocolate cookies of the same size. DAS; HDAS; IHAT; MDWPO.

OSAGE APPLE   *See* Osage Orange.

OSAGE ORANGE   *an Osage orange.* The noncitrus fruit of the Osage orange tree. MWCD: 1817. Source ORANGE. MWCD: 14th cent. The Osage orange tree is so called because its fruit is large and round, the bare roots are bright orange, and the gnarly wood was once used by Osage Indians to make bows. (The French call the tree *bois d'arc* "bow wood," which the English pronounced *bodark* or *bodock*.) The bare wood, however, is yellow, and the fruit is first green and then greenish yellow. When Lewis and Clark encountered the tree on their expedition in 1804, they named it for the fruit, which they thought resembled an apple: the *Osage apple*. Beginning in the 1840s, farmers and ranchers used Osage orange trees to make hedgerows, and they referred to the fruit as *hedge apples*. The Osage orange tree is a member of the mulberry family, and the Osage orange fruit is no doubt the largest fruit of that family. It is the size of a large grapefruit—but lumpy and inedible (except to cattle, which seem to like it). People prob. called it an *apple* or an *orange* because it was big and round and the large grapefruit was not yet well known outside of Florida. Osage orange hedgerows have pretty much been cleared away now, but farmers recall how much the wood was like hickory: dense, hard, smooth, resistant to rot and insects, perfect for making tool handles and ladder rungs; and archers, who made their own bows out of billets of Osage orange, remember how strong and resilient the wood was, how nice it smelled, and how beautiful the bow looked when it was polished. EWPO; NSOED.

OUT OF THE FRYING PAN INTO THE FIRE   *to go out of—or from—the frying pan into the fire.* To go from bad to worse. DC: 1528. (Sir Thomas More.) Source: FRYING PAN. MWCD: 14th cent. It's bad enough for a poor fish—Sir Thomas specified a flounder—to be placed in a low-sided pan, perhaps with a little oil, and sautéed until golden brown over a roaring fire. It's even worse for the fish to "jump" or "leap" out of the pan, perhaps while it is being shaken, into the fire itself, where it will become blackened and "consumed." People *go from* *the frying pan to the fire* when they manage to escape one difficult situation only to find themselves in an even worse one—the old "good news, bad news" scenario. The expression, in one form or another, goes back to the ancient Greeks, who wrote of going "out of the smoke into the flame." AID; BDPF; CE; CI; DAI; DAP; DEI; HI; HND; MDWPO; MS; NSOED.

OUT OF YOUR GOURD   *See* Gourd.

OUT TO LUNCH   *See* Business Lunch.

OVAL (adj., n)   *See* Love.

OVO-VEGETARIAN   *See* Vegetarian.

OX ROAST   *See* Barbecue (v).

OYSTER COCKTAIL   *See* Shrimp Cocktail.

P

PABLUM   *See* Cereal.

PACKED IN LIKE SARDINES   *See* Packed like Sardines.

PACKED LIKE SARDINES   *to be packed (in) like sardines*. To be crowded in a small enclosure. DC: 1894. Source: SARDINE. MWCD: 14th cent. The *sardine* is a small or immature fish that is caught commercially in the waters off the coast of Europe (the pilchard) and North America (the herring) for the purpose of preserving them as food. As might be expected, the sardine was named for the Italian island of Sardinia, where the fish swim in schools in the Mediterranean Sea. Once netted, the sardines are either preserved "dry"—i.e., smoked or salted—or canned in oil, mustard sauce, or tomato sauce. The metaphor refers to the fact that the tiny fish are packed in a flat tin in such a way—head to tail— that as many as possible can be accommodated. Humans experience this same pressure when they are crowded together in enclosures such as small rooms, elevators, automobiles, buses, subway cars, trolleys, and trains; and the enclosure itself is sometimes referred to as a *sardine can*. AID; CE; CI; DAFD; DEI; FLC; HND; NSOED; SA.

PACKING PEANUTS   *See* Work for Peanuts.

PACKING POPCORN   *See* Popcorn Shrimp.

PALATABLE   Agreeable to the sense of "taste." MWCD: 1669. Source: PALATE. MWCD: 14th cent. The *palate*, or "roof of the mouth," was erroneously believed to be the organ of taste in the 17th cent. Consequently, a number of terms relating to taste involve the word *palate*: e.g., *please the palate, pleasing to the palate*, and *palate-pleasing*. We now know that the tongue—or, more specifically, the thousands of *taste buds* (MWCD: 1879) on its upper surface—is the true organ of taste; but the word *tongue* has provided us with no taste metaphors, whereas the word *palate* has furnished us with several. *Palate*, for example, can refer to intellectual taste (a *sophisticated palate*); and *palatable* can mean "agreeable to the mind" (a *palatable work*). It is unclear where the word *toothsome* (MWCD: 1551), which has approx. the same meaning as *palatable*, fits into this picture. Is it possible that before both the tongue and the palate were believed to be taste sensors, the teeth enjoyed this honor? CE; NSOED; WNWCD.

PALATE-PLEASING   *See* Palatable.

PAN (n)   *See* Pan out.

PAN (v)   *See* Pan out.

PANCAKE (n)   *a pancake.* A form of bread—not "cake"—that was orig. fried in a pan. MWCD: 14th cent. Source: PAN (MWCD: O.E.); CAKE (MWCD: 13th cent.). The pancake was the first food to be called a *cake* (in the 13th cent.), although it was unleavened, unsweetened, fried rather than baked, and turned over when the bottom side was brown. After a cent. or so (in the 14th cent.), *cake* was redefined as a leavened, sweetened, baked, and unturned food, and the original "cake" was renamed a *pancake*. The same pattern of development has held throughout the world, with pancakelike breads preceding both loaf breads and sweet breads: e.g., the Mexican *tortilla*, the Jewish *latke*, the Slavic *blintz*, and the French *crêpe*. In America, the *pancake* has gone by many different names: *Indian cake* (1607), *hotcake* (1683), *johnnycake* (1739), *hoe cake* (1745), *buckwheat cake* (1740s), *wheat cake* (1772), *griddle cake* (1783), *slapjack* (1796), *flapjack* (1830s), *battercake* (1830s), and *flannel cake* (1870s). BDPF; DAFD; FLC; HDAS; IHAT; NSOED. *See also* Cake.

PANCAKE (v)   *to pancake.* For a series of horizontal structures to fall down on top of each other during an earthquake or explosion. Source: PANCAKE. MWCD: 14th cent. Pancakes are usu. served in a stack of three or four. (A "short stack" has only two.) The stack of pancakes on a plate looks very much like the floors of a building that have fallen, one on top of the other, during an earthquake. The same resemblance can be seen in the collapsed levels of a multilevel highway ("full stack") or bridge ("short stack") as a result of a California tremor. The verb *pancake* is also used, intransitively, to describe the vertical drop of a stalled plane in a horizontal position (MWCD: 1928). This sort of occurrence, called a *pancake landing* (MWCD: 1928), doesn't happen much anymore, but it must have been common back in the early days of aviation. It was prob. caused by a light plane stalling on takeoff about twenty feet in the air, losing its forward motion, and then falling *flat as a pancake* (q.v.) on the runway. The scene must have resembled the fall of a real pancake that had been flipped and was on its way down toward the griddle. Transitively, the verb *pancake* is used in college football to describe what an offensive lineman hopes to do to his opponent: *pancake him*, knock him *as flat as a pancake* (q.v.). NSOED; WNWCD.

PANCAKE AWARD   *See* Flat as a Pancake.

PANCAKE BLOCK   *See* Flat as a Pancake.

PANCAKE DAY   *See* Pancake Tuesday.

PANCAKE ICE   *See* Flat as a Pancake.

PANCAKE LANDING   *See* Pancake (v).

PANCAKE MAKEUP   Theatrical makeup in cake form. Source: PANCAKE. MWCD: 14th cent. Pancake makeup was invented in 1935 by Hollywood makeup artist Max Factor, Sr., who created a "cake" of compressed powder that could be applied to an actor's face in order to keep the skin from looking green in the new Technicolor movies. He then marketed the makeup under the name Pan-Cake Make-Up for cosmetic use by theater actors and ordinary citizens, esp. women. The makeup was named after the caked powder in the "pan," rather than the flat, round sponge used to apply it. NSOED; WNWCD.

PANCAKE SYRUP   *See* Cough Syrup.

PANCAKE TUESDAY (Or *Pancake Day*.)   The day before Ash Wednesday in the Christian calendar. Source: PANCAKE. MWCD: 14th cent. *Pancake Tuesday* was once an alternative name for "Shrove Tuesday" (MWCD: 15th cent.), the equivalent of Fr. *Mardi Gras* "Fat Tuesday" (MWCD: 1699). It was the last day before the beginning of Lent, the last chance to "load up" before forty days—and nights—of fasting. Pancakes may have been selected for this purpose because though they were fried in fat, they contained no meat and were a transition from excess to denial. Each ingredient of the batter—eggs, flour, milk, and salt—was regarded as a symbol of Christianity. BDPF; DAFD; MDWPO.

PAN FISH   *See* Have Other Fish to Fry.

PAN-FRY   *See* Fried.

PANHANDLE (n)   *a panhandle*. A narrow extension of land from a larger territory. MWCD: 1856. Source: PAN. MWCD: O.E. An important feature of many stovetop cooking pans, such as the *frying pan* (q.v.), is the handle, which is used to move the pan and its contents to the burner, to shake up the contents, to remove the pan from the stove, and to slide or pour the contents onto a plate. The handle of an old-fashioned *skillet* (q.v.), which was used in an open hearth in Colonial days, was very long, sometimes even longer than the pan was wide, but the handles of modern frying pans are usu. not even as long as the diameter of the pan. The term *panhandle* was applied in 1856 to part of Texas, which looks a little like an uneven pan, seen from above, with the "handle" on top, and to part of Florida, which looks more like a butterfly net with a very long handle on the left. (Both of these states were admitted to the Union in 1845.) The term was later used for Nebraska (admitted in 1867) and Oklahoma (admitted in 1907), which have a broader pan and a shorter handle. (The states of Louisiana, Mississippi, and Alabama all have "panhandles," but they are not referred to as such.) Derived from the noun *panhandle* is another noun, *panhandler* "a beggar," so called either because he/she extends a cup or bowl (sometimes called a *begging bowl*) with his/her hand and arm (the "handle") to beg for alms, or, if there is no cup or bowl, because his/her body is the "pan." Derived from the noun *panhandler*, by back-formation, is the verb *to panhandle* (MWCD: 1903), which simply means "to beg," with or without a "pan." EWPO; WNWCD.

PANHANDLE (v)   *See* Panhandle (n).

PANHANDLER   *See* Panhandle (n).

PAN OUT   *to pan out.* To turn out as planned, hoped, or expected. MWCD: ca. 1868. Source: PAN (n). MWCD: O.E. *Pan out* is derived from the verb *to pan* (MWCD: 1839), as for gold, which involves "washing" potential gold-bearing sand or gravel in a large, deep pie pan, allowing the lighter matter to "float" over the edge of the tilted pan, leaving the heavier gold in the bottom. When such an event occurs, the affort is said to *pan out*, or "succeed." In the broader metaphor, the phrase is usu. used in the negative: The merger didn't *pan out*; the marriage didn't *pan out*. The verb *pan*, which is derived from the noun *pan*, is also used to mean "to criticize severely" (NSOED: early-20th cent.) as when a movie critic *pans* a film, or a music critic *pans* a concert. From this usage the noun *pan* has come to mean "a harsh criticism," as in *picks* (approval) and *pans* (disapproval). The original meaning of the noun *pan* was "a shallow metal container used for baking" (e.g., a cake pan) "or frying" (e.g., a frying pan). Other meanings that the noun *pan* has acquired are the primer receptacle on a flintlock musket; a natural or artificial depression in the ground; a flat slab of floating ice; a hard stratum of compacted earth (*hardpan*—MWCD: 1817); and a person's face. *Pan* meaning "face" occurs in the adj. *deadpan* (HDAS; 1928) and the phrase "a *deadpan expression*," which denotes a total lack of facial expression, as in a *deadpan comedy*, which is played with a "straight face." DAS; WNWCD.

PAP   Oversimplified writing; simplistic ideas. NSOED: mid-16th cent. Source: PAP. MWCD: 15th cent. Literally, *pap* is "baby food": soft, strained food for infants and invalids. The word is poss. derived from infant babbling of the syllable *pap*, which mothers interpret to mean "mealtime" (as in M.E. *pappe* "nipple") and fathers interpret to mean "father" (as in Brit. *papa* "father" or "grandfather"). To other adults, such pasty pulp is bland, tasteless, insipid, worthless, and lacking in substance, exactly like the language in which adults "talk down to," or patronize, children. The word *pap* is very similar to the word *pablum* "infant cereal," although the two words come from different sources. Somehow, *pap* has also acquired the meaning "political patronage," i.e., favors given to or by someone in political office, even though such favors could be far from "worthless." PT; WNWCD. *See also* Cereal.

PAPAW   *See* Papaya.

PAPAYA   *a papaya.* A "tree melon"; a "custard apple." Source: PAPAYA. MWCD: 1598. *Papaya*, fr. Arawak Indian *papaia*, is the name of a tropical, palmlike tree, first discovered in the Caribbean, that produces large, melonlike fruit that are a staple of the region. The papaya fruit are yellow in color (both the skin and the flesh), oblong in shape, juicy and sweet, and weigh up to two pounds or more. The six-inch-long fruit can be eaten raw, pressed for juice, or used as an exotic flavoring for other fruit juices. Unfortunately, the word *papaya* has also been used to describe an unrelated tree that grows not only in the tropics but in the subtropical and temperate parts of eastern North America as well, from the Gulf to the Great Lakes, and produces a fruit that is very much like the true papaya in color, shape, and texture. The Native American name for this mainland fruit was *papaw* (MWCD: 1624)—*pawpaw* or *paw paw* in the Eng. rendition—and its name survives in at least two towns in the Great Lakes area: Paw Paw, Mich., and Paw Paw, Ill. Unlike the papaya, which is sometimes referred to as a *tree melon*, the *pawpaw* has been identified more closely with the apple—the *custard apple* (MWCD: 1657) and the *sugar apple* (MWCD: 1738)—and with the banana: the *Indiana banana* and the *Michigan banana* The profusion of metaphors results from the fact that *pawpaws* come in two basic shapes: apple-shape and banana-shape. *Pawpaws* have not become a staple of the Midwestern diet; in fact, they are not available in stores or markets. DAFD; EWPO; FLC; IHAT; NSOED; WNWCD.

PARASITE   *a parasite.* A plant or animal that depends on an organism of another species for its sustenance or protection but provides no benefit to its host in return. NSOED: early-18th cent. Source: EAT. The original *parasite* (NSOED: mid-16th cent.) wasn't a plant or animal but a human—one who ate at the table (fr. Gk. *para* "beside" + *sitos* "food") of a wealthy patron but offered nothing more than false praises and flattery in return (MWCD: 1539). Today, both types of parasites exist, but the human parasite is sometimes called a *toady* (because he/she will do anything to please), a *sponge* (because he/she soaks up the substance from others), or a *freeloader* (HDAS: 1936—because he/she loads up his/her plate with free food). In fact, to *sponge off* and to *freeload* (MWCD: ca. 1934) have become popular alternatives to the technical term *parasitize* when it applies to humans. DAI; DAS; LCRH; SA. *Compare* Toadeater.

PARCHING CORN   *See* Popcorn Shrimp.

PARE (v)   *See* Pare down.

PARE DOWN   *to pare down the budget; to pare down the speech.* To reduce the size of the budget or the length of a speech (etc.). Source: PARE. MWCD: 14th cent. In cooking, *to pare* is almost synonymous with *to peel*, although the former always requires a knife (a *paring* knife), whereas the latter can sometimes be done with the hands (e.g., to *peel* an orange). *Pare* is the basis for the verb *prepare* (as in "*to prepare*—or *prep*—food for cooking or serving"). Outside of the kitchen, to *pare* expenses is to cut back on spending; and to *pare* your nails is to cut them back or trim them. FLC; NSOED; WNWCD. *See* Peel off.

PAREVE   *See* Cream in My Coffee.

PARFAIT   *a parfait.* An ice-cream sundae in a glass. MWCD: after-1894. Source: SUNDAE. An American *parfait* consists of alternating layers of syrup (or fruit) and ice cream (or yogurt) topped with fruit, nuts, and whipped cream. The sundae is served in a tall, footed glass (often a disposable one made of clear plastic) called a "*parfait* glass." However, the original *parfait* (MWCD: 1894) was a French dessert consisting of a frozen custard containing eggs, cream, and flavored syrup. The French thought it was "perfect" (i.e., *parfait*), but the Americans thought that they could do it one better. DAFD; FLC; NSOED.

PASTA   *See* Antipasto.

PASTE   *See* Antipasto.

PASTRAMI   *See* Corned Beef.

PASTRY   Sweet baked goods. NSOED: mid-16th cent. Source: PASTRY. MWCD: ca. 1538. *Pastry* orig. referred to the high-fat dough used to make pie crust. Later, it came to refer not to the dough itself but to the products that are made from that dough, such as pies, cakes, and sweet rolls. One of these sweet rolls is a *Danish* (MWCD: ca. 1928). Danish pastry is rich in butter, light in weight, filled with goodies, and usu. topped with icing. The "goodies" include fruit (e.g., a prune Danish), cheese (e.g., a cream-cheese Danish), and nuts (e.g., an almond Danish). Another imported sweet roll is the *napoleon*, an oblong roll with a sweet filling. The Emperor Napoleon is said to have had the habit of carrying one of these individual-sized pastries in his breast pocket (Is that what he was reaching for in his portrait?), but that is not how it got its name. The *napoleon* is so called because it was a product of Naples, Italy (*Napolitano* in It., *Napolitain* in Fr.), not because it was a favorite of the French Emperor. Napoleons are usu. filled with cream, custard, or jelly and coated with sugar icing or powdered sugar. DAFD; EWPO; FLC; WNWCD.

PASTY   *a pasty*. A meat-and-potato "pocket pie." (Fr. M.Fr. *paste* "dough.") MWCD: 13th cent. Source: PIE. The *pasty*, also known as a *Cornish pasty* and a *mule ear*, originated in Cornwall, Britain, where Cornish tin miners carried into the mines a lunch consisting of a meat-and-vegetable stew wrapped in a sheet of bread dough and partially baked. The *pasty* was transported to the Upper Peninsula of Michigan in the late-19th cent. by Cornish immigrants who worked in the copper mines there. The recipe remained essentially the same, except that the vegetable was usu. potato rather than turnips. Today, with the copper mines in the Upper Peninsula long closed, the *pasty* is sold at roadside stands to hungry tourists, who mistakenly pronounce the name *paste-y*, like the nipple covers worn by burlesque strippers, rather than the correct *past-y*. As for the name *mule ear*, the pasty somewhat resembles the ear of a mule in size (large), texture (soft), and shape (long). DAFD; FLC; NSOED; SA. *See also* Turnover. *Compare* Elephant Ear.

PAT-A-CAKE   *See* Patty-cake.

PÂTÉ DE FOIE GRAS   *See* Antipasto; Chopped Liver.

PATTY   *See* Antipasto.

PATTY-CAKE   A clapping game usu. played by a mother and child. MWCD: 1889. Source: CAKE. MWCD: 13th cent. *Patty-cake*—or *pat-a-cake*—is played by two participants, who sit, or kneel, facing each other, and alternate touching their extended palms and clapping their own hands in time with the nursery rhyme of the same name, the first stanza of which goes as follows: "*Patty-cake, patty-cake, baker's man; / Bake me a cake as fast as you can*" [italics added]. There is no winner to the game, but you can embarrass yourself by clapping when you should be touching (or vice versa) or by forgetting the words. It is one of the first games taught to a young child of, say, two years of age. The game mimics the action that a baker performs while kneading and slapping bread—not cake!—dough. DAI.

PAWPAW   *See* Papaya.

PEA BEAN   *a pea bean*. A bean the size of a pea. MWCD: 1887. Source: PEA (MWCD: 1611); BEAN (MWCD: O.E.). The *pea bean*, the one used to make Boston baked beans, is the smallest of the white beans, slightly smaller than the navy bean. The pea that this bean is compared to is prob. the English pea (the *garden* or *green* pea) rather than the French pea (*le petit pois*), which is even smaller. The word *pea* has been used liberally to describe the size of other small objects, such as *peanut* (q.v.), *peabrain* "having a brain the size of a pea," *pea gravel* "small-stone gravel," *pea-shooter* "a small and ineffective shotgun," and *pea-size hail* (q.v.). In the compound *pea bean*, *pea* is used to modify *bean*. However, in other cases the word *pea* replaces the word *bean*, leading to all sorts of confusion. For example, a *black-eyed pea* (MWCD: 1728), or *cowpea* (MWCD: 1776), is not a pea at all but a relative of the mung bean that was brought to America by African slaves and is still grown in the South. (It is called *black-eyed* because the black outline of an eye appears on the inner curve of the beige bean; if the "eye" happens to be yellow, the bean is called a *yellow-eyed pea*.) A *chickpea* (MWCD: ca. 1722) is not a pea but a *garbonzo bean* (MWCD: 1944); and a *sweet pea* (MWCD: 1646) is not a pea either, although it is a legume, like the rest. Finally, (1) the *pea* in *peacock* (MWCD: 14th cent.) refers not to the legume but to a "peafowl," so *peacock* lit. means "male peafowl"; and (2) the *pea* in *peajacket* (MWCD: 1721) refers not to the vegetable but to "coarse wool cloth," so *peajacket* (or Amer. *peacoat*) lit. means "woolen jacket" (or coat). CE; DAFD; EWPO; FLC; HF; LA; MDWPO; NSOED; PT; THT; WNWCD.

PEABRAIN   *See* Pea Bean.

PEACH   *a peach.* A friendly and generous member of either sex; a beautiful young woman (IHAT: 1865). Source: PEACH. MWCD: 14th cent. Saying to some-one "You're a *peach*!" is like saying that he or she is as nice as a peach is to eat, or as attractive as a peach is to look at. Granted, the fruit has its drawbacks: (1) The skin is covered with *peach fuzz* (which is also a metaphor for a young man's beard before it is long enough or obvious enough to be shaved), so many people prefer to eat peaches peeled, or peeled and cut up; and (2) the flesh of some peaches—called *clingstone peaches* (MWCD: 1705)—clings to the pit (or "stone"), making it easy to eat them peeled but not to cut them up. The solution to the latter problem is to buy *freestone peaches*, such as the Elberta (EWPO: ca. 1870), which are ideal for either eating peeled or eating cut up. Cut-up peaches are excellent with cream or ice cream, and the expression *peaches and cream* can refer either to an excellent combination (to *go together like peaches and cream*) or to an excellent complexion (a *peaches-and-cream complexion*). Peaches are delicious when baked in pies and cobblers, and the expressions *just peachy* ("fine" NSOED: early-20th cent.) and *peachy-keen* ("dandy") reflect the regard that people have for this ancient fruit. The Romans called the peach *malum persicum* "persian apple" because it was about the size of an apple and came from Persia—and before that from India and ultimately China. CE; DAFD; DAP; DAS; DEI; FLC; NSOED; PT.

PEACHES AND CREAM   *See* Peach.

PEACHES-AND-CREAM COMPLEXION   *See* Peach.

PEACH FUZZ   *See* Peach.

PEACH MELBA   *See* Melba Toast.

PEACHY   *See* Peach.

PEACHY-KEEN   *See* Peach.

PEACOAT   *See* Pea Bean.

PEACOCK   *See* Pea Bean.

PEA GRAVEL   *See* Pea Bean.

PEA JACKET   *See* Pea Bean.

PEANUT   *a peanut.* A pealike "nut." MWCD: 1802. Source: PEA (MWCD: 1611); NUT (MWCD: O.E.). A peanut is neither a pea nor a nut, but it resembles both. (That's what makes its name a metaphor.) The peanut is like a pea because both are legumes, both grow on a low plant or vine, and both develop with others in a casing. However, peas grow above ground, not under it; they are soft, not hard; and their pod is edible. The peanut is like a nut because it is hard and snappy; its shell is inedible; and it comes only two or three to the "pod." "True" nuts, however, grow on trees or shrubs, not on vines; and nuts have never been grown underground. Nevertheless, the *peanut* is the quintessential nut: the basic "nut" to which all others are compared; and its history is almost as complicated as its biology. It may have first developed in Brazil, first been cultivated in Peru, first discovered by the Spanish in Mexico, first transported to Africa by the Portuguese, and first introduced to America by African slaves, who called it *nguba*, which was later interpreted in the South as *goober* (MWCD: 1833). A test of your knowledge of things Southern, right after the question "What is a grit?" is this: *Do goobers eat gophers, or do gophers eat goobers?* (Gophers eat goobers.) The earliest Eng. name for the peanut was *groundnut* (MWCD: 1602), which has survived mainly in England. Other early names for the peanut were *earth nut, ground-pea, goober pea,* and *monkey nut* (q.v.) (which is also more likely to be heard in England than in America). DAFD; EWPO; FLC; HF; IHAT; LA; MDWPO; SA; WNWCD.

PEANUT-BRAINED   *See* Work for Peanuts.

PEANUT BUTTER   A spread consisting of ground roasted peanuts and peanut oil. FLC: ca. 1900. Source: PEANUT (MWCD: 1802); BUTTER (MWCD: O.E.). Peanut butter is not "real" butter (processed from milk or cream), but it *spreads* like real butter (esp. "smooth" or "creamy" peanut butter); and though not yellow, it is yellowish brown in color. Peanut butter also mixes well with jelly in a sandwich, just as dairy butter does. WNWCD. *Compare* Apple Butter; Cocoa Butter; Crab Butter; Maple Butter.

PEANUT BUTTER RAREBIT　　*See* Welsh Rabbit.

PEANUT GALLERY　　*See* Work for Peanuts.

PEANUTS　　*See* Work for Peanuts.

PEA PICKERS　　*See* Like Two Peas in a Pod.

PEARL DIVER　　*See* Taste like Dishwater.

PEARL ONION　　*See* Onionskin Paper.

PEAR-SHAPED　　Bell-shaped. NSOED: late-16th cent. Source: PEAR. MWCD: O.E. The most popular American pear, the Bartlett, is shaped like a bell (but rounded off at the bottom). This shape has also been described as resembling the profile of a woman in a wasp-waisted, full-length dress, or a Rubens nude. In the music world, a singer who produces *pear-shaped tones* has a voice that is full-bodied and resonant. The pear, a pome fruit like the apple, has been enjoyed for many centuries, but unlike the apple, it cannot be stored for many months—or even weeks. Its soft, juicy flesh and short life have prob. added to its mystique. The history and popularity of a fruit are reflected in the fact that other fruits, discovered later, have been named after it. One example is the *prickly pear* (MWCD: 1612), also known as a *cactus pear*; another is the *alligator pear* (q.v.), or avocado, which got its name in 1763. Both fruits are the same size (approx. four inches long), the same color (green, at some stage of development), and the same shape (bell-shaped) as pears. DAFD; EWPO; FLC; WNWCD.

PEAR-SHAPED TONE　　*See* Pear-shaped.

PEASE PORRIDGE　　*See* Grueling; Like Two Peas in a Pod.

PEA-SHOOTER　　*See* Pea Bean.

PEA-SIZE HAIL　　*See* Grapefruit-size Hail.

PEA SOUP　　*See* Soup.

PEA-SOUP FOG　　*See* Soup.

PECK OF TROUBLE   *See* In a Peck of Trouble.

PEEL (n)   *See* Peel off.

PEEL (v)   *See* Peel off.

PEEL DOWN   *See* Peel off.

PEEL OFF   *to peel off.* To remove an outer layer of something; for a thin outer layer to fall away. Source: PEEL (v). MWCD: 13th cent. The original Eng. meaning of the verb *peel* was to remove, by hand, the outer layer of a fruit, such as an orange. (The Lat. source of *peel, pilare,* meant "to remove the hair.") Since the 13th cent., the transitive sense of the verb has broadened to include the *peeling* of both fruits and vegetables, either by hand or with a knife (e.g., to *peel* a potato), the removal of paint from a wall (to *peel off* old paint), the removal of skin from a sunburn (to *peel off* dead skin), the removal of labels (to *peel* the label *off* a can), the removal of a bill from a roll (to *peel off* a dollar bill), and the removal of clothes (to *peel off* your wet clothes, or *peel down*). An intransitive sense has also developed: for paint to *peel (off)*, for skin to *peel (off)*, for an airplane to *peel off* from its formation, and for a car to *peel out* of the driveway. Wherever danger lurks, you would be well advised to *keep your eyes peeled* (DC: 1853), based on the earlier expression *to keep your eyes skinned* (DC: 1833), i.e., to keep your eyes wide open, with the lids drawn back. The noun *peel,* meaning "the skin or rind of a fruit," did not develop until the 14th cent. Now we can *peel* an orange and throw away the *peel.* Incidentally, the term *orange peel* (MWCD: ca. 1909) refers, metaphorically, to "a slightly bumpy surface." DAI; DAP; EWPO; FLC; HND; MS; NSOED; WNWCD. *See also* Fruit with Appeal.

PEEL OUT   *See* Peel off.

PEEL RUBBER   *See* Peel off.

PEMMICAN   *See* Chipped Beef.

PEP (n)   Vim, vigor, and vitality. MWCD: 1912. Source: PEPPER. MWCD: O.E. Although *pep* is a shortened form of the noun *pepper,* it was based not on the original meaning of *pepper,* i.e., the black or white seasoning that came to Europe from the East Indies, but on the meaning that was added to the word in the 17th cent., i.e., the red, green, or yellow capsicum pod that was discovered by the Spanish in Mexico in the 16th cent. (Earlier, the word *pepper* had also been applied to the red, green, or yellow "sweet" pepper that was discovered in the West Indies in the late-15th cent.) In Mexico, the Nahuatl word for this pungent pod was *chilli,* which became *chile* in Spanish and *chili* (or *chile*) in English (MWCD: 1604). Because the term *chili pepper* is a redundancy, the term *hot pepper*

(MWCD: 1945) was created to distinguish the pungent pepper from the *sweet pepper* (MWCD: 1814). Anyone who has eaten the Mexican dish called *chili*, which is spiced with hot peppers, knows that it can wake you up—or fire you up—in a hurry; i.e., it can give you *pep*, *pep you up* (MWCD: 1925), or make you feel *peppy* (MWCD: ca. 1918). The *pep talk* (MWCD: 1925) is a speech given by a coach to his/her team before a game—or between periods—in order to inspire them to play their best in the upcoming encounter; and the *pep rally* is a gathering on the night before a homecoming game at which the students demonstrate their support for the team. (If things get out of hand at the pep rally, *pepper spray*, which contains an extract of hot peppers, may have to be used.) The *pep pill* (MWCD: 1937) contains no hot pepper extract but achieves its stimulant effect through drugs such as amphetamines. Someone who is *peppery* (MWCD: 1699) has either a hot temper or a pungent vocabulary; and if you like *pepperoni* (MWCD: 1821) on your pizza, you must like *cayenne peppers* (MWCD: 1756), which are the major seasoning of the sausage. CE; DAFD; EWPO; FLC; NSOED; PT; WNWCD.

PEPPER (n)   The dried, ground berry of a pepper plant; the sweet or hot fruit of a capsicum plant. Source: PEPPER. MWCD: O.E. One of the most unfortunate events in the history of food was the naming of the newly discovered West Indian sweet (or "garden") pepper after the long-enjoyed East Indian black pepper— followed only by the naming of the Chilean hot (or "chili") pepper after the West Indian sweet pepper. Keeping the peppers straight has not been an easy task, as evidenced by the rationale for the name *pepper steak*. There are two quite different recipes for this entrée, one featuring beefsteak covered with coarse-ground black pepper, sautéed in butter, and set on fire, and the other consisting of slices of beef cooked or stir-fried with green peppers and other vegetables in a soy sauce (sometimes called *green pepper steak*). The *pepper pot* is another dish that can go either way. In the West Indies it is a meat or fish stew seasoned with hot chili peppers, whereas in Philadelphia it is a tripe and vegetable soup flavored with ground *peppercorns* (MWCD: O.E.), the dried berries of the East Indian pepper plant. Suffice it to say that if the "pepper" dish makes you sneeze, it's prob. East Indian pepper, and if it makes you reach for the nearest glass of water, it's prob. a Chilean pepper. The term *pepper pot* (MWCD: 1679) orig. meant a *pepperbox* (MWCD: 1546), or what we now call a *pepper shaker* (MWCD: 1895)—i.e., a container for finely ground flakes of dried black peppercorns. In the 18th cent., a revolving-barrel pistol was also referred to as a *pepperbox*, prob. because it scattered shots the way a pepperbox scattered pepper. A *pepper mill* (MWCD: ca. 1858) is a hand-held grinder used for crushing peppercorns, either by yourself at home or by the waiter in a restaurant: "Would you like pepper on your yogurt?" In Britain, *peppercorn rent* (NSOED: early-17th cent.) is rent so small that it amounts to almost nothing, like an individual peppercorn. In American baseball, *pepper* is a pregame warm-up in which a batter faces four or five fielders, only twelve to fifteen feet away, who throw the ball back to the batter after he/she has bunted it to him/her. During the game, the same players may *pepper* the park with hits, just as (1) a boxer *peppers* his/her opponent with blows, (2) a drive-by shooter *peppers* a house with bullets (NSOED: late-19th cent.), (3) a reporter *peppers* a celebrity with questions, and (4) a speech-writer *peppers* an address with jokes. All of these metaphors involve the verb *pepper* (MWCD: 1538), which is derived from the noun *pepper*, and they all relate to the action of sprinkling pepper from the holes in a pepper shaker onto your food. BDPF; DAFD; DEI; EWPO; FLC; PT; WNWCD.

PEPPER (v)   *See* Pepper (n).

PEPPER-AND-SALT   *See* Salt-and-pepper.

PEPPERBOX   *See* Pepper (n).

PEPPERCORN   *See* Pepper (n).

PEPPERCORN RENT   *See* Pepper (n).

PEPPER MILL   *See* Pepper (n); Through the Mill.

PEPPERMINT PATTY   *See* Antipasto.

PEPPERONI   *See* Pep (n); Sausage Dog.

PEPPER POT   *See* Pepper (n).

PEPPER SHAKER   *See* Pepper (n).

PEPPER SPRAY   *See* Pep (n).

PEPPER STEAK   *See* Pepper (n).

PEPPERY   *See* Pep (n).

PEP PILL   *See* Pep (n).

PEPPY   *See* Pep (n).

PEP RALLY   *See* Pep (n).

PEP TALK   *See* Pep (n).

PEP UP   *See* Pep (n).

PERSISTENT VEGETATIVE STATE   *See* Vegetable.

PERSON OF GOOD TASTE   *See* Good Taste.

PETIT FOUR   *a petit four*. A miniature, bite-size cake, covered with frosting, decorated with icing, and served at teas and receptions. MWCD: 1884. Source: OVEN. The *four* in *petit four* means "oven" (fr. Lat. *furnus*). Therefore, a *petit four* is a "little (*petit*) oven," i.e., a little piece of baked goods from the oven. Petits fours are made by cutting square, rectangular, triangular, or diamond-shaped pieces from a sheet of sponge cake or pound cake—although very low "layer" cakes are sometimes used—and then frosting and decorating them. FLC; NSOED; PT; WNWCD.

PETROLEUM JELLY   *See* Jelly.

PFEFFERNUSSE   *See* Mexican Wedding Cake.

PHONEY BALONEY   *See* Baloney!

PICKLE (n)   *(a) pickle*. Cold salt brine (or vinegar) for preserving foods; a difficult situation; a small or medium cucumber preserved in brine (or vinegar). Source: PICKLE (n). MWCD: 15th cent. When Americans see or hear the word *pickle*, they usu. think of the cucumber rather than the brine, whereas in Europe it is the brine that they think of. That is because the meaning of the word has expanded further in America, and *pickle* as a "cucumber preserved in brine" is an Americanism. (Ironically, this meaning of the word follows, rather than precedes, the metaphorical *pickle* as "a difficult situation" NSOED: mid-16th cent.). However, the existence of terms such as *cucumber pickle* and *watermelon pickle* remind us that in the 18th cent. the noun *pickle* could refer to any food preserved in brine. There are as many different types of pickles as there are types of sauce— more than one hundred—but the H. J. Heinz Company settled on approx. half that number in 1896 when it boasted of *Heinz 57 Varieties*, a phrase that has unfortunately become a slang term for "a mongrel dog of mixed or uncertain parentage" (HDAS: 1950). A *picklepuss* is a person with a puckered-up mouth who looks as if he/she just ate a sour pickle; and *dill pickles and ice cream* are what women are said to crave the most during pregnancy, perhaps because the two are such an odd combination of sweet and sour. DAFD; DAS; EWPO; FLC; LA. *See also* Bread and Butter Pickles; In a Pickle; Pickle (v).

PICKLE (v)   *to pickle something*. To preserve food in "pickle" (MWCD: 1522); to clean metal or preserve wood. Source: PICKLE (n). MWCD: 15th cent. The first food to be *pickled*, or preserved in brine or vinegar, was prob. the herring (*pickled herring*) in 14th cent. Holland. Since that time, meats such as pig's feet, "vegetables" such as cucumbers, and fruit such as watermelons have been pickled. Peter Piper once did the impossible by picking peppers that were already pickled. Even humans can be *pickled*, i.e., intoxicated; and a person who is *pickled to the gills* is totally drunk. Metal can be *pickled*, or cleared of scale, by dipping it in a chemical bath. Wood can be *pickled*, or preserved, by dipping it in a similar bath, and its finish can be *pickled*, or lightened, by bleaching. BDPF; DAS; FLC; IHAT; MDWPO; PT; WNWCD.

PICKLED   *See* Pickle (v).

PICKLED BEETS   *See* Red as a Beet.

PICKLED HERRING   *See* Red Herring.

PICKLED TO THE GILLS   *See* Pickle (v).

PICKLEPUSS   *See* Pickle (n).

PICKS AND PANS   *See* Pan Out.

PICK UP THE TAB   *See* Dutch Treat.

PICNIC HAM   *See* No Picnic.

PIE   *a pie.* An entrée consisting of meat and vegetables in or under a pastry crust; a dessert consisting of fruit or custard in or on a pastry crust (IHAT: 18th cent.). Source: PIE. (MWCD: 14th cent.) When a meat stew was first baked in a pot with a pastry crust on top, it was named after the "magpie," or *pie,* for one or both of the following reasons: (1) the magpie is a notorious "pack rat," collecting and hoarding all kinds of odds and ends of food that make up a "stew"; (2) the magpie builds a huge nest, up to three feet in diameter, that features a large dome, like the bulging top crust of a meat pie. For the next four cents., including the cent. of the first settlement of the English colonies in North America, the word *pie* referred to what is now called a *potpie* (MWCD: 1792). However, in the mid-1700s *pie* was applied to "sweet" pies—filled with fruits, berries, preserves, jams, and custards—as well as to the earlier "savory" pies, filled with various meats and vegetables. Since that time the meaning of the word *pie* has been stretched both lit.—e.g., *Boston cream pie* (a creamy cake)—and fig.—e.g., *to have a finger in the/every pie* (to be active in social affairs) or *to have a slice of the pie* (to share in the wealth)—all of which *see.* In addition, *pie* appears in two compound adjs. describing the human eyes and face: (1) *pie-eyed* (MWCD: 1904), which orig. meant "wide-eyed," i.e., with *eyes as big as saucers* (or round pies), but now means "drunk," perhaps because alcohol causes the pupils to dilate, making the eyes appear larger; and (2) *pie-faced* (MWCD: ca. 1912), i.e., having a round, smooth, or blank face such as can be found on the Cabbage Patch Kid, a cloth doll with a round, smooth, flat face. (Of course, some pies are square.) ATWS; BDPF; DAFD; DAS; FLC; IHAT; MDWPO; NSOED; SA; WNWCD. *Compare* Doughface.

PIECE BETWEEN MEALS   *See* Comfort Food.

PIÈCE DE RÉSISTANCE   *the pièce de résistance.* The chief attraction; the main event. MWCD: 1839. Source: MEAL. In a formal dinner in America, the *pièce de résistance* is the *main course* of the meal—usu. the third course, following *soup* (the first course) and *fish* (the second course). The chief dish of the main course consists of meat or poultry, e.g., a beef roast or a baked turkey—something that diners can *sink their teeth into* (q.v.), thus the "resistance." The *pièce de résistance* is also known as the *entrée* in America (DAFD: 1954), although that term has a somewhat different meaning in Western Europe, where it refers to the course (also the third course) occurring between the *fish* (the second course) and the *meat* (the fourth course). Regardless of its placement in the dinner, the *pièce de résistance* has become a global metaphor for a showpiece or showcase—the featured person or thing at an event, such as a banquet: "And now, Ladies and Gentlemen, the *pièce de résistance!*" FLC.

PIECE OF CAKE   *See* Cakewalk.

PIECE OF MEAT   *See* Meat.

PIE CHART   *a pie chart.* A circle graph. MWCD: 1922. Source: PIE. MWCD: 14th cent. A pie chart is a graph in the shape of a circle (a "pie"), divided into wedge-shaped portions (the "slices") of varying sizes (and colors and shadings). Pie charts are most often used to illustrate economic conditions, such as sources of income and types of expenses. When introduced to pie charts, employees sometimes discover that they need a larger *slice of the pie* (HND: 1967)—i.e., a larger share of the profits. In addition, states may want a larger slice (or "piece") of the lottery pie, the sales tax pie, the casino pie, or the federal grant pie. Before *slice of the pie* became popular in America, the expression was *slice of the melon*, which has just about disappeared. In England, the expression is *slice of the cake*. CI; DEI; NSOED; PT.

PIE-EYED   *See* Pie.

PIE-FACED   *See* Pie.

PIE IN THE SKY   Unrealistic hopes and dreams. MWCD: 1911. Source: PIE. MWCD: 14th cent. Most sources attribute this metaphor to a song written in 1911 by labor organizer Joe Hill for the International Workers of the World (the

"Wobblies") that parodied the unrealistic promises that preachers and politicians were making to workers in the early-20th cent. The last line, "You'll get *pie in the sky* when you die" [italics added], is critical of the denial of such benefits to workers during their lifetimes. Since 1911 the meaning of the phrase has broadened considerably, not limiting itself to church and labor but covering unfulfillable promises made by anyone, including laborers themselves. Today, *pie-in-the-sky* promises are regarded as "pipe dreams," like promising yourself—or someone else—the sun or the moon. In fact, the sun and the moon, not the Wobblies, may have been the inspiration for the metaphor in the first place. Consider the song "That's Amore," in which the moon is said to look like a big *pizza pie*, and the child's remark when it notices the moon for the first time: "Look, Mommy! There's a big *pie in the sky!*" AID; BDPF; CE; CI; DAI; DAS; DC; DEI; HND; LCRH; MS; PT. *Compare* Moon Pie.

PIE-IN-THE-SKY   *See* Pie in the Sky.

PIEPLANT   *See* Rhubarb.

PIEROGI   *See* Dumpling.

PIE SHELL   *See* Shell out.

PIGEON MILK   Predigested food that is regurgitated from the throat of an adult pigeon into the throat of one of the nestlings. Source: MILK. MWCD: O.E. *Pigeon milk* is not really milk—pigeons are birds, not mammals—but it resembles milk in color and consistency. Food is secreted in the crop of the male and female parents, where it is stimulated to produce "milk" by the same hormone that produces real milk in mammalian mothers. (The method of transfer is quite different, of course.) BDPF states that in England, children are sometimes sent on a wild goose chase to bring back some "pigeon milk" from a neighbor.

PIG MONTH   *See* Pork.

PIG OUT   *See* Eat like a Pig.

PIGS IN THE BLANKET   *See* Angels on Horseback; Everything but the Oink.

PINCH OF JEALOUSY   *See* For Good Measure.

PINEAPPLE   *a pineapple.* A hand granade. NSOED: early-20th cent. Source: APPLE. MWCD: O.E. The apple has been a stand-in for "fruit in general" since Classical times. The "fruit" of the pine tree is a bristly cone, and the original English name for it was *pineapple* (DAFD: 1398). When Columbus discovered a large bristly fruit in Guadalupe in 1493, he called it the "pine of the Indies," but by the mid-17th cent. the British were calling it a *pineapple* (MWCD: 1664). In WWI, Allied soldiers applied the name *pineapple* to the new hand grenades that they were issued, and in the 1920s the hand grenades used by the mob in Chicago were called *pineapples*. The "pineapple" grenades became so identified with Chicago that a pineapple sundae was nicknamed a *Chicago sundae*. However, the enduring association of *pineapple* with America has been in Hawai'i, where the fruit was introduced by Captain Cook in 1790. Dishes featuring pineapple on the mainland are often called "Hawai'ian-style," and the *pineapple express* is a trade wind of hot air that blows directly from Hawai'i to the Continental United States. EWPO; FLC; IHAT; LCRH; PT.

PINEAPPLE EXPRESS   *See* Pineapple.

PINT-SIZED   *See* Half-pint.

PIPING HOT   *See* Tempest in a Teapot.

PITS   *the pits*. The worst. DC: ca. 1975. Source: PIT (*). MWCD: O.E. The expression *It's the pits*, meaning "It's the worst," seems, at first hearing, to relate to drupaceous fruit, or *drupes*, whose single seed is sometimes called a *pit*, as in *cherry pit*. Furthermore, the pits of such fruits are usu. discarded, either because they are inedible or because they are poisonous (as is the case with apricot pits); and the plural form *pits* is sometimes used in contrast to *berries*, as in "It's not the *berries* (q.v.), it's the *pits*." However, there is strong evidence that *It's the pits* derived from heroin-addict slang of the 1970s, when a user discovered that the only unscarred part of his/her body was the armpits—also one of the most sensitive parts. Injecting heroin there became known as *the pits*, and eventually anything painful to endure became known as *the pits*. When the expression passed into general usage in the late-1970s, anything unenjoyable or of inferior quality came to be known as *the pits*. However, most people have no idea where the term came from, although they may suspect fruit pits or the pits on a racetrack where the drivers make a quick "pit stop." CE; EWPO; FLC; HND.

PIZZA-FACED   *See* Pizza Pie.

PIZZA PIE   *a pizza pie*. A pizza (fr. It. *pizza* "pie"). Source: PIZZA (MWCD: 1935); PIE (MWCD: 14th cent.). *Pizza pie* was an informal name given by American soldiers to the dish that they experienced for the first time during and after WWII in Naples, Italy. The dish was round, had a bottom crust, and was filled with meat and vegetables—just like a topless *meat pie*. (Italians in the large cities on the East Coast of the United States had been familiar with *pizza* since the early 1900s.) Eventually, the term *pizza pie* was shortened to the more authentic *pizza*, and *pizzerias* (MWCD: 1943), or "pizza parlors," sprang up across the country. When the craze hit Chicago, that city came up with a variation of its own, perhaps influenced by its Sicilian bakers: thick-crusted, deep-dish, pan-baked, "Chicago-style" pizza. Today, pizza vies with burgers and tacos as the most popular fast food in the nation, and the word *pizza* has figured in at least two other metaphors: *pizza-faced*, for someone whose face has been scarred by acne; and *road pizza*, for "road kill." CE; DAFD; DAS; FLC; NSOED; PT.

PIZZERIA   *See* Pizza Pie.

PLAIN-VANILLA   Basic, bland, boring, dull, ordinary, uninteresting. NSOED: mid-19th cent. Source: VANILLA. MWCD: 1662. There is nothing uninteresting about the flavoring called *vanilla*. It comes from the seeds (or beans) in the pod of a tropical orchid, orig. discovered in Central America by Spanish Conquistadors and named by them for the resemblance of the pod to the sheath (Sp. *vaina*) in which they carried their swords. *Vanilla* ("little sheath") from the New World became a popular flavoring in Europe and America, but Madagascar is now the principal supplier. The use of vanilla to flavor vanilla ice cream, the most basic of ice creams (milk-colored, no fruit or fruit juice, and no nuts or seeds—although vanilla beans are now added to some varieties), has led to the association of *vanilla* with "plain." The phrase *plain-vanilla* "undistinguished," however, may also have been influenced by the term *plain manila*, as in "The magazine arrived in a *plain manila* wrapper." DAFD; DAS; FLC; PT; WNWCD. *Compare* White Bread.

PLASTIC SILVERWARE   *See* Silverware.

PLATE GLASS   *See* Full Plate.

PLATE IS FULL   *See* Full Plate.

PLATE IS OVERFLOWING   *See* Full Plate.

PLATTER   *See* Full Plate.

PLEASE THE PALATE   *See* Palatable.

PLEASING TO THE PALATE   *See* Palatable.

PLUM   *a plum*. An unexpected prize; a generous reward. NSOED: early-19th cent. Source: PLUM. MWCD: O.E. The figurative *plum* orig. meant "a large sum of money" in England, but now, in America, it can mean anything that is desirable, superior, admired, or highly coveted. An example is a *political plum* (EWPO: 1887), a government job that involves little work but pays lots of money; and any easy job with good pay is *quite a plum*. The term *plum* is also applied to a new car that is perfect in every way, as opposed to a *lemon* (q.v.); and *plum* is an appropriate name for the *sugarplum* (MWCD: ca. 1668), a small ball of candied fruit covered with a sugar coating, even though it contains no plum fruit. Another "plum" dessert is *plum pudding* (MWCD: 1711), which also contains no plums but does have raisins or currants, both of which were referred to as *plums* as far back as the 1600s. *Plum* is also used attributively in the expression *plum role*, a good part in a movie or theater production: "to land a *plum role*." A *plum tomato* (MWCD: ca. 1900), however, is not an outstanding tomato but one that is midway in size between an average tomato and a *cherry tomato* (q.v.); it is special because it is oblong. A person who is *sloe-eyed* (MWCD: 1867) does not have lazy eyes but has irises the color of blackthorn plums, or *sloes* (MWCD: O.E.): dark blue or purplish black. BDPF; CE; DAFD; DAS; DEI; FLC; MS; PT.

PLUM PUDDING   *See* Plum.

PLUM ROLE   *See* Plum.

PLUM TOMATO   *See* Plum; Tomato.

POACH   *See* 'Coddle.

PO' BOY   *See* Submarine Sandwich.

POCKET PIE   *See* Pasty.

POKER POT   *See* Potbelly.

POLISH THE APPLE   *See* Apple-polisher.

POLITICAL PLUM   *See* Plum.

POMEGRANATE   *a pomegranate.* A "grainy apple." MWCD: 14th cent. Source: APPLE. The word *pomegranate* derives fr. Lat. *panum grenatum* "grainy apple," via M.Fr. *pomme grenate* "seedy apple." (The pomegranate is actually not a "pome" fruit, like the apple, but a berry, like the orange; however, Lat. *pome* "multiseeded fruit" and Fr. *pomme* "apple" have virtually merged in Mod. Fr., with *pomme* carrying the sense of both.) The pomegranate has been called "Nature's most labor-intensive fruit" (FLC) because it is basically inedible, and to get any nutrition from it you must cut it open, extract the seed sac, suck the juice from the sac, and spit out the seeds. (Then repeat the process.) To go to all that trouble doesn't seem worth it; and that is the opinion of most Americans, who have never even seen a pomegranate, let alone eaten one, although connoisseurs value them highly. *Grenadine* (MWCD: 1852) is a syrup made from the pomegranate that is used to flavor mixed drinks; and *garnet* (MWCD: 14th cent.), a modification of M.Fr.

grenat "the color of a pomegranate," denotes both a color (dark red) and a semi-precious stone of that color in English. DAFD; EWPO; FLC; THT. *See also* Grenade.

POOR BOY   *See* Submarine Sandwich.

POP (n)   *See* Pop Your Cork.

POP (v)   *See* Pop Your Cork.

POPCORN BALL   *See* Popcorn Shrimp.

POPCORN COTTAGE CHEESE   *See* Popcorn Shrimp.

POPCORN FISH   *See* Popcorn Shrimp.

POPCORN SHRIMP   Breaded, deep-fried baby shrimp—or bite-size pieces of adult shrimp. Source: POPCORN (MWCD: 1823); SHRIMP (MWCD: 14th cent.). The size of popcorn has increased over the years. The popcorn—or *popped corn*—that the Native Americans brought to the first Thanksgiving dinner in 1621 was prob. the size of the baby shrimp that are sold at some fast-food restaurants today, whereas modern popcorn is closer to the size of the shrimp pieces that are available in the frozen-food sections of supermarkets. *Popping corn* and *parching corn* were early names for the tiny, ricelike kernels of a variety of small-eared corn that is native to both North America (esp. Mexico) and South America (esp. Peru). By the early 1820s, popcorn, prepared in a covered pan in the fireplace, had become a popular Saturday or Sunday evening snack, and at Christmastime it was used—unbuttered and unsalted—to make Christmas tree "ropes." The late-19th cent. saw the invention of the *popcorn ball* (DAFD: 1870), the *popcorn machine* (DAFD: 1885), and *Cracker Jack* (DAFD: 1896). Popcorn has always been the most popular snack at movie theaters, and in various forms, popcorn has overtaken peanuts at the ballpark. Other bite-size foods that have been named for popcorn are *popcorn fish* (small, battered, deep-fried pieces of whitefish), *Cajun popcorn* (DAFD: 1980s—battered, deep-fried, shelled crayfish), and *popcorn cottage cheese* (the largest-curd cottage cheese available). Little pieces of potato-starch packing material are sometimes referred to as *packing popcorn*, although this does not imply that real popcorn was ever used for packing. (It's too crumbly.) EWPO; LA; WNWCD.

POP FLY   *See* Pop Your Cork.

POPGUN   *See* Pop Your Cork.

POP IN   *See* Pop Your Cork.

POPPED CORN   *See* Popcorn Shrimp.

POP PILLS   *See* Pop Your Cork.

POPPING CORN   *See* Popcorn Shrimp.

POP THE QUESTION   *See* Pop Your Cork.

POP-TOP   *See* Pop Your Cork.

POP UP   *See* Pop Your Cork.

POP YOUR CORK   *to pop—or blow—your cork.* To go wild or crazy. HDAS: 1938. Source: POP (v) (MWCD: 15th cent.); CORK (MWCD: 14th cent.). *To pop your cork* is to release your anger or frustration, just as a bottle of fermented or carbonated beverage suddenly releases its bottled-up gas when the cork or cap is removed. (Bottles sometimes *pop their cork* spontaneously, as during an earthquake or heat wave.) The verb *pop* is an imitative word for the sound of the explosion that takes place under these circumstances, and it, or the noun derived from it, *pop* (MWCD: 1591), is the basis for such terms as *popgun* (MWCD: 1622) "a toy gun that fires a cork (on a string) that goes 'Pop!' when it exits the barrel"; *soda pop* (MWCD: 1863) "a soft drink of soda water, sweet syrup, and flavoring"; a *pop fly* (MWCD: 1887) "a baseball that is hit high into the infield or short outfield"; and a *pop-top* (MWCD: 1965) "a can top that can be opened by pulling back a ring with your finger." The verb *pop* sometimes retains the imitative sense, as in the name Pop-Tart; however, it more often borrows the suddenness, rather than the sound, of the explosion, as in *to pop the question* "to propose marriage," *to pop in* "to stop by to say hello," and *to pop pills* "to take pills as if throwing them in your mouth." The proper method of uncorking a bottle of wine—except for champagne bottles with round-headed corks—is with a *corkscrew* (MWCD: 1720) "a pointed metal spiral that is screwed into the cork and then pulled out slowly." The spiral nature of the corkscrew is so unusual that it has been used to describe both a crooked person ("as crooked as a corkscrew") and a twisting, turning, looping roller coaster ride; and the expression *to uncork a wild pitch* (in baseball) reflects the unpredictable behavior of the ball. Some bottles and jugs can be recorked after opening, and that is prob. the source of the expression *Put a cork in it!* "Shut your mouth!" AID; DAFD; DAS; FLC; NSOED; WNWCD.

PORK   Political patronage. MWCD: 1879. Source: PORK. MWCD: 14th cent. Before the days of electrical refrigeration, the standard way to preserve pork was to "cure" it with salt, either by rubbing the salt directly on the meat or by soaking the meat in salt brine. (This process could optionally be followed by smoking the pork to produce hams and bacon.) Regardless of which "cure" was used, the pork was then packed into barrels for use throughout the year—esp. during the summer months (May through August), when fresh pork could not be kept for more than a few days. (During the months of September through April—the months with an *r* in them, or the *pig months*—the cooler weather helped to keep the pork fresh a little longer.). Whenever the householders retrieved *salt pork* (MWCD: 1723) from the barrel, they were taking back what was rightfully theirs; and people who gave away portions of the cache did it either out of charity or to impress or reward the recipients. *Pork* first came to be associated with political patronage during the Reconstruction period following the Civil War. The term *pork barrel* appeared in the early-20th cent. (MWCD: 1909), and *pork-barrel legislation* appeared four years after that (MDWPO: 1913). All of these terms can be summed up as *pork-barrel politics*, under which a legislature operates by permitting legislators to sponsor bills that reward the groups that got them elected in the first place. The process is a kind of "log-rolling": You scratch my back (i.e., do me a favor), and I'll scratch your back (i.e., do you a favor). The critics who keep track of the patronage in Congress use a *bacon barometer*. BDPF; HB; LCRH; MS; NSOED; SA; SHM.

PORK BARREL   *See* Pork.

PORK-BARREL LEGISLATION   *See* Pork.

PORK-BARREL POLITICS   *See* Pork.

PORK CHOP   *See* Chopping Block.

PORK OUT   *See* Eat Like a Pig.

PORKPIE HAT   *a porkpie hat*. A men's cloth hat with a flat top and a narrow brim. MWCD: 1860. Source: PORK; PIE. MWCD: 14th cent. The *porkpie hat* is so called because it bears some resemblance to a *meat pie* (in this case, pork), the first dish that was to go by the name *pie*. A casserole-type cooking bowl is filled with chopped meat (e.g., pork), vegetables, and gravy; baked in the oven until almost done; covered with a topping of mashed potatoes or pastry crust; and baked until brown. (If beef is used, the dish is called a *cottage pie*; if venison is used, it is called a *lumberjack pie*; and if lamb or mutton is used, it is called a *shepherd's pie*). In the *porkpie hat* analogy, the top of the hat represents the crust, the round sides of the hat represent the bowl, and the brim of the hat represents the plate on which the bowl is served. DAFD; FLC; SA; WNWCD.

POTATO   *a potato*. A sweet potato–like tuber. Source: POTATO. MWCD: 1565. The potato and its name have had a complicated history. The name is derived fr. Taino *batata*, the Haitian Indian word for an orange-fleshed tuber, or what is now called a *sweet potato*. The batata was discovered by Columbus in the late-15th cent. and taken back to Europe, where its name was altered to *patata* in Spanish, *patate* in French, and *potato* in English. The batatas were easy to grow, there was almost no waste, they could be roasted or boiled, and the orange-colored flesh was delicious. However, in the late-16th cent. the Spanish discovered another tuber, smaller and white fleshed, that was being cultivated by the Incas of Peru, who called it a *papa*. This tuber was not related to the batata, but it was related to the poisonous nightshade, which meant that it was prob. poisonous (as green potato skins are now known to be). At first the *papa* was called by its Inca name in Spain; but eventually the name of the sweet potato, *patata*, was extended also to the white potato. The somewhat euphemistic names for the white potato in French and German are, respectively, *pomme de terre* and *Erdapfel*, both meaning "earth apple." If it had not been for the Irish, the *white potato* (or *Irish potato*— MWCD: 1664) might never have reached North America during the Colonial period. American colonists were aware of the sweet potato, which they ate and enjoyed in the 17th cent., but they had no knowledge of the fact that Sir Walter Raleigh had introduced the white potato to his farmland in Ireland, where it was grown for human consumption, not as in England, where it was grown only for fodder. The first white potatoes were introduced into Boston in the early-18th cent. (LA: ca. 1719) by Irish settlers, but because of custom and the continuing fear of poison, the English colonists used them only as cattle feed. (The Irish and the Pennsylvania "Dutch" both fed white potatoes to their families.) Gradually, over the next century (LA: ca. 1719 to ca. 1819), the Americans accepted the white potato as human food—and to eliminate confusion with the "other" potato, labeled the orange-fleshed potato the *sweet potato* (MWCD: 1750). Neither of these unrelated potatoes is related to the *yam* (q.v.). BDPF; DAFD; DAS; EWPO; FLC; MDWPO; NSOED; THT.

POTATOHEAD   *a potatohead (or potato head)*. A fool. LA: 1930s. Source: POTATO. MWCD: 1565. A *potatohead* is someone who has a potato for a head—or at least for a brain. That was lit. the case with the original *Mr. Potato Head*, a child's toy that first appeared in 1952 and, with some modifications, has been in production ever since. The first model was actually a kit of plastic parts consisting of a headless torso (with attachable hands and feet) and eyes (with eyebrows), ears, nose (with pince-nez), mouth (with a large mustache), and a tiny bowler hat. These parts were intended to be stuck into a large russet potato (not included). When all of the parts were attached to the potato, the head appeared to be about twice the size of the body, the man looked a lot like a clown, and the toy had to be kept in the refrigerator at night to prevent spoilage and sprouting. (A cartoon of Mr. Potato Head in the October 1991 *Smithsonian* magazine showed a large Idaho potato lying in a single bed, under the covers, with a pair of plastic feet on the floor beside the bed and a set of plastic eyes, ears, nose, and lips on the nightstand!) Mr. Potato Head got married in 1953, and he underwent a major change in 1964, when the real potato was replaced by a plastic one and the figure became all plastic and all head, with the hands attached to arms, the pince-nez replaced by "shades," and the bowler hat much enlarged. Mr. Potato Head's big break came in 1995, when he starred in the computer-animated film *Toy Story*, in which he proved that he was not a stupid *potatohead* but was really a warm and funny guy—though a little "flaky." DAS.

POTATO FLOUR   *See* Take the Starch Out.

POTATO STARCH   *See* Take the Starch Out.

POTAYTO/POTAHTO   *See* Mashed Potato.

POTBELLIED   *See* Potbelly.

POTBELLIED STOVE   *See* Potbelly; Slave over a Hot Stove All Day.

POTBELLY   *a potbelly.* A protruding abdomen. MWCD: ca. 1714. Source: POT. MWCD: O.E. A *potbelly*, the curse of middle-aged men, is a large belly that somewhat mirrors the abdomen of a pregnant woman. It is so called because it resembles a round-bottom pot—or, more precisely, a bowl, kettle, or wok—that seems to be attached, bottom-side out, to the man's "stomach." The condition was recognized in the mid-17th cent., when the adj. *potbellied* (MWCD: 1657) was first recorded, over half a cent. before the noun *potbelly*. More recently, the adj. has been applied to a wood-burning, space-heating stove: a *potbellied stove* (MWCD: 1933) that resembles a large bowling pin more than a "pregnant" man. Most *pot* metaphors, however, relate to the *inside* of the vessel, the part that actually holds water (etc.). For example, the *pothole* (MDCD: 1826) started out as an underwater hole in the rocky bottom of a riverbed and is now a hole in a road, street, or highway that fills up with water during a rainstorm. A *pot bunker* is a small, steep-sided sand trap, usu. near a green, that fills up with golf balls and frustrates golfers. A *pot of gold* is what people hope to find at the end—the *other* end—of the rainbow; and a *melting pot* (MWCD: 1912) is what American schools were once thought to be, serving to integrate students of different races, religions, and ethnic background, although that myth has pretty much been shattered. There are also *lobster pots* (MWCD: 1764), which are placed in the water but do not hold it, and *poker pots*, which hold either chips or money. A *potwalloper* (LA: ca. 1860) used to be a kitchen helper who wrestled with the pots in a cheap restaurant. A *pothead* (MWCD: 1959) is not a person whose head is the shape of a pot but one who smokes *pot* (MWCD: 1938—i.e., marijuana), which is not derived fr. Eng. *pot*. BDPF; DAS; DEI; FLC; NSOED; WNWCD.

POTBOILER   *See* Keep the Pot Boiling.

POT BUNKER   *See* Potbelly.

POT CALLING THE KETTLE BLACK   *See* Like the Pot Calling the Kettle Black.

POT CHEESE   *See* Cottage-cheese Thighs.

POTHEAD   *See* Potbelly.

POTHOLE   *See* Potbelly.

POTLIDS   *See* Blow the Lid off.

POTLIKKER   *See* Crock.

POT LIQUOR   *See* Crock.

POTLUCK   *See* Take Potluck.

POTLUCK SUPPER   *See* Take Potluck.

POT OF GOLD   *See* Potbelly.

POT PIE   *See* Pie.

POTSHOT   *See* Go to Pot.

POTWALLOPER   *See* Potbelly.

POUND CAKE   *a pound cake*. A loaf cake made with equal proportions of four main ingredients. MWCD: 1747. Source: CAKE. The original recipe for a pound cake called for one pound each of flour, butter, sugar, and eggs—hence the name. The result was a cake that was heavy both in weight—approx. four pounds— and in the proportion of butter, sugar, and eggs. Modern recipes for pound cake do not respect the original measurements—cutting the weight approx. in half— and usu. call for a flavoring, such as vanilla or lemon. DAFD; FLC; IHAT.

POWER BREAKFAST   *See* Breakfast (n).

POWER LUNCH   *See* Business Lunch.

PRAIRIE COCKTAIL   *See* Lamb Fries.

PRAIRIE OYSTERS   *See* Lamb Fries.

PRAWN   *See* Little Shrimp.

PRESERVE   *a preserve.* An area of usu. wooded land set aside for the protection of wild animals and plants. Source: PRESERVE. MWCD: 1600. The "nature preserve" derives from the preservation of fruit by cooking it whole or in chunks with sugar and pectin. The resulting *preserve* is unlike a *jelly*, which is made of clear fruit juice, or a *jam*, which is made of pureed fruit. The *preserve* "preserves" the shape of the fruit of which it is made, allowing it to be identified when spread on bread. If a mixture of fruits is used in the production of a preserve, it can be called a *conserve* (MWCD: 15th cent.); and if the chunks of fruit are candied and brandy is added, it can be called *tutti-frutti* (q.v.), Italian for "all fruit." *See also* Marmalade.

PRESSURE COOKER   *a pressure cooker.* A tense situation; an emotion-packed environment; a stressful job. Source: PRESSURE COOKER. MWCD: 1915. A person who describes his/her life this way feels as if he/she were food being cooked *in a pressure cooker: taking the heat, getting all steamed up,* and occasionally being forced to *let off steam.* Unlike the electric *crock pot* (q.v.), which cooks food slowly, with low heat, the pressure cooker is a stove-top utensil, cooking food over high heat, under great pressure, operating principally on the basis of steam. When the pressure of the steam gets too high, some of it is vented off through a valve on the tightly fitting cover; if it gets *much* too high, and the hot steam cannot exit quickly enough, the cover *hits the ceiling.* Pressure-cooker jobs are ones that are demanding, fast-paced, hectic, and frantic—as in the emergency room of a hospital, the floor of the stock exchange, the bench of a professional sports team, the lockup of a city jail, a boot camp for the U.S. Army or Marines, and the romper room of a neighborhood nursery school. DAFD; FLC; PT.

PRETTY KETTLE OF FISH   *See* Kettle of Fish.

PRETZEL BOW   *See* Human Pretzel.

PRETZEL KNOT   *See* Human Pretzel.

PRICE OF TEA IN CHINA   *See* Not for All the Tea in China.

PRICKLY PEAR   *See* Pear-shaped.

PRINTING PLATE   *See* Full Plate.

PRIX FIXE   *See* Menu.

PROGRESSIVE DINNER   *See* Dinner (2).

PROOF IS IN THE PUDDING   *See* Proof of the Pudding Is in the Eating.

PROOF OF THE PUDDING IS IN THE EATING   *The proof of the pudding is in the eating.* The success of a person or product can only be measured by his/her/its performance; the success of a plan or project can only be measured by its outcome. DAP: ca. 1300. Source: PUDDING (MWCD: 13th cent.); EAT (v) (MWCD: O.E.). A pudding, which was orig. the first, rather than the last, dish at dinner, may look delicious, but the only way to find out for sure is to taste it. The proverb has been mistakenly altered in modern times to *The proof is in the pudding,* which prob. has the same meaning to the person who utters it, although the person who hears it, if he/she is familiar with the original, may become either confused or amused. BDPF; CE; CI; CODP; DC; DEI; HND; MS.

PROPOSE A TOAST   *See* Toast (n) (1).

PRUNE   *See* Full of Prunes.

PTOMAINE DOMAIN   *See* Cafeteria.

PTOMAINE PALACE   *See* Cafeteria.

PUDDING   Soft-cooked food. NSOED: mid-16th cent. Source: PUDDING. MWCD: 13th cent. Foods that go by the name *pudding* range from *Indian pudding* (water-based baked cornmeal) to *hasty pudding* (milk-based boiled cornmeal) to *plum pudding* (fruit-based steamed cake) to *Yorkshire pudding* (popovers baked with roast beef) to *custard pudding* (milk-based cooked dessert). About all that these dishes have in common is that they are soft and cooked. (A hard, uncooked "pudding" is *puddingstone*—MWCD: 1753—a geological conglomerate of stones and pebbles that were bonded together by clay in ancient times.) The word *pudding* derives fr. O.Fr. *boudin* "sausage," and the first pudding was what is now called *blood pudding,* or *blood sausage* (MWCD: 1868), a sausage that contains a high percentage of blood. Today, the only "pudding" that contains meat is the Brit. *steak and kidney pie,* which is sometimes referred to as *steak and kidney pudding.* DAFD; WNWCD.

PUDDINGHEAD   *See* Puddingheaded.

PUDDINGHEADED (adj.)   Soft-headed; stupid. LA: 1726. Source: PUDDING. MWCD: 13th cent. Someone who is *puddingheaded*—i.e., is a *puddinghead* (LA: 1849)—has pudding for brains, or at least is thought to. In Mark Twain's novel *Pudd'nhead Wilson* (1894), the townspeople call local lawyer David Wilson by this name because of his eccentricity. However, the pithy sayings in "Pudd'nhead Wilson's Calendars," from this novel and the subsequent *Following the Equator,* reveal that Wilson was not only smart but funny. (Examples: "Cauliflower is nothing but cabbage with a college education"; "Put all your eggs in one basket— and WATCH THAT BASKET!"; and "Man is the only animal that blushes . . . or needs to.") Wilson was an obvious role model for later aphorists such as Will Rogers and Forrest Gump. CE; DAS; IHAT; NSOED; PT. *Compare* Cabbage Head; Chowderhead; Meathead; Mutton Head.

PUDDINGSTONE   *See* Pudding.

PUFFBALL MUSHROOM   *See* Spring up like Mushrooms.

PULL SOMEONE'S CHESTNUTS OUT OF THE FIRE   *to pull someone's chestnuts out of the fire.* To bail someone out of trouble, usu. at considerable hardship to yourself. HND: 18th cent. Source: CHESTNUT. MWCD: 14th cent. This metaphorical expression alludes to an ancient Aesop fable about a monkey, a cat, and some chestnuts roasting on an open fire. Cats don't eat chestnuts, but monkeys do, and this one wanted the chestnuts, which had fallen into the coals, so badly he could taste them. Knowing, however, that if he reached into the embers he would burn his own paw, the monkey convinced the cat to do the job for him. Result? The cat got a singed paw, and the monkey got the roasted nuts. The moral to the story has focused on the stupidity of the cat rather than the cleverness of the monkey, and the term *cat's paw* (also 18th cent.) has come to mean a dupe, a pawn, a sucker, a tool—i.e., someone "dumb" enough to get "conned" into doing someone else's dirty work. ATWS; CI; DEI; HB; MDWPO; MS; SA; SHM; WNWCD.

PUMPKIN   (or *Punkin.*) A term of endearment and address for a child (usu. a girl). NSOED: mid-20th cent. Source: PUMPKIN. MWCD: 1654. The pumpkin (fr. Fr. *pompon*—not to be confused with the flower) is the fruit of a North American vine that was introduced to the English colonists by the Native Americans but was regarded by the English as a squash—and still is—leaving it up to the French explorers to give it the name *pompon*, meaning "melon," and the Dutch to add *-kin*, giving it the meaning "little melon." Melon or squash, the pumpkin is a member of the gourd family, the members of which are variously classified as fruits (e.g., the watermelon) or vegetables (e.g., the cucumber), with the pumpkin (and squash) falling among the vegetables. Like most of the vegetable "gourds," pumpkins are brilliantly colored. When they are ripe, they are bright orange (orangish yellow or yellowish orange), both inside and out. The attractiveness of the pumpkin is prob. what led to its selection as a term of endearment and address for a young girl. An older girl might be described as being *some pumpkin* (or *some punkins*), i.e., someone special (NSOED: mid-19th cent.). Like Cinderella, the young lady would be warned to be home by midnight or her conveyance would *turn into a pumpkin*; and if that happened, she might refer to her driver as a *pumpkin head* (LA: 1841) "a stupid person." DAFD; DAS; EWPO; FLC; PT; WNWCD. *Compare* Cabbage Head; Chowderhead; Puddinghead.

PUMPKIN HEAD   *See* Pumpkin.

PUMPKIN SHELL   *See* Shell Out.

PUNKIN   *See* Pumpkin.

PURE GRAVY   *See* Ride the Gravy Train.

PURE VEGETARIAN   *See* Vegetarian.

PUT A BUN IN THE OVEN   *See* Have a Bun in the Oven.

PUT A CORK IN IT   *See* Pop Your Cork.

PUT A LID ON   *See* Blow the Lid Off.

PUT ALL YOUR EGGS IN ONE BASKET   *to put all your eggs in one basket.*
To foolishly put all your trust in one plan, one individual, one company, one
bank, etc. HND: 1710. Source: EGG. MWCD: 14th cent. The classic case of
"putting all of your eggs in one basket" is the Aesop fable of the eggmaid who
carried the day's production of eggs to market in a single basket. Distracted by
thoughts of what she might do with the money that she would receive for the
eggs, she dropped the basket, and all of the eggs broke. If the "foolish" girl had
divided up the eggs between two baskets, half of them might have survived, and
half of her dreams might have come true. For this reason, the advice—or warning—is usu. *Don't put all your eggs in one basket* (DAP: 1666), i.e., don't gamble
everything on a single venture: Diversify! An alternative, according to Mark
Twain's *Pudd'nhead Wilson* (1894), is to *Put all your eggs in one basket—and
WATCH THAT BASKET!* AID; ATWS; CE; CI; DAI; DC; DEI; MS; NSOED; PT;
SA. *Compare* Don't Count Your Chickens before They Hatch.

PUT ALL YOUR EGGS IN ONE BASKET—AND WATCH THAT BASKET!
See Put All Your Eggs in One Basket.

PUT FOOD ON THE TABLE   *See* Keep the Wolf from the Door.

PUT IN COLD STORAGE   *See* Put on Ice.

PUT ON ICE   *to put something on ice.* To set something aside; to hold something
in reserve; to postpone or delay something. HDAS: 1875. Source: ICE. MWCD:
O.E. In Colonial America, one of the best methods of preserving food, at least in
the northern colonies, was to cut blocks of ice from the lake during the winter
months, place them in the cellar of an *icehouse* (MWCD: 1687), put the food to
be preserved on top (i.e., "on ice"), and cover everything with straw, wood shav-

ings, or sawdust. An improvement on this system occurred in the early-19th cent. with the invention of the *refrigerator* (MWCD: 1803), which was not an electrical appliance but an insulated wooden *icebox*, located inside the house, that could keep a small amount of food cold for a short period of time—until the water was drained and the ice was replaced. On the farm, the farm boy or girl emptied the water, and the farmer or hired man carried in the block of ice from the icehouse. In town, artificially made ice was delivered in a horse-drawn *ice wagon* (LA: 1844), carried into the house on the shoulder of an *iceman* (LA: 1844), and lowered into the top of an *ice box* (MWCD: 1846). The expression *to stink on ice* (HDAS: 1927) means that something is both intensely and inherently bad because if it has been kept *in cold storage* (MWCD: 1877), i.e., "on ice," it must have been bad to start with. The metaphor *to cut no ice* (DC: 1897), as in "That *doesn't cut any ice* with me," meaning that you are not impressed with or convinced by an argument, hearkens back to the difficult and dangerous days of sawing blocks of ice out of the lake. Persons who did this must have *had ice water in their veins*, in the sense of being "courageous and stoic," although the expression is also used of killers who are "cold-blooded and cruel." The expression *on the rocks* (DAFD: ca. 1945) refers to a beverage served with *ice cubes* (LA: 1920), provided in the new electrical home *refrigerator* (LA: 1916), although *on the rocks* can also be used to describe a marriage or an institution that is in serious trouble, based on the original nautical meaning of a ship "gone aground" on the rocks. Crushed ice scooped into a large paper cone and doused with flavored syrup is known as a *snowcone* (MWCD: 1964) in some parts of the country, esp. at ballparks, where a *snowcone* is a catch of the baseball in the fingertips of the glove, so that the white ball stands out like crushed ice in a paper cone. *Ice* is also a slang term for diamonds (HDAS: 1905), since (1) clear diamonds look a lot like frozen water (i.e., *ice*), and (2) the clarity of diamonds is described by jewelers in terms of *water*: "a diamond of the *first water*." CI; DAFD; DAI; DAS; DC; DEI; EWPO; FLC; HB; HND; MS; NSOED. *See also* Icebox Cookies; Long Drink of Water.

PUT ON THE BACK BURNER   *See* Slave over a Hot Stove.

PUT ON THE FEED BAG   *to put—strap, or tie—on the (old) feed bag.* To eat. HDAS: 1906. Source: FEED (n). MWCD: 1576. A *feed bag* is a short canvas bag for holding feed (esp. oats) that is strapped onto the muzzle of a horse during a rest stop so that the animal can eat while it is in harness and hitched to a load. If the feed bag had not been invented, the driver would have had to feed the horse out of his/her hat or unhitch it and let it graze on the nearest grass, a time-consuming process. People don't eat oats out of a bag, but someone with farm experience transferred this colorful phrase to the human behavior of stuffing a napkin into your collar and food into your mouth. Likewise, a horse that has lost its appetite and appears sluggish and listless is said to be "off its feed," and the same phrase is used to describe the condition of a human being who is "under the weather" or "down in the dumps," i.e., *off your feed*. The cure for the horse may be to change its diet; the cure for the human may require a visit to the physician or psychologist. AID; ATWS; DAI; DAS; SA; WNWCD.

PUT SOME MEAT ON YOUR BONES   *See* Meat.

PUT THROUGH THE MILL   *See* Through the Mill.

PUT WORDS INTO SOMEONE ELSE'S MOUTH   *See* You Said a Mouthful.

Q

QUIT COLD TURKEY *to quit cold turkey.* To terminate a harmful addiction suddenly, without gradual withdrawal. MWCD: 1941. Source: TURKEY. MWCD: 1555. It is not at all certain why *cold turkey* (MWCD: 1921) has become a metaphor for abrupt cessation of drug use, although it has been suggested that the association may lie in the similarity between the bumpy skin of a plucked turkey and that of a shivering addict undergoing withdrawal symptoms. To *quit cold turkey* orig. meant to kick a drug, alcohol, or tobacco habit, but now it can also be applied to a cessation of gambling, cheating on your income tax, or exceeding the speed limit—and even to ceasing to eat chocolate, junk food, or red meat. AID; ATWS; DAI; DAS; DC; DEI; HDAS; HND; IRCD; LCRH; MS; PT; SA.

QUITE A PLUM *See* Plum.

R

RABBIT FOOD   Salad greens and raw vegetables. DAFD: 1960s. Source: RAB-BIT (MWCD: 14th cent.); FOOD (MWCD: O.E.). Because they are herbivorous, wild rabbits feast on all of the roots (such as carrots), stalks (such as celery), and leaves (such as lettuce) in your garden. Most humans are omnivorous, and they can be expected to feed not only on raw vegetables but on rabbits as well. How-ever, for some strange reason, many children and grown men have a dislike for the food that rabbits love so much, referring to it by the pejorative term *rabbit food* (or *roughage*), as if it were unfit for human consumption. Unfortunately, therefore, they miss out on all green salads and have no idea how good carrot sticks and celery stalks can taste when they are dipped into salad dressing. In contrast, almost all humans like *squirrel food*, i.e., "nuts," although the term is also used pejoratively for people who are themselves *nuts* (q.v.) or at least a little *nutty* (q.v.). DAS; IRCD; MDWPO; NSOED; SA.

RACING SHELL   *See* Shell out.

RAISIN   *a raisin*. A dried grape. MWCD: 14th cent. Source: GRAPE. *Raisin* entered English from French, where it meant, and still means, "grape." At about the same time, the word *grape* also entered English from French, where it referred to the *grappling* hook used to harvest grape clusters. *Grape* prevailed in English for the fresh fruit, whereas *raisin* prevailed for the dried fruit. In modern times, grapes are dried either in the sun or by artificial heat. If large Thompson seedless or Muscat grapes are used, the dried products are called *raisins*; if tiny Zante grapes are used, the products are called *currants*. (Concord grapes are not used to make raisins.) Raisins are often packaged in very small cardboard boxes, which has led to the expression "a *raisin-box size* theater (etc.)" for a theater (etc.) that is no bigger than a box of raisins, i.e., extremely small. DAFD; FLC; NSOED. *Compare* Prune.

RAISIN-BOX SIZE   *See* Raisin.

RASPBERRY   *a raspberry.* A Bronx cheer; a colorful bruise. HDAS: 1927. Source: RASPBERRY. MWCD: ca. 1616. The Bronx cheer, which is really a jeer rather than a cheer, originated at Yankee Stadium, where the fans of the Bronx Bombers (the New York Yankees) gave *raspberries* to the umpires, the opposing players, and even their own team in the early part of the 20th cent. The Bronx cheer, or *raspberry*, is made by closing your lips, sticking your tongue out between them, and blowing hard enough to produce a slobbery trill. (In this sense, the word *raspberry* is short for *raspberry tart* —NSOED: late-19th cent.— which is Cockney rhyming slang for "fart.") Another baseball *raspberry* is the bruise that a player acquires by being hit by a ball or bat or by running into a wall or an opposing player; when the bruise turns red, it looks like a giant red raspberry (or *strawberry*). Unlike a *strawberry mark* (q.v.), however, the *raspberry* is only temporary. Wild raspberries come in two forms, red and black, both of which grow on thorny canes that give the fruit its name: a *berry* that grows on a *rasp* (or "coarse file"). The black raspberry looks like a smaller version of the blackberry, but one that is more tender and more refined. The red raspberry looks like no other fruit and is generally regarded as the more elegant—and is also the more expensive—of the two. Both berries go well with milk, cream, and ice cream and are processed for use in jams, jellies, and dessert sauces. BDPF; CE; DAFD; DAS; DEI; EWPO; FLC; PT.

RASPBERRY TART   *See* Raspberry.

RAT TRAP CHEESE   *cheddar cheese.* MWCD: 1927. Source: CHEESE. MWCD: O.E. In the 1920s, American cheddar was the favorite bait to use in rattraps (and mousetraps). When customers at the grocery store asked for *rat trap cheese*, the grocer knew exactly what they wanted because cheddar was the cheapest, most pungent, and most popular cheese on hand. Tastes have changed, however, and rats (and mice) now prefer *peanut butter.* Another kind of "rat" is still a cheese-eater: an informer (or "rat fink") who squeals on his/her partner(s) in crime like the "dirty rat" that he/she is. DAS; LA; SA.

RAVENOUS APPETITE   *See* Appetite.

RAVIOLI   *See* You Can't Get Blood from a Turnip.

RAZORBACK   *See* The Other White Meat.

REACH THE BOILING POINT   *to reach the boiling point.* For matters to reach the point of crisis; for anger to become uncontrollable. Source: BOIL (v). MWCD:

13th cent. The *boiling point* of water (MWCD: 1773) is 212° Fahrenheit (or 100° centigrade) at sea level. This is the temperature at which bubbles begin to rise to the surface and burst into steam. This point is preceded by a period of development of tiny bubbles that produce little or no steam. The progression is like that of an individual or a group that starts out calm, develops a small amount of anger, then lets that anger erupt into a violent outburst (equivalent to a "full rolling boil" in cooking terms). A person who *has a low boiling point*—i.e., who angers very easily—is like water that boils at a temperature lower than the boiling point at sea level (e.g., at approx. 200° Fahrenheit on top of a 7,000-foot mountain). Regardless of the altitude, a person who *reaches the boiling point* is *boiling mad* (MWCD: 1607), *boiling (over) with anger or rage*, or *seething inside*. AID; BDPF; CE; DAI; DAS; FLC; MS.

REAL MEN DON'T EAT QUICHE   Quiche is for sissies. Source: EAT (MWCD: O.E.); QUICHE (MWCD: 1941). When quiche first appeared in American restaurants in the early-1940s, Americans didn't quite know how to react to it. Because these little custard pies arrived from France at about the same time as the larger pizza pies from Italy, the quiche may have been regarded as the weak sister of the two. Furthermore, the quiche was too small to fill the role of entrée, as a pizza could, but was treated as a side dish of the regular meal, or as an hors d'oeuvre before the meal. Such dainty dishes were not the sort of food that "real men" required—e.g., meat and potatoes, or beer and brats—hence the saying. Quiche originated in the region of Lorraine in northeastern France, across the Rhine from Germany, and the word *quiche* is fr. Ger. *Küche* "cake." The basic *quiche Lorraine* (MWCD: 1941) consists of a custard made of eggs, onion, and bacon bits baked in a straightsided pastry shell. American variations on the recipe add such ingredients as cheese, other vegetables (e.g., mushrooms, peppers, spinach), and other meats (e.g., ham, sausage, seafood). Quiches are not as popular now as they were in the 1970s, at the height of their popularity, but, then again, neither are "real men." DAFD; EWPO; MDWPO; NSOED; WNWCD.

RECEIPT   *See* Recipe.

RECEIPT BOOK   *See* Recipe.

RECIPE   *a recipe.* A set of instructions for making something from a set of ingredients. Source: RECIPE. MWCD: 1584. In the earliest American *cookbook* (DAFD: 1796), the ingredients were integrated into the instructions, but in Fannie Farmer's *Cook Book* of 1921 the set of instructions and the set of ingredients were separated, with the ingredients listed first. Eighteenth-century cookbooks were called *recipe books* (or *receipt books*); they consisted mostly of handwritten *recipes* (or *receipts*) that had been passed down from grandmothers to mothers and would be passed on, with additions, to daughters. The word *recipe*, as it applies to cooking, is derived from the noun *recipe*, meaning "prescription," which is often abbreviated as "Rx" and is sometimes written and pronounced *Rex*. The medical term *recipe* is from Lat. *recipe* "Take!" the imperative of Lat. *recipere* "to take"; and the folk term *receipt* is from the past part. of the same Lat. verb. It is uncertain whether such extended metaphors as *recipe for success* "a formula for success" and *recipe for disaster* "a formula for disaster" are based on the medical term or the cooking term. The most famous recipe was the one for cooked hare, which appeared in an 18th cent. cookbook and began with the following instruction: *First catch your hare*. The second most famous recipe contained an instruction for behavior further along in the procedure: *Stand facing the stove*. BDPF; CODP; DAP; EWPO; MS; NSOED; PT. *See also* Cookbook.

RECIPE BOOK   *See* Recipe.

RECIPE FOR DISASTER   *See* Recipe.

RECIPE FOR SUCCESS   *See* Recipe.

RED AS A BEET   *to be as red as a beet*. To be redfaced with anger, embarrassment, fever, or sunburn. Source: BEET. MWCD: O.E. The roots of most garden beets are *beet red* on both the outside and the inside, and they "bleed" when you pick them. (So you really *can* get "blood" from a "turnip"!) However, some beets are white, and some, like the *sugar beet* (MWCD: 1817), which weighs several pounds and is used to make *beet sugar* (q.v.), are light brown. *Harvard beets* (MDWPO: ca. 1930s) were prob. so named by a cook at, or in the shadow of, Harvard University who noticed the similarity between the deep red color of the beets that he/she was slicing and the color most associated with the University: crimson. The name *Harvard beets* caught on so quickly and so firmly that it has almost replaced the earlier term, *pickled beets*, and it is recognized as far west as Stanford University. Harvard beets are made by slicing raw red beets as if they were apples for a pie, cooking them in a sweet (sugar)-and-sour (vinegar) sauce thickened with cornstarch, and serving them hot, as a side dish with meat and mashed potatoes. Beets are "mange-tout" food: You can eat everything, including the leafy greens. CE; DAFD; DEI; EWPO; FLC; NSOED; PT.

RED AS A LOBSTER   *See* Look like a Boiled Lobster.

RED FLANNEL HASH   *See* Hash (n).

RED HERRING   *a red herring*. A deliberate diversion, distraction, or false clue. HND: 1890. Source: HERRING. MWCD: O.E. The literal "red herring" is a herring that has been smoked, salted, and dried until it turns a reddish brown color and acquires a strong and distinctive odor. (It is known as a *bloater* in Britain and is also called a *kippered herring* and a *kipper* in America.) The deceitful nature of the red herring comes from its association with hounds in the 17th cent. Fox hunters discovered that they could train their fox hounds to follow a scent by dragging a red herring behind a horse and leaving a trail so powerful that the hounds would follow nothing else. Opponents of fox hunting then discovered that if they *dragged a red herring across the path* of the fox, the hounds would be set "at fault" and would follow the false scent; and criminals pursued by bloodhounds discovered that they could set the hounds "at fault" by *dragging a red herring across their path* (NSOED: late-19th cent.) and then tossing it away for the dogs to follow. Metaphorically, the last-mentioned phrase has come to refer to (1) a mystery writer dragging false clues in order to deceive the readers, and (2) a politician creating a straw man to divert the voters' attention from the real issues. ATWS; BDPF; CI; DAFD; DC; DEI; EWPO; FLC; HI; HND; IRCD; LCRH; MDWPO; MS; SA; SHM.

RED HOT *See* Hot Dog.

RED MEAT *See* Beef (n).

REFRIGERATOR *See* Icebox Cookies; Put on Ice.

REFRIGERATOR ART *See* Icebox Cookies.

REFRIGERATOR COOKIES *See* Icebox Cookies.

REHASH *See* Hash (v).

RELISH (n) Enjoyment, delight, satisfaction; inclination, desire, fondness. Source: RELISH (n). MWCD: 1530. *Relish* as an abstract noun meaning "pleasure" derives from the early-16th cent. noun *relish*, with the semiabstract meaning "flavor," esp. a pleasing or zestful flavor. The earlier *relish* derives from M.E. *relis* "taste," from O.Fr. *relais* "something remaining or left behind," specif. a trace of taste or flavor left on the palate after eating. Also derived fr. *relish* "flavor," but later than *relish* "pleasure," is the concrete noun *relish*, meaning a food with a zesty flavor, such as a pickle-based condiment (DAFD: 1798). Consequently, when someone says that he/she *ate their hot dog with relish*, you don't know whether the hot dog was eaten with pleasure (NSOED: mid-17th cent.) or with chopped pickles—or both. The abstract *relish* can also allude to a strong desire, as when someone says that he/she *has little relish for something*, such as hot dogs— or relish. Derived from the abstract noun *relish* is the verb *relish* "to enjoy" (NSOED: late-16th cent.), esp. to enjoy something pleasurable in the past (*to relish the memory of*), the present (*to relish the moment*), or the future (*to relish the thought of* something that is about to happen). CE; DAFD; DAP.

RELISH (v) *See* Relish (n).

RELISH THE MEMORY OF *See* Relish (n).

RELISH THE MOMENT   *See* Relish (n).

RELISH THE THOUGHT OF   *See* Relish (n).

RENDER   *See* Tub of Lard.

RESTAURANT   *a restaurant.* A refueling station for the body. MWCD: 1827. Source: RESTAURANT. A *restaurant* is lit. a place for "restoring" the body (fr. the pres. part. of Fr. *restaurer* "to restore"). The name was first used for an eating establishment in France in the late-18th cent. (LA: 1782), when a Parisian cook began serving food to paying customers at separate tables. From France, the term passed directly to America, where it was applied first to a small coffee shop and then to a full-service dining establishment, both in New York City and both named for the Swiss brothers who founded them: Delmonico's (1831–1923). However, in most other large cities the finest "restaurants" were located in hotels (where they were called *dining rooms*), an arrangement that was convenient for the hotel guests but not as convenient for the nonguests, who found it necessary to dress up for every meal. In the 20th cent., *restaurant* became the generic term for all eating establishments that permit members of the general public to purchase meals and eat them on the spot—i.e., that are not simply *take-out* (MWCD: 1965) or *carryout* (MWCD: 1965) shops. Consequently, buffets are "restaurants," as are cafeterias, diners, eateries, grills, hash houses, inns, joints, lunchrooms, and parlors. Restaurants can be found on trains (*dining cars*) and ships (*dining salons*); however, the cabin of an airplane does not automatically become a restaurant when food is served, although your car *does* become a part of the restaurant when you visit a *drive-in* (MWCD: 1937). When you attend a *catered* affair (MWCD: 1600), you eat food that may have been prepared in a kitchen miles away. To *cater* to someone else's tastes or whims is to satisfy them, regardless of your personal feelings. DAFD.

REUBEN (SANDWICH)   *See* Dagwood Sandwich.

RHUBARB   *a rhubarb.* A heated argument; a noisy controversy. Source: RHU-BARB. MWCD: 15th cent. The modern *rhubarb*, as at a meeting of the governing body of almost any organization, is tame compared with the earlier sense of the word. In the early-20th cent., a *rhubarb* was a brawl among baseball players (and coaches and umpires), during a game, in which participants were often roughed up or seriously injured. In other words, they acted like "barbarians," which is precisely what the *barb* in *rhubarb* orig. meant: Gk. *rha* "rhubarb" + *barbaron* "barbarian"—Lat. *rhabarbarum* "barbarian rhubarb." The baseball rhubarb was descended, in turn, from the tamest rhubarb of all: the use of the word itself in the theater in the late-19th cent. It seems that there was something about the word's sound that made it perfect for simulating a crowd muttering to each other, either onstage or off. The audience couldn't tell what they were saying—and that was the whole idea—but they could sense that they were upset about something. Later, in the early-20th cent., the trick was employed in films and on radio and television: "Just say *rhubarb*, over and over again." Botanically, rhubarb is a vegetable; but horticulturally it is treated as a fruit. The only part of the plant that is used is the long stalk, which turns from green to red as it matures. (The huge green leaves are poisonous.) However, because the stalks are so tart, they must either be cooked with plenty of sugar in a compote or baked with sweeter fruit (such as strawberries) in a pie. Rhubarb is such a popular ingredient in pies that it is sometimes called *pieplant* (MWCD: ca. 1847). CE; DAFD; DAS; EWPO; FLC; MDWPO; NSOED; PT; THT; WNWCD.

RICE PAPER   Edible cooking paper. MWCD: 1832. Source: RICE. MWCD: 13th cent. Rice paper isn't really paper, and it isn't really made of rice. It is so called because it is thin, flat, and translucent, like waxed paper, and it resembles real paper that is made out of rice straw. Rice paper is made from the pith of a rice-paper plant, mixed with water, rolled, and dried. It is used for wrapping foods before deep-frying them and as a no-stick lining for baking sheets. (It sticks to the baked goods but can be eaten along with them.) Real rice is grown in paddies in East Asia and Southeast Asia, as it was in the Carolina and Virginia colonies in the 17th and 18th cents. However, Thomas Jefferson brought back a rice from Italy in the late-18th cent. that required no flooding and led to the expansion of rice cultivation in most of the Southern states during the 19th cent. *Wild rice* (MWCD: 1748) existed in America when the colonists arrived, but it was not a true rice, and it was not really wild, having been cultivated by the Native Americans for some time. Besides *wild rice*, this aquatic grass was called by such names as *Indian rice* (LA: 1843) and *water rice* (LA: 1817). What do you do if you run out of rice? You use a *ricer* (MWCD: 1886) to make ricelike particles by pressing food such as boiled potatoes through a perforated screen. What do you throw at the wedding couple as they leave the church? Not rice, because pigeons—and other birds—eat the kernels, the kernels swell in the birds' crops, and the birds die. DAFD; FLC. *Compare* Onionskin.

RICER   *See* Rice Paper.

RICOTTA   *See* Cottage-cheese Thighs.

RIDE THE GRAVY TRAIN   *to ride the gravy train*. To have it "made"; to be living on easy street. HDAS: 1917. Source: GRAVY. MWCD: 14th cent. The savory sauce called *gravy* is either (1) the juices remaining in the pan after cooking meat, or (2) meat juices and seasonings combined with milk and thickened with flour. It is not a primary food but a condiment, poured over meat, mashed potatoes, and vegetables to enhance their flavor—and perhaps hide their imperfections. The superficial nature of gravy has led to its metaphorical sense of something— such as money, a position, or an award—that is obtained without working for it or even expecting it (DAFD; ca. 1900). It is *pure gravy*: a bonus, a gift, a lagniappe, pennies from heaven (NSOED: early-20th cent.). What you work for is meat and potatoes: *Everything else is gravy*. The metaphor *gravy train* (HDAS; 1914) is a combination of *gravy*, in the sense of "easy living," and *train* (of the railroad variety). It orig. referred to an "easy run," with little to do and good pay for doing it. By another metaphorical step, *to ride the gravy train* equates the train with life, and the easy work with a position of luxury. Naturally, everyone would like to *get on the gravy train* and snare these comforts, but some people have to settle for a *gravy boat*: a boat-shaped pitcher used for serving gravy. AID; CE; CI; DAFD; DAS; DC; DEI; EWPO; FLC; HB; HND; MS; PT.

RIPE   Advanced, appropriate, mature, mellow, odoriferous, offensive, prepared. Source: RIPE. MWCD: O.E. A fruit or vegetable is "ripe" when it has fully matured and is ready to be picked and eaten. Some products, such as tomatoes, ripen on the vine, whereas others, such as pears, must be picked green and allowed to ripen on the shelf. Timing is everything. A person is *ripe for the picking* when he/she is just asking to be "fleeced"; a bank is *ripe for the picking* when it is just asking to be robbed; and a corporation is *ripe for the picking* when it is just asking to be taken over. Instead of saying "when the time is *right*" (to take action), we say "when the *time is ripe*," as if time were a green olive that we were patiently waiting to turn black. Shakespeare was one of the first authors to use this expression (albeit minus *the*) in *Henry IV, Part I* (ca. 1598), Act I, Scene 3. Thomas Percy, Earl of Worcester, says to his relative, Henry Percy ("Hotspur"): "Cousin, farewell. No further go in this / Than I by letters shall direct your course. / *When time is ripe*, which will be suddenly, / I'll steal to Glendover" [italics added]. Like fruit and vegetables, cheese is said to be *ripe* (or "mellow") when it has been aged (or "cured") and has developed a proper body, color, flavor, odor, and texture; and beef is said to be *ripe* when it has been aged (in the cooler) and has developed a proper flavor and tenderness. Young women are said to be *ripe* when they begin to fill out and "blossom"; both young women and young men are said to smell *ripe* when they come off the basketball floor; both are exposed to *ripe* language on the big and little screens; and both expect to live to a *ripe old age*. AID; CE; CI; DAI; DAS; DC; DEI; HND.

RIPE FOR THE PICKING   *See* Ripe.

RIPE OLD AGE   *See* Ripe.

ROAD APPLE   *See* Apple.

ROAD HOG   *See* Hog.

ROAD PIZZA   *See* Pizza Pie.

ROAST   *See* Toast (n) (2).

ROCK CANDY   *See* Candy.

ROCK SALT   *See* Old Salt.

ROCKY MOUNTAIN OYSTERS   *See* Lamb Fries.

ROLLING IN DOUGH   *See* Dough.

ROMAINE LETTUCE   *See* Lettuce.

ROOM AND BOARD   *See* Boardinghouse Reach.

ROOT BEER   *See* Moxie.

ROTTEN APPLE   *See* One Rotten Apple Spoils the Barrel.

ROTTEN EGG   *a rotten egg.* A despicable person (usu. male). HDAS: 1848. Source: EGG. MWCD: 14th cent. Hens' eggs give off an offensive odor if they are allowed to remain too long without refrigeration. Despicable adult males do not give off an offensive odor, but their deeds "stink to high heaven." Younger males are usu. called "stinkers" rather than *rotten eggs*, but the expression *Last one in is a rotten egg!* is popular in their play. It is uttered by one child in the group as a challenge to the other children to dive into the water, get on the bus, climb on a carnival ride, etc. The last one to do so—and everyone knows which one that will be—will be reminded that he is a *rotten egg.* DAS; DAI; LA; SA. *See also* Bad Egg; One Rotten Apple Spoils the Barrel.

ROTTEN TO THE CORE   *See* One Rotten Apple Spoils the Barrel.

ROUGHAGE   *See* Rabbit Food.

ROUGH AS A COB   *See* Corn.

ROYAL ICING   *See* Icing on the Cake.

RUBBER CHICKEN   *See* Rubber-chicken Circuit.

RUBBER-CHICKEN CIRCUIT   *the rubber-chicken circuit.* The series of speeches and lectures required of political candidates, authors of best sellers, and other celebrities. Source: CHICKEN. MWCD: 14th cent. A *rubber chicken* (DAFD: 1950s) is a rubberized version of a dead, plucked chicken, with head and feet attached in the anatomically correct locations but neck and legs much longer than usual. Comics used to use such stage props in vaudeville and burlesque shows, and clowns still use them in the circus. In the opinion of politicians, authors, and other celebrities, the meals served at the fundraisers and banquets always seem to feature chicken (because it's the cheapest), and the chicken always tastes rubbery—like a rubber chicken. SA.

RUB IT IN   *See* Salt away.

RUB SALT INTO SOMEONE'S WOUNDS   *See* Salt away.

RUMINATE   *See* Chew Your Cud.

RUMOR MILL   *See* Grist for the Mill.

RUMP   *your rump.* Your bottom. Source: RUMP. MWCD: 15th cent. The use of *rump* as a name for the human buttocks is almost as old as its use for the upper hindquarters of a bovine. The rump of a steer is the largest part of the *round*, which includes all of the flesh on the rear legs. A "rump roast" is a triangular section of meat cut from the rump, and "rump steaks" are "fillets of beef" sliced from the rump roast. *Rump* has also been used to refer to what is left after everything else has been removed, as was the case with the British *Rump Parliament*, which was purged in 1648 but allowed to function for five more years in its reduced state. (It was disbanded in 1653, recalled in 1659, and disbanded again in 1660; and that was the end of the Rump Parliament.) ATWS; FLC; SA; WNWCD.

RUMP PARLIAMENT   *See* Rump.

RUN-OF-THE-MILL   *See* Through the Mill.

RUSK   *See* Biscuit.

RUSSIAN TEA CAKE   *See* Mexican Wedding Cake.

RUSTLE UP   *See* See What I Can Rustle up.

RUTABAGA   *See* You Can't Get Blood from a Turnip.

SACCHARINE (adj.)   Overly sweet, friendly, or sentimental. Source: SAC-CHARINE (adj). MWCD: ca. 1674. The adj. *saccharine*, whose literal meaning is simply "sugarlike," or "sweet as sugar," is derived from the Lat. noun *saccharum* "sugar," which derives from Gk. *sakcharon* and Skt. *śarkarā*, both of which also meant "sugar." The metaphorical use of *saccharine* to characterize behavior that is overly sweet (nauseating), overly friendly (ingratiating), or overly sentimental (mawkish) is an American achievement, as is the coining of the word *saccharin* (MWCD: 1885) for the world's first artificial sweetener. This *sugar substitute* was discovered by accident in 1879 in a chemistry laboratory at Johns Hopkins University, but the name was not applied until six years later. In spite of the fact that saccharin is three-to-five-hundred times as sweet as sugar, contains no calories, and has been used in diabetic diets, questions about its safety have led the FDA to require warning labels on all foods containing it. CE; DAFD; FLC; WNWCD.

SALAD   *a salad*. A heterogeneous mixture: a hodgepodge; a potpourri. NSOED: early-17th cent. Source: SALAD. MWCD: 14th cent. The original salad was not a mixture at all but simply lettuce, seasoned with *salt* (Lat. *sal*), from which the name derives. The first new ingredient came in the 16th cent., when *salad oil* (MWCD: 1537) was added to flavor the pieces of lettuce and hold them together. The first combination of lettuce, salad oil, vegetables, eggs, meats, and cheeses appeared in the form of the 17th cent. *salmagundi* (MWCD: ca. 1674), which was popular in Colonial America. The modern version of salmagundi is prob. the *chef's salad*, an entrée that contains approx. the same ingredients except for the dressing. Both *salad* and *salmagundi* now function like *potpourri*: "a hodgepodge or heterogeneous mixture." Today, the *salad bar* (MWCD: 1973), a self-service counter of various (usu.) cold ingredients, is an important part of the dining experience, even at midscale restaurants. However, the American salad no longer need contain lettuce (or salt!) at all; *macaroni salad* and *taco salad* don't, and the sandwich fillings called *chicken salad, egg salad,* and *ham salad* don't either. *Fruit salad* need not even contain fruit (the term is a metaphor for the ribbons worn on the left chest of an American serviceman or woman—HDAS: 1943), and *word salad* is a metaphor for "gobbledygook." DAFD; FLC; MDWPO; PT. *See also* Hold the Mayo!; Salad Days.

SALAD BAR   *See* Salad.

SALAD DAYS   A time of youth; a time of happiness and prosperity. MWCD: 1606. Source: SALAD. MWCD: 14th cent. The term *salad days* occurs in Shakespeare's *Antony and Cleopatra* (Act I, Scene 5), when Cleopatra, now head-over-heels in love with Mark Antony, refers to the time of her youthful affair with Julius Caesar as "my *salad days,* when I was green in judgment, cold in blood" [italics added]. Cleopatra means that she was impetuous and fearless at that earlier time, and Shakespeare employs the word *green* to liken her to a young plant. Under other circumstances, *salad days* can refer to a time in a your life (not necessarily youth) when things were better than they are now—a period of great success and acclaim, when you were sitting on top of the world, and the money was flowing in. Now you are *beyond your salad days,* but at least you still have pleasant memories. The word *salad* developed in O.Prov. as the past part., *salada,* of the verb *salar* "to salt," a word that was not present in Classical Latin. *Salada* then passed into It. as *insalate* and into Sp. as *ensalada,* both words referring to "salad" only, and into Fr. as *salade* and Ger. as *Salat,* both meaning either "salad" or "lettuce." In Mod. Eng., *salad* denotes primarily a cold dish of lettuce leaves tossed with sliced garden "vegetables" (such as cucumbers and tomatoes) and covered with oil or *salad dressing* (MWCD: ca. 1839). The popular *Caesar salad* (DAFD: 1924) is not named after Cleopatra's former lover, Julius Caesar, but for Caesar Cardini, an Italian chef and restaurant owner in Tijuana, Mexico, who combined romaine lettuce with olive oil, Worcestershire sauce, lemon juice, garlic, Parmesan cheese, croutons, and a coddled egg. (Anchovies were added to the recipe by others.) BDPF; CE; CI; DAFD; DC; EWPO; FLC; HND; LCRH; MDWPO; NSOED; PT. *See also* Salad.

SALAD DRESSING   *See* Salad Days.

SALAMI   *See* Sausage Dog.

SALARY   *See* Salt of the Earth.

SALISBURY STEAK   An individual-size meat loaf. MWCD: 1897. Source: STEAK. MWCD: 15th cent. *Salisbury steak* does not come from Salisbury, England, and it is not really a steak. The dish is named for James H. Salisbury, an

English health food advocate. What Salisbury advocated was that people eat ground beef—enriched and enhanced with milk, eggs, bread crumbs, and seasonings and fried or broiled in the form of a patty—three times a day. The practice caught on in America, which was ripe for food and eating fads at the turn of the 19th cent. Both Salisbury steak and hamburger steak are thought to have been the forerunners of the modern hamburger patty. During WWI, when businesses were afraid to make any mention of Germany in their advertising, the term *Salisbury steak* was used as a convenient substitute for *hamburger steak* (named after Hamburg, Germany). Now, hamburger steak is usu. advertised as *chopped steak* in restaurants, and Salisbury steak is touted as a personal-size meat loaf. Another steak with a proper name is *Swiss steak* (MWCD: 1924): pounded round steak coated with flour, braised on both sides, covered with ground vegetables (carrots, onions, etc.), and baked. Swiss steak is not a dish from Switzerland but a steak that has been tenderized by pounding or rolling (called "swissing") before baking. In England, it is called "smothered steak," presumably because the meat is smothered with vegetables. The word *steak* comes fr. O.N. *steik*, meaning "stick" or "stake," suggesting that the original *steak* (MWCD: 15th cent.) was an integral slice of meat, like Swiss steak, rather than chopped-up meat, like Salisbury steak. DAFD; DEOD; EWPO; FLC; IHAT; LA; MDWPO; PT. *Compare* Fletcherize.

SALMAGUNDI   *See* Salad.

SALMON LOAF   *See* Meat Loaf.

SALSA   *See* Sauce.

SALT (n)   *See* Old Salt.

SALT (v)   *See* Salt Away.

SALT AND PEPPER   *See* Salt-and-pepper.

SALT-AND-PEPPER   Having a mixture of white and black—or light and dark—colors. MWCD: 1915. Source: SALT; PEPPER. MWCD: O.E. White salt and black pepper are the two main seasoning agents in American homes and restaurants. (In lunch-counter jargon, the salt and pepper shakers were called *Mike and Ike*, or *The twins*.) The compound adj. *salt-and-pepper* has been used to describe (1) clothes (e.g., a *salt-and-pepper* suit—a suit with a check or hourdstooth weave having alternating white and black colors); (2) hair (*salt-and-pepper* hair—gray or graying hair having a mixture of white and black strands); and (3) relationships (a *salt-and-pepper* marriage—a white woman married to a black man, or a black woman married to a white man). In addition, a black-and-white police car can be referred to as either a *black and white* or a *salt and pepper*. However, the original order of the seasonings was *pepper* and *salt* (as it is today in Brit.

Eng.), as in the adj. *pepper-and-salt* (MWCD: 1774), which was prob. a translation of Fr. *poivre et sel* "pepper and salt," a Mod. Fr. metaphor for "gray-haired." BDPF; DAS; IHAT; NSOED; PT.

SALT AWAY   *to salt something away*. To put money (etc.) aside for future use. MWCD: ca. 1890. Source: SALT (v). MWCD: O.E. Keeping money safe for later use is like preserving and storing food for future meals. One ancient method of preserving meat or fish was to rub it with salt and/or pack it in salt or salt brine. *Salt pork*, for example, one of the staples on ocean-going sailing ships, consisted of pork-belly fat cured with salt, which had a shelf (or barrel) life of an entire voyage; and *pickled herring*, i.e., herring that had been dry-salted and then cured in salt brine, must have lasted just as long. Salt had another purpose on board ship: to rub into a sailor's wounds in order to kill infection and "preserve" the sailor's life. However, the modern expression *to rub salt into someone's wounds* means to add insult to injury: to kick someone while they're down. The allusion is to the extreme pain that salt causes when it touches raw flesh—almost as bad as dousing with alcohol or cauterizing with a hot poker (and it lasts a lot longer). The shortened phrase *to rub it in* is not so violent; it simply means to remind someone of an embarrassing mistake he/she made at the last office party. A good place to *salt away* your valuables might be an abandoned salt mine—constant 50° temperature, low humidity, no bugs or vermin. Money ought to last there for a long time. AID; BDPF; CE; CI; DAFD; DAI; DAP; DEI; FLC; HND; MS; NSOED; PT. *See also* Old Salt.

SALTCELLAR   *See* Salt of the Earth.

SALT HAS LOST ITS SAVOR   *See* Salt of the Earth.

SALTINES   *See* Drive Someone Crackers.

SALT MINES   *See* Old Salt.

SALT OF THE EARTH   *the salt of the earth*. The light of the world. Source: SALT. MWCD: O.E. In the Sermon on the Mount (Matthew, chapters 5–7), following the eight Beatitudes (the "Blessed are's"), Jesus refers to his disciples as *the salt of the earth* (5:13), implying that they are like the salt that is mined from the earth: beneficial, dependable, irreplaceable, invaluable. A world without salt (the disciples), or in which *the salt has lost its savor*, would be like a world without light, where the candles are all hidden under bushel baskets. Salt was so valuable in Ancient Rome that soldiers were first given a ration of salt and then, later, money for buying salt: "salt money," Lat. *salarium*, today's *salary* (MWCD: 13th cent.). To be *worth your salt* (DC: 1830) means to be "worth your salary," i.e., to earn your pay; and *not to be worth your salt* is not to be earning it. To *eat someone's salt* is to enjoy someone's hospitality, and *to sit above the salt* is to enjoy a higher status than others. This last expression derives from the late-medieval custom among noble families in England of placing a *saltcellar* (MWCD: 14th cent.—lit. "salt salter") in the center of a long table and using it as a dividing line between the family members and the hired help. On the occasion of a royal banquet, the saltcellar became a dividing line between the guests of higher status, who sat with the host and hostess, i.e., *above the salt*, and those of lower status, who sat *below the salt*. AID; BDPF; CE; CI; DAI; DAP; DAS; DEI; EWPO; HB; HI; HND; LCRH; MDWPO; MS; NSOED; PT; THT.

SALT PORK   *See* Salt Away.

SALT WATER TAFFY   *See* Taffy.

SALTY   *See* Old Salt.

SALVER   *See* First Come, First Served.

SAND IN YOUR CRAW   *See* Stick in Your Craw.

SANDWICH (n)   *a sandwich.* A slice of meat, cheese, etc., between two slices of bread. Source: SANDWICH (n). MWCD: 1762. The *sandwich* is named after the Fourth Earl of Sandwich, who, as First Lord of the Admiralty, also gave his (title) name to the Sandwich Islands (now called the *Hawai'ian Islands* or *Hawai'i*). The Earl, John Montague, was an avid card player, and during an all-nighter at the gaming table in 1762 he ordered so many of the as-yet-unnamed snacks that they came to be identified with him. One of the advantages of the *sandwich* was that the bread protected his hands—and cards—from the greasy, juicy filling inside the bread, illustrating that the sandwich, in the 18th cent., was already a *finger food* (q.v.). The Earl's sandwich was prob. made with slices of roast beef between slices of bread, but the most popular "sandwich" in America is now the *hamburger sandwich* (or *hamburger*, or *burger*), made with ground beef in a kaiser roll, followed at some distance by the *submarine sandwich* (or *submarine*, or *sub*), made with a meat, cheese, and vegetable filling in a small loaf of French or Italian bread. The definition of *sandwich* has also been expanded to include (1) the *club sandwich* (MWCD: 1903), sometimes called a *double-decker*, which consists of one sandwich (minus its lower slice of bread) on top of another, each containing slices of chicken or turkey and ham between slices of (usu. toasted) bread (three slices altogether); and (2) the *open-face(d) sandwich*, which is served inside-out, i.e., with the two (usu. toasted) slices of bread separated, covered with the sliced meat and vegetable contents, and left to the diner to put together. For some reason, a *hot beef* (or pork or turkey) *sandwich*, consisting of meat between untoasted slices of white bread, cut diagonally, separated by a scoop of mashed potatoes, and covered altogether with the appropriate gravy, is also called an *open-face(d) sandwich*. DAFD; EWPO; FLC; IHAT; LA; MDWPO; NSOED; PT. *See also* Jam Sandwich.

SANDWICH (v)   *to sandwich between or around*. To place object A between two object Bs; to place two object Bs around one object A. MWCD: 1861. Source: SANDWICH. MWCD: 1762. A sandwich is made by *sandwiching* a slice of meat (etc.) *between* two slices of bread, or by *sandwiching* two slices of bread *around* a slice of meat (etc.). It all depends on whether you are focusing on the meat or the bread. Metaphorically, anything that is placed between two of something else is *sandwiched between* them, e.g., a sheet of copper between two sheets of stainless steel in the construction of a cooking pot; and two of the same things that surround one of something else are *sandwiched around* it, e.g., two three-pointers by Team A separated by a two-pointer by Team B (in basketball). A *sandwich man* (*sic*) (MWCD: 1864) is lit. and fig. *sandwiched between* the two parts of a *sandwich board* (MWCD: 1897), which is really two boards hung lengthwise, front and back, by connecting leather straps over the person's shoulders. The boards contain advertisements and menus for the restaurant or store in front of which the man is parading, and they can be set up, by themselves, in front of the business while the person is resting. You don't see many *sandwich men* or *boards* in America anymore, but the tradition is being carried on by picketers wearing printed cardboard signs fore and aft. BDPF; CE; DEI; FLC; NSOED; PT.

SANDWICH AROUND   *See* Sandwich (v).

SANDWICH BETWEEN   *See* Sandwich (v).

SANDWICH BOARD   *See* Sandwich (v).

SANDWICH BREAD   *See* Finger Sandwich.

SANDWICH COOKIE   *See* Oreo.

SANDWICH ISLANDS   *See* Sandwich (n).

SANDWICH LOAF   *See* Sandwich Bread.

SANDWICH MAN   *See* Sandwich (v).

SANDWICH MEAT   *See* Variety Meats.

SANDWICH SPREAD   *See* Sandwich Bread.

SARDINE CAN   *See* Packed like Sardines.

SASSY   *See* Saucy.

SATELLITE DISH   *See* Dish (n).

SAUCE   Impudence or impertinence; alcohol. Source: SAUCE. MWCD: 14th cent. The word *sauce* is derived fr. Lat. *salsa* "salted" (which is now the Sp. word for "sauce") and ult. fr. Lat. *sal* "salt." In medieval times, salt was used not only to preserve foods (e.g., in brine) but to mask the taste of spoiled foods (e.g., those containing meat stock). Salt is no longer the primary ingredient in sauces, which now take the form of condiments and relishes, dressings and toppings, and stewed or preserved fruit. The association of *sauce* with "rudeness" is attributable to the sharpness of the taste of some of the early sauces; and the connection between *sauce* and alcohol prob. reflects the powerful effect of some of the more recent *hot sauces*. Some examples of the alcohol-sauce connection are *sauce parlor* ("a bar"), *on the sauce* ("drinking regularly"), *hit the sauce* ("to drink heavily"), *sauced* ("drunk"), and *lost in the sauce* ("totally out of it"). BDPF; DAFD; DAI; DAS; FLC; NSOED; PT; WNWCD. *See also* Saucy.

SAUCED   *See* Sauce.

SAUCE PARLOR   *See* Sauce.

SAUCER   *See* Flying Saucer.

SAUCY   Rude; pert; smart. NSOED: early-16th cent. Source: SAUCE. MWCD: 14th cent. The adj. *saucy* is derived from the noun *sauce* "a thick, liquid condiment served with food to add to or enhance its flavor." Just as sauce spices up food, *saucy* behavior (such as impertinence or impudence), a *saucy* smile (somewhat forward and flippant), and *saucy* clothes (modern and stylish) spice up your appearance and personality. *Saucy* was first recorded in the literal sense of "having the consistency of sauce" in the early-16th cent. (MWCD: 1508), and the alternative pronunciation *sassy*, with an identical meaning, was first recorded in the mid-19th cent. The metaphorical *saucy* appeared sometime in between. CE; PT; WNWCD.

SAUERKRAUT   *See* Cabbage.

SAUSAGE DOG   *a sausage dog*. A dachshund. Source: SAUSAGE. MWCD: 15th cent. The dachshund is called a *sausage dog* because it looks like a long, fat sausage with tiny legs, a medium-size head, and a short tail. "*Do you know how sausage is made?*" "No. How?" "Don't ask." Sausage is made by grinding up lean trimmings of pork (and/or beef, lamb, veal, venison, or fowl) with fat, salt, seasonings, and preservatives; curing or smoking it; and cooking it (or not). The word *sausage* derives fr. Lat. *salsus* "salted" by way of L.Lat. *salsicia*, O.N.FR. *sausiche*, and M.E. *sausige*. Therefore, linguistically speaking, the key ingredient in sausage is not the lesser cuts of meat but the salt and other preservatives. Some sausages, such as *summer sausage*, are preserved so well that they do not even require refrigeration. Sausages that are not so well preserved may cause food poisoning such as *botulism*

(MWCD: 1887), a paralytic disease whose name is derived fr. Lat. *botulus* "sausage," presumably because it was first identified with improperly stored food of this sort. The name of one of the most popular sausages, *salami* (MWCD: 1852), is, like *sausage*, derived fr. Lat. *sal* "salt," by way of It. *salare* "to salt." Salami is different from many of the other types of sausage because although it is neither cooked nor smoked, it is safe to eat "as is." One of the best-known salami-type sausages is *pepperoni* (MWCD: 1921), which is a favorite topping for American pizza. Sausages are also very popular in eastern Europe—e.g., *kielbasa* (MWCD: ca. 1939) "Polish sausage"—and central Europe—e.g., *Bratwurst* (MWCD: ca. 1888) "fresh pork sausage" and *Knockwurst* (MWCD: ca. 1929) "smoked beef and pork sausage." DAFD; EWPO; FLC; MDWPO; PT.

SAVE YOUR BACON   *to save your bacon.* To save your career, life, marriage, reputation, skin, etc. HDAS: 1666. Source: BACON. MWCD: 14th cent. The simplest explanation for the development of this metaphorical expression is that it grew out of the custom of hanging meat, such as a slab of bacon, high in the rafters of a house or smokehouse in order to protect it from dogs and other animals. Another explanation for the transfer of *bacon* from pig to person is the existence of such expressions as "You saved my ass" and "You saved my butt." Granted, bacon comes from the side (or back) of a pig, not from the "rump"; still, the association is close—and clear—enough. However, the best explanation of all may be the definition of *bacon* in a 1725 Eng. dictionary of thieves' cant as "loot, or prize." In other words, the spoils of a successful robbery would have been lost if you had not been around to *save my bacon*. And where did the thieves get the idea of associating "booty" with *bacon*? Perhaps from the offering of a prize consisting of a side of bacon at the Dunmow Flitch, which was still going on in 1725. BDPF; CI; DEI; HI; MS; NSOED; SA. *See also* Bring Home the Bacon.

SAY A MOUTHFUL   *See* You Said a Mouthful.

SAY CHEESE   *Say "Cheese"!* Smile for the camera! NSOED: mid-20th cent. Source: CHEESE. MWCD: O.E. Photography has been around since 1839, but the first smile was not photographed until the 20th cent. Apparently no one could figure out what to do to make the subjects show their teeth. Then an Eng.-speaking photographer hit upon the idea of telling them to moisten their lips and *say cheese*, which spread their lips and exposed their ivories. It worked, for Eng.-speakers; and photographers of persons speaking other languages soon worked out their own magic words. Another pronouncement of *cheese* occurs when a crook, about to be caught committing a crime, tells his/her fellow crooks: *Cheese it!* (LA: 1870s)—i.e., "Let's get out of here! The cops are coming!" Before being adopted by criminals, and altered to suit their own purposes, *Cheese it!* was a command used by the police (MWCD: ca. 1811). It meant something like "Stop it! or "Cease it!"—the latter being the probable source rather than the milk product. BDPF; DAS; EWPO; HDAS; MDWPO. *Compare* Say When.

SAY WHEN!   *See* Cream in My Coffee.

SCALLION   *See* Onionskin Paper.

SCARF DOWN   *See* Devour.

SCAVENGER   *See* Bottom Feeder.

SCHMALTZ   Sticky sentimentality. MWCD: 1935. Source: CHICKEN; FAT. *Schmaltz* is the Ger. spelling of a Yid. word, *shmaltz*, which has the same general meaning as the Ger. word, "rendered animal fat," but refers more specif. to "chicken fat." In kosher cooking, chicken fat, which is yellow, is used as a substitute for butter, either as a lard or a spread, whenever meat is part of the meal. The fact that chicken fat is sticky, mushy, and yellow prob. also led to its association with *corny*—or overly sentimental—writing, music, art, film, and television. Any of these endeavors that fits this bill is considered *schmaltzy*. DAFD; DAS; EWPO; FLC; LCRH; MDWPO; NSOED; SA.

SCHMALTZY   *See* Schmaltz.

SCOOP   *See* Ice-cream Cone.

SCOOP NECK   *See* Ice-cream Cone.

SCOTCH RABBIT   *See* Welsh Rabbit.

SCOTCH WOODCOCK   Scrambled eggs on toast with anchovy paste. MWCD: 1879. Source: EGG. *Scotch woodcock* is a glamorous name for a rather pedestrian meal (except for the anchovy paste!). A woodcock is a small game bird with a large breast of tasty dark meat. Such birds are very difficult to catch, and it would take more than one of them to make a meal. The name is reminiscent of *Welsh rabbit* (q.v.), i.e., toast covered with melted cheese and seasoned. Celtic dishes seem to receive more than their share of humorous names in English cookbooks. FLC; MDWPO.

SCRAMBLED EGGS   The gold oak leaves (Brit.) or gold braid (Amer.) on the bill of the cap of a high-ranking military officer. Source: EGG. MWCD: 14th cent. The golden leaves or braids were called *scrambled eggs* because they resembled the food in both color (yellow) and shape (jumbled). The color of the decorations also led to the coining of the term *brass hat* (MWCD: 1893) for a top-ranking officer and the term *top brass* for the collective officers of such rank. (*Fruit salad* is a term for the service and combat ribbons worn on the left *chest* by both officers and enlisted persons.) The scrambling of eggs—i.e., the stirring of an egg-milk mix while frying—may have led to the use of *scramble* in the expression *to scram-*

ble signals, i.e., to distort electronic transmissions for security reasons. The signals are *unscrambled* (q.v.) for legitimate customers. The "signal" that a lunch-counter waitress [sic] used to call out to the cook for an order of scrambled eggs was *Wreck a pair!* Punchdrunk boxers are sometimes described as having *scrambled eggs* for brains. BDPF; DAS; MDWPO.

SCRAMBLE SIGNALS   *See* Scrambled Eggs.

SCRAPE THE BOTTOM OF THE BARREL   *to scrape the bottom of the barrel*. To be forced to use whatever is left, even if it is of unsatisfactory quality. Source: BARREL. MWCD: 14th cent. The expression is very old (HND cites Cicero), but it can't be older than Chaucer's time in English. The container in question is prob. a wine barrel, at the bottom of which are the dregs that have settled there over the years. These sediments are compared to the least desirable products of nature or society, which, if it were a matter of choosing sides, would be the last ones picked. AID; CI; DAI; DAS; DEI; MS.

SCRAPE UP   *See* See What I Can Dig up.

SCRATCH BREAD   *See* Make from Scratch.

SCRATCH CAKE   *See* Make from Scratch.

SEA BISCUITS   *See* Biscuit.

SEA COOK   *See* Son of a Sea Cook.

SEAFOOD COCKTAIL   *See* Shrimp Cocktail.

SEA SALT   *See* Old Salt.

SEASON (v)   *to season*. To make more suitable or agreeable. Source: SEASON (v). MWCD: 14th cent. The verb *to season* (fr. M.Fr. *assaisonner* "to ripen") is derived fr. the noun *season* (fr. M.Fr. *saison*, fr. Lat. *sation* "the action of sowing"). The literal meaning of modern *season* (v) is "to add condiments, herbs, and spices to food in order to improve its flavor or taste" (NSOED: late-M.E.); the literal meaning of modern *season* (n) is "the time at which fruits, grains, vegetables, etc., are removed from the plant or tree for use as food" (NSOED: M.E.). Some of the more popular *seasonings* (MWCD: 1580) also come in the form of a liquid (vinegar), grains (salt), and flakes (pepper). Just as *seasonings* add savor to food, *seasoning* can add life to cast-iron pots and pans (coated with vegetable oil and heated in a 350° oven for approx. one hour) and lumber (aged, cured, dried, or otherwise treated). More abstractly, advice can be made more agreeable if it is *seasoned* with sympathy, a lecture can be made more interesting if it is *seasoned* with humor, and discipline can be made more effective if it is *seasoned* with kindness. Baseball players are sent to the minor leagues for *seasoning*, i.e., improving their all-around skills; and if they graduate to the majors, they may someday become *seasoned veterans*. FLC; WNWCD.

SEASONED VETERAN   *See* Season (v).

SEASONING   *See* Season (v).

SECOND BANANA   *See* Top Banana.

SEEDED   *See* Go to Seed.

SEEDY   *See* Go to Seed.

SEEFOOD DIET   *a seefood (sic) diet.* An unrestricted diet—i.e., no diet at all. Source: SEAFOOD (MWCD: 1836); DIET (MWCD: 13th cent.). *Seefood* is a play on the word *seefood*, which refers to *fish* (with interior skeletons), *shellfish* (with exterior skeletons), and *cephalopods* (with no skeletons at all) that live in the *sea*. A regular *seafood diet* consists of the eating of flesh only from those creatures and not from any others. A *seefood diet*, in contrast, consists of a single prescription: "You *see food*, you *eat* it." The word *diet*, which orig. meant "a regular provision or consumption of food and drink" is now also used metaphorically to mean "a regular provision of pitches" (The pitcher threw the batter a *steady diet* of curve balls) or "a regular consumption of entertainment" (The man put his date on a *steady diet* of clubs and shows.) *See also* Glutton for Punishment.

SEERSUCKER   Light, striped, puckered fabric. MWCD; 1722. Source: MILK; SUGAR. *Seersucker* has nothing to do with seeing or sucking. It is derived from Hindi *śīrsakar* "milk and sugar," which in turn is a modification of Persian *shir-o-shakkar* (same meaning). Milk and sugar have nothing to do with "puckering," either, but that's what the compound meant when the British brought it home from India in the early-18th cent. The fabric was orig. linen but later cotton and rayon. It is still popular for summer suits, esp. in alternating blue and white or beige and white stripes. EWPO; NSOED. *Compare* Goatsucker.

SEETHE   *See* Simmer down.

SEETHING INSIDE   *See* Reach the Boiling Point.

SEE WHAT I CAN DIG UP   *I'll see what I can dig—rustle, or scrape—up.* I'll see what I can throw together for dinner. Source: COOK (v). This statement is the typical reply of a homemaker to the typical question of a spouse arriving home from work: "What's for dinner?" (The reply *really* means "Let's go out to a restaurant.") When the food is ready to eat, the cook says *Dig in!* Literally, *to dig up* (MWCD: 14th cent.) means to "unearth," and the kind of food that could be unearthed is either vegetables, which normally grow in the ground, or meat that has been buried there. Early humans prob. learned the trick of burying meat to preserve it from wild dogs and cats. In the northern climes, both wolves and mountain lions bury part of their kill in the snow for future use. *Rustle up* implies a search for meat, specif. beef, and derives from the rustling, or stealing, of steers in the Wild West. "I'll see what I can *scrape* up" implies that the dinner will consist of leftovers, further encouraging a trip to the restaurant. AID; DAI; SA.

SEE WHAT I CAN RUSTLE UP   *See* See What I Can Dig up.

SEE WHAT I CAN SCRAPE UP   *See* See What I Can Dig up.

SELL LIKE HOTCAKES   *to sell like hotcakes*. To sell fast and in great quantities. DC: 1860. Source: PANCAKE. *Hotcake* (MWCD: 1633) is one of the numerous alternative names for the generic *pancake*. In the mid-19th cent., before the appearance of the hot dog, hamburger, ice-cream cone, and pizza pie, hotcakes were the best-selling hot food at carnivals, circuses, and fairs. They sold so fast that they became the basis for the metaphor: "How's the new model doing?" "It's *selling like hotcakes*." BDPF; CE; CI; DEI; EWPO; HND; MDWPO. *See also* Hot off the Griddle.

SELL THE FAMILY SILVER   *See* Silverware.

SELL YOUR BIRTHRIGHT FOR A MESS OF POTTAGE   *See* Fine Mess.

SERVE UP   *See* First Come, First Served.

SET A GOOD TABLE   *See* Set the Table.

SET THE TABLE   *to set the table for someone or something*. To lay the groundwork or prepare the way for someone or something. Source: TABLE. MWCD: O.E. Lit., to "set the table" is to cover it with a linen tablecloth; supply each "place" with the proper "setting" of dishware, silverware, glassware, and linenware; and furnish the table with butter plates and knives, salt and pepper shakers, bowls of condiments and sauces, and large serving plates and bowls. From this activity has come the expression "to *set the table* for someone or something," i.e., to prepare the way, or lay the groundwork, as the introducer does for a speaker at a banquet, or as the first three men in a baseball lineup try to do (by filling the bases) for the "cleanup" hitter (who bats fourth). The speaker takes over once *the table is set*, and so does the cleanup hitter, who is expected to hit a grand-slam home run under these circumstances. *Another table with the same setting* refers to a "Here-we-go-again" situation: a different occasion for the same old arguments.

At the end of an elegant dinner, one might make the compliment, "He/she *sets a good table*," i.e., he/she knows how to follow the rules and serve a magnificent meal. When the guests have left, it is time to *clear the table*, i.e., to remove everything, except perhaps the tablecloth, from the table, an expression that has become a metaphor for *starting over from scratch* (q.v.). AID; BDPF; DEI.

SETTLE SOMEONE'S HASH *See* Hash (n).

SET YOUR TEETH ON EDGE *to set your teeth on edge*. For something to sound, or taste, so unpleasant that it causes you great discomfort; i.e., it lit. causes you to close your eyes, grit your teeth, and perhaps even utter a hissing sound (on ingressive air). Source: SOUR (adj.). Historically, this phrase is associated with sour taste, partic. of *sour grapes* (q.v.). In the Old Testament book of Jeremiah (31:29–30), God promises to improve the lot of the children of Israel and Judah: (29) "In those days they shall say no more, the fathers have *eaten a sour grape*, and the children's *teeth are set on edge*." (30) "But every one shall die for his own iniquity: every man that *eateth the sour grapes*, his *teeth shall be set on edge*." In Shakespeare's *Henry IV, Part I* (ca. 1598), Act III, Scene 2, Hotspur states that halting verse has the same effect on him: "I had rather hear a brazen canstick turn'd [a brass candlestick turned on a lathe] / Or a dry wheel grate on the axletree,/ And that would *set my teeth nothing on edge*, / Nothing so much as mincing poetry" [italics added]. Currently, the fruit usu. associated with *setting your teeth on edge* is the lemon, and the sound is that of fingernails scraping an old-fashioned slate blackboard. AID; BDPF; CI; DAI; HI; LCRH; MS. *See also* Sour Grapes.

SEVILLE ORANGE *See* Orange.

SHAKE *See* Milk Shake.

SHALLOT *See* Onionskin Paper.

SHATTER LIKE AN EGGSHELL *See* Walk on Eggs.

SHAVETERIA *See* Cafeteria.

SHELF LIFE The extent of someone's popularity or marketability. Source: SHELF. MWCD: O.E. The notion of *shelf life* comes from the grocery store, where the grocer has to know approx. how long a product can remain on the shelf without spoiling, rotting, molding, mildewing, souring, fermenting, etc. The grocer knows that some foods have a long shelf life (e.g., canned, bottled, or frozen foods), some have a medium shelf life (such as boxed, bagged, or refrigerated foods), and some have a very short shelf life (e.g., uwrapped bread, rolls, cookies, etc.). It is the same with people. Everyone can expect fifteen minutes of fame, but very few of us can expect to remain in the spotlight for fifteen months, or even weeks. Most new actors, artists, authors, dancers, musicians, singers, etc., will have a very short shelf life: They will be *flashes in the pan* (q.v.). What does it take to have a long shelf life? A good work ethic, a good agent, and a lot of luck. In another *shelf* metaphor, a project or proposal is *shelved* when it is abandoned, postponed, or set aside for an indefinite period. In this case, spending a lot of time on the shelf appears to be a *bad* thing—until you consider that preparing for the future can be a pretty good idea. Squirrels *squirrel away* nuts for the winter; i.e., they store them in hollow trees in expectation of the time when the ground will be frozen and the nuts that they have buried will no longer be available. (Smart.) ATWS; DAFD; DAI; DEI; MS; NSOED; SA.

SHELL (n)   *See* Shell out.

SHELL (v)   *See* Shell out.

SHELL COMPANY   *See* Shell out.

SHELL GAME   *See* Shell out.

SHELL OUT   *to shell out money* (etc.). To pay out cash for something. MWCD: 1801. Source: Shell (v). MWCD: 1562. *Shelling out money* derives from shelling beans or peas from their pods, i.e., removing the food from the covering in which it has grown—although bean pods and pea pods are also used as food. This process is the basis for *shelling out money* from your purse or wallet, i.e., removing the cash (orig. coins) from its cloth or leather covering. The verb *shell* also applies to shelling peanuts, i.e., removing the nuts from their shells, and to shelling corn, i.e., removing the kernels from the cob to which they are attached. (Removing the leafy covering from an ear of corn is called *shucking* it, and the verb *shuck* is also applied to removing the body of an oyster or clam from its shell.) The noun *shell* (MWCD: O.E.) orig. referred to the hard covering of an animal, such as a crustacean, mollusk, or turtle; then it was applied to the egg of a bird or reptile; and finally it was applied to the covering of a nut or gourd. A *shell game* is a con game that was orig. played with three English walnut half-shells and one dried pea; the larger plastic "shells" now used are made to look like the nutshells. A carved *pumpkin shell* is a familiar sight at Halloween. Metaphorically, *shell* is now used in *pie shell*, *gun shell*, *racing shell*, *band shell*, and *shell company* (a phony or nonexistent company). AID; BDPF; EWPO; FLC; LCRH; SA.

SHELL OUT MONEY   *See* Shell Out.

SHELVE A PROPOSAL   *See* Shelf Life.

SHEPHERD'S PIE   *See* Porkpie Hat.

SHISH KEBAB   *See* Spit.

SHIT ON A SHINGLE   *See* Chipped Beef.

SHOOFLY PIE   *a shoofly pie.* A pie so sweet that it is like a magnet to flies. MWCD: 1926. Source: PIE. MWCD: 14th cent. Shoofly pie is of Pennsylvania "Dutch" origin, although the original Ger. name for it is not known. It is an "open," or bottom-crusted pie, filled with a sticky sweet mixture of molasses, brown sugar, and butter. When baked, the pie looks very much like a Southern pecan pie— minus the pecans. *Shoofly pie* is apparently so called because anyone who sits down to eat one first has to *shoo* away the *flies*: "Shoo, fly!" However, some people believe the pie was deliberately designed to serve as a kind of "attractive nuisance," attracting the flies away from the rest of the food. DAFD; FLC; IHAT; IRCD; LCRH; MDWPO; SA.

SHOOTER   *See* Biscuit Shooter.

SHORT AND SWEET   *See* Sweet Tooth.

SHORTBREAD   *See* Shortcake.

SHORTCAKE   *a shortcake.* A dessert consisting of a biscuit, fruit, and whipped cream. NSOED: late-16th cent. Source: CAKE. MWCD: 13th cent. A shortcake is neither "short" (in height or length) nor a *cake* (i.e., made of cake dough). Instead, it is a large, round *biscuit*—baked, sliced horizontally, and buttered. The bottom half is placed, butterside up, in a large soup bowl; covered with whole or sliced strawberries; covered with the top half of the biscuit, butterside down; and topped with more strawberries and whipped cream. The *short* in *shortcake* refers to the fact that the biscuit dough contains a large amount of fat, or shortening. Ironically, if you can't bake a biscuit, you can substitute a sponge-cake shell, which contains no shortening at all; and if you have no whipped cream, you can substitute an artificial whip, which contains no cream at all. (Artificial strawberries have not yet been invented.) A related term, *shortbread* (NSOED: early-18th cent.), refers to neither a cake nor a bread but a cookie. Shortbread cookies are so called because the ratio of fat to flour in their dough has been greatly increased by adding more fat, which causes the cookies to become rich, firm, crumbly, and crisp. Shortbread cookies, like those sold by the Girl Scouts, are often "pressed," i.e., forced into a mold, baked upside down, and then righted when the cookies are turned out of the mold. *Shortnin' bread* really *is* a loaf of bread, made with plenty of lard and popular in the South. Vegetable fat gradually overtook animal fat in kitchens and bakeries during the second half of the 20th cent. because it is light, smokeless, longer storing, and more politically correct. However, fat is fat, and either type can make pie crust flaky, croissants crispy, and cookies crumbly. DAFD; FLC; IHAT; WNWCD.

SHORTENING   *See* Shortcake.

SHORTNIN' BREAD   *See* Shortcake.

SHORT-ORDER RESTAURANT   *See* Fast Food.

SHRIMP COCKTAIL   *a shrimp cocktail*. A cold appetizer consisting of shelled, pealed, deveined, boiled shrimp with a ketchup- or chili-based dip. Source: SHRIMP (MWCD: 14th cent.); COCKTAIL (MWCD: 1806). In the early-19th cent. a *cocktail* was an aperitif consisting of a mixed alcoholic drink and a flavoring ingredient. By the middle of the 19th cent. the meaning of the term was extended to include *food* appetizers such as the *seafood cocktail*: the *clam cocktail* and the *oyster cocktail* (DAFD: ca. 1860). The early-20th cent. saw the development of a new aperitif, the *champagne cocktail*, and two new appetizers: the *shrimp cocktail* and the *fruit cocktail* (DAFD: 1922—mixed fruit in a cup). Why nonalcoholic food dishes were named after an alcoholic drink has been explained as follows: (1) Both products consist of a mixture of ingredients. (This is true of mixed drinks and fruit cocktails but not of the champagne cocktail and the seafood cocktails.) (2) Both products are served either before the meal (the aperitifs) or as the first course (the appetizers). (3) Since 1900, both the champagne cocktail and the seafood cocktail have been served in a wide-mouthed, stemmed glass. In the case of the shrimp cocktail, the "bell" of the glass is quite large, and it is filled with crushed ice, into which a small metal tub of dip is embedded, and the shrimp are hung from the glass's edge. DAFD; FLC; NSOED; PT.

SHUCK (v)   *See* Shell Out.

SIEVE   *See* Leak like a Sieve.

SIFT THROUGH EVIDENCE   *See* Leak like a Sieve.

SIGN OF THE FIG   *See* Sycophant.

SILVER   *See* Silverware.

SILVER PLATE   *See* Full Plate.

SILVERWARE   Eating utensils. Source: SILVERWARE. MWCD: 1860. The meaning of the word *silverware* orig. included *flatware* (i.e., eating and serving utensils) and *hollowware* (such as pots and bowls) that were made of or plated with silver and were used at the table (i.e., were "silver tableware"). However, this definition has pretty much been taken over by the word *silver*, whereas *silverware* has both narrowed its coverage of "wares" (to eating and serving utensils only) and broadened its composition (to include gold, stainless steel, and even plastic).

If you read a newspaper report that a burglar had broken into a wealthy person's house and stolen the *silver*, you would prob. have assumed that the haul included both silver knives, forks, and spoons and silver pots and bowls. If you read a report that a burglar had broken into a wealthy person's house and stolen the *silverware*, you would prob. have assumed that the haul included only knives, forks, and spoons, most likely plated with either silver or gold. If you read a report that a burglar had broken into a *poor* person's home and stolen the *silverware*, you would prob. have assumed that the haul included both silver-plated utensils and utensils made of stainless steal. If you read a report that a burglar had broken into a fast-food, drive-through restaurant and stolen silverware, you would know for certain that the haul included only plastic knives, forks, and spoons (i.e., *plastic silverware*, an oxymoron). *Hide the silverware!* is a warning given (sometimes in jest) before a larcenous relative comes to visit, and *Count the silverware!* is a reminder given after he/she has left. *To sell the family silver* is to take the most drastic of steps to avoid ruin. CE; DEI; MS; NSOED; WNWCD.

SIMMER   *See* Simmer Down.

SIMMER DOWN   *to simmer down*. To calm or quiet down. MWCD: 1871. Source: SIMMER. MWCD: 1653. Metaphorically, *to simmer down* is to control your temper, often as ordered by the command "Simmer down!" In cooking, to simmer down is what the food in a pot of water does when it is reduced from a hard—or rolling—boil to a temperature at which the contents are relatively quiet and only a few tiny bubbles appear, i.e., a *simmer*. Without the adv. *down*, *to simmer* is also a figure of speech, meaning "to foment," like ideas taking shape in the back of your mind; and *to seethe* (NSOED: late-16th cent.) is to hold your anger inside until you *reach the boiling point* (q.v.) again. A *simmering dispute* is one that can erupt at any time. AID; FLC; PT.

SIMMERING DISPUTE   *See* Simmer.

SING FOR YOUR SUPPER   *See* Supper.

SINKER   *See* Doughnut.

SINKERS AND SUDS   *See* Lunch-counter Jargon.

SINK YOUR TEETH INTO   *to sink—or get—your teeth into something*. To tackle a job or a problem that is both difficult and rewarding. HND: early-20th cent. Source: TEETH. MWCD: O.E. When a wild predator sinks its teeth into a prey, that prey is about to become the predator's next meal. Stalking the prey, chasing it, and dragging it to the ground are necessary preliminaries; but the real reward comes from taking that first bite of warm flesh. On the same literal level, people— perhaps even vegetarians?—grow tired of a diet of *rabbit food* (q.v.) and yearn for something they can really *sink their teeth into*, such as a thick, juicy steak. On a metaphorical level, people who are underchallenged yearn for *something they can sink—or get—their teeth into*, something challenging, substantial, worth doing. AID; CI; DAI; DAS; DEI; EWPO; MS. *See also* Pièce de Résistance.

SIRLOIN   *the sirloin*. The "royal" portion of beef above the flank and forward of the rump and round. MWCD: 1554. Source: LOIN. MWCD: 14th cent. *Sirloin* is an early Mod. Eng. misspelling of M.E. *surloin*, which was a misspelling of M.Fr. *surlonge* "upper loin." This etymology was clear to the Fr.-speaking Normans in England in the 12th and 13th cents.; but by the 14th and 15th cents., as French again became a foreign language, the association of *sur-* with "over" or "above" was lost on the Eng.-speaking population. In the 16th cent., when Eng. spelling was phonetic at best and chaotic at worst, *sur* came to be spelled *sir*. By the 17th cent., folk etymologies had arisen to account for how a lean and tender cut of beef had come to be knighted and referred to as "Sir Loin" by Henry VIII, James I, and Charles II! The rationalizations were false, but the attempt was understandable because *sirloin* is *a cut above the rest* (q.v.) only if you are a butcher and the beef is hanging from its hind legs. In that position, the *sirloin* is above the lower, or short, loin, which includes the porterhouse, tenderloin, and T-bone. When the steer was alive and standing on its four legs, the sirloin portion was above only a very shallow portion of flank. BDPF; DAFD; EWPO; MDWPO; PT; THT.

SIR LOIN   *See* Sirloin.

SIT ABOVE THE SALT   *See* Salt of the Earth.

SIT BELOW THE SALT   *See* Salt of the Earth.

SIZZLE (v)   *to sizzle*. To suddenly reach a higher level of performance; to "get hot." Source: SIZZLE (v). MWCD: 1603. The verb *sizzle* is imitative of the sound that foods make when they get hot enough for their fat or liquids to expand and burst—or when food or liquid is suddenly dropped onto a hot grill or into a hot frying pan or deep fryer. When an athlete suddenly starts to *sizzle* in a game, he/she is making shots, getting hits, or scoring points as if "in a zone." However, this higher level of performance is not necessarily accompanied by sizzling sounds or sounds of any kind (although grunts have become popular among tennis players). The similarity between "noisy" bacon and "hot" performances is that both are about ready to become what we want them to be: perfect specimens. NSOED; WNWCD.

SKILLET   *See* Spider.

SKUNK CABBAGE   *See* Cabbage.

SLAM DUNK   *See* Dunk a Basketball.

SLAPJACK   *See* Pancake (n).

SLAVE OVER A HOT STOVE ALL DAY   *to slave over a hot stove all day*. To work as hard as a housewife-cook did during the 19th and early-20th cents. Source: STOVE. MWCD: 1591. The earliest Eng. "stove" (O.E. *stofa*) was not a cooking stove but a heated room (or "sauna") for steam bathing, the heat for which was prob. provided by a fireplace that was separate from the main fireplace of the house. It was not until the late-18th cent. that the word *stove* was applied to a wood-burning "furnace" that was located apart from the fireplace but was attached to the fireplace's chimney by a sheetmetal pipe. This *Franklin stove* (MWCD: 1787), invented by Benjamin Franklin and designed only for heating, not cooking, served the country well until it was replaced by the *potbellied stove* (MWCD: 1933) a century and a half later. The cooking stove, or *cookstove* (MWCD: 1824), was a modification of the Franklin stove for cooking, although it, too, was replaced by the *range*, a combination stove and oven operated by gas and, later, by electricity, in the period between WWI and WWII. Gas and electric ranges are well insulated and don't allow much heat to escape into the room, but woodburning cookstoves were like furnaces, esp. on a hot day. The housewife-cook who started the day by fixing breakfast on the stove and continued it by baking bread in the morning, fixing a huge dinner at noon, baking cakes, cookies, and pies in the afternoon, and fixing a light meal of leftovers on the stove at suppertime was not exactly thrilled to hear her farmer husband say that he needed one more "hand" to help milk the cows: "You mean I slave over a hot stove all day and you want me to milk the cows too?" Today, the expression is more likely to be facetious, as when a husband says, "I slave over a hot computer all day and you want me to help fix dinner too?" Other *stove*-related terms and expressions are *stove-pipe hat*, a tall, black, narrow-brimmed, formal dress hat that resembled a short (approx. one-foot) length of stove pipe and was made famous by President Abraham Lincoln; *turn up the heat* (HB: ca. 1917) or *make it hot for someone*, as by "grilling them on the stand"; and *put something on the back burner* (HND: ca. 1930) "to postpone action or consideration of something indefinitely." CE; CI; DAS; DC; EWPO; HDAS; HI; LA; MS; PT; WNWCD.

SLICE OF LIFE   *a slice of life*. An accurate representation of actual life. MWCD: 1895. Source: SLICE (n). MWCD: 1613. *Slice of life* is a translation of Fr. *tranche de vie*, which was coined in the late-19th cent. to describe a drama, or a portion of a drama, that realistically portrayed events in everyday life. Since that time, the phrase has been applied also to other types of creative writing, such as novels, short stories, films, and television shows. Literally, a *slice* is either a small, thin piece that is cut (or *sliced*, MWCD: 1551) from a long or spherical object (e.g., a slice of bread or fruit) or a wedge-shaped piece cut from a flat or cylindrical object (e.g., a slice—or piece—of pie or cake). Each slice is representative of the rest of the food from which it is taken—the real thing. WNWCD. *See also* Best Thing since Sliced Bread; Slice of the Cake; Slice of the Melon; Slice of the Pie.

SLICE OF THE CAKE   *See* Pie Chart.

SLICE OF THE MELON   *a slice of the melon.* A piece of the action; a percentage of the profits; a share of the spoils. HND: early-20th cent. Source: MELON. MWCD: 14th cent. The melon in question is prob. the *watermelon* (MWCD: 1615) because it is usu. so large that it has to be sliced for eating out of hand. The watermelon is one of the divisions of the melon group, the other being the *muskmelon* (MWCD: 1573), which in turn is divided into two subdivisions: "netted-surface" muskmelons, such as the *cantaloupe* (MWCD: 1739), and "smooth-surface" muskmelons, such as the *honeydew melon* (MWCD: 1916). Melons make up one of two divisions of the gourd family (not including the gourd itself, which is inedible): gourds cultivated as fruit, i.e., melons; and gourds cultivated as vegetables, i.e., cucumbers and pumpkins (or squash). All gourds grow on vines, although watermelons are so heavy that they spend most of their life resting on the ground. The watermelon is thought to have been brought to America, in the form of seeds, by African slaves, and the stereotype of a Black child eating a slice of watermelon while his/her parents labor in the fields developed early in the 19th cent. Later in the 19th cent., the melon—again, prob. the watermelon—acquired the figurative sense of "earned profit surplus" or "unearned financial windfall." For several decades, also, *melons* has been a slang term for women's breasts; and little girls have been warned that *if they swallow watermelon seeds they'll grow in their stomach.* (Little boys are usu. the ones who are warned that if they don't wash thoroughly, "they'll *have potatoes growing in—or behind—their ears.*") CE: DAFD; DC; FLC; NSOED.

SLICE OF THE PIE   *See* Pie Chart.

SLIP ON A BANANA PEEL   *See* Fruit with Appeal.

SLOE   *See* Plum.

SLOE-EYED   *See* Plum.

SLOP   *See* Taste like Dishwater.

SLOPPY JOE   *See* Make Hamburger of.

SLOW AS MOLASSES IN JANUARY   *to be as slow—or thick—as molasses in January.* To be dilatory, lethargic, or sluggish. HND: ca. 1880. Source: MOLASSES. MWCD: 1582. Molasses is a by-product of sugar production. Sugar cane is crushed to extract its juices; the juices are boiled down to a mixture consisting of crystals and syrup; the sugar crystals are removed from the mixture, leaving what is known as *light molasses*, a thin table syrup for pouring on pancakes and waffles; a second boiling produces *dark molasses*, a thick cooking syrup used for making *molasses cookies* (soft) and *gingerbread cookies* (hard); and a third boiling results in an even darker and thicker syrup called *blackstrap molasses*, which is mixed with cattle feed in most of the country but with rum in New England. The molasses-rum connection dates back to the days of slavery, when molasses, produced from sugar cane in the West Indies, was shipped to New England, where it was fermented into rum, which was then shipped to Africa to be exchanged for slaves, who were then shipped to the West Indies for relocation: the so-called triangular trade, esp. of the 18th cent. Although molasses was first extracted from dates in the 16th cent., it was named for the syrup it most closely resembled at that time: *honey* (fr. Port. *melacao*, fr. Lat. *mel* "honey"). *Molasses* has persisted in America as the name for the syrup associated with the production of sugar from any source (sugar cane, sugar beets, sorghum, etc.); however, it was replaced in Britain in the late-17th cent. by the word *treacle*, which, since the 14th cent., had referred to a poison remedy that was sweetened with molasses. Now, in America, *treacle* has become a metaphor for anything that is excessively sentimental or cloying. Of the three popular sweeteners in America in 1900—maple syrup, molasses, and sugar—sugar is now by far the most popular; maple syrup runs a distant second, and molasses is barely running at all, as is its condition on a cold January day. BDPF; CE; DAFD; DC; FLC; LA; PT; SA; THT; WNWCD.

SLOW BURN   *to do a slow burn*. For anger to build up slowly within you. Source: BURN. MWCD: O.E. A literal "slow burn" is what is required to barbecue the whole carcass of an animal on a *spit*, as at a pig roast or an ox roast. When humans do a *slow burn*, they are not being roasted on a spit but feel as if they are. Their anger heats up until they are seething with a silent fury. Other cooking-related expressions with *burn* are (1) *to get your fingers burned* "to get caught meddling in someone else's affairs" (perhaps by trying to *pull someone's chestnuts out of the fire*, q.v.); (2) *to be burned to a crisp* "to receive a severe sunburn from too much time in the summer sun" (prob. from the neglect of sunscreen or sun block); and (3) *to burn one* "to throw another hamburger on the grill" (from lunch-counter jargon shouted by waitresses [sic] to the cook). AID; BDPF; DAI; DAS; EWPO; IHAT; WNWCD. *See also* Can't Boil Water without Burning It.

SLUGFEST   *See* Feast.

SLUSH   *See* Slush Fund.

SLUSH FUND   *a slush fund*. A contingency fund within a congressional budget; a political fund for financing illegal activities. Source: GREASE. *Slush* was a 19th cent. sailor's term for the grease that was drained off from baked, broiled, or fried meat—so called because it resembled partly melted snow. Among the sailors, a *slush fund* (MWCD: 1869) was an accumulation of money raised by the sale of the *slush* when the voyage was over and used at the pleasure of the crew. Shortly after the origination of the term *slush fund*, it was applied to a "rainy day" fund set aside within a larger budget allocated by the U.S. Congress (EXPO: 1866). Later in the 19th cent., a *slush fund* became popularly known as a fund established by a political party for bribing public officials and financing certain other corrupt activities. *Slush* is still collected by cooks on many U.S. Navy, Coast Guard, Merchant Marine, and cruise ships, and it is prob. still sold to manufacturers of soap and candles; but it is unlikely that the sailors get a share of the profits for a homecoming spree. LCRH; MDWPO.

SMACK OF   *to smack of.* To have the distinctive features of. NSOED: late-16th cent. Source: TASTE. In O.E. the noun *smæc* meant "a distinctive taste or flavor." In early-M.E. *smæc* became a verb meaning "to *have* a distinctive taste or flavor." Later, with the addition of the prep. *of*, the verb came to mean "to have the distinctive taste or flavor of" (something else). Currently the expanded verb can apply to subjects other than food and drink: e.g., *to smack of treason* "to have some of the characteristics of treason" or *to smack of sarcasm* "to carry some of the flavor of sarcasm." This verb is not related to another *smack*, as in "to smack your lips" (MWCD: 1557), which is an imitative word based on the sound of closed lips breaking suction when the lower jaw is suddenly dropped. This sound is now a substitute for a kiss, or a signal that you're hungry. WNWCD.

SMACK OF SARCASM   *See* Smack of.

SMACK OF TREASON   *See* Smack of.

SMACK YOUR LIPS   *See* Make Your Mouth Water; Smack of.

SMALL-FRY   *See* Small Fry.

SMALL FRY   Unimportant people (MWCD: 1817); young children (EWPO: 1852); minor organizations (SA: late-19th cent.). (NSOED gives a late-16th cent. date for Britain.) Source: FRY (n). MWCD: 14th cent. The noun *fry* has been used to describe young fish since the 1300s, and young children since the 1600s (EWPO: 1697). In America, the adj. *small-fry* appeared in 1817 to describe an unimportant politician; Harriet Beecher Stowe introduced the noun *small fry* to describe young children in her novel *Uncle Tom's Cabin* in 1852; and the noun *small fry* was first used to describe small businesses in the late-1800s. The 14th cent. noun *fry* referred to the hatchlings of fish (esp. salmon), which develop from fish eggs, looking like pollywogs and numbering in the hundreds. (The numerous young of frogs and bees are also called *fry*.) The age, size, and numbers of the fry are the basis for the metaphor when applied to children—young, small, and numerous. It is unlikely that there is a link between *small fry* and a *fish fry* (q.v.) involving small fish or a small catch of fish. It is uncertain whether the noun *fry* derives from O.N. *frjo* "seed" or O.N.Fr. *fri* "spawn"—or possibly a merger of the two words in the mouths of Eng.-speakers. ATWS; CI; DAI; DAS; DEI; HI; WNWCD.

SMALL POTATOES   Insignificant; trivial; unimportant; worthless. MWCD: 1831. Source: POTATO. MWCD: 1565. White potatoes that are small are either immature (and hard) or mature (and tender) but are genetically too small to market. Regardless of the reason, small potatoes are not worth bothering with or even digging up. (Leave them to the animals, or let them rot in the ground!) Small countries are *small potatoes*, compared to large countries, because they lack political clout. Small cities are *small potatoes*, compared to large cities, because they can't attract dollars or tourists the way metropolitan areas can. Small companies are *small potatoes*, compared to large companies or corporations, because they can't compete with them in production or sales. Office workers are *small potatoes*, compared to the management of a company, because they are out of the loop. Poor people are *small potatoes*, compared to rich people, because they lack economic clout. Etc. If you *work for small potatoes*, you *work for peanuts* (q.v.), i.e., for practically nothing: You're a nobody. BDPF; CE; DAP; DAS; LCRH; MS.

SMART APPLE   *See* How Do You Like Them Apples?

SMART COOKIE   *a/one smart cookie*. A very smart or clever person. DC: 1948. Source: COOKIE. MWCD: 1703. *Smart cookies* are gender neutral: "He is a *smart cookie*"; "She is *one smart cookie*." How intelligence or cleverness came to be associated with a cookie is not certain. DC suggests that the origin may lie in the name traditionally given to chuck wagon cooks in the Wild West of the late-19th cent.: "Cookie" (or "Cookee"). It is easier to understand the source of a similar term, *tough cookie* "a tough or durable person," because cookies that are intended to be chewy but are baked too long can be very tough indeed. CE; DAFD; DAS; HDAS.

SMEARCASE   *See* Cottage-cheese Thighs.

SMELL FISHY   *See* Fishy.

SMOKE EATER   *See* Fire-eater.

SMOOTH AS CREAM CHEESE   *See* Cheesecake.

S'MORES   Campfire cookies. Source: COOKIE. *S'mores* are unusual in that they are childhood foods that are also enjoyed by adults. All that is required is a campfire (for roasting a marshmallow), a bar of thin, flat, milk chocolate, and two large graham crackers. On top of one of the graham crackers place a piece of chocolate of about the same size; on top of the chocolate, place the roasted marshmallow; and on top of the marshmallow, place either the other graham cracker or another piece of chocolate (if you're *really* hungry) and *then* the other cracker. Then you press the whole "sandwich" together, eat it, and make some more *s'mores*. It is not known how old the practice is, but the first thin, flat, milk chocolate was certainly Hershey's, and that company regularly publishes the recipe and even includes directions for preparation in the microwave (on rainy days). An adult who likes s'mores (and campfires and children) is sometimes called a *marshmallow*, i.e., a "softy" (HDAS: 1966). DAFD. *See also* Graham Cracker.

SMORGASBORD   *a smorgasbord*. A heterogeneous mixture or mélange. ("The weather today will be a veritable *smorgasbord* of . . .") NSOED: mid-20th cent. Source: SMORGASBORD. MWCD: 1893. When the Swedish smorgasbord arrived in America in the late-19th cent., it consisted pretty much of what the word meant in Swedish: "a bread and butter table." That is, it featured Swedish rye bread (and butter), Swedish meatballs (and other meats for making a sandwich), Swedish smoked or pickled herring, and Swedish desserts. Today, the smorgasbord is a luncheon or dinner *buffet* (see below) that includes not only Swedish specialties but also hors d'oeuvres, hot or cold meats, hot or cold vegetables, and the makings for a salad. The word *smorgasbord* is now virtually synonymous with the word *buffet* in American English—both words having the sense of a variegated spread of hot and cold foods set out on tables by which the diner passes and either fills his/her plate, or has it filled, at each stop. The word *buffet* (MWCD: 1718) derives fr. Fr. *buffet* "sideboard" (the *-bord* in *smorgasbord*), on which food is set out for self-service. Some restaurants now function entirely as buffets or smorgasbords, charging a flat fee and allowing the diner to eat as much as he/she wants. DAFD; FLC; MS.

SNACK (n)   *See* Snack Bar.

SNACK (v)   *See* Snack Bar.

SNACK BAR   *a snack bar*. A small diner that serves the same menu of light food throughout the day. MWCD: 1930. Source: SNACK (n). NSOED: late-17th cent. A *snack* is a light meal, taken at any time of the day or night, that does not require a great deal of preparation, may not involve the use of a conventional oven or stove, does not take a long time to eat, may be eaten off the premises, and is intended to relieve hunger pains rather than substitute for a regular meal. Although the term *snack bar* dates from only the early-1930s, snack bars have been around since the late-19th cent. (DAFD: 1895), often located in factories, hospitals, office buildings, and college dormitories and student centers—sometimes just across from a cafeteria. The snack bar was designed for the person in a hurry, who needed to get in and out without waiting at a table, standing in line, or pushing a tray along a counter. A typical *snack* in the 1930s was a ham salad sandwich, some potato chips, and a milk shake. (Some soda fountains also functioned as snack bars in the 1930s.) Snacks taken—or "snatched" (the sense of the original source, Du. *snacken*)—at home may be heavier or lighter than the kind offered at a snack bar. Dagwood Bumstead's *midnight snack* practically emptied the refrigerator, but his daytime *snack food* at work was prob. much lighter, consisting of a candy bar, some popcorn, and a soda pop—the sort of snack that people enjoy at the movies. *Snack foods* are also known as *munchies*, and someone who craves them is said to *have the munchies* (HDAS: 1971) or to *have the hungries* (HDAS: 1970). To eat between meals is to *snack* (MWCD: 1807), to *piece* (q.v.), or to *nosh* (MWCD: 1956), the last-mentioned verb deriving from M.H.G. *naschen* "to eat on the sly," by way of Yiddish. A *nosher* (HDAS: 1947) is someone who *noshes* (HDAS: 1947) on *nosh* (HDAS: 1951) "snack food." BDPF; DAS; EWPO; LA.

SNACK FOOD   *See* Snack Bar; Twinkie Defense.

SNICKERDOODLES   Soft sugar cookies sprinkled with cinnamon. DAFD: 19th cent. Source: COOKIE. The name for these New England cookies is a nonsense word, prob. coined to make sugar cookies sound more attractive to children. The original New England recipe called for fruits (such as raisins) and nuts, but most modern cookbooks omit these ingredients. Another cookie with an unusual name is the *hermit* (DAFD: 1896), which is a lumpy brown cookie that also may contain nuts and raisins. The lumps in the hermits are attributable to the raisins and nuts; the brown color comes from the use of molasses—or brown sugar—as a sweetener. The name seems to derive not from either of these features but from the fact that hermit cookies can keep for a very long time—like a fruitcake—and can be baked ahead of time and hidden away for later use. FLC; MWCD.

SNOW CONE   *See* Put on Ice.

SNOW PEA   *See* Like Two Peas in a Pod.

SODA   *a soda.* A carbonated soft drink; a carbonated ice-cream drink. Source: SODA. MWCD: 1558. A carbonated drink is one that contains water charged with carbon dioxide—i.e., *soda water* (MWCD: 1802). In the early-19th cent., flavored soda water was sold under the name "(soda) *pop*" (DAFD: 1809). In the mid-19th cent. vanilla-flavored soda water was marketed as *cream soda* (DAFD: 1854), and in the late-19th cent. ice cream was added to cream soda to produce the first *ice-cream soda* (DAFD: ca. 1870). Because of the various forms of soda water in the past—straight, flavored, containing ice cream—the word *soda* means different things to different people in different places and under different circumstances. For example, in the finest restaurants, a *soda* means a glass of "club soda" (or "soda water"); in the Northeastern states a *soda* is a "soft drink"; and in the rest of the country a *soda* is an "ice-cream soda." To avoid confusion, people in Boston call a soft drink a *tonic*, people in the Midwest call it (a) *pop*, and almost everybody calls it a *Coke* (a trademark of the Coca-Cola Company). It is still wise, however, to specify *soda pop* or *ice-cream soda* in order to be sure you get what you really want. EWPO; FLC; IHAT; NSOED.

SODA CRACKER   *See* Drive Someone Crackers.

SODA JERK   *a soda jerk.* A preparer and dispenser of carbonated soft drinks—as well as ice-cream sodas, malts, shakes, and sundaes—at a *soda fountain* in a drug store or ice-cream parlor. MWCD: 1922. Source: SODA. MWCD: 1558. The *soda jerk*—or *soda jerker* (IHAT: 1880s)—was so called because he (*sic*) was the one who pulled the ball-topped lever down to shoot carbonated water into a soft drink or ice-cream soda. In addition, the soda jerk performed tasks that did not involve soda water, such as scooping ice cream into a stainless steel "glass" for mixing malted milks and milk shakes—or into a glass bowl for preparing ice-cream sundaes and banana splits. With the disappearance of soda fountains from drug stores, and even ice-cream parlors, the soda jerk pretty much works in anonymity now in the kitchens of restaurants. DAFD; DAI; HF; NSOED; WNWCD.

SODA JERKER   *See* Soda Jerk.

SODA POP   *See* Pop Your Cork; Soda.

SODA WATER   *See* Soda.

SOFA SPUD   *See* Couch Potato.

SOFT TACK   *See* Biscuit.

SO HOT YOU COULD FRY AN EGG ON IT   *See* Fried Egg.

SO HUNGRY YOU COULD EAT A HORSE   *See* Eat like a Horse.

SOME APPLES   *See* How Do You Like Them Apples?

SOME CRUST   *See* Crust.

SOME DISH   *See* Dish (n).

SOME PUMPKINS   *See* Pumpkin.

SOMETHING YOU CAN SINK—OR GET—YOUR TEETH INTO   *See* Sink Your Teeth into Something.

SONGFEST   *See* Feast.

SON-OF-A-BITCH STEW   *See* In a Stew.

SON-OF-A-GUN STEW   *See* In a Stew.

SON OF A SEA COOK   *You son of a sea cook!* You stinker! Source: COOK. MWCD: O.E. There once *was* such a thing as a *sea cook*—a cook on an oceangoing sailing ship—and it was possible to be the son of one of them. However, this *cook* has nothing to do with the sea: *Sea cook* is a corruption of the Algonquian Indian word *segonku* "polecat," from which the English word *skunk* (MWCD: 1634) is derived. The Native American word was first pronounced *sea-konk* by the English colonists, then anglicized to *sea cook*. Therefore, the *son of a sea cook* is a "stinker" all right: He's the son of a skunk. EWPO; SA.

SOPHISTICATED PALATE   *See* Palatable.

SOP TO CERBERUS   *See* Milksop.

S.O.S.   *See* Chipped Beef.

SO TENDER YOU COULD CUT IT WITH A FORK   *See* Fork in the Road.

SO THICK YOU COULD CUT IT WITH A KNIFE   *See* Cutting Edge.

SOUFFLÉ   *See* Flat as a Cheese Soufflé.

SOUL FOOD   The traditional Southern food enjoyed by African Americans. MWCD: 1964. Source: FOOD. MWCD: O.E. *Soul food* includes such items as black-eyed peas, chitterlings, collard greens, ham hocks, and hominy grits—all of which are part of the traditional Southern diet. What makes these foods special is their association with Black heritage and culture and how they symbolize Black spirit and pride. The year in which the term *soul food* was first recorded (1964) reflects the height of Black activism in this country. DAFD; FLC. *Compare* Brain Food.

SOUND FISHY   *See* Fishy.

SOUP   Dense fog; a liquid mixture; power; sentimentality; trouble. Source: SOUP. MWCD: 14th cent. Soup is a food that has spawned many metaphors. Literally, soup is (1) a clear, thick, or creamy liquid that can be either spooned or drunk ("Drink your soup!") or (2) a combination of a liquid base with meat, fish, fowl, or vegetables that must be eaten with a spoon. Weather that is *soupy* (MWCD: 1869) is like a thick soup in which the spoon diappears from sight. *Soupy* weather can be either rainy, drizzly, or foggy, and in the last-mentioned case it can be described as *pea soup* (NSOED: mid-19th cent.), as in *a pea-soup fog* or *as thick as pea soup*. *Soupy* is also used to characterize a piece of art, literature, or music as being overly sentimental. The word *soup* is also the basis for metaphors in which it represents clear liquids, such as nitroglycerin ("liquid dynamite"), or liquids mixed with other substances, such as concrete (a mixture of cement, sand or gravel, and water). The combination of ammonia and water has been described as the "chemical *soup of life*." Just as hot soup fuels the human body on a cold day, a higher-octane gasoline can add *soup*, or "power," to an automobile; and a racing car can be *souped up* (MWCD: 1933) in various ways to improve its performance. To be *in the soup* is to be in serious trouble, like the fly that is drowning in your tomato bisque. ("Waiter! *There's a fly in my soup!*") AID; BDPF; CE; CI; DAI; DAS; DEI; EWPO; FLC; MS; PT.

SOUP AND FISH   *See* Everything from Soup to Nuts.

SOUP DU JOUR   *See* Menu.

SOUP OF LIFE   *See* Soup.

SOUP-STRAINER   *a soup-strainer*. A large mustache. Source: SOUP; STRAIN (v). MWCD: 14th cent. A mustache that qualifies as a *soup-strainer* is big and bushy—large and thick enough to allow the liquid part of soup to pass through, while rejecting the solid part. This is absurd, of course, as is the use of *strain* in *to strain out gnats and swallow camels*—i.e., lit. to let huge camels pass through the strainer while not allowing tiny gnats to do so. Metaphorically, the passage in Matthew 23:24 "Ye blind guides [the Scribes and Pharisees], which *strain at a gnat*, and *swallow a camel*," [italics added] really means to ignore important matters while focusing on trivial ones. ATWS; DAS; DEI; FLC; HB; NSOED; SA.

SOUP TO NUTS   *See* Everything from Soup to Nuts.

SOUP UP   *See* Soup.

SOUPY   *See* Soup.

SOUR   *See* Hit a Sour Note.

SOUR BALL   *See* Sourpuss.

SOUR CHERRY   *See* Cherry (n); Sourpuss.

SOUR DEAL   *See* Lemon.

SOUR DISPOSITION   *See* Sourpuss.

SOURDOUGH   *a sourdough*. A prospector for gold in California ca. 1850 or the Yukon Territory ca. 1890. Source: SOUR; DOUGH. MWCD: O.E. Prospectors were nicknamed *sourdoughs* because they made their bread (*sourdough bread* NSOED: mid-19th cent.) from dough that did not contain a leavening (or "raising") agent such as baking powder (invented in 1850). Instead, they brought "starter" dough with them to their prospecting site and from then on saved some of the dough as a "starter" for the next batch of bread or biscuits. Some of the sourdough starters are said to have been passed on through many generations and may still be around in rural California or in the wilds of the Yukon Territory. DAFD; FLC; IHAT; MDWPO.

SOURDOUGH BREAD   *See* Sourdough.

SOUR GRAPES   Disparagement of something that is desirable but unattainable. MWCD: 1760. Source: SOUR (MWCD: O.E.); GRAPE (MWCD: 14th cent.). In Aesop's animal fable "The Fox and the Geese," the fox tries to jump up and grab a mouthful of luscious-looking grapes that are hanging from an arbor. After several unsuccessful attempts, he turns away, muttering to himself that the grapes are prob. sour anyway. Such a *sour-grape attitude* is also assumed by humans who, after several failures to achieve a personal goal, console themselves with the rationalization that the goal wasn't worth fighting for anyway. *Sour grapes!* is also something that other people say to persons who exhibit the behavior—i.e., who give up too easily and disparage the value of the thing sought. The motivation for the fox's remark was frustration, but the motivation for people's *sour grapes* is often envy, jealousy, or resentment of the person who *did* get the "grapes." ATWS; BDPF; CI; DC; EWPO; HI; HND; LCRH; MDWPO; MS; NSOED; PT; SA.

SOUR-GRAPES ATTITUDE   *See* Sour Grapes.

SOUR NOTE   *See* Hit a Sour Note.

SOUR OIL   *See* Sourpuss.

SOURPUSS   *a sourpuss*. A grouch. MWCD: 1937. Source: SOUR (adj). MWCD: O.E. A *sourpuss* has a *puss* (or "face") that always seems to wear a frown, as if the owner has just eaten a sour pickle, sucked on a sour lemon, or drunk some sour milk. The adj. *sour* denotes one of the four basic taste sensations, the others being *bitter*, *salt*, and *sweet*, although many people group *bitter* and *salt* with *sour* and recognize only a single opposition: *sweet* vs. *sour*. The adj. *tart* is frequently used synonymously with *sour*, and the bright red "cooking cherry" is known as either a *sour cherry* (MWCD: ca. 1884) or a *tart cherry*—as opposed to the dark eating cherry, known as a *sweet cherry* or a *black cherry*. A *sour ball* (MWCD: ca. 1909) is a ball of hard candy that has a sharp, biting, acid, or tart flavor. *Sweet and sour* pork or shrimp is both sweet and sour at the same time. Some nonfood items that can be described as *sour* are *sour soil* (high in acids), *sour oil* (high in sulphur), and, getting back to the *sourpuss*, a *sour disposition* (high in negativity). DAFD: DAS; FLC; NSOED; WNWCD. *See also* Set Your Teeth on Edge; Sour Grapes. *Compare* Picklepuss.

SOUR SOIL   *See* Sourpuss.

SOUS-CHEF   *See* My Compliments to the Chef.

SOW YOUR WILD OATS   *See* Feel Your Oats.

SOY MILK   *See* Milk (n).

SPAGHETTI   *See* Spaghetti Squash.

SPAGHETTINI   *See* Spaghetti Squash.

SPAGHETTI SQUASH   *a spaghetti squash.* A large, oval squash whose flesh forms little strings when baked. MWCD: 1975. Source: SPAGHETTI (NSOED: mid-19th cent.); SQUASH (MWCD: 1634). "Little strings" is the Eng. translation of the It. word *Spaghetti*, the pl. of It. *spaghetto*, which is the dim. of It. *spago* "string." (*Spaghetti straps* are thin cords holding up a woman's dress.) The "spaghetti" from the spaghetti squash is not quite as bland looking as real spaghetti (the color of its flesh is yellow-gold), but it is just as bland tasting; consequently, like spaghetti, it is served on a plate with an appropriate sauce. Real spaghettis are solid strings, strands, or cords of pasta that are classified by their diameters when cooked. Spaghetti per se has a diameter of approx. one-eighth of an inch; *spaghettini* (MWCD: 1923) is slightly thinner; *vermicelli* (MWCD: 1669), lit. "little worms," is thinner yet; and *angel-hair pasta* (MWCD: 1981, fr. It. *capelli d'angelo* "angel hair") is the thinnest of all. Except for *vermicelli* (1669), the names for the various types of spaghetti date from no earlier than 1888; before that time, they were classified as types of *macaroni* (MWCD: 1599). Regardless of the type, spaghetti is tested for "doneness" by lifting a strand from the boiling water with a fork, biting into it, and determining the amount of resistance "to the tooth" (i.e., *al dente*—MWCD: 1935). If the spaghetti is soft and limp, it is overdone; if it is tough and chewy, it is underdone; but if it is only somewhat firm, it is just right. DAFD; EWPO; FLC; SA; WNWCD.

SPAGHETTI STRAPS   *See* Spaghetti Squash.

SPAGHETTI WESTERN   *a spaghetti western.* A "western" movie made in Europe, in Italian, with an Italian producer, director, and supporting cast. MWCD: 1969. Source: SPAGHETTI. MWCD: 1888. Spaghetti, of course, is almost synonymous with Italy, and that's why the Italian version of the American "western" is called a *spaghetti western*. However, the film was not always shot in Italy, and the star was not usu. an Italian. *The Good, the Bad, and the Ugly* (1968) was directed by Sergio Leone, an Italian, and the dialogue was in Italian; but the movie was shot in Spain, and it starred Clint Eastwood, an American. (The Italian of the cowboys and Indians was later dubbed into English for American audiences.) How was Italy able to attract American movie stars to the Continent in the 1960s? That's not entirely clear, but it prob. had something to do with the higher salaries, the greater exposure to the European market, and the chance to work with some of the world's greatest directors. NSOED; WNWCD.

SPANISH FIG   *See* Not Worth a Fig.

SPANISH GARLIC   *See* Onionskin Paper.

SPEAK WITH FORKED TONGUE   *See* Fork in the Road.

SPECIALTY MEATS   *See* Variety Meats.

SPICE UP YOUR LIFE   *See* Variety Is the Spice of Life.

SPICY   *See* Variety Is the Spice of Life.

SPIDER   *a spider*. A cast-iron skillet. NSOED: late-18th cent. Source: SKILLET. *Spider* is a Colonial Americanism based on the resemblance between a four-legged *skillet* (MWCD: 15th cent.) and a four-legged (counted in pairs) arachnid. In Colonial times, when most cooking was done in an open hearth (a large fireplace), utensils were fashioned to accommodate such use. For example, cast-iron kettles (Brit. *skillets*) had a "bail" for hanging from an "arm" that could swing in and out of the hearth, and (usu.) four short legs (or "feet") that allowed them to sit at the edge of the hearth over the coals. (The modern Salvation Army kettle is a smaller but otherwise close duplicate.) Likewise, Colonial *frying pans* (q.v.), which were also called *skillets*, sat above the coals and, because they never hung from a swinging arm, had to have very long handles. When removed from the fire, the round-bottomed kettles and skillets could sit upright on the hearth to cool, without tipping over. A different device that supports *flat-bottomed* pots and pans at the table is a *trivet* (MWCD: O.E.), which is so called because it has *three* short legs (fr. Lat. *triped* "three-footed"). FLC; IRCD; MDWPO; WNWCD.

SPILL THE BEANS   *to spill the beans*. To divulge information that was supposed to be kept secret. LA: 1919. Source: BEAN. MWCD: O.E. The beans in question are prob. dried beans, which must be immersed in liquid at least twice before eating. First, the beans are soaked in cold water overnight to rehydrate them; then they are cooked slowly in hot water, or baked slowly in hot water and molasses, to soften them up. At either of these stages, spilling them on the kitchen floor would create quite a mess, but the mess would be even greater at the second stage, when the beans are soft and the liquid is sticky. Spilling the beans is an unfortunate mistake, resulting in spoiled dinners and disappointed diners. In the metaphor, the *beans* or (secrets) that are *spilled* (or revealed) are not always of any great consequence, as when some friends are planning a surprise birthday party for one of their group and another member of their group inadvertently lets the plans slip to the birthday person, thus spoiling the surprise. However, metaphorically *spilling the beans* can be serious business in the fields of law enforcement (where it amounts to telling all you know about a crime that has been, or is about to be, committed), big business (where it consists of blowing the whistle on your employer for illegal or immoral practices), and government (where it involves turning traitor and revealing your country's deepest and darkest secrets to the enemy). BDPF; CE; DAS; DC; DEI; EWPO; HI; HND; LCRH; MS; PT.

SPILL THE MILK   *See* Cry over Spilled Milk.

SPINACH   Money; folding money. Source: SPINACH. MWCD: 15th cent. Like the leaves of *cabbage* (q.v.) and *lettuce* (q.v.), the leaves of the spinach plant are long and green and resemble American *greenbacks*; however, spinach leaves are darker than the others and more wrinkled or rumpled, like an unpressed handkerchief. Spinach leaves are also bitter-tasting, so they are usu. cut up, boiled or steamed, and served with plenty of butter and salt, although they can be eaten raw (at least by adults) if they are thoroughly washed, several times, to remove grit. Most children never liked spinach very much until the appearance of the *Popeye* cartoon in 1919. Popeye was an *old salt* (q.v.), with one eye (the other had "popped" out), huge forearms, tattoos, and an ever-present corncob pipe. Most of the other characters had names or appetites that were associated with food: Popeye's girlfriend, Olive Oyl; the orphan, Sweet Pea; and his friend, Wimpy, who craved hamurgers. Popeye himself had a favorite vegetable, spinach, which he ate raw, straight from the can, by pouring it directly into his mouth when he needed strength to defeat his perennial foe, Bluto. Parents explained that Popeye's added strength came from the large amount of iron that spinach contained, although it is now known that a can of peas would provide more iron than a can of spinach of the same size. Nevertheless, Popeye explained, in his theme song, which he sang himself, that he was "strong to the finish" because he ate his spinach; and that was enough to convince parents and children alike. The only problem with spinach these days is that it can become a social embarrassment if it gets stuck between your front teeth. You smile, and everyone gasps, as if you had something unbuttoned or unzipped. DAFD; DAS; EWPO; FLC; PT.

SPINELESS JELLYFISH   *See* Jellyfish.

SPIT   *a spit*. A narrow point of sand or gravel projecting into a large river, lake, or sea. Source: ROAST (v). MWCD: 13th cent. The sand or gravel *spit* is a metaphor derived from the roasting *spit* (MWCD: O.E.), a wooden pole or metal rod used to roast a whole hog (or pig), ox (or steer), or sheep (or lamb) over an open fire (or pit). The carcass is impaled on the pointed rod or bar, which is turned during the roasting process; and the meat is basted with pan drippings throughout the process. On a smaller scale is the *shish kebab* (MWCD: 1914—fr. Turk. for "spit-roast"), which consists of alternating chunks of meat and vegetables skewered on a metal rod and turned over a raised fire until done. In either case, the broiled or roasted meat is said to be *done to a turn*—i.e., to the final turn of the spit or skewer. FLC; MDWPO; PT. *See also* Barbecue. *Compare* Do up Brown.

SPOILAGE   *See* Spoiled Rotten.

SPOILED ROTTEN   Coddled, pampered, overindulged. (Said of a child who behaves like a brat.) MWCD: 1880. Source: SPOIL (MWCD: 14th cent.); ROTTEN (MWCD: 13th cent.). *Spoiled rotten* is a redundancy as well as a metaphor: If something is spoiled, it must be rotten; and if it's rotten, it must have spoiled. *Spoilage* (MWCD: 1597) is the process by which food decays, or becomes rotten, as the flesh of a wild animal does when its hide (Lat. *spolium*) is removed and the carcass is abandoned. The noun *spoil* (MWCD: 14th cent.) orig. meant "the loot or plunder taken in a battle" (the *spoils of war*), and the verb *spoil* developed the meaning "to rob or pillage." Eventually the verb came to mean "to damage or ruin," as in to ruin a child's character through excessive attention or praise. In food preparation, a cook can *spoil* a meal by under- or overcooking it; and food can *spoil* on its own if it is improperly processed or preserved. In a sense that hearkens back to the original one, a person can be *spoiling for a fight*, i.e., itching for one. The adj. *rotten* orig. described meat that had decayed to the point of becoming putrid, i.e., producing an extremely foul odor; but it soon became a metaphor for anything corrupt (*Something is rotten in the state of Denmark*), unpleasant (*rotten weather*), unfortunate (*rotten luck*), or just plain bad (a *rotten movie*). In the metaphor *spoiled rotten*, *rotten* is simply an intensifier meaning "to the extreme" (MWCD: 1880). CE; DAS; NSOED; SA. *See also* Rotten Egg.

SPOILING FOR A FIGHT   *See* Spoiled Rotten.

SPOILS OF WAR   *See* Spoiled Rotten.

SPOIL YOUR DINNER   *See* Sweets to the Sweet.

SPOON (n)   *See* Spoon-fed.

SPOON (v)   *See* Spoon-fed.

SPOON-FED   Overindulged, spoiled, pampered. Source: SPOON. MWCD: 14th cent. To *spoon-feed* an infant (MWCD: 1615) is to feed it baby food with a spoon. To *spoon-feed* an older child, however, is to treat him/her like a baby, as if he/she could not think or act for him/herself. When a high school or college teacher *spoon-feeds* his/her students, he/she does their thinking for them; and when a government *spoon-feeds* a particular group of constituents, it overindulges them to the detriment of the majority. Spoon-feeding of children of wealthy families in the late medieval period may have been done with the silver *apostle spoons* (q.v.) that they received at their christening; but in poorer (esp. rural) families in the 14th cent. it was more likely done with a wooden spoon. (The wooden spoon was orig. a long-handled stirring spoon for pots and kettles; then it progressed to the table, where it became a serving spoon and later an eating spoon.) In the average family, however, *pewter* (MWCD: 14th cent.), an alloy of tin and lead (!), was the material of choice because it was cheaper than silver but, though dull, had a silverlike color. Pewterware competed with silverware until the early-20th cent., when chromed steel and stainless steel made it unnecessary to eat with utensils either containing lead or costing several pretty pennies. Unlike the knife and the fork, the spoon has become the most important kitchen utensil, providing exact measurements for cooking, such as the teaspoon (tsp), or *teaspoonful*, and the *tablespoon* (tbsp), or *tablespoonful*. (The *spoonful of sugar* in the Mary Poppins song—the one that makes the medicine go down—is prob. a *teaspoonful*.) The noun *spoon* has also left the kitchen and dining room to serve as the name for a spoon-shaped fishing lure (which wobbles when drawn through the water) and an old-fashioned three-wood in golf (which had a long wooden "handle" like the old stirring spoon). The verb *spoon* "to transfer with a spoon" did not appear until the early-18th cent. (MWCD: 1715); but in the following cent. it developed a most interesting metaphorical meaning: "to make love by caressing, embracing, kissing, necking, or petting" (IHAT: late-1850s), perhaps based on the way spoons are nestled against each in the silver chest. BDPF; CE; CI; DAS; DEI; IHAT; NSOED; PT; WNWCD. *Compare* Spoiled Rotten.

SPOON-FEED   *See* Spoon-fed.

SPRING UP LIKE MUSHROOMS   *to spring up like mushrooms*. To multiply rapidly. EWPO: 1787. Source: MUSHROOM. MWCD: 1533. The mushroom is a fungus that pops up ("springs up") in the spring in dark, damp, wooded areas and expands very rapidly—sometimes, as with the *puffball mushroom* (MWCD: 1649), reaching a weight of fifty pounds. (Children love to step on dried-up puffballs and watch them explode in a shower of spores.) The original Eng. name for the *mushroom* (fr. M.Fr. *mousseron*) was *toad's hat*, which, in the modified form *toadstool*, is now the name for an inedible fungus (although some *mushrooms* are also inedible). The most prized American mushroom is the *morel* (MWCD: 1672), the *truffle of the North*, whose "cap" is like a brown flame rising from the stem, and whose dark flesh is delicious when sautéed in butter and a little wine. *Magic mushrooms* (HDAS: 1967) are fungi that cause halucinations when eaten. The expression *to spring up like mushrooms* orig. referred to cities in England that were popping up all over during the Industrial Revolution in the late-18th cent.; and, in fact, such cities were referred to as *mushrooms*. At about the same time, the verb *mushroom* developed, with the meaning "to grow or multiply rapidly," like wildfires. In the 20th cent., the verb was employed to describe what happened when a volcano erupted or an atomic bomb exploded: It *mushroomed*—i.e., the ash and smoke rose up in a column and then flattened out into a dome. (Actually, it looked more like a toadstool than a mushroom.) The shape was called a *mushroom cloud* (MWCD: ca. 1909), although in some cases it took the form of something quite unnatural: a double mushroom, one on top of the other. BDPF; DAFD; DAS; DEI; EWPO; FLC; HF; MS; NSOED; PT; SA.

SPRINKLE SALT ON THEIR TAILS   *See* Take with a Grain of Salt.

SPROUT   *See* Go to Seed.

SPROUT ANTLERS   *See* Go to Seed.

SPROUT WINGS   *See* Go to Seed.

SPUD   *See* Couch Potato.

SQUARE MEAL   *See* Meal.

SQUEEZE ONE   *See* O.J.

SQUIRREL AWAY   *See* Shelf Life.

SQUIRREL FOOD   *See* Rabbit Food.

STAFF OF LIFE   *See* Bread and Water.

STAND FACING THE STOVE   *See* Recipe.

STARCH   *See* Take the Starch out of.

STARCHY   *See* Take the Starch out of.

STARVE   *to starve.* To suffer or die from lack of food. MWCD: 15th cent. Source: STARVE. MWCD: O.E. In O.E., the verb *steorfan* simply meant "to die," of whatever cause, not necessarily from a shortage of food. In Mod. Eng. the verb has both broadened its meaning (to either "die" or "suffer") and narrowed it (to "die from a particular cause"). The expressions *I'm starving!* (or *I'm starving to death!*) and *I'm starved* (or *I'm starved to death*) refer to the pangs of hunger "suffered" as a result of having missed a meal or having deliberately skipped one in anticipation of an upcoming "special" repast. The "suffering" sense has been extended further to include the deprivation of affection (to be *starved for affection*) or attention (to be *starved for attention*). In the early part of the 20th cent., children who took more food than they could eat were reminded of the *starving Armenians*, who had none at all, and were told that anything left on their plate would be put in their pocket. If adults rather than children were the guilty parties, they were told that they were *taking food out of the mouths of children*. On a less serious note, no one has been able to figure out whether we should *starve a cold and feed a fever* or *feed a cold and starve a fever*. (To play it safe, we should prob. feed both.) CODP; DAP; MDWPO; MS; NSOED.

STARVE A COLD, FEED A FEVER   *See* Starve.

STARVED FOR AFFECTION   *See* Starve.

STARVED FOR ATTENTION   *See* Starve.

STARVED TO DEATH   *See* Starve.

STARVING ARMENIANS   *See* Starve.

STARVING TO DEATH   *See* Starve.

STEADY DIET   *See* Glutton for Punishment.

STEAK   *See* Salisbury Steak.

STEAK AND KIDNEY PIE   *See* Pudding.

STEAK AND KIDNEY PUDDING   *See* Pudding.

STEAK TARTARE   Coarsely ground beef, highly seasoned, eaten raw. MWCD: 1911. Source: STEAK. *Steak tartare*—also called *tartar steak* and *beef tartare*—gets its name from the Tartars (or Tatars) of Tartary (or Tatary), a vast region extending from eastern Siberia to southern Russia that was settled by Turkic and Mongolian peoples during the late Middle Ages in Europe. As the Tartars moved into eastern Europe, they brought with them the (alleged) custom of placing a large piece of beefsteak under their saddle at the beginning of a long day's ride. At the end of the day, they would remove the steak, which was by then shredded and tenderized, and eat it raw. The practice of eating raw, shredded beef caught on in the Baltic region, whence it was brought by German sailors to Hamburg. There, the steak was chopped up, seasonings were added, and the meat was cooked in the form of a large patty. The result was what we now call a *hamburger steak*—the precursor to the modern *hamburger*, which is more finely ground and to which the seasonings are added *after* the cooking, in the form of condiments. The condiment *tartar sauce* (MWCD: 1855) is so named because the ingredients—mayonnaise, chopped pickles, capers, olives, onions, etc.—are similar to those used with the original German version of *steak tartare*, although the sauce is now usu. served with fish. EWPO; FLC; IHAT; NSOED; PT; WNWCD. *See also* Make Hamburger of.

STEAL SOMEONE'S LUNCH   *See* Lunch (n).

STEP ON THE JUICE   *See* Juice.

STEWED   *See* Stew in Your Own Juice.

STEWED TO THE GILLS   *See* Stew in Your Own Juice.

STEW IN YOUR OWN JUICE   *to stew in your own juice*. To suffer from the consequences of your own actions. DC: 1885. Source: STEW; JUICE. MWCD: 14th cent. *Stewing in your own juice* is what you have to do when you bring something on yourself and other people refuse to bail you out (i.e., they *leave you to stew in your own juice*). (The expression was orig. *to fry in your own grease*—DC: 14th cent.—which was used to describe someone who was being burned at the stake.) Meat and vegetables do not become a "stew" simply because they are placed—or layered—in a covered pot. The mixture must be heated lowly and slowly until the juices seep out of the solids and form a liquid. From that point on, the ingredients are allowed to lit. "stew in their own juice," with only a minimum of stirring required to prevent the vegetables from sticking to the bottom of the pot. If a person is *stewed* (MWCD: 1739), he/she is drunk; if that person is *half-stewed*, he/she is almost drunk; and if the person is *stewed to the gills* (LA: 1925), he/she is extremely drunk, with alcohol reaching from his/her stomach to his/her neck (or "gills"). AID; BDPF; CE; CI; DAP; DAS; DEI; FLC; HI;ʾ HND; IHAT; MS; NSOED; PT.

STICK A FORK IN HIM AND SEE IF HE'S DONE   *See* Fork in the Road.

STICK IN YOUR CRAW   *for something to stick in your craw*. For something to anger, annoy, bother, "bug," disgust, or repel you. HND: late-17th cent. Source: CRAW. MWCD: 14th cent. "That really sticks in my craw" is something a bird might want to say if it swallowed grit consisting not of sand or pebbles but stones. The stones might be small enough to pass through the bird's gullet (or "throat") but not through its craw (or "crop")—and certainly not through its gizzard (or "stomach"). When something sticks anywhere in a bird's alimentary canal, it is fatal. People don't die from having something *stick in their gullet, craw,* or *gizzard* (DC: 1679), but they can become very upset about it if the matter is disagreeable, objectionable, or repugnant. People also don't swallow grit to aid in their digestion, but they use the expression *to have sand in your craw* (or *gizzard*—DC: 1867), i.e., not large pabbles or stones, to indicate that they are plucky or gutsy and raring to go. AID; ATWS; BDPF; DAI; EWPO; SA.

STICK IN YOUR GIZZARD   *See* Stick in Your Craw.

STICK IN YOUR GULLET   *See* Stick in Your Craw.

STICK TO YOUR RIBS   *See* Hidebound; Meal.

STILL TIED TO YOUR MOTHER'S APRON STRINGS   *See* Tied to Your Mother's Apron Strings.

STINK ON ICE   *See* Put on Ice.

STIR THINGS UP   *See* Stir up Trouble.

STIR UP A HORNET'S NEST   *See* Stir up Trouble.

STIR UP A POT OF TROUBLE   *See* Stir up Trouble.

STIR UP THE POT   *See* Stir up Trouble.

STIR UP TROUBLE   *to stir up trouble*. To cause trouble to occur. Source: MWCD: O.E. The verb *stir*, without *up*, orig. meant "to arise from sleep" or "to arouse someone from sleep." Later, it was applied, transitively, to the agitating of a liquid or semisolid mass, in a pot, with an implement, such as a large spoon. This is what the three witches were doing in Shakespeare's *Macbeth* (Act IV, Scene 1), when they stirred the boiling cauldron full of a newt's eggs, frog's toes, dog's tongue, etc. The witches were both lit. and fig. *stirring up trouble*, a job that is much easier now because no physical equipment is required. The same is true of an expression with a similar meaning, *to stir up a hornet's nest*, which derives from the disturbing of a paper wasp's nest, hanging from a tree limb, with a long stick. Although no liquid is involved, and the implement is pointed up rather than down, the hornet's nest is equivalent to the pot, and the circular movement of the stick is similar to that of the stirring spoon. Other "stirring" expressions are *to stir things up* and *to stir (up) the pot*. AID; DAI; IRCD; MS; SA.

STOMACH SWEETBREAD   *See* Sweetbread.

STONED OUT OF YOUR GOURD   *See* Gourd.

STONE SOUP   St. Bernard's soup: a free meal. BDPF: 16th cent. Source: SOUP. MWCD: 14th cent. The unusual name for this soup derives from an old folk tale about a starving man (St. Bernard?) who, having been denied a handout at the kitchen of a wealthy person's home, asked if he could at least boil a stone in a pot of water. The servants agreed, and the man then asked for and got some salt and pepper to season the "soup" with and some vegetables and scraps of meat to flavor it with, until he had what amounted to a hearty pot of soup—with a stone in it. The story is supposed to be either humorous (the laugh being on those who denied him food in the first place) or moralistic (if someone gives you a stone, make stone soup); however, this sort of thing happens in roadside diners almost every day, when a penniless drifter asks the waitress for a bowl of hot water, adds to it some crackers from the counter, pours in some ketchup from the ever-present bottle, stirs it up, and voilà!: *stone soup*. PT.

STOP FOR A BITE   *See* Bite (n).

STORM IN A TEACUP   *See* Tempest in a Teapot.

STOVE   *See* Slave over a Hot Stove All Day.

STOVE-PIPE HAT   *See* Slave over a Hot Stove All Day.

STRAIN AT A GNAT   *See* Soup-strainer.

STRAINER   *See* Leak like a Sieve.

STRAIN OUT GNATS AND SWALLOW CAMELS   *See* Soup-strainer.

STRAP ON THE OLD FEED BAG   *See* Put on the Feed Bag.

STRAWBERRY   *See* Strawberry Mark.

STRAWBERRY BLONDE   *See* Strawberry Mark.

STRAWBERRY MARK   *a strawberry mark*. A red birthmark. MWCD: 1347. Source: STRAWBERRY MWCD: O.E. A *strawberry mark* is usu. small, red, slightly elevated from the surrounding skin, and found on the head or face. The color, which is usu. a light to medium red, derives from the blood vessels that fill the "tumor." (If the birthmark is large, uneven, and dark red, like that on the right side of the head of Mikhail Gorbachev, it is sometimes called a "wine stain.") Although strawberries—the fruit—were popular in Europe during the Middle Ages, pregnant women were warned against eating them for fear that they would give birth to children with such marks. The color of strawberries has been applied to the coat of a horse—a *strawberry roan* (MWCD: 1955) "a horse with a light (i.e., *strawberry*) red (i.e., *roan*) coat"—and to the "mane" of a woman—a *strawberry blond(e)* (ca. WWII) "a woman with light red hair." Finally, the elegance of strawberries, esp. with milk or cream, prob. led to the euphemisms *Alaska straw-berries* (DEOD: 19th cent.) and *Boston strawberries* for "dried beans" in the mining camps of the Yukon. The *straw* in *strawberry* (O.E. *strawberige*) refers either to (1) the straw that was used as a mulch around the plants or (2) the strawlike bristles surrounding the seeds on the surface of the fruit. (A strawberry is an "inside-out" fruit.) Besides being covered with milk or cream, strawberries can be dipped in chocolate, can serve as a filling for pies and tarts, can serve as a topping for cakes and ice cream, and, when processed and canned, can serve as a spread for toast and a filling for cookies. BDPF; CE; DAFD; DAS; EWPO; FLC; HDAS; HF; IHAT; NSOED; WNWCD. *Compare* Raspberry.

STRAWBERRY ROAN   *See* Strawberry Mark.

STRAWBERRY TOMATO   *See* Tomato.

STRICTLY FOR THE BIRDS   *See* Chicken Feed.

STRICT VEGETARIAN   *See* Vegetarian.

STRIKE A SOUR NOTE   *See* Hit a Sour Note.

STRING BEAN   *See* Bean Pole.

STUDMUFFIN   *See* Muffin.

STUFFED TO THE GILLS   *See* Have a Bellyful.

STYLING MOUSSE   *See* Mousse.

SUB   *See* Submarine Sandwich.

SUBMARINE   *See* Submarine Sandwich.

SUBMARINE SANDWICH   *a submarine sandwich—or submarine, or sub.* A sandwich made with an entire (small) loaf of French or Italian bread, split length-wise, and filled with meat and vegetables. Source: SANDWICH. MWCD: 1762. The *submarine* (which has become a generic term for this type of sandwich) is so called because the half-size loaf of bread resembles a toy submarine of the sort that children like to play with in the bathtub. Such a sandwich has also been called a *bomber* in upstate New York and a *torpedo, zeppelin,* or *zep* in Los Angeles. The *submarine sandwich* developed in the northeastern United States before, dur-ing, and after WWII, primarily in the cities of Boston, New York, and Philadelphia, where it went by various names: *hero,* the original "sub," in New York City (EWPO: 1920s); *grinder* (from the amount of chewing necessary to finish one?)

in Boston (DAFD: 1954); *hoagie* (for Hoagie Carmichael?) in Philadelphia (MWCD: 1955); and *wedgie* (from cutting the filled roll diagonally?) in Connecticut and Rhode Island. Adopted by many American cultures, the submarine has been called a *Cuban sandwich* in Florida, a *Garibaldi* (after the 19th cent. Italian patriot) in Wisconsin, and an *Italian sandwich* (or *Italian beef sandwich*) in Illinois. It has even been suggested that *hero* may be a corruption of Gk. *gyro* "a pita bread sandwich containing lamb or beef, tomato, and onion," and that *poor boy* (or *po' boy*), the "big" sandwich of New Orleans (MWCD: 1941), may be derived from the Fr. word *pourboire* "tip." DAFD; FLC; HDAS; LA; MDWPO; PT.

SUCK (v)   To form a vacuum; to extract by means of a vacuum; to become vacuous. Source: SUCK (v). MWCD: O.E. The most basic form of sucking is the baby's attempt to draw milk from its mother's nipple. At a certain age, the child is introduced to the nipple on a bottle, and, when that is not available, to a nipple on a pacifier (or its own thumb). Children eventually learn to suck juice directly from an orange, liquid indirectly from a glass (by means of a straw), sugar from a lollipop, etc. Adults learn how to *suck dirt* from a floor or carpet (by means of a vacuum cleaner) and to *suck up to* a boss; and they learn that big business can *suck the life out of* small business and that *life* (or a band, a book, a course, or a film) sometimes *sucks*. A person whose fate is to *suck the hind teat* is, like the piglet in a litter that exceeds the number of available nipples, always getting the short— or dirty—end of the stick. DAS; HB; NSOED; SA.

SUCK DIRT   *See* Suck (v).

SUCKER   *a sucker*. A leech, a fish; a lollipop; a dupe, a pushover; a "shoot." Source: SUCK (v). MWCD: O.E. The leech (or bloodsucker) and the fish (a bottom-feeder) really are "suckers" in the sense that they obtain their food by sucking: the leech sucking blood from a fish or human, the fish sucking leftovers from the floor of the lake. The *lollipop* (q.v.) is a *sucker* only in the sense that it is sucked on by children until the candied sugar dissolves. The dupe and the pushover are *suckers* because they can't resist temptation. The dupe's temptation is to accept an offer that sounds too good to be true—and is. The pushover's temptation is a fondness for something to which he/she is almost addicted, such as hang gliding or bullfighting. The "shoot" known as a *sucker* is a new vertical growth on the top side of an older branch. Several shoots lined up next to each other resemble piglets nursing a sow. An *air-sucker* is a jet airplane (HDAS: 1964). ATWS; DAP; SA.

SUCK THE HIND TEAT   *See* Suck (v).

SUCK THE LEMON DRY   *See* If Life Hands You a Lemon, Make Lemonade.

SUCK THE LIFE OUT OF   *See* Suck (v).

SUCK UP TO   *See* Suck (v).

SUGAR   *Sugar*. (A term of address and endearment: e.g., "Hi, Sugar!") Source: SUGAR. MWCD: 14th cent. Until the 19th cent., sugar was the sweetest thing on earth. Cane sugar was introduced to the Iberian peninsula by the Moors in the 9th cent., and Columbus brought sugar cane plants to the Caribbean in 1494. In North America, *Indian sugar* (i.e., brown maple sugar) and honey were the sweeteners of choice until the mid-19th cent., when *store-bought sugar* (i.e., white cane sugar) decreased in price and became more affordable. (*Beet sugar* did not become available until the 1880s.) However, unlike *Honey*, which became a metaphor for "a loved one" as early as the 14th cent., *Sugar* did not become a term of endearment for a lover, a spouse, or a child (esp. a girl) until the 20th cent. (LA: 1920s). Among African Americans, *sugar* has come to mean "a show of affection or love," specif. a hug or a kiss, prompted by the request "Give me some *sugar!*" In high society, a *sugar daddy* (MWCD: 1926) is an elderly man who lavishes *sugar* (i.e., "money"—LA: 1859) on a much younger woman, although the object of his affections—and gifts—could also be a perfectly worthy Broadway production. A *sugar pill* is a placebo, sweet but harmless; to *sugar the pill* is to make something more acceptable, attractive, or pleasant; and to *sugarcoat* something, such as bad news, is to make it seem better than it really is. We all know what adding a little bit of sugar can do to medicine, thanks to the 20th cent. *Mary Poppins*, but other phrases and expressions seem much older: e.g., *sugar and spice, and everything nice*, which is what little girls are made of (little boys are made of snips—or rats—and snails and puppydog tails); and *sugar is sweet*, from the valentine rhyme: "Roses are red, / Violets are blue, / *Sugar is sweet*, / And so are you" [italics added]. BDPF; CE; CI; DAFD; DAI; DAP; DAS; DEI; FLC; MS; PT; WNWCD.

SUGAR AND SPICE   *See* Sugar.

SUGAR APPLE   *See* Papaya.

SUGAR BUSH   *See* Cough Syrup.

SUGAR CANDY   *See* Candy.

SUGARCOAT   *See* Sugar.

SUGAR CONE   *See* Ice-cream Cone.

SUGAR DADDY   *See* Sugar.

SUGAR IS SWEET   *See* Sugar.

SUGARLOAF   *See* Meat Loaf.

SUGAR MAPLE   *See* Cough Syrup.

SUGAR PEA   *See* Like Two Peas in a Pod.

SUGAR PILL   *See* Sugar.

SUGARPLUM   *See* Plum.

SUGAR SHACK   *See* Cough Syrup.

SUGAR SUBSTITUTE   *See* Saccharine (adj.).

SUGAR SYRUP   *See* Cough Syrup.

SUGAR THE PILL   *See* Sugar.

SUMMER SAUSAGE   *See* Sausage Dog.

SUNDAE   *a sundae.* A bowl of ice cream topped with syrup and (optionally) crushed fruit, nuts, and whipped cream. MWCD: 1897. Source: ICE CREAM. There is no question about the contents of a *sundae.* The question is why it is called by that name. The answer is that either (1) the dish was so rich and special that it was prepared only on *Sunday* or (2) the dish was created in response to moralists' objections to selling ice-cream *sodas* on *Sundays* (soda water being the common denominator in many alcoholic drinks). At any rate, the word *sundae* developed from the word *Sunday* in a city north of Chicago (either Evanston, Ill., or Manitowoc, Wisc.) in the 1890s. The most popular sundae is the *hot fudge sundae*, which consists of a small bowl of vanilla ice cream topped with hot chocolate syrup. If the hot fudge is poured over chocolate ice cream, the concoction is called a "double-chocolate sundae" or a *black-bottom sundae* (DAFD: after-1926), prob. after the 1926 dance of the same name. If vanilla ice cream is topped with crushed pineapple, it can be called a *Chicago sundae* (IHAT: mid-1920s) because waitresses at lunch counters in Chicago during the Roaring Twenties drew a connection between the pineapple topping and the slang term *pineapple* (q.v.) for the small bomb used by Chicago gangsters. (*Pomegranate,* q.v., might have been a better choice.) The term stuck, but like the lunch counter itself, it eventually faded away. DAFD; EWPO; FLC; MDWPO. *See also* Banana Boat; Houseboat; Parfait. *Compare* Black-bottom Pie.

SUNDAY BRUNCH   *See* Brunch.

SUNNY-SIDE UP   *See* Fried Egg.

SUPPER   A light evening meal; an evening meal accompanying a social gathering. Source: SUPPER. MWCD: 13th cent. Eng. *supper* derives fr. Fr. *souper* "to sup" (which has also become a noun, meaning "supper," in Mod. Fr.). To *sup* suggests a light meal, and that is exactly what *supper* meant for over three centuries in America, where the daily meals were *breakfast* (medium size, at daybreak), *dinner* (large size, at noontime), and *supper* (light, at twilight). Only a handful of Americans retain this triad of meal terms with their original meanings, namely, those who grew up on a farm that had a herd of dairy cattle. For everyone else, the term *dinner* has now replaced *supper* for the evening meal—now the heaviest meal of the day—and *supper* has been relegated to the status of (1) a late (and light) evening meal—a *late supper*, such as a *buffet supper*, perhaps at a *supper club* (MWCD: 1925)—following a regular dinner and an evening at the theater or (2) a light meal in the evening served at a church (school, or community center) in connection with a fund raiser—a *church supper*—and often named for the featured dish: a *pancake supper*, a *spaghetti supper*. (If the food is brought in by the members, rather than prepared in the church kitchen, it is called a *potluck supper* because no one person knows precisely what the overall menu will be, so they must trust the "luck of the pot.") The expression *to sing for your supper* (HND: 1609) derives from the life of the wandering minstrels in England in the medieval period who traveled from tavern to tavern singing in exchange for a meal, as Little Tommy Tucker did in the nursery rhyme: "Little Tommy Tucker / *Sings for his supper*. / What shall we give him? / White bread and butter" [italics added]. *To sing for your supper* is now simply to work for money. DEI; EWPO; LA; MS; PT; WNWCD.

SUPPER CLUB   *See* Supper.

SWALLOW CAMELS   *See* Strain out Gnats and Swallow Camels.

SWALLOW HOOK, LINE, AND SINKER   *See* Hard to Swallow.

SWALLOW YOUR PRIDE   *to swallow your pride.* To admit your mistake and accept your punishment. DC: at least 1821. Source: SWALLOW. MWCD: O.E. In this metaphorical expression, pride is treated as if it were distasteful or disgusting food—something that no one in his/her right mind would eat. In that sense, the metaphor is similar in meaning to (1) *to eat crow* (q.v.) and *to eat humble pie* (q.v.), both of which involve foods that demand an *acquired taste* (q.v.); (2) *to eat your hat* (q.v.), in which the entrée is not ordinarily regarded as a food but is potentially edible; and (3) *to eat your words* (q.v.), where only the written or recorded words could conceivably be consumed. The expression *to swallow your words* is quite different from *to eat your words*: The former means "to speak words unclearly or indistinctly," whereas the latter means "to take back what you just said." AID; CI; DAI; DAS; DEI; HND; MS.

SWALLOW YOUR WORDS   *See* Swallow Your Pride.

SWEDISH TEA CAKE   *See* Mexican Wedding Cake.

SWEET AND SOUR   *See* Sourpuss.

SWEET-AND-SOUR   *See* Sweet Tooth.

SWEET AS HONEY   *See* Honeymoon; Mealymouth.

SWEET AS PIE   *See* Sweetie Pie.

SWEETBREAD   The thymus or pancreas of a calf (etc.) when prepared as food. MWCD: 1565. Source: SWEET; BREAD. MWCD: O.E. *Sweetbreads* are not sweet loaves of bread but two of the internal organs of a calf, lamb, or pig: the thymus gland, or *throat sweetbread*, and the pancreas gland, or *stomach sweetbread*. In this compound, the element *bread* is used in one of its earlier senses of "food," and *sweet* is apparently euphemistic. Sweetbreads are regarded as gourmet food by some but are considered as a little too exotic by most. DEOD; FLC; NSOED; PT; WNWCD.

SWEET BUTTER   *See* Sweet Tooth.

SWEETCAKES   *See* Cupcake.

SWEET CHERRY   *See* Cherry (n).

SWEET CHOCOLATE   *See* Sweet Tooth.

SWEET CIDER   *See* Applejack.

SWEET CORN   *See* Sweet Tooth.

SWEET CRUDE   *See* Sweet Tooth.

SWEET DEAL   *See* Sweeten the Kitty.

SWEETEN THE DEAL   *See* Sweeten the Kitty.

SWEETEN THE KITTY   *to sweeten the kitty*. To increase the stakes or incentives. EWPO: late-19th cent. Source: SWEETEN. MWCD: ca. 1552. The term *kitty* derives from the game of faro, which was orig. played in Chinese gambling houses where liquor was served, thereby earning them the name *blind tigers*. *Tiger* then became the name of the house bank but was soon replaced by *kitty*, in the language of the gamblers, just as faro was soon replaced by poker. In poker, *kitty* became the name of the "pot," or the chips anteed up, usu. in the center of the table, for the next hand. To *sweeten—or feed—the kitty*, or *sweeten the pot*, was to raise the stakes in the *kitty* after the ante had already taken place, the idea being to make the pot *sweeter*, or more attractive, to the potential winner. From poker, the expression passed into business and finance, where to *sweeten the pot*, or *sweeten the deal*, is to make an offer more attractive to a potential buyer or lender by adding concessions or inducements so that the buyer or lender will say, "That was a *sweet deal*." CE; DAS; HB; MS; SA.

SWEETEN THE POT   *See* Sweeten the Kitty.

SWEETHEART CONTRACT   *a sweetheart contract.* A privately arranged "contract" between an employer and a union official. MWCD: 1942. Source: SWEET. MWCD: O.E. A *sweetheart* (MWCD: 14th cent.) is someone who is both loved and loving, such as a spouse, a lover, or a child. The word is used as both a term of endearment and a term of address ("Sweetheart, would you bring me a glass of water?") and is equivalent to "Darling." The implication is that the heart is the seat of love, and that a person so addressed has an abundance of it. A *sweetheart contract*, however, involves a pair of rather odd "lovers": the boss of the company and the boss of the workers, who are carrying on a secret "affair" for their mutual benefit. The unwritten "contract" allows management to get away with actions that are forbidden by law or by the written contract without the shareholders or the rest of the employees knowing anything about it. *Sweetheart contracts* are also made at the government level, between public officials and executives of private companies, often involving favoritism by the former and kickbacks for the latter. A *sweetheart deal* (EWPO: ca. 1900) between two friends is expected to profit both of them, provided that the law and their relatives don't get wind of it. If it works, however, it is regarded as a *sweetheart of a deal*. DAP; DAS; DEOD; MS. *See also* Sweet Deal.

SWEETHEART DEAL   *See* Sweetheart Contract.

SWEETHEART OF A DEAL   *See* Sweetheart Contract.

SWEETIE PIE   *a sweetie pie.* A sweetheart. (Usu. female.) MWCD: 1928. Source: SWEET (MWCD: O.E.); PIE (MWCD: 14th cent.). A *sweetie pie* is a girl or woman whom a boy or man is *sweet on*—or whom the boy or man finds to be *as sweet as pie*. *Sweetie pie* is also a term of endearment or address for a girl or woman ("*Sweetie pie*"—or the abbreviated form *Sweetie*—"would you pass me the butter?"), and *sweet as pie* is sometimes used sarcastically of a woman in whose mouth butter would not melt ("She was *as sweet as pie* to my face"). A similar phrase, *cutie pie*, is used both as a term of address for a pretty young child (not necessarily known to the speaker) and as a term of address for a pretty young woman (definitely not known to the speaker). Presumably, the child and the woman are as cute as a fancy pie. AID; BDPF; CE; DAI; DAS; DEI; PT.

SWEETMEATS   *See* Meat; Sweets to the Sweet.

SWEET MILK   *See* Sweet Tooth.

SWEET NOTHINGS   *See* Sweet Tooth.

SWEET ON   *See* Sweetie Pie.

SWEET PEA   *See* Pea Bean.

SWEET PEPPER   *See* Pep (n).

SWEET POTATO   *a sweet potato.* An ocarina. Source: SWEET POTATO. MWCD: 1750. An *ocarina* (MWCD: 1877) is not really a sweet potato, but it seemed to Eng. speakers of the late-19th cent. that it looked like one. To the Italians, who created the word *ocarina*, it looked more like a "little goose" (It. *oca* "goose" plus the dim. suffix *-ina* "little"). The ocarina is a small, oval-shaped, wind instrument that consists simply of a hard body with a mouthpiece and approx. eight finger holes. (The fact that the tones that it produces are soft and *sweet*, like those of an Irish pipe, may also have influenced the selection of the name.) Not only is an ocarina not really a sweet potato, neither is a *yam* (MWCD: 1657), even though the dark-orange-fleshed sweet potato goes by that name, colloquially, in the southeastern United States and, commercially, throughout the country. The reason for the confusion in the United States between these two unrelated tubers is that the West African name for the yam, *nyam-* (fr. Fulani *nyami* "to eat"), was brought to America by African slaves, who applied the name to the sweet potatoes that they encountered in the Caribbean. (True yams, which can grow over seven feet long and weigh over one hundred pounds, have never been grown commercially in the Western Hemisphere.) The confusion was supposedly cleared up in the mid-18th cent., when the true sweet potato, which is native to this hemisphere, was distinguished from both the African yam and the Irish (or "white") potato, which Americans experienced here for the first time in the early-18th cent. Candied sweet potatoes are a traditional dish at Thanksgiving time, and *sweet potato pie* is popular throughout the year. DAFD; EWPO; FLC; WNWCD. *See also* Yummy.

SWEET POTATO PIE   *See* Sweet Potato.

SWEET REVENGE   *See* Sweet Tooth.

SWEET SIXTEEN   *See* Sweet Tooth.

SWEETS OF VICTORY   *See* Sweets to the Sweet.

SWEET SPOT   *See* Sweet Tooth.

SWEETS TO THE SWEET   Sweet treats for a sweet person. DAP: 1600.
Source: SWEET (n) (MWCD: 14th cent.); SWEET (adj.) (MWCD: O.E.). Modern
sweets are either "candy" (or some other confection high in sugar content) or
"rewards" (as in *the sweets of victory*). However, Queen Gertrude had something
else in mind when she spoke this line in Shakespeare's *Hamlet* (Act V, Scene 1),
as she scattered sweet-smelling flowers on the grave of sweet Ophelia, who had
lost her mind and (presumably) drowned herself over the rottenness in the state
of Denmark: "*Sweets to the sweet!* Farewell. / I hop'd thou shouldst have been my
Hamlet's wife; / I thought thy bride-bed to have deck'd, sweet maid, / And not
have strew'd thy grave" [italics added]. When the line is spoken or written in
America today, however, it is usu. on the occasion of someone giving a box of
chocolates to a lover. In England, the word *sweets* more likely refers to hard candy,
whereas the word *sweetmeats* (MWCD: 14th cent.) more likely refers to soft candy
(or what are called "creams" in America). American children are cautioned not to
fill up on sweets—including not only candy but cookies, small cakes, and ice-
cream bars—because they will *spoil their dinner*. FLC; LA; NSOED.

SWEET SWING   *See* Sweet Tooth.

SWEET TALKER   *See* Mealymouthed.

SWEET TOOTH   *a sweet tooth*. A fondness for sweet food. MWCD: 14th cent.
Source: SWEET. MWCD: O.E. *To have a sweet tooth* is to have a craving for any
food with a high sugar content, such as candy, cakes, pies, and ice cream. (Mrs.
Jack Spratt had a "fat tooth": She craved fat.) *Sweet* is combined with food names
to indicate that the foods are either not bitter (e.g., *sweet chocolate*, *sweet corn*,
sweet pea) or not sour (e.g., *sweet butter*, *sweet corn*, *sweet milk*). However, some
foods are allowed to be both bitter (or sour) and sweet at the same time—e.g.,
bittersweet chocolate and *sweet-and-sour pork and shrimp*. The phrase *to take the
bitter with the sweet* means to accept unpleasant things along with the pleasant.
Unlike the other three taste sensations (bitter, salty, and sour), which gen. have
a negative connotation, *sweet* has a positive connotation in almost every respect.
Purified crude oil is "sweet" (*sweet crude*); whispered intimacies are "sweet" (*sweet
nothings*); turning sixteen is "sweet" (*sweet sixteen*); revenge is "sweet" (*sweet revenge*); a smooth baseball, golf, or tennis swing is "sweet" (a *sweet swing*); the ideal
place on the bat, club head, or racket to hit the ball is "sweet" (the *sweet spot*);
time is "sweet" (*take your own sweet time*); a short speech is "sweet" (*short and
sweet*); and life is "sweet" (*You bet your sweet life*). *How sweet it is!* (Jackie Gleason).
AID; BDPF; CI; DAFD; DAI; DAP; DAS; DC; DEI; FLC; HND; MS; NSOED.

SWISS-CHEESE INFIELD   *See* Holey as Swiss Cheese.

SWISS STEAK   *See* Salisbury Steak.

SYCOPHANT   *a sycophant.* A fawning flatterer; a clinging parasite; an obse-quious apple-polisher. MWCD: 1575. Source: FIG. In ancient Greece, a *syko-phantēs* was lit. a "maker of the *sign of the fig*" (fr. *sykon* "fig" + *phanein* "to show"); i.e., he was an accuser or informer—one who "fingered" people who were committing crimes by directing at them a thumb thrust between the first two fingers. This is the most obscene of all gestures in the Mediterranean countries, suggesting either copulation or defecation. However, there is a possible confusion here between *sykon*, the native Gk. word for "fig," and *ficus*, the native Lat. word. *Sykon* is unambiguous, but as PT notes, Lat. has a fem. form, *fica*, which refers to the female pudenda. The "making of the *sign of the fig*" in ancient Greece may simply have been a legal "pointing to the defendant" rather than a combination legal-obscene gesture. EWPO; WNWCD. *See also* Not Worth a Fig. *Compare* Spanish Fig.

SYRUPY   *See* Cough Syrup.

T

TABLE D'HÔTE   *See* Menu.

TABLE IS SET   *See* Set the Table.

TACO   *See* Tortilla.

TACO CHIPS   *See* Tortilla.

TACO SALAD   *See* Salad.

TAFFY   Cajolery; flattery. Source: TAFFY. MWCD: ca. 1817. *Taffy* is a Scottish English and American English word for a popular candy that is made with the simplest ingredients and techniques: Boil sugar (white or brown), butter, and flavorings in a pot until the mixture thickens slightly; pour the taffy onto a marble slab until it cools slightly; pull it back and forth until it becomes elastic; and cut it up into bite-size pieces. This procedure, called a *taffy pull*, was a social occasion in mid-19th cent. America in which all of the members of a family—or all of the young people in a church or school group—would participate. The metaphorical senses of "arm-twisting" and "leg-pulling" may have derived from the twisting and stretching of the candy during the taffy pull. The Brit. Eng. version of taffy, called *toffee* (MWCD: ca. 1825) or *toffy*, is also popular in the United States but is harder than American taffy and often contains nuts. *Salt water taffy* (DAFD: ca. 1885), which was created in Atlantic City, N.J., and is sometimes called *Atlantic City Taffy*, was so called because a little salt water was once part of the recipe. FLC; NSOED; PT; WNWCD.

TAFFY PULL   *See* Taffy.

TAILGATE PICNIC   *See* No Picnic.

TAKE ANOTHER BITE OF THE APPLE   *See* Two Bites of the Cherry.

TAKE ANOTHER BITE OF THE CHERRY   *See* Two Bites of the Cherry.

TAKE A POTSHOT   *See* Go to Pot.

TAKE FOOD OUT OF THE MOUTHS OF CHILDREN   *See* Starve (v); Take the Bread out of Someone's Mouth.

TAKE-OUT   *See* Restaurant.

TAKE POTLUCK   *to take potluck (or pot luck)*. To take what is offered to you. NSOED: late-16th cent. Source: POT. MWCD: O.E. Unannounced guests who show up at a friend's home at dinnertime are likely to be invited to stay for dinner but are reminded that they will have to *take potluck*, i.e., to eat whatever the family is eating. This notion of the *luck of the pot* goes back to Elizabethan times, when an unannounced guest was invited to share *potluck* (MWCD: 1592), i.e., the contents of the large cast-iron pot on the hearth, with the rest of the family. The guest might not like what was cooking in the pot on that particular evening, but those were the chances that he/she would have to take. This take-your-chances notion of *potluck* has developed in modern times into a more general meaning of *to take potluck*, i.e., to take whatever comes your way—whatever is available at that particular time or place. For example, you might tell the agency to send you any temporary employee who is available, or order whatever the "special" is that evening at the restaurant, or vote for any of the candidates whose last name begins with C. The surprise-me aspect of *potluck* has increased with the invention of the *potluck supper* (NSOED: late-19th cent.), to which each invitee is expected to bring a "dish to pass" or a "dish to share," although sometimes the expected guests are told that if their last name begins with a letter from *A* to *E* they are supposed to bring a casserole, *F* to *J* a salad, *K* to *O* a dessert, etc. Such meals are popular at churches, schools, and fund-raisers because they capitalize on individual specialties and minimize individual costs. (In some parts of the country a potluck supper is called a *covered-dish supper*.) CE; CI; DAFD; DAI; DC; DEI; EWPO; LCRH; MS.

TAKE THE BITTER WITH THE SWEET   *to take the bitter with the sweet*. To accept the bad with the good. Source: BITTER; SWEET. MWCD: O.E. *Bitter* and *sweet* are two of the four basic taste sensations (the other two being salt and sour). *Bitter* is defined lit. as "acrid, astringent, disagreeable, distasteful, sharp, or severe," and *sweet* as "agreeable or pleasant." The metaphor, however, refers not to sensations arising from the taste buds but to feelings arising from the mind. Each person's life experiences go into his/her definition of "good" and "bad," and whatever they are, they are at least slightly different from those of anyone else. *Bitter* ("bad") and *sweet* ("good") are diametrically opposed, and it would seem impossible for something to be both bitter and sweet at the same time. Nevertheless, that is exactly what occurs with *bittersweet* (MWCD: 1511). *Bittersweet chocolate* is both bitter (from the chocolate) and sweet (from the small amount of sugar); and a *bittersweet victory* is one that is both happy and sad. AID; DAP; DC; HND. *See also* Sweet Tooth. *Compare* Sweet and Sour.

TAKE THE BREAD OUT OF SOMEONE'S MOUTH   *to take the bread out of someone's mouth.* To rob someone of his/her livelihood. Source: BREAD. MWCD: O.E. One person can *take the bread out of someone else's mouth* by depriving that other person of his/her job or by depriving him/her of the tools, supplies, facilities, or time necessary to do that job. A person who is so deprived may complain that the depriver is *taking the bread out of his family's mouth.* A similar expression is *to take food out of the mouths of children,* i.e., to cut off support for the poor or to ignore the plight of hungry children. BDPF; DAI; MS; NSOED.

TAKE THE CAKE   *to take the cake.* To be the best (DC: 1884); to be the worst (EWPO: 20th cent.). Source: CAKE. MWCD: 13th cent. The literal meaning of *take the cake* dates back to the mid-19th cent., when the couple who performed the fanciest *cakewalk* (q.v.) won the prize—a cake. The first metaphorical use of the phrase occurred in the late-19th cent., when a North Dakota farmer was said by a newspaper to *take the cake* for being the first one to harvest his wheat that year. A second metaphorical use of the phrase, exactly contrary to the first, developed in the early-20th cent. *That really takes the cake* means that the person, group, or institution that committed a certain action really takes the prize for stupidity. In other words, instead of winning a valuable prize, they should win the booby prize. AID; BDPF; CE; CI; DAI; DEI; HDAS; HI; HND; IHAT; LCRH; MDWPO; MS; NSOED; PT.

TAKE THE HEAT   *See* Pressure Cooker.

TAKE THE STARCH OUT OF   *to take the starch out of someone.* To loosen someone up; to make someone act less stiff and formal. Source: STARCH. MWCD: 15th cent. Someone who has a *starchy* manner (MWCD: 1802) is stiff and unbending, the way a military officer is expected to be. That stiffness is reflected in the dress uniform that the officer wears—achieved partly by laundering it with starch (or spraying it with starch before pressing) and partly by using "sizing" to stiffen the mesh that maintains the form of the hat or cap. Starch is obtained from vegetables, esp. grains (such as corn) and tubers (such as potatoes). Because it is odorless, tasteless, and virtually colorless, it can be used to thicken foods such as gravies, sauces, and puddings without altering their flavor, aroma, or appearance. It is also used as an adhesive, as a base for cosmetics, as a "sizing" for paper, and as a thickening additive for medicines. *Cornstarch* (MWCD: 1853), obtained from corn, is one of the most popular types of cooking starch, replacing the former favorite, *arrowroot* (MWCD: 1696), which was obtained from a tuber by the same name. *Potato starch* (also called *potato flour*), which is obtained by cooking, drying, and milling potatoes, is used as a moistener and thickener in sponge cakes and fried cakes. AID; DAFD; FLC; NSOED; PT; WNWCD.

TAKE THE WORDS RIGHT OUT OF MY MOUTH   *See* You Said a Mouthful.

TAKE TWO BITES OF THE CHERRY   *See* Two Bites of the Cherry.

TAKE WITH A DOSE OF SALTS   *See* Take with a Grain of Salt.

TAKE WITH A GRAIN OF SALT   *to take something with a grain of salt.* To react to a spoken or written statement with considerable skepticism. DC: 1647. Source: GRAIN (MWCD: 14th cent.); SALT (MWCD: O.E.). The Romans knew that not only tasteless food but also questionable statements were easier to swallow if taken with even a single grain of salt: *cum grano salis* (Pliny). The Eng. version of that phrase has remained faithful to the Lat. original in America, but in Brit. Eng. it has been increased to a *pinch of salt*, the amount that you can hold between your thumb and forefinger. However, if the questionable statement is a ridiculous charge or accusation, both Americans and Britishers can *take it with a dose of salts*—referring to *Epsom salts* (MWCD: 1876), the crystalline "salt" (magnesium sulphate) refined from the mineral waters of Epsom, Surrey, England, and used as a cathartic or purgative. Because common salt (sodium chloride) has long been associated with religious rituals by Jews and Christians, a superstition has developed that it is unlucky to spill salt—and that if you *do* spill it, you must pick up a pinch of it with your right hand and throw it over your left shoulder—or else something bad will happen. This custom has been practiced for so long that most people who follow it have no idea why they are doing it (to ward off evil) or which hand or shoulder to use. (Spilled *pepper* should be "pinched" with the *right* hand and thrown over the *right* shoulder.) Salt also has the magical quality of getting wild birds to slow down long enough for you to catch them—or at least that's what big kids tell little kids: "Just *sprinkle salt on their tails.* Works every time." (Of course it works: If you're close enough to a bird to sprinkle salt on its tail, you're close enough to grab it.) AID; ATWS; BDPF; DAI; DEI; EWPO; HI; HND; IRCD; LCRH; MDWPO; MS; NSOED; PT; SA.

TAKE WITH A PINCH OF SALT   *See* Take with a Grain of Salt.

TAKE YOUR OWN SWEET TIME   *See* Sweet Tooth.

TALK GARBAGE   *See* Garbage in, Garbage out.

TALK TRIPE   *See* Tripe.

TALL DRINK OF WATER   *See* Long Drink of Water.

TANGERINE   *See* Mandarin Orange.

TANTALIZE   *to tantalize someone.* To tease someone by showing them something they want and then denying them access to it. MWCD: 1597. Source: HUNGER; THIRST. The verb *tantalize* is named for King Tantalus of Greek mythology, who was sentenced to an eternity of hunger and thirst for revealing to humans the secrets of the gods. In Hades, Tantalus was confined to a pool of cool water, over which hung a tree with delicious fruit. However, whenever Tantalus bent over to drink the water, it would recede; and whenever he reached up to pluck the fruit, the wind would blow the branch away. Thus, he was tormented not only with unending thirst and hunger but with constant frustration as well. Modern humans are still *tantalized* by cool water (esp. when the beach is closed) and fresh fruit (esp. when it is out of reach in a tree), but they also find *tantalizing* (MWCD: ca. 1683) the showgirls in Las Vegas ("Look, but don't touch!") and the male strippers at the local bar ("Touch only with money!"). EWPO; LCRH.

TANTALIZING   *See* Tantalize.

TAPIOCA PUDDING   *See* Caviar to the General.

TART (n)   *a tart.* A prostitute. Source: TART. MWCD: 15th cent. It did not take *tart* "a sweet, open-faced pie" (MWCD: 15th cent.) long to broaden its meaning to include "prostitute" (16th cent.). Perhaps the basis for the metaphor was the fact that prostitutes were "as sweet as a tart" or that they were sometimes as topless as the bottom-crusted pie. The major differences between a pie and a tart are that (1) the pie is sometimes sweet, whereas the tart always is; (2) the pie is sometimes top-crusted, whereas the tart never is; (3) the pie is usu. large, whereas the tart seldom is; and (4) the pie is usu. served as a dessert, whereas the tart (or "tartlet") is often used as a snack or hors d'oeuvre. The noun *tart* is not related to the adj. *tart* "sharp-tasting," but it prob. is related to the noun *torte* (q.v.). CE; FLC; IHAT; PT.

TARTAR SAUCE   *See* Steak Tartare.

TARTAR STEAK   *See* Steak Tartare.

TART CHERRY   *See* Cherry (n).

TASTE   *a taste of success (etc); to taste success (etc).* A sample of what success (etc.) is really like; to experience success (etc.) for the first time. Source: TASTE. MWCD: 14th cent. Both the noun *taste* and the verb *taste* were borrowed from O.Fr. in the early-14th cent., at which time the words referred to the test (identification, recognition) of something by touching it. It was not until the middle of the 14th cent. that the words were applied to the identification or recognition of food or drink by touching it with the tongue, which contains the *taste buds* (MWCD: 1879). Therefore, what are now the "literal" meanings of *taste* (n) (the flavor and aroma of food and drink) and *taste* (v) (to identify or recognize a food or drink by its flavor or aroma) were once the derived meanings; and what are now the "figurative" meanings (a sample or experience, to sample or experience) were once the basic meanings. The meaning of the noun has also become broader than that of the verb, referring to such things as judgment and propriety. CE; EWPO; NSOED; WNWCD. *See also* Good Taste; In Good Taste.

TASTE BUDS   *See* Palatable.

TASTE FISHY   *See* Fishy.

TASTEFUL   *See* In Good Taste.

TASTELESS   *See* In Good Taste.

TASTE LIKE DISHWATER   *to taste (just) like dishwater.* To taste weak and watery; to have no flavor at all. Source: TASTE (v) (MWCD: 14th cent.); DISHWATER (MWCD: 15th cent.). *Dishwater* is the water in which dishes are washed. It is usu. thin, gray, and lukewarm, like weak coffee with too much water and not enough beans. *Dull as dishwater* (HND: 20th cent.) is an Americanism used to describe a person or event that is boring, although the source of the simile is the Brit. expression "dull as *ditchwater*" (HND: 18th cent.). A *dishwater blond* is a girl or woman who is a natural blond, not a "bottle blond," but whose hair is a dark grayish brown rather than a light yellowish brown. Dishwater—or laundry water—is the basis for *hogwash* (MWCD: 15th cent.): the *swill* (MWCD: 1553), or *slop,* fed to hogs. *Hogwash* has also come to stand for anything that is worthless or otherwise unfit for human consumption, from cheap liquor to misleading propaganda (EWPO: late-17th cent.). Even the *dishrag* (MWCD: 1839) that is used to wash the dishes has provided us with figurative language. A person who *feels like a wet dishrag,* or is *as limp as a dishrag,* is weak and exhausted, as after a bout with the flu or a high fever. The person who wields the dishrag in a restaurant is known as a *pearl diver* because he/she is constantly plunging his/her hands and arms into the water, looking for things of value (such as knives, forks, and spoons). Before the advent of indoor plumbing, kitchen sinks, and automatic dishwashers, dishes were washed in a pan—a *dishpan* (MWCD: 1872)—filled with hot water (from the reservoir of the cookstove) and lye soap. The action of the hot water, the caustic soap, and the amount of time it took to wash all of the dinner dishes usu. gave the housewife a daily case of *dishpan hands* (MWCD: 1944), a condition in which the skin on the hands becomes red, wrinkled, and exceedingly dry, although today people claim to have *dishpan hands* when they simply wash the car or the dog. ATWS; DAP; DAS; DEI; HDAS; NSOED; SA. *See also* Chief Cook and Bottlewasher; Pot-walloper. *Compare* Tastes Just like Chicken.

TASTES JUST LIKE CHICKEN   *It tastes just like chicken*. You're going to love it! Source: TASTE (v); CHICKEN. MWCD: 14th cent. Never trust anyone who tries to get you to eat the meat of an animal that you have never seen up close, say nothing about tasted. "What does rattlesnake meat taste like?" "You like chicken, don't you?" "Yes." "Well, it tastes just like chicken." Chicken is used as an exemplar because just about every culture of the world is familiar with it, likes the taste of it, and knows that people are supposed to prefer the white meat over the dark meat. Among fish, the same is true of the albacore tuna, which is sometimes called the *chicken of the sea* because of its large amount of tender white meat. (The *alba* in *albacore* does not mean "white"; the word is from Ar. *al-bakurah*.) Some "exotic" animals actually *do* taste like chicken, e.g. frogs' legs. DAFD; FLC; PT.

TASTE TESTER   *See* Try It on the Dog.

TEA   *a tea*. A late afternoon family or social gathering at which refreshments, including tea, are served. Source: TEA. MWCD: ca. 1655. The introduction of Chinese tea into England in the mid-17th cent. led to a tremendous demand for the product that has never ceased. In America, the Boston Tea Party of 1773 marked the beginning of the end of easy access to tea by the colonists, and the Revolution put an end to British shipping of tea to the new United States. Therefore, England was the location of the development of the *tea*—not as an occasional party or dance but as a regular snack or meal. In that country, *tea* became a late afternoon (ca. 3–6 P.M.) snack, prob. inspired by the English housewives' practice of serving their husbands a light meal when they got home from their blue-collar jobs. Eventually, late afternoon *tea* was adopted by the middle classes (DAFD: early-1800s) and expanded by the upper classes into *high tea* (MWCD: 1831). A regular *tea* offered finger sandwiches, tea cakes, petits fours, scones and crumpets, lots of jams and jellies, and plenty of hot tea. A *high tea*, served in the early evening, was a social replacement for dinner at home alone or at a restaurant. It became a substantial meal, usu. served in buffet style, of roast beef, baked ham, sausages, fish, vegetables, breads and rolls, and not only tea but coffee and ale as well. DAFD; DAS; FLC; MDWPO; PT.

TEACH YOUR GRANDMOTHER TO SUCK EGGS   *to teach your grandmother (how) to suck eggs*. To presume to give advice to an expert. HI: ca. 1700. Source:

SUCK (MWCD: O.E.); EGG (MWCD: 14th cent.). Sucking eggs is a lost art, but if anyone would know how to do it, it would be an old farmer's wife who collected the chickens' eggs and occasionally poked a few holes in one, inserted a straw in one of the holes, and sucked out the liquid white and yolk. If her grandchildren read about the procedure and tried to explain it to their grandmother, they would be telling her something she already knew. Although the art of sucking eggs is lost, some other egg-sucking expressions survive: (1) *egg-sucker* (HDAS: 1838— a "brown-noser") and (2) *Go suck an egg!* (an order to "Get lost!"). ATWS; BDPF; CI; CODP; DAP; DAS; DEI; EWPO; LCRH; MS; SA. *See also* Go Fry an Egg; Go Lay an Egg.

TEAKETTLE   *See* Kettledrum; Tempest in a Teapot.

TEAPOT   *See* Tempest in a Teapot.

TEAR UP THE PEA PATCH   *See* Like Two Peas in a Pod.

TEMPEST IN A TEACUP   *See* Tempest in a Teapot.

TEMPEST IN A TEAPOT   *a tempest in a teapot.* Much ado about nothing. DC: late-19th cent. Source: TEAPOT. MWCD: 1705. A *teapot* is the vessel in which tea leaves are brewed and from which the brewed tea is poured into cups. Unlike the *teakettle* (MWCD: 1705), in which the water for tea is brought to a violent and noisy boil, the teapot is quite peaceful and quiet. In this metaphor, the "tempest" of the teakettle is transferred to the calmness of the teapot, where it obviously does not belong. The original form of the metaphor, in England, was—and is— *a storm in a teacup*, which goes back to the mid-19th cent. (CI: 1854). In America, the expression was first altered to *a tempest in a teacup* (HB: 1872) and then, perhaps in imitation of the initial consonants of the two syllables of *tempest* (*t-, p-*), to *a tempest in a teapot*. Children, esp. young girls, like to play "tea party," and they should be quite familiar with the teapot; however, the nursery rhyme illustrates that they sometimes confuse a placid teapot with a whistling teakettle: "I'm a little teapot, short and stout. / [The child is standing.] Here is my handle, here is my spout. / [The child puts one arm akimbo and extends the other to the side like a goose neck and head.] When I get all steamed up, then I shout, / Tip me over and pour me out. [The child bends sideways in the direction of the goose neck.]" The "shouting" of the *teakettle* indicates that the water is *piping hot* (MWCD: 14th cent.) and ready to join the tea leaves in the *teapot*. Another reference to children and vessels is the proverb *Little pitchers have big ears* (CODP: 1699—"Kids hear the darnedest things"), in which the children are the "little *pitchers*" (MWCD: 13th cent.), and the *big ears* are the pitcher's (double) handles. (The size of the pitchers may change, but the handles must always be big enough to accommodate a human hand.) AID; BDPF; CE; CI; DAI; DAP; DEI; EWPO; HND; MDWPO; MS; PT.

TEMPLE ORANGE   *See* Mandarin Orange.

TENDERLOIN   *the tenderloin.* The most attractive assignment for a Manhattan police officer in the 1870s. Source: TENDERLOIN. MWCD: ca. 1828. The tenderloin, or short loin, is regarded as the leanest, tastiest, and tenderest cut of beef. It would be called *a cut above the rest* (q.v.) if it were not for the fact that when the beef is hung up by its hind legs, the *sirloin*—a "royal" cut—is above the short loin. The tenderloin includes boneless cuts such as filet mignon, chateaubriand, and tournedos and such bone-in cuts as T-bone and porterhouse. Because of its reputation as the choicest part of the beef, *tenderloin* has also become a metaphor for the choicest assignment for a crooked police officer—the section of a city where graft and corruption are so rampant that an officer can make a fortune simply by looking the other way and keeping his/her mouth shut. The silence is enough for the officer to switch to eating tenderloin instead of the *chuck* (shoulder) or *rump* (hip) that he/she was used to on a prior assignment. The first *tenderloin district* (DAFD: 1876) of this sort was the area of Manhattan covered by the 29th Precinct. When a new commanding officer was brought in, the captain, who was well aware of the 29th's reputation, commented that he would now be *eating tenderloin*—i.e., going on the take and making a pile of money. The *tenderloin district* of Manhattan was cleared up long ago, but the name remains—not only in New York City but in San Francisco—to remind people of what it was like once upon a time. DAFD; EWPO; MDWPO; NSOED; PT.

TENDERLOIN DISTRICT   *See* Tenderloin.

TEN LASHES WITH A WET NOODLE   *See* Wet Noodle.

TEXAS TURKEY   *See* Cape Cod Turkey.

THANKSGIVING DINNER   *See* Dinner (1).

THAT DOESN'T FEED THE BULLDOG   *See* Feed the Bulldog.

THAT (REALLY) TAKES THE CAKE   *See* Take the Cake.

THAT'S THE WAY THE COOKIE CRUMBLES   That's the way it is; that's life. HDAS: 1956. Source: COOKIE. MWCD: 1703. Cookies crumble, unexpectedly, into an unpredictable number of pieces of unpredictable shape and size. The only thing predictable about this is that it *will* happen, sooner or later. This modern proverb is usu. uttered by someone trying to comfort or console someone else who has been a victim of an unfortunate occurrence. The speaker could have chosen a different Eng. expression, such as "That's the way the ball bounces" or "That's the way the Mercedes-Benz," or he/she could have used a Fr. phrase, such as "C'est la vie" or "C'est la guerre." AID; CE; CI; DAI; DAS; DC; HND; MS; SA.

THEN LET THEM EAT CAKE!   *See* Let Them Eat Cake!

THE OTHER WHITE MEAT   (A trademark of the Pork Council of America.) Pork. Source: PORK. MWCD: 14th cent. Pork meat is not pure white, like a breast of chicken; but when cooked, it is lighter in color than the *red meat* (q.v.) of beef, and it resembles veal in many ways. (Pork fat, however, *is* pure white, the whitest of all fats, as reflected in the word *porcelain*.) It is interesting that people need to be reminded of the attractive qualities of pork, considering the fact that pork has been the meat of choice around the world—except in Semitic cultures—for several centuries. In America, the pig was introduced by Columbus to the Caribbean Islands, where it competed with the native *peccary* (MWCD: 1613), which was referred to by the Spanish as a *javelina* (MWCD: 1822—fr. Sp. "wild pig"). European pigs were introduced into Florida in the mid-16th cent. and into the English colonies in the early-17th cent. Pigs that escaped from the Spanish colony of Florida roamed wild throughout the South and are now referred to as *razorbacks* (MWCD: 1849). Domesticated pigs are desirable farm animals for several reasons: (1) they eat just about anything, including garbage; (2) they can carry a lot of weight on their long, low bodies; (3) they don't need to be milked or sheared; (4) they are susceptible to few diseases; (5) they produce large litters of young; and (6) their meat is tender and tasty and surrounded by a lot of fat, which makes the best lard for cooking. When pork is cured and smoked, it becomes "the other *red* meat": *ham* (q.v.). BDPF; DAFD; DAS; DEOD; FLC; MDWPO; PT; WNWCD.

THERE IS ALWAYS ONE ROTTEN APPLE IN THE BARREL   *See* One Rotten Apple Spoils the Barrel.

THERE'S A FLY IN MY SOUP   *See* Soup.

THERE'S MANY A SLIP TWIXT THE CUP AND THE LIP   *See* Cup (n).

THERE'S NO ACCOUNTING FOR TASTE   *See* Everyone to His Own Taste.

THERE'S NO SUCH THING AS A FREE LUNCH   You can't get something for nothing. CODP: 1967. Source: LUNCH. MWCD: 1812. There may be no such thing as a "free lunch" today, but there used to be—in American saloons, barrooms, and beerhalls at the turn of the 19th cent. The term *free lunch* dates back to the early-19th cent. (DAFD: 1830), but at that time it consisted only of salted peanuts, salted popcorn, and salted pretzels—the salt being designed to make the patrons so thirsty that they would have to order more drinks. The practice was so successful that the customers began to demand more food, and by the late-19th cent. (IHAT: 1880s) a *free lunch* consisted of soup and chowder, beef and ham, smoked herring and oysters, baked beans and chili, cole slaw and potato salad, cheese and pickles, and even caviar. In the 20th cent., because of Prohibition (1920–1933), the saloons, barrooms, and beerhalls were closed for almost fourteen years; but after its repeal, during the Great Depression, the full *free lunch* was reinstated until WWII, when the offerings were reduced again to peanuts, popcorn, and pretzels. So there is no longer a literal *free lunch*, but it has provided us with a modern proverb to remind us that "There is no free ride." HDAS.

THICK AS MOLASSES IN JANUARY   *See* Slow as Molasses in January.

THICK AS PEA SOUP   *See* Soup.

THIRST (n)   *a thirst.* A craving or longing. NSOED: M.E. Source: THIRST. MWCD: O.E. Literally, *thirst* is either (1) a conscious desire of the individual for liquid refreshment or (2) an unconscious need of the body for rehydration. Metaphorically, *thirst* can be a conscious desire of the individual for things such as blood or knowledge. A *bloodthirsty* person (MWCD: 1535) is one who, like Count Dracula, is thirsty for blood; and a *bloodthirsty* crime is one that has been committed by such a person. A *thirst* for knowledge is a craving for the facts of life— esp. when they are not readily available—by someone who is *thirsty* for information. Even inanimate objects can be *thirsty*—e.g., absorbent cloth or paper towels that soak up liquids in a hurry, and dry ground that has already soaked up all the water available and is *thirsty* for more. MS; SA; WNWCD. *Compare* Hungry for Affection; Starved for Affection.

THIRST (v)   *See* Thirst (n).

THIRSTY   *See* Thirst (n).

THIS CAR IS A LEMON   *See* Lemon.

THREE-MARTINI LUNCH   *See* Business Lunch.

THREE SQUARE MEALS   *See* Meal.

THREE SQUARES   *See* Meal.

THROAT SWEETBREAD   *See* Sweetbread.

THROUGH THE MILL   *to have been—or been put—through the mill.* To have experienced difficulty and hardships that have contributed positively to your development. HND: 19th cent. Source: MILL. MWCD: O.E. *Grist* (or grain) is put through the stones of a water mill, windmill, or animal-powered mill to produce meal or flour. Someone who has had rough treatment—and obviously survived— feels as if he/she has been chewed up by and spit out of a "grist mill" (MWCD: 1602), emerging different but wiser. Such persons are better able to *grind it out* (DC: 1801)—i.e., to survive the *daily grind*. Someone who has not undergone hardship has had a *run-of-the-mill* existence (MWCD: 1930): average and uneventful, like the typical grind of a batch of grain between the millstones. Oxen have become so associated with the *daily grind* of walking around in a circle, yoked to a pole to which the grinding wheel is attached, that when we see cattle moving about the pen in a circle, we say that they are *milling about*. The noun *mill*, which was once attached only to the grain mill, now describes many different types of factories that cut, crush, groove, press, or stamp everything from metal to vegetables; and every restaurant has a *coffee mill* (MWCD: 1691) and a *pepper mill* (MWCD: ca. 1858). BDPF; DAS; DC; EWPO; FLC; HDAS; MS; NSOED.

THROW IT TO THE DOGS   *See* Try It on the Dog.

THROW SOMEONE A BONE   *See* Go to the Dogs.

THROW SOMEONE A FEW CRUMBS   *See* Crumb.

TIED TO YOUR MOTHER'S APRON STRINGS   *to be tied to your mother's apron strings*. For a man to be completely dominated by, and dependent on, his mother. DC: 1848. Source: APRON. MWCD: 15th cent. This expression is often preceded by *still*: i.e., *still tied to your mother's apron strings* (even at the age of forty!), implying that young children were once so tethered in order for their mother to keep track of them. Although that may not have been the case, since the 16th cent. *apron strings* have been a symbol of dominance by females—the ones who wore the aprons—over males, both children and adults. In fact, the original form of the expression was "tied to your *wife's* apron strings," referring to the 17th cent. English law of "apron-string tenure," which allowed a husband to enjoy the property that his wife had inherited only as long as she lived. During that period of time, the husband was financially dependent on his wife, who, in our modern sense, "wore the pants in the family." The word *apron* itself has undergone a strange twist, though one of form rather than meaning. The original form of the word in early-M.E. was *napron* (fr. M.Fr. *naperon*); however, by a process called "misdivision," *a napron* became *an apron*, just as *a numpire* became *an umpire*. (The misdivision also worked in reverse, producing *a nickname* from earlier *an ekename* "an 'also' name.") BDPF; CI; DAI; DEI; EWPO; HB; HND; MDWPO; MS; PT.

TIE ON THE (OLD) FEED BAG   *See* Put on the Feed Bag.

TIGHTEN YOUR BELT (ANOTHER NOTCH)   *See* Have Something under Your Belt.

TIME IS RIPE   *See* Ripe.

TIN   *See* In the Can.

TIN CAN   *See* In the Can.

TIN FOIL   *See* Freezer Burn.

TIP   *See* Dutch Treat.

TOADEATER   *a toadeater.* A parasite; a sycophant. NSOED: early-17th cent. Source: EAT. MWCD: O.E. A 17th cent. *toadeater* really did eat toads, which were thought to be poisonous at that time. He was a boy who traveled the English countryside with his master—a mountebank, charlatan, or quack—who was a purveyor of panaceas, cure-alls, and patent medicines. Once the audience had assembled beside the wagon, the mountebank extolled the medicinal virtues of his elixir, instructed the boy to eat a "poisonous" toad, and administered his magic medicine to the boy, who recovered completely. By the early-19th cent., an adult (esp. a male) who behaved like the toadeating boy—i.e., who was willing to do anything, regardless of how disgusting or demeaning, in order to please his superior—came to be called by a shortened form of *toadeater*: *toady* (MWCD: 1826). Today, a *toady* is a fawning flatterer, a clinging parasite, an obsequious brownnoser; and the verb *toady* (MWCD: ca. 1859) has developed to describe his actions. ATWS; BDPF; CE; EWPO; IRCD; LCRH; MDWPO; SA; THT; WNWCD.

TOAD'S HAT   *See* Spring up like Mushrooms.

TOADSTOOL   *See* Spring up like Mushrooms.

TOADY   *See* Toadeater.

TOAST (adj.)   *See* Toast (n) (1).

TOAST (n) (1)   *a toast.* An expression of honor accompanied by a raised glass. NSOED: mid-18th cent. Source: TOAST (n). MWCD: 15th cent. How a wish for good health, good luck, and long life came to be named after a piece of browned bread is not certain, but there are several theories, all of them pointing to the time of Shakespeare: (1) after a glass of wine was raised, and the words of honor spoken, each person dipped a piece of toast into his wine and ate it; (2) before the glasses of wine or ale were raised, a small piece of toast was put in the bottom of each to trap the dregs; (3) before the good wishes were spoken and the drinks drunk, a piece of spiced toast was placed in each glass to add flavor to the wine. The toast was first associated with the drink (a *toast*), then with the speech (to *toast* someone—MWCD: 1640), then with the person *proposing the toast* (a *toastmaster*) and finally with the person being toasted (the *toast of the town*). The practice of touching (or "clicking") glasses after a toast goes back to an ancient custom by which a host and a guest each poured a little wine into the other's cup to ensure that if one had poisoned the other, they would both *become toast* (i.e., "die"). This may have been the inspiration for modern expressions such as "The flooded town was *toast*" (i.e., totally destroyed) and "They *toasted* her" (i.e., killed off her character on the TV soap opera). BDPF; CE; MDWPO; WNWCD. *See also* Toast (n) (2).

TOAST (n) (2)   *a toast.* A banquet in honor of a single individual or group. Source: TOAST (n). MWCD: 15th cent. A ceremony called a *toast* is presided over by a *toastmaster* (MWCD: 1749) or *toastmistress* (MWCD: 1921), who acts as a master (or mistress) of ceremonies, calling on numerous after-dinner speakers who say complimentary things about—and *propose a toast* (q.v.) to—the guest of honor (the *toast* of the banquet). In contrast, if the purpose of the ceremony is to poke fun at the guest of honor, the banquet is called a *roast* (NSOED: mid-18th cent.), and the speakers drag out all of the uncomplimentary things they can think of, just short of causing the guest to become angry and leave the room. At the end of his/her *roast*, each speaker makes a complimentary *toast*—but it is not called a "roast," and the toastmaster is not called a "roastmaster." The fun part of all this is when the guest thinks he/she is being invited to a *toast* but is actually being invited to a *roast*. MDWPO; FLC; NSOED; PT; WNWCD. *See also* Toast (n) (1).

TOAST (v)   *See* Toast (n) (2).

TOASTED   *See* Warm as Toast.

TOASTMASTER   *See* Toast (n) (1), (2).

TOASTMISTRESS   *See* Toast (n) (2).

TOAST OF THE TOWN   *See* Toast (n) (1).

TOASTY   *See* Warm as Toast.

TO EACH HIS OWN   *See* Everyone to His Own Taste.

TOFFEE   *See* Taffy.

TOFFY   *See* Taffy.

TOFU   *See* Milk (n).

TOIL IN THE VINEYARDS   *See* Wither on the Vine.

TOMATILLO   *See* Tomato.

TOMATO   *a tomato.* An attractive young woman. LA: 1920. Source: TOMATO. MWCD: 1604. The connection between a plump red tomato and an attractive young woman may be the fact that the tomato was once called a *love apple*, an Eng. translation of Fr. *pomme d'amour*, which in turn was a mistranslation of It. *pomodoro* "golden apple," which in turn was a mistranslation of the earlier It. *pomo da moro* "Moorish apple," i.e., the fruit that had been brought to Spain from Mexico by way of North Africa. Fortunately, Spanish settled on a version of Nahuatl *tomatl, tomate*, which English and most other languages have used as a model for their own names for the fruit/vegetable. Ironically, the tomato is a fruit, of the subclass "berry," but horticulturally, and legally—according to an 1893 decree of the U.S. Supreme Court—it is treated as a vegetable. Some of the Sp. pronunciation, [tomahtay], is retained in the Eng. pronunciation, which was orig. [tomahto], and remains so in Britain, but is now [tomayto] in all of the United States except Boston. This contrast in Amer. pronunciations of *tomato* was highlighted in the 1937 film *Shall We Dance*, starring Fred Astaire and Ginger Rogers, in which they complained that since one of them said [tomayto] and the other said [tomahto], they ought to call the whole relationship off. Because the tomato is a member of the nightshade family, Americans believed that it was poisonous and refused to eat it until the early 1800s (EWPO: ca. 1830). Even today, except in the South, Americans have a suspicion that *fried green tomatoes* are unpalatable, although the green *tomatillo* (MWCD: ca. 1913), or *Mexican green tomato*, has been eaten in the Southwest for some time. Nowadays, of course, the red tomato is essential to American—Mexican-American and Italian-American—cooking, both as a sauce and as a condiment for hamburgers and hot dogs. A *beefsteak tomato* (MWCD: 1968) is a very large tomato, a slice of which resembles a beefsteak in color and size; a *plum tomato* (MWCD: ca. 1900) is a tomato that is about the size of a plum; and a *strawberry tomato* (MWCD: ca. 1847) is not a tomato at all but an edible, globular, yellow fruit. *Tomato* is also the *T* in *BLT* (q.v.). CE; DAFD; DAS; FLC; HF; IHAT; NSOED; PT; WNWCD. *See also* Mashed Potato.

TOMATO KETCHUP   *See* Catsup.

TOMAYTO/TOMAHTO   *See* Mashed Potato; Tomato.

TOM TURKEY   *See* Tough Old Bird.

TONIC   *See* Moxie; Soda.

TOO MANY COOKS SPOIL THE BROTH   A successful outcome can be achieved only if there is a single person in charge. DC: 1575 ("pottage"). Source: COOK (n); BROTH. MWCD: O.E. This proverb applies to organizations of all kinds, but it is usu. uttered by a homemaker at Thanksgiving time, when visiting relatives are drawn to the kitchen to check on the progress of the turkey and "fixins." They may even be tempted to taste some of the works in progress, such as the stuffing, the mashed potatoes, the sweet potatoes, the cranberry sauce, and, of course, the turkey neck and giblets simmering in the pot. The trouble is that the visitors get in the cook's way, they all have opinions on the quality of the food, and they may even add their own favorite ingredients. Here's where the cook must put his/her foot down and order everyone to *Get out of my kitchen!* because only one person can be in charge of preparing a dinner, and everyone else must defer to him or her. The proverb also applies to a situation in baseball when all of the infielders, including the catcher, unsuccessfully attempt to catch a pop fly that should have been caught by the pitcher in the first place. AID; CI; CODP; DAP; FLC; MS; PT.

TOO OLD TO CUT THE MUSTARD   *See* Cut the Mustard.

TOOTHSOME   *See* Palatable.

TOP BANANA   *the top banana.* The chief member of a comedy team; the top official of a business or organization. MWCD: 1952. Source: BANANA. MWCD: 1597. The title *top banana* comes from American burlesque—and, later, vaudeville—where there was once a skit (or "routine") that featured several comedians trying to top each other by giving the best punch line to a joke—and getting a banana as a prize. The one who gave the best punch lines—and won the most bananas—was declared the *top banana*. However, looking back at three outstanding comedy teams—Laurel and Hardy, Burns and Allen, and Abbott and Costello—most people would prob. name Oliver Hardy, George Burns, and Bud Abbott as the "top bananas," whereas the real *top bananas* were Stan Laurel, Gracie Allen, and Lou Costello—the ones who gave the punch lines. Hardy, Burns, and Abbott were *second bananas* (MWCD: 1953)—the straight men (*sic*) who fed jokes to the *top bananas*. Modern executives who are called *top bananas* are prob. misnamed. They are the ones who establish the framework in which the others operate. They are really the *second bananas*. CE; DAI; DAS; EWPO; HDAS; MDWPO.

TOP-SEEDED   *See* Go to Seed.

TOQUE   *See* My Compliments to the Chef.

TORPEDO   *See* Submarine Sandwich.

TORTILLA   *a tortilla.* A little cake. (Sp. dim. of *torta* "cake," fr. Lat. for "round loaf of bread.") Source: TORTILLA. MWCD: ca. 1699. The Mexican tortilla, a thin, flat, round "pancake," was orig. made of cornmeal but is now made of either cornmeal or wheat flour. It is a staple of Mexican and Mexican-American cooking and is the basic "bread" from which *enchiladas* (q.v.), *tamales* (q.v.), and many other "wrapped" foods are prepared. A *taco* (MWCD: 1934) is a folded tortilla that functions as a Mexican "sandwich," coming in two varieties—"soft shell" (wheat flour) and "hard shell" (cornmeal)—filled with ground meat, vegetables, cheese, and salsa. The cornmeal taco shell can also be eaten alone or broken up into pieces called *nachos* (MWCD: 1969), *taco chips, tortilla chips*, or *tostadas*. A *burrito* (MWCD: 1934—fr. Sp. for "little burro") is a Mexican dish consisting of a soft, wheat-flour tortilla with a filling of meat, vegetables, cheese, and sour cream, rolled into a "log" (which must have resembled the torso of a little burro to the coiner of the word), baked, and served "wet" (i.e., covered with salsa and eaten with a knife and fork) or "dry" (without salsa and ready to eat out of hand). A *chimichanga* (MWCD: 1982) is a burrito that is deep-fried, rather than baked, and is served in the fashion of a wet burrito. DAFD; FLC; NSOED; PT; SA; WNWCD.

TORTILLA CHIPS   *See* Tortilla.

TOSS YOUR COOKIES   *to toss your cookies.* To throw up. Source: COOKIE. MWCD: 1703. It is uncertain why the cookie was chosen to illustrate this unfortunate act, but it may simply have been the semiassonance of the rounded vowels of *toss* and *cook*. (Note the consonant alliteration employed in two similar expressions: *to feed the fishes* "to vomit over the side of a boat or ship" and *to lose your lunch* "to throw up soon after eating a meal.") An inspiration may also have been the practice of tossing cookies, or pieces of a cookie, to fish at a lake or stream. AID; BDPF; DAS; DEI; SA; WNWCD.

TOSTADAS   *See* Tortilla.

TO THE BITTER END   *See* Bitter End.

TOUGH COOKIE   *See* Smart Cookie.

TOUGH EGG   *See* Hard-boiled.

TOUGH NUT TO CRACK   *See* In a Nutshell.

TOUGH OLD BIRD   *a tough old bird.* An elderly person who hangs onto life despite all odds. Source: TURKEY. A North American wild turkey leads a difficult life—scrounging for food in the daytime and roosting on a tree limb at night. The females (or "hens") are fairly small and well camouflaged, but the males (or "toms") are large and brilliantly colored. Turkeys are everybody's prey, and a seventy-pound tom can feed a small family for a week, although an older bird can be pretty tough. Domestication of turkeys in Europe, and reintroduction of them to America, has produced smaller, more tender birds, with the weight distributed more to the breast. The turkey has been the centerpiece of holiday dinners in England since 1550—five years before it received its present name (it was first called a "guinea fowl") and seventy years before the Pilgrims' first Thanksgiving. During the Victorian period, the offensive word *breast* (of the bird) was replaced by the euphemism *white meat*; and during WWII the obscene expression *tough shit* "too bad" was replaced by the euphemism *tough turkey*. DAFD; FLC; PT; SA.

TOUGH TURKEY *See* Tough Old Bird.

TRAIL FOOD *See* Chipped Beef.

TREACLE *See* Slow as Molasses in January.

TREAD ON EGGS *See* Walk on Eggs.

TREAT LIKE A PIECE OF MEAT *See* Meat.

TREAT LIKE GARBAGE *See* Garbage in, Garbage out.

TREE IS KNOWN BY ITS FRUIT *A tree is known by its fruit.* A person is judged by his/her words and deeds. Source: FRUIT. MWCD: O.E. The original version of this proverb appears in Matthew 12:33: "Either make the tree good, and his (*sic*) fruit good; or else make the tree corrupt, and his fruit corrupt: for *the tree is known by his fruit.*" This chapter condemns both evil deeds and evil words; however, in an earlier chapter (7), Matthew attacks evil words specifically, likening them to the fruit of a tree, and warns against false prophets: "*Ye shall know them by their fruits.* Do men gather grapes of [i.e., *from*] thorns, or figs of thistles?" (7:16); "Wherefore *by their fruits* [i.e., their words] *ye shall know them*" (7:20) [italics added]. CODP; DAP.

TREE MELON *See* Papaya.

TRIM THE FAT *See* Fat (n).

TRIPE Nonsense. IHAT: 1924. Source: TRIPE. MWCD: 14th cent. Tripe is the lining of the second stomach of a ruminant animal, esp. an ox, that is used as food. Although expensive to buy and difficult to prepare, it is considered a delicacy in northern England. Elsewhere, esp. in America, where tripe is gen. regarded as offensive and worthless, the word has appeared in such expressions as *to talk tripe* "to talk nonsense" and *a bunch of tripe* "a bunch of crap." By itself, *tripe* comes close to matching American "B.S.," as in Q. "What did you think of the movie?" A. "I thought it was *tripe*." CE; DAFD; DAS; DEI; DEOD; FLC; PT; SA.

TRIVET *See* Spider.

TRUCK FARM *See* Truck Garden.

TRUCK GARDEN   *a truck garden.* A commercial vegetable farm. Source: GAR-
DEN. MWCD: 13th cent. New Jersey, the Garden State, is famous for its *truck
gardens* or *truck farms* (MWCD: 1866), where vegetables are raised for sale in the
large metropolitan markets. People prob. assume that these farms or gardens are
so called because the produce is hauled to the city in trucks; however, the term
truck comes from the O.Fr. word *troque*, meaning "barter," which is how the
farmers were compensated for their labors. In the "good old days" every family
had a garden, and they all grew the same vegetables, a fact that led to the rise of
the term *garden-variety* (MWCD: 1928) for anything that was "commonplace,
ordinary, or run-of-the-mill" (e.g., "That's no *garden-variety* squirrel! Look at him
ride that water ski!"). A *hothouse* (MWCD: 1511), *hotbed* (MWCD: 1626), or *greenhouse* (MWCD: 1664) is a glass-(or plastic-) enclosed structure—an indoor garden—in which plants are either "started" in the spring (with the structure being
razed during the summer) or planted during the fall and nourished during the
winter (or year-round). A *hothouse* was orig. a bordello; *hotbed* has given us the
metaphor *a hotbed of activity* (crime, rumors, etc.); and *greenhouse* has given us
the *greenhouse effect* (MWCD: 1937). A gardener who can grow plants without
fail, inside or outside, winter or summer, is said to have *a green thumb* (MWCD:
1943) in America or "green fingers" in Britain. CI; DAFD; DAS; DEI; EWPO;
MDWPO; MS.

TRUFFLE   *a truffle.* A ball of soft, rich chocolate candy. Source: TRUFFLE.
MWCD: 1591. Literally, a *truffle* is a dark, round fungus that grows underground
among the roots of oak and other nutbearing trees in southern France, northern
Italy, and Spain. Despite its unappealing appearance and pungent taste, the truffle
is regarded as a supreme delicacy and sells for a very high price, partly because
it must be located by scent and rooted out by the snouts of specially trained pigs.
It is the *caviar* (q.v.) of fungi. At up to one thousand dollars (for the rare white
variety), truffles are used primarily to flavor sauces and omelettes or to sprinkle
over pasta dishes. The candy *truffle*, a confection that resembles the fungus in
shape and color, but not in size, is also regarded as a delicacy. It is made of
chocolate, butter, and sugar—sometimes filled with whipped chocolate—and is
usu. coated with cocoa or powdered chocolate to make it look like the real thing.
DAFD; EWPO; FLC; WNWCD.

TRUFFLE OF THE NORTH   *See* Spring up like Mushrooms.

TRY IT ON THE DOG   *to try it on the dog.* To try out a new play in a smaller
market before taking it to Broadway. HB: late-19th cent. Source: TASTE. *Trying
it on the dog* was what taste testers once did when they suspected that a piece of
meat was spoiled to the point of endangering the lives of humans: They *threw it
to the dogs*, and if the dogs survived, the people prob. would too. In the metaphorical sense, the "meat" is the play, and the "dog" is the city that will judge its
quality. Cities that served this purpose in the late-1800s were Boston, Hartford,

New Haven, and Philadelphia, all of which were called "dogtowns." The practice was modeled after the one used in the London theater, where new plays were first "shaken down" in the provinces. ATWS; SA.

TRY OUT   *See* Tub of Lard.

TUBE STEAK   *See* Hot Dog.

TUB OF LARD   *a tub of lard.* A fat person. Source: LARD (n). MWCD: 14th cent. Technically, *lard* is not *human* fat but rendered and clarified *animal* fat, specif. that of a hog. Pork fat is *rendered* (MWCD: 14th cent.), or *tried out*, by melting it down over low heat, straining it, and storing it in cans or tubs. A byproduct of rendering is *cracklings*: the bits of meat and rind that settle to the bottom of the kettle and are browned in the process (NSOED: mid-19th cent.). In modern times the word *lard* has been used in combinations such as *lard ass* "a fat person" (or a term of address for a fat person) and *lardhead* "a stupid or foolish person," one who has lard in his/her head instead of brains (or a term of address for such a person). (*Compare* Fathead.) The source of Mod. Eng. *lard* is Lat. *lardum* "fat," which developed in French as neither "fat" nor "rendered fat" but "bacon." In early medieval times, before pork fat was rendered for use in cooking, bacon was fried with other meats or wrapped around (and/or sandwiched between) pieces of lean meat for baking or roasting. This preparation was done in the *larder* (MWCD: 14th cent.), now simply a "pantry" but orig. a separate room for curing, *larding* (MWCD: 14th cent.—fr. the noun *lard*), and storing meats. From the practice of placing strips of fat between slices of lean meat—to make it more tender and juicy—has come the metaphor *to interlard* (MWCD: ca. 1587—fr. M.Fr. *entrelarder*), or simply to *lard*, "to mix irrelevant matter with relevant matter," as to intersperse anecdotes in a narrative or epithets in a speech. BDPF; DAI; DAS; FLC; NSOED; PT.

TURKEY BACON   *See* Canadian Bacon.

TURKEY JERKY   *See* Chipped Beef.

TURN INTO A PUMPKIN   *See* Pumpkin.

TURNIP GREENS   *See* You Can't Get Blood from a Turnip.

TURN SOUR   *See* Hit a Sour Note.

TURN UP THE HEAT   *See* Slave over a Hot Stove.

TURN UP THE JUICE   *See* Juice.

TURN YOUR STOMACH   *See* Have No Stomach for.

TUTTI-FRUTTI   Ice cream containing pieces of several different fruits. MWCD: 1834. Source: FRUIT. MWCD: O.E. *Tutti-frutti* is an Italian name (meaning "all fruits") for an American product: ice cream containing a mixture of chopped, diced, or minced pieces of candied, dried, or fresh fruits. The idea, which prob. originated in New York City, was soon broadened to include preserves that contained a variety of fruits—also called *tutti-frutti*—and also gum, gum balls, and candies that were flavored, synthetically, with the tastes of "all fruits." The name *tutti-frutti* has faded somewhat in recent years, but the spirit of "all fruits" has been revived in Polaner All Fruit, the trademark for a sweet fruity spread for bread and crackers. DAFD; FLC; WNWCD.

TV DINNER   *See* Dinner (2).

TWINKIE   *See* Twinkie Defense.

TWINKIE DEFENSE   *a Twinkie defense*. A "temporary insanity" defense. NSOED: late-20th cent. Source: TWINKIE. (A trademark of the Hostess Company.) A *Twinkie* is a small, individually wrapped, oblong sponge cake with a vanilla creme (orig. banana creme) filling. Although it is only one of many sweet treats classified as *snack foods* (q.v.), its popularity since the 1940s led the news media to seize upon it as a symbol of *junk food* (q.v.) at a 1978 trial in San Francisco. The defendant claimed that his act of killing the mayor of the city and a supervisor was the result of temporary insanity brought on by the prior and prolonged consumption of sugar-rich snacks. The defense was successful (getting manslaughter instead of murder one), the nickname has stuck, and the term *Twinkie defense* has gone on to be applied to the case of a person charged with committing a crime while sleepwalking. *Twinkie* is also slang for (1) a young woman who is the mistress of a much older man and (2) an Asian American who congregates with Caucasians more than with Asians, also known as a *banana* (HDAS: 1970): "yellow on the outside, white on the inside." DAFD. *Compare* Oreo.

TWINS   *See* Salt-and-pepper.

TWO BITES OF THE CHERRY   *to get (or have)—or to make (or take)—two bites of the cherry*. To get (or have) a second chance to succeed where you have previously failed; to make a job last twice as long as necessary (or to take twice as long as necessary to do a job). Source: BITE (MWCD: O.E.); CHERRY (MWCD: 14th cent.). A cherry is so small that it doesn't usu. require more than one bite to eat it. To do so would make you seem to be too dainty, to be cutting things too fine, to be splitting hairs—hence the warnings: *Don't make (or take) two bites of the cherry* and *You only get one bite of the cherry*. If, however, you actually found a cherry so large that it could afford you two bites, you would consider yourself lucky—as if you had received an unearned bonus or a new lease on life—and you would prob. take a second bite. The expression is sometimes also extended to the apple, as in *to have a second bite of the apple* or *to take another bite of the apple*, both meaning "to have a second chance," even though apples *always* require a second bite. BDPF; CI; EWPO; MS; NSOED.

TWO HEADS ARE BETTER THAN ONE   *See* Cabbage.

TWO-MARTINI LUNCH   *See* Business Lunch.

U

UGLI FRUIT   *See* Mandarin Orange.

UNCORK A WILD PITCH   *See* Pop Your Cork.

UPPER CRUST   *the upper crust.* The highest class of society: the elite; the aristocracy. MWCD: 1836. Source: CRUST. MWCD: 14th cent. The crust is the exterior of a loaf of baked bread or the pastry shell of a baked pie, and there is some question as to whether the metaphor derives from bread crust or pie crust. If it comes from bread crust, it refers either to the attractive appearance of the top of the loaf or to the fact that the *upper crust* once preferred to eat only the top half, which was sliced off by the servants. (Nowadays, the favored part of the bread is the soft insides, without any crust at all, used for finger sandwiches and fussy children.) If, however, the metaphor comes from pie crust, it is the visible top crust that is being referred to, the one that bears no weight but sits on the other ingredients. (The upper crust of pie, as opposed to the bottom crust, is also sometimes decorated with attractive air vents or latticing.) Of the two Brit. dictionaries in the Works Cited that express an opinion on this subject, BDPF supports the bread, whereas CI supports the pie as a metaphor for the English population: the upper crust representing the upper class, the lower crust the lower class, and the filling the middle class. DAI; DEI; DC; EWPO; HND. *See also* Crust.

UPSET THE APPLECART   *to upset the applecart.* To ruin someone's carefully laid plans. MWCD: 1788. Source: APPLE. MWCD: O.E. An applecart was once a pushcart in which fresh apples were displayed for sale in the tray on top. In the 19th and early-20th cents., vendors of apples in the streets of large cities were the frequent victims of juvenile pranksters who amused themselves by tipping over the carts, thereby bruising and scattering the apples. Nowadays, in metaphor, *to upset someone's applecart* is to overturn their hard work, to dash their hopes and dreams. A milder form of mayhem is warned against in the negative imperative form of the metaphor *Don't upset the applecart*, which means something like "Don't make waves" or "Don't rock the boat." AID; BDPF; CE; CI; DAI; DC; DEI; EWPO; HDAS; HI; HND; LCRH; MS; PT.

USE THE OLD BEAN   *See* Bean.

V

VALENCIA ORANGE   *See* Orange.

VANILLA   *See* Plain-vanilla.

VANTAGE LOAF   *See* Baker's Dozen.

VARIETY IS THE SPICE OF LIFE   Diversity is what makes life interesting.
HND: 1785. (From a poem, "The Task," by William Cowper: "Variety's the very
spice of life, / That gives it all its flavour.") Source: SPICE. MWCD: 13th cent.
Spice is what makes food interesting: It seasons it, flavors it, colors it, and even
perfumes it. Unlike herbs, which come from the leaves of plants, spices come
from the roots (e.g., ginger), bark (e.g., cinnamon), seeds (e.g., nutmeg), buds
(e.g., cloves), pods (e.g., paprika), and even stigmas (e.g., saffron) of plants. Just
as turmeric "spices up" mustard and gives it its yellow color, a change in scenery
can *spice up a person's life*, adding zest and spirit. Meatballs flavored with sage, an
herb, are considered *spicy* (MWCD: 1562); and gossip flavored with scandal is
considered *spicy* as well. CE; CI; CODP; DAP; FLC; HF; NSOED. *See also* Sugar
and Spice and Everything Nice.

VARIETY MEATS   The edible parts of mammals other than the skeletal meat.
MWCD: ca. 1946. Source: MEAT. MWCD: O.E. Variety meats are of two types:
organs (such as brains, heart, kidneys, liver, pancreas, stomach, and thymus) and
extremities (such as ankles, feet, lips, tail, and tongue). *Variety meats* is a euphemism for *meat by-products*, which includes everything other than muscle and fat
(i.e., *flesh*). Another euphemism is *specialty meats*, which consists of skeletal meat
and (optional) extremity meats ground up fine, baked or boiled, formed into

loaves, and sliced for use as *cold cuts* (MWCD: 1945) or *sandwich meat. Fragrant meat* (DEOD: 1973) was a euphemism for dog meat on the menus of some Chinese restaurants in New York City in the 1970s. (The term *dog meat* is also a metaphor, similar to *dead meat* (q.v.), i.e., "You say that one more time and you're *dog meat.*" HDAS: 1977.) *Mystery meat* is not a euphemism but a child's term for unidentifiable cafeteria food: Parent: "What did you have for lunch at the cafeteria today?" Child: "*Mystery meat.*" ATWS; DAFD; DAS; FLC; NSOED; WNWCD.

VEAL CHOP   *See* Chopping Block.

VEGAN   *See* Vegetarian.

VEGETABLE   *a vegetable.* A person who has permanently lost the ability to move, feel, or respond and is being kept alive by machines. NSOED: early-20th cent. Source: VEGETABLE. MWCD: 1582. The garden vegetable was prob. selected for this metaphor because although it is "alive," it is incapable of voluntary movement, it has no sense of feeling, and it lacks a spontaneous communication system. A person who resembles a vegetable in these ways is described clinically as being in a *persistent—or chronic—vegetative state,* although the general public uses terms such as "brain dead" and "living dead." Even though a *vegetative state* can be created by physical trauma or a drug overdose, some people actually *choose* to enter a more passive existence, to exert their mind and body as little as possible, to *vegetate*—in other words, to become *couch potatoes* (q.v.). It is ironic that the ancestor of the words *vegetable, vegetate,* and *vegetative,* i.e., M.Lat. *vegetare,* meant "to grow" or "to grow exuberantly," i.e., "to animate" or "to proliferate," and that the source of *vegetare* was Lat. *vegetus* "lively," which was fr. Lat. *vegere* "to enliven." These are not exactly inert sources. It is also interesting to note that the adj. *vegetable* (MWCD: 15th cent.), as in *vegetable stew,* appeared at least a century before the noun *vegetable.* (Was that because of the problem of defining exactly what a vegetable is?) Currently, a vegetable is any plant or plant part (such as the leaves, stalks, tubers, and roots) that is not cultivated as a fruit. (The rhubarb stalk is regarded as a fruit.) And a fruit is any plant (such as drupes, pomes, berries, or gourds) that is not treated as a vegetable. (Tomatoes, which are berries, and cucumbers, pumpkins, and squash, which are gourds, are sold as vegetables.) Any questions? CE: DAS; DEI; EWPO; MS; WNWCD.

VEGETARIAN   *a vegetarian.* A person who eats only fruits and vegetables. MWCD: 1839. Source: VEGETABLE. MWCD: 1582. In animal terms, a vegetarian is an herbivore; however, just as an animal herbivore, such as a black bear, sometimes eats cheese and eggs when it encounters them in the garbage of its human neighbors, vegetarians sometimes eat dairy products and eggs when they encounter them on the menu of their favorite restaurant. Such vegetarians are called *lacto-ovo-vegetarians*—or if they eschew one or the other, *lacto-vegetarians,* who eat dairy products but not eggs, and *ovo-vegetarians,* who eat eggs but not dairy products. *Strict—or pure—vegetarians* eat no animal products of any kind, dairy or poultry, juice or lard, gravy or honey. The strictest vegetarian of all is the *vegan* (MWCD: 1944), who not only abstains from *eating* animal products of any kind but refuses to *wear* animal products such as leather and fur. *Veggies* (MWCD: 1955) is not only a colloquial form for *vegetables* but also a slang term for vegetarians, of any degree of strictness. A *veggie burger* is a vegetarian "hamburger," made with a base of textured soy protein. *Veggie* is a back-formation from *veggies*, which is baby talk for "vegetables," as in "Eat your veggies!" To *veg out* (MWCD: 1980) is to take it easy, relax, "cocoon," *vegetate* (NSOED: mid-18th cent.): i.e., to stay home and do nothing but eat, sleep, and watch TV. To be *vegged out*, however, is to be intoxicated with alcohol or drugs. DAFD; DAS; EWPO.

VEGETATIVE   *See* Vegetable.

VEGETATIVE STATE   *See* Vegetable.

VEGGED OUT   *See* Vegetarian.

VEGGIE   *See* Vegetarian.

VEGGIE BURGER   *See* Vegetarian.

VEGGIES   *See* Vegetarian.

VEG OUT   *See* Vegetarian.

VERMICELLI   *See* Spaghetti Squash.

VINAIGRETTE   *See* Vinegar.

VINE APPLE   *a vine apple.* A squash. Source: VINE (MWCD: 14th cent.); APPLE (MWCD: O.E.). Apples don't grow on vines, but the apple has long been regarded as the most basic fruit. Roger Williams, the founder of the Rhode Island Colony, had prob. never seen a squash when he applied this name to one of them that was round, like an apple, and either immature or naturally small. The roundness of Williams' "vine fruit" prob. eliminates "summer" squash from consideration because they are usu. cylindrical, like the cucumber or zucchini. However, a number of "winter" squash, such as the *acorn squash* (q.v.) and the *pumpkin* (q.v.) are possibilities because the former are small and reasonably round when mature, and the latter are perfectly round at every stage of their development. Nevertheless, the name *vine apple* didn't stick, giving way to a shortening of the Narragansett Indian word *askutasquash*, lit. "eaten raw." The "eaten raw" translation presents a problem: Did the Native Americans actually eat squash (or pumpkins) raw, or did the colonists mistakenly narrow the meaning of the Narragansett word to "squash" (or "pumpkin") when it was really meant to apply to something much broader, such as "gourd," a classification that would include melons, which everyone eats raw? Roger Williams and the Narragansett Indians may have been talking about two different things, however—he of an acorn squash and they of a muskmelon. At least the situation in America isn't as bad as it is in Britain, where all of the vegetable gourds are known as *marrow*. DAFD; EWPO; FLC; HF; PT.

VINEGAR   Sourness or disagreeableness; vim and vigor. NSOED: early-17th cent. Source: VINEGAR. MWCD: 14th cent. A person who is ill-humored or ill-tempered is said to be *full of vinegar*, and a person who is coltish and frisky is said to be *full of piss and vinegar*. Literally, the former person is behaving appropriately, but the latter person should not be feeling that good. *Vinegar* (fr. Fr. *vinaigre*, fr. *vin* "wine" + *aigre* "sour" and playfully referred to as "eager wine") was orig. "wine turned sour," i.e., wine whose alcohol had been converted into a weak solution of acetic acid by bacterial activity. Nowadays, vinegar can be made from all sorts of alcoholic beverages (fruit brandy, hard cider, malt liquor, etc.); if made from grain alcohol, it is called "white vinegar." Vinegar is used as a condiment, as on fish and chips; as a flavoring, as in sauces and marinades; and as a preservative, as in pickling brine. One well-known use of vinegar is in the salad dressing known by its Fr. name, *vinaigrette* (MWCD: 1699), i.e., "vinegar sauce," a combination of oil and vinegar (at a three-to-one ratio) plus various seasonings. Such a sauce is called *Italian dressing* by some American bottlers and *French dressing* by others. For some reason, the name *vinaigrette* has also been applied to an ornamental box containing smelling salts, perhaps because the smell of the salts is just as repulsive as the taste of pure vinegar. *Mother of vinegar* (MWCD: 1601), or simply *mother*, is the bacterial substance that causes alcoholic beverages to change into vinegar. BDPF; DAFD; FLC; HF; WNWCD. *See also* You Can Catch More Flies with Honey than with Vinegar.

VIRGIN   *See* Cherry (adj.).

VORACIOUS APPETITE   *See* Appetite.

W

WAFFLE (n)   *See* Waffle (v).

WAFFLE (v)   *to waffle.* To vacillate on an issue. NSOED: early-19th cent. Source: WAFFLE (n). MWCD: 1744. (From Du. *wafel* "wafer.") The noun *waffle* seems like a natural source for the verb *waffle*. To *waffle* is to be indecisive, to be unable to make up your mind, to move your position to and fro, to straddle the fence, to flip-flop, to yo-yo. That is exactly what it would be like, if you were two inches tall, to walk across the surface of a fresh, crisp, steaming waffle, just out of the *waffle iron* (MWCD: 1794). Your journey would certainly have its ups and downs, regardless of which direction you took; and if you selected a *Belgian waffle* (DAFD: 1964), with deeper valleys and higher peaks, you might not even be able to reach the other side. However, the verb *waffle* may not have come from the Dutch bread baked on a griddle but from M.E. *waffen* "to wave or waver." Regardless of the correct source, Garry Trudeau's portrayal of President Clinton as a steaming, airborne, square waffle was instantly clear. CE; DAS; FLC; IHAT; LCRH; MDWPO; PT.

WAFFLE CONE   *See* Ice-cream Cone.

WAFFLE IRON   *See* Waffle (v).

WAITER   *See* Menu.

WAKE UP AND SMELL THE COFFEE!   (The title of a 1996 book by advice columnist Ann Landers.) Wise up! Get real! Source: COFFEE. MWCD: 1598.

People have been waking up to the smell of brewing coffee for thousands of years, ever since the beans were first cultivated, picked, roasted, and brewed in Ethiopia. The Eng. word *coffee* derives ultimately from the name of the Ethiopian port of *Kaffa*, from which the beans were shipped to Arabia, where the beverage was called *qahwa*, then to Turkey, where it was called *kahve*, and eventually to Italy, where it got its familiar name, *caffè*. Coffee, which reached England in 1598, and tea, which reached England in 1655, coexisted there, and in Colonial America, for many years. However, after the Boston Tea Party of 1773 and the subsequent Revolution, Americans, esp. the males of the lower classes, turned to coffee, whereas the women of the upper classes stuck with tea. In modern America, both men and women drink coffee, but tea, except for iced tea, appears to be drunk more by women than by men. *Coffee, tea, or me?* is a parody of the question that stewardesses used to ask passengers on an airplane: "Coffee, tea, or milk?" *To come up for a cup of coffee* (HDAS: 1908) is a baseball expression ("He *came up for a cup of coffee* in the mid-eighties") referring to a minor leaguer who is called up to the parent team to replace a major leaguer who has gone on the disabled list for a few days. The temporary replacement is around only long enough to have a cup of coffee before being sent back to the minors. DAFD; EWPO; LA; MDWPO; PT. *See also* Wet Noodle.

WALK ON EGGS *to walk on eggs (or eggshells)*. To watch your step. EWPO: 1734. (The Brit. version, *to tread on eggs*, dates from 1591. DC.) Source: EGG. MWCD: 14th cent. Weasels have no trouble walking on eggs as they enter a henhouse looking for a late supper, and they may even be able to walk out of the henhouse on the shells of the eggs that they have sucked dry. However, humans are too heavy to actually walk on eggs (to say nothing about eggshells), so the analogy is more to the danger that the weasel faces from the farmer's gun as it exits the scene of the crime. Humans figuratively *walk on eggs* when they try to "negotiate a minefield" of dangers, such as blowing a deal or offending a client. Parents *walk on eggs* when they try to go about their business without waking their children. Eggshells figure in such expressions as *to shatter like an eggshell* (in reference to what could happen to a motorcycle helmet in a serious accident) and the color *eggshell* (a yellowish white). Christmas eggshell decorations may have been the inspiration for the famous "*Fabergé* eggs" of the 19th cent., and Easter eggs may have been the inspiration for the *L'eggs* (trademark) pantyhose sold in a plastic egg. ATWS; BDPF; CE; DAS; DEI; HND; LA; NSOED; SA.

WALK ON EGGSHELLS *See* Walk on Eggs.

WALNUT-SIZE HAIL *See* Grapefruit-size Hail.

WANT YOUR BREAD BUTTERED ON BOTH SIDES *See* Butter Your Bread on Both Sides.

WARM AS TOAST   *to be as warm as toast*. To be warm and comfortable. Source: TOAST. MWCD: 15th cent. Toast is made by subjecting a slice of bread to dry heat until it is brown and crisp. In the process, the bread becomes quite warm, though hopefully not hot enough to burn. (To *burn the toast*, usu. at breakfast, is to experience the beginning of a bad day.) To be *toasty* (MWCD: 1953) is to feel warm and comfortable by a roaring fire. (However, if you get too close you could *become toast*, q.v.) To be *toasted* is to be "drunk." DAS; DEI; WNWCD.

WARM OVER   *See* Look like Death Warmed over.

WARM UP   *See* Look like Death Warmed over.

WATCHED POT NEVER BOILS   *A watched pot never boils*. Impatience never hastens progress. CODP: 1848. Source: POT (MWCD: O.E.); BOIL (v) (MWCD: 13th cent.). Water boils in the amount of time it takes to reach 212° Fahrenheit. The time is affected only by (1) the altitude (it boils faster at higher altitudes); (2) the container (it takes longer to reach its boiling point in a heavy container); (3) the quantity of the contents (a gallon of water takes longer to boil than a pint or a quart); and (4) the density of the contents (plain water boils faster than stew). Regardless of the conditions, however, trying to get a pot of water to boil faster by giving it your full attention is about as effective as trying to get a bowling ball to hit the pocket by using body English. Of course, a watched pot *does* eventually boil—usu. when the phone rings or someone knocks on the door—but not because of your anticipation. This proverb cautions against impatience and anxiety. The moral seems to be "Let nature take its course. There's nothing you can do about it." AID; BDPF; DAP; HND.

WATCH THE DOUGHNUT, NOT THE HOLE   *See* Doughnut Hole.

WATER CARNIVAL   *See* Carnival.

WATER CHESTNUT   *See* Chestnuts.

WATER DOWN   *See* Water, Water, Everywhere, but Not a Drop to Drink.

WATERING HOLE   *See* Water, Water, Everywhere, but Not a Drop to Drink.

WATERMELON   *See* Slice of the Melon.

WATERMELON PICKLE   *See* Pickle (n).

WATER MILL   *See* Grist for the Mill.

WATER RICE   *See* Rice Paper.

WATER, WATER, EVERYWHERE, BUT NOT A DROP TO DRINK We are surrounded by an abundance of riches that are just beyond our reach. Source: WATER; DRINK. MWCD: O.E. These words are a modification of lines 121–122 of Samuel Taylor Coleridge's "Rime of the Ancient Mariner" (1798): "*Water, water, everywhere, / Nor any drop to drink*" [italics added]. The water that was "everywhere" was the warm water of the Pacific Ocean, on the equator, midway between Southeast Asia and South America. However, the ship was becalmed, the fresh water on board was depleted, and, of course, the salt water surrounding the ship was undrinkable. The situation was much like the one faced by King Tantalus, of Greek mythology, who was confined to a pool of fresh water but was unable to drink from it because whenever he bent over, the water would recede. A more friendly *watering hole* (MWCD: 1955), a term based on the place where wild animals gather to have a drink of water, is the establishment where people go to drink something a little stronger, such as "bourbon and branch," the favorite drink of J. R. Ewing on the TV show *Dallas*, which consisted of bourbon whiskey and *branch water*, the *branch* referring to the original source of such water: a "branch," or stream. (Nowadays, tap water or bottled water is used.) The purpose of the water is to dilute the whiskey so that its effect will not be as strong, and this process of *watering down* has become a metaphor (MWCD: 1850) for weakening a regulation or standard. DAFD; FLC.

WAY TO A MAN'S HEART IS THROUGH HIS STOMACH *The (quickest) way to a man's heart is through his stomach.* The quickest way to get a man to fall in love with you is to prove to him that you are the greatest cook in the world. HND: mid-19th cent. Source: STOMACH. MWCD: 14th cent. Just as *an army marches on its stomach* (q.v.), a man's affections ride on the quality and quantity of food that a female suitor can fill his stomach with—or at least that seems to have been the way it was back in the 1850s. It is no surprise that a musical question at that time was *Can she make a cherry pie?* (q.v.). CODP; DAP.

WEDGIE *See* Submarine Sandwich.

WEENIE *a weenie.* A young boy's penis; a high school or college-age nerd; a sissy. Source: WIENER. MWCD: 1900. *Wiener* is short for *Wienerwurst* (MWCD: 1889) "Vienna sausage." However, several decades before the sausage was called a *wiener*, it was dubbed a *wienie* (IHAT: 1867), and this form, respelled, became the basis for the word *weenie* (MWCD: ca. 1906), also meaning "sausage." *Weenie* has always referred to the sausage alone, without a bun, as in the term *weenie* (or *wienie* or *wiener*) *roast* (LA: 1920s). Its resemblance to the juvenile penis was recognized in the 1930s, and it was first applied to socially inept nerds in the 1950s. The *wiener* is sometimes equated with the *frankfurter* (MWCD: 1894), although the former was orig. much smaller and made of both beef and pork, whereas the latter was orig. much larger and made only of beef. Both words have pretty much been replaced by *hot dog* (q.v.), although "cocktail franks" and "Vienna sausages" are still identified as such at cocktail parties (even though they are the same thing); and people still refer to a dachshund as either a *sausage dog* or a *wiener dog*. CE; DAI; DAS; EWPO; FLC; NSOED.

WELL HAS RUN DRY   *See* You Can Lead a Horse to Water, but You Can't Make It Drink.

WELSH ONION   *See* Onionskin Paper.

WELSH RABBIT   Melted cheese on toast. MWCD: 1725. Source: Rabbit. MWCD: 14th cent. There is no rabbit in *Welsh rabbit*. The name appears to be a cruel joke perpetrated on the poor people of Wales by the more affluent people of England in the early-18th cent. What the English may have wanted the world to believe was that the Welsh could not afford to buy rabbit, so they substituted cheese and called it *rabbit*. However, the term is English, not Welsh, and the English may have done the same thing to the Scots, naming their version of the dish *Scotch rabbit*. Yet we can't blame the English for what happened next. Sixty years after the appearance of *Welsh rabbit*, the term *Welsh rarebit* (MWCD: 1785) began to appear in recipes—and later in cookbooks and on restaurant menus. This modification was not another cruel joke but an attempt, prob. by American cooks and innkeepers, to correct the impression that they were serving rabbit meat—and, at the same time, to emphasize that what they were serving was "rare bits" of tasty food. Later still, it was prob. Americans who created the dishes *Mexican rarebit* (add onions, peppers, and tomatoes to the cheese) and *peanut butter rarebit* (substitute peanut butter for cheese). BDPF; DEOD; EWPO; FLC; HF; LCRH; MDWPO; NSOED; PT; SA.

WELSH RAREBIT   *See* Welsh Rabbit.

WESTERN BARBECUE   *See* Barbecue.

WET NOODLE   *ten lashes with a wet noodle*. The mildest possible punishment. Source: NOODLE. MWCD: 1779. Ann Landers, the newspaper advice columnist, seems to have invented the *wet noodle* as a form of punishment for herself when she has made a mistake or given bad advice in one of her columns. A wet noodle— i.e., one that is soft from being boiled—is about the gentlest weapon that could be used for self-flagellation. It is several steps below a slap on the wrist. As food, the noodle is one of the three major types of pasta: *macaroni* (tubular or shaped), *spaghetti* (long and stringy), and *noodles* (soft and flat). The noodle is the only one of the three that is made with eggs, and it is the only one that does not have an Italian name. (Its name is fr. Ger. *Nudel* "noodle.") However, noodles are eaten in Italy as well as in Germany and America, and their recipe may have come from China, though long before Marco Polo. *Noodle* as a slang term for "head" is not from the pasta but from *noddle*, a M.E. word for "the back of the head"; and the verb *to noodle* "for a musician to warm up, practice, or improvise" (MWCD: ca. 1937) is also not from the pasta but from *noodle* "head." CE; DAFD; DAS; FLC; HDAS; PT; WNWCD. *See also* Wake up and Smell the Coffee.

WHAT AM I, CHOPPED LIVER?   *See* Chopped Liver.

WHAT ARE YOU FRETTING ABOUT?   *See* Fret (v).

WHAT DOES THAT HAVE TO DO WITH THE PRICE OF TEA IN CHINA?
See Not for All the Tea in China.

WHAT DO YOU WANT, EGG IN YOUR BEER?   Why don't you stop complaining! DC: 1946. Source: EGG (MWCD: 14th cent.); BEER (MWCD: O.E.). This question was in common use among American troops during WWII as a putdown for someone who was always griping or complaining. The question was based on an actual practice of cracking open a raw egg and depositing the contents in a glass of beer. The egg was presumably thought to work as an aphrodisiac, but the question prob. focused on the fact that eggs were scarce in the combat zone, since there was no way to refrigerate them, whereas beer was plentiful. The practice of putting an egg in an alcoholic drink may also relate to the much older practice of adding an egg to a pot of coffee (DAFD: 1896). HND.

WHAT IT ALL BOILS DOWN TO   *See* Boil down to.

WHAT'S COOKING?   What's happening? What's up? HDAS: 1940. Source: COOK (v). MWCD: 14th cent. *What's cooking?* was prob. first asked of a home-maker by the children returning from school or the spouse returning from work. It may simply have meant "What's cooking on the stove?" and it may have alternated with "What's for dinner?" However, the existence of the slang expression of the 1930s *What's cookin', Good Lookin'?*—asked by a man of a woman—suggests that the cook may have been the "lady of the house." Another "cooking" expression, *to be cooking with gas* "to be making great progress or performing magnificently," may go back to the early 1900s, when gas stoves began to replace wood or coal stoves. This latter expression is sometimes shortened to *Now you're cooking!* or *Now you're really cooking!* AID; BDPF; CE; CI; DAI; DAS; DEI; HI; MS; PT.

WHAT'S COOKIN', GOOD LOOKIN'?   *See* What's Cooking?

WHAT'S EATING YOU?   *See* Eat Your Heart out; Fret.

WHAT'S FOR DINNER?   *See* Dinner (2).

WHAT'S GOOD FOR THE GOOSE IS GOOD FOR THE GANDER   *See* What's Sauce for the Goose Is Sauce for the Gander.

WHAT'S SAUCE FOR THE GOOSE IS SAUCE FOR THE GANDER   What's good (fair, fitting, right) for one person is good (fair, fitting, right) for the other. DC: 1670. Source: SAUCE (MWCD: 14th cent.); GOOSE (MWCD: O.E.). Because of the distinction between *goose* (the female goose) and *gander* (the male goose), this proverb was prob. orig. intended to apply to wife and husband, with the emphasis on the husband: "If you can buy a new outfit (take a vacation, fool around), so can I." The sauce in question was prob. a tart fruit sauce because domesticated geese have a high percentage of fat, and something is needed to cut the taste. That the Amer. version of the original Brit. proverb is now *What's good for the goose is good for the gender* (DAP: 1670) prob. reflects the fact that goose—male or female—is no longer very popular in this country, and neither is the sauce. AID; BDPF; CI; CODP; DEI; HND; IRCD; MS; SA.

WHEATCAKE   *See* Pancake (n).

WHEN THE TIME IS RIPE   *See* Ripe.

WHERE'S THE BEEF?   *See* Beef (n).

WHET YOUR APPETITE   *See* Appetite.

WHEY   *See* Curds and Whey.

WHEY-FACE   *See* Curds and Whey.

WHICH CAME FIRST, THE CHICKEN OR THE EGG?   Which of two things was the cause, and which was the effect? Source: CHICKEN (MWCD: O.E.); EGG (MWCD: 14th cent.). This question is an example of a conundrum. Though supposedly unanswerable, the *chicken-and-egg question* (MWCD: 1959) has led to numerous speculations: (1) In the book of Genesis, God created "every winged fowl after his kind" and commanded them to "be fruitful and multiply" (1:21–22); therefore, the chicken came before the egg. (2) In early folk legends about eggs, there is no mention of chickens having produced them; therefore, the egg came before the chicken. (3) In both the question and the derived modifier, *chicken-and-egg*, the word *chicken* appears first; therefore, the chicken came before the egg. In other words, no one really knows, or ever will know. FLC; MS; SA.

WHITE BACON   *See* Canadian Bacon.

WHITE BREAD   People who live in the suburbs but work in the inner city. Source: BREAD. MWCD: O.E. Bleached-flour bread was introduced in the 1860s in grocery stores ("store-bought bread") and bakeries ("bakery bread"), but it was regarded by housewives as being too soft and bland for their hardworking husbands. By the 1880s it had become the standard not only in groceries and bakeries but in homes as well and was simply called *white bread* (or *sandwich bread* or simply "bread"). The adj. *white-bread* (MWCD: 1979), as in a "*white-bread* image" or a "*white-bread* town," retains the features of blandness and softness and links the term with the white middle class, who are characterized as being plain, dull, aloof, and WASPish. It is possible, however, to shed a *white-bread* image. DAS; IHAT. *Compare* Plain-vanilla.

WHITE-BREAD   *See* White Bread.

WHITE CHOCOLATE   (An oxymoron.) White-colored, vanilla-flavored "chocolate." MWCD: 1923. Source: CHOCOLATE. MWCD: 1604. The word *chocolate* refers not only to a food but to a color ("brown"), a flavor ("sweet"), and a texture ("buttery"). *White chocolate*, which actually does contain some cocoa butter, is buttery, and it is sweet; but it is neither dark brown, like bittersweet chocolate, nor light brown, like milk chocolate. Nevertheless, white chocolate has been around for a long time, and it can be used as a substitute for brown chocolate in just about every way possible: in sheet candy, candy bars, creams, ice-cream bars, cookies, mousses, etc. The introduction of white chocolate has confused the century-old contrast of *black* (chocolate) and *white* (vanilla) in the menu of the old-fashioned soda fountain. A *black-and-white* used to mean any combination of chocolate and vanilla in an ice-cream-based dish, such as a chocolate soda with vanilla ice cream or a vanilla sundae with chocolate syrup. Nowadays, "chocolate" and vanilla can form a "white on white." CE; DAFD; FLC.

WHITE COW   *See* Milk Shake.

WHITE MEAT   *See* Drumstick; Tough Old Bird.

WHITE POTATO   *See* Potato.

WHOLE ENCHILLADA   *See* Chili Today, Hot Tamale.

WHOLE NOTHER KETTLE OF FISH   *See* Kettle of Fish.

WIENER   *See* Weenie.

WIENER DOG   *See* Weenie.

WIENIE   *See* Weenie.

WILD OATS   *See* Feel Your Oats.

WILD RICE   *See* Rice Paper.

WINDFALL   *See* Manna from Heaven.

WINDMILL   *See* Grist for the Mill.

WINE AND DINE   *See* Dine (v).

WINTER CARNIVAL   *See* Carnival.

WISHBONE   *a wishbone.* An offensive formation in football. LA: 1960s. Source: WISHBONE. MWCD: 1853. A team in the *wishbone formation* has the fullback lined up directly behind the quarterback and the halfbacks positioned even further back and on either side. From the air, this alignment looks very much like the wishbone of a chicken or turkey, from which the name derives. The wishbone of a fowl is its fork-shaped breastbone, or *furcula* (Lat. for "little fork"), which resembles a two-tined fork with a very short handle. It has been the custom in America since the mid-19th cent. to set aside the furcula of the Thanksgiving or Christmas bird until it dries, then to play a game called *Make a wish.* The game is played by two contestants, who stand facing each other, each holding one of the two tines of the breastbone, make a silent wish, and pull upward on the pieces until the bone breaks. The one with the longer piece is the winner, and his/her wish will most certainly be fulfilled. (In England, where the practice goes back to at least 1600, the wishbone is called a "merrythought," and the winner is supposedly going to be the first of the two contestants to get married.) HF; MDWPO; SA; WNWCD.

WISHBONE FORMATION   *See* Wishbone.

WITH A GRAIN OF SALT   *See* Take with a Grain of Salt.

WITHER ON THE VINE   *to wither—or die—on the vine.* To fail, in the planning stage, from lack of interest or involvement. Source: VINE. MWCD: 14th cent. The vine that is the basis for this metaphor is the *grapevine* (q.v.), a climbing vine that produces berries that are used for eating and for pressing into grape juice and wine. Grapes "wither on the vine" when the weather is too hot or cold, or the ground is too moist or dry: They lit. shrivel up and die. Projects may also die such a "natural" death, as a result of changing financial and social conditions, but the metaphor implies a lack of attention from the laborers in the vineyard. Those who *toil in the vineyards* of Congress were accused of letting the deficit-reduction bill *wither on the vine* in late-1995 and early-1996. Another "vine" metaphor is *clinging vine*: a woman who is heavily dependent on her husband for encouragement and love. Literally, a clinging vine is a climbing vine that runs up walls and trees, adhering tightly to the brick or bark, but bears no fruit. (An example is poison ivy.) AID; DAFD; DAI; HND; MS.

WITH GUSTO   *See* Gusto.

WOLF DOWN   *See* Devour.

WONTON   *See* Dumpling.

WORD SALAD   *See* Salad.

WORK FOR CHICKEN FEED   *See* Chicken Feed.

WORK FOR PEANUTS   *to work for peanuts*. To work for practically nothing. LA: 1830s. Source: PEANUT. MWCD: 1802. The humble peanut, a legume that grows underground after the plant's flower-laden stem dips down and buries itself in the earth, has long been regarded as something small and insignificant: a trifle. It's what the organ grinder's monkey works for—one coin at a time, which is used to buy the little simian its favorite snack—and what the monkeys and elephants in the zoo beg for: one unshelled "nut" at a time, which looks pretty tiny next to the hulking pachyderm. The term *monkey nuts*, which was a nickname for Spanish peanuts (the small, round peanuts that still have their brown "skin" on) in the early decades of the 20th cent., was prob. based on the practice of buying peanuts for children to throw to the monkeys at the zoo. *Peanut* also became a metaphor for a small or insignificant person (LA: 1919) and was used as a term of endearment by a father for his daughter. (It was sometimes adopted by the entire family and used even after the child became an adult.) In the 1940s, the term *peanut gallery*—which had been applied since the 1880s to the upper balcony, or "cheap seats," of a theater, from which unshelled peanuts, the "popcorn" of the time, were thrown at unpopular actors or characters—was borrowed for a children's audience, on stage, sitting on bleachers, during a morning TV show, such as the *Howdy Doody Show* (1947–1960). Children—and small animals—are the *Peanuts* of the Charles Schulz comic strip (LA: 1950), and adults who behave like children are said to be *peanut-brained*. Lightweight blobs of Styrofoam that are used to protect goods during shipping are called *packing peanuts* because they sometimes resemble unshelled peanuts. AID; CE; DAS; DEI; EWPO; MDWPO; MS; SA.

WORK FOR SMALL POTATOES   *See* Small Potatoes.

WORM-EATEN   *See* Moth-eaten.

WORM FOOD   *See* Food for Worms.

WORTH YOUR SALT   *See* Salt of the Earth.

WRECK A PAIR   *See* Scrambled Eggs.

WRINKLED AS A PRUNE   *See* Full of Prunes.

Y

YAM   *See* Sweet Potato.

YEAST   *See* Yeasty.

YEASTY   Frivolous, superficial; restless, unsettled. NSOED: late-16th cent. Source: YEAST. MWCD: O.E. Bread dough is *yeasty* (MWCD: 1598) when the fungus in it begins to ferment and the dough begins to rise. The fermentation, which begins even before the dough enters the oven, results from the conversion of the starch in the flour into alcohol and carbon dioxide gas, which become trapped in the fibers of the dough and cause it to expand. (Baking destroys both the yeast and the alcohol.) The change in the size and shape of the bread dough may have led to the "restless" and "unsettled" part of the *yeasty* metaphor, and the change in the lightness and density may have led to the "frivolous" and "superficial" part of it. However, because the fermentation that goes on inside the dough is gradual and unseen, the metaphor may have been influenced by the use of *brewer's yeast* (MWCD: 1871) in the making of beer, where the action is more exciting. DAFD; FLC; WNWCD.

YELLOW-EYED PEA   *See* Pea Bean.

YESTERDAY, TODAY, AND TOMORROW   *See* Hash (n).

YOU ARE WHAT YOU EAT   If you eat healthful food, you'll lead a healthy life. CODP: 1930. Source: EAT. MWCD: O.E. Some ancient warriors believed that if they ate the livers of their dead enemies, they would acquire their strength. Fortunately, *cannibalism* (q.v.) has not survived in most cultures, and no traditions have developed for eating brains for wisdom, hearts for courage, tongues for eloquence, etc. In modern times, there has been some suspicion that eating red meat promotes violent behavior, whereas eating white meat or vegetables promotes peaceful behavior. Mr. and Mrs. Jack Sprat were persons of such opposite tastes who managed to remain happily married in spite of their differences: "Jack Sprat could eat no fat, / His wife could eat no lean; / And so, betwixt the two of them, / They licked the plotter clean." Can we gather from this nursery rhyme that Mr. Sprat was a lean, mean, fighting machine, whereas Mrs. Sprat was a fat, happy peacemaker? DAP. *See also* Brain Food; Food Chain; Food Pyramid. *Compare* Cannibalize; Eat Someone Alive.

YOU BET YOUR SWEET LIFE   *See* Sweet Tooth.

YOU CAN CATCH MORE FLIES WITH HONEY THAN WITH VINEGAR   *See* Honey.

YOU CAN DISH IT OUT, BUT YOU CAN'T TAKE IT   *See* Dish It out.

YOU CAN LEAD A HORSE TO WATER, BUT YOU CAN'T MAKE IT DRINK   You can't make someone do what he/she doesn't want to do. BDPF: 1546. Source: WATER; DRINK. MWCD: O.E. Before a hard day's work in the fields, a horse—or mule—must drink a lot of water; but if it refuses, you must wait until it's ready. (The bigger problem with watering a horse comes *after* the day's work, when it wants to drink itself sick, without cooling off first. Mules are smart enough to know that they have to wait a while.) Stubborn people are like the stubborn draft animal in the morning: They don't want to cooperate, and there's no way to force them to. Yet some people, like the horse in the evening, can *go to the well once too often*; i.e., they can take advantage of a good thing, or ask for one favor too many. As a result, they may discover that *the well has run dry* (HND: 1757) and develop a greater appreciation for the value of our natural resources, esp. water. ATWS; CI; CODP; DAP; DC; IRCD; SA.

YOU CAN TAKE IT, BUT YOU CAN'T DISH IT OUT   *See* Dish It out.

YOU CAN'T EAT YOUR CAKE AND HAVE IT TOO   You can't have it both ways. DC: 1546. Source: EAT (MWCD: O.E.); CAKE (MWCD: 13th cent.). This was the original—and logical—form of the proverb. It simply means that you can't both use up your resources and possess them at the same time. However, an alternative—and illogical—form, *You can't have your cake and eat it too*, has developed which has competed with the original for about the same length of time. It is said to be illogical because if you *have* a cake, you can *eat* it any time you want to. Someone who wants to *eat his/her cake and have it too* wants the best of both worlds—the real world and the imaginery one. In the 1930s, women were warned by advertisers that they couldn't eat their cake and have "IT" (i.e., the sex appeal of Clara Bow, the "IT" girl) too. AID; BDPF; CE; CI; CODP; DAI; DAP; HND; MDWPO; MS; NSOED.

YOU CAN'T GET BLOOD FROM A TURNIP   You can't do the impossible. DAP: 1666. Source: TURNIP. MWCD: 1533. You may not be able to get blood from—or out of—a turnip, but you can get "blood" (i.e., red juice) from a beet if you cut off the stem close to the body. The flesh of the turnip is not red but either white (the "common" turnip) or yellow (the rutabaga, also known as the "Canadian turnip" or the "Swedish turnip"). The common turnip was introduced into the Virginia Colony in the early-17th cent. (DAFD: 1609), and it became popular throughout the English colonies. The *rutabaga* was introduced into America in the late-18th cent. (DAFD: 1799) and became esp. popular in the South, where the root is boiled and mashed like a potato, and the leaves are cooked with bacon or ham hocks and served as *turnip greens*. In fact, the relationship between the closely related turnip and rutabaga (both are roots) is much like that between the unrelated white potato and sweet potato (both are tubers). Although, according to its etymology, the turnip is a round root (a "well-turned" one), turnips also come in flat and cylindrical shapes; and it was presumably the flat shape that was the model for It. *ravioli* (dim. pl. of It. *rava* "turnip"), i.e., "little turnips." The familiarity of the American colonists with the recently introduced turnip, and the familiarity of the Native Americans with another edible root in their midst, is reflected in the term *Indian turnip* for "jack-in-the-pulpit." The identification of a turnip with a stone—you can't get blood from either one of them—is unfortunate for the turnip; but it is even more unfortunate for a *person* to be linked with a turnip, as in the expression *I didn't just fall off the turnip—or cabbage—truck*, meaning "I wasn't born yesterday" or "I'm not a hick from the sticks." CODP; DC; EWPO; FLC; HDAS; HF; HND; MS; NSOED; WNWCD.

YOU CAN'T HAVE YOUR CAKE AND EAT IT TOO   *See* You Can't Eat Your Cake and Have It too.

YOU CAN'T MAKE AN OMELETTE WITHOUT BREAKING EGGS   You can't achieve a difficult goal without hurting somebody's feelings. EWPO: 1859. Source: OMELETTE. (MWCD: ca. 1611); EGG (MWCD: 14th cent.). This maxim is a direct translation of an earlier Fr. saying, suggesting that French cooks may once have had to justify to the mistress of the house the slaughter of unborn chickens for the sake of haute cuisine. (Mork, at least, notified the next of kin.) Metaphorically, the maxim has undoubtedly been useful to army generals who have had to explain why so many troops were killed in the taking of an objective— or by football or ice hockey coaches explaining why there were so many injuries en route to the league championship. An omelette (or *omelet*) starts out with the same basic ingredients as scrambled eggs (eggs and milk); but many more ingredients are added, and the resulting mixture is allowed to settle, rather than being stirred, while frying. BDPF; CODP; HND; MS; SA. *Compare* You Can't Unscramble an Egg.

YOU CAN'T UNSCRAMBLE AN EGG   (Also *You can't unscramble an omelette.*) You can't undo what you have done. DAP: 1928. Source: SCRAMBLE (MWCD; ca. 1586); EGG (MWCD: 14th cent.). Once an egg is mixed with milk, poured into a pan, and stirred while frying, it cannot be restored to its original state. Lady Macbeth recognized this truth when she said, "What's done cannot be undone" (*Macbeth*, Act V, Scene 2), and Eastern philosophers have observed, "You can't unring a bell." A more recent saying, "You can't turn back the clock," is contradicted every fall in the United States when residents turn their clocks back one hour to observe the end of daylight savings time. DEI; MS.

YOU CAN'T UNSCRAMBLE AN OMELETTE   *See* You Can't Unscramble an Egg.

YOU GET ONLY ONE BITE OF THE CHERRY   *See* Two Bites of the Cherry.

YOU'LL NEVER EAT LUNCH IN THIS TOWN AGAIN   *See* Business Lunch.

YOUNG SPROUT   *See* Go to Seed.

YOU'RE THE CREAM IN MY COFFEE   *See* Cream in My Coffee.

YOUR GOOSE IS COOKED   *See* Cook Someone's Goose.

YOU SAID A MOUTHFUL   Your comments hit the nail right on the head. DC: 1934. Source: MOUTH. MWCD: O.E. A literal *mouthful* (MWCD:: 15th cent.) is as much as a mouth can hold of food or drink. A figurative *mouthful* is as much truth as a mouth can utter in one statement. A person who *puts words into someone else's mouth* is either a ventriloquist or someone who accuses someone else of saying something that he/she didn't actually say. A person who *takes the words right out of someone else's mouth* (DC: 1530) says something that the other person would have said if he/she had been given a chance to finish his/her remarks. AID; CE; CI; DAS; DEI; MS. *See also* Do You Eat with That Mouth?; Garbage Mouth; Make Your Mouth Water.

YOU SHALL KNOW THEM BY THEIR FRUIT(S)   *See* Tree Is Known by Its Fruit.

YUMMY   Delicious; delightful. MWCD: 1899. Source: TASTE. *Yum-yum* (MWCD: 1878) is the sound that babies make when they are nursing or being fed with a spoon. Adults make the same sound when they see or smell something delicious—or in between bites, when they are allowed to taste or eat it. When the adult is finished eating and is asked how it was, he/she may declare that it was *yummy*. Adolescents sometimes also use the term *yummy* to describe things that are not food but are attractive in some other way: a *yummy* room, a *yummy* car, a *yummy* vacation, a *yummy* teacher, a *yummy* girl or boy. They also sometimes say *Yummy!* when they recall the good time that they had at the movie, the concert, the game, etc. (Eng. *yummy* may derive fr. Fulani *nyami* "to eat," which in turn may derive fr. *njam* "Yam.") *See also* Sweet Potato.

YUM-YUM   *See* Yummy.

Z

ZEP *See* Submarine Sandwich.

ZEPPELIN *See* Submarine Sandwich.

ZWIEBACK *See* Biscuit.

CLASSIFICATION OF TERMS ACCORDING TO SOURCE

ACORN

Acorn Doesn't Fall far from the Tree

Acorn Squash

Mighty Oaks from Little Acorns Grow

ALE

Cakes and Ale

Ginger Ale

Life Is Not All Cakes and Ale

No More Cakes and Ale

AMBROSIA

Ambrosia

Nectàr

Nectarine

APPETITE

Appetite

Appetizer

Appetizing

Beer-belly Pocketbook

Bulimia

Canapé

Canine-Appetite

Champagne Appetite

For Starters

Hit the Spot

Hors d'Oeuvre

Lick Your Chops

Lose Your Appetite

Make Your Mouth Water

Mouth-watering

Mouth Waters

Ravenous Appetite

Smack Your Lips

Voracious Appetite

Whet Your Appetite

APPLE

Adam's Apple

American as Apple Pie

Apple

Apple a Day Keeps the Doctor away

Apple Brandy

Apple Brown Betty

Apple Butter

Applecart

Apple-cheeked

Apple Doesn't Fall Far from the Tree

Apple for the Teacher

Applejack

Apple-knocker

Apple of Discord

Apple of Love

Apple of Your Eye

Apple Orchard

Apple-pie Bed

Apple-pie Order

Apple-polish

Apple-polisher

Apple-polishing

Apples and Oranges

Applesauce!

As American as Apple Pie

As Sure as God Made Little Green Apples

Bad Apple

Big Apple

Candy Apple

Candy-apple Red

Cider

Cider Vinegar

Compare Apples and Oranges

Custard Apple

Don't Upset the Applecart

Faux Apple Pie

Hard Cider

Have a Second Bite of the Apple

Hedge Apple

How Do You Like Them Apples?

In Apple-pie Order

John Barleycorn

Like Apples and Oranges

Little Apples

Love Apple

Mock Apple Pie

Oak Apple

One Rotten Apple Spoils the Barrel

One Smart Apple

Osage Apple

Pineapple

Polish the Apple

Pomegranate

Road Apple

Rotten Apple

Rotten to the Core

Smart Apple

Some Apples

Sugar Apple

Sweet Cider

Take Another Bite of the Apple

There Is Always One Rotten Apple in the Barrel

Upset the Applecart

Vine Apple

APRON

Apron

Apron Strings

Still Tied to Your Mother's Apron Strings

Tied to Your Mother's Apron Strings

AVOCADO (*See* Pear)

BACON

Back Bacon

Bacon Barometer

Beef Bacon

Belly Bacon

BLT

Bring Home the Bacon

Canadian Bacon

Save Your Bacon

Turkey Bacon

White Bacon

BAG

Bowser Bag

Brown Bagger

Brown-bag It

Brown Bagging

Brown-bag Lunch

Doggie Bag

BAGEL

Bagel

Bagel out

Lox and Bagel

BAKE

Bake (v)

Baked Alaska

Bake in the Sun

Bake into the Budget

Baker's Dozen

Baker's Knees

Clambake

Done up Brown

Do up Brown

Half-baked

Vantage Loaf

BALONEY (*See* Bologna)

BANANA

Banana

Banana Boat

Banana Pepper

Banana Republic

Banana-republic Politics

Banana Seat

Banana Split

Canoe

Cooking Bananas

Go Bananas

Drive Someone Bananas

Fruit with Appeal

Houseboat

Indiana Banana

Indian Banana

Lady's Finger Bananas

Michigan Banana

One Banana

Second Banana

Slip on a Banana Peel

Top Banana

BANQUET (*See* Feast)

BAR

Bar and Grill

Snack Bar

BARBECUE

Barbeque (n)

Barbeque (v)

Bar-B-Q

Ox Roast

Western Barbecue

BARLEY

John Barleycorn

BARREL

One Rotten Apple Spoils the Barrel

Scrape the Bottom of the Barrel

There Is Always One Rotten Apple in the Barrel

BEAN

Bean (n)

Bean (v)

Beanball

Bean Counter

Beaneater

Bean Eater

Beanery

Beanie

Beano

Bean Pole

Black Jelly Bean

Full of Beans

Garbanzo Bean

Hill of Beans

Jellies

Jelly Bean

Jelly Bellies

Know Beans (about)

Know How Many Beans Make Five

Musical Fruit

Not Amount to a Hill of Beans

Not Have a Bean

Not Know from Beans

Not Worth a Bean

Not Worth a Hill of Beans

Not Worth Beans

Pea Bean

Spill the Beans

String Bean

Use the Old Bean

BEAT

Beat the Stuffing out of

Eggbeater

BEEF

Albany Beef

Beef (n)

Beef (v)

Beef about

Beefalo

Beef Bacon

Beefcake

Beefeater

Beef Jerky

Beefsteak

Beefsteak Tomato

Beef Tartare

Beef up

Beefy

Bully Beef

Chipped Beef

Corned Beef

Creamed Chipped Beef on Toast

Have a Beef with

Jerk (v)

Jerkin Beef

Jerky

Pastrami

Pemmican

Red Meat

Shit on a Sningle

Sirloin

S.O.S.

Where's the Beef?

BEER

Beer-belly Pocketbook

Ginger Beer

Root Beer

What Do You Want, Egg in Your Beer?

BEET

Beet Red

Beet Sugar

Harvard Beets

Pickled Beets

Red as a Beet

Spinach Beet

Sugar Beet

BERRY

Berries

Blackberries Are Red When They're Green

Blackberry Summer

Blackberry Winter

Blueberry

Boysenberry

Brown as a Berry

Chinese Gooseberry

Dewberry

Huckleberry

It's the Berries

Loganberry

BIRD

Birdseed

Early-bird Special

For the Birds

Strictly for the Birds

Tough Old Bird

BISCUIT

Biscotti

Biscuit

Biscuit Roller

Biscuit Shooter

Clinkers

Hardtack

Rusk

Sea Biscuits

Shooter

Soft Tack

Zwieback

BITE

Bite (n)

Bite (v)

Bite off More than You Can Chew

Bite Someone's Head off

Bite the Hand That Feeds You

Can't Eat Another Bite

Don't Make/Take Two Bites of the Cherry

Geek

Get Your Teeth into

Have a Bite

Have a Second Bite of the Apple

Stop for a Bite

Take Another Bite of the Apple

Two Bites of the Cherry

You Get Only One Bite of the Cherry

BITTER

Bitter

Bitter Cold

Bitter Contempt

Bitter Death

Bitter End

Bitter Enemies

Bitter Fruits

Bitter Pill to Swallow

Bittersweet

Bittersweet Chocolate

Bittersweet Victory

Bitter Terms

Take the Bitter with the Sweet

To the Bitter End

BLANCH

Blanch (v)

BLOOD

Blood Pudding

Blood Sausage

Bloodthirsty

Get Blood from a Turnip

Make Someone's Blood Boil

You Can't Get Blood from a Turnip

BOARD

Bed and Board

Bed and Breakfast

Board (n)

Board (v)

Boarder

Boardinghouse

Boardinghouse Reach

Cupboard

Room and Board

BOIL

Boil down to

Boiling Mad

Boiling Point

Boiling (over) with Anger

Boiling (over) with Rage

Boil Water without Burning It

Can't Boil Water without Burning It

Can't Even Boil Water

Have a Low Boiling Point

Hard-boil

Hard-boiled

Hard-boiled Egg

Keep the Pot Boiling

Look like a Boiled Lobster

Low Boiling Point

Make Someone's Blood Boil

Potboiler

Reach the Boiling Point

Seethe inside

Watched Pot Never Boils

What It All Boils down to

BOLOGNA

Baloney!

Baloney Dollar

Bologna

Bologna Sausage

Boloney

Bunch of Baloney

Full of Baloney

Globaloney

No Matter How You Slice It, It's Still Baloney

Phoney Baloney

BOLONEY (*See* Bologna)

BONE

Bone of Contention

Bone to Pick

Bonfire

Cut to the Bone

Have a Bone to Pick

Make a Wish

Make No Bones about It

Put Some Meat on Your Bones

Throw Someone a Bone

Wishbone

Wishbone Formation

BORSCHT

Borscht Belt

Borscht Circuit

BOTTLE

Bottle Gourd

Bottleneck

Bottle up

Buttery (n)

Chief Cook and Bottle Washer

BOWL

Begging Bowl

Bossy in a Bowl

Bowl of Cherries

Finger Bowl

Life Is Just a Bowl of Cherries

No Bowl of Cherries

BOX

Box Lunch

Lunch Box

BRAN

Bran Muffin

BREAD

Best Thing since Sliced Bread

Bigger than a Breadbox

Bread

Bread Always Falls Butterside Down

Bread Always/Never Lands Butterside up

Bread and Butter (1)

Bread and Butter (2)

Bread-and-butter (1)

Bread-and-butter (2)

Bread-and-butter Letter

Bread and Circuses

Bread and Water

Breadbasket

Breadbasket of America

Breadwinner

Break Bread

Brown Bread

Butter Your Bread on Both Sides

Cast Your Bread upon the Waters

Companion

Cry with a Loaf of Bread under Your Arm

Daily Bread

Gingerbread

Gingerbread Cookie

Gingerbread House

Gingerbread Man

Graham Bread

Greatest Thing since Sliced Bread

Have Your Bread Buttered on Both Sides

Heavy Bread

Hit Someone in the Breadbasket

Is It Bigger than a Breadbasket?

Know Which Side Your Bread Is Buttered on

Long Bread

Man Cannot Live by Bread Alone

Sandwich Bread

Scratch Bread

Shortbread

Shortnin' Bread

Staff of Life

Sweetbread

Take the Bread out of Someone's Mouth

Want Your Bread Buttered on Both Sides

White Bread

White-bread

BREAKFAST

Bed and Breakfast

Breakfast (n)

Breakfast Buffet

Breakfast for Your Head

Breakfast Nook

Continental Breakfast

Eat Someone for Breakfast

English Breakfast

Most Important Meal of the Day

Power Breakfast

BRIM

Brimful

Brim over

Filled to the Brim

BROTH

Too Many Cooks Spoil the Broth

BROWSE

Browse (v)

Browse through

BRUNCH

Brunch

Champagne Brunch

Sunday Brunch

BUFFALO

Beefalo

Buffalo Chip

BUN

Crumb Bun

Have a Bun in the Oven

Honey Bun

Honeybun

Put a Bun in the Oven

BURN

Boil Water without Burning It

Burned to a Crisp

Burn One!

Can't Boil Water without Burning It

Freezer Burn

Get Your Fingers Burned

Hay Burner

Put on the Back Burner

Slow Burn

BURRITO

Burrito

Chimichanga

BUTCHER

Butcher (n)

Butcher (v)

BUTTER

Apple Butter

Bread Always Lands Butterside up

Bread and Butter (1)

Bread and Butter (2)

Bread-and-butter (1)

Bread-and-butter (2)

Bread-and-butter Letter

Butter (n)

Butter-and-egg Man

Butter-and-egg Money

Butterball

Buttercup

Butterfingered

Butterfingers

Butterfly

Buttermilk

Butternut

Butternut Squash

Butter up

Butter Wouldn't Melt in Your Mouth

Buttery (adj.)

Buttery (n)

Butter Your Bread on Both Sides

Cocoa Butter

Crab Butter

Have Your Bread Buttered on Both Sides

Know Which Side Your Bread Is Buttered on

Like a Hot Knife through Butter

Lobster Butter

Look as if Butter Wouldn't Melt in Your Mouth

Maple Butter

Melt in Your Mouth

Peanut Butter

Want Your Bread Buttered on Both Sides

CABBAGE

Brussels Sprouts

Cabbage

Cabbagehead

Cabbage with a College Education

Cold Slaw

Cole Slaw

Come to a Head

Fall off the Cabbage Truck

Liberty Cabbage

Sauerkraut

Skunk Cabbage

Two Heads Are Better Than One

CABINET

Kitchen Cabinet

CAFÉ

Café

Café Society

CAFETERIA

Cafeteria

Cafeteria-style

Cafetorium

Drugeteria

Ptomaine Domain

Ptomaine Palace

Shaveteria

CAKE

Angel Cake

Angel Food Cake

Babycakes

Beefcake

Brownie

Cake (n)

Cake (v)

Cakes and Ale

Cakewalk

Cheesecake

Cupcake

Devil's Food Cake

Eat Your Cake and Have It Too

Fried Cake

Frosting on the Cake

Fruitcake

Girdle Cake

Griddle Cake

Have Your Cake and Eat It Too

Hoecake

Honeycakes

Hotcake

Johnnycake

Journey Cake

Ladyfinger

Layer-cake Effect

Let Them Eat Cake!

Life Is Not All Cakes and Ale

Mexican Wedding Cake

Mississippi Mud Cake

No More Cakes and Ale

No Piece of Cake

Nuttier than a Fruitcake

Nutty as a Fruitcake

Pancake (n)

Pancake (v)

Pat-a-cake

Patty-cake

Petit Four

Piece of Cake

Russian Tea Cake

Scratch Cake

Shortcake

Slice of the Cake

Swedish Tea Cake

Sweetcakes

Take the Cake

That (Really) Takes the Cake

Then Let Them Eat Cake!

You Can't Eat Your Cake and Have It Too

You Can't Have Your Cake and Eat It Too

CALF

Calf Fries

Kill the Fatted Calf

CAN

Can It

Canned Applause

Canned Laughter

Canned Music

Canned Sales Pitch

Canned Speech

Can of Corn

Get Canned

Home Canning

In the Can

Sardine Can

Tin

Tin Can

CANDY

Candy

Candy Apple

Candy-apple Red

Candy-ass

Candy-coated

Candy Man

Candy Store

Candy Striper

Cotton Candy

Cotton-candy Clouds

Ear Candy

Easy as Taking Candy from a Baby

Eye Candy

Happy as a Kid in a Candy Store

Like a Kid in a Candy Store

Like Taking Candy from a Baby

Needle Candy

Nose Candy

Rock Candy

Sugar Candy

CANNIBAL

Cannibal

Cannibalism

Cannibalize

CARROT

Like a Carrot to a Donkey

Like Holding out a Carrot to a Donkey

Carrot-and-stick Approach

Carrot-and-stick Policy

Carrottop

CAULIFLOWER

Broccoli

Cabbage with a College Education

Cauliflower Ear

CAVIAR

Caviar to the General

Fish Eggs

Tapioca Pudding

CEREAL

Cereal

Granola

Pablum

CHEESE

Big Cheese

Big Wheel

Blue Cheese

Cheesecake

Cheese-eater

Cheesehead

Cheese It!

Cheese Soufflé

Cheese Stands Alone

Cheesy

Cheshire Cat

Cottage Cheese

Cottage-cheese Thighs

Cream Cheese

Dutch Cheese

Farmer Cheese

Green Cheese

Grin like a Cheshire Cat

Headcheese

Head Cheese

Holey as Swiss Cheese

Moon Is Made of Green Cheese

Popcorn Cottage Cheese

Pot Cheese

Rat Trap Cheese

Ricotta

Say "Cheese!"

Smearcase

Smooth as Cream Cheese

Swiss-cheese Infield

Tofu

Welsh Rabbit

Welsh Rarebit

CHEF

Chef de Cuisine

Cordon Bleu

My Compliments to the Chef

Sous-chef

Toque

CHERRY

Bing Cherry

Black Cherry

Bowl of Cherries

Can She Make a Cherry Pie?

Cherries Jubilee

Cherry (adj.)

Cherry (n)

Cherry Angioma

Cherry Bomb

Cherry Farm

Cherry Lips

Cherry-pick

Cherry Picker

Cherrystone Clam

Cherry Tart

Cherry Tomato

Come up Cherries

Cooking Cherry

Desert Cherry

Dessert Cherry

Don't Make/Take Two Bites of the Cherry

Eating Cherry

Have a Second Bite of the Cherry

Have Two Bites of the Cherry

Life Is Just a Bowl of Cherries

Maiden's Delight

Make Two Bites of the Cherry

Maraschino Cherries

No Bowl of Cherries

Sour Cherry

Sweet Cherry

Take Another Bite of the Cherry

Take Two Bites of the Cherry

Tart Cherry

Two Bites of the Cherry

Virgin

You Get Only One Bite of the Cherry

CHESTNUT

Castanets

Cat's Paw

Chestnut

Chestnuts

Old Chestnut

Pull Someone's Chestnuts out of the Fire

Water Chestnut

CHEW

Bite Off More than You Can Chew

Chew Face

Chew on

Chew out

Chew over

Chew Someone out

Chew Someone up and Spit Them out

Chew the Fat

Chew the Rag

Chew up the Scenery

Chew Your Cud

Fletcherism

Fletcherize

Ruminate

CHICKEN

Chicken-and-egg Question

Chicken Coffee

Chicken Feed

Chicken in Every Pot

Chicken of the Sea

City Chicken

Count Your Chickens before They Hatch

Don't Count Your Chickens before They Hatch

Mock Chicken

Rubber Chicken

Rubber-chicken Circuit

Schmaltz

Schmaltzy

Tastes Just like Chicken

Which Came First, the Chicken or the Egg?

Work for Chicken feed

CHILI

Chile

Chili Con Carne

Chili-dip

Chili Dip

ChiliDog

Chili Powder

Chili Sauce

Chili Today, Hot Tamale

CHIP

Buffalo Chip

Cow Chip

Taco Chips

Tortilla Chips

Tostadas

CHOCOLATE

Bittersweet Chocolate

Black-and-white

Chocoholic

Hershey Bar

Sweet Chocolate

White Chocolate

CHOP

Chop-Chop

Chop House

Chopped Liver

Chopper

Chopping Block

Chopsticks

Chop Suey

Have Your Head on the Chopping Block

Lamb Chop

Lick Your Chops

Mutton Chops

Pork Chop

Veal Chop

What Am I, Chopped Liver?

CHOW

Chow

Chowchow

Chow Down

Chow Hound

Chow Line

Chow Mein

Chow Time!

Come and Get It!

CHOWDER

Chowderhead

Clam Chowder

CHUCK

Chuck Wagon

CHURN

Churn

Churn in/out/up

CIDER

Apple Cider

Applejack

Cider

Cider Vinegar

Hard Cider

Sweet Cider

CLAM

Cherrystone Clam

Clambake

Clam Chowder

Clam Cocktail

CLARIFY

Clarify

COCKTAIL

Clam Cocktail

Cocktail Table

Fruit Cocktail

Oyster Cocktail

Prairie Cocktail

Seafood Cocktail

Shrimp Cocktail

COCOA

Cocoa Butter

COCONUT

Coconut Cream

Coconut Milk

CODDLE (*See* Egg)

COFFEE

Battery Acid

Café

Café Society

Cafeteria

Chicken Coffee

Chicory Coffee

Coffee

Coffee Break

Coffee Grinder

Coffee Hour

Coffeehouse

Coffee Klat(s)ch

Coffee Mill

Coffee Room

Coffee Shop

Coffee Table

Coffee-table Book

Coffee, Tea, or Me?

Come up for a Cup of Coffee

Cup of Coffee

Dishwater

Espresso

Here's Mud in Your Eye

Hot Stuff

Java

Joe

Kaffeeklatsch

Mock Coffee

Mud

Sinkers and Suds

Wake up and Smell the Coffee

CONE

Ice-cream Cone

Snow Cone

Sugar Cone

Waffle Cone

COOK (n)

All Hands and the Cook!

Chief Cook and Bottle Washer

Sea Cook

Son of a Sea Cook

Too Many Cooks Spoil the Broth

COOK (v)

Concoct

Cookbook

Cookbook Approach

Cook from Scratch

Cooking Banana

Cooking Oil

Cooking with Gas

Cook Someone's Goose

Cook Something up

Cook the Books

Cook up

Goose Is Cooked

Hard-cooked

Liaison

Made from Scratch

Make from Scratch

Now You're (Really) Cooking

Pressure Cooker

Rustle up

Scrape up

See What I Can Dig up

See What I Can Rustle up

See What I Can Scrape up

What's Cooking?

What's Cookin', Good Lookin'?

Your Goose Is Cooked

COOKIE

Animal Crackers

Caught with Your Hand in the Cookie Jar

Cookie

Cookie-cutter

Cookie-cutter Houses

Cookie Pusher

Death Cookie

Elephant Ear

Fortune Cookie

Get Caught with Your Hand in the Cookie
  Jar

Gingerbread Cookie

Hermit

Icebox Cookies

Mexican Wedding Cake

One Smart Cookie

Oreo

Refrigerator Cookies

Russian Tea Cake

Sandwich Cookie

Smart Cookie

S'Mores

Snickerdoodles

Swedish Tea Cake

That's the Way the Cookie Crumbles

Toss Your Cookies

Tough Cookie

CORK

Corkscrew

Pop Your Cork

Put a Cork in It!

Uncork a Wild Pitch

CORN

Can of Corn

Corn

Cornball (adj.)

Cornball (n)

Corn Bread

Corn Dodger

Corn Dog

Corned Beef

Cornfed

Corn Fritter

Corn Milk

Cornpone

Corn Pone

Cornrow

Corn Snow

Corny

Hush Puppy

Indian Corn

John Barleycorn

Maize

Parching Corn

Peppercorn

Peppercorn Rent

Popcorn

Popped Corn

Popping Corn

Rough as a Cob

COW

Black Cow

Bossy in a Bowl

Brown Cow

Cash Cow

Cow Chip

Cow Pat

Cow Patty

Cowpea

Cow Pie

Milk a Cash Cow

White Cow

CRAB

Crab Butter

CRACKER

Animal Crackers

Cracker-barrel Philosopher

Cracker Jack

Crackerjack (adj.)

Crackerjack (n)

Crackerjack Shot

Crackers

Drive Someone Crackers

Graham Cracker

Saltines

Soda Cracker

CRAW

Have Sand in Your Craw

Sand in Your Craw

Stick in Your Craw

CREAM

Boston Cream Pie

Chocolate Cream

Coconut Cream

Cream (n)

Cream (v)

Cream Always Rises to the Top

Cream Cheese

Cream-colored

Creamed

Creamer

Cream of Society

Cream of Tartar

Cream of the Crop

Cream Puff

Cream Rinse

Cream Soda

Creamware

Creamy

Crème de Cacao

Crème de la Crème

Crème de Menthe

Egg Cream

Go Together like Peaches and Cream

Ice Cream

Maple Cream

Nondairy Creamer

Peaches and Cream Complexion

Say When!

Smooth as Cream Cheese

You're the Cream in My Coffee

CROCK

Crock

Crocked

Crockery

Crock of Shit

Crock Pot

Crock-Pot

Half-crocked

CROW

Eat Crow

CRUMB

Crumb

Crumb Bum

Crumb Crust

Crumble

Crumbly

Crummy

Throw Someone a Few Crumbs

CRUMPET

Crumpet

CRUST

Crumb Crust

Crust

Crusty

Some Crust

Upper Crust

CUCUMBER

Cold as a Cucumber

Cool as a Cucumber

Cucumber Eyes

Cucumber Slices

CUD

Chew Your Cud

CUISINE

Cajun Cuisine

Creole Cuisine

Cuisine

Culinary Arts

French Cuisine

Haute Cuisine

New American Cuisine

Nouvelle Cuisine

CUP

Athletic Cup

Brassiere Cup

Buttercup

Come up for a Cup of Coffee

Cup (n)

Cup (v)

Cupboard

Cupcake

Cup of Java

Cup of Joe

Cup of Tea

Cuppa Joe

Cups Runneth over

Cup Your Hands

In the Cup

In Your Cups

Loving Cup

Not My Cup of Tea

Tempest in a Teapot

There's Many a Slip twixt the Cup and the Lip

CURDLE

Bloodcurdling Scream

Bonnyclabber

Curdle Your Blood

Curds and Whey

CURE

Cure (v)

CUSTARD

Custard

Custard Apple

CUT

Can't Cut It

Can't Cut the Mustard

Center Cut

Cookie-cutter Houses

Cut above the Rest

Cut It Close

Cut No Ice

Cut out the Fat

Cut the Feed

Cut the Mustard

Cutting Edge

Cut to the Bone

French-cut

On the Cutting Edge

So Tender You Could Cut It with a Fork

So Thick You Could Cut It with a Knife

Too Old to Cut the Mustard

DAIRY

Nondairy Creamer

DESSERT

Get Your Just Desserts

Jiggly Dessert

Junket

Just Desserts

DEVIL

Deviled Eggs

Deviled Ham

Devil's Food Cake

Devils on Horseback

DIET

Seefood Diet

Steady Diet

DIG

Dig Your Grave with a Knife and Fork

See What I Can Dig/Rustlé/Scrape up

DIGEST

Digest (n)

Digest (v)

DINE

Desktop Dining

Dine

Dine out

Diner

Dinette

Dining Car

Dining Room

Dining Salon

Wine and Dine

DINNER

Din Din

Dinner (1)

Dinner (2)

Dinner Jacket

Dinner Pail

Dinner Theater

Dinnertime

Dinnerware

Don't Forget to Call Me for Dinner

Early Dinner

Frozen Dinner

Late Dinner

Progressive Dinner

Spoil Your Dinner

Thanksgiving Dinner

TV Dinner

What's for Dinner?

DIP

Chili-dip

Dip into

Double-dipper

DISH (n)

Covered-dish Supper

Dish (n)

Dishpan Hands

Dishrag

Dish Ran away with the Spoon

Dishwater

Feel like a Wet Dishrag

Limp as a Dishrag

Satellite Dish

Some Dish

DISH (v)

Dis

Dish (v)

Dish Dirt

Dish It out

Dish off

Dish Someone

Dish up

You Can Dish It out, but You Can't Take It

You Can Take It, but You Can't Dish It out

DISHWATER

Dishwater

Dishwater Blond(e)

Dull as Dishwater

Hogwash

Pearl Diver

Slop

Swill

Taste like Dishwater

DOG

Bowser Bag

Chili Dog

Corn Dog

Dachshund Sausage

Dog-eat-dog

Doggie Bag

Dog Meat

Go to the Dogs

Hot Dog

Hush Puppy

It's a Dog-eat-dog World

It's Dog-eat-dog out there

Sausage Dog

Throw It to the Dogs

Try It on the Dog

Wiener Dog

DONE

Stick a Fork in Him/Her and See If He/She's
  Done

DOUGH

Dough

Doughboy

Doughface

Dough-faced

Doughnut

Make a Lot of Dough

Rolling in Dough

Sourdough

DOUGHNUT

Bet Dollars to Doughnuts

Donut

Doughnut

Doughnut Hole

Fastnacht

Fried Cake

Hush Puppy

Sinker

Sinkers and Suds

Watch the Doughnut, Not the Hole

DRESSING

Dressing

Stuffing

DRINK

Drink of Water

Eat, Drink, and Be Merry, for Tomorrow
  We Die

Eat, Sleep, and Drink

Let Us Eat, Drink, and Be Merry, for
  Tomorrow We Die

Long Drink of Water

Meat and Drink

Tall Drink of Water

Water, Water, Everywhere, but Not a Drop
  to Drink

You Can Lead a Horse to Water, but You
  Can't Make It Drink

DUCK

Bombay Duck

Cold Duck

Duck's Egg

Duck Soup

Easy as Duck Soup

Lay a Duck's Egg

Mock Duck

DUMPLING

Apple Dumpling

Dumpling

Dumpling Culture

Matzo Ball

Pierogi

Wonton

DUNK

Dunk (n)

Dunk (v)

Dunk a Basketball

Slam Dunk

DUTCH

Dutch Oven

Dutch Treat

Go Dutch

EAT

Bean Eater

Beefeater

Big Fish Eat Little Fish

Bolt Down

Can't Eat Another Bite

Cheese-eater

Corrode

Devour

Dig in

Dog-eat-dog

Do Goobers Eat Gophers, or Do Gophers Eat Goobers?

Don't Eat Yellow Snow

Don't Eat Your Heart out

Do You Eat with That Mouth?

Eat a Bullet

Eat a Horse

Eat a Sour Grape

Eat away at

Eat Crow

Eat Dirt

Eat, Drink, and Be Merry, for Tomorrow We Die

Eat Face

Eat High on/off the Hog

Eat Humble Pie

Eat It up

Eat It up with a Spoon

Eat like a Bird

Eat like a Horse

Eat like an Ox

Eat like a Pig

Eat Nails

Eat out of Your Hands

Eat Punches

Eat, Sleep, and Drink

Eat Someone Alive

Eat Someone for Breakfast

Eat Someone for Lunch

Eat Someone out of House and Home

Eat Someone's Dirt

Eat Someone's Lunch

Eat Someone's Salt

Eat Someone up and Spit Them out

Eat Tenderloin

Eat Your Cake and Have It Too

Eat Your First Peach

Eat Your Gun

Eat Your Hat

Eat Your Heart out

Eat Your Words

Erode

Fire-eater

Fire-eating

Floor Looks Clean Enough to Eat off/on

Freeload

Freeloader

Garlic Eater

Gobble up

Hand-to-mouth

Have Someone Eating out of the Palm of Your Hand

Have Someone Eating out of Your Hand(s)

Have Your Cake and Eat It Too

Inhale Your Food

It Must Have Been Something I Ate

Know Where Your Next Meal Is Coming from

Lead a Hand-to-mouth Existence

Let Them Eat Cake!

Let Us Eat, Drink, and Be Merry, for Tomorrow We Die

Look Good Enough to Eat

Look like the Cat That Ate the Canary

Lotus-eater

Lotusland

Mad Enough to Eat Nails

Make a Pig of Yourself

Make Someone Eat Crow

Make Someone Eat Dirt

Make Someone Eat Their Words

Mange-tout

Man Who First Ate a Peach

Moth-eaten

Not Know Where Your Next Meal Is Coming from

Oat-eater

Parasite

Pig out

Proof of the Pudding Is in the Eating

Real Men Don't Eat Quiche

Scarf down

Smoke Eater

So Hungry You Could Eat a Horse

Then Let Them Eat Cake!

Toadeater

Toady

What's Eating You?

Wolf down

Worm-eaten

You Are What You Eat

You Can't Eat Your Cake and Have It Too

You Can't Have Your Cake and Eat It Too

You'll Never Eat Lunch in This Town Again

EGG

Adam and Eve on a Raft

Bad Egg

Butter-and-egg Man

Butter-and-egg Money

Chicken-and-egg Question

Coddle

Curate's Egg

Darning Egg

Deviled Eggs

Don't Put All Your Eggs in One Basket

Duck's Egg

Easter Egg

Easter-egg Hunt

Easter-egg Roll

Eggbeater

Egg Cream

Egghead

Egg in Your Beer

Eggnog

Egg on

Egg on Your Face

Eggplant

Egg Rolling

Egg-shaped

Eggshell

Egg-sucker

Egg-white

Fabergé Egg

Fish Egg

Fried Egg

Go Fry an Egg

Go Lay an Egg

Good Egg

Goose Egg

Go Suck an Egg

Ham and Egg It

Hard-boiled

Hard-boiled Egg

Have Egg on Your Face

Have Scrambled Eggs for Brains

Hen Fruit

Hobo Egg

If You Break an Egg, Make an Omelette

Kill the Goose That Laid the Golden Eggs

Lacto-ovo-vegetarian

Last One in Is a Rotten Egg

Lay a Duck's Egg

Lay a Goose Egg

Lay an Egg

Like the Curate's Egg

Love

Nest Egg

Oval

Ovo-vegetarian

Poach

Put All Your Eggs in One Basket

Put All Your Eggs in One Basket—and
WATCH THAT BASKET

Rotten Egg

Scotch Woodcock

Scrambled Eggs

Shatter like an Eggshell

So Hot You Could Fry an Egg on It

Sunny-side up

Teach Your Grandmother to Suck Eggs

Tough Egg

Tread on Eggs

Walk on Eggs

Walk on Eggshells

What Do You Want, Egg in Your Beer?

Which Came First, the Chicken or the Egg?

Wreck a Pair!

You Can't Make an Omelette without
Breaking Eggs

You Can't Unscramble an Egg

ENCHILADA

Big Enchilada

Whole Enchilada

FAMINE

Feast or Famine

FARM

Truck Farm

FAST

Breakfast

Feast or Fast

Mardi Gras

FAT

Chew the Fat

Cut out the Fat

Fat (adj.)

Fat (n)

Fat as a Pig

Fat Book

Fat Cat

Fat Chance

Fat Contract

Fat Farm

Fathead

Fat Is in the Fire

Fat Lip

Fat Lot of

Fat of the Land

Fat Part

Fat Part of the Bat

Fat Pitch

Fat Profit

Fat Role

Fatted Calf

Fatten (up)

Fat Tone

Fat Wallet

Fat Year

Grow Fat

Kill the Fatted Calf

Live off the Fat of the Land

Mardi Gras

Schmaltz

Trim the Fat

FEAST

Banquet

Feast

Feast for the Eyes

Feast or Famine

Feast or Fast

Feast Your Eyes on

Fest

Festival

Festive

Gabfest

Immovable Feast

Movable Feast

Slugfest

Songfest

FEED

Birdseed

Bite the Hand that Feeds You

Bottom Feeder

Chicken Feed

Cornfed

Cut the Feed

Delayed Feedback

Fed up

Fed up to Here

Fed up to the Back Teeth

Fed up to the Gills

Feed (n)

Feed (v)

Feed a Cold, Starve a Fever

Feedback

Feed Bag

Feeding Frenzy

Feed Someone a Line

Feed the Ball

Feed the Bulldog

Feed the Fire

Feed the Fishes

Feed the Imagination

Feed the Kitty

Feed Your Face

Fish Food

For the Birds

Have a Lot of Hungry Mouths to Feed

Lose Your Feed

Off Your Feed

Put on the Feedbag

Scavenger

Spoon-fed

Spoon-feed

Starve a Cold, Feed a Fever

Strap on the (Old) Feed Bag

Strictly for the Birds
That Doesn't Feed the Bulldog
Tie on the (Old) Feed Bag
Work for Chicken Feed
FIG
Fig
Fig Leaf
Not Care a Fig
Not Give a Fig
Not Worth a Fig
Sign of the Fig
Spanish Fig
Sycophant
FINGER
Butterfingered
Butterfingers
Finger Bowl
Finger Food
Finger in Every Pie
Finger Sandwich
Fingers Were Made before Forks
Get Your Fingers Burned
Have a Finger in Every Pie
Have a Finger in Many (Different) Pies
Have a Finger in the Pie
Ladyfinger
Lady's Fingers
FIRE
Bonfire
Fat Is in the Fire
From the Frying Pan to the Fire
Go from the Frying Pan to the Fire
Go out of the Frying Pan into the Fire
Grape Balls of Fire
Out of the Frying Pan into the Fire
FISH
Another Kettle of Fish

Big Fish Eat Little Fish
Catch of the Day
Chicken of the Sea
Different Kettle of Fish
Fed up to the Gills
Feed the Fishes
Fine Kettle of Fish
Fish Boil
Fish Eggs
Fish Food
Fishy
Have Bigger Fish to Fry
Have More Important Fish to Fry
Have Other Fish to Fry
Jellyfish
Kettle of Fish
Look Fishy
Mess of Fish
Neither Fish nor Fowl
Neither Fish nor Fowl nor Good Red
    Herring
One Man's Meat Is Another Man's Poisson
Pan Fish
Popcorn Fish
Pretty Kettle of Fish
Red Herring
Smell Fishy
Sound Fishy
Soup and Fish
Spineless Jellyfish
Taste Fishy
Whole Nother Kettle of Fish
FLAVOR
Flavor
Flavor of the Month
FLESH
Carnival
Carny

Water Carnival

Winter Carnival

FLOUR

Flour

Flower

Graham Flour

FODDER

Cannon Fodder

Farrago

Fodder

FOOD

Angel Food Cake

Brain Food

Chow

Comfort Food

Creature Comforts

Devil's Food Cake

Fast Food

Fast-food Restaurant

Finger Food

Food Chain

Food for Thought

Food for Worms

Food Guide

Food Guide Pyramid

Food of Love

Food Pyramid

Good for You

Grub for Food

Junk Food

Kosher Food

Leftovers

Lion's Share

Low on the Food Chain

Manna

Manna from Heaven

Put Food on the Table

Rabbit Food

Roughage

Snack Food

Soul Food

Squirrel Food

Stick to Your Ribs

Take Food out of the Mouths of Children

Trail Food

Windfall

Worm Food

FORK

Dig Your Grave with a Knife and Fork

Fingers Were Made before Forks

Forkball

Fork in the Road

Forklift

Fork over Your Money

Fork-tender

So Tender You Could Cut It with a Fork

Speak with Forked Tongue

Stick a Fork in Him/Her and See If He/She Is Done

FOWL

Breast

Dark Meat

Drumstick

Eat like a Bird

Neither Fish nor Fowl

Neither Fish nor Fowl nor Good Red Herring

White Meat

FREEZE

Freezer Burn

FRENCH

French-cut

French-fried Onion Rings

French-fried Potatoes

French Fries

FRET

Don't Fret about It

Fret (v)

What Are You Fretting about?

FRITTER

Corn Fritter

FROSTING

Frosting

Frosting on the Cake

FRUIT

Bear Fruit

Be Fruitful, and Multiply

Bitter Fruits

By Their Fruits You Shall Know Them

First Fruits

Forbidden Fruit

Fruit

Fruit Boat

Fruitcake

Fruit Cocktail

Fruitful

Fruition

Fruitless

Fruit of the Loom

Fruit of the Womb

Fruit Salad

Fruits of Your Labors

Fruit with Appeal

Fruity

Grapefruit

Hen Fruit

Kiwifruit

Musical Fruit

Nuttier than a Fruitcake

Nutty as a Fruitcake

Tree Is Known by Its Fruit

Tutti-frutti

Ugli Fruit

You Shall Know Them by Their Fruit(s)

FRY

Brain Is Fried

Calf Fries

Deep-fry

French-fried Onion Rings

French-fried Potatoes

French Fries

Fried

Fried Cake

Fried Egg

Fries

From the Frying Pan to the Fire

Fry (n)

Fry (v)

Frying Pan

Fry in Your Own Grease

Go from the Frying Pan to the Fire

Go Fry an Egg

Go out of the Frying Pan into the Fire

Have Bigger Fish to Fry

Have More Important Fish to Fry

Have Other Fish to Fry

Lamb Fries

Lamb's Fries

Out of the Frying Pan into the Fire

Pan-fry

Sizzle (v)

Small fry

Small-fry

So Hot You Could Fry an Egg on It

FUDGE

Fudge (n)

Fudge (v)

Fudge!

Fudge Brownies

Fudge Factor

Fudge Frosting

Fudge the Figures

Fudge the Issue

Fudge the Rules

Hot Fudge Sundae

Oh, Fudge!

GARBAGE

Bunch of Garbage

Garbage

Garbage in, Garbage out

Garbage Mouth

Garbologist

Go to the Dogs

Talk Garbage

Treat Someone like Garbage

GARDEN

Garden (n)

Garden State

Garden-variety

Greenhouse

Greenhouse Effect

Green Thumb

Have a Green Thumb

Hotbed

Hotbed of Activity

Truck Garden

GARLIC

Cloves

Garlic

Garlic Breath

Garlic Eater

Italian Perfume

Shallot

Spanish Garlic

GARNISH

Garnish (n)

Garnish (v)

Garnishee (n)

Garnishee (v)

Garnishment

GELATIN

Gel (n)

Gel (v)

Gelatin

GINGER

Ginger

Ginger Ale

Ginger Beer

Gingerbread

Gingerbread Cookie

Gingerbread House

Gingerbread Man

GIZZARD

Have Sand in Your Gizzard

Sand in Your Gizzard

Stick in Your Gizzard

GLASS

Crystal

Drinking Glass

Glass Is Half Empty

Glass Is Half Full

Milk Glass

Plate Glass

GLUTTONY

Glutton

Glutton for Punishment

Gluttony

No Glutton for Punishment

GOOSE

Cook Someone's Goose

Goose Egg

Goose Hangs High

Goose Is Cooked

Kill the Goose That Laid the Golden Eggs

Lay a Goose Egg

Ocarina

What's Good for the Goose Is Good for the Gander

What's Sauce for the Goose Is Sauce for the Gander

Your Goose Is Cooked

GORGE

Gorge Yourself

Make Your Gorge Rise

GOURD

Bottle Gourd

Calabash

Gourd

Out of Your Gourd

Stoned out of Your Gourd

GRAIN

Grain of Salt

Take with a Grain of Salt

With a Grain of Salt

GRAPE

Grape

Grape Balls of Fire

Grape Caesar's Ghost

Grapefruit

Grape-Nuts

Grapeshot

Grapes of Wrath

Grape Sugar

Grapevine

Raisin

Sour Grapes

Sour-grapes Attitude

GRAPEFRUIT

Grapefruit

Grapefruit League

Grapefruit-size Hail

GRAPEVINE

Grapevine

Grapevine Telegraph

Hear It through the Grapevine

GRATE

Grate (v)

Grate on Your Nerves

Have Your Nerves Grated

GRAVY

Everything Else Is Gravy

Get on the Gravy Train

Gravy Boat

Gravy Train

Pure Gravy

Ride the Gravy Train

GRAZE

Graze (v)

Grazing Restaurant

GREASE

Bear Grease

Elbow Grease

Fry in Your Own Grease

Grease

Greasepaint

Greaser

Greasy

Greasy Clothes

Greasy/Greazy Line

Greasy Smile

Greasy Spoon

Slush

Slush Fund

GREEN

Green Onion

Greenhouse Effect

Green Thumb

Have a Green Thumb

GRIDDLE

Girdle Cake

Griddle Cake

Hot off the Griddle

GRILL

Bar and Grill

Grill (n)

Grill (v)

Grill a Suspect

Hot off the Grill

Mixed Grill

GRIND

Coffee Grinder

Daily Grind

Grinder

Grind It out

Mills of the Gods Grind Slowly

GRIST

Grist for the Mill

GRITS

Chinese Grits

Cornmeal Mush

Cornpone

Corn Pone

Georgia Ice Cream

Grits

Hominy Grits

Mush(y)

GRUB

Grub (n)

Grub (v)

Grub for Food

Grubstake

GRUEL

Gruel (n)

Gruel (v)

Grueling

GULLET

Stick in Your Gullet

HAM

Deviled Ham

Ham (1)

Ham (2)

Ham Actor

Ham-and-egg

Ham and Egg It

Hamfatter

Ham-fisted

Ham-handed

Ham It up

Ham Loaf

Ham Radio

Ham Radio Operator

Ham Radio Station

Imported Ham

HAMBURGER

Burger

Hamburger

Hamburger Bun

Hamburger Steak

Liberty Sandwich

Make Hamburger of

Sloppy Joe

Veggie Burger

HASH

Hash (n)

Hash (v)

Hash Browns

Hash House

Hashhouse Greek

Hash Marks

Hash out

Hash over

Hash Slinger

Hash up

Make a Hash of

Red Flannel Hash

Rehash

Settle Someone's Hash

Yesterday, Today, and Tomorrow

HEAT

If You Can't Stand the Heat, Get out of the Kitchen

Take the Heat

Turn up the Heat

HEN

Hen Fruit

HERB

Herb of Grace

HERRING

Drag a Red Herring across Someone's Path

Kipper

Kippered Herring

Neither Fish nor Fowl nor Good Red Herring

Red Herring

HOG

Eat High on/off the Hog

Gas Hog

Hog

Hog the Limelight

Hoover Hog

Live High on/off the Hog

Razorback

Road Hog

HONEY

Catch More Flies with Honey than with Vinegar

Honey

Honeybun

Honey Bun

Honeybunch

Honeycakes

Honey Child

Honeycomb

Honeymoon

Honeymoon Is over

Honeysuckle

Land Flowing with Milk and Honey

Land of Milk and Honey

Maple Honey

Mealymouthed

Mellifluous

Sweet as Honey

Sweet Talker

You Can Catch More Flies with Honey than with Vinegar

HORSE

Angels on Horseback

Devils on Horseback

Eat a Horse

Eat like a Horse

Horse Chestnut

Horse Radish

Lead a Horse to Water

Oat-eater

So Hungry You Could Eat a Horse

You Can Lead a Horse to Water, but You Can't Make It Drink

HOT

Be in Hot Water

Drop like a Hot Potato

Hotbed of Activity

Hotcake

Hot Dog

Hot off the Griddle

Hot off the Grill

Hot Pot

Hot Potato

Hot Sauce

In Hot Water

Like a Hot Knife through Butter

Like a Hot Potato

Make It Hot for

Piping Hot

Red Hot

Slave over a Hot Stove All Day

Too Hot to Handle

HOT DOG

Chili Dog

Coney Island

Corn Dog

Dachshund Sandwich

Hot Diggity Dog!

Hotdog

Hot Dog

Hot Dog!

Hotdogger

Pigs in the Blanket

Red Hot

Tube Steak

HUNGER

Bulimia

Have a Lot of Hungry Mouths to Feed

Have the Hungries

Hungry as a Bear

Hungry for Affection

Hungry for Attention

Hungry for Money

Hungry for Praise

Keep the Wolf from the Door

Money-hungry

So Hungry You Could Eat a Horse

Tantalize

Tantalizing

ICE

Cuts No Ice

Have Ice Water in Your Veins

Ice

Icebox

Icehouse

Iceman

Ice Wagon

Ice Water in Your Veins

Icing

In Cold Storage

On the Rocks

Pancake Ice

Put on Ice

Snow Cone

Stink on Ice

ICEBOX

Icebox

Icebox Cookies

Icebox Pie

Refrigerator

ICE CREAM

Black-bottom Sundae

Dill Pickles and Ice Cream

Double-dipper

Flavor of the Month

Georgia Ice Cream

Ice Cream

Ice-cream Chair

Ice-cream Cone

Ice-cream Pants

Ice-cream Sandwich

Ice-cream Sociable

Ice-cream Social

Ice-cream Soda

News Scoop

Scoop

Scoop Neck

Sundae

ICING

Frosting

Icing on the Cake

Royal Icing

JAM

In a Jam

It Must Be Jelly, 'Cause Jam Don't Shake like That

Jam (n)

Jam (v)

Jampacked

Jam Sandwich

Jelly's Last Jam

JELL-O

Jell-O

Jiggly Dessert

Like Trying to Nail Jell-O to a Tree

Nervous Pudding

JELLY

Black Jelly Bean

It Must Be Jelly, 'Cause Jam Don't Shake like That

Jell (v)

Jellied Gasoline

Jellies

Jelly

Jelly Bean

Jelly Bellies

Jellyfish

Jelly Roll

Jelly's Last Jam

Legs Turn to Jelly

Like Trying to Nail Jelly to a Wall

Petroleum Jelly

Spineless Jellyfish

JUICE

Creative Juices

Get the Creative Juices Flowing

Juice

Juice up

Juice up the Engine

Juice up the Plot

Juicy Contract

Juicy Details

Juicy Gossip

Juicy Passages

Juicy Role

Leave You to Stew in Your Own Juice

Lime-juicer

Step on the Juice

Stew in Your Own Juice

Turn up the Juice

JUNKET

Junket

KETCHUP

Cat Soup

Catsup

Ketchup

Tomato Ketchup

KETTLE

Another Kettle of Fish

Ass over Teakettle

Ass-over-teakettle in Love

Different Kettle of Fish

Fine Kettle of Fish

Kettledrum

Kettle of Fish

Knock Someone Ass over Teakettle

Like the Pot Calling the Kettle Black

Pot Calling the Kettle Black

Pretty Kettle of Fish

Teakettle

Whole Nother Kettle of Fish

KIDNEY

Steak and Kidney Pie

Steak and Kidney Pudding

KITCHEN

Culinary Arts

Everything but the Kitchen Sink

Get out of My Kitchen!

If You Can't Stand the Heat, Get out of the
    Kitchen

Kitchen Cabinet

Kitchen Police

Kitchen-sink

Kitchen Spanish

Kosher Kitchen

KP

Soup Kitchen

KNEAD

Lady

KNIFE

Dig Your Grave with a Knife and Fork

Like a Hot Knife through Butter

So Thick You Could Cut It with a Knife

KOSHER

Kosher

Kosher Food

Kosher Kitchen

Kosher Laws

Kosher Meat

Kosher Pickles

Kosher Restaurant

Not Kosher

Pareve

LAMB

Lamb Fries

Lamb's Fries

Prairie Cocktail

LARD

Cracklings

Interlard

Lard (n)

Lard (v)

Lard Ass

Larder

Lardhead

Render

Try out

Tub of Lard

LEAVEN

Leaven

LEEK

Garlic

LEMON

Go Suck a Lemon

If Life Hands You a Lemon, Make
    Lemonade

Lemon

Lemon-laundering

Lemon Law

Suck the Lemon Dry

This Car Is a Lemon

LETTUCE

BLT

Head Lettuce

Leaf Lettuce

Lettuce

Lettuce Spray

Lettuce, Turnip, and Pea!

Romaine Lettuce

LICORICE

Licorice Stick

LID

Blow the Lid off

Flip Your Lid

Hit the Ceiling

Keep the Lid on

Potlids

Put a Lid on It

LIME

Hog the Limelight

Key Lime

Key Lime Pie

Limeade

Lime-juicer

Limelight

Limey

LIVER

Braunschweiger

Chopped Liver

Foie Gras

Liverwurst

Pâté de Foie Gras

What Am I, Chopped Liver?

LOAF

Cry with a Loaf of Bread under Your Arm

Half a Loaf Is Better than None

Ham Loaf

Lady

Lord

Meat Loaf

Salmon Loaf

Sandwich Loaf

Sugarloaf

Vantage Loaf

LOBSTER

Be in Hot Water

Crayfish

In Hot Water

Lobster Butter

Lobster Pot

Look like a Boiled Lobster

Red as a Lobster

LOIN

Eat Tenderloin

Sirloin

Sir Loin

Tenderloin

Tenderloin District

LOLLIPOP

Lollipop

Lollipop Dress

Lollipop Man

Lollypop

Never Wave to a Lollipop Man

Sucker

LUNCH

Box Lunch

Brown-bag Lunch

Brunch

Business Lunch

Businessman's Lunch

Do Lunch

Eat Someone for Lunch

Eat Someone's Lunch

Free Lunch

Let's Do Lunch

Lose Your Lunch

Lunch (n)

Lunch (v)

Lunch Box

Lunch Counter

Lunch-counter Jargon

Luncheon

Luncheonette

No Such Thing as a Free Lunch

Out to Lunch

Power Lunch

Steal Someone's Lunch

There's No Such Thing as a Free Lunch

Three-martini Lunch

Two-martini Lunch

You'll Never Eat Lunch in This Town Again

MACARONI

Macaroni

Macaronic Verse

MAÎTRE D'HÔTEL

D'

Maître d'

Maître d'Hôtel

MALT

Malt

Malted

Malted Milk

Malted Milk Shake

Malt Shop

Mud Shake

White Cow

MANNA (*see* Food)

MAPLE

Maple Butter

Maple Cream

Maple Honey

Maple Sugar

Maple Syrup

Sugar Bush

Sugar Maple

Sugar Shack

MARGARINE

Margarine

Oleo

Oleomargarine

MARKET

Meat Market

MARSHMALLOW

Marshmallow

S'mores

MASH

Mashed

Mashed Potato

Masher

Mash Your Thumb

MAYONNAISE

Hold the Mayo!

Mayo

Mayonnaise

MEAL

À la Carte

American Plan

Chow

Entrée

European Plan

Know Where Your Next Meal Is Coming from

Main Course

Meal

Meals-on-wheels

Meal Ticket

Most Important Meal of the Day

Not Know Where Your Next Meal Is Coming from

Piece between Meals

Pièce de Résistance

Prix Fixe

Square Meal

Table d'Hôte

Three Square Meals

Three Squares

MEASURE

And One for Good Measure

And One for the Pot

Bushel and a Peck

Bushel of Trouble

Bushels of Money

Dash of Humor

Dollop of Satire

For Good Measure

Half-pint

In a Peck of Trouble

Just for Good Measure

Mind Your P's and Q's

One for Good Measure

One for the Pot

Peck of Trouble

Pinch of Jealousy

Pint-sized

MEAT

All That Meat and No Potatoes

Buzzard Meat

Dark Meat

Dead Meat

Dog Meat

Feel like a Piece of Meat

Forcemeat

Fragrant Meat

Kosher Meat

Meat

Meat and Drink

Meat and potatoes

Meat and Potatoes

Meat-ax Approach

Meat By-products

Meat Hand

Meathead

Meatheaded

Meat Hooks

Meat Loaf

Meat Market

Meat Wagon

Meaty

Mincemeat

Mystery Meat

Nutmeat

One Man's Meat Is Another Man's Poison

One Man's Meat Is Another Man's Poisson

Piece of Meat

Put Some Meat on Your Bones

Red Meat

Sandwich Meat

Specialty Meats

Sweetmeat

The Other White Meat

Treat like a Piece of Meat

Variety Meats

White Meat

MELON

Cantaloupe

Honeydew Melon

Melon

Melons

Muskmelon

Slice of the Melon

Tree Melon

Watermelon

MELT

Butter Wouldn't Melt in Your Mouth

Look as if Butter Wouldn't Melt in Your Mouth

Melting Pot

Melt in Your Mouth

MENU

À la Carte

Babe du Jour

Catch of the Day

Early-bird Special

Hunk du Jour

In the Alley

Menu

Menu-driven

Prix Fixe

Soup du Jour

Table d'Hôte

MESS

Fine Mess

Make a Mess

Mell of a Hess

Mess (around) with

Mess Call

Messed up

Mess in

Mess Hall

Messmate

Mess of Fish

Mess of Peas

Mess of Pottage

Mess Tent

Mess up

Officers' Mess

Sell Your Birthright for a Mess of Pottage

MILK

Buttermilk

Coconut Milk

Corn Milk

Cry over Spilled Milk

Cry over Spilt Milk

Don't Cry over Spilled Milk

Lacto-ovo-vegetarian

Lacto-vegetarian

Land Flowing with Milk and Honey

Land of Milk and Honey

Malt

Malted

Malted Milk

Malted Milk Shake

Malt Shop

Milk (n)

Milk (v)

Milk a Cash Cow

Milk a Mine

Milk a Snake

Milk Dry

Milk Glass

Milk of Human Kindness

Milk of Magnesia

Milk Run

Milk Shake

Milk Snake

Milksop

Milk the Clock

Milk Toast

Milk Tooth

Milkweed Milk

Milky

Milky Way

Milquetoast

Mother's Milk

Pigeon Milk

Seersucker

Sop

Sop to Cerberus

Soy Milk

Spill the Milk

MILL

Been through the Mill

Coffee Mill

Daily Grind

Diploma Mill

Grind It out

Grist for the Mill

Mill

Mill about

Mills of the Gods Grind Slowly

Pepper Mill

Put through the Mill

Rumor Mill

Run-of-the-mill

Through the Mill

Water Mill

Windmill

MINCE

Mince (n)

Mince (v)

Mincemeat

Mince Words

Mincing Steps

Not Mince Words

MINCEMEAT

Make Mincemeat of

Mincemeat

Mincemeat Pie

MOLASSES

As Slow as Molasses in January

As Thick as Molasses in January

Blackstrap Molasses

Dark Molasses

Light Molasses

Molasses Cookies

Slow as Molasses in January

Thick as Molasses in January

Treacle

MOUSSE

Mousse

Styling Mousse

MOUTH

Bad Taste in Your Mouth

Born with a Silver Spoon in Your Mouth

Butter Wouldn't Melt in Your Mouth

Do You Eat with That Mouth?

Garbage Mouth

Hand-to-mouth

Have a Lot of Hungry Mouths to Feed

Lead a Hand-to-mouth Existence

Leave a Bad Taste in Your Mouth

Live from Hand to Mouth

Look as if Butter Wouldn't Melt in Your Mouth

Make Your Mouth Water

Mealymouthed

Melt in Your Mouth

Mouthful

Mouth-watering

Put Words into Someone Else's Mouth

Say a Mouthful

Take Food out of the Mouths of Children

Take the Bread out of Someone's Mouth

Take the Words Right out of Someone's Mouth

You Said a Mouthful

MUD

Here's Mud in Your Eye

Make Mud Pies

Mud Pie

MUFFIN

Bran Muffin

English Muffin

Graham Muffin

Meadow Muffin

Muffin

Muffins

Studmuffin

MUSHROOM

Magic Mushrooms

Mushroom (n)

Mushroom (v)

Mushroom Cloud

Puffball Mushroom

Spring up like Mushrooms

Toad's Hat

Toadstool

Truffle of the North

MUSTARD

Ballpark Mustard

Can't Cut It

Can't Cut the Mustard

Cut the Mustard

Must

Mustard

Mustard Gas

Mustard-seed Shot

Too Old to Cut the Mustard

MUTTON

Cold Shoulder

Give Someone the Cold Shoulder

Mutt

Mutton Chops

Muttonhead

Muttonheaded

NECTAR (*see* Ambrosa.)

NEST

Nest Egg

NOODLE

Noodle (n)

Noodle (v)

Ten Lashes with a Wet Noodle

Wet Noodle

NUT

Academia Nut

Butternut

Butternut Squash

Chestnuts

Doughnut

Drive Someone Nuts

Earth Nut

Everything from Soup to Nuts

From Soup to Nuts

Go Nuts

Grape-Nuts

Groundnut

Hard Nut to Crack

In a Nutshell

Monkey Nuts

Nut

Nutcase

Nut Factory

Nuthouse

Nutmeat

Nut of the Matter

Nuts (adj.)

Nuts (n)

Nuts!

Nuts about

Nuts to You!

Nuttier than a Fruitcake

Nutty

Nutty as a Fruitcake

Off Your Nut

On the Nut

Pfeffernüsse

Soup to Nuts

Tough Nut to Crack

Walnut-size Hail

OAT

Feel Your Oats

Know Your Oats

Oat-eater

Oater

Sow Your Wild Oats

Wild Oats

OIL

Cooking Oil

Salad Oil

Vegetable Oil

OLEOMARGARINE (*see* Margarine)

OLIVE

Crown of Olives

Extra Virgin

Green Olive

Groves of Academe

Hold out an Olive Branch

OD Gravy

ODs

Oil

Oleaginous

Olive (adj.)

Olive (n)

Olive Branch

Olive Complexion

Olive Drab

Olive Drab Gravy

Olive Drabs

Olive Green

OMELETTE

If You Break an Egg, Make an Omelette

You Can't Make an Omelette without
    Breaking Eggs

You Can't Unscramble an Omelette

ONION

Chives

French-fried Onion Rings

Green Onion

Know Your Onions

Onionskin

Onionskin Paper

Pearl Onion

Scallion

Shallot

Welsh Onion

ORANGE

Apples and Oranges

Compare Apples and Oranges

Juice

Like Apples and Oranges

Mandarin Orange

O.J.

Orange

Orangeade

Orange Peel

Osage Orange

Seville Orange

Squeeze One

Tangerine

Temple Orange

Ugli Fruit

Valencia Orange

OVEN

Dutch Oven

Have a Bun in the Oven

Nuke It!

Petit Four

Put a Bun in the Oven

OX

Bulimia

Eat like an Ox

Ox Roast

OYSTER

Angels on Horseback

Devils on Horseback

Man who First Ate an Oyster

Mountain Oysters

On the Half Shell

Oyster Cocktail

Oyster Shooter

Prairie Oyster(s)

Rocky Mountain Oysters

PAIL

Dinner Pail

PALATE

Palatable

Palate-pleasing

Please the Palate

Pleasing to the Palate

Sophisticated Palate

PAN

Deadpan

Dishpan Hands

Flash in the Pan

From the Frying Pan to the Fire

Frying Pan

Go from the Frying Pan to the Fire

Go out of the Frying Pan into the Fire

Hardpan

Out of the Frying Pan into the Fire

Pan (n)

Pan (v)

Pancake (n)

Pancake (v)

Pan Fish

Panhandle (n)

Panhandle (v)

Panhandler

Pan out

Picks and Pans

PANCAKE

Buttercake

Buckwheat Cake

Fall Flat as a Pancake

Flannel Cake

Flapjack

Flat as a Pancaké

Flatter than a Pancake

Girdle Cake

Griddle Cake

Hoecake

Hotcake

Indian Cake

Johnnycake

Knock Flat as a Pancake

Pancake (n)

Pancake (v)

Pancake Award

Pancake Block

Pancake Day

Pancake Ice

Pancake Landing

Pancake Makeup

Pancake Syrup

Pancake Tuesday

Sell like Hotcakes

Slapjack

Wheat Cake

PAP

Pablum

Pap

PAPAYA

Papaw

Papaya

Pawpaw

Paw Paw

PARE

Pare

Pare down

PARFAIT (*see* Sundae)

PASTA

Angel-hair Pasta

Antipasto

Pasta

Paste

Pastry

Pasty

Pâté de Fois Gras

Patty

PASTRY

Danish

Napoleon

Pastry

PASTY

Cornish Pasty

Mule Ear

Pasty

PATTY

Cow Pat

Patty-cake

PEA

Alike as Two Peas in a Pod

Black-eyed Pea

Chickpea

Cowpea

Goober Pea

Ground Pea

Hide the Pea

Lettuce, Turnip, and Pea

Like Two Peas in a Pod

Mess of Peas

Pea Bean

Peabrain

Peacoat

Peacock

Pea Gravel

Pea Jacket

Peanut

Pea Pickers

Pease Porridge

Pea-shooter

Pea-size Hail

Pea Soup

Pea-soup Fog

Snow Pea

Sugar Pea

Sweet Pea

Tear up the Pea Patch

Thick as Pea Soup

Yellow-eyed Pea

PEACH

Clingstone Peach

Eat Your First Peach

Freestone Peach

Go Together like Peaches and Cream

Just Peachy

Peach

Peaches and Cream

Peaches and Cream Complexion

Peach Fuzz

Peach Melba

Peachy

Peachy Keen

PEANUT

Do Goobers Eat Gophers, or Do Gophers
    Eat Goobers?

Earth Nut

Goober

Goober Pea

Groundnut

Ground-pea

Monkey Nut

Packing Peanuts

Peanut

Peanut-brained

Peanut Butter

Peanut Gallery

Peanuts

Work for Peanuts

PEAR

Alligator Pear

Avocado

Cactus Pear

Guacamole

Pear-shaped

Pear-shaped Tones

Prickly Pear

PECK (*See* Measure)

PEEL

Keep Your Eyes Peeled

Keep Your Eyes Skinned

Orange Peel

Peel (n)

Peel (v)

Peel down

Peel off

Peel out

Peel Rubber

PEPPER

Banana Pepper

Cayenne Pepper

Chili Pepper

Green Pepper Steak

Hot Pepper

Mike and Ike

Pep

Pepper (n)

Pepper (v)

Pepper-and-salt

Pepperbox

Peppercorn

Peppercorn Rent

Pepper Mill

Peppermint Patty

Pepperoni

Pepper Pot

Pepper Shaker

Pepper Spray

Pepper Steak

Peppery

Pep Pill

Peppy

Pep Rally

Pep Talk

Pep up

Pfeffernüsse

Salt and Pepper

Salt-and-pepper

Sweet Pepper

Twins

PICKLE

Brine

Cucumber Pickle

Dill Pickles and Ice Cream

Heinz 57 Varieties

In a Pickle

In a Pretty Pickle

Kosher Pickles

Pickle (n)

Pickle (v)

Pickled

Pickled Beets

Pickled Herring

Pickled Pig's Feet

Pickled to the Gills

Picklepuss

Watermelon Pickle

PICNIC

No Picnic

No Picnic in the Park

Picnic Ham

Tailgate Picnic

PIE

American as Apple Pie

Apple-pie Bed

Apple-pie Order

As American as Apple Pie

Black-bottom Pie

Boston Cream Pie

Can She Make a Cherry Pie?

Cornish Pasty

Cottage Pie

Cow Pie

Cutie Pie

Easy as Pie

Eat Humble Pie

Faux Apple Pie

Finger in Every Pie

Finger in the Pie

Have a Finger in Every Pie

Have a Finger in Many (Different) Pies

Have a Finger in the Pie

Have a Slice of the Pie

Humble Pie

Icebox Pie

In Apple-pie Order

Key Lime Pie

Lumberjack Pie

Make Mud Pies

Meat Pie

Mincemeat Pie

Mississippi Mud Pie

Mock Apple Pie

Moon Pie

Mud Pie

Pasty

Pie

Pie Chart

Pie-eyed

Pie-faced

Pie-in-the-sky

Pie in the Sky

Pieplant

Pie Shell

Pizza Pie

Pocket Pie

Porkpie Hat

Potpie

Refrigerator Pie

Shepherd's Pie

Shoofly Pie

Slice of the Pie

Steak and Kidney Pie

Sweet as Pie

Sweetie Pie

Sweet Potato Pie

PIG

Eat like a Pig

Everything but the Oink

Fat as a Pig

Make a Pig of Yourself

Pig Month

Pig out

Pigs in the Blanket

PINEAPPLE

Chicago Sundae

Pineapple

Pineapple Express

PINT (*See* Measure)

PIT

It's the Pits

Pits

PITCHER

Little Pitchers Have Big Ears

PIZZA

Pizza-faced

Pizza Pie

Pizzeria

Road Pizza

PLANT

Eggplant

PLATE

Blue Plate Special

Dental Plate

Flatware

Full Plate

Hand It over on a Silver Plate

Have a Full Plate

Have a Lot on Your Plate

Have Enough/Too Much on Your Plate

Home Plate

License Plate

Plate Glass

Plate Is Full

Plate Is Overflowing

Platter

Printing Plate

Silver Plate

PLUM

Plum

Plum Pudding

Plum Role

Plum Tomato

Political Plum

Quite a Plum

Sloe

Sloe-eyed

Sugarplum

POACH (*See* Egg)

POD

Alike as Two Peas in a Pod

Like Two Peas in a Pod

POMEGRANATE

Garnet

Grenade

Grenadier

Grenadine

Hand Grenade

Pomegranate

PONE

Cornpone

Corn Pone

POP

Lollipop

Pop (n)

Pop (v)

Popcorn

Pop Fly

Popgun

Pop in

Popped Corn

Pop Pills

Popping Corn

Pop the Question

Pop-top

Pop up

Pop Your Cork

Soda Pop

POPCORN

Cajun Popcorn

Packing Popcorn

Parching Corn

Popcorn

Popcorn Ball

Popcorn Cottage Cheese

Popcorn Fish

Popcorn Shrimp

Popped Corn

Popping Corn

PORK

Bacon Barometer

Pork

Pork Barrel

Pork-barrel Legislation

Pork-barrel Politics

Pork Out

Porkpie Hat

Salt Pork

The Other White Meat

PORRIDGE

Pease Porridge

POT

And One for the Pot

Chicken in Every Pot

Crackpot

Crock Pot

Fill the Pot

Go to Pot

Hodgepodge

Hotchpot

Hotchpotch

Hot Pot

Keep the Pot Boiling

Like the Pot Calling the Kettle Black

Lobster Pot

Luck of the Pot

Melting Pot

Mess of Pottage

One for the Pot

Pepper Pot

Poker Pot

Potbellied

Potbellied Stove

Potbelly

Potboiler

Pot Bunker

Pot Calling the Kettle Black

Pothead

Pothole

Potlids

Potlikker

Pot Liquor

Potluck

Pot of Gold

Potshot

Potwalloper

Sell Your Birthright for a Mess of Pottage

Stir up a Pot of Trouble

Stir up the Pot

Take a Potshot

Take Potluck

Teapot

Watched Pot Never Boils

POTATO

All That Meat and No Potatoes

Couch Potato

Drop like a Hot Potato

French-fried Potatoes

Have Potatoes Growing in Your Ears

Hot Potato

Irish Potato

Like a Hot Potato

Mashed Potato

Meat and Potatoes

Meat-and-potatoes

Mouse Potato

Mr. Potato Head

One Potato

Potato

Potato Flour

Potatohead

Potato Starch

Potayto/potahto

Small Potatoes

Sofa Spud

Spud

Sweet Potato

White Potato

Work for Small Potatoes

POTLUCK

Covered-dish Supper

Potluck Supper

Take Potluck

POULTRY (*See* Fowl)

PRESERVE

Conserve

Preserve

Tutti-frutti

PRESSURE COOKER

All Steamed up

Get All Steamed up

Hit the Ceiling

In a Pressure Cooker

Let off Steam

Pressure Cooker

Take the Heat

PRETZEL

Bend Your Mind into a Pretzel

Big Pretzel

Human Pretzel

Pretzel Bow

Pretzel Knot

PRUNE

Full of Prunes

Old Prune

Prune

Wrinkled as a Prune

PUDDING

Apple Brown Betty

Betty

Blood Pudding

Brown Betty

Custard Pudding

Hasty Pudding

Indian Pudding

Jell-O

Nervous Pudding

Plum Pudding

Proof Is in the Pudding

Proof of the Pudding Is in the Eating

Pudding

Puddinghead

Puddingheaded

Puddingstone

Steak and Kidney Pudding

Tapioca Pudding

Yorkshire Pudding

PUMPKIN

Pumpkin

Pumpkin Head

Punkin

Some Pumpkins

Turn into a Pumpkin

QUICHE

Quiche Lorraine

Real Men Don't Eat Quiche

RABBIT

First Catch Your Hare

Mexican Rarebit

Peanut Butter Rarebit

Rabbit Food

Roughage

Scotch Rabbit

Welsh Rabbit

Welsh Rarebit

RADISH

Horse Radish

RAISIN

Currant

Raisin

Raisin-box-size

RASPBERRY

Raspberry

Raspberry Tart

RECIPE

First Catch Your Hare

Receipt

Receipt Book

Recipe

Recipe Book

Recipe for Disaster

Recipe for Success

Stand Facing the Stove

REFRIGERATOR

Fridge

Icebox

In Cold Storage

Put in Cold Storage

Refrigerator

Refrigerator Art

Refrigerator Cookies

RELISH

Eat with Relish

Have Little Relish for

Relish (n)

Relish (v)

Relish the Memory

Relish the Moment

Relish the Thought

RESTAURANT

Automat

Bus (v)

Bus Boy

Bus Girl

Carryout

Cater

Coming up

Drive-in

Dutch Treat

Fast-food Restaurant

Go Dutch

Grazing Restaurant

Greasy Spoon

Hash House

In Short Order

Kosher Restaurant

Lunch Counter

Maître d'Hôtel

Pick up the Tab

Restaurant

Take-out

Tip

Short-order Restaurant

RHUBARB

Pieplant

Rhubarb

RICE

Indian Rice

Rice Paper

Ricer

Water Rice

Wild Rice

RIPE

Ripe

Ripe for the Picking

Ripe Old Age

Time Is Ripe

When the Time Is Ripe

ROAST

Done to a Turn

Roast

Ox Roast

Shish kebab

Spit

ROLL

Danish

Jelly Roll

Napoleon

Roll

Rolling in Dough

ROTTEN

Last One in Is a Rotten Egg

One Rotten Apple Spoils the Barrel

Rotten

Rotten Apple

Rotten Egg

Rotten to the Core

Spoiled Rotten

There Is Always One Rotten Apple in the Barrel

RUMP

Rump

Rump Parliament

SACCHARIN

Saccharin (n)

Saccharine (adj.)

SALAD

Beyond Your Salad Days

Caesar Salad

Chef's Salad

Chicken Salad

Egg Salad

Fruit Salad

Ham Salad

Macaroni Salad

Salad

Salad Bar

Salad Days

Salad Dressing

Salad Oil

Salmagundi

Taco Salad

Word Salad

SALMON

Lox and Bagel

Salmon Loaf

SALT

Above the Salt

Back to the Salt Mines

Below the Salt

Black-and-white

Earn Your Salt

Eat Someone's Salt

Grain of Salt

Mike and Ike

Mined Salt

Not Worth Your Salt

Old Salt

Pepper-and-salt

Rock Salt

Rub It in

Rub Salt into Someone's Wounds

Salad

Salary

Salt (n)

Salt (v)

Salt and Pepper

Salt-and-pepper

Salt away

Saltcellar

Salt Has Lost Its Savor

Saltines

Salt Mines

Salt of the Earth

Salt Pork

Salty

Sea Salt

Sit above the Salt

Sit below the Salt

Sprinkle Salt on Their Tails

Take with a Dose of Salts

Take with a Grain of Salt

Take with a Pinch of Salt

Twins

With a Grain of Salt

Worth Your Salt

SANDWICH

Bomber

Cuban Sandwich

Dagwood

Dagwood Sandwich

Denver Sandwich

Double-decker

Finger Sandwich

Garibaldi

Grinder

Gyro

Hamburger Sandwich

Hero

Hoagie

Hot Sandwich

Ice-cream Sandwich

Idiot Sandwich

Italian Beef Sandwich

Italian Sandwich

Jam Sandwich

Knuckle Sandwich

Leather Sandwich

Monte Cristo

Open-faced Sandwich

Po' Boy

Poor Boy

Reuben Sandwich

Sandwich (n)

Sandwich (v)

Sandwich around

Sandwich between

Sandwich Board

Sandwich Bread

Sandwich Cookie

Sandwich Islands

Sandwich Loaf

Sandwich Man

Sandwich Spread

Sub

Submarine

Submarine Sandwich

Torpedo

Wedgie

Zep

Zeppelin

SARDINE

Packed (in) like Sardines

Sardine Can

SAUCE

Applesauce!

Hit the Sauce

Hot Sauce

Lost in the Sauce

Melba Sauce

On the Sauce

Salsa

Sassy

Sauce

Sauced

Sauce Parlor

Saucer

Saucy

Tartar Sauce

What's Sauce for the Goose Is Sauce for the Gander

SAUCER

Eyes as Big as Saucers

Flying Saucer

Saucer

SAUSAGE

Blood Sausage

Botulism

Bratwurst

Dachshund Sausage

Kielbasa

Knockwurst

Pepperoni

Pigs in the Blanket

Salami

Sausage Dog

Summer Sausage

SAVOR

Salt Has Lost Its Savor

Savor

SCAVENGER

Scavenger

SCHMALTZ

Schmaltz

Schmaltzy

SCOOP

News Scoop

Scoop

Scoop Neck

SCRAMBLE

Scrambled Eggs

Scramble Signals

Wreck a Pair!

You Can't Unscramble an Egg

You Can't Unscramble an Omelette

SCRAPE

Scrape the Bottom of the Barrel

Scrape up

SCRATCH

Cook from Scratch

Made from Scratch

Make from Scratch

Scratch

Scratch Bread

Scratch Cake

SEAFOOD

Seafood Cocktail

Seefood Diet

SEASON

Season (v)

Seasoned Veteran

Seasoning

SEED

Birdseed

Go to Seed

If You Swallow Watermelon Seeds, They'll
        Grow in Your Stomach

Mustard-seed Shot

Number-one Seed

Seeded

Seedy

Strictly for the Birds

Top-seeded

SEETHE

Seethe inside

SERVE

Come and Get It!

Credenza

Dresser

First Come, First Served

Lazy Susan

Salver

Serve up

SHAKE

Frappé

Malted Milk Shake

Milk Shake

Mud Shake

Shake

White Cow

SHELF

Shelf Life

Shelve a Proposal

SHELL

Band Shell

Eggshell

Gun Shell

In a Nutshell

On the Half Shell

Pie Shell

Pumpkin Shell

Racing Shell

Shatter like an Eggshell

Shell (n)

Shell (v)

Shell Company

Shell Game

Shell out Money

Shuck (v)

Walk on Eggshells

SHORTENING

Shortbread

Shortcake

Shortening

Shortnin' Bread

SHRIMP

Jumbo Shrimp

Little Shrimp

Popcorn Shrimp

Prawn

Shrimp Cocktail

Shrimp Creole

SIEVE

Colander

Have a Memory like a Sieve

Leak like a Sieve

Memory like a Sieve

SIFT

Sift through Evidence

SILVERWARE

Born with a Silver Spoon in Your Mouth

Count the Silverware!

Flatware

Hide the Silverware!

Plastic Silverware

Sell the Family Silver

Silver

Silverware

SIMMER

Simmer Down

Simmering Dispute

SINK

Everything but the Kitchen Sink

Kitchen-sink

SIZZLE

Sizzle (v)

SKILLET

Skillet

Spider

SLICE

Best Thing since Sliced Bread

Cucumber Slices

Greatest Thing since Sliced Bread

Have a Slice of the Pie

Slice of Life

Slice of the Cake

Slice of the Melon

Slice of the Pie

SMELL

Wake up and Smell the Coffee

SMORGASBORD

Buffet

Smorgasbord

SNACK

Have the Munchies

Midnight Snack

Munchies

Nosh (n)

Nosh (v)

Nosher

Piece between Meals

Snack (n)

Snack (v)

Snack Bar

Snack Food

SODA

Black-and-White

Black Cow

Boston Cooler

Brown Cow

Cream Soda

Have a Lot of Moxie

Ice-cream Soda

Moxie

Mud Fizz

Root Beer

Soda

Soda Fountain

Sodá Jerk

Soda Jerker

Soda Pop

Soda Water

Tonic

SOP

Milksop

Sop

Sop to Cerberus

SOUFFLÉ

Cheese Soufflé

Fall Flat as a Cheese Soufflé

Flat as a Cheese Soufflé

Soufflé

SOUP

Alphabet Soup

Cat Soup

Chicken Soup

Duck Soup

Easy as Duck Soup

Everything from Soup to Nuts

Fly in My Soup

For Starters

From Soup to Nuts

In the Soup

Jewish Penicillin

Mess of Pottage

Mock Turtle Soup

Pea Soup

Pea-soup Fog

Sell Your Birthright for a Mess of Pottage

Soup

Soup and Fish

Soup Kitchen

Soup of Life

Soup-strainer

Soup to Nuts

Soup up

Soupy

Stone Soup

There's a Fly in My Soup

Thick as Pea Soup

SOUR

Go Sour (on)

Hit a Sour Note

Sauerkraut

Set Your Teeth on Edge

Sour (v)

Sour Ball

Sour Cherry

Sour Deal

Sour Disposition

Sourdough

Sourdough Bread

Sour Grapes

Sour-grapes Attitude

Sour Note

Sour Oil

Sourpuss

Sour Soil

Strike a Sour Note

Sweet and Sour

Sweet-and-sour

Turn Sour

SOY

Soy Milk

Tofu

SPAGHETTI

Spaghetti

Spaghettini

Spaghetti Squash

Spaghetti Straps

Spaghetti Western

Vermicelli

SPICE

Spice up Your Life

Spicy

Variety Is the Spice of Life

SPINACH

Spinach

Spinach Beet

SPOIL

One Rotten Apple Spoils the Barrel

Rotten to the Core

Spoilage

Spoiled Rotten

Spoiling for a Fight

Spoils of War

Spoil Your Dinner

SPOON

Apostle Spoon

Born with a Silver Spoon in Your Mouth

Eat It up with a Spoon

Greasy Spoon

Spoon (n)

Spoon (v)

Spoon-fed

Spoon-feed

SPREAD

Sandwich Spread

SPROUT

Brussels Sprouts

Sprout (n)

Sprout (v)

Sprout Antlers

Sprout Wings

Young Sprout

SQUASH

Butternut Squash

Spaghetti Squash

Vine Apple

SQUIRREL

Squirrel away

Squirrel Food

STARCH

Arrowroot

Cornstarch

Potato Starch

Starch

Starchy

Take the Starch out of

STARVE

Feed a Cold, Starve a Fever

Hidebound

Keep the Wolf from the Door

Starve (v)

Starve a Cold, Feed a Fever

Starved for Affection

Starved for Attention

Starved to Death

Starving Armenians

Starving to Death

STEAK

Beefsteak Tomato

Chopped Steak

Hamburger Steak

Pepper Steak

Salisbury Steak

Steak

Steak and Kidney Pie

Steak and Kidney Pudding

Steak Tartare

Swiss Steak

Tartar Steak

Tube Steak

STEAM

All Steamed up

Let off Steam

STEW

Bossy in a Bowl

Graveyard Stew

Half-stewed

In a Stew

Jambalaya

Leave You to Stew in Your Own Juice

Mulligan Stew

Son-of-a-bitch Stew

Son-of-a-gun Stew

Stewed

Stewed to the Gills

Stew in Your Own Juice

STIR

Stir Things up

Stir up a Hornet's Nest

Stir up a Pot of Trouble

Stir up the Pot

Stir up Trouble

STOMACH

Army Marches on Its Stomach

Beer-belly Pocketbook

Can't Stomach Something

Eyes Are Bigger than Your Stomach

Have a Bellyful

Have a Strong Stomach

Have No Stomach for

Have Something under Your Belt

If You Swallow Watermelon Seeds, They'll Grow in Your Stomach

Potbellied Stove

Potbelly

Tighten You Belt (Another Notch)

Turn Your Stomach

Way to a Man's Heart Is through His Stomach

STORE

Candy Store

Happy as a Kid in a Candy Store

Like a Kid in a Candy Store

STOVE

Franklin Store

Potbellied Stove

Put on the Back Burner

Range

Slave over a Hot Stove All Day

Stand Facing the Stove

Stove-pipe Hat

STRAIN

Soup-strainer

Strain at a Gnat

Strainer

Strain out Gnats and Swallow Camels

STRAWBERRY

Alaska Strawberries

Boston Strawberries

Strawberry

Strawberry Blond(e)

Strawberry Mark

Strawberry Roan

Strawberry Tomato

STUFF (v)

Beat the Stuffing out of

Dressing

Forcemeat

Had It up to Here

Knock the Stuffing out of

Stuffed to the Gills

Stuffing

SUCK

Air-sucker

Egg-sucker

Go Suck a Lemon

Go Suck an Egg

Honeysuckle

Life Sucks

Suck (v)

Suck Dirt

Sucker

Suck the Hind Teat

Suck the Lemon Dry

Suck the Life out of

Suck up to

Teach Your Grandmother to Suck Eggs

SUGAR

Beet Sugar

Grape Sugar

Indian Sugar

Maple Sugar

Saccharine (adj.)

Seersucker

Sugar and Spice

Sugar Apple

Sugar Beet

Sugar Bush

Sugar Candy

Sugarcoat

Sugar Cone

Sugar Daddy

Sugar Is Sweet

Sugarloaf

Sugar Maple

Sugar Pill

Sugarplum

Sugar Shack

Sugar Substitute

Sugar the Pill

SUNDAE

Banana Split

Black-bottom Sundae

Chicago Sundae

Hot Fudge Sundae

Houseboat

Parfait

Sundae

SUPPER

Buffet Supper

Covered-dish Supper

Potluck Supper

Sing for Your Supper

Supper

Supper Club

SWALLOW

Bitter Pill to Swallow

Find Something Hard to Swallow

Hard to Swallow

If You Swallow Watermelon Seeds, They'll
   Grow in Your Stomach

Look like the Cat That Swallowed the
   Canary

Strain out Gnats and Swallow Camels

Swallow a Camel

Swallow It Hook, Line, and Sinker

Swallow Your Pride

Swallow Your Words

SWEET

Bittersweet

Bittersweet Chocolate

Bittersweet Victory

Fill up on Sweets

Have a Sweet Tooth

How Sweet It Is!

Short and Sweet

Sweet and Sour

Sweet-and-sour

Sweet as Pie

Sweetbread

Sweet Butter

Sweetcakes

Sweet Chocolate

Sweet Corn

Sweet Crude

Sweet Deal

Sweet Milk

Sweet Pea

Sweeten the Deal

Sweeten the Kitty

Sweeten the Pot

Sweetheart Contract

Sweetheart Deal

Sweetheart of a Deal

Sweetie Pie

Sweetmeat

Sweet Nothings

Sweet on

Sweet Pea

Sweet Potato

Sweet Revenge

Sweet Sixteen

Sweets of Victory

Sweet Spot

Sweets to the Sweet

Sweet Swing

Sweet Talker

Sweet Tooth

Take the Bitter with the Sweet

Take Your Own Sweet Time

You Bet Your Sweet Life

SWEETBREADS

Stomach Sweetbread

Throat Sweetbread

SWEET POTATO

Ocarina

Sweet Potato

Sweet Potato Pie

Yam

SYRUP

Birch Syrup

Cane Syrup

Corn Syrup

Cough Syrup

Maple Syrup

Pancake Syrup

Sugar Syrup

Syrupy

TABLE

Another Table with the Same Setting

Clear the Table

Cocktail Table

Coffee Table

Coffee-table Book

Put Food on the Table

Set a Good Table

Set the Table

Table d'Hôte

Table Is Set

TACO (*See* Tortilla)

TAFFY

Atlantic City Taffy

Salt Water Taffy

Taffy

Taffy Pull

Toffee

Toffy

TAMALE

Chili Today, Hot Tamale

TANGERINE (*See* Orange)

TAPIOCA

Tapioca Pudding

TART

Cherry Tart

Tart (n)

Tart Cherry

TASTE

À Chacun Son Goût

Acquire a Taste for

Acquired Taste

Bad Taste

Bad Taste in Your Mouth

Chacun à Son Goût

Distasteful

Everyone to His Own Taste

Good Taste

Good Taste in

Gusto

Have Gusto

In Bad/Poor Taste

In Good Taste

Leave a Bad Taste in Your Mouth

Palatable

Savor

Smack of

Smack of Sarcasm

Smack of Treason

Smack Your Lips

Taste (n)

Taste (v)

Taste Buds

Tasteful

Tasteless

Taste like Dishwater

Tastes Just like Chicken

Taste Tester

There's No Accounting for Taste

Throw It to the Dogs

To Each His Own

Toothsome

Try It on the Dog

With Gusto

Yummy

Yum-yum

TEA

Ass over Teakettle

Ass-over-teakettle

Coffee, Tea, or Me?

Cup of Tea

For All the Tea in China

High Tea

Knock Someone Ass over Teakettle

Not for All the Tea in China

Not My Cup of Tea

Price of Tea in China

Storm in a Teacup

Tea

Teakettle

Teapot

Tempest in a Teacup

Tempest in a Teapot

What Does That Have to Do with the Price of Tea in China?

TEAPOT

I'm a Little Teapot

Teapot

Tempest in a Teapot

TEETH

Al Dente

Fed up to the Back Teeth

Have a Sweet Tooth

Milk Tooth

Set Your Teeth on Edge

Sink Your Teeth into

Something You Can Sink Your Teeth into

Sweet Tooth

Toothsome

TENDER

Fork-tender

So Tender You Could Cut It with a Fork

TENDERLOIN

Eat Tenderloin

Tenderloin

Tenderloin District

THIRST

Bloodthirsty

Tantalize

Tantalizing

Thirst (n)

Thirst (v)

Thirsty

THROAT

Throat Sweetbread

TOAST

Adam and Eve on a Raft

Become Toast

Bottoms up!

Burn the Toast

Down the Hatch!

Here's Mud in Your Eye!

Lampoon

Melba Toast

Milk Toast

Milquetoast

Propose a Toast

Roast

Scotch Woodcock

Toast (adj.)

Toast (n) (1)

Toast (n) (2)

Toast (v)

Toasted

Toastmaster

Toastmistress

Toast of the Town

Toasty

Warm as Toast

Welsh Rabbit

Welsh Rarebit

TOMATO

Beefsteak Tomato

BLT

Cherry Tomato

Fried Green Tomatoes

Love Apple

Mexican Green Tomato

Plum Tomato

Strawberry Tomato

Tomatillo

Tomato

Tomato Ketchup

Tomayto/Tomahto

TONGUE

Speak with Forked Tongue

Taste Buds

TORTILLA

Burrito

Nachos

Taco

Taco Chips

Tortilla

Tortilla Chips

Tostados

TRIPE

Bunch of Tripe

Talk Tripe

Tripe

TRIVET

Trivet

TRUFFLE

Truffle

Truffle of the North

TURKEY

All the Trimmings

Cape Cod Turkey

Cold Turkey

Do the Honors

Irish Turkey

Make a Wish

Quit Cold Turkey

Texas Turkey

Tom Turkey

Tough Turkey

Turkey Bacon

Turkey Jerky

Wishbone

Wishbone Formation

TURNIP

Fall off the Turnip Truck

Get Blood from a Turnip

Indian Turnip

Lettuce, Turnip, and Pea

Ravioli

Rutabaga

Turnip Greens

You Can't Get Blood from a Turnip

TURTLE

Caribbean Buffalo

Mock Turtle Soup

TWINKIE

Twinkie

Twinkie Defense

VANILLA

Plain-vanilla

Vanilla

VEGETABLE

Chronic Vegetative State

Lacto-ovo-vegetarian

Lacto-vegetarian

Ovo-vegetarian

Persistent Vegetative State

Pure Vegetarian

Strict Vegetarian

Vegan

Vegetable

Vegetable Oil

Vegetarian

Vegetate

Vegetative

Vegetative State

Vegged out

Veggie

Veggie Burger

Veggies

Veg out

VINE

Clinging Vine

Die on the Vine

Grapevine

Toil in the Vineyards

Vine Apple

Wither on the Vine

VINEGAR

Catch More Flies with Honey than with Vinegar

Cider Vinegar

Full of Piss and Vinegar

Full of Vinegar

Mother of Vinegar

Vinaigrette

Vinegar

You Can Catch More Flies with Honey than with Vinegar

WAFFLE

Belgian Waffle

Waffle (n)

Waffle (v)

Waffle Cone

Waffle Iron

WAITER

Dumb Waiter

Waiter

WALNUT

Walnut-size Hail

WARM

Feel like Death Warmed over

Leftovers

Look like Death Warmed over

Warm as Toast

Warm over

Warm up

WATER

Be in Hot Water

Boil Water without Burning It

Branch

Bread and Water

Can't Boil Water without Burning It

Can't Even Boil Water

Cast Your Bread upon the Waters

Dishwater

Drink of Water

First Water

Go to the Well Once Too Often

Have Ice Water in Your Veins

Ice Water in Your Veins

In Hot Water

It Must Be the Water

Lead a Horse to Water

Long Drink of Water

Make Your Mouth Water

Mouth-watering

Salt Water Taffy

Soda Water

Tall Drink of Water

Water Chestnut

Water down

Watering Hole

Watermelon

Water Rice

Water, Water, Everywhere, but Not a Drop to Drink

Well Has Run Dry

You Can Lead a Horse to Water, but You Can't Make It Drink

WATERMELON

If You Swallow Watermelon Seeds, They'll Grow in Your Stomach

Watermelon

WHEY

Curds and Whey

Whey-face

WIENER

Frankfurter

Weenie

Wiener

Wiener Dog

Wienie

WINE

Wine (v)

Wine and Dine

WORM

Food for Worms

Worm Food

YAM

Yam

Yummy

Yum-yum

YEAST

Brewer's Yeast

Yeasty

About the Author

ROBERT A. PALMATIER is Professor Emeritus of Linguistics, Western Michigan University.